THE
SECOND FIRESIDE BOOK
OF
BASEBALL

Edited by
CHARLES EINSTEIN

With an Introduction by
TED WILLIAMS

19 — 58

SIMON AND SCHUSTER · NEW YORK

ACKNOWLEDGMENTS

THE EDITOR wishes to express his gratitude to the following individuals and publishers for permission to include in this volume material from the following sources:

The American Weekly for "They Gave Him the Bat" by John M. Ross, © 1957 by The Hearst Publishing Co., Inc.

Argosy Magazine for "A Bat and a Prayer" by Howard Breslin, © 1945 by Popular Publications, Inc.; and "Stick It in His Ear" by Ray Robinson, © 1957 by Popular Publications, Inc.

The Atlantic Monthly for "I'd Rather Catch" by Birdie Tebbetts, © 1949 by The Atlantic Monthly Company.

A. S. Barnes & Company for "The Pioneers" from *Baseball's Hall of Fame* by Ken Smith, © 1952 by Ken Smith; "The Real Iron Man" from *Baseball's Greatest Pitchers* by Tom Meany, © 1951 by A. S. Barnes & Company; "A Letter to Mrs. Gilligan" and "Guess Who" (reprinted from *Baseball* Magazine) from *The Hot Stove League* by Lee Allen, © 1955 by A. S. Barnes & Company.

Baseball Digest for "All by Themselves," © 1957 by *Baseball Digest;* "Mid-Career Tragedies" by Bill Bryson, © 1958 by *Baseball Digest;* "California Always Was in the Majors" by Harold Sheldon, © 1958 by *Baseball Digest.*

Jim Bishop for "Sunny Morning at Spring Training," © King Features Syndicate, Inc.

Clem Boddington for "Bugs," reprinted from *Real* Magazine.

Boston *Globe* for "Pitcher's Pa" by Roger Birtwell; "Double-X" by Bob Holbrook; "Stuffy and the Error" by Harold Kaese.

Boston *Record* for "The Barrymore of Baseball" by Dave Egan. Howard Brubaker for "The Milk Pitcher" from *A Treasury of Sports Humor,* edited by Dave Stanley, © 1946 by Howard Brubaker.

Bennett Cerf for "Two-Top Grushkin" from *Try and Stop Me,* © 1944 by Bennett Cerf.

University of Chicago *Law Review* for "Baseball, Sport or Commerce?" by John Eckler from the Chicago *Law Review,* vol. 17, no. 1, 1949.

The Chicago *Daily News* for "The Prince of Pitchers" by Lloyd Lewis; "1932: New York Yankees 5, Chicago Cubs 2" by Lefty Gomez as told to John Drohan; "1938: Chicago Cubs 6, Pittsburgh Pirates 5" by Gabby Harnett as told to Hal Totten; "1908: Chicago White Sox 3, Cleveland Indians 2" by Ed Walsh as told to Francis J. Powers; "1930: Philadelphia Athletics 7,8, Washington Senators 6,7" by Al Simmons as told to John P. Carmichael. M. W. (Bill) Corum for "1948: Leo Changes Jobs" from the New York *Journal-American.*

Cosmopolitan Magazine for "Major vs. Minor Leaguers" by Amram Scheinfeld, © 1957 by *Cosmopolitan* Magazine.

Cupples and Leon for "The Winning Throw—

Conclusion" by Lester Chadwick from *Baseball Joe of the Silver Stars,* © 1912 by Cupples and Leon.

Dell Publications for "Let's Bring Back the Spitball" by Joe Reicher, © 1958 by Dell Sports—*Baseball Stars Magazine.*

University of Denver Press for selections from "Small Town Note" by Sherwood Anderson from *Sherwood Anderson, His Life and Works* by James Schevill.

The Detroit *Free Press* for "Busher" by Lyall Smith.

E. P. Dutton & Co., Inc., for "I Was a Bad Kid" from *The Babe Ruth Story* by Babe Ruth as told to Bob Considine, © 1958 by George Herman Ruth.

Esquire for "Nine Ladies *vs.* Fate" by Lynn Montross, © 1935 by Esquire, Inc.

Farrar, Straus and Cudahy, Inc., for "braves 10, giants 9" from *Raising Demons* by Shirley Jackson, © 1957 by Shirley Jackson.

James T. Farrell for "He Got a Raw Deal" published originally in August 1957 issue of *Baseball Digest,* © 1957 by James T. Farrell.

Ben Foote and the Phoenix *Gazette* for "The Road to Cananea."

Frank Music Corp. for "The Game" from *Damn Yankees* by Jerry Ross and Richard Adler, © 1955 by Frank Music Corp.

Zane Grey, Inc., for "Old Well Well" by Zane Grey.

Harcourt, Brace and Company for selection from *The Natural* by Bernard Malamud, © 1952 by Bernard Malamud; "Goodwood Comes Back" from *The Circus in the Attic and Other Stories* by Robert Penn Warren, © 1941 by Robert Penn Warren.

Pat Harmon and the Cincinnati *Post* for the column "How to Pitch to Ted Williams."

Harper & Brothers for "How to Keep Score" from *How to Watch a Baseball Game* by Fred Schwed, Jr., © 1957 by Fred Schwed, Jr.

Ernie Harwell for "A Letter to Joseph A. Whitacre" by Adrian C. Anson; "A Letter to Edward B. Talcott" by James Whyte Davis.

W. C. Heinz and *True, The Man's Magazine* for "The Rocky Road of Pistol Pete," © 1958 by Fawcett Publications, Inc.

International News Service for "See, Doc, It's Like This" by John Barrington; "The 1957 All-Star Game" by Howard Sigmand.

Mike Jackson and the Laguna Beach *Post* for the column "Take Me Out to the Ball Game, I Can Get Home by Myself."

Roger Kahn for "Intellectuals and Ballplayers" from *The American Scholar,* Summer 1957.

Walt Kelly for "The Whirled Series" from *I Go Pogo,* © 1951, 1952 by Walt Kelly.

Alfred A. Knopf, Inc., for selection from *Bang the Drum Slowly* by Mark Harris, © 1956 by Mark Harris.

Little, Brown & Co. and Atlantic Monthly Press for selection from *God's Country and Mine* by Jacques Barzun, © 1954 by Jacques Barzun.

Marianne Moore for "Hometown Piece for Messrs. Alston and Reese," reprinted from the New York *Herald Tribune.*

The McCall Corp. for "The Sleeper" by Charles Einstein, © 1954 by the McCall Corp.

McGraw-Hill Book Company for "How to Play the Outfield" by Joe DiMaggio from *Baseball for Everyone,* © 1948 by the McGraw-Hill Book Company, Inc.

Minneapolis Star and Tribune Company for "The Man" by Dick Gordon, © 1957 Minneapolis Star and Tribune Company.

William Morrow & Co. for selection from *Mister Shortstop,* © 1954 by Duane Decker.

Moynihan & Wachsmith for "My Roomy" by Ring Lardner, © 1912, 1942 by Ellis A. Lardner.

New York *Daily News* for "1957: Milwaukee Braves 5, New York Yankees 0" by Joe Trimble; "Dateline: Miami" by Dick Young.

New York *Herald Tribune* and Red Smith for "1950: Philadelphia Phillies 4, Brooklyn Dodgers 1," © 1950 New York *Herald Tribune.*

New York *Mirror* and Bill Slocum for "Gentlemen, This Is a Man."

New York *Post* for "Jim Thorpe Bats 7-for-7" by Jerry Mitchell, © New York Post Corp.; "1947: Brooklyn Dodgers 5, Boston Braves 3" by Jimmy Cannon, © 1947 New York Post Corp.; "Long Ride Home" by Milton Gross, © 1956 New York Post Corp.

The New York Times for "Casey in the Box" by Meyer Berger; "1938: Cincinnati Reds 6, Brooklyn Dodgers 0" by Roscoe McGowan; "1905: New York Giants 2, Philadelphia Athletics 0"; "1926: St. Louis Cardinals 3, New York Yankees 2" by James R. Harrison; "1934: St. Louis Cardinals 11, Detroit Tigers 0" by John Drebinger.

The New Yorker Magazine for "Old Reliable" by Richard O. Boyer, © 1949 by The New Yorker Magazine, Inc.

Pageant Magazine for "Jimmy Piersall's Greatest Day" by Al Hirshberg from *Pageant,* October 1957.

Kenneth Patchen for "The Origin of Baseball."

George E. Phair for "The Magic Number" from the New York *American.*

G. P. Putnam's Sons for "How I Lost the World Series" by Grover Cleveland Alexander and "A Tip for Teddy" by Grantland Rice from *The Best of*

Contents

INTRODUCTION by Ted Williams   xvii

PREFACE   xix

SAMUEL HOPKINS ADAMS [AUTOBIOGRAPHY]   1
    Baseball in Mumford's Pasture Lot: *A great "Grandfather Story"*

GROVER CLEVELAND ALEXANDER [AUTOBIOGRAPHY]   7
    How I Lost the 1915 World Series: *By the pitcher who won his team's only game*

HYDER ALI [POETRY]   10
    How Old Is Anson?: *"The stars were present at his birth"*

LEE ALLEN [HISTORY]   11
    A Letter to Mrs. Gilligan: *"How far is it from home to second?" "I never ran that way."*

SHERWOOD ANDERSON [AUTOBIOGRAPHY]   16
    From *Small Town Note: Perhaps someone like Babe Ruth was at bat*

ADRIAN C. ANSON [HISTORY]   18
    A Letter to Joseph A. Whitacre: *"I can not play to empty benches"*

JOHN BARRINGTON [GENERAL]   19
    See, Doc, It's Like This: *Where is everybody?*

JACQUES BARZUN [GENERAL]   20
    From *God's Country and Mine: Why baseball fans don't bring hip flasks to the ball park*

BASEBALL DIGEST [GENERAL]   22
    All by Themselves: *How unassisted triple plays are made*

BASEBALL HEROES MAGAZINE [SPOT REPORTING]   24
    The 1941 All-Star Game: *Remember the one Ted hit at Detroit?*

BASEBALL MAGAZINE [POETRY]   25
    Guess Who?: *". . . and bottles inundate his back . . ."*

MEYER BERGER [SPOT REPORTING]   26
    1941: Casey in the Box: *Mickey Owen drops the third strike*

ROGER BIRTWELL [GENERAL]   28
    Pitcher's Pa: *A great moment for the Bearden family*

Contents

JIM BISHOP [GENERAL]   30
    Miss Wattles: *by the author of* The Day Lincoln Was Shot

CLEM BODDINGTON [PROFILE]   32
    Bugs: *The legendary Mr. Raymond*

RICHARD O. BOYER [PROFILE]   36
    Old Reliable: *The masterful Mr. Henrich*

BOBBY BRAGAN *as told to* STANLEY FRANK [GENERAL]   46
    What Percentage Percentage?: *A manager sounds off real good*

HOWARD BRESLIN [FICTION]   55
    A Bat and a Prayer: *What to say when at bat*

WARREN BROWN [HISTORY]   60
    From *Don't Believe Everything You Read: How many double plays* were *Tinker-to-Evers-to-Chance?*

HOWARD BRUBAKER [FICTION]   62
    The Milk Pitcher: *Could this conceivably have anything to do with a cow? Yes*

BILL BRYSON [HISTORY]   69
    Mid-Career Tragedies: *A sad recounting*

JIMMY CANNON [SPOT REPORTING]   76
    1947: Brooklyn Dodgers 5, Boston Braves 3: *Jackie Robinson's first day in the majors*

BENNETT CERF [ENTERTAINMENT]   77
    Two-Top Gruskin: *A neoclassic routine*

LESTER CHADWICK [FICTION]   78
    The Winning Throw—Conclusion: *From one of the deathless Baseball Joe books*

BILL CORUM [SPOT REPORTING]   82
    1948: Leo Changes Jobs: *A real inside story*

ROBERT CREAMER [GENERAL]   84
    Stars in Their Eyes: *What the All-Star Game really means*

ARTHUR DALEY [GENERAL]   85
    Baseball's Human Comedy: *A bunch of stories—one better than the next*

DANIEL M. DANIEL [SPOT REPORTING]   89
    1949: DiMag Returns to the Lineup: *And hits four home runs in three games!*

JAMES WHYTE DAVIS [HISTORY]   90
    A Letter to Edward B. Talcott: *"I desire to be buried in my baseball suit"*

DUANE DECKER [FICTION]   91
    From *Mister Shortstop: A chapter from the famous Blue Sox series*

Contents

JOE DIMAGGIO [GENERAL]
How to Play the Outfield: *Detailed advice from the master himself* — 94

JOHN DREBINGER [SPOT REPORTING]
1934: St. Louis Cardinals 11, Detroit Tigers 0: *The Gas House Gang at its crazy best* — 100

FINLEY PETER DUNNE [GIN'RAL]
Mr. Dooley on Baseball: *"Inside baseball, th' pa-apers calls it"* — 104

JOHN ECKLER, ESQ. [GENERAL]
Baseball—Sport or Commerce?: *Complete with 93 footnotes* — 107

DAVE EGAN [GENERAL]
The Barrymore of Baseball: *Mr. Hornsby, of course* — 121

CHARLES EINSTEIN [FICTION]
The Sleeper: *A brand-new kind of night baseball* — 123

BERGEN EVANS *and* CORNELIA EVANS [GENERAL]
From *A Dictionary of Contemporary American Usage*: *The meaning of "pinch-hitter"* — 126

JAMES T. FARRELL [HISTORY]
"He Got a Raw Deal": *The fabulous Buck Weaver* — 127

ROBERT FONTAINE [AUTOBIOGRAPHY]
God Hit a Home Run: *A delightful excerpt from* The Happy Time — 133

BEN FOOTE [GENERAL]
The Road to Cananea: *Bus breakdown south of the border* — 140

WHITEY FORD *as told to* EDWARD LINN [GENERAL]
The Great American Pitchers' Union: *Where Macy's always tells Gimbel's* — 142

BILL FURLONG [PROFILE]
Billy Pierce: *An uncommonly gifted left-hander of today* — 149

LEFTY GOMEZ *as told to* JOHN DROHAN [AUTOBIOGRAPHY]
1932: New York Yankees 5, Chicago Cubs 2: *An uncommonly gifted left-hander of yesterday* — 153

DICK GORDON [PROFILE]
The Man: *An uncommonly gifted left-hander of all time* — 155

FRANK GRAHAM [HISTORY]
The Window Breakers: *The start of the Yankee Dynasty* — 157

ZANE GREY [FICTION]
Old Well-Well: *Here, at last, a fan who is immortal* — 164

MILTON GROSS [SPOT REPORTING]
The Long Ride Home: *A story you will not easily forget* — 169

Contents

PAT HARMON [EXCLUSIVE]   172
How to Pitch to Ted Williams: *The secret: Tell the truth at all times*

MARK HARRIS [FICTION]   173
From *Bang the Drum Slowly*: *Henry Wiggen dictates the terms*

JAMES R. HARRISON [SPOT REPORTING]   181
1926: St. Louis Cardinals 3, New York Yankees 2: *Old Pete strikes out Lazzeri*

GABBY HARTNETT *as told to* HAL TOTTEN [AUTOBIOGRAPHY]   185
1938: Chicago Cubs 6, Pittsburgh Pirates 5: *The "home run in the gloaming"*

ERNIE HARWELL [HISTORY]   188
Baseball among the Headhunters: *Or, Ladies' Day in the Philippines*

W. C. HEINZ [PROFILE]   190
The Rocky Road of Pistol Pete: *An incredible story—and every wonderful word the truth!*

AL HIRSHBERG [GENERAL]   199
Jimmy Piersall's Greatest Day: *Sequel to another story*

BOB HOLBROOK [PROFILE]   202
Double X: *The brilliant Jimmy Foxx*

MIKE JACKSON [GENERAL]   204
Take Me Out to the Ball Game (I Can Get Home by Myself): *All about mountain climbing . . . and one of the funniest pieces in the book*

SHIRLEY JACKSON [SPOT REPORTING]   206
braves 10, giants 9: *Small type used on purpose*

HAROLD KAESE [HISTORY]   212
Stuffy and the Error: *Whom did McInnis hit? Rooney or Shannon? And why?*

ROGER KAHN [GENERAL]   214
Intellectuals and Ballplayers: *About a one-sided romance*

HOWARD L. KATZANDER [GENERAL]   218
Case History of Joey J., Baseball Player: *Father figures, burial grounds, women caged, and Freud*

JOHN LARDNER [PROFILE]   222
The One and Only Bobo: *The slightly unbelievable saga of Louis Norman Newsom*

RING LARDNER [FICTION]   230
My Roomy: *Lardner's nuttiest character*

Contents

LLOYD LEWIS [SPOT REPORTING]   240
  1911: Philadelphia Athletics 4, New York Giants 2: *How Home Run Baker got his name*

BERNARD MALAMUD [FICTION]   243
  From *The Natural: A bat named Wonderboy*

ROSCOE McGOWEN [SPOT REPORTING]   254
  1938: Cincinnati Reds 6, Brooklyn Dodgers 0: *Vander Meer's second consecutive no-hitter*

TOM MEANY [PROFILE]   256
  The Real Man of Iron: *The fabulous Joe McGinnity*

D. J. MICHAEL [ENTERTAINMENT]   260
  Dice Baseball: *Time of game: about 20 minutes*

JERRY MITCHELL [GENERAL]   263
  Jim Thorpe Bats 7-for-7: *Did you know Thorpe was a professional ballplayer too?*

LYNN MONTROSS [FICTION]   264
  Nine Ladies *vs.* Fate: *Six ladies, that is—and three men*

MARIANNE MOORE [POETRY]   270
  Hometown Piece for Messrs. Alston and Reese: *Has Los Angeles developed any Dodger fans like Miss Moore?*

THE NEW YORK TIMES [SPOT REPORTING]   271
  1905: New York Giants 2, Philadelphia Athletics 0: *Series shutout number 3 for Matty*

JACK ORR [GENERAL]   274
  The Worst Team of All: *The 1916 A's*

KENNETH PATCHEN [POETRY]   276
  The Origin of Baseball: *". . . he wanted to throw something . . ."*

GEORGE E. PHAIR [POETRY]   277
  The Magic Number: *Philosophy in four lines*

BABE PINELLI *as told to* AL STUMP [AUTOBIOGRAPHY]   278
  Kill the Umpire? Don't Make Me Laugh!: *Babe should know*

SHIRLEY POVICH [SPOT REPORTING]   284
  1956: New York Yankees 2, Brooklyn Dodgers 0: *The prize-winning story of Don Larsen's perfect game*

JOE REICHLER [GENERAL]   287
  Let's Bring Back the Spitball: *Why not? The spray lingers anyway*

GRANTLAND RICE [POETRY]   290
  A Tip to Teddy: *Job advice to the President of the United States*

MILTON RICHMAN [SPOT REPORTING]   292
  1957: Pittsburgh Pirates 9, New York Giants 1: *The end of something (see Bob Stevens below)*

Contents

RAY ROBINSON [GENERAL]   294
Stick It in His Ear!: *The noble art of bench jockeying*

BILL ROEDER [PROFILE]   299
The Dodger They Don't Boo: *About that most happy fella, Gil Hodges*

JERRY ROSS *and* RICHARD ADLER [ENTERTAINMENT]   303
The Game: *Complete lyrics of a marvelous number in* Damn Yankees

JOHN M. ROSS [PROFILE]   305
They Gave Him a Bat: *About Cincinnati's Frank Robinson—and a man named George Poles*

BABE RUTH *with* BOB CONSIDINE [AUTOBIOGRAPHY]   307
I Was a Bad Kid: *A much misunderstood boyhood*

AMRAM SCHEINFELD [GENERAL]   313
From "Looking into People": *The difference between bush-leaguers and big-leaguers*

FRED SCHWED, JR. [GENERAL]   314
How to Keep Score: *More or less*

DICK SEAMON [PROFILE]   319
The Whole Story of Pitching: *Control—which is another name for Robin Roberts*

HAROLD SHELDON [GENERAL]   325
California Always Was in the Majors: *With assembled proof, of course*

HOWARD SIGMAND [SPOT REPORTING]   327
The 1957 All-Star Game: *Remember that madcap ninth inning?*

AL SILVERMAN [PROFILE]   329
Hank Aaron: *How do you get him out? Pitch* under *the plate*

AL SIMMONS *as told to* JOHN P. CARMICHAEL [AUTOBIOGRAPHY]   333
1930: Philadelphia Athletics 7,8, Washington Senators 6,7: *Old Foot-in-the-Bucket's Greatest Day*

HARRY SIMMONS *and* WILLARD MULLIN [GENERAL]   335
So You Think You Know Baseball!: *Knotty problems, in word and picture—answers, too*

BILL SLOCUM [PROFILE]   337
Gentlemen, This Is a Man!: *An unusual story about an unusual ballplayer*

KEN SMITH [HISTORY]   339
The Pioneers: *Cartwright, Chadwick, Bulkeley, and the nonflying Wright Brothers*

LYALL SMITH [PROFILE]   342
Busher: *Nearly forty when he hit the big time*

Contents

RED SMITH [spot reporting]   343
> 1950: Philadelphia Phillies 4, Brooklyn Dodgers 1: *How to waltz to a pennant—backwards*

ROBERT SMITH [history]   345
> The Freshest Man on Earth: *Giving it the Arlie Latham*

BOB STEVENS [spot reporting]   350
> 1958: San Francisco Giants 8, Los Angeles Dodgers 0: *The beginning of something (see Milton Richman above)*

BIRDIE TEBBETTS [autobiography]   353
> I'd Rather Catch: *About a lot of things people don't realize*

JOE TRIMBLE [spot reporting]   358
> 1957: Milwaukee Braves 5, New York Yankees 0: *Lew Burdette pitches the clincher*

FRANK C. TRUE [history]   361
> Bridegrooms Wallop Beaneaters: *How ball clubs came to get their names*

ED WALSH *as told to* FRANCIS J. POWERS [autobiography]   363
> 1908: Chicago White Sox 3, Cleveland Indians 2; *The greatest spitball artist on the mound—and Nap Lajoie at bat!*

ROBERT PENN WARREN [fiction]   365
> Goodwood Comes Back: *A distinguished short story*

JOE WILLIAMS [general]   371
> Managers Are a Dime a Dozen: *Do you agree?*

HERBERT WARREN WIND [fiction]   376
> The Master's Touch: *A famous golf writer uses a golflike title for a baseball story*

YOMIURI MORNING PRESS [spot reporting]   384
> 1955: New York Yankees 6, Japanese All-Stars 1: *Here comes another one of those Oriental box scores*

DICK YOUNG [general]   386
> Dateline: Miami: *A bitter piece*

INDEX   389

List of Illustrations

FRONT ENDPAPER: PAINTING by EDMOND KOHN, *The Long Ball Hitter*

CARTOON by JOHN GALLAGHER   6

CARTOON by CHON DAY   15

CARTOON by JOHN GALLAGHER   17

CARTOON by JIMMY HATLO   23

CARTOON by JOHN GALLAGHER   25

CARTOON by JOHN GALLAGHER   29

CARTOON by VIRGIL PARTCH   31

CARTOON by DAVID PASCAL   43

CARTOON by HANK KETCHAM   44

CARTOON by JOHN GALLAGHER   54

CARTOON by JIMMY HATLO   61

CARTOON by WALT KELLY   73

PHOTOGRAPHS, THE GRAND OLD MEN   76A

PHOTOGRAPHS, WHAT?!?!   76B

CARTOON by JOHN GALLAGHER   93

CARTOON by HARRY LYONS   103

CARTOON by CHARLES SCHULZ   106

PHOTOGRAPHS, A DAY IN THE LIFE OF MICKEY MANTLE   108A

CARTOON by TED KEY   139

PHOTOGRAPHS, GREAT MOMENTS   140A

PHOTOGRAPHS, PISTOL PETE   140B

PHOTOGRAPHS, HELLO AND GOODBYE!   140C

PHOTOGRAPHS, DON LARSEN PITCHING   140C

CARTOON by JOHN GALLAGHER   152

CARTOON by WALT DITZEN   171

PHOTOGRAPHS, BROTHER ACT   172A

PHOTOGRAPHS, LADIES' DAY   172B

CARTOON by JOHN GALLAGHER   180

CARTOON by DAVE HIRSCH   187

CARTOON by ELDON DEDINI   189

CARTOON by MARTY LOWE   201

PHOTOGRAPHS, SLUGGERS!   204A

PHOTOGRAPHS, FIGHT!!   204B

PHOTOGRAPHS, . . . AND AFTER THE FIGHT . . .   204D

CARTOON by JIM KIERNAN   213

CARTOON by JOE TRECENO   221

PHOTOGRAPHS, BIG DAYS FOR THE BROWNS   236A

PHOTOGRAPH, AFTER THE BALL WAS OVER   236B

PHOTOGRAPHS, THE SHORTSTOP FLIES HIGH   236C

PHOTOGRAPHS, PAY DAY FOR THE BABE   236D

EDITORIAL CARTOON by REG MANNING   251

EDITORIAL CARTOON by H. M. TALBURT   251

EDITORIAL CARTOON by BURRIS JENKINS, JR.   252

EDITORIAL CARTOON by HERBLOCK   252

EDITORIAL CARTOON by BRUCE RUSSELL   253

EDITORIAL CARTOON by DAN DOWLING   253

CARTOON by DON TOBIN   255

CARTOON by DICK CAVALLI   269

CARTOON by JOHN GALLAGHER   275

CARTOON by BILL YATES   289

CARTOON by BEN THOMPSON   291

CARTOON by JOHN GALLAGHER   293

PHOTOGRAPHS, HAPPY DAYS   300A

PHOTOGRAPHS, BENCH JOCKEYS   300B

PHOTOGRAPHS, THE GASHOUSE GANG   300D

PHOTOGRAPH, LAST GAME IN BROOKLYN   300F

CARTOON by PETER ARNO   300H

CARTOON by JOHN GALLAGHER   324

CARTOON by WALT DITZEN   332

CARTOON by JOHN GALLAGHER   338

CARTOON by HARRY LYONS   347

CARTOON by BILL FREYSE   348

CARTOON by JOHN GALLAGHER   352

CARTOON by HAL SHERMAN   370

BACK ENDPAPER: PHOTOGRAPH, DAWN OF A NEW ERA

Introduction

BASEBALL PLAYERS *like myself share a rather incurable habit: When they are not playing the game they like to read, look at, and listen to accounts of the game in word and picture.*

Fortunately, the amount of literature and illustrative material on our great American game is large indeed, in the off season as well as the on.

Nevertheless, I think it fair to say that before Charlie Einstein's first Fireside Book of Baseball *came along, no publication had really taken the sport in hand the way that one did. If you are like me, you wanted one thing after reading it; that one thing was a lot more of the same.*

So The Second Fireside Book of Baseball *is pretty much the logical answer. Charlie Einstein, for many years baseball editor of the International News Service, has taken the right approach in this sequel volume. He has not brought out a "different" anthology; instead, he has taken his cue from the enjoyment not only the readers and reviewers but we ballplayers ourselves got from the first* Fireside *book, and enlarged upon the same idea with a vast amount—certainly, I'd guess, equal in size to the first book—of new material, but along the same wonderful lines.*

Let me say one thing "against" this book: You don't take it to the ball park with you. I think that's the great thing about baseball—nobody's ever invented a substitute for it.

But in between sessions at the ball park—let alone those long winters —this is a book I think you'll admire for its looks, treasure for its contents.

Having glanced through these contents, I can't help but think it might even settle three or four dozen "hot stove" arguments!

TED WILLIAMS

Preface

The Second Fireside Book of Baseball follows its predecessor volume, The Fireside Book of Baseball, by the brief interval of two years, and the aims and the format of the second book duplicate those of the first. Any prolonged discussion in this space would therefore be largely no more than a restatement of the preface to the original collection.

A word in one direction does seem proper: Since the first book was published, baseball has of course become richer not only in performance but in accompanying word and picture. And we have tried to include here some of the highlights of the past two years, and some of the fine writing and notable illustrations. But it was never the purpose, once this second book was proposed, to make it merely an "updating" of the first one. Once again you will find that the contents span the whole range of baseball history; but even that is fairly accidental. In every instance we have tried to be guided by quality and by interest —in performer, writer, event, picture— rather than by specific date. Baseball has a marvelously timeless nature to it, and fans of all ages like to hear about memorable players and contests no matter when they happened to come along. Sometimes the accounts themselves were not written until years later.

Finally, any editor who became date-conscious in selecting the contents of an anthology like this one would have to face the practical possibility that baseball is no respecter of book publishers. On the day the first Fireside Book of Baseball was published, Art Larsen pitched his perfect World Series game.

I do wish to say that so many of the writers whose contributions appear here have helped in additional ways in the production of this book that to list them would be in great measure to recite over again the table of contents. In addition, I am grateful to Frank Slocum, Knox Burger, Gene Roguski, Seymour Berkson, Robert G. Begam, Jim Bagley, Lurton Blassingame and the staff of his office, Peter Schwed, Paul Fisher, Arnold Hano, Ed Fitzgerald and all of the reviewers of the first book, the latter not only for their unfailing kindness but because what they had to say so often initiated hunches, ideas, inspirations and follow-ups that led to the inclusion in this new book of things I hope you'll like.

Once again I wish to reserve a special acknowledgment for Dick Kaplan, through whose judgment and unstinting help the photographic sections of this volume were largely brought into being.

Of course there would be no second Fireside Book like this if the first had not been a gratifying success. But I believe the matter goes deeper than that.

Some books of the anthology type, like *The Settlement Cook Book* or John James Audubon's *Birds of America,* have done very well without the need for sequel volumes as big as the originals.

The answer may lie in the character of baseball itself. There may be 627 ways to cook an egg, but the number of ways to lose a ball game approaches infinity. Somebody is always coming up with a new one. Only recently I heard a story told by Charley Dressen, about one day when he was managing the Dodgers and, on exceedingly short notice, needed a new pitcher from the bullpen. The new pitcher, whom we shall call Jones, was a warmhearted, naïve fellow who, among other things, had not had sufficient time to warm up properly. Dressen therefore decided to stall, to give Jones the time for more practice throws once he reached the mound.

First the manager entered into a lengthy discussion with infielders Reese and Robinson over such germane topics as where they intended to dine that night. Then, when the umpire finally broke it up, Dressen took Reese aside and said in a low voice, "Look—when you get back to shortstop call time and tell them you have something in your eye. Then while you're nutsing around, Jones can keep on throwing."

Reese nodded, returned to his position, and, just as the umpire cried, "Play ball!", held up his hand for time.

"What is it now?" the umpire asked.

"Something in my eye," Reese said.

"Here," said the ever solicitous pitcher Jones, setting down ball and glove and coming off the mound. "Let me take it out."

Batter up!

Scottsdale, Arizona, 1958   CHARLES EINSTEIN

THE ACCIDENT of alphabetical order gives us a great leadoff man—
with one of his marvelously delightful "Grandfather Stories."

Baseball in Mumford's Pasture Lot

———————— **SAMUEL HOPKINS ADAMS** ————————

A SMART SINGLE RIG drew up to the hitching post of No. 52 South Union Street as we three boys approached. Out of it stepped a short, red-faced, dapper man who secured his horse and then addressed us.

"Does Mr. Myron Adams live here?"

"Yes, sir," John said.

"We're just going in to see him," Sireno added. "He's our grandfather."

"Well, you can wait," the stranger said. "I've got private business with him."

"If you're trying to sell him a colored enlargement of a photograph . . ." John began but got no further.

"I ain't," the caller interrupted. "My name is Phillips and I represent the Rochester Baseball Club."

"There isn't any," I said glumly.

It was cause for humiliation to every right-thinking inhabitant of the city, young and old, that in the spring of the baseball-mad year of 1879, Rochester was represented by no professional team whatever.

"There will be if I can sell fifty of these here tickets, good for the whole season and only ten dollars," Mr. Phillips said. "D'you think he'll pony up? How's he on baseball?"

"He wouldn't know a Dollar Dead from a Young America if it hit him in the snoot," Reno answered. The Dollar Dead was the standard amateur ball, the Young America the twenty-five-cent junior favorite.

"I'll have a crack at him anyway," Mr. Phillips decided. He vanished into the cottage, and in a few minutes we heard Grandfather, in his deep and resonant voice, putting an end to the interview. "What?" he cried. "Money? To witness what should be a *gentleman's* pastime? Nonsense! Fustian! Good day to you!"

The crestfallen visitor came out, silently climbed into his buggy, and drove away. We went in to pay our duty call.

A week later, the three of us ran upon Mr. Phillips again, this time in Livingston Park, and heard from him tidings of great joy. In spite of Grandfather's recalcitrance, Rochester was to have its team. Mr. Asa T. Soule, the patent-medicine magnate, had just come forward with an offer to finance a club out of his private pocket, provided it should bear the name of Hop Bitters, the cure-all he manufactured.

The news spread fast and, as the opening of the season drew near, Rochester glowed with restored pride. In its first game the new club swamped an amateur nine, fourteen to six.

Next, an exhibition game was scheduled against Rochester's ancient and bitter rival, the Buffalos, who were in the National League and therefore supposedly a cut above us. It was to be the event of the year, and the admission was fifty cents. John, being ten years old and our senior member, put the painful question to Reno and me.

"Where are we going to get half a dollar apiece?"

"Grandpa Adams," I suggested doubtfully.

"In your mind, baby mine!" Reno said, using the most emphatic negation of the time.

"What other chance have we got?" I asked. Nobody had an answer. Fifty cents was unthinkably hard for a small boy to come by in those days. Grandfather was our only hope.

In preparation for the desperate attempt upon his purse, we all three devoted the next week or so to attending him with great assiduity. We mowed his lawn. We weeded the vegetable patch. We suffered errands gladly. When but two days remained before the game, we decided the time had come. We washed our hands and brushed our hair, and since none of us coveted the honor of putting the momentous question, I plucked three timothy heads for the purpose of drawing lots.

"Shortest straw pulls the skunk's tail," I said. This was formula; no disrespect was intended.

John drew the short one, and, led by him, we went to face our grandfather. John opened cautiously, speaking of the importance of the coming event to Rochester and the Hop Bitters Club. "You know, Grandpa, our team's named for the medicine," he said brightly.

The old gentleman glanced at the mantel, where stood a dark-amber bottle containing the spirituous and inspiriting "Invalid's Friend & Hope."

"Why, yes," he said. "A superior restorative. Very comforting to the system," a sentiment shared by thousands of the old gentleman's fellow teetotalers.

"It's a dandy ball team," Reno gloated.

"I assume that you refer to its costume?" Grandfather said coldly. He did not countenance slang on our lips.

"Yes, sir," Reno agreed hastily. "You ought to see their uniforms."

"I am willing to believe that they present a macaroni appearance," the old gentleman said. "But what is the precise connection between this remedy and the projected contest?"

"Mr. Soule is giving the money for the club," John explained.

"Mr. Asa T. Soule? I was not aware that he had sportive proclivities."

"Oh, he's not really a sporting man," John hastened to disclaim. "No, sir! He—he's quite religious. Why, he won't have a player on his team who ever played on Sunday."

I saw that Grandfather, a strict Sabbatarian, was impressed. "They've got a rule against Sunday games in the National League," I said, opportunely recalling an item in the *Democrat & Chronicle*.

"Baseball is a very Christian game, sir," John added.

"I daresay, I daresay," the old gentleman conceded. "But it is not, by all accounts, what it was in my day. When I first came here, the Rochester Baseball Club met four afternoons a week. We had fifty members. That was in 1827."

"I play first base on the Livonia Young Eagles," Reno said eagerly. "Where did you play, sir?"

"In Mumford's pasture lot, off Lake Avenue."

"Reno means what position, Grandpa," I explained.

"Batter, for choice," said the old gentleman.

"You couldn't bat all the time," Reno demurred.

"No," Grandfather said. "But I preferred to. I frequently hit the ball over the fence."

"When your side was in the field, where did you play?" John asked.

"Wherever I thought the ball most likely to be batted, naturally," the alumnus of Mumford's pasture lot replied, manifestly annoyed at the stupidity of the question.

"That's a funny kind of a game," Reno muttered.

"I see nothing humorous in it," Grandfather retorted. "The cream of Rochester's Third Ward ruffleshirts participated in the pastime."

"Lots of the nicest boys in town go to baseball games now," I said hopefully.

"Well, well." Our grandfather's deep accents were benevolent. "I see no reason why you should not attend. You are old enough to go by yourselves, I suppose."

"It isn't that exactly, Grandpa," John said. "You see, sir—"

"It costs money to get in," Reno blurted.

"So I was informed by the person with the inflamed nose," said Grandfather dryly.

"Only fifty cents," John said with admirable casualness; then he added, "We thought, sir, that perhaps you would like to come along with us and see how they play it now, just for once."

There was a breathless pause. Then Grandfather said, "Fetch me the emergency cashbox from the desk."

Hardly able to believe our ears, we fell over one another to obey.

*   *   *

During the next forty-eight hours, John, Reno and I debated long and seriously as to whether we should brief Grandfather on modern baseball, which he was about to see for the first time. All of us were, of course, experts, although we had never seen a professional game. We knew the rules and the etiquette of the diamond and could have passed perfect examinations on the quality and record of every wearer of a Hop Bitters uniform. Reno and I were for giving Grandfather the benefit of our erudition, but John outargued us. Older generations, he pointed out, did not take kindly to instruction from younger.

"He'd just tell us that he played the game before we were born," he said.

On the great day, Grandfather and the three of us arrived early at Hop Bitters Park and found good places in the fifth row directly back of the plate. Before our enchanted eyes there stretched the greensward of the diamond, bounded by the base paths. It was close-cut, but the outfield was practically in a state of nature, its grass waving gently in the breeze. We had heard that the Buffalo manager had entered a protest against the outfield's unmown state, complaining that he had not brought his players all the way to Rochester to have them turned out to pasture.

The stand filled up promptly. There must have been as many as three hundred people present, mostly of the prosperous classes. Mr. Mudge, the undertaker, and Mr. Whittlesey, the Assistant Postmaster, took seats in front of us and were presently joined by Mr. Toogood, the Troup Street livery-stable man. Two clerks from Glenny's China Emporium crowded past us, while on the aisle side the manager of Reynolds Arcade took his place, accompanied by Professor Cook, the principal and terror of No. 3 School. Back of us sat a red-necked, hoarse-voiced canalman. Mr. Mudge addressed our grandfather.

"A pleasure and a surprise to see you here, Mr. Adams."

"The young must have their day," Grandfather replied amiably. "*Maxima debetur puero reverentia*, you know."

"Yes, sir; I don't doubt it for a minute," the liveryman said earnestly. "I hear those Buffalos are tough."

"We can lick 'em," I said loyally.

"Rochester boasted a superior club in my day, also," Grandfather said.

"Did you play on it, Mr. Adams?" inquired Professor Cook.

"I did, sir, for two seasons."

"I assume that the game as then played differs from the present form."

"You are justified in your assumption, sir," said Grandfather, who then entered upon an informative discourse regarding the baseball of 1827.

The play at Mumford's pasture lot, he set forth, was open to all fifty active members of the club. The pitchers, who were ex officio the captains, chose up sides. Twelve to a team was considered a convenient number, but there might be as many as fifteen. A full turnout of members would sometimes put three teams in the field. Mr. Mudge expressed the belief that this must result in overcrowding. Where did they all play?

Pitcher, catcher and baseman, Grandfather said, remained in their positions. The basemen

stood touching their bases with at least one foot until the ball was hit. The remainder of the out team formed a mobile defense, each man stationing himself where he foresaw the best opportunity of making catches. Mr. Toogood wished to know what the third team did while two were in the field. It waited, the veteran explained. At the close of each inning, when three batters had been put out—whether on flies, fouls, or by being touched or hit with the ball—the runs were totted up and the side with the lower score was supplanted by the third team. This continued until the hour agreed upon for stopping, which was usually sunset. Then the team with the largest total was adjudged the winner.

"Sounds like three-old-cat gone crazy," Reno muttered in my ear.

Further elucidation of the baseball of Grandfather's day was cut short by a shout of "Here they come!" as, amidst loyal clamor, the home team strode forth in neat gray uniforms, the name of the sponsoring nostrum scarlet across their breasts. They were a terrifically masculine lot, with bulging muscles and heavy whiskers. Eagerly we boys identified our special heroes, having often trailed them through the streets to the ball-park entrance. "That's Meyerle, the first base," John said. "He can jump six feet in the air and catch the ball with his left hand."

"The little, dumpy one is Burke," said Mr. Toogood. "He's shortstop. You oughta see him handle daisy-cutters! Oh, my!"

"McGunnigle, our right fielder, batted pretty near three hundred with Buffalo last year," Mr. Mudge told Grandfather proudly.

"Three hundred runs?" Grandfather asked with evident skepticism.

The reply was drowned by the loudest shout of all. "There he comes! Tinker! Tinker!" A hundred voices chorused, "What's the matter with Tinker!" and three hundred antiphonal howls responded, "HE'S ALL RIGHT!"

The canaller leaned over and spoke confidentially in Grandfather's ear. "You watch that fellow Tinker, Mister. If a high fly goes out to left field, he'll git under it and do the prettiest back flip ever you seen before he catches it. You wouldn't see nothing like that in the League. Used to be a circus man."

"I shall make it a point to observe him," Grandfather said.

Out came the enemy at a carefree trot. They were even more muscular-looking than our heroes and sported whiskers at least as luxuriant. They lined up near the plate, faced the stand, and saluted the crowd grimly, fingers to the peaks of their green caps. We boys joined lustily in the chorus of opprobrious hoots that was the response. A man in street clothes appeared and took a stand a yard behind the catcher, who stood five yards back of the plate.

"On which side does that person play?" Grandfather asked.

"He doesn't play," Mr. Mudge answered. "He's the umpire. He makes the decisions."

"In our game, we had no need of such intervention," Grandfather said. "If a point of dispute arose, the captains consulted and came to a composition."

"Suppose they disagreed?" Professor Cook suggested.

"Then, sir, they skied a copper for heads or tails and abode by arbitrament of the coin, like gentlemen and Corinthians," Grandfather replied. He turned his attention to the scene below. "Why is the tall man throwing the ball at the short man?" he inquired.

"That's our pitcher, Critchley, soopling his arm up," Mr. Toogood said.

Grandfather frowned. "That is *throwing*, not pitching," he said. "He should keep his arm down."

"He's only got to keep it as low as his waist," Reno said.

The old gentleman shook his head obstinately. "Knuckles should be below the knee, not the waist. A highly improper procedure."

The Hop Bitters team had now taken their positions and were standing, crouched forward, hands upon knees, in the classic posture. A burly Buffalo player stalked to the plate, rang his bat upon it, and described threatening arcs in the air.

"High ball," he barked at the umpire.

The umpire shouted to the pitcher, "The batsman calls for a high ball."

Grandfather addressed the universe. "What in Tophet is this?"

We boys were glad to enlighten him. "He wants a pitch between his shoulder and his belt," John said.

"If he'd called for a low ball, it'd have to be between his belt and his knee," Reno added.

"Do you mean to say that he can choose where the pitch is to come?" Grandfather asked incredulously.

"Yes, sir. And if it doesn't come there, it's a ball, and if he gets eight balls, he can take his base," I said.

"I should admire to bat in such circumstances," said Grandfather.

"Maybe it wouldn't be so easy," Reno said. "Critchley's got a jim-dandy curve."

"Curve?" asked the old gentleman. "What may that be?"

"Outcurve or incurve," Reno told him. "It starts like this, then it goes like this or like this—sorta bends in the air—and whiff! One strike!"

"Bends in the air!" An indulgent smile appeared on Grandfather's visage. "These young folk will accept any absurdity," he said to Professor Cook.

"Some do hold it to be an optical illusion," the principal said diplomatically.

"Certainly," Grandfather said. "Anything else would be contrary to the laws of God and nature. Let me hear no more of such fahdoodle," he concluded sternly, turning his back upon Reno.

The first inning was uneventful, as were the second and third. Pitcher Critchley's optical illusions and those of the opposing pitcher were uniformly and dully successful. Grandfather fidgeted and commented sharply upon the torpor of the proceedings.

"Lackadaisy-dido!" he said. "Why does not someone hit the ball?"

"A couple of goose eggs is nothing, Grandpa," John said. "Just let our team once get a start and you'll see."

The last of the fourth inning supplied a momentary stir. A high foul came down just in front of us, and the Buffalo catcher raced after it. The ball slithered from his outstretched fingers. We boys shrieked with delight. He glared at us and Grandfather addressed him kindly.

"Young man, that was ill-judged. You would have been well advised to wait and take it on the first bounce."

We held our collective breaths, but the wrath died out of the upturned face.

"Look, Mister," the catcher said, earnestly argumentative, "that ball was a twister. How'd I know where it would bound?"

The canaller back of us raised a jeering voice. "Butterfingers! Whyncha catch it in your cap?"

"You can't catch a ball in your cap any more," John said to the canaller. "It's in this year's rules."

"Back to the berm, fathead!" the catcher added.

The umpire walked up, lifting an authoritative hand. "No conversation between players and spectators," he snapped, and the game was resumed.

4

Later, there was a considerable delay when a foul sailed over the fence. Both teams went outside to search for the ball, and Grandfather took the occasion to expatiate upon the superiority of the old-time game.

"Our Saturdays," he said, "were very gala affairs. Ladies frequently attended and refreshments were served."

"Did you have uniforms, Grandpa?" I asked.

"Uniforms? We had no need of them. We removed our broadcoats, hitched our braces, and were prepared."

John said, "Our nine has militia caps with brass buttons."

"Fabricius Reynolds played catcher in a canaller's tall castor," Grandfather recalled. "It was of silky beaver, gray, with a picture of the *Myron Holley* passing through Lock Twenty-three painted on the front. Very bunkum."

"I've got a fifteen-cent Willow Wand with 'Home Run' on it in red letters," Reno said proudly.

"Hamlet Scrantom's bat was of polished black walnut with his initials on a silver plate," the old gentleman went on. "He was a notorious batsman."

The quest for the lost ball was eventually abandoned, Mr. Soule reluctantly tossed out a new one, the umpire called "Play ball, gents!" and the dull succession of runless innings continued. Then, in the opening half of the sixth, with two Buffalos out and two on base, a break came. A towering fly to left field brought a yelp of anticipatory delight from the admirers of the accomplished Tinker. Fleet of foot, he got beneath the ball while it was still high in air. His back flip was a model of grace and exactitude. Down came the ball into his cupped and ready hands—and broke through. Amid howls of dismay, he chased it, scooped it up, and threw it home. It went four feet above the catcher's reach, and the Buffalo runners galloped merrily in.

"Boggle-de-botch!" Grandfather exclaimed.

John plucked at his sleeve. "I want to go home," he said brokenly.

"Do not show yourself such a milksop," the old gentleman said. "How far is our own club behind?"

"Three runs," John groaned.

"And there's another," I added, almost in tears, as the Buffalo shortstop sent the ball over the left-field fence.

"Pooh!" said Grandfather. "Four runs is not an insuperable advantage. Why, I once saw Hamlet Scrantom bat in more than that at one stroke."

We stared at him. "How could he, Grandpa?" John asked. "Even if there were three men on base—"

"There were. I was one of them."

"—that would be only four runs."

"Seven, in this instance," the old gentleman said cheerfully. "Hamlet knocked the ball into a sumac thicket, and we continued to run the bases until it was found and returned."

From then on, the Hop Bitters were a sad spectacle. They stumbled and bumbled in the field, and at bat, as the embittered Reno said, they couldn't have hit a rotten punkin with the thill of a four-horse bob. On their side, the enemy fell upon Pitcher Critchley's offerings with dire effect. They dropped short flies over the basemen's heads. They slashed swift daisy-cutters through the impotent infield. They whacked out two-baggers and three-baggers with the nonchalance of assured victory. Grandfather assayed the situation.

"The Buffalos appear to have the faculty of placing their strokes where the Rochesters are not," he said sagely, a comment later paralleled by Willie Keeler's classic recipe, "Hit 'em where they ain't."

We boys and the Rochester rooters around us became silent with gloom. Only Grandfather maintained any show of interest in the proceedings. He produced a notebook from the pocket of his ceremonial Prince Albert coat and, during what was left of the game, wrote in it busily. We were too depressed even to be curious. It was a relief when the agony ended, with a pop fly to the pitcher.

"Three out, all out," the umpire announced. "The score is Buffalos eleven, Hop Bitters nothing. A game will be played in this park . . ."

But we had no heart in us to listen.

We went back to Grandfather's cottage, and over a consolatory pitcher of raspberry shrub in the sitting room he delivered his verdict.

"The game is not without merit," he said thoughtfully, "but I believe it to be susceptible of improvement."

❖   ❖   ❖

Surprisingly, the Hop Bitters nine beat both Worcester and Washington in the following fortnight. On the strength of their improvement, a return game with Buffalo was scheduled for August, and we boys resumed what Grandfather would have called our "officiousness" at Union Street; we were sedulous in offers to mow, to weed, to fetch and carry. On the last Saturday in July, when a less important game, with Syracuse, was on the card, we found the front door locked and our step-grandmother out back, tending her hollyhocks.

"Where's Grandpa?" I asked.

"You'd never guess," the old lady said with a twinkle.

"Gone canalling," John surmised.

"Mr. Adams is attending the baseball game, if you please," his wife said, "and no more thought of the fifty cents expense than if it was so many peppercorns. This is the second time since he took you boys. I do believe he has ideas."

Grandfather did, indeed, have ideas. We learned of them later. The notes made while the Buffalos were swamping the wretched Hop Bitters were the groundwork of a comprehensive plan which turned up among his papers after his death. It was a design for the betterment of baseball and was addressed to Mr. Soule, the Hop Bitters Baseball Club and the Citizens of Rochester, New York. A prologue, which still seems to me to have its points, introduced it.

The purport and intent of the game of baseball, as I apprehend, is to afford healthful exercise to the participants and harmless entertainment to the spectators. In its present apathetic and supine form it fulfills neither desideratum. A scant dozen runs for an afternoon's effort is a paltry result, indeed. I have seen twice that number achieved in a single inning when the game was in its prime. I therefore have the honor, sir, to lay before you a prospectus for the rejuvenescence of the pastime and its reclamation from the slough of inertia and monotony wherein it is engulfed as practiced in your ball park.

The plan provided for an extra shortstop between first and second bases and two additional outfielders to take care of long flies. But the really revolutionary proposal dealt with the pitching. The expert of Mumford's pasture lot approved of one innovation he had witnessed, the right of the batter to call his ball. But this did not go far enough. Grandfather's rule proscribed the pitcher from "any motion or pretense delusive of or intended to delude the eye of the batter."

"Such practice," he wrote, "savors of chicanery and is subversive of true, Corinthian sportsmanship." So much for curves!

Whether Mr. Soule ever received the memorial I don't know. Certainly he did not act upon it. A Rochester team took the field in the following spring with the usual complement of nine players and Grandfather never went to another ball game.

JOHN GALLAGHER

Courtesy *Sport* Magazine. ©

"Huh?—Oh, a happy Fourth of July doubleheader to you too, dear."

HERE IS a fascinating piece, so modern-sounding it might have been written yesterday. It appeared in *Baseball* magazine in the winter following the 1915 World Series (a Series which started the Phils off to baseball's worst World Series record; as of today, they have played in two World Series, lost them both; won one game, lost eight. Those eight were—and are—consecutive). But as time wore on, perhaps Old Pete felt a little less unhappy. After all, he did win thirty-one games during the 1915 season. He did pitch the Phils' only Series win. And eleven years afterward, he became known for all time not as a pitcher who lost a Series but as a pitcher who won one (see the James Harrison piece farther on in the book).

How I Lost the 1915 World Series

—————————— **GROVER CLEVELAND ALEXANDER** ——————————

THE WORLD SERIES was a disappointment to me. It was not so much the result, which went against my team, Philadelphia, but my own individual showing, which was so far from what I hoped it might be. Everyone knows by now that the Boston Red Sox beat us with four victories to our one, but I feel it might have been considerably different if I had lived up to expectation.

I have never yet given alibis and I am not going to begin now. But I would like to explain to my fans and friends why I think I failed in the series.

Let me begin with a day during the last month of the pennant race. It was Labor Day. We opened a crucial series with Brooklyn. The club was right on our heels and our manager Pat Moran and his boys felt, with good reason, that we must come out on the winning side of this encounter. I believe no one on our team even considered that we might not win a single contest. That is, of course, exactly what happened.

I was picked to pitch the opener. Moran depended a great deal upon winning that game. If we won, we'd have that one on ice and we'd be confident besides. It is my own feeling that Moran did not exaggerate the importance of winning that first game. I always feel that a visiting team should put its best foot forward. The home team has obvious advantages, and

it is important for a visiting manager to balance those advantages as soon as he possibly can.

Larry Cheney was on the mound for the Brooks. He was lately acquired from the Cubs, and I detected an unusual determination on his part to justify the move that had brought him from Chicago.

Brooklyn scored one run off me in the first inning. After that the game settled down into one of those contests where neither team will budge an inch and the pitcher must work his heart out. Cheney, while wild, as is natural with spitball pitchers, was invincible. We could not make a single hit off him for six innings. In the seventh, he strained himself and was obliged to leave the box. It was then that our boys fell on the opposition and drove in three runs.

We began the eighth with a two-run lead. Moran felt that the game was won. I hoped it was myself when Jake Daubert went out on the first ball pitched. But then something happened. I have never been able to understand it, but in some way I strained my shoulder and the muscles in my back. I have the misfortune of getting a blister on my middle finger from throwing the ball. I remember I had a blister on that finger Labor Day, and it bothered me considerably. The ball player doesn't pay much attention to minor injuries, but try as he will a twirler can hardly get normal results from his pitching hand when his fingers are sore. I know that I unconsciously tried to humor that blistered finger. In doing so I brought the muscles of my shoulder into play in an unusual manner. Pitching a fast ball to the next man up, I strained my shoulder. I immediately felt it, and I couldn't seem to control the ball so well. When I put forth all my strength and tried to get the ball over the plate, it would go outside. When I cut down a little on the stuff I was serving up, the Brooklyn batters would hit me.

I remember that I overheard a loud-voiced rooter in the stand when that inning began. The Brooklyn crowd seemed discouraged when we piled up those three runs. This particular rooter yelled out: "Never mind, boys. Go at Alexander. He's human like the rest of us."

He was certainly right. I felt human enough when they started to pound me around the lot. And I felt extremely human when at the end of that inning they had scored five runs off my delivery and snatched away a game that I had considered as good as won.

It was a bitter blow to Moran—and that Brooklyn series never got any better. We lost all three games. The third defeat ended in an accident to our first-string catcher, Reindeer Bill Killefer. My own thoughts as to the prospects for the pennant were gloomy. I worked my best with Killefer. He understood me and knew how to handle my peculiarities. However, on that score my pessimism was unnecessary. Ed Burns, Killefer's replacement, did a fine job through the closing laps of the pennant race.

I didn't tell Moran that I wrenched my shoulder during the Labor Day game. I knew he had enough on his mind without thinking about me. I was lucky enough to pitch a one-hit game against the Braves that clinched the pennant. That gave me, momentarily, the feeling that the shoulder might not disrupt me through the most important games of my career—the World Series.

It has never been my disposition to worry about things, but if there was one time in my whole life when I wanted to be in best pitching form it was for those World Series games. I would willingly have given my share of the receipts to have been able to pitch my team to a championship of the world. That is my answer to the oft-repeated suggestion that we ball players think only of the money that there is in the game.

The papers, unconsciously no doubt, added to the burden of my position. Many pitchers can work in great form when nothing in particular is at stake but crumple badly in a pinch. I do not believe I have ever faltered when I was asked to carry a heavy load, but it is human nature to feel responsibilities and to be weighted down by them. The papers spoke of Christy Mathewson and what he did in the famous series of 1905 (Matty pitched three shutouts). They said he won the series singlehanded. Some of my friends were good enough to predict equal success for me.

It is a fine thing to have friends who are confident in you, but I may say the responsibility of pitching in the World Series is enough in itself without the added consideration of living up to high expectations.

They said I was nervous in the first game. All right, I was. They hit me pretty hard, but that didn't worry me. There was a time when I used to burn up all my stuff on every ball pitched, but the pitcher grows wiser as he grows older. The fact that Boston was hitting me didn't worry me as long as I was able to keep the hits well scattered. What worried me most was the fact that our boys didn't seem to be able to hit Ernie Shore as much as the Red Sox were hitting me. At that, they only put their hits together in a single inning. They scored one run. However, I must admit in fairness that Shore had very hard luck and the breaks went badly against him. We won, 3-1.

The pitcher knows when he is not right. It is a miserable experience to know you are not at your best when you are facing a pennant winner and the world's championship is at stake.

That thought came to me with overwhelming force in the first contest, and I had to fight against it all through the series. Perhaps I allowed too much for it. As I look back upon the series now, I can criticize myself because at times I was too careful, too exact, too conscious of myself. When I am at my best I can get the ball to break as I want it to, instinctively, with little effort. And I can get my fast ball to sweep across the plate just where I tell it to go. The pitcher can always work best when he has to use the least thought and care. The more he tries to supplement tired muscles or aching joints by mental effort, the more he loses the edge he may have had on the opposition. I tried to foresee every contingency, to guard against every accident, because I was not right. Had I been in my best form, I would have given those things scarcely a second thought. I would have pitched the best I could and trusted the ability of my fielders.

Again, the pitcher in a World Series game has none of the assurance that he may have during the season. In the short series he has to do whatever he is going to do then or never at all. If a slip occurs it is too late to change it. He has one or two, or at the most three chances to deliver, and if he fails it is too late. During the season if he loses a game or two successive games it doesn't matter so much. He feels that he will have time later on to redeem himself and comforts himself with the thought that the best of them can't win all the time.

In my second game, and the game that was destined to be my last, I had hoped I might feel in perfect shape. It was the third game of the series. Boston had taken the second game 2-1.

We got off to an early lead with a run in the third, but Boston came back with a score in the fourth. From the fourth until the ninth Dutch Leonard and I were knotted in a pitcher's duel. I think I was pitching better than I did in the first game, but as fate would have it Leonard was pitching even better.

The crucial point for me came in the last of the ninth. With the potential winning run on base I elected to pitch to Duffy Lewis. My critics contend that I should have elected to pass Lewis, a .291 hitter in the regular season, and pitched instead to Larry Gardner, who had a season's mark in the neighborhood of .250. That thought occurred to me, too, but I decided to pitch to Lewis for several reasons. In the first place, he had been going great guns in the series, and I figured the percentages were bound to catch up with him. Besides, I had faced him in twelve games in a previous All-Star tour, and he had made only two hits off me. On one occasion I had struck him out four straight times. Furthermore, I estimated Gardner as a far more dangerous man in a pinch.

All my reasons notwithstanding, I was wrong. It was Lewis' hit that won the game. However, had I passed Lewis and Gardner hit me safely, I'm sure these same critics would have leveled the same complaint. The ball player becomes accustomed to the second guess, in which the press writer seems to find a delight.

I have no desire to take anything away from the reputation of Duffy Lewis. He had a wonderful series. But regardless of the results, I still feel that I was right in pitching to him. It may have been the most disastrous decision of my career, but even in defeat my reason compels me to stick by it.

After my loss in the third game, I know our team felt down and out. That depression may very well have made the difference in the score of the fourth game, which Boston won, 2-1. It was Ernie Shore who won that one for Boston. It is an interesting note that he gave us seven hits in this game, which he won, compared to the five hits he gave us in the first game, which he lost.

Behind three games to one, our hopes were all but shattered. A great deal has been written about the fifth game. I was slated to pitch and, in fact, intended to pitch up till the last moment. I never wanted to pitch a game so much in my life. How I would have loved to beat Boston in that fifth game and put us back in the series!

But I knew when I started to warm up that I wasn't right. Once again I had to make a decision. I had to choose between my own instinctive desire to pitch and my knowledge that I was in no condition to properly represent my team. I decided to tell Moran how I felt. I must give him credit for taking this information without any great demonstration of disappointment.

"If you are not right, Alex," he said, "the rest of us will have to carry it."

Moran expressed a fine sentiment, but unfortunately it didn't work out so well. It was Mr. Lewis again who was our nemesis. He belted a lusty home run into the bleachers and Harry Hooper put the game on ice with his second home run of the contest. Again, it was a game decided in the ninth inning and Boston won, 5-4.

I do not wish to disparage the work of our pitchers, Jim Mayer and Jeptha Rixey. They did a fine job. Had the fates of the game been kinder in the ninth, they would have gained a deserved victory. But be that as it may, as long as I live I will always wonder how I might have fared had I pitched that fatal fifth game of the '15 series.

I shall always think of this series as a great personal disappointment. I was unable to live up to the expectations of my friends, and I didn't come through for my team. No matter what anyone else may say, I know the reason I lost the 1915 World Series was that I **was not** in the proper physical condition to **give it my** best.

LONGEVITY in ballplayers is a thing to be admired, and occasionally it moves fans to lyric heights. Of the famous Adrian ("Cap" or "Pop") Anson, Lee Allen wrote that he was "a man who once seemed destined to play the game forever." As Anson started his twenty-seventh season of big-league play in 1897, "an admiring fan signing himself Hyder Ali penned a long verse that appeared in *The Sporting News*." Two of its stanzas follow.

How Old Is Anson?

HYDER ALI

How old is Anson? No one knows.
I saw him playing when a kid,
When I was wearing still short clothes,
And so my father's father did;
The oldest veterans of them all
As kids, saw Anson play baseball.

How old is Anson? Ask the stars
That glisten in the hair of night
When day has drawn her golden bars
To shut the sunbeams from our sight;
The stars were present at his birth—
Were first to welcome him to earth.

LEE ALLEN of Cincinnati is, I think without doubt, baseball's foremost historian, and his book *The Hot Stove League* is from first to last, again I believe, one of the two or three most enjoyable in the literature of the game. Where else can we learn, for example, that in 1903 the Cincinnati *Enquirer* decided to give professional advice to drunk batsmen? The advice was:

Whenever a ball looks like this:

O

O

O

Take a chance on the middle one.

Or for that matter, L. H. Addington's limerick:

The Dodgers have Del Bissonette,
No meal has he ever missed yet;
The question that rises
Is one that surprises,
Who paid for all Del Bissonette?

Well, enough. Go buy the book. Here is one of its chapters:

A Letter to Mrs. Gilligan

LEE ALLEN

ALTHOUGH BRANCH RICKEY, the learned chief executive of the Pittsburgh Pirates, has a deserved reputation for manipulating the English language to suit his purposes, it is doubtful that he will ever achieve the heights of rhetoric reached by James (Orator Jim) O'Rourke, the player who caught an entire game for the New York Giants at the age of fifty-two in 1904. O'Rourke was one of the first clubhouse lawyers, and his command of the English tongue was astonishing and bizarre.

When an outfielder named Louis Sockalexis, a Penobscot Indian, signed a contract containing a clause that forbade drinking, O'Rourke read about it, then turned to a friend and said, "I see that Sockalexis must forgo frescoing his tonsils with the cardinal brush; it is so nominated in the contract of the aborigine."

On another occasion, when Orator Jim was a manager, one of his players, John Peters, asked for a ten-dollar advance. "I am sorry," O'Rourke replied sympathetically, "but the exigencies of the occasion and the condition of our exchequer will not permit anything of the sort at this period of our existence. Subsequent developments in the field of finance may remove the present gloom and we may emerge into a condition where we may see fit to reply in the affirmative to your exceedingly modest request." Understandably, Peters did not try again.

The most remarkable document attesting to O'Rourke's powers appeared in the New York *Sporting Times*, a short-lived journal of the trade, in its issue of November 23, 1890. It seems that a widow named Gilligan who lived in Bridgeport, the Orator's home town, heard a disturbance in the barn where she kept a calf. Not knowing that the intruder was a lion which had just escaped from Barnum's winter headquarters, she rushed into the fray with a pitchfork, routing the beast. The newspapers then made her a sensation. O'Rourke, reading about her feat and overcome with admiration, wrote her as follows:

DEAR MRS. GILLIGAN:

The unparalleled bravery shown by you, and the unwavering fidelity extended by you to your calf during your precarious environment in the cowshed, when a ferocious, carnivorous beast threatened your total destruction, has suddenly exalted your fair name to an altitude much higher than the Egyptian pyramids, where hieroglyphics and other undecipherable mementos of the past are now lying in a state of innocuous desuetude, with no enlightened modern scholar able to exemplify their disentangled pronunciation. The exuberance of my verbosity is as natural as the chrysanthemums exhibited at the late horticultural exhibition, so in reality it cannot be called ostentation, even though the sesquipedalian passages may seem unintelligible to an untutored personality. The lion—or it may have been a lioness—but you, of course, in the impending predicament could only make a cursory and rather unsatisfactory investigation— must have discerned your courageous eye (a trait so characteristic of the Celtic Micks and Biddys), which shows, beyond peradventure, that you are possessed of undeniable hypnotical mesmerization qualities, as well as the diabolical intricacies of legerdemain and therapeutics. We should arise, Phoenix-like, and show our appreciation of your unswerving loyalty. We should extol your bravery to the coming generation in words more lofty than my unprepared efforts can faithfully depict, for your name hereafter will be synonymous with fearlessness in all that the word can unconsciously imply. Standing before a wild, unrestrained pitcher with a mellifluous and unconquerable courageousness is as of nothing compared with the indomitable fortitude exhibited by you when destruction seemed inevitable—when pandemonium rent the oxygenic atmosphere asunder with the tragic vociferation of Barnum's untamed and inhospitable intruder. A thousand blessings to you!

Yours admiringly,
James O'Rourke

Take it away, Mr. Rickey!

Ballplayers differ widely in temperament but are more apt to be laconic than verbose, and there are few O'Rourkes in the profession. Two of the quietest performers of all time were Clyde Barnhart, an outfielder, and Charles (Whitey) Glazner, a pitcher, who roomed together at Pittsburgh from 1920 to 1923. Barnhart never talked at all and Glazner was hard of hearing. One night Johnny Morrison, a pitcher whose name still bobs up in Hot Stove League circles because of his amazing curve ball, visited their room. Only once during his stay was there any attempt at conversation at all. Barnhart opened his mouth to ask the time, but the question was never answered because Whitey failed to hear him.

Charlie Gehringer, the great second baseman of the Tigers, and Elon Hogsett, an Indian pitcher at Detroit, formed another taciturn pair. Like Barnhart and Glazner they roomed together. One morning Hal Walker, a writer for the Toronto *Globe* and *Mail*, had breakfast with them. Hogsett turned to Gehringer and said, "Pass the salt, please." Gehringer obliged, but said in reproach, "You might have pointed."

The stupidity of certain players was acknowledged long before Ring Lardner painted his classic pictures of bushers, alibi artists, boneheads and bores. Pete Browning, a favorite in Louisville and one of the greatest hitters of the 1880s, is supposed to have said, upon hearing of the assassination of James A. Garfield, "Yeah? What league was he in?"

Lardner's creations, by the way, were not at all exaggerated. He is believed to have received the inspiration for one of his more pleasant characters, the busher, after watching Butcher Boy Joe Benz pitch an exhibition game for the White Sox while wearing hip boots. But just as the automobile has helped destroy baseball interest in some sections of the country it has helped destroy provincialism, and the rookie that Lardner knew so well, the kid with his badger haircut and straw suitcase, has disappeared from the scene. The cultural level of players has been raised greatly in the past thirty years. Today's businessman-ballplayer is at ease before the television cameras and in the dining rooms of the snootiest hotels. He buys stocks and bonds and sends his children to private schools. There are still a few who confine their reading to comic books and box scores but their number is decreasing, and it will be a sad day for the game when they disappear entirely because they supply the few splotches of color in the fabric of a game that sometimes approaches the monotony of near-perfection.

Almost every anecdote about the illiteracy of players dates back to the period before World War I when Lardner was using his genius to describe the genus. Shoeless Joe Jackson, greatest of natural hitters and one of the unfortunates who became involved in the Black

Sox scandal of 1919, had little or no education and the fact that he could not spell was known to the galleries. Once, after Joe had delivered a resounding triple and was perched on third base, a fan shouted from the grandstand, "Heh, Joe. Spell 'cat.'" Jackson glared at him, squirted a stream of tobacco juice out the side of his mouth and retorted, "Spell 'hit.'"

But long before Jackson certain players were celebrated for their lack of formal learning. William (Blondie) Purcell, a pitcher and outfielder, was a popular member of the first Phillies team in the National League in 1883. One night he was invited to a party at the home of an affluent admirer and arrived late. "Why, hello there, Blondie," his hostess greeted him. "Do come right in; we're having tableaux." "I know," Blondie replied. "I smelt 'em when I come in."

Connie Mack, who witnessed players of every variety in his unparalleled career, once conducted a clubhouse meeting in which he carefully went over the batting weaknesses of every opposing player. After he finished, a rookie rose to his feet and said, "Mr. Mack, there's one fellow you forgot; this man Totals. I looked at the box score and seen that he got four hits yesterday."

Quite similar is the story, probably apocryphal, about the National League outfielder who could neither read nor write. Each morning he used to sit in the hotel lobby and have other players read the box score to him. One morning he listened patiently while a mate read the box score of one game in its entirety, even the summary, and concluded by saying, "Time of game, one fifty-three. Umpires, Messrs. Klem and Emslie." Hearing this, the rookie jumped to his feet, shouting, "Don't tell me that Messrs. is in this league! He umpired in the Southern League last year and he was terrible!"

But perhaps the most ridiculous of all these stories is the one involving Heinie Zimmerman, who played second and third for the Cubs and Giants from 1907 through 1919. Zim, so the story goes, was limbering up at third one day in Chicago during batting practice. A boy who worked on the pass gate approached him and said, "Heinie, there's a guy out there from Rockford, Illinois, named Kelly who wants you to leave a pass for him."

"Never heard of him," Heinie grunted. "The hell with him."

But in a few minutes the boy was back. "Heinie, this guy says you will remember him all right. Name's Kelly, from Rockford."

"Look," Heinie insisted. "I don't know any Kelly from Rockford. Now, go away."

When the boy returned the third time, he was almost in tears. "Please, Heinie," he begged. "Help me out. This guy swears he knows you. He said for me to ask you about that hotel episode in Rockford."

"Now I know he's a four-flusher," Zim sneered. "I know Rockford like a book and there ain't no Hotel Episode there."

There is apparently no connection between formal education and success on the diamond, although native intelligence is a great asset. But Moe Berg, the most erudite player the game has ever seen, had a batting average that persisted at the .250 level. Berg is a graduate of Princeton, the Columbia Law School and Sorbonne. He speaks English, Latin, Greek, French, Italian, German, Spanish, some Russian, Japanese, Hebrew and Sanskrit. His thesis on Sanskrit is a valuable work of reference at the Library of Congress.

But when Moe was catching for Washington, the player on the team he most admired was Dave Harris, a hard-hitting outfielder whose schooling had stopped somewhere in the vicinity of the seventh grade. "There's a fellow who really had the pitchers licked," Berg once told Shirley Povich of the Washington *Post*. "He wasn't burdened with too much imagination; he'd just step up there and take a beautiful cut. He used to rib me about my own batting average and say I was too smart to be a good hitter. He may have been right because I liked to try to guess with the pitcher. Once Harris hit a home run and I followed him to the plate. 'Moe, you go on and try your best,' he told me, 'but don't forget, none of them seven languages you know is gonna help you.'"

The best players, educated or otherwise, seem to be those who concentrate completely on the job at hand and who believe absolutely that they can control the outcome of the game. They take baseball seriously and do not exhibit such indifference as was shown by Frank Woodward, a pitcher on the Phillies in 1918. A writer once stopped in the Phillies' clubhouse and asked Woodward, "Who's going to work today?" Frank, who was scheduled to pitch that day, replied, "Who's gonna work? Me and the outfielders."

Woodward may have been an irresponsible kid but he was not lacking in imagination. Two years after leaving the Phillies he found himself a member of the Cardinals in training at Brownsville, Texas. One evening he wanted to go to the movies but did not have the price of admission. After thinking over his problem at some length, he finally strolled down to the theater, sought out the manager and said, "I was sent here by Branch Rickey. Mr. Rickey has called a meeting of the players and he wants all those who are here at the movies to go back to the hotel right away."

This information was immediately flashed on the screen, and the players filed out. Watching the proceedings from under a tree across the street, Woodward waited until a decent interval had passed, then walked back to the theater and said to the ticket-taker, "Meeting's over. Now to watch the rest of the picture."

There is no way you can safely generalize about the personalities of players. They can be as verbose as Jim O'Rourke, as quiet as Charlie Gehringer, as ignorant as the Lardner prototype or as erudite as Moe Berg. There are players from the mountains of Tennessee and West Virginia who are as suspicious as moonshiners. There are the college boys with the crew haircuts who collect swing records. There are the Oklahomans, bronzed by the sun, who look older than their years. Club owners have long claimed that baseball, absorbing all these men, is a great social leveler, that it is democracy in action. The claim is not without merit. Charlie Devens was a pitcher who joined the Yankees in 1932. He had attended Groton and Harvard, where he had been a member of the Hasty Pudding Club. His mother was a Vanderbilt. But when he reported to the big stadium across the Harlem, he found that his new team's greatest star, Babe Ruth, was an alumnus of a different institution, a graduate of the St. Mary's Industrial School, a semireform school at Baltimore, Class of '14.

Rookies are supposed to be brash and confident. When Billy Gleason, a young second baseman on the 1921 Browns, was asked the distance between home plate and second base, he quipped, "I don't know. I never ran that way." Such answers are given to cover up any insecurity the player might feel.

Ernie Sulik certainly did not indicate that he felt insecure when he reported to the Phillies as a young outfielder in 1936. In his first game he was called upon to face Dizzy Dean, who was then at the height of his pitching fame with the Cardinals. In his first time at bat Sulik looked at three blistering strikes, tossed his bat away and muttered, "That guy ain't shown me much." When his fellows on the bench looked at him in amazement, he confided, "Just watch me when I go to bat again; I'll hit that ball between the outfielders." Strange to say, that is exactly what he did, splashing a triple into right center. "How is it you looked at those three strikes the first time up?" Ernie was asked after the game. "I wanted to see what Dean had," he explained. "That's how I knew he didn't have anything."

One of the few players who ever achieved more than average success despite the lack of confidence was Emerson (Pink) Hawley, a pitcher from Beaver Dam, Wisconsin, who won 182 major league games in a decade starting in 1892. Hawley was in constant need of reassurance. One day, when he was pitching for St. Louis, he called time and motioned to his catcher, Heinie Peitz, to join him in a conference. "Heinie," he said. "Do you like to catch me?" Peitz was so astonished he had to grope for words, and when he was finally able to mumble that there was nothing he would rather do than catch Pink Hawley, the pitcher seemed reassured and went back to the job of throwing at the hitters.

Charles (Chief) Zimmer was a National League catcher who owned a cigar store and one day, in the dead of winter, Hawley strolled in, walked up to Zimmer and said, "Chief, will you forgive me?" "Certainly," replied the Chief, not having the slightest notion of what Pink was talking about, as the two players, in years of acquaintance, had never had cross words.

Early during the following season Zimmer came up to bat in a game against Hawley, who was leading in the late innings, 12 to 0, and just toying with the opposition. "Chief, what's your batting average?" Hawley asked.

"Oh, about .214 I guess," Zimmer admitted.

"Well, boost it a little," Pink said, and when the next pitch was down the middle Zimmer connected for a home run and his team's only score.

Ballplayers simply do not follow any pattern of personality. It is even possible to find some who are genuinely modest. Eddie Moore, for instance. Eddie was an infielder with the Pirates, and during the season of 1924 a Pittsburgh paper hired him to write his daily impressions of the games. He refused to use a ghost. One day, after winning a 3 to 2 contest by delivering a late-inning home run, Moore did not refer to the feat or even mention his name in the copy. On the other hand, shortly after the Phillies had released a pitcher named Pete Sivess to Milwaukee, a Philadelphia baseball writer received a wire that read, "Please send Milwaukee papers full sketch of Pete Sivess and send pictures." The message was signed by Pete Sivess.

There are even players with a romantic

streak. Ed Kenna was a pitcher with the Athletics in 1902. The son of John E. Kenna, a United States Senator from Virginia, he attended West Virginia University and became a hero of sorts when he kicked three field goals in a football game against Grove City. He was a fair pitcher, but his heart really was not in the game, for his principal interest in life was in poetry. They called him the "Pitching Poet" and he could be found scribbling verses in the clubhouse before and after games. Here is a sample of his wares taken from his published book of verse, *Lyrics of the Hills,* written while he was employed to pitch at Wheeling, West Virginia:

Fall time in the country, when the
  Sunshine filters down
The tangled maze of cloudland
  And through the beeches brown;
In the golden rays it scatters
  On the dear, old dirty sod
I can trace in wondrous letters
  The mystic word of God
And the goodness of the master,
  Who willed that it should be—
Oh, the olden, golden autumn
  Is the best of times for me.

Play ball!

CHON DAY

LADIES

It is difficult to categorize this small vignette, which is from *Hello Towns*, a collection of editorials that Sherwood Anderson wrote for two Virginia weeklies. The following is from an editorial that, according to Anderson's biographer James Schevill, concerned a visit Anderson made to a photographer who secretly wanted to be a professional baseball player.

From *Small Town Note*

SHERWOOD ANDERSON

HE DID NOT know I was coming. . . . The man was in his house alone and had become in fancy a ball player. I saw what happened through a window. The man was squatting, with his hands on his knees, in the living room of his house. He had become a shortstop and was all alert. I dare say some one like Babe Ruth was at bat. When the man had gone to the cities to see the professionals play he had noted how the infielders kept talking to each other.

"Now, Ed. Careful now, Ed. Watch him, Ed!" I heard the photographer cry. He spoke sharply to the pitcher. "Get it over the plate, Bill!" he cried.

It was evident the batter had made a hit. I saw him dash across the room for second base. He had knocked over a chair on the way, but he did not care. He had made the play.

I saw him receive the ball and throw to first. There was an intent look in his eyes. Would the ball get to first ahead of the runner? It did. "Ah," I heard him sigh with relief.

It goes without saying that I went away and returned on the next day to see him about taking the photographs we wanted.

NERVOUS HABIT

Now THAT you have read the Hyder Ali poem on page 10—the one that asks "How Old Is Anson?"—let us hear from Anson himself. This was in Anson's postplaying days. The slogan at the top of the letter, and the letter itself, tell the rest of the story.

A Letter to Joseph A. Whitacre

ADRIAN C. ANSON

"A Better Actor Than Any Ball Player, A Better Ball Player Than Any Actor."

CAPT. ADRIAN C. ANSON
"THE GRAND OLD MAN OF BASE BALL"

PERMANENT ADDRESS
320 EAST THIRTIETH STREET
CHICAGO

JOSEPH A. WHITACRE
MARSHALLTOWN, IOWA

MY DEAR SIR

I am in receipt of your letter of July 29th, 1912, and consider it an honor to have you ask for my autograph. Inclosed you will find the autograph and I will mail you a photograph later. I have had some correspondence with G. Walter Thompson in regard to booking me at the Colonial Theater but he does not think he can pay my price (One hundred dollars for four days.) I suggested that he raise the price to fifteen cents and give me the five cents per head. I would like to have your judgment if you think I could do as well by taking the five cents per head. I would like very well to play my home town and feel that my good old friends and base ball fans would turn out and root for me. Would the Times Republican boost my game? If I make up my mind that my old friends would like to see me in my new line I would be tempted to come, but I must be reasonably sure of good houses as I can not play to empty benches. Yours truly

ADRIAN C. ANSON.

John Barrington's popular sports column, *Fair or Foul*, never was more wrong—nor, at the same time, more horrifyingly close to being right—than in this topical moment (July 22, 1957). For "Doc's" reaction, see Howard L. Katzander's story farther on.

See, Doc, It's Like This

JOHN BARRINGTON

I've never been on the couch before, Doc, but this dream I had—well, it's sort of got me going, and maybe you can tell me what it all means.

You see, Doc, it was like this. There were these two distinguished-looking gentlemen in this office, pretty plush layout, too. One of them, Ford, seemed to have been out of touch for awhile, and he was getting a briefing on the baseball situation from his assistant, Charley.

"So the Dodgers and Giants moved to the West Coast, eh, Charley?" said Ford. "I remember, the newspaper fellows asked me about it at the All-Star Game, but I told them I didn't know any more than they did."

"Well, not exactly, sir," replied Charley. "The Dodgers went to Los Angeles, all right, but after all that talk about San Francisco, the Giants finally stopped in Minneapolis. They're called the Millers, now."

"But then . . . you mean New York—our biggest city—doesn't have National League ball any more?"

"Oh, sure. The Cincinnati Redlegs moved in."

"But Cincinnati . . . that's the cradle of professional baseball. Cincinnati not in the majors any more? That's indecent, that's what."

"Yes, sir. That's what people said. So the Washington Senators shifted over there."

"But, Charley, you mean the nation's capital doesn't have a team? After all, the national pastime and all that."

"Oh, that's taken care of. The Indians weren't doing so well in Cleveland, so they're in Washington now."

"Charley, that's too bad. About the Indians, I mean. Why, I remember when Bill Veeck had the club in Cleveland. The other owners didn't like some of the things he did, but he sure packed the fans in."

"Yes, I know, and Bill's back there now. He bought the Chicago Cubs and moved 'em to Cleveland."

Ford shook his head numbly. "All these changes . . . but about the Giants. You say they're in Minneapolis and called the Millers, but I'm sure I read about the San Francisco Giants . . ."

"Well, yes, but that's the Tokyo Giants, or used to be. San Francisco got sore about not getting a franchise, so it imported a club. Lefty O'Doul, the man in the green suit, is managing it."

"But wait. That makes too many clubs. Surely there aren't nine teams in one league?"

"No, the Giants are replacing the Yankees. The State Department sent the Yankees on a world-wide good-will tour."

"But . . . but . . . but who's in Yankee Stadium? Billy Graham?"

"Oh, no, the Yankees moved in their farm club. You know, the Athletics. They've got a deal like the Dodgers had with Jersey City. Play seven home games in Kansas City and the rest at Yankee Stadium."

Well, Doc, that's it. I know it's only a dream, but, Doc . . .

FRENCH-BORN Jacques Barzun, the distinguished historian, puts it very simply: "Whoever wants to know the heart and mind of America had better learn baseball . . ."

From *God's Country and Mine*

JACQUES BARZUN

PEOPLE WHO CARE less for gentility manage things better. They don't bother to leave the arid city but spend their surplus there on pastimes they can enjoy without feeling cramped. They follow boxing and wrestling, burlesque and vaudeville (when available), professional football and hockey. Above all, they thrill in unison with their fellow men the country over by watching baseball. The gods decree a heavyweight match only once in a while and a national election only every four years, but there is a World Series with every revolution of the earth around the sun. And in between, what varied pleasure long drawn out!

Whoever wants to know the heart and mind of America had better learn baseball, the rules and realities of the game—and do it by watching first some high-school or small-town teams. The big-league games are too fast for the beginner and the newspapers don't help. To read them with profit you have to know a language that comes easy only after philosophy has taught you to judge practice. Here is scholarship that takes effort on the part of the outsider, but it is so bred into the native that it never becomes a dreary round of technicalities. The wonderful purging of the passions that we all experienced in the fall of '51, the despair groaned out over the fate of the Dodgers, from whom the league pennant was snatched at the last minute, give us some idea of what Greek tragedy was like. Baseball *is* Greek in being national, heroic, and broken up in the rivalries of city-states.

And that it fitly expresses the powers of the nation's mind and body is a merit separate from the glory of being the most active, agile, varied, articulate, and brainy of all group games. It is of and for our century. Tennis belongs to the individualistic past—a hero, or at most a pair of friends or lovers, against the world. The idea of baseball is a team, an outfit, a section, a gang, a union, a cell, a commando—in short, a twentieth-century setup of opposite numbers.

Baseball takes its mystic nine and scatters them wide. A kind of individualism thereby returns, but it is limited—eternal vigilance is the price of victory. Just because they're far apart, the outfield can't dream or play she-loves-me-not with daisies. The infield is like a steel net held in the hands of the catcher. He is the psychologist and historian for the staff—or else his signals will give the opposition hits. The value of his headpiece is shown by the ironmongery worn to protect it. The pitcher, on the other hand, is the wayward man of genius, whom others will direct. They will expect nothing from him but virtuosity. He is surrounded no doubt by mere talent, unless one excepts that transplanted acrobat, the shortstop. What a brilliant invention is his role despite its exposure to ludicrous lapses! One man to each base, and then the free lance, the trouble-shooter, the movable feast for the eyes, whose motion animates the whole foreground.

The rules keep pace with this imaginative creation so rich in allusions to real life. How excellent, for instance, that a foul tip muffed by the catcher gives the batter another chance. It is the recognition of Chance that knows no argument. But on the other hand, how just that the third strike must not be dropped. This points to the fact that near the end of any struggle, life asks for more than is needful in order to clinch success. A victory has to be won, not snatched. We find also our American innocence in calling "World Series" the annual games between the winners in each big league. The world doesn't know or care and couldn't compete if it wanted to, but since it's us children having fun, why, the world is our stage. I said baseball was Greek. Is there not a poetic symbol in the new meaning—our meaning—of "Ruth hits Homer"?

Once the crack of the bat has sent the ball skimmering toward second, between the infielder's legs, six men converge or distend their defense to keep the runner from advancing along the prescribed path. The ball is not the center of interest as in those vulgar predatory games like football, basketball, or polo. Man running is the force to be contained. His getting to first or second base starts a capitalization dreadful to think of: every hit pushes him on. Bases full and a homer make four runs, while the defenders, helpless without the magic power of the ball lying over the fence, cry out their anguish and dig up the sod with their spikes.

But fate is controlled by the rules. Opportunity swings from one side to the other because innings alternate quickly, keep up spirit in the players, interest in the beholders. So does the profusion of different acts to be performed —pitching, throwing, catching, batting, running, stealing, sliding, signaling. Hits are similarly varied. Flies, Texas Leaguers, grounders, baseline fouls—praise God the human neck is a universal joint! And there is no set pace. Under the hot sun, the minutes creep as a deliberate pitcher tries his drops and curves for three strikes called, or conversely walks a threatening batter. But the batter is not invariably a tailor's dummy. In a hundredth of a second there may be a hissing rocket down right field, a cloud of dust over first base—the bleachers all a-yell—a double play, and the other side up to bat.

Accuracy and speed, the practiced eye and hefty arm, the mind to take in and readjust to the unexpected, the possession of more than one talent and the willingness to work in harness without special orders—these are the American virtues that shine in baseball. There has never been a good player who was dumb. Beef and bulk and mere endurance count for little, judgment and daring for much. Baseball is among group games played with a ball what fencing is to games of combat. But being spread out, baseball has something sociable and friendly about it that I especially love. It is graphic and choreographic. The ball is not shuttling in a confined space, as in tennis. Nor does baseball go to the other extreme of solitary whanging and counting stopped on the brink of pointlessness, like golf. Baseball is a kind of collective chess with arms and legs in full play under sunlight.

The team is elegance itself in its striped knee breeches and loose shirts, colored stockings and peaked caps. Except for brief moments of sliding, you can see them all in one eyeful, unlike the muddy hecatombs of football. To watch a football game is to be in prolonged neurotic doubt as to what you're seeing. It's more like an emergency happening at a distance than a game. I don't wonder the spectators take to drink. Who has ever seen a baseball fan drinking within the meaning of the act? He wants all his senses sharp and clear, his eyesight above all. He gulps down soda pop, which is a harmless way of replenishing his energy by the ingestion of sugar diluted in water and colored pink.

Happy the man in the bleachers. He is enjoying the spectacle that the gods on Olympus contrived only with difficulty when they sent Helen to Troy and picked their teams. And the gods missed the fun of doing this by catching a bat near the narrow end and measuring hand over hand for first pick. In Troy, New York, the game scheduled for 2 P.M. will break no bones, yet it will be a real fight between Southpaw Dick and Red Larsen. For those whom civilized play doesn't fully satisfy, there will be provided a scapegoat in a blue suit—the umpire, yell-proof and even-handed as justice, which he demonstrates with outstretched arms when calling "Safe!"

And the next day in the paper: learned comment, statistical summaries, and the verbal imagery of meta-euphoric experts. In the face of so much joy, one can only ask, Were you there when Dogface Joe parked the pellet beyond the pale?

Now, FRIENDS, for a quick major-league history of that most improbable event—the unassisted triple play. You ever see one?

All by Themselves

BASEBALL DIGEST

WORLD SERIES

Bill Wambsganss, 2 B.   Cleveland vs. Brooklyn, Oct. 10 1920

• In the fifth inning of the fifth game, Wamby took Clarence Mitchell's line drive, stepped on second to retire Pete Kilduff and then wheeled around and tagged Otto Miller coming on from first base.

LEAGUE PLAY

Neal Ball, SS.   Cleveland vs. Boston, July 19   1909

• In the second inning of the first game of a double-header, Ball speared Amby McConnell's liner, came down on second base to retire Heinie Wagner and then tagged Jake Stahl as he came into second base from first.

George Burns, 1 B.   Boston vs. Cleveland, Sept. 14   1923

• In the second inning, Burns caught Frank Brower's line drive, reached out and tagged Walter Lutzke, who had been on first, and then dashed to second base and slid into the bag before Joe Stephenson, who had broken from second to third, could return.

Ernie Padgett, SS.   Boston N. L. vs. Phila., Oct. 6   1923

• Padgett, a rookie, snared a line drive off Walter Holke's bat in the fourth inning of the second game, tagged second base to double Cotton Tierney, who had been there, and then tagged Cliff Lee coming on from first base.

Glenn Wright, SS.   Pittsburgh vs. St. Louis, May 7   1925

• In the ninth inning Wright took Jim Bottomley's line drive, touched second, retiring Jim Cooney, who had started for third, and then tagged Rogers Hornsby, who was on his way from first to second.

Jim Cooney, SS.   Chicago vs. Pittsburgh, May 30   1927

• In the fourth inning of the morning holiday game, Cooney caught Paul Waner's liner, stepped on second to double Lloyd Waner and then tagged Clyde Barnhart, coming on from first base.

Johnny Neun, 1 B.   Detroit vs. Cleveland, May 31   1927

• With runners on first and second in the ninth inning, Neun took Homer Summa's liner and tagged first to retire Charlie Jamieson. Looking up, Neun saw Glenn Myatt close to third and, ignoring the cries of Shortstop Jackie Tavener for the ball, decided to run him down, tagging Myatt before he could return to second base.

JIMMY HATLO

THEY'll DO IT EVERY TIME

For the greatest finish in All-Star Game annals, we take you to Detroit and—

The 1941 All-Star Game

BASEBALL HEROES MAGAZINE

There were 54,675 persons packed into Detroit's Briggs Stadium for the ninth annual All-Star game. They were American League rooters and they had come to see the established clouters like Hank Greenberg and Joe DiMaggio. But they also wanted a long look at the latest sensation of the league, a lean, nervous 22-year-old hitter named Ted Williams. Ted had come up with a hot bat from Minneapolis during the 1939 season and the major-league pitchers were still looking for some way to cool it off. Going into the midseason classic, Williams was hitting .405 and was hitting with fearful consistency.

Manager Del Baker named Bob Feller as his starting pitcher and he was opposed by Brooklyn's Whitlow Wyatt. For the first three innings the pitchers were in complete control but the American Leaguers managed to get a run off big Paul Derringer in the fourth and take the lead. Then Arky Vaughan, the Pittsburgh infielder, got hot and slammed two homers to put the National League in front, 5-2, by the top of the eighth. Williams had driven in the American League's second run with a double in the sixth inning.

With Claude Passeau, a crafty Chicago Cubs pitcher, coming in to hold the lead in the last of the eighth, the American Leaguers strained mightily but could come up with only one run. Passeau avoided serious trouble by getting Williams on a called third strike. Edgar Smith was able to hold the National League scoreless in the top of the ninth and the American League came up for its last inning, still two runs in arrears.

The first man to face Passeau went out and, with the pitcher due to bat next, Cleveland's Ken Keltner was sent up as a pinch hitter. He managed to scratch a single off shortstop Eddie Miller. Cecil Travis was the next batter and the Washington third baseman waited out a base on balls, sending Keltner to second.

That brought up Joe DiMaggio and he smashed a scorching grass-cutter at Eddie Miller as the crowd moaned, sensing a double play. Miller deftly scooped the ball to second base, forcing Travis, but the relay to first baseman Frank McCormick pulled him off the bag and DiMaggio was safe.

Now it was up to Williams, with two men on and two out. He went through his patented little ritual as he stepped into the batter's box: scuffing a little depression with his left foot; bouncing on the balls of both feet; twitching his neck and shoulders and squeezing the handle of his slender bat until his knuckles turned white. Then he was ready.

The first pitch was in and Ted swung, fouling it off. The next two were wide and Williams refused to bite. The next one was a fast ball around the knees and the wonderful reflexes suddenly came alive as the bat flashed at the last possible instant and sent a towering drive to right field that was a home run from the crack of the bat.

With an ear-to-ear grin, Williams leaped into the air and clapped his hands like a little boy before sheepishly trotting around the bases. The crowd roared and loved "The Kid." Not so defeated manager Bill McKechnie. "Ted," he muttered later in the jammed locker room, "you're just not human."

THE FOLLOWING appeared in the January 1926 issue of *Baseball*.

Guess Who?

BASEBALL MAGAZINE

Though sticks and stones his bones may crack
And bottles inundate his back,
The harshest names
From men and dames
Won't jar his self-possession.

Though folks all call him "Jesse James"
And "crook" and "yegg" and such like names,
And say he's blind,
He doesn't mind.
Now, what is his profession?

JOHN GALLAGHER

Courtesy *Sport* Magazine. ©

. . . "And furthermore, that pitch wasn't even near the strike zone . . ."

IN THE FIRST *Fireside Book of Baseball* there appeared the famous Ernest Thayer poem "Casey at the Bat," and it was classified as poetry, of course. This one here we classify as spot reporting, which it is. Done by a Pulitzer Prize winner, too—Mr. Berger of *The New York Times*.

1941: Casey in the Box

MEYER BERGER

The prospects seemed all rosy for the Dodger nine that day.
Four to three the score stood, with one man left to play.
And so when Sturm died, and Rolfe the Red went out,
In the tall weeds of Canarsie you could hear the Dodgers' shout.

A measly few got up to go as screaming rent the air. The rest
Were held deep-rooted by Fear's gnaw eternal at the human breast.
They thought with only Henrich, Hugh Casey had a cinch.
They could depend on Casey when things stood at the pinch.

There was ease in Casey's manner as he stood there in the box.
There was pride in Casey's bearing, from his cap down to his sox.
And when, responding to the cheers, he took up his trousers' sag,
No stranger in the crowd could doubt, he had them in the bag.

Sixty thousand eyes were on him when Casey toed the dirt.
Thirty thousand tongues applauded as he rubbed his Dodger shirt.
Then while the writhing Henrich stood aswaying at the hip,
Contempt gleamed high in Casey's eye. A sneer curled Casey's lip.

And now the leather-covered sphere came hurtling through the air,
And Henrich stood awaiting it, with pale and frightened stare.
Close by the trembling Henrich the ball unheeded sped.
"He don't like my style," said Casey. "Strike One!" the umpire said.

From the benches black with people there went up a muffled roar,
Like the thunder of dark storm waves on the Coney Island shore.
"Get him! Get him, Casey!" shouted someone in the stand.
Hugh Casey smiled with confidence. Hugh Casey raised his hand.

With a smile of kindly charity Great Casey's visage shone.
He stilled the Faithful's screaming. He bade the game go on.
He caught Mickey Owen's signal. Once more the spheroid flew,
But Henrich still ignored it. The umpire bawled, "Strike Two!"

"Yay!" screamed the maddened thousands, and the echo answered, "YAY!"
But another smile from Casey. He held them under sway.
They saw his strong jaws tighten. They saw his muscles strain,
And they knew that Hughie Casey would get his man again.

Pale as the lily Henrich's lips; his teeth were
clenched in hate.
He pounded with cruel violence his bat upon
the plate.
And now Great Casey held the ball, and now
he let it go.
And Brooklyn's air was shattered by the whiff
of Henrich's blow.

But Mickey Owen missed this strike. The ball
rolled far behind,
And Henrich speeded to first base, like Clipper
on the wind.
Upon the stricken multitude grim melancholy
perched.
Dark disbelief bowed Hughie's head. It seemed
as if he lurched.

DiMaggio got a single. Keller sent one to the
wall.
Two runs came pounding o'er the dish and oh,
this wasn't all.
For Dickey walked and Gordon a resounding
double smashed.
And Dodger fans were sickened. And Dodger
hopes were hashed.

Oh somewhere North of Harlem the sun is
shining bright.
Bands are playing in The Bronx and up there
hearts are light.
In Hunts Point men are laughing, on the Con-
course children shout.
But there is no joy in Flatbush. Fate had
knocked their Casey out.

THE boy had a moment of glory. So did his dad. This is from the Boston *Globe* of October 9, 1948.

Pitcher's Pa

———————— **ROGER BIRTWELL** ————————

A BIG MAN in a brown overcoat sat quietly in a crowd of 70,000 here yesterday and saw the dream he'd sacrificed his career for come true.

Twenty-seven years ago this autumn, the man in the brown overcoat had faced a golden chance. He was a youngster of 25, and he had just been sold by Fort Worth to the Pittsburgh Pirates. After years of struggling in the bushes, his chance to be a big-leaguer had come.

But he turned it down—in order to work for $2.78 a day as a brakeman on the Missouri Pacific railroad.

For baseball offered a hazardous, uncertain future. It might find him jobless at 35. And he had other things to consider. There was his wife. Also there was a tiny golden-haired girl and a scrawny little boy named Gene.

Yesterday that scrawny little boy—now a decorated war hero with plates of aluminum in his knee and skull—took the mound in Cleveland's Municipal Stadium and shut out the Boston Braves in the third game of the World Series.

It was the boy's eighth straight victory in a series of pitching performances that included a stretch drive for a pennant, a playoff for the American League championship and the World Series.

And, in his last 38 innings of pitching, the boy had allowed only one earned run.

The big man in the brown overcoat, Henry Bearden, 62, came down to the Cleveland dressing room after the game. Quietly, with just a suspicion of tears in his eyes, he shook hands with his son. Then while the son was taking a shower, the man reviewed his own, and his son's career.

He told of his three years as a catcher for Fort Worth in the Texas League, of his weigh-ing the Pittsburgh chance and turning it down, of his six-day week as a brakeman at $16.68 per week.

But he spoke more glowingly of his son. He told how he used to take Gene out in the back yard at Memphis and have the boy pitch to him.

"But Gene never pitched as a youngster. He was tall, left-handed and a good hitter," Henry Bearden said, "so he became a first baseman. I didn't make him a first baseman. He just took to it naturally because he had the qualifications.

"Gene played first base all through high school. He was a good football player too. He was All-City end."

He spoke of the time he spent $50 to send Gene, then near the end of his high-school days, to a baseball school in Little Rock, Ark.

It was then that the father and Ross Williams, head of the baseball school and brother of Dibrell Williams, one-time shortstop of the Philadelphia Athletics, talked Gene into becoming a pitcher.

"I thought he had the stuff and I knew he had the control," the father said, "but it wasn't until he picked up his knuckleball under Casey Stengel at Oakland, after the war, that he really arrived."

It was at that point that the reporter asked Mr. Bearden for his first name.

"Henry," he said.

"I suppose they called you Hank," the reporter remarked.

"No," said Mr. Bearden, who must weigh at least 235 pounds, "they used to call me 'Slim.' I was—then."

"How did the railroading career work out?" the reporter inquired.

The man who had gone to work at $2.78 a

day proudly drew his railroad pass from his pocket. It was made out in the name of Henry Bearden, general yard superintendent of the Missouri Pacific at Poplar Bluff, Mo.

"That worked out all right, too," he said.

Then the son came out from the shower bath and—rubbing a towel back and forth over his shoulders—stood beside his father.

Just then a sturdy middle-aged man shouldered his way through the milling crowd of reporters, photographers, ballplayers and Cleveland fans.

"How do you do, you old rubber-arm," exclaimed the new arrival, grabbing the younger Bearden by the hand. "You are a truly wonderful pitcher."

Then the man walked away.

Gene Bearden looked after him, curiously.

"Who was that fellow?" he asked.

"Bill Killefer," someone explained.

"Who's he?" inquired Gene Bearden.

It was Tris Speaker who answered.

"He's the man who caught Grover Cleveland Alexander."

JOHN GALLAGHER

Courtesy *Sport* Magazine. ©

"Toughest manager in the league."

WHAT do those ladies do who wander out to the ball park during the early stages of spring training and just sit there watching? What do they talk about? Jim Bishop, author of *The Day Lincoln Was Shot* and *The Day Christ Died*, decided to find out. He found out.

Miss Wattles

JIM BISHOP

SHE TALKED. I nodded. We sat in the morning sun at Phoenix Stadium and I could listen and still watch Dusty Rhodes miss two pitches and slam the next one through second so hard that he almost tore an infielder's arm off.

She was pleasant and pretty, and the wattles were just beginning to show on her neck. Her eyes looked sun-squinted even in the shade.

She could talk. She never saw a play. The hair was dark and it lifted slightly every time she turned her head. The tone was sincere and she told me how often she went to church. She had been married once, but it was all over. Men are no good, even the best of them.

Her slim curving brows were about 5 feet from the spiked heels. In between were a size-10 dress and two strands of choker pearls.

Willie Mays leaned against the batter's cage and said, "I gotta hit. Somebody gotta let me hit," and Hank Sauer said, "Well, get in there and hit."

Her trouble, she said, was that she was too goodhearted. A soft touch. The hands were long and bony and the blue veins made little forks in the skin. If she hadn't been so good to everybody, she wouldn't be such a nervous wreck now.

Everybody took advantage of her. Take Dot. Dot had been her girl friend for oh, maybe 15 years. They had more on each other than a pair of bank robbers.

Dot, she told me, was a wonderful girl. She had looks and figure and she came from a fine family. But drink? Brother! You know how mixed up a girl can get when she's confused.

Dot was born confused. She liked men but the men she liked always turned out to be married three months later. Then she would start drinking and it was up to our Miss Wattles to wring her out. Goodhearted? Too much so, she said, if you don't mind me saying it.

"One time I gave her $80 because the bank threatened to throw her in jail for writing checks."

Another time she wanted to move out of a hotel but they held her luggage until Miss Wattles gave her $120. Always a touch. Always a desperate touch. And always Dot said she was about to begin a new life.

The kid, Peter Burnside, was pitching and he had that nice even poetry of the arm, and the ball came in like a blur.

This new-life routine almost drove Miss Wattles crazy, she said. Over the years, Dot fell into her arms many times, always weeping, always promising, always borrowing money, always meeting a new man.

She asked if she was boring me, and, without looking away from Burnside, I said no. She talked on and on, pulling the hem down a half-inch, fingering the watch, wringing the hands, brushing away an imaginary fleck of hair.

The last time Dot asked for $50, Miss Wattles gave it and said it was final. Dot said I'm no good. Miss Wattles said oh yes you are, you're going to start a new life. The tears came to Dot's eyes and she said I will I will. This time I will.

My companion lowered her voice a little. The words were still flowing, but the tone was low and the lips kept peeling away from the snowy teeth. Dot went out and blew the $50 on a new dress. Miss Wattles heard about it and became angry.

She phoned Dot just to let her know that she knew.

"You and your new life," she said. "Well, I hope the dress does you a lot of good. Wear it in health, kid. Just don't bother me any more, no matter what happens. From now on, you're on your own."

Then she went to bed in good conscience. She was a good woman. A faint flush of pink stood over the Superstition Mountains when the police tapped on the door. Did she know Dot? Yes, she did.

Well, the cops said, Dot had just killed herself and had left a note for Miss Wattles.

She opened it and the hands shook.

"I told you," it said, "that I could start a new life."

VIRGIL PARTCH

Courtesy *True, The Man's Magazine.* ©

The TITLE to this article just about says it all.

Bugs

CLEM BODDINGTON

THE WORD "pitcher" has two entirely different meanings. This may account for some
of the confusion in the short, moist life of
Arthur Lawrence Raymond. As a baseball
pitcher in the early 1900s, Raymond was a performer of near-legendary accomplishment. He
could throw a spit ball at three different speeds,
something not even the renowned Spittin' Ed
Walsh of the Chicago White Sox could do.
But as an eager consumer whenever liquid refreshment was poured from pitcher, bottle or
vat, Raymond also could get himself thrown
out of saloons at three different speeds. There
is no record that Walsh could do that, either.

Raymond was known to the outer world, in
the simplest of terms, as "Bugs." The nickname was intended to mean just what you
think, but it dismayed its wearer. Though occasionally he walked to and from the pitcher's
mound on his hands, and once was seen traveling comatose through the streets of Charleston, South Carolina, in a wheelbarrow piloted
by the bemused manager of the Charleston Sea
Gulls, Raymond exhibited a marked distaste
for eccentric behavior.

Once, when news reached him that fellow
pitcher Rube Waddell was permitting small
boys to jump up and down on his chest in a
demonstration of physical strength, Bugs
opined that Waddell was only trying to lure
attention away from the forthcoming Gotch-
Hackenschmidt wrestling match. "He's just a
crazy show-off," Raymond said.

On another occasion, when Raymond was
with the New York Giants, he heard that a
trade was brewing that would bring Cincinnati's big, fun-loving catcher, John Bannerman
McLean, to the New York club. "I wouldn't if
I were you," Raymond advised Giant Manager
John J. McGraw. "McLean's nuts."

The advices that Raymond and McGraw exchanged are among some of the most famous

utterances in baseball archives. The relationship of the carefree pitcher, whose method of
arguing with umpires was to shake with helpless laughter, and the Napoleonic McGraw,
whose determination to thwart Bugs's affinity
for the grape rose to missionary heights,
evolved in a series of brilliant skirmishes, with
tactical triumphs on both sides.

For one season McGraw held the upper
hand, with the result that his tall right-hander
won 18 games, but Raymond's inventive nature
could not be long suppressed. He had an un-
earthly capability for smuggling alcohol into
the ball park despite McGraw's elaborately
mapped defenses. For a time, Raymond's technique was to toss baseballs over the fence from
the bull pen, in return for which eager con-
federates supplied the needed beverage. Mc-
Graw then placed a ring of guards around the
park, blocking all gates, only to find Raymond
happily lowering an empty bucket containing
money from the outer window of the clubhouse, with an agent, stealthily crouched on
the sidewalk below, ready to fill the bucket
with beer. In final desperation, McGraw deprived the pitcher of money, sending his salary
check direct to Raymond's wife. The technique
worked only until it was Raymond's next turn
to pitch, an assignment which Bugs declined.

"If my wife gets the money," he told Mc-
Graw, "let *her* pitch."

Leaving no stone unturned, McGraw even
hired a private detective to shadow Raymond
and steer him away from cocktail lounges.
When Raymond learned of this, he was indignant to the point of quitting the team for a
few days. He changed his mind, however, upon
meeting the shamus, a gentleman named Fuller.
"He's a nice fellow," Raymond told McGraw
as he returned voluntarily from his self-imposed exile. "He needs the work." Happily, on
bar-room occasions that followed, Raymond

would introduce the private eye to friends and acquaintances. "This is my keeper," Bugs would say. "I'm full but he's Fuller." Mr. Fuller seemed something less than grateful to Raymond for giving him what amounted in likelihood to a lifetime job. Their companionship ended one day when Fuller punched Raymond in the eye. Bewildered at such treatment, Raymond went to the ball park to complain to McGraw, who then promptly punched him in the other eye.

It is not inaccurate to state, as indeed this narrative has so far suggested, that McGraw went to fantastic lengths to master the ingenious Mr. Raymond. The iron-fisted manager even took his players off the American Plan at the hotel where they stayed during spring training one year. He had heard that Bugs not only was drinking the cocktails that automatically came with everybody's meal, but was loitering after dessert to scoop up the tips his teammates left and buy more cocktails.

From McGraw's evangelistic dedication, it can be assumed that Mr. Raymond must have been a pretty good pitcher, worth saving. He was.

A 21-year-old Chicago sandlotter in 1903, Raymond earned a trial with the Waterloo team of the Iowa State League. He won 19, lost only seven, and the following season was signed by the Atlanta Crackers of the Southern Association. It was here that the first signs of his indubitably convivial nature began to assert themselves. The result was that despite a good season, he was not retained for service with the Crackers in 1906, but he found manager Wilson Matthews of the lowly Savannah team in the South Atlantic League ready to take on almost any kind of talent in an attempt to bolster the fortunes of his slumping Club.

"Sign me up," Raymond told him.

"You have a reputation," Matthews responded, a little sadly. "I know you can pitch, but . . ."

"Not only can I pitch," Raymond interrupted. "I shall pitch Savannah to the pennant."

It was this statement that earned Raymond the nickname of Bugs. The cognomen clung to him from then on, even though, true to his word, Raymond won 18 games and Savannah won the pennant.

The following season, the hypnotized Mr. Matthews became manager at Charleston and brought Raymond along with him. The pitcher felt constrained to establish social contacts in the aristocratic old Southern city and did not show up at the ball park until the season was a week old. When he finally did take the mound, he hurled a winning shutout. Ten days later he had already won five games of seven pitched, including two shutouts. By June 4, his assortment of pitching weapons, by no means limited to the spit ball alone, but including a splendid fast ball and an estimable curve, had recorded 17 triumphs. He pitched and won the first game of a July 4 double-header, a morning-afternoon affair that enabled Raymond to relax with a group of railroaders in the friendly surroundings of a saloon during the noon hour. The railroad men, strong in their admiration of the great pitcher, plied him with cheese, unripe bananas and tankards of beer. They then bethought themselves of the hour, guided the amiable Raymond to the door, pointed him in the direction of the ball park and let him go. Raymond arrived at the stadium in time to pitch a perfect no-hit, no-run game in the afternoon half of the double-header.

Delighted and awed by this performance, Manager Matthews threw his arms around the tall, lanky pitcher. "Take a couple of days off, Bugs," he said. "You've earned a rest." Something in the listening Raymond's expression gave the manager momentary pause. "However," he amended, tapping Raymond significantly on the lettering of his baseball shirt, "I want to see this uniform sitting on the bench three days from now."

"You will," Raymond swore. He was true to his word. Three days later Raymond's uniform *was* sitting on the bench. Raymond, to be sure, was not in it. He had met, under the customary circumstances, a traveling salesman from his native Chicago, who bemoaned the dull life he led and confided to Raymond that he had always wanted to be a ballplayer.

This seemed to Raymond a most suitable ambition, and he undertook to help his new friend by outfitting him with his own uniform and dispatching him to the ball park.

Raymond stayed behind in mufti to entertain the customers of the saloon by standing on a chair and delivering a learned discourse, with gestures, on the subject of umpires. One of the gestures brought Raymond's pitching hand in contact with the rotating blades of an electric fan. Three days later, with hand encased in bandage and his salesman friend having failed in his tryout, Raymond donned his uniform and pitched and won an 11-inning four-hitter. His record on the year was 35 victories, enough to provide Charleston with the pennant and earn for the ace pitcher a major-league berth.

Raymond's pitching achievements with the St. Louis Cardinals in 1908 were notable. He tossed a brilliant one-hitter against the Cubs, coming up with an added delivery—an underhanded slow ball, no less—to be blended in his assortment of pitches.

One sports writer had this to say:

"Arthur 'Bugs' Raymond is a wonder. When he is well supported he can pitch as great ball as anyone in the National League. He has everything a pitcher could wish for. There are those who declare that without his spit ball he would be a failure. Just to convince the public that he does not rely solely on it, he mixes up a puzzling assortment of curves, fast and slow balls. His slow ball is most deceiving. His curve sometimes starts back of his collar and then, at others, down near his shoe tops."

Another observer wrote:

"Raymond can usually win any time his team gives him two runs to work on. He brims with confidence and at times actually lets the opposing batters know what kind of ball he would throw, then dares them to hit it. He seldom kicks at umpires, preferring to chuckle at what he considers an umpire's mistake. This humiliates the umpire more than if Bugs were to curse him."

Having won 15 games for a last-place club, Raymond at season's end took himself to his favorite watering place in St. Louis, a bar and grill named The Bucket of Blood, where a reporter sought to interview him as to his plans for the winter.

"I am in doubt," Raymond said to the newspaperman. "I may either run a locomotive for the Great Northern Railroad or become a newspaperman."

Raymond's destiny, however, took a less visionary turn with the news that he had been traded to the Giants. His reputation preceded him, but Manager McGraw was flushed with pride at having been able to control Mike Donlin, another extreme individualist, and he volunteered he could do the same for Raymond.

The discipline began early—in spring training of the following season, in fact, when McGraw forced Raymond to pitch the full nine innings of an exhibition game as a form of punishment for what one writer described as "undue liberties with liquids." The experience dulled neither Raymond's thirst nor his confidence. Arriving in New York, he announced to sports writers that he would defeat the Bostons in his first encounter with them or "never moisten a ball again." He beat Boston, 5 to 3, and, thus encouraged, he issued subsequent pronouncements which did not delight opposition clubs. In one game, he was felled by a duster pitch while at bat, causing one reporter to write archly:

"Bugs Raymond was downed by one high ball. This unprecedented incident occurred while the Giants were playing the St. Louis Cardinals. The disgrace was deeply felt by Mr. Raymond, although he absorbed this particular high ball behind his left ear instead of through his usual channel. After he was resuscitated, Mr. Raymond described the effect as similar to the absorption of his usual high balls, but quicker. St. Louis pitcher Bachman served."

The Giants finished third in 1909, with Raymond having won 18 games, but he was slipping away from McGraw. Word reached the fiery manager that Raymond, lunching at a New York tavern, had been asked by a waiter to demonstrate how he threw his spitter. Eager to oblige, Bugs arose from his chair and gripped a glass tumbler. "Follow me closely," said he to his taut audience. "I wet these two fingers like so." Then, with appropriate windup, he threw the glass through a window. "Notice," he murmured, as he sat down again, "the break."

McGraw's fears were further enlarged by events of the spring training trip the following year. Bugs's tolerance for alcohol made itself so manifest that at one stopover, McGraw angrily ordered the pitcher off the team. Raymond went quietly, but returned two hours later and ran around the outfield ten times to demonstrate his excellent physical state.

It was then that McGraw hit upon the idea of withholding funds from Raymond as a means of regulating the pitcher's buying power. At one port of call, McGraw even insisted on buying Raymond a suit of clothes rather than trusting him to spend the money on his own. The manager learned later that Raymond had returned the suit to the store, exchanged it for a cheaper one and invested the cash difference in drink. Angrily, McGraw cut off all funds and warned the other Giants against lending any money to the thirsty right-hander. Raymond met this new challenge by writing out free passes to Giant exhibition games as the team toured northward and giving them to bartenders in exchange for sustenance. The passes were spurious, of course, but legend states that there was not a bartender between Marlin, Texas, and New York who did not get turned away at the ball-park gates that spring. By the time the club reached home, orders from McGraw had reached the sweeping point of denying Raymond even an unopened package of cigarettes.

But not even the watchfulness of Mr. Fuller, the private detective, was a match for Raymond's thirst. As a final move, before the 1911 season, the Giant management arranged for Bugs to take a cure for alcoholism. The effects of the cure lasted only until June of that year, when he finally was suspended by McGraw. Writing in the New York *Telegram*, John B. Foster said:

"At least the New York National League Baseball Club, through its owner and manager, can take credit for trying to make a man out of Arthur Raymond.

"He got through the season this year as far as the middle of June before he was suspended. There has been a great deal of sympathy for Raymond in some channels of baseball and little in others. His ability is unquestioned. When he began to play baseball as a young man, he had $50,000 in his right arm. Had he taken strict care of himself he would have been one of the best pitchers in the history of the major leagues.

"It was the desire of John T. Brush (owner of the Giants) that Raymond be sent to Dwight, Ill., in the winter of 1910 to see if it were not possible to cure him of what is considered to be a disease as well as a misfortune.

"Raymond took the treatment and for a time behaved admirably. The change in his physical appearance and his general deportment was noticeable, but Raymond, throughout the various cities of the United States, had cultivated an acquaintanceship with many who called him friend. Their mistaken ideas of friendship were to put temptation in his path rather than to keep him away from it. From pitching good ball he began to pitch uncertainly, without the assurance that he had in

the early part of the season, and was foolish enough to believe that he could conceal from others the cause of his retrogression."

Raymond subsequently drifted into semipro baseball. Early in 1912 he wired McGraw, seeking one last chance. The Giant manager wired back:

"I have my own troubles."

Bugs returned to his native Chicago, there to sign with the local club in the outlawed United States League, which in turn folded within two months.

In early September, Raymond emerged, the worse for grog, from a South Side saloon. His feet, remembering perhaps what his mind no longer remembered, carried him the few blocks to that same sandlot ball field where nine years before he had caught the eye of a professional scout. There, a neighborhood sandlot game was in progress. Feelings among the onlookers, small in number though they were, ran high. Someone picked up a broken piece of pottery and threw it through the air. It struck Raymond in the face. A young man, standing a few feet away from Raymond, laughed out loud. Bugs Raymond turned on him.

He did not win the fight. He wound up on the ground, trying to shield his head as his adversary kicked at him.

Moaning, he finally was led away to the small hotel where he was staying.

Six days later, he was found dead in his hotel room. At the coroner's inquest it was reported that he had died of a cerebral hemorrhage, caused in turn by a fractured skull.

Pallbearers at Raymond's funeral were his former teammates from the disbanded Chicago team of the United States League. Pete Noonan, who had caught for pitcher Raymond in a happier day, said: "Bugs paid too much, too soon, for too many drinks."

It was indeed too much too soon. Raymond was 30 when he died.

PHRASES LIKE "Old Reliable," to describe ballplayers, usually are invented by newspapermen. But the men in the game themselves applied this one phrase to just one player: Tommy Henrich. This article appeared in 1949, when the Yankees, despite something like seventy different injuries, won the pennant on the last day of the season. If I may be permitted a personal reminiscence, it was that year that I took my wife to her first big-league game, early in the season, at Comiskey Park in Chicago. The White Sox were hot, and they were playing the Yankees. I told my wife, "In the seventh inning, Henrich will hit a homer and the Yanks will win." In the seventh inning, Henrich hit a homer and the Yanks won. As for this article's reference to the "lately incapacitated" Joe DiMaggio, see Dan Daniel's piece elsewhere in this collection.

Old Reliable

RICHARD O. BOYER

WHEN THOMAS DAVID HENRICH, left-handed right fielder and reserve first baseman for the New York Yankees, went on a hunting trip the week before Pearl Harbor, he was not an exceptional marksman, but, in his own words, "I saw two deer, fired two shots, and killed two deer." The animals were such handsome creatures that when Henrich came upon their prostrate bodies, he contritely resolved that whatever wildlife he might shoot in the future he would shoot with no weapon more lethal than a motion-picture camera. To date, he has kept that resolve to the extent of not shooting anything with anything, but he plans to accompany some friends to Maine on a hunting trip next fall, and may well return with some footage of color film of game instead of a head and antlers. It is in keeping with Tommy Henrich's character that when the precise moment came to nail the deer, he did so expertly and with dispatch, just as it is that in renouncing guns in favor of cameras he chose the quieter, less showy way of doing things. Throughout his career in baseball, he has conducted himself in much the same manner. Now thirty-three years old and beginning his thirteenth season under contract to the Yankees, he is, except for the lately incapacitated Joe DiMaggio, the most valuable player on the team, as well as the highest-paid (which is not necessarily the same thing), yet

few people who don't follow the game would be likely to recognize his name. Henrich is conscientious and hard-working, and he possesses an unusual grasp of the technical aspects of his trade, but, whether on the field or off, he has little of the flair for showmanship that made the names of men like Hornsby, Cobb, and Ruth familiar to even those indifferent to baseball. His exploits, rarely spectacular, are confined mostly to good, solid work on the ball field, and he cuts few, if any, capers. Sportswriters, who delight in coining titles like Sultan of Swat and Brown Bomber for their heroes, long ago despaired of making a colorful figure out of Henrich and, with a tired sigh, nicknamed him Old Reliable, to which they occasionally add, with what is perhaps, for once, unconscious alliteration on their part, "the baseball players' ballplayer."

When the Yankees' regular first baseman suffered a protracted batting slump last summer, Henrich uncomplainingly took over the position and played it competently from mid-season on, although he is really happy only when playing in the outfield. If the team should fail to develop an adequate first baseman this year, he may be obliged to take over again, but he hopes not. He regards himself as a right fielder and thinks like one. In that position, his primary job is, of course, to catch or retrieve all balls that are hit into his territory. He worries a great deal about such things as wind currents, shadows, sun glare, the condition of the ground, which if overly dry can make a ball hop crazily and if wet can cause it to plop quickly to a standstill, and about cigarette haze, which sometimes drifts out of the stands behind the plate to form a mist against which it is difficult to see either ball or batter. Henrich maintains that mental condition is as important to a player as physical condition. A big-league outfielder, he points out, must know, among a good many other things, how to play the walls in all eight ball parks the teams of his league compete in; that is, in order to be in the right place at the right moment, he must know the angles, different in each park, at which batted balls will carom off the outfield walls. During a game, Henrich applies himself so earnestly to matters of this nature, as he stares intently all the while at the batter, some three hundred feet distant, that he seldom hears the roar of the crowd and is only dimly conscious of the great encircling blur of faces peering from grandstand and bleachers. "I'm listening for the crack of that bat," he says. "You got to get the jump on the ball. You got to get started to where it's going as soon as it leaves the bat."

Other players often admiringly call Henrich the smartest outfielder in the big leagues. They also admire him for certain respectable, steady-going, burgherlike qualities, which are more highly regarded in professional baseball than in many other sports. Ever since the Black Sox scandal of 1919, when the World Series was deliberately lost by some Chicago players for the benefit of a ring of professional gamblers, organized baseball has made a studied effort to appear and to be virtuous. As a general rule, even poker playing is forbidden the ballplayers. Because of his zeal for rectitude, Henrich is particularly valued by his employers, who like to present him as an exhibit of clean living for the inspiration of American youth. His contract stipulates not only that he shall receive forty thousand dollars for this season's work—not quite half what DiMaggio is getting—but that this work shall include making public appearances off the field whenever his employers request it. A few years ago, as a speaker, he was known to his teammates as "strictly a bow man." He would bob up from his place at a banquet, acknowledge the applause with a bow, and sit down without attempting any spoken word. As the result of practice and determination, he is now able to deliver rather halting, painfully sincere speeches at such affairs

as Boy Scout dinners, father-and-son banquets, and Holy Name Society Communion breakfasts.

Henrich doesn't like making speeches, but he makes them anyway, with the same dogged persistence that he shows on the field. Some of his colleagues regard him as a triumph of brain and morality rather than of natural ability. They feel that strength of will, more than instinctive talent, has made him a great ballplayer. A Henrich partisan enthusiastically declared not long ago that he should be known as Plain Joe Citizen. Another, paying tribute to his stolid, regular ways, described him as "strictly Massillon, Ohio." Henrich was confused by this, because, although he and his family recently moved to Ridgewood, New Jersey, he still thinks of Massillon, Ohio, where he was born and brought up, as his home town, and not as a compound adjective. Like many another citizen of Massillon, past or present, Henrich smokes cigars, enjoys cold beer and ham sandwiches, reads and believes everything in the newspapers, plays hearts (he rules bridge out as too serious), and is fond of group singing.

The Yankee manager, Casey Stengel, has summed Henrich up by saying, "He's a fine judge of a fly ball. He fields grounders like an infielder. He never makes a wrong throw, and if he comes back to the hotel at three in the morning when we're on the road and says he's been sitting up with a sick friend, he's been sitting up with a sick friend." One of Henrich's predecessors in the Yankee right field was Babe Ruth, who endeared himself to fans not only by hitting as many as sixty home runs in a season but by consistently returning to his hotel at three in the morning when he had not been sitting up with a sick friend. The catholicity of Yankee fans is such that they esteem Henrich's impressive virtue almost as much as they used to Ruth's hell-raising—or heck-raising, as Henrich would say.

Henrich often tires of hearing his character exalted. He feels it is not right that virtue should be its own penalty. Because of his moral excellence, he has to work harder than his more sinful associates, as, for instance, when he is making speeches while grosser players are relaxing. His character is not his fault, he says—he was brought up to be the way he is by honest, religious, old-fashioned parents of German descent—and if he conducts himself with moderation and restraint, it is because he would be hard put to it to do otherwise. He is a genial, unpretentious man, fond of harmless banter and of adding his baritone to any impromptu burst of song in the Yankee clubhouse, and he finds it puzzling that he should be looked upon as an inspiration to American youth simply because he acts as he feels like acting. It saddens him when fans speak of his sterling attributes as a family man—he is married and has three children—instead of the strength and accuracy of his throwing arm, one of the best in baseball. He fears that Henrich the inspiration may overshadow Henrich the ballplayer. Last year, with a thoroughly creditable batting average of .308 (third highest on the Yankee team), Henrich scored a hundred and thirty-eight runs, more than any other major-league player, and drove in a hundred. He hit fourteen triples—the 1948 record for the American League—and forty-two doubles, exceeding by sixteen the number of any one of his teammates. In the matter of home runs, he hit twenty-five, which was well under the thirty-nine of DiMaggio, who led the League, but an impressive total, nonetheless, and among them were four he knocked out when the bases were loaded. Only five other major-leaguers—Lou Gehrig, Rudy York, Ruth, Frank Schulte, and Vince DiMaggio—have ever hit so many four-run homers in a season.

A member of the Yankee team since 1937, with the exception of three war years he spent in the Coast Guard as an athletic instructor with the rank of specialist first class, Henrich has helped the team win the American League pennant on six occasions and the World Series on four. He is the only player who ever saved a World Series game for his team after swinging on a third strike with two out in the ninth inning, thus apparently ending and losing the contest. He performed this feat in the fourth game of the World Series against Brooklyn in 1941, with the Dodgers leading, 4-3. The score by games was 2-1 against the Dodgers, and it looked as if they were about to tie it. As every follower of baseball knows, Mickey Owen, the Brooklyn catcher, muffed what would otherwise have been the last pitch of the game. Under the circumstances, Henrich was privileged to try to reach first base ahead of the ball. He did so, and the Yankees went on to win the game and, ultimately, the series. The episode is by no means typical of Henrich's batting ability, but it is characteristic of him to save a game at the last minute. His colleagues call him "a real pro" and "a good money player." His batting average under the terrific pressure of the seesaw World Series with Brooklyn in 1947 was .323, thirty-six points higher than his average for the regular season. Henrich frequently goes hitless until a game's climax in some late inning,

and then starts the winning rally, or drives in the winning run, or even makes the winning run himself, as he did in this season's opening game when he hit a homer with two out in the ninth inning. Hence "Old Reliable."

There are not many ways in which Henrich's good-natured calm can be shattered, but whenever he hears a remark disparaging the general intelligence of baseball players, his mild blue eyes turn icy, his manner becomes frigid, and it is clear why no one during the whole time he has been playing baseball has ever picked a fight with him. He contends that baseball is as complicated as chess, and much more difficult, inasmuch as most of the outfielders' decisions must be made instantly and often while running at full speed. On many plays, there are a number of places to which an outfielder can throw the ball, but only one is the right one. A fielder must know when to play safe by intentionally taking a line drive on the hop, or bounce, rather than making a speculative attempt to catch the ball before it touches the ground. If such a liner is hit with a runner on first, it may be better to take the ball on the hop and try to throw the runner out as he advances, but if it's the last half of the ninth inning, say, and there are two out, the outfielder may make a desperate effort to catch the ball on the fly and retire the side.

Henrich is the only outfielder currently in action who makes a specialty of "trapping" the ball. In this play, the outfielder pretends he is going to catch a fly, thus holding the runners on their bases, and then backs away and lets the ball bounce once before scooping it up, a very risky procedure. Each of the runners thus finds himself in the position of being forced to try to advance a base. Henrich is generally credited with having brought the trapped-ball play to its present advanced state of development. He started working on it in 1941, with the help of Joe Gordon, who was then a Yankee second baseman and is now with Cleveland; Gordon's part in the play consisted of running into the outfield, adding to the deception by pretending that he, too, was going to try to catch the ball. Since Gordon left the Yankees, his successor, George Stirnweiss, has been helping Henrich bring off this stunt. On three occasions last year, Henrich started a double play by trapping the ball. This is regarded as one of the fanciest defensive plays in baseball.

In further support of his contention that a good ballplayer has to have a mind, Henrich points out that every member of a big-league team is expected to memorize the hitting propensities of each of the hundred and seventy-five players who comprise the seven opposing squads in his league. He must learn whether each of these potential batters can place a hit or whether he usually hits the ball in the same direction, whether he is fast or slow on the bases, what kind of pitching he likes and what kind he dislikes, and whether he is a pull hitter, a straightaway hitter, or a power hitter. A pull hitter hits away from the direction he is facing; that is, a left-handed batter who pulls the ball hits to right field. The direction in which a straightaway batter hits depends more on the type of pitch he is thrown than on his swing. Power hitters are precisely that, and when one of them walks up to the plate, the outfielders move back. If a non-power hitter is able to place his hits, the outfielders may converge toward the infield, fearful lest he punch the ball "through the box"—meaning past the pitcher and through the gap between shortstop and second, or through some other hole in the infield defense. But, Henrich says, that isn't all a ballplayer must know about opposing hitters. A good batter hits differently in different situations. If there is no one out and no one on base, he may try for a long power hit, but if there is a man on first and none out, he may try for a hit-and-run play by punching a hit through to the outfield. Or, another time, the same man may bunt, to advance a player from first to second.

One evening recently, after a dinner at which Henrich had been the principal speaker, a fan asked him what he thought about while out in right field. Using a game the Yankees had played a few days before with Detroit as an example, Henrich, with his customary painstaking thoroughness, gave him an answer. "Well," he said slowly, "Lake, the second baseman, leads off. I know he hits a long ball to left field. But strictly left field. I come in quite a bit on him unless a hit-and-run is on. Then Lipon comes up. He's grown to be a better hitter. He's getting a good piece of the ball. Power mostly to left but pretty good power in any direction. I move back on him. The percentage is to give way a little bit, and I move back on him. Kell comes up next. He's changed a little bit. Used to hit a lot of balls to right field, but he's pulling a lot more. He had me scared last year and he used to back me up in right center field. But occasionally he'd hit a Texas Leaguer, or what we call a humpbacked liner. I don't recall having run many of his back to right center field all last year, though, so now I don't play him so deep. Wertz is next.

He's a left-handed power hitter. I don't expect him to pull too much because he swings a little late. Most of his go through the middle, over second base to center. I play him for power, but I don't shade him too much over toward the foul line. Then comes Wakefield, one of their left fielders. Lots of power. He's one of the few power hitters that isn't a definite pull hitter. I play him deep and move away from the right-field line. But Robinson—he's next—*he's* a pull hitter, and with pretty good power. I play him as an ordinary left-handed hitter. Now comes Groth. He's a rookie, so I don't know too much about him yet. I saw him take one little slap at a ball down in Lakeland and it went like a bullet. As strong as *he* is, you can tell he's got power. Can't play him cheap on any field. I figure on playing him a few feet deeper than Kell. Then up comes Vico. I don't play him as a pull hitter. The percentage is for him to hit through the middle, so I move to my right a little bit."

In view of all this, and much more, Henrich is in a sweat of concentration during every minute of every game that he stands guard at his distant outpost. Many fans do not notice him as he constantly shifts his position in accordance with the characteristics of the man at bat and with the way an inning or the game itself is shaping up; the attention of the crowd is mostly focused on the infield, and particularly on the batter and the pitcher. Few spectators realize that Henrich is mentally, if not physically, exhausted at the end of a game. "Baseball is work," he says. But he enjoys the game when he has a good day at bat. When he goes hitless—or, as he puts it, "goes for the horsecollar"—he is inclined to think it a hard life. "I like to play baseball at a picnic—married men against the single, or something like that," he has remarked after a disappointing game, "but when you're out there against clubs like Cleveland or Boston, it's not all fun. Especially when you go for the horsecollar."

It was the speechmaking in which Henrich reluctantly indulges that led him to settle in Ridgewood when he decided, a couple of years ago, that Massillon was too far from his center of operations. ("The kids were getting old enough to go to school, spring and fall," he says, "and the only answer was to live near where I'm in business.") One day in the course of the 1947 season, a friend of Henrich's named Bob Willaman—a former resident of Canton, Ohio, which is adjacent to Massillon, who now lives in Hohokus, New Jersey, which is adjacent to Ridgewood—persuaded him to come out to Hohokus and speak at a banquet sponsored by St. Luke's Catholic Church. Henrich found he liked the neighborhood, and rented a house in Ridgewood for his family during last year's season, at the close of which he bought a house there. "It's nice in Ridgewood," he says. "It's just like Massillon. You wouldn't know you were within a thousand miles of New York." The Henrich house is of recent construction and is in the best suburban tradition—four bedrooms, plastic doorknobs with synthetic flowers embedded in them, first floor of brick, upper story of shingle, painted white. When the Yankees are playing at home, Henrich ordinarily gets up between nine and ten in the morning and eats an unusually large breakfast, knowing that he will not have another full meal until dinner, after the game. "I really pack it in good," he says. At eleven-forty-five, he gets into his car, a Buick, and, driving swiftly and expertly, arrives at the Yankee Stadium, in the Bronx, half an hour later. By the time he enters the sumptuous Yankee dressing room, under the stands, several players are likely to be already there, mostly in various states of undress, some of them waving bats slowly in the air as they face imaginary pitchers, others studiously autographing baseballs sent in by fans, and still others massaging new bats with pieces of broken glass, in order to take off the sheen and make them less slippery to the grip.

In the dressing room—which is usually called the locker room, although it has no lockers—Henrich sometimes feels a touch of pride. At such a moment, he may recall his days in minor-league baseball, when he had to put on his uniform in a cheap boarding house in whatever town he was playing in and keep the sweat-soaked garments on after the game until he had got back to his quarters. The Yankees' dressing room, sometimes referred to as the Yankee clubhouse, has the appearance of the lounge of a private club. Deep green leather chairs fill one wing of it, and there are smoking stands, thick rugs, a small library, telephones, attendants to answer them and respectfully notify the players of their calls, and writing desks with stationery bearing the Yankee letterhead. The light is subdued, a radio is generally tuned in to soft music, hunting prints hang on the apple-green walls. Instead of the rows of battered iron lockers that line many dressing rooms, even in the big leagues, the Yankees enjoy spacious dressing booths, one for each player, which flank three walls of the room. There is a good deal of horseplay in the

dressing room. The younger players occasionally wrestle and shove one another about, but the veterans know that there is a greater chance of getting hurt in this kind of fooling around than there is on the field. Henrich undresses and puts on his uniform in a leisurely manner, pausing now and again to chat with teammates. Not long ago, at such a time, Cliff Mapes, who occasionally substitutes for Henrich, asked him for some advice on playing the wall. "The sharper the angle the ball hits the wall," Henrich said with the serious air of a professor, "the farther back it bounces." As he spoke, he withdrew one arm from his shirt and, with the garment still dangling from the other, jumped back and pretended to be playing a ball off the wall. "You're getting too good out there, Cliff," he said with a smile. "If you get any better, I'll have to protect my position by breaking your arm." A young newspaper reporter from Winnipeg came in and requested an interview. Henrich talked long and earnestly with him. "I always try to catch a fly with my hands just about even with my head," he said, "so I'll be in the best position for a throw." Then he went through the motions of running, without really running, and suddenly looked back over his shoulder. "If a fielder can turn his back on a ball and run like heck to just a certain point and then turn at the right second and catch the ball—why, then he can do anything," he said.

At one o'clock, when the team takes the field for batting practice, an hour before a game, Henrich excused himself from the interview. Out on the field, he turned and looked briefly at the half-filled stands, then, while waiting his turn at the plate, he picked up two bats, swung them around a few times, and tossed one aside. Presently he yelled at the player who had preceded him at the plate, "Come on, goldarn it! You gonna spend all weekend there?" Just before stepping up to the plate, Henrich pulled his cap down, hitched up his pants, and rubbed his hands in the dirt. Then, taking his stance, he planted his spikes firmly in the ground. "I like to dig in deep," he said later, "so you get real leverage on the ball. Pitchers always try to uproot you. They try to brush you back." He hit a high fly, and as he prepared to meet the next throw, one of his teammates on the sidelines shouted, "Screech one, Tommy!" Henrich had been in good form lately, and he swung at one ball after another with casual confidence. He never forgets, though, that he may at any moment inexplicably become the victim of a batting slump. All players, even the greatest—even Ruth and Cobb and DiMaggio—have, of course, suffered periodically from such slumps, and when they are in this pitiful state, they get so snappish that none of their teammates dares speak to them about it, and their friends try to steer clear of them for the duration. Players in a slump almost invariably decide that they are all through, that they are washed up and have lost their stuff. Henrich is no exception. "I try to pretend it doesn't worry me," he says, "but it does."

As the first batter of the visiting team goes to the plate and the crowd begins its roar, Henrich may hear someone in the stands nearest him yell, "Oh, Tommy, you punk!" or "Tommy, the bum!" He pays no attention to this normal concomitant of baseball; he is quiet on the field, and he does not attempt to retaliate when the players of an opposing team try to ride him from the dugout. This is in keeping with the customary deportment of the Yankee club, whose members do not constitute what is known as a holler team. Some clubs, while on the field, keep up a constant squall of encouragement to their pitchers and insults to opposing batters. "We play heads-up baseball," Henrich says, "but we keep our mouths shut. Crosetti—he used to be our shortstop—was a holler guy, but now we don't holler much."

If the Yankees win, Henrich is in jovial spirits as he charges into the dressing room. If they lose, he is sometimes despondent, but he recovers within a couple of hours. Attendants hand out refreshments to the players after the game. As Henrich pulls off his uniform, he stops from time to time to take a swig from a bottle of beer or a bite from a ham sandwich. Recently, after the Yankees had lost a tough contest that went into extra innings, Henrich, who was standing before a mirror with his mouth full, knotting his tie, said morosely, "A game like that makes an old man of you." Several of his teammates, equally morose, nodded.

Massillon, Ohio, has no more fervent booster than Henrich, whose birth occurred there on February 20, 1916. He is proud of the fact that it is the town in which Lillian and Dorothy Gish were raised and of which Jacob Sechler Coxey, the head of Coxey's Army, was once mayor. Then, too, Cy Rigler, for twenty years an umpire in the National League, was the son of a Massillon fire chief, and the Massillon Tigers, an early professional-football team, numbered Knute Rockne as a member. Henrich's father, a plasterer—and a good one, ac-

cording to his son—was a great baseball fan and took Tommy to his first game when he was five. The boy began playing baseball, or trying to, when he was six or seven, and from the start, he says, "the Yankees were my team. When they won, I was happy." He recalls that all during his boyhood he yearned with a painful intensity to be a big-league player, and he remembers well certain fruitless plans he had to go to Cleveland and see the Yankees play. Because he has not forgotten his own youthful ardor for baseball, he is unusually patient with the small fry who hang around outside the Yankee dressing room after a game. As a player emerges, the boys swarm about him, yipping and pushing, waving pencils and paper, and screaming for autographs. No big-league player of any importance can appear anywhere, from a hotel lobby to a soda fountain, without attracting something of a crowd, and most of them delight in such attention. Good players draw handsome salaries, but, even so, fans consider it a privilege to contribute to funds that are raised from time to time to buy their heroes fancy cars and other expensive gifts, which are presented at special ceremonies before a game. A group of factory workers in, say, New London will decide that some player from that city, whom they may never have spoken to and have probably seldom seen, should have a "day," to be observed by the pressing of lavish gifts upon him. One of the most famous examples of a day of this sort was Pepper Martin Day, some ten years ago, when admirers of the Cardinal third baseman stocked his farm for him; pigs and geese were herded to the plate in an unusual celebration that included the presentation of a tractor, which Pepper mounted and, to the accompaniment of wild cheers, drove about the park. On July 17th last year, Tommy Henrich Day was observed at Yankee Stadium, and he was presented with the Buick he now drives and a Steinway spinet, the gifts of almost a thousand admirers, who had contributed from twenty-five cents to fifty dollars apiece.

Henrich was a pupil in the parochial schools of Massillon and Canton, and a parishioner of St. Mary's Catholic Church, in Massillon. He attended St. Mary's until he moved to New Jersey, where he now attends St. Luke's. He sang in the choir at St. Mary's and expects to try out for the one at St. Luke's next fall. He graduated from St. John's Catholic High School, in Canton, in 1933, when he was seventeen. During his last two years there, he played on the softball team of the Hoffman Drugs Company, in Massillon, an amateur outfit that won eighty of the eighty-seven games on its schedule during one of the seasons he was with it. He is one of the few big-leaguers who have ever been offered a contract in organized baseball on the basis of their showing in softball. He began his full-time baseball career in 1934, when he was eighteen, by joining the Zanesville, Ohio, team, a Cleveland farm club. A year later, he was sent to New Orleans, then also a Cleveland property. In 1936, he batted .346, which made him feel that he was entitled to a trial with the big-league Cleveland Indians. Instead, at the end of the 1936 season he was ordered to report to Milwaukee, still another Cleveland farm club.

During that winter, Henrich came to realize that a baseball player is a property that can be sold or traded anywhere, any time, without having any voice in the matter. He read a sports-page story to the effect that he was to be sold to the Boston Braves, or Bees, as they were then called, and it was news to him. Not long afterward, he read one saying he had been traded to the St. Louis Browns. He grew annoyed. What he had wanted was a tryout with the Cleveland Indians, and now he didn't even know whether he still belonged to Cleveland. He wrote a letter to the late Kenesaw Mountain Landis, baseball's first commissioner, describing his bafflement and declaring that he didn't know who owned him. Landis held two hearings on the Henrich case early in 1937, found that Cleveland had "prevented [Henrich's] advancement to a major-league club under the selection rules," and ruled that no club owned him and that he was a free agent, entitled to deal for himself. Henrich's New Orleans record had been so good that eight big-league clubs at once sought to sign him up. The Yankees won out, with an offer of ten thousand dollars for his first season's play and a twenty-thousand-dollar bonus for signing. He got off to a fine start with the team, and then, in August, tore a cartilage in his left knee while, as he explains, "running to the right and trying to throw to the left." This retired him for the season, except for pinch-hitting. He had an excellent year in 1938, and played in his first World Series.

In 1940, on the last day of August, Henrich again injured his left leg, and spent twenty-eight days in St. Elizabeth's Hospital, in upper Manhattan, where he regained the use of his leg and met Miss Eileen O'Reilly, one of the nurses on the floor, when she stopped in at his room to listen to his radio. They were married the following year. Their three children—Patricia, Ann, and Thomas David, whom they call T.D.—are aged six, five, and three, respectively. Henrich is acutely conscious of the fact that the average playing life of a big-league ballplayer is about seven years. "I might break a leg out there any day," he says. He is a thrifty man, and it is the opinion of his friends that he has saved a hundred thousand dollars or so. He plans to buy a dairy farm in Ohio when he retires. He is explicit on one point concerning dairy farming. "Look," he says. "My idea is to have a guy to do the heavy stuff. The guy who gets up at four in the morning, that ain't me."

Henrich finds his chief relaxation in playing the piano and singing. In Massillon, he was an active member of the Society for the Preservation and Encouragement of Barber Shop Quartet Singing in America. He still wears its pin in his lapel. Only the other day, he was delighted to discover that the Society has a chapter in Ridgewood, and he is looking forward to joining it in the fall, when he has a little leisure. He used to be a member of the Massillon Tomcat Quartet, a barbershop group that practices twice a week during the winter in the American Legion Hall there. It won the state championship in 1946 by its rendition of "Down by the Old Mill Stream" and "Carolina in the Morning." Henrich has hopes of helping Ridgewood's vocalists achieve comparable honors in New Jersey.

When the Yankees are on the road, Henrich usually spends his evenings—those, that is, on which no night game is scheduled—at the movies or studying books on dairy farming. The Yankees are playing thirty-five night games this season, out of a total of seventy-seven road games. In 1947, Henrich was elected by the Yankee players as their representative to confer with the management, pursuant to a new procedure in the league, and in this position, he has voiced their objections to certain aspects of night playing. Their principal complaint is that lighting conditions vary from park to park and that in some cities the lighting is so inadequate that the players can't see a low, fast pitched ball. The players would like to have uniform lighting systems at all parks.

Henrich asserts that he owes much of his success in baseball to the fact that his wife is not interested in it. He likes to tell a story about an old-time baseball player, one Jay Kirke, whose wife was in the habit of following baseball so closely that every afternoon she would greet her husband as he returned home with this little verse:

Well, my honey, well, my Jay,
How many hits did you get today?

"That was all right when old Jay was getting hits," Henrich says, "but when he wasn't, it wasn't. Finally, one afternoon, he waited till she got through and then hollered, 'Look, you take care of the cooking in this family and I'll take care of the hitting!' Heck of a situation." At this point, Henrich pauses, and then adds, with quiet satisfaction, "My wife takes care of the cooking."

DAVID PASCAL

Courtesy *Sport* Magazine. ©

"We promise you won't catch him stealing candy again. Won't you let him go this time, Mr. Bromley? He's our star pitcher. Honest, Mr. Bromley . . ."

45

THIS PIECE, written while Mr. Bragan was managing Pittsburgh, has a fascinating topic—and it also has a fascinating by-product: an actual explanation (some of it between the lines) of what makes one manager better than another.

What Percentage Percentage?

BOBBY BRAGAN

as told to STANLEY FRANK

DON LARSEN had just pitched the greatest game in the history of baseball and now a bunch of us were master-minding it at World Series headquarters. It wasn't so much the fact that he'd just pitched the only no-hitter ever hung up in the Series and the first perfect game in the majors since 1922 that excited the deep thinkers—we were all raving about a technical gimmick. "Imagine changing a guy's pitching style during the Series and seeing him put down 27 hitters in a row," someone said. "That Stengel must be a genius or the luckiest stiff alive."

I could have said something, but I didn't. A freshman manager doesn't go around claiming membership in the genius club, especially when his team has just finished in seventh place. But at the Pirates' training camp that spring I had experimented with having my pitchers deliver the ball to the plate without a windup or a stretch on the mound. I had George Munger, a veteran on the staff, teach the rookies to fire from the hip—just as the Yankees' Larsen and Bob Turley did with such spectacular success seven months later—but my kids wanted no part of the newfangled method. They argued that pitchers had been taking big windups since the dawn of time to get more stuff on the ball, and they refused to listen when I proved all that hocus-pocus was so much wasted motion. Ballplayers are as hidebound as most people in this business.

Casey had done the same thing that I tried to do—he had challenged the value of an old practice handed down from the past and discovered that it served no practical purpose—but the difference was that his players had listened. Believe me, nobody's talking me out

of any of my ideas this season. I'm bringing baseball up to date, and nobody's going to stop me.

With the conspicuous exceptions of Stengel, Paul Richards and Leo Durocher, practically all managers in recent years have been playing safety-first, old-fashioned baseball. They're so afraid of criticism from the fans and the sportswriters that they rarely pull anything unorthodox. Whenever they're confronted with a choice of making a routine or a daring decision, they generally resort to the "book"—the percentage play which is supposed to work in the majority of cases. That's the easy way of getting off the hook. Worse yet, it has kept the strategy of the game in a deep freeze since the 1890s, when the original Baltimore Orioles introduced most of the maneuvers that still pass for "modern" baseball.

In the years since the war, vastly improved techniques have brought a radical upheaval in the tactics of every sport except baseball. The emphasis in all games today is on sudden explosions of scoring power. The T formation in football is built around the long-gainer, the play that can go all the way, instead of the old, three-yards-off-tackle system. If you're old enough to be reading this you'll realize that the fast break in basketball and the jump shot have practically killed the old possession game. In tennis, the "big" game—a cannonball service and strong net play—is a must for any sort of national ranking. The great Bobby Jones wouldn't place within the first ten today with the same scores that captured major golf tournaments a quarter of a century ago. Top golfers now shoot boldly for the pin instead of merely trying to land on the green, an approach that has cut fully 20 strokes off a 72-hole match score.

A similar revolution in playing conditions and individual skills should be effecting a drastic overhauling in the basic concept of baseball. The lively ball and bats with a lot more whip have brought the fences within range of practically every hitter who goes up to the plate. A comparison of fielding records shows that infielders today reel off twice as many double plays as were racked up years ago and commit only one third as many errors, yet most managers still are dominated by the old Oriole strategy of playing for one-run innings. It's high time the outmoded "book" was thrown into the ashcan and superseded by tactics geared to more exciting and imaginative baseball.

The manager who goes with the percentages and loses always has a convenient excuse. He can merely say: "I don't have the ballplayers to make the percentages stand up." If he had tried to cross up the opposition and his idea had backfired, he'd have been a sitting duck for the second-guessers. I should know. During the 10 years I've been managing in the Texas, Cuban, Pacific Coast and National Leagues, I've been torn apart by the wolves as much as anyone in the business because I've thrown away the book consistently. I've often been caught with my foolish face hanging wide open and I've got the scars to prove it. But I've never regretted it. If I had stuck to the book, I'd probably be back trying to make a living as a 40-year-old, second-string catcher in the bushes. I'm convinced it's not safe to "play it safe."

I've tried to pattern myself after Stengel, Richards and Durocher, the managers I admire most. They've never hesitated to go out on a limb and take chances that exposed them to second-guessing, as I'll show later by citing chapter and verse on their gambles. Too many managers run their teams to please the fans and sportswriters, an approach that inhibits their decisions. The good manager takes full responsibility for actions that originate with him and says the hell with the consequences.

Here's how I see it. There are very few upsets in baseball over the course of a season. Sure, a tail-ender occasionally scrambles the dope by taking a series from a pace-setter, but in the final analysis the teams that figure to finish 1-2-3 invariably wind up in that order, give or take one position. You didn't have to be an expert this year to pick the Dodgers, Braves and Redlegs to make the strongest run for the National League pennant or to predict that the

Yankees would get their toughest competition from the Indians and White Sox. By the same token, teams earmarked for the second division always need radar to keep within sight of the leaders come September. A weak sister occasionally goes crazy with the heat for a while and threatens to upset the dope, but it's all a snare and a delusion.

Last season the Pirates had everyone turning nipups by leading the league in mid-June. Dale Long set an all-time record by belting homers in eight straight games and his average was better than .400. Bob Friend and Ronnie Kline were pitching as though they had invented the game. We were eating high off the hog and I wanted to believe stories touting me as the new boy wonder, but I couldn't kid myself.

Scores of reporters put me on a ticklish spot by bombarding me with the same question: Could the Pirates stay up there? I couldn't tear down the confidence of my players and say we didn't have a chance to finish in the first division, much less make a serious pass at the pennant. At the same time, I had to be honest with myself and the fans to cushion them against disappointment when the rug was eventually pulled under the Pirates.

"It's hard for me to get excited when there still are a hundred games to play," I answered. That was a diplomatic way of saying, "No—we can't win or even come close." The Pirates finished 27 games out of first place. The net result of our great getaway was that we escaped the cellar for the first time in five years.

You can bet the family jewels on one maxim in baseball: Class always tells in the long run. Two or three men on a team may have unusually good seasons, but they can't lift the other 20-odd players more than a notch or so above the normal level of their performance. Conversely, a good team doesn't go to pieces overnight unless the front office gets complacent and neglects to replace key men who are over the hill.

All right. You can't beat the percentages. But it's foolish for a manager involved in the long, painful process of building a pennant-winner to play conservative baseball, because the percentages will beat him down over the course of 154 games. If both sides go by the book, superior class will assert itself every time.

But a manager can throw a monkey wrench into the percentages now and then by pulling surprises and devising measures that will squeeze the last drop of talent from the manpower at his disposal. What has he got to lose? He's like the atheist who suddenly dropped to his knees and began to pray when he was told he was suffering from an incurable disease and had only a few months to live. He's got to try *something*.

Take the batting order I introduced last year, which kicked up such a rumpus in the National League. I had Long, my Number 1 slugger, leading off. He was followed by Bill Virdon and Bob Clemente, who had the best batting averages on the team. After them I went down the line placing the players in descending order of their batting marks. That setup ran absolutely counter to the traditional custom of putting a team's best hitters in the middle of the batting order where they are in a position to drive in runs when they connect.

Critics called the innovation "Bragan's brainstorm," but I had been thinking about it for 10 years and I did a good deal of research before I decided to spring it. My bird dog in the research department was Dick Hall, a pitcher who had a sore arm that put him on the shelf for two months last season. Hall, a Phi Beta Kappa from Swarthmore, dug up information that was more valuable than the pitching of a Newcombe or a Roberts.

Most importantly, Hall found that a man has 17 more times at bat over the course of a season for every notch he advances in the lineup. In other words, the lead-off man gets 51 more whacks than the player hitting in the Number 4 spot.

Let me show how the 1956 National League race might have been changed drastically had the close runners-up used my lineup. Milwaukee's Number 4 hitter was Joe Adcock and Cincinnati's was Ted Kluszewski. Adcock hit 38 homers in 454 chances, or one in every 12. Kluszewski teed off at the rate of one homer in every 15 turns at the plate. If they had been leading off they would have each gone to bat 51 more times. Translated in terms of Adcock, that would have meant four more homers and for Kluszewski three more. Milwaukee missed the pennant by one game, Cincinnati by two. A lot of prize money could have gone down the drain with those extra homers Adcock and Kluszewski never had a chance to deliver.

Every team from the deepest bush to the majors adheres to the same formula for its batting order. A fast man with a good eye is picked to lead off, followed by a player who can bunt and work the hit-and-run. In the meat of the batting order the power guy is sandwiched between the men who hit for the best averages. The poorer hitters fill out the last four spots.

That setup is rooted so deeply in custom that everyone forgets—or ignores—one significant fact: *It hasn't been changed in 75 years.* Strategy governing the batting order dates from the days of the dead ball, the horse-and-buggy era of baseball that was knocked into a cocked hat nearly 40 years ago by Babe Ruth and the lively ball.

Miller Huggins, the Yankee manager who won six pennants in the 1920s, was the first to realize that the old system of playing for one run at a time was revolutionized by the increasing frequency of home runs. Huggins had a theory that the winning team scores more runs in *one* inning than the losers score in the *entire* game. If the final score is 5-2, let's say, the odds are in favor of the winning side having a three- or four-run inning—and you'd be surprised how often it works out that way. I'm told there are professional gamblers who have been making a good living for years just betting on Huggins' theory.

What inning usually produces the outburst that puts a game on ice? Hold your hats for a surprise. Despite all the stories you've read of late rallies pulling ball games out of the fire, the most runs, by far, are scored in the *first* inning. Conclusive proof is provided by Allan Roth, my old buddy who is the Dodgers' statistician. Roth compiled an inning-by-inning breakdown of the runs scored by the Dodgers and the combined opposition in 1956. Here are the figures:

	Dodgers	Opponents
1st	129	93
2nd	62	53
3rd	77	79
4th	84	57
5th	76	47
6th	81	65
7th	79	87
8th	83	62
*9th	49	49

(*Ninth-inning totals are so low because the home team does not take its last licks when the game already has been won. Making due allowances for that, increase the runs by 50 per cent. The ninth still will be just about the same as any other inning, except the first.)

The reason why the first inning is marked by heavy scoring will be obvious to any fan who gives it a moment's thought. Pitchers generally have some trouble with their control at the start. They're more apt to groove the ball for the hitters than when they settle down later. Tough competitors like Robin Roberts, Sal

Maglie and Whitey Ford get tougher as the game progresses. If you're going to beat them you've got to put the boots to them early.

How can a manager take full advantage of the knowledge that the first inning represents his best chance to wrap up the decision? To answer this, I'll ask another question: To put pressure on a shaky pitcher from the start, do you want your two best hitters facing him or a .260 speedboy followed by a fellow who seldom comes through with more than a single?

Anyone in his right mind has to go with the best power and punch he can wheel up to the plate. There's one valid objection against leading off with a slugger. If he hits one on the nose, the blast will come with the bases empty and will not drive in a run. Granted. But I can counter that argument by pointing out that when your powerhouse is the first man up you can be certain he won't be passed purposely. Sure, he may get a walk, but it won't be intentional because the team's top percentage hitter is on deck.

Theory goes for Sweeney unless it is supported by results. The only payoff in baseball is the won-and-lost column. On August 18, 1956, I sprang the new batting order and stayed with it for the final 41 games of the season. In that stretch the Pirates won 16, lost 24 and tied one. In the preceding 41 games, when I used the standard batting order, the team won 14, lost 26 and tied one. Just to satisfy the skeptics, we played the identical number of games (25) against first-division clubs during both periods.

Now a difference of two games in 41 may seem picayune, but projected over a full season it adds up to more than seven games—and that can make all the difference in the world to a contender. Since World War II, only two pennants in the National League and three in the American League have been captured by margins greater than seven games.

Figures on first-inning scoring justify Bragan's brainstorm, but there is an added clincher —*the hitters it brings up in the ninth inning*. Late last season the Pirates gave Milwaukee an awful jolt by winning two straight games by one run. On both occasions the Braves' final out was made by Johnny Logan, the Number 2 man in the lineup. The thought struck me then that the last hitter in tight games is usually from the top of the batting order. It was nothing more than a hunch, but it was confirmed by demon statistician Allan Roth.

"I've been analyzing box scores for ten years," Roth says, "and close, low-scoring games follow a definite pattern. Eleven men usually get on base in the first eight innings on hits, walks and errors. Going into the ninth inning, 24 men have been retired, making a total of 35 who have gone to bat. The first man up in the ninth, therefore, completes the fourth complete swing through the batting order and then come the two top men. In tight games, hitters below the second slot seldom get five chances to hit."

I'll ask a variation on the question I posed a few paragraphs ago. Suppose you're managing the Braves and you can choose two players who will get to bat five times in a game. Whom will you take, O'Connell and Logan or Adcock and Mathews? You've got to pick Adcock and Mathews, the muscle guys who can break up a game with one swish of their bats.

In case anyone is interested, if I were managing other teams in the league I'd have Duke Snider lead off for the Dodgers, Frank Robinson for the Reds, Ed Mathews for the Braves, Stan Musial for the Cardinals, Willie Mays for the Giants, Richie Ashburn for the Phillies and Ernie Banks for the Cubs. I'm not familiar with American League teams, but I know for sure I'd want Mickey Mantle up there for me scaring pitchers to death right off the first crack of the bat.

I suppose I'm hipped on the idea because I'm convinced it contributed to my becoming a manager. I suggested it in 1947 to Manager Burt Shotton when I was with the Dodgers, but he gave me a polite brushoff. "I'll stick with a winning lineup," he said. "Try it yourself when you get your own ball club." Sportswriters traveling with the Dodgers heard of my proposal and gave it a big play which Branch Rickey, the Dodgers' general manager, must have seen. Looking back, I believe that was the turning point of my career.

Rickey unquestionably is the most imaginative executive the game ever has known. He introduced the farm system, which every major-league team since has copied. He was the first to scout players scientifically and, through the years, practically the only front-office man constantly seeking improvements on techniques. Gabe Paul, Cincinnati's general manager, told me last year that Rickey himself suggested putting a team's best hitters at the top of the batting order a quarter of a century ago. The similar idea I popped must have brought me to his attention. Lord knows there was no other reason for him to take special notice of me.

I broke into organized ball as a shortstop in

1937 when I was 20 and went up to the Phillies three years later. I don't suppose one Philadelphia fan in 100 remembers I played 154 games at shortstop in 1941, and no wonder. I was too slow to be a competent big-league shortstop and my .251 batting average didn't send off Roman candles either. The next year the Phillies suddenly were left without a catcher when Benny Warren was hurt and Mickey Livingston was called away by his wife's illness. Manager Hans Lobert asked for someone to fill in behind the bat and I volunteered. I had caught a little for an American Legion team in Birmingham, my home town, when I was a kid, but I wanted to have a go at the job because I knew it was the only position where my lack of speed would not be a handicap.

That day I caught in an exhibition game at Lancaster, Pa., and the next night I was in there for a regular game with the Reds. I twice threw out Lonnie Frey, a fast man, on attempted steals of second base and decided my future, if any, was as a catcher. In 1943 I was traded to the Dodgers and for the next two years I was a utility catcher and infielder until I went into the Army.

When I rejoined the Dodgers two years later the handwriting on the wall was spelled out in neon lights. Brooklyn had Bruce Edwards, who was rated the best young catcher in the business until he hurt his arm. Behind him was Gil Hodges, who hit the ball so hard he made it bleed. And there already was talk of another coming catcher in the Dodger farm system—a kid named Roy Campanella. In 1947 I was used in only 25 games. My most significant contribution to the team was a pinch double in a four-run rally that won the sixth World Series game. The hit gave me a piece of a record that will never be broken—a 1.000 batting average in World Series play—but it hardly gave me the bargaining power of a Mickey Mantle when I discussed salary terms with Rickey in the winter of '48.

Rickey offered me $9,000 and I accepted immediately. It was a generous salary under the circumstances, but I couldn't help thinking that Peewee Reese, who had come up to the big leagues the same year I did, was getting about $25,000. And nobody had to tell me the difference between Reese's earning power and mine was an accurate reflection of the difference in our ability. I took a deep breath and summoned up the nerve to make a little speech I had been rehearsing mentally for four months.

"Mr. Rickey, I know I have limited value as a player," I blurted. "I believe, though, my experience can be useful to the Brooklyn organization as a manager. I'll be grateful if you'll consider me a candidate when an opening develops."

I waited for Rickey to give me the horse-laugh, but he looked at me silently for a long minute. Maybe he remembered the new batting order I had suggested to Shotton. Maybe he recalled that he too had been a mediocre catcher 40 years before when he asked for a chance to remain in baseball in another capacity.

I'm merely guessing, of course. All I know is that he finally nodded and said, "I can't promise anything, Bragan, but I'll keep you in mind."

Five months later, in June 1948, Rickey decided to change the manager at Fort Worth, the Dodger farm in the Texas League, and I was given the job and held it for five years. In the meantime, Rickey had shifted to Pittsburgh as the general manager. In 1953, when Fred Haney was appointed manager of the Pirates, Rickey selected me as his successor at Hollywood in the Pacific Coast League. I followed Haney to Pittsburgh when he resigned at the end of the '55 season.

As Rickey's protégé, I try to run a team with the imagination which always has characterized his attitude toward baseball. That means, among other things, a willingness to find improvements on plays that are mildewed with age.

To my mind, the most overworked—and overrated—plays in baseball are the hit-and-run and the sacrifice bunt, the basic strategy of most managers. In the hit-and-run, as you probably know, the batter tries to hit the ball behind the runner on first base, who takes off with the pitch. The purpose is to reduce the possibility of a double play or, in the event of a single, to advance the runner to third. It's a fine play—with two serious drawbacks. It sharply reduces the batter's chances of a base hit and it succeeds in pushing up the runner on a ground ball only 30 per cent of the time, and then at the cost of a big out.

The hit-and-run is a typical example of an old-fashioned stratagem that has long outlived its usefulness. I don't doubt it was a hot-shot idea when John J. McGraw, Willie Keeler and Hughey Jennings dreamed it up some 60 years ago. In that low-scoring era when games generally were decided by one run, giving away an out to advance a runner a base might have been a good trade. Today it's a lousy swap, especially in an early inning, because it cuts heavily into a team's potential for getting a big cluster of runs.

In the majority of instances, the batter is saddled with pretty severe handicaps. He's obliged to swing at the ball, whether the pitch is good or bad, to protect the runner going down to second. Too often that results in easy outs. And if he is a right-handed hitter, he cramps his natural power by pushing the ball to right field, the opposite direction of his free swing.

The most stereotyped play in the game is the sacrifice bunt in two common situations. Most managers feel they can't go wrong calling for it when a runner is on first with none out or there are men on first and second with less than two out and the pitcher is the hitter. In my book, a manager hardly can do worse than give away an out to advance the runners one base.

There has been a lot of talk about the lively ball revamping offensive strategy, but I've never heard anyone mention its effect on the art of bunting. It's an inescapable fact that the jackrabbit used today travels so fast even when it is tapped that good infielders are racking up more force plays on bunts all the time. I have no authoritative statistics to support that statement, but it's my definite impression that the runner on first is cut down at second on one out of three attempted sacrifices.

In 1947, the last full season I was with the Dodgers, Burt Shotton had his pitchers lay down the ball on 23 occasions when there were runners on first and second. As I recall, both runners were advanced only three times. The other 20 times somebody was forced at second or third. Pitchers as a group are terrible hitters, to be sure, but they're bound to produce collectively at least three hits in 23 chances if they swing away. That's a batting average of only .130 and most pitchers manage to hit 50 points higher.

Let's examine for a moment the setup when a bunt is successful with a man on first. The big idea in sacrificing is to avoid a double play and put the runner in position to score on a single. Assume a good hitter is the next man up. What does the opposing manager do? He gives him an intentional walk, setting up an easier double play. The offensive team still needs a hit, but by giving away an out its run-making potential has been reduced by one third.

Since I'm sticking my neck out, I might as well go all the way and say most National League managers put undue emphasis on bunting. If I had Duke Snider, Willie Mays, Ed Mathews, Joe Adcock, Ted Kluszewski, Frank Robinson, Stan Musial or Ernie Banks they'd never lay down a sacrifice. My equivalents of those players are Dee Fondy and Frank Thomas. Day in and day out Fondy and Thomas will do more for the team swinging from the heels. Any time either of them bunts I'm sacrificing 50 per cent of my power, a concession I can't afford to give to the opposition.

After the Pirates went into a tailspin last year and dropped into the second division, I was panned for pulling too much cute and clever stuff. My biggest fault was that I didn't experiment enough. I'm not making the same mistake this season. There are several new dodges I already have sprung or intend to unveil in the proper spot. I don't mind tipping my mitt. Advance notice of trick plays may rob them of the element of surprise, but it will accomplish something more important. The threat of them will keep the other side guessing.

The one instance in which the hit-and-run can possibly be utilized is when there is a man on third base with one out and two strikes on a hitter who usually gets a piece of the ball. It may look like a squeeze play—with the runner taking off at full speed for the plate on the pitcher's delivery—but there is one major difference. The hitter takes a full cut at the ball instead of bunting.

You may say it's crazy to gamble with a man on third and one out because the odds are all in favor of the run scoring. If the batter misses the ball the runner is a dead duck at the plate and the inning is ended with a double play. That's absolutely true—but there is one glaring flaw in that line of reasoning. The odds are all *against* the run scoring.

Most fans assume a run is in the bag when a man is on third with one out. Any fairly long fly or a deep grounder will get him home, they say. Managers who have gone along on that cozy assumption have been dying for years with the guy on third. Pushing the run home is a good deal tougher than the layman suspects.

I can get rich betting the average fan will overestimate outlandishly the number of scoring fly balls a hitter produces in any given season. I'll give you one of the best, the Dodgers' Gil Hodges, a long-ball hitter on a club which always has men on the bases. Well, sir, two years ago Hodges *topped the league with a grand total of 10 sacrifice flies* and last season he had only two.

I heard through the grapevine that Walter Alston held a special batting practice a few years ago after the Dodgers had dropped a raft of close games by stranding runners on third. The regulars on the best team in the league were told to concentrate on hitting the ball in the air to the outfield—and they were able to do it on the average of only *twice in 10 attempts*. The odds were 5 to 1 against a reasonably long fly, and don't forget the pitchers weren't bearing down as hard as they do in regular games.

My chances of scoring with the run-and-hit are much better than 5 to 1, provided I consider two factors. The opposing pitcher must be a fellow who has good control and, with two strikes on the batter, figures to throw the ball close to the plate. Then, the batter must be someone like Dick Groat, Bill Mazeroski or Johnny O'Brien—a punch hitter who generally gets a piece of the ball. In the event of a fly, the runner has time to backtrack, tag up and score. On a grounder, his big jump enables him to beat the throw home even when the infield is playing up on the grass.

Another maneuver I will be stressing in Pittsburgh this season is the steal of third base, the mostly grossly neglected play in baseball. People carry on as though a guy has pulled a job as daring as the Brinks holdup when he swipes third. Nuts. It's infinitely harder to steal second base, a stunt that doesn't get a ripple from the customers. Yeah, I'm fully aware that the catcher's throw to third base is 90 feet compared to 127 feet down to second. But that extra distance is covered in *less than half a second* once the catcher cuts loose.

Every sandlotter knows bases are stolen on the pitcher, not the catcher. A runner's lead from first is limited to about 5 feet because the pitcher can pick him off with a snap throw, but an agile man can take as much as 15 feet at second with perfect safety. There's little danger of a pickoff since the pitcher has to wheel and make a complete turn on the mound before throwing the ball. A dozen men in the majors are faster than Willie Mays, but he's the only one today fully exploiting the big lead he can take from second base. Last season Willie attempted 13 steals of third base and made it every time.

This gimmick is a prime example of a double-edged weapon. The shortstop can reduce the runner's lead by moving over toward second and holding him closer to the bag, but that leaves a wider hole in the infield and, as a consequence, weakens the defense. The third baseman has a headache, too. To guard against the threat of a steal, he's got to play even with the bag to take the catcher's peg, making him a pushover for a bunt.

A team with a reputation for bold baserunning collects dividends that are not always apparent in the box score by keeping the opposing pitcher and infield off balance. This prediction may look silly by the time it appears, but I believe Gil Hodges will miss Jackie Robinson more than any other Dodger. Robinson's antics on the baselines distracted pitchers to such a degree that they couldn't concentrate on Hodges, the next man in the batting order. All of us could go on a Caribbean cruise if we had 10 bucks for every time a jittery pitcher, who was giving Robinson the anxious eye, fell behind Hodges on the balls-and-strikes count and then had to groove a fat pitch.

The only achievement that gave me any satisfaction last year was that the Pirates were involved in 54 games decided by one run and won 25, an unusually high percentage for a seventh-place team. Daring tactics turned the issue in our favor in many of those tossups. At a guess, I'd say we tried the squeeze play 20 times, twice as much as any other National League team. If the truth must be known, we would've been better off had I called it 40 times.

I'll also confess I chickened out on a number of occasions when my first impulse was to shoot the works and try to pull a rabbit out of the hat. Baseball people raise such a holler against any deviation from routine that I was reluctant in my first year to adopt a gimmick like Birdie Tebbetts' four-man outfield. Tebbetts once put his third baseman in the outfield when Stan Musial was the hitter and the Cardinals needed a long belt to win the game. That was a reverse switch on the 5-man infield Branch Rickey dreamed up many years ago and which I've used in the minors.

It's entirely logical to bring in an outfielder and station him between the pitcher and the first baseman when a bad hitter is up in one of two situations. If a runner is on first and you anticipate a bunt, the extra man can field the ball normally handled by the first baseman. He stays back to hold the runner close to the bag, increasing the possibility of a force play at second. If a runner is on third, your tighter defense has a better chance of cutting him off at the plate on a grounder. Of course, there's an element of risk in the whole thing. A fly ball may drop in the outfield—and when it does you wind up with knots in your head and the grandstand managers have a field day.

A manager who refuses to let sentiment influence his judgment gets nothing but the worst of it from second-guessers. I was given the business in Pittsburgh last year in a game with the Reds when, with the score tied in the ninth, the bases loaded with one out and two strikes on Frank Thomas, I sent in Bob Skinner as a pinch hitter. Thomas is a local boy and the fans were highly indignant that I didn't give him a chance to break up the game. My main concern at the moment was that Thomas strikes out a lot, like most sluggers, and I wanted someone up there who was a better bet to get a piece of the ball. Skinner connected solidly but lined to the shortstop, leaving the bases full. Fortunately, Jack Shepard came through with a single that got me off the hook, but it didn't pipe down completely the criticism fired at me for lifting Thomas.

One of the funniest cracks I've ever heard in baseball came from a second-guesser. Maybe I think it's amusing because it happened to Fred Haney, my predecessor at Hollywood, instead of me. During a wild-scoring game Haney used a slugger named Frank Kelleher as a pinch hitter in the sixth inning with the bases loaded and Frank responded nobly by unloading a four-run homer. San Francisco bounced back and went ahead, 9-7, but in the ninth Hollywood filled the bases. Lightning didn't strike again for Haney. His pinch hitter fanned, ending the game. A flannel-mouthed fan got up on his hind legs and bellowed, "See, meathead. You could've won if you saved Kelleher."

❉   ❉   ❉

It's strictly a sucker play for me to give aid and comfort to the enemy, but the vicious yapping of grandstand wolves intimidates managers more than most of us care to admit. The exceptions are Stengel, Richards and Durocher.

Richards pulled a gambit that's hard to top for sheer courage of convictions. When he was piloting Buffalo in the International League, Sam Jethroe, Montreal's leadoff man, set an all-time record for the loop by stealing 89 bases. Richards found the one way, short of a shotgun, to stop Jethroe. He purposely passed the pitcher to clog up the base paths ahead of Jethroe—and damned if it didn't work.

That's too rich for my blood, but I do in-

tend to copy another Richards scheme. He first used it against the Red Sox when he was managing the White Sox. Billy Pierce, his fine southpaw, was pitching a strong game but got into a bit of a jam when a right-handed batter, who hit him like a cousin, came up with a couple of men aboard. Richards didn't want Pierce to pitch to his nemesis and he didn't want to take him out of the game. He solved the dilemma by bringing in Harry Dorish, a right-hander, and having Pierce play first base. After Dorish retired that one man, Pierce returned to the mound and nailed down his victory.

Durocher's utter disregard for attacks by second-guessers was epitomized for me by one stroke he pulled in the opening game of the 1951 World Series. That was the year the Giants beat the Dodgers in the famous playoff for the pennant and then picked up where they left off by tearing into the favored Yankees the next day in the first inning. They had a run in, men on second and third with two out and Bobby Thomson at bat. On his last appearance the previous day, Thomson had walloped his epic homer. The Yankee pitcher was Allie Reynolds, who in his previous start had fashioned his second no-hit, no-run game of the season.

Reynolds was having trouble with his control this day, though, and the Giants had a chance to apply the crusher with Thomson, who was hotter than a two-dollar pistol. It was no time to get fancy, but Durocher always played every angle for all it was worth. He alone noticed that Reynolds was bearing down so hard on Thomson that he was letting Monte Irvin take a huge lead off third base. Durocher gave Irvin the high sign to go all the way—and Irvin got away with the first steal of home seen in the World Series in 30 years. Just for the sake of the record, Thomson did not get a hit. Irvin's dash for the plate was the winning run.

The palm for originality and independent thinking, however, must be awarded to the Old Master, Casey Stengel. He's the oldest manager in the majors and he's got it made, yet no one in the business has experimented and defied the percentages more than Casey.

When Phil Rizzuto was nearing the end of his brilliant career, Casey consistently lifted him for a pinch hitter as early as the second inning if he thought a rally was on the fire. Rizzuto probably didn't like it and I know darn well the sportswriters resented such treatment of a longtime favorite, but that didn't stop Casey from making the move. The same goes for his two-platoon system, which ballplayers dislike because it tends to cut down their salaries. I remember reading that Casey used 71 different lineups one year, manipulating his men to get the most out of the talent at his command.

Managers who are slaves to the strategy laid down by the book inevitably make the discouraging discovery that percentage baseball is no substitute for good ballplayers. After all, you can't think a man into a base hit or break a third strike over the plate while you're sitting on the bench. Then there is a small complication known as the psychological factor which can make a genius look like a bum every time.

I've often felt like using a ballplayer's head for fungo practice and I came awful close to obeying that impulse last season in a game we lost by one run. Bob Clemente, the third best hitter in the league, went up there with two out and none on and proceeded to end the game by getting thrown out tamely on a bunt.

"Bunting with nobody on base when we needed a run to tie was the dumbest play I've ever seen," I raved. "You must be loco to pull a boner like that. There was only one thing for you to do. You had to be up there swinging for a home run."

Clemente looked me squarely in the eye and shrugged. "Boss, me no feel like home run," he said.

Does anybody know an answer to that one?

JOHN GALLAGHER

"You're not angry because I called that pitch a strike—subconsciously you rebel against all authority. Think back—you hated your father . . ."

THERE ARE two things to be said about this story, and they do not concern either the fact that it deals in a sense with religion or that it appeared in *Argosy* magazine during World War II. The two things are: (1) it has a surprise ending; (2) you won't guess what it is.

A Bat and a Prayer

HOWARD BRESLIN

ALL THIS TALK about training in the North hurting baseball is just so much bench babble to me. Of course it's a long time since I pitched for the Katydids, but we trained in Virginia and I never saw the day when I couldn't reach home plate with the ball. The Katydids were a real ball club, too. The likes of them haven't set spikes on a diamond since Connie Mack was a rookie. These DiMaggios and Beazleys and Walkers play a pretty fair brand of ball—for youngsters. But, without bragging, I'd take my chances against them all tomorrow, and I'd still be on the mound when the ninth inning rolled around. What with the draft and the Manpower Commission I might get the chance, too. Imagine. "Now pitching—Hooks Goodhue."

Not that I've had any offers exactly, but there've been a couple of hints. I can't be so much older than some of the boys Rickey's dug up for Brooklyn. I'll pitch to any batter living provided it isn't Dinny Hanrahan. Hanrahan of the old Katydids.

So maybe you never heard of Hanrahan, and maybe you never heard of the Katydids. Well, brother, it's time your education was improved. Hanrahan and me, we played in a series that would have made last year's disturbance between the Cardinals and the Yankees look like a checker tournament. Just settle back in the bleacher seats now, while old Hooks throws a few curves.

When Dinny Hanrahan came to the Katydids he was straight from Brother Chrysostom's orphanage. Hanrahan was a grinning Irishman, tall and big-shouldered. Pat Boyle, who was managing the Katydids, stuck him in the outfield the minute he showed up at the training camp.

The kid didn't do much in his first turn at bat, and everybody figured we'd drawn a blank. But the next time Hanrahan caught hold of one and it probably hasn't come down yet. Boyle's face got as red as a sunset. He stopped the game and sent our best pitchers in against Hanrahan. Dinny hit them all. He sent one back at me that nearly took my head off.

Everybody was excited. You see, the Katydids were a field club. We had a sweet infield and pitching staff. But hit! The whole outfit combined couldn't hit hard enough to knock the foam off a beer. These Chicago Hitless Wonders were sluggers compared to the Katydids.

Naturally, the sight of Hanrahan had us all hipped. I remember Sarsfield, the catcher, took off his mask and came over to Pat Boyle.

"Hey, Chief," he said. "Funny thing."

"What?" Boyle snapped, still looking at Hanrahan.

"That Hanrahan—he says a prayer or something when he takes his cut."

Boyle's mouth dropped open. "A prayer?"

"So help me," said Sarsfield. "I heard him."

Well, Boyle grabbed hold of Sarsfield and shoved his face close. "Listen, I don't give a damn if he gets down on his knees, as long as he keeps powdering that ball!"

From that moment Dinny Hanrahan was regular center fielder for the Katydids—and he was the best center fielder, hit, catch and throw, in the business.

I think it was the catcher of the Batwings that nicknamed Dinny "Holy Hanrahan." Of course everybody in baseball soon knew about that habit of saying a little prayer just before he swung. They kidded Hanrahan, but he just grinned. And he kept hitting.

Some people said we had no right to win the pennant that year—even with Hanrahan. If the Batwings hadn't all gotten hoof-and-mouth disease in August, it might have been a different story. But they did get it, and we did win, and anybody who says that poisoned beer barrel came from the Katydids is a dirty liar.

Anyway, there was the Katydids due to face the Tornados in the series, and the Tornados just licked their lips. Iron-fist McManus was the manager of the Tornados and he'd hated Pat Boyle for years. The Tornados had slaughtered their own league. They were hard hitters and their pitchers were every bit as good as ours, and it's no wonder the newspapers were saying we didn't want to show up for the series.

It was to be the best four out of seven games. Two at the Tornados' park, three at the Katydids' and the last two back at the Tornados'. But nobody thought we'd have to take the train west twice.

Boyle decided to pitch Dawson in the first game. He was the best we had. Just before we took the field Pat gathered the whole club around him. "Boys," he said, "don't let the big talk worry you. They can't win if they can't score. We'll show them that tight, smart baseball can whip slugging every time."

The Tornados beat us 11 to 1. The one Katydid run was a homer by Hanrahan.

In the second game they shut us out 6 to 0. Hanrahan got all three of our hits.

Back in our own park I was supposed to pitch the third game. You could cut the gloom with a knife. I didn't feel too good standing out there. We had a packed crowd—the Katydid fans evidently showing up with the same feeling that made the Christians go watch their buddies wrestle with the lions. Hanrahan stopped on his way to the outfield.

"Hooks, lad," he said, "it's only a game. Take it easy."

Now, I'm a Methodist myself, and I was christened John Wesley Goodhue, but, after all, I had to pitch that ball game.

"Dinny," I said, "I know you pray while you're hitting. But have you got a prayer for pitchers, too?"

Hanrahan shook his head. I guess the Papists only look out for batters. But I noticed Rosy Rosenberg, our first baseman, staring after Hanrahan as he trotted out on the grass.

"Hooks, you maybe have a thought," said Rosy. He spat in his glove. "You hold them. Maybe we get you some hits."

The Tornados were so cocky it wasn't hard to get past the first inning. When it came to our turn at bat the first two men popped out. You could hear McManus hee-hawing on the Tornado bench. But he stopped when Dinny Hanrahan picked up his bat.

"Wait, Dinny." Rosy Rosenberg put out a hand and grabbed him by the arm. "Can you hit this lefty they got in there?"

Hanrahan smiled, running his big hand up and down the bat. "I'll tell you better in a minute," he said. He walked out to the batter's box.

McManus jumped in front of the Tornado bench and waved the fielders back. He cupped his hands to his mouth and bellowed, "This is the holy one, Lefty. Strike him out!"

They had a big, string-bean, left-handed spitballer in there, and his jaws worked as if he was having a fit. He's seen Hanrahan bat and he took his time, throwing one leg up in the air and bringing his arm back till you thought he touched the right-field wall.

Hanrahan looked at two, a ball and a strike. But when the next one came down there—bam! He slapped a line drive right over second base. It wasn't three feet off the ground and going like a bullet. The Tornado shortstop dove for it but missed. Lucky for him, because it would have made a hole in his hand.

Hanrahan pulled up at first and the crowd gave him a cheer. But that was the end of the inning as far as it mattered. The southpaw struck out the next man swinging.

I was set to pitch when I noticed that Rosenberg was talking it up. There hadn't been a sound behind me in the first inning, but now Rosy was chattering away.

"Feed it in, Hooks," he chanted. "Feed it in."

"Are you crazy?" I asked. "Don't make them sore!"

But it was too late. McManus was waving his arms and roaring at his boys to get some runs. He swore at Rosenberg and I nearly balked when Rosy laughed in his face.

Somehow I got through the inning. I was slow-balling them to death, but even at that Hanrahan saved me by going up the center-field fence like a monkey and spearing a ball that had homer written all over it.

When we got to the bench, I was shaking like a leaf. Pat Boyle looked at me, grunted, and sent two lads out to the bull pen. Rosenberg was the first man to bat.

"Hanrahan," he said. "Can I maybe use your bat?"

"Sure."

"And listen." Rosy put his nose in Hanrahan's ear and whispered to him. Suddenly Hanrahan began to laugh. He threw back his head and roared. Then he whispered something back to Rosy.

"What's so funny, Hanrahan?" growled Pat Boyle.

Hanrahan gave Rosy a pat on the back and shoved him toward the plate. He turned to Boyle, grinning. "Watch," said Hanrahan.

Rosenberg stood there in the box. The lanky southpaw reared back and pitched. To this day the Tornado catcher swears that Rosy shut his eyes tight, muttered something, and swung with all his might. There was a crack and the ball screamed into left field. Pat Boyle fell off the bench, and he was still sitting on the ground, staring, pop-eyed, when Rosy came into second.

"Glory be to God," said Boyle in a whisper.

Even the crowd in the stands wasn't making any noise. All the Katydids except Hanrahan were gasping like hooked fish. Little Pinky Tremont, our third baseman, dropped the three bats he was holding and scrambled for the one Rosy'd used.

"Gimme that bat," Tremont stuttered, his eyes popping.

"It ain't the bat," said Hanrahan, seeing that Pinky could hardly lift it. "Listen." He bent down and whispered in Tremont's ear.

Pinky nodded grimly, swung around and started for the box like a man going to his death. He tapped his bat on the plate, swung it back and forth, and bellowed, "Come on, you big bum. Pitch!"

This was like a rabbit taking a shotgun away from the hunter and slapping him with it, and McManus nearly exploded. He ripped out with an oath that made the umpire swing around. McManus choked, coughed, and said hoarsely, "One hit was luck, Lefty. Get on with it!"

The pitcher was scratching his head and watching Rosenberg dance on second. Finally he shrugged his shoulders and faced the batter. I give him credit, he wasn't worried any.

Little Tremont worked him to three and two, fouling both strikes. Then, as smooth as Cobb, he slapped a single along the first baseline. Rosenberg was crossing third at the crack of the bat, and he walked home.

"Everybody hits," yelled Hanrahan. He grabbed Rosy and waltzed him around. Boyle wasn't saying a word. He kept slapping his face with a glove, and staring.

Sarsfield stood in front of Hanrahan. "Tell me, Dinny." He begged like a kid after candy. "Tell me."

Hanrahan whispered something to him, too, and Sarsfield walloped a liner against the Yellow Kid sign on the bleachers. Tremont was fast and he came all the way in from first.

The Tornados went to pieces. McManus was raging like a wild man, the pitcher hit the next batter, and when Sarsfield and the other guy worked a double steal, their catcher threw the ball into the outfield.

By that time I was at the plate myself and trying to remember what Hanrahan said. "Hooks, you watch that pitcher. And when his foot starts to come down, you say, 'Saint-Denis-pray-for-us.' Say it fast but be sure and say it all. Then—swing!"

I was torn between wanting a hit and thinking my father would haunt me if I asked a popery saint for a favor. But the left-hander was a wreck. He walked me and McManus took him out. We made seven runs that inning before they retired the side.

With that behind me, I pitched the best game of my life. Slow and hooking the corners, and slipping the fast one past them now and then because they were still rattled over what had given us the needle. Incidentally, I remember I kept saying that Saint-Denis thing on every pitch.

My next time up I found out from Hanrahan that we were using Saint Hilary on the new Tornado pitcher. Saint Hilary did all right by us, too. The game ended with a score of 14 to 3, in favor of the Katydids.

McManus, who'd been thrown out for indecent language when Hanrahan tripled in the fifth, came storming into our dressing room afterward. His face was purple.

"Witchcraft!" he kept yelling. He shook his fist at Pat Boyle. "You haven't the decency to keep the saints out of this and fight like men!"

Pat Boyle grinned from ear to ear. "The likes of you wouldn't understand, McManus. You're too cheap to light a candle once in a while."

"That's a lie!" McManus said, looking guilty. "And anyway, we're still a game ahead. It'll take more than praying to beat us tomorrow."

Rosy Rosenberg was sitting on a trunk taking off his spikes, but he stood up in his stocking feet. "McManus," said Rosy, "such talk is not nice. You go to your church, we go to ours."

McManus' lantern jaw dropped, his tongue hung out. Hanrahan chuckled, and the Tornado manager whirled on him.

"Okay, Hanrahan!" he said, snarling. "You're behind this. But there's two can play the game!" He went out and slammed the door.

There must have been some wild telegrams sent that night because when we came out of the clubhouse the next afternoon, McManus was crowing like a bantam, and the Bishop of Tornado City was sitting next to him on the Tornado bench.

Pat Boyle scowled. He muttered, "Bringing the clergy in."

"Is that bad, Dinny?" Rosenberg asked Hanrahan, casting a worried look at the bishop. "Is the reverend maybe better than you?"

Hanrahan was watching Dutch Brubaker warm up for the Tornados. Brubaker had beat us the first game, and the Katydids were scared. But Hanrahan grinned.

"Sure," he said. "I've got this bird's number. It's 'Saint-Stanislaus-pray-for-us'—and swing."

Well, that fourth game was probably the politest ball game ever played. Having the bishop on the bench did wonderful things to those roughneck Tornados. But not being able to cuss made them uneasy, and the Katydids, taking their cue from Hanrahan, were fairly bursting with pep.

Saint Stanislaus was evidently a slow starter because we didn't get to the Dutchman until the fourth. Their first baseman dropped an easy out with two away, and Dutch threw his glove down and glared. But the whole Tornado team yelled, "Shhh!" and glanced at the bishop. The Katydids had three runs before the Tornados had pulled themselves together.

Dawson, pitching, had trouble every inning, but the Katydids were 'way over their heads. The infield pulled three double plays—and Hanrahan! Well, Hanrahan just about played all the positions in the outfield.

They pushed over two runs in the seventh and it looked bad. A man was on third with one out. But the next batter lifted a long fly to Hanrahan, and he threw a perfect strike from deep center. The Tornado made a dive for the plate, but the umpire's thumb jerked up. "Out!"

"Out!" McManus bounced from his seat beside the bishop. "Out? Why you—" The bishop coughed; McManus swallowed hard. Then he smiled sort of sickly, and said in a weak voice, "Yeah. Of course. Out."

That broke the Tornado spirit and we didn't have any more trouble. We won, 5 to 2. You should have heard those Tornados in the clubhouse. They let go with everything they'd kept back all afternoon, and a few besides.

With the series even, the fifth game broke the attendance record. I guess the only people who didn't pay to get in were the two bishops in their boxes. For by that time Pat Boyle had dug up a bishop who was a Katydid rooter, and they both sat together. McManus wasn't making the mistake of having his bishop on the bench this time.

The Tornados were wearing so many charms and medals and rabbits' feet that they clanked when they walked. But the Katydids were still sticking to Hanrahan's saint. The papers had spread the whole story; there was even a picture of McManus coming out of a church. Rosy Rosenberg tried to corner the candle market to keep the Tornados from lighting any, but Hanrahan made him stop, much to Rosy's disappointment.

Nothing could hold the Katydids. You know how it is when folks are sure they've got God on their side. We trimmed the pants off them— 9 to 0.

Iron-fist McManus was still game, and still snarling. "It'll be different when we get back to our park," he said. "There's a curse on this place! A devil's curse!"

The Katydids just laughed. Pat Boyle said, "McManus, you don't live right. How can you expect any luck?"

* * *

There was a mob at the Tornado City station when we got off the train. And their newspapers had accused us of everything from selling our souls to the devil, to trying to put the Pope in the White House. Folks took their ball games serious in those days. But when McManus tried to get the Bishop of Tornado City to excommunicate Hanrahan, the bishop threw him out on his ear.

The Katydids were a little upset because Hanrahan's saints were now off their home grounds, but Hanrahan fixed that. Just before the game he brought a little chubby-faced man with spectacles around to the bench.

"Boys," said Hanrahan, "this is Brother Chrysostom. He's come from the orphanage for this game. Brother taught me to bat."

We all took off our caps. Roman collar or no Roman collar, I'll tip my hat to a man who can teach anybody to hit like Hanrahan.

"Brother," said Rosy Rosenberg, "would you maybe run your hands over our bats?"

Brother Chrysostom frowned. "You're a superstitious lot," he said. "But Hanrahan, here, is my boy, and I've been a Katydid rooter for years. If it'll keep you hitting, I'll do it." And he touched every bat we had.

There's no sense in telling you about that last game. You wouldn't believe it. But it was the greatest game anyone will ever see. It was nip and tuck till the last man was out.

McManus tried everything. They walked Hanrahan every time. Wouldn't put the ball anywhere near him. And I swear McManus paid the man who threw that pop bottle from the bleachers. Another inch and it'd have killed Hanrahan.

Pat Boyle used four pitchers. He told them each to give out with everything as long as they were in there. I pitched the first three innings myself. I gave them four hits and one run.

It was four to four going into the ninth. Hanrahan was up first and he walked. The place was a bedlam. Brother Chrysostom, in the box with the bishops, was so excited that he hammered his glasses on the railing and finally threw them away.

Hanrahan went down on the first pitch. He hooked into the bag, but it was close. The Tornado shortstop went crazy when he heard the ump yell, "Safe!" He tried to spike Hanrahan, threw the ball away, and took a poke at the umpire, all in one motion.

Hanrahan was on his feet and streaking for third before the dust had even settled over second. He slid in safe a foot ahead of the ball.

After about fifteen minutes, McManus agreed to go on with the game. There was Hanrahan on third, and the Tornado shortstop out of the game, and nobody out. McManus sent in a new pitcher.

The Katydid at bat took three lusty cuts. The air was blue around the plate but he didn't hit anything else. One out, Rosenberg at bat.

Rosy nearly broke his back, he swung so hard at the first pitch. "Strike!" said the umpire.

Hanrahan, on third, held up a hand and yelled, "Time!"

"No!" screamed McManus. "No! No!" And that cost him the game, because the umpire got sore and called time.

Hanrahan ran down the baseline and Rosy went halfway to meet him. McManus figured that Hanrahan was giving Rosy the prayer for the new pitcher, and when they whispered together he was sure of it. So he waited till Rosy got back in the batter's box, and then he sent in still another pitcher.

Pat Boyle swore but there was nothing he could do. The pitcher wound up and Hanrahan started in with the pitch. Every Katydid was screaming, and so was the crowd.

Rosy bunted, of course. Any other time you could have seen that coming a day ahead, but nobody'd been thinking of anything but slugging since Hanrahan brought in the saints. It was as much of a surprise to us as it was to the Tornados. And McManus passed out cold.

We turned them back in their half of the inning, and it was all over. Katydids—5; Tornados—4.

Brother Chrysostom fought his way into the dressing room. He grabbed Hanrahan's hand and pumped it. "Hanrahan," he said, "is it a miracle you worked making these boys hit?"

Hanrahan laughed. "Well, now, Brother. Remember how, when we played at the orphanage, you'd tell us, 'Swing at it—say a little prayer to Saint Chrysostom, and swing'? Sure, it got to be a habit with me. But Saint Chrysostom was too long for a fast-ball pitcher. And I used to change saints for each pitcher."

"A grand thing," said Pat Boyle.

"It's all a matter of timing," said Hanrahan. "And a few of the boys timed it the same way when I told them. Sure, the rest of it was easy because they believed I was giving them supernatural help."

"You mean you wasn't?" asked Rosy Rosenberg.

Hanrahan clapped him on the shoulder. "Do you think the good saints have nothing to do but take care of your base hits?"

Brother Chrysostom peered around. He said, "Faith is wonderful."

I'd never believed in that stuff for a minute, but, just the same, you should see the chapel we built for Brother Chrysostom's orphanage. There was quite an argument, but we finally named it All Saints.

"THESE ARE the saddest of possible words, Tinker-to-Evers-to-Chance."
So run the deathless opening lines of Franklin P. Adams' poem "Base-
ball's Sad Lexicon" (you'll find it in the first *Fireside Book of Baseball*).
Nobody ever questioned their skill at the double play—not, that
is, till that masterful sports writer Warren Brown did a little digging.
Whatever you think of the following, it ain't quite as poetic as Mr.
Adams' version.

From *Don't Believe Everything You Read*

WARREN BROWN

I DARESAY even those whose education on sports affairs, past and present, has been fostered by the inspired outpourings of writers for the stars of radio and television would agree with the accepted baseball truism that where Tinker to Evers to Chance went, there went the double play. I know this to be so, since I have asked opinions of many people well acquainted with baseball's present and past. Some of them, still active, dated back to the days of the spitball. Some of them saw Tinker and Evers and Chance play with the Cubs in the days of their glory, 1906 through 1909. I did not. I came in time to appreciate the double-play-making artistry of Bill Jurges, Billy Herman and Charlie Grimm of another set of Cubs. What they could do, and it was wondrous, indeed, I decided others, later on, could do better. Among them I would list Frank Crosetti and Joe Gordon of the Yankees, and a bit later, Gordon with Lou Boudreau of the Indians, and more recently, Phil Rizzuto with Jerry Coleman and/or Billy Martin of the Yankees. In the case of these, it didn't seem to matter who happened to play first base. Then one day, my curiosity about this immortal Tinker-to-Evers-to-Chance combination started bothering me. Existing record books were of no help. I did find out that Ferris Fain, with the Athletics in 1949, had figured in 194 double plays for the season. In one game, he figured in six, as had several other major-league first basemen. I learned that Jerry Priddy, Detroit second baseman in 1950, figured in 150 double plays. He was in five in one game, as others had been. I found that Lou Boudreau, while with Cleveland in 1944, had a

hand in 134 double plays. He also was in five in one game.

But nowhere in the record books did I turn up the names of Tinker (ss), Evers (2b) or Chance (1b) as having done anything extraordinary.

I enlisted the offices of Charley Segar, aide-de-camp to Ford Frick, then the National League president. "I'd like to know," I said, "how many double plays that combination, Tinker to Evers to Chance, made in a season."

"So would I," said Segar. He went to work on the official scoring records of 1906 through 1909. When he had completed the check, the result was startling.

Armed with his findings, I began asking around and about: "How many double plays do you think the combination, Tinker to Evers to Chance, turned in during a season?" The answers I got ranged from 100 to what we mathematicians are pleased to term infinity.

Then I began lowering the boom. The official box scores of the National League, 1906 through 1909, revealed that Tinker to Evers to Chance (or 6-4-3 in scoring parlance) made exactly 29 double plays! They made eight in 1906, Tinker playing in 148 games, Evers in 154, and Chance in 136. They made seven in 1907, Tinker playing in 113 games, Evers in 151, and Chance in 109. They made eight in 1908, Tinker playing in 157 games, Evers in 123, and Chance in 126. They made six in 1909, Tinker playing in 143 games, Evers in 126, and Chance in 92.

Charley Segar did not want to be the complete iconoclast. He also presented the figures on their double-play activity on the basis of Evers to Tinker to Chance (or 4-6-3). In 1906, they made nine; in 1907, they made six; in 1908, they made eight; and in 1909, they made two for a total of 25.

Whether you take them in their more metrical Tinker-to-Evers-to-Chance sequence or in the Evers-to-Tinker-to-Chance sequence, these Hall of Fame dwellers, as a trio, accounted for just 54 double plays in the four seasons when they caused FPA to start twanging his lyre. To be sure, there were many double plays of the Tinker-to-Chance and Evers-to-Chance nature, but then, no one ever committed them to verse.

JIMMY HATLO

© 1957 Courtesy King Features Syndicate, Inc.

THEY'LL DO IT EVERY TIME

IN THE FIRST *Fireside Book of Baseball,* there was a story about a horse who played third base. Now all we need is one in which the hero winds up saying, "There'll be plenty more ball games, but there'll never be another cow like Dolly."

And here it is.

The Milk Pitcher

HOWARD BRUBAKER

THE FULLERS named their son "Philip" after his maternal grandfather. That was an error in judgment because the time came when the name Phil Fuller aroused chuckles and snickers among the pleasure-loving faces of the countryside. At the age of one Phil had practically settled upon red as the best color for hair. Sometime in his third year the truth was established that he was left-handed. When given something he did not want, he threw it away with violence.

This act seemed to set up pleasurable emotions in his young soul. His simple face widened into a grin, and before long he was heaving things around for the sheer love of heaving.

At four Phil sprouted a genuine freckle on his nose, the forerunner of a bumper crop, and even his prejudiced mother had to admit that his ears were large for their age.

The youth spent his fourth summer in the society of a Jersey calf named Lily, who was tethered in the orchard. Phil had nothing to do except to throw green apples at a tree with his left hand, and Lily's time was also her own. The child learned not to wince when she licked his pink nose with her rough tongue, and the calf put up with some pretty rowdy conduct too. Both infants cried when separated for the night. The tender attachment between Phil and Lil was the subject of neighborhood gossip as far away as the Doug Morton place at the bend of Squaw Creek.

When Phil was six he threw a carriage bolt from the wagon shed into the water trough, and he laughed so boisterously over this feat that Mr. Harrington heard the noise while passing in a light spring wagon.

Phil had a misguided sense of humor. It seemed to him that throwing things was the world's funniest joke. As he picked up a stone and let it fly, the freckles on his face arranged themselves into a pleasure pattern, his features widened, and he grinned expansively, showing vacant spots where he was changing teeth.

By this time his love for the cow stable had become a grand passion. Horses, dogs, cats, and pigs meant rather less in his young life than they do to most farm boys, but cows meant more. Phil attended all the milkings with his father, dealt out bran, and threw down hay. He wandered in and out among the bovine legs without fear; hoofs, horns, and teeth had no terrors for him. He was soon old enough to drive the cattle to pasture and bring them back.

At the age of eight he was probably the ablest redheaded cowboy and left-handed stone thrower in Clinton Township. At this date in history he had drunk enough milk to float a battleship and thrown enough stones, sticks, bones, horseshoes, apples, corncobs, and baseballs to sink one. He was now the owner in fee simple of Lily's knock-kneed daughter, Dolly. This white-faced blond flapper followed Phil around with adoration and bleated at the barnyard gate until her playmate came home from school.

That fount of knowledge was Clinton Township, District No. 5, known locally as Tamarack School. There he absorbed a reasonable quantity of booklore and learned to pitch a straight ball with speed and control. He is still remembered in educational circles as the southpaw who hurled the Tamarackers to glorious victory over the Squaw Creek outfit, while unveiling the broadest grin ever seen on the lot and issuing many unnecessary noises. Although he had a lot of influence over a baseball, he could not make his face behave.

Baseball was the great joy of Phil's school years. Every spring when the frost came out of the ground his flaming head sprang up on the soggy field like a tulip. He had never learned to bat well, but he was a thrower of great ability and a laugher and yeller of great audibility. In school when asked to give the boundaries of Baluchistan he could scarcely make the teacher hear, but on the diamond his disorderly conduct was noted and deplored as far away as Grandma Longenecker's cottage.

The game uncorked his inhibitions and released his ego. His habitual shyness vanished and gave place to vociferous glee. He did frolicsome things with his feet; his arms went round like a windmill wheel; sometimes he burst into what he wrongly believed to be song. Miss Willikans, the teacher, testified that Phil had easily the worst singing voice that had attended District No. 5 in her time—which would be nineteen years if she lived through this term, as seemed highly unlikely.

Inevitably there came an afternoon in late May when Phil's career as a Tamaracker had run its course. He twisted a button almost off his new coat, whispered a graduating piece about Daniel Webster, took his books and his well-worn right-hand glove, and went back to the cows.

At five o'clock the following morning the fourteen-year-old Phil became the vice-president and general manager of the dairy department of the Fuller farm. His father was overworked; help was scarce and expensive; and the graduate of Tamarack was judged strong enough to handle the job. He milked all the cows that summer, cleaned the stalls, helped to get in the hay and fill the silo. He ran the separator, he churned, he carried skim milk to the pigs. The end of the summer found him a stocky lad of rather less than normal height but with a rank growth of feet, arms, and ears. He had the complexion of a boiled beet and hair exactly the shade of a two-cent stamp. His hands were large and fully equipped with freckles, calluses, bumps, cracks, warts, knuckles, and rough, red wrists.

Phil could lift with one hand Dolly's new calf, Molly; he could throw a ten-pound sledgehammer over the hay barn; he could sing like a creaky pump; and he shattered all known speed records from the stable to the dining room. He was an able performer with the table fork as well as with the pitchfork.

In September he took all these assets and liabilities and his first long pants and went to Branford to live with Aunt Mary and Uncle Phineas and attend high school. As he was winding up his affairs preparatory to this great adventure, it was clear that he had something on his mind. It came out one night at supper in the hiatus between the fifth and sixth ears of Golden Bantam.

"It's too bad they don't keep a cow," he said, apropos of nothing.

"Oh, sakes alive, child!" Mother exclaimed in surprise. "They wouldn't want to be bothered with a cow."

Phil's ears went red. He polished off his corncob and returned to the attack. "They wouldn't need to be bothered much. They have no horse any more and there's room in the barn. I could feed her and milk her and everything. I bet Aunt Mary would be glad to have lots of nice milk and cream. We could tie her behind the buggy and take her in with us."

"Tie who—Aunt Mary?" asked Father with ill-timed facetiousness.

"Dolly," said Phil.

A dozen objections were raised and disposed of. Aunt Mary and Uncle Phineas were consulted by telephone, and after the first shock they agreed to the outrageous plan. And thus it came about that Phil Fuller was the first case in recorded history of a boy who went to Branford High School accompanied by a private and personal cow.

During those first months of strangeness and homesickness, Dolly was his comfort and his joy, his link with the familiar. He brushed and polished that blond cow until her upholstery was threadbare, pampered her with choice viands and clean bedding, scrubbed and whitewashed the interior of the old barn, put in window sashes to give Dolly more sunlight and a better view. Often when the day was fair he led her around the block to take the air and see a little city life.

At six o'clock of a dark, bitter morning the neighbors could hear distressing noises issuing from Phineas Rucker's lantern-lit barn, and they knew from sad experiences of the past that another day was about to dawn and the redheaded Fuller boy was singing to his heart's true love.

Dolly was now in the full flush of her splendid young cowhood, and home was never like this. Phil plied her with experimental mixtures —beet pulp, ground oats, cottonseed meal—and carefully noted the results. The contented cow responded gratefully to this treatment. Before long she exceeded the needs of the Rucker family, and Phil was doing a pleasant little milk business with the neighbors. His immaculate barn, his new white overalls, his vocal excesses, and his free street parades all helped trade. The milk inspector passed Dolly with high honors, and doctors recommended her for ailing babies. Presently she was one of Branford's leading citizens, a self-supporting twenty-quart cow commanding a premium of three cents over the market price. Phil had discovered his lifework.

His second great discovery did not come until spring. On a blustery March day he was out on the diamond behind the high-school building warming up his left wing and chuckling over his favorite joke when Mr. Huckley, chemistry teacher and baseball coach, came along.

"Southpaw, eh!" he demanded. "Let's see what you've got, Fuller."

Phil gave a brief exhibition of his wares with Dinky Doolittle holding the catcher's glove.

"Plenty of steam and good control," the teacher said, "and your footwork is terrible. Now show us your curve."

"I haven't got any," Phil answered. "Nobody ever showed me how to pitch a curve."

"Somebody will now," Mr. Huckley said. "Whether you can do it or not is another question."

That was the beginning of a beautiful friendship and a new era in the life of Philip Fuller.

Mr. Huckley had pitched on the team of Athens University, of which he was a graduate. He liked Phil, admired his able hands, his abnormally developed forearms, his keen joy in the game. The coach saw great possibilities in this piece of raw material, and he spent a patient hour teaching Phil some of the rudiments of curve pitching, and in time they achieved a perceptible out curve. At the height of his exultation, the boy pulled out a nickel-plated watch and said:

"I ask you to excuse me now. It's time to milk my cow."

After a week of such instruction, Mr. Huckley handed down this decision: "You have the makings of a good pitcher, Phil, if you're willing to learn. You have a couple of fine qualities and not over twenty-five or thirty serious faults."

Phil's ears flushed with pleasure and embarrassment.

"Well, maybe I can get shut of some of them —I mean those—faults. I've got four years to do it in."

"Right-o. You have good control of your fast one; you have a nice little out; and you have the worst style of windup these eyes have ever seen."

Four years of study, dairying, and baseball, with summers of hard work on the farm made Phil a different boy—different and yet curiously the same. His shoulders were broader, his arms stronger, but he did not add many inches to his stature. He knew more mathematics, science, and history, but Latin was still Greek to him. Although he took on some of the manners and customs of his town contemporaries, he still had the gait of one walking over a plowed field. In time he learned to talk with girls without being distressed, but as a social light he was a flickering flame in a smoky chimney. He was a conspicuous success on the barn floor but a brilliant failure on the dance floor. His voice changed, but not for the better. His matin song to Dolly now sounded like a bullfrog with a bad attack of static. He wrote a creditable little rural farce for the senior dramatic class and further distinguished himself as the worst actor on the American stage.

Though much ridiculed, he was universally liked and genuinely respected. On the ball field he was a source of low comedy to friend and foe because of the eccentric behavior of his face and feet, but in his succeeding seasons on the mound he pitched the Branford High School out of the cellar position into respectable company, into select society, and finally, in his senior year, into the state championship of the small-town division.

At the joyfest in the assembly hall in celebration of this final triumph, Phil was forced to make a speech. He fixed his eyes upon his third vest button and informed it in confidence that it was Mr. Huckley who had made him what he was today—which wasn't so very much.

When his turn came, the chemist and coach arose and told the world a great secret about this Phil Fuller who had now pitched his last game for dear old B. H. S. Phil, he said, owed his success as a pitcher to his having been brought up in a cow barn. Constant milking had developed his forearm muscles to surprising strength, and the knots and knobs on his good left hand had enabled him to get a spin on the ball that produced his deadliest curves.

"I therefore propose," he said, "that Phil's girl friend, Dolly, be elected an honorary member of the team."

This motion was seconded with a will and carried with a whoop, and Dolly became, as far as anyone could learn, the only cow that ever belonged to a ball club.

"Phil has told you," Mr. Huckley went on, "that he got some help from my coaching. If so, he has chosen a rotten way to pay his debt. Instead of going to a high-class and fancy culture factory like Athens, he has decided to enter Sparta Agricultural College. Athens and Sparta are deadly enemies in athletics, and some day Phil may use what I have taught him against my own alma mater. There is no use trying to keep Phil from running after the cows, but this is a sad blow to me. I didn't raise my boy to be a Spartan."

It was the county agricultural agent who had first put Sparta into Phil's head. The boy had naturally assumed that his education would cease with high school, but this Mr. Runkleman came into Dolly's palatial quarters one day and spoke an eloquent piece in favor of his own Sparta.

"A boy who intends to be an expert dairy farmer," he said in part, "ought to learn all there is on the subject. You have a natural gift for taking care of cows, but what you don't know about scientific dairying would fill a ten-foot shelf."

"That's so," Phil answered, "but I haven't got much money."

"You don't need much money. Lots of the boys are working their way through. I'll guarantee that you get a job in the college dairy barn. The work will pay your board, teach you the practical side, and you'll meet the nicest cows in the world."

This was a weighty inducement, and one crisp day in late September found Phil knocking at the door of the higher education. He was a youth of five feet five with fiery hair and complexion, with ears that stuck out like red semaphores: a homely, awkward, likable boy, full of hope, inexperience, diffidence, and whole raw milk. His only regret was that he could not take Dolly with him to college.

Because of Mr. Runkleman's hearty recommendation, he got his job in the dairy barn, and he took a room in a house near by. His days sped by in a new kind of eternal triangle—boardinghouse, dairy, and classroom—and he was happy in all three places.

Every morning at the ghastly hour of four he trudged through windy blackness to the big concrete barn. Now followed several hours of milking, feeding, currying, and stable-cleaning in company with half a dozen other cow students, then home to breakfast and to class. In the late afternoon there was a repetition of these chores, followed by dinner, some study, and an early bed. Such was the wild college life of his flaming youth.

Football, the great autumn obsession, meant little to him. Basketball was more fun, but a habitual early riser makes a poor customer of night life. In fact, Phil made up his mind that, for the first year, he would waste no time on athletics.

Sibyl Barnett Samboy, the wife of Kenneth Samboy, director of Sparta athletics, said after Phil had been introduced to her at the fresh-man reception: "That's the first time I ever shook hands with a Stillson wrench."

Although he honestly intended to keep out of baseball, the first warm afternoon in March brought on an attack of the old spring fever. There was no harm, he thought, in getting out a ball and glove and tossing a few to "Spider" Coppery behind the barn while waiting for milking time. Before long it was a regular practice among the "cowboys" to beguile their idle moments with playing catch and knocking up flies, and presently there was talk of forming a team to play a game with the students of the horticultural department, otherwise the "greenhouse gang."

An insulting challenge was given and taken, and the game took place on a pleasant Saturday.

This contest was held upon the old ball grounds. The new stadium was built upon a better site, and the former athletic grounds with their little grandstand were given over to the general use of the students. Samboy was a firm believer in athletics for everybody. He loved to stir up little wars between classes, dormitories, fraternities, and departments. Often these little home-brew contests developed and uncovered talent for the college teams.

Along about the fifth inning of this ragged ball game an uninvited guest appeared among the handful of spectators in the grandstand. Phil was on the mound at the time.

So Mr. Samboy's eyes were gladdened by the sight of a stocky, freckled, redheaded southpaw who burned them over with power, who laughed from head to foot and uttered unfortunate noises.

Samboy talked with him after the game, poked his nose into his past, and urged him to try for the college team.

Phil protested that he was too busy with his classes and his cows. It was a long argument, but Samboy won.

"Report to Donnigan on Monday," said the director, "and tell him I suggested that he look you over. Every coach has a free hand with his own team, you know, but if he turns you down let me know, and I'll give you a tryout on the freshman team. I'll speak to Professor Weatherby, if you like, and ask him to let you shift hours at the dairy while you're trying your luck on the diamond."

"You don't suppose—" Phil was visibly embarrassed—"there wouldn't be any danger of me losing that job—or anything? I wouldn't do that for all the baseball there is."

"Not a chance, Fuller. We don't give fellows

positions here because they are good athletes, but we don't fire 'em either."

H. B. Donnigan—"Hardboiled Donnigan"—had learned his trade under the great Tim Crowley of the Eagles. Donnigan's big-league days were over, and he was making a living coaching college teams. He used the Crowley method and the Crowley philosophy. All ballplayers were worms and should be treated as such.

He had spent his boyhood among the tin cans and bottles of a vacant lot in New York's gashouse district, and he never really believed that ballplayers could be grown in the country.

One trouble with his policy was that it did not work at all. It was rumored that when his contract expired at the end of the season Samboy would let him go. A sense of his failure did not improve the coach's technique—or his temper. It was to this man-eating tiger that Samboy had cheerfully thrown the redheaded rookie from the cow barn.

"And now who let you in?" was Hardboiled Donnigan's address of welcome."

"Mr. Samboy said would you please look me over."

The phrase was perhaps an unfortunate one. The coach did exactly that.

"All right. Tell him I've done it, and if you're Lillian Gish I'm Queen Marie."

"I'm a pitcher—southpaw." Phil's hard-earned grammar fled in this crisis. "I done good in high school."

"Oh, all right, stick around," said the testy coach. "When I get time, I'll see if you've got anything."

He seemed to forget all about Phil—who had not the slightest objection. The boy had a bad case of stage fright, partly from Donnigan's ill-nature, but more from the immensity of the empty stadium. He had almost made up his mind to sneak back to his beloved cows when he realized that he was being addressed.

"Hey, you—carrots—come out to the box and pitch to the batters." Donnigan took his place behind the plate. "Murder this guy," he muttered to Risler, a senior and the captain of the team.

Risler murdered, instead, the bright April sunshine in three brutal blows. The old miracle had happened again. The moment Phil took hold of the ball and faced the batter he forgot his fears; he remembered only that throwing a baseball was the greatest fun in the world.

"Hey, wipe that grin off your map," yelled the coach. "What do you think this is, a comic opery?"

Phil controlled his features with an effort while two more batters showed their futility. Donnigan handed his catcher's glove to "Swede" Olson.

"Gimme that stick," he growled. "You birds belong in a home for the blind!"

There were two serious mistakes that Phil could make in this crisis, and he made them both without delay. He struck out Hardboiled Donnigan, and he laughed. Of course he knew better than to ridicule the coach, but there was something irresistible about the way Donnigan lunged for that last slow floater.

"All right, now you've done your stuff, get out!" yelled the offended professional. "And stay out. I can't monkey with a guy who won't take his work serious. Laugh that off."

A few snickers were thrown after the defeated candidate, but the players knew that Donnigan had committed a manager's unpardonable sin of turning down a promising recruit on a personal grudge—and he knew that they knew.

As for Phil, he left the stadium with genuine relief. The more he saw of Donnigan, the better he liked cows. He had kept his promise to Samboy; now he would just sink out of sight and stick to business.

In reply to an inquiry, Samboy got a letter from Mr. Huckley stating that, in the opinion of an old Athens pitcher, Phil Fuller was the best that Branford High School had ever produced. The director showed this tribute to Donnigan.

"Oh, that's the sorreltop. He hasn't got anything but a giggle."

"Are you sure, Hank? We could use a good southpaw."

"I know, but he ain't the answer. This Athens bird is trying to frame us."

"I'll wish him on the freshmen then."

"Sure—give the kid a chanst, Ken," said Donnigan with affected good will. "He might show something if he ever gets over the idea it's all a big wheeze."

Phil was heartily welcomed into the freshman squad. In the presence of Samboy, he performed ably in a practice game. His fast ball, well-controlled curve, and change of pace made the inexperienced batters helpless; and his strange conduct landed him in the public eye with a bang.

The college comic paper, *The Cutup*, had a fine time over Phil. It discovered that the eccentric left-hander was a cow-barner, and it almost died of laughter at this joke.

"Phil Fuller, the Milk Pitcher," was the title

of the piece. He was one of the wide-open faces from the wide-open spaces, the wit said, and sure winner of the standing broad grin. Also he proved the truth of the old saying, "Little pitchers have big ears."

But the result of the publicity was that the crowd at the freshman-sophomore game was the largest of the season. Among those present were old President Whitman, Professor Weatherby, and Mr. and Mrs. Kenneth Samboy.

The assembled underclassmen laughed until they ached at the grinning, gesticulating, noisy southpaw with the red-thatched roof. They greeted his queer, awkward windup with a yell invented by the sophomore cheerleader, a long, rhythmic "So—o—o, boss." But when he had won the game handily for the freshmen, the jeers turned to cheers.

Sibyl Samboy looked at her husband.

"And why," she asked, "is this infant phenomenon not on the varsity?"

"Hank can't see him somehow, and if I butt in, it upsets my whole system of government. Personally I'd pitch him in a game or two to season him and then try him on Athens. But it isn't worth a rumpus, Sib. After all, Fuller will be with us a long time yet, and Donnigan won't."

"Poor old Hank! I wonder what he's got against the boy."

"It's incompatibility of temperament, I guess. Hank thinks baseball is cosmic and Phil thinks it's comic."

"And you," said Sibyl, "think you're a wisecracker on *The Cutup.*"

In the next issue of that little weekly there was a marked difference in tone. The frosh cowboy, it said, was showing ability as well as risibility. It was time Donnigan tried him out on the team.

There was something inevitable about the Phil Fuller movement. Donnigan did not want him on the team. Samboy was committed to keep his hands off, and Phil himself had no craving to appear in that big stadium. But the team was limping through a disastrous season, and there were signs of disaffection among the players. The crowds dwindled, finances were suffering, and the all-important Athens game, the schedule's climax, was approaching like the day of doom.

Donnigan resisted as long as he could, but, schooled as he was in the professional game, he recognized one power greater than players, managers or owners—the customer. And when white-haired Doctor Whitman called him into the president's office and intimated ever so

gently that it might be just as well to give the public what it wanted, he gave in.

He did not surrender, but he retreated inch by inch. He gave Phil a uniform and let him practice with the team and learn the signals, then he put him in at the end of game that was already hopelessly lost. On the eve of the Athens contest he announced that he would pitch Hagenlaucher with Graybar and Fuller in reserve.

Any contest with the traditional foe always brought out the largest crowd of the season, but this year there was a novelty in the situation. The freshmen were out in full force prepared to make an organized nuisance of themselves on behalf of their favorite character. When he appeared on the field for practice they gave him a tremendous ovation.

Just before the game started, Phil realized that somebody was calling to him from the edge of the stand. To his great delight, this proved to be Mr. Huckley, who had traveled all the way from Branford to see the game.

"Phil," he said, "if you get a chance today, I want you to do your darnedest."

"I'd kinda hate to play against Athens after all you did for me."

"I know. That's why I spoke. Forget all that, Phil. If they put you in, pitch as you did last year against Milltown, Three Falls, Oderno, and Jefferson. Good luck!"

"Thank you, Mr. Huckley. I'll meet you right here after it's over. I've got something to tell you."

As he took his seat on the bench his smile faded and he lapsed into gloom. "He's scared stiff," thought Donnigan. "I won't dare to stick him in if Haggy blows."

But Hagenlaucher was not blowing up; he was pitching his best game of the season. The Athens moundsman was doing well, too, and there was promise of a tight pitchers' battle. But in time the game grew looser, the pitchers faltered, Haggy was getting wobbly.

The score stood 6 to 5 in favor of the visitors in the fifth when the umpire made the momentous announcement, "Greenwich batting for Hagenlaucher." At the same moment Graybar and Fuller left for the bull pen to warm up. The next inning would see a new face in the box.

Whose face? That was what all Sparta wanted to know; that was what Samboy wanted to know as he stepped out of the stand and walked up to Donnigan.

"Graybar," said the coach. "Fuller is scared to death. I guess he's got a yellow streak."

Samboy hesitated. The teams were changing sides now, and the embattled freshmen were booming in unison, like a bass drum: "Phil! Phil! Phil!"

"All right, you're the doctor, Hank. But I'll go and talk to the boy."

The new pitcher did his best, but he was a broken reed. A base on balls, a single, and a hit batter filled the bags with nobody out, and the air was full of disaster. Captain Risler stepped to the box as if to steady the wobbly pitcher; Swede Olson, the catcher, joined this conference, which was further enriched by the presence of the lanky first baseman, Keeler.

Now Graybar handed the ball to Risler, who made a sign toward the bench. There was an instant of suspense, and then out of the dugout appeared the gaudy head of Phil Fuller.

An avalanche of sound slid down upon the field. From the freshman bloc came the long, rhythmic yell, "So-o-o, boss." In the general confusion, Hardboiled Donnigan was scarcely seen emerging from the dugout. He seemed to shrink before the wave of noise; then he disappeared through an opening out of the field and out of the athletics department of Sparta.

Scarcely anyone in the audience knew that Donnigan had not ordered the change of pitchers, nor had Samboy. It was Risler, backed by Olson, Keeler, and the whole team. It was mutiny; it was rebellion.

But this was not the familiar Phil Fuller who had laughed and danced his way into the hearts of the fans. This was a serious Phil, a gloomy Phil. Life was now real; life was earnest. He took his long queer windup, and he threw the ball high, far too high. Olson made a jump for the ball, missed it, and landed in a heap. Before he could recover the ball two runs had come over, and Athens rocked with laughter.

But so, to the amazement of the uninformed, did Phil Fuller. It suddenly seemed to the misguided youth that it was the funniest thing in the world that he should have thrown away the ball and let in two runs. The infield laughed in imitation. Philip was himself again.

Now the tension under which the team had been working suddenly relaxed as if a tight band had snapped and brought relief. The nervous, eager, do-or-die spirit suddenly disappeared, leaving the natural instinct of youth to have a good time. With the utmost ease the pitcher and the infield disposed of the next three batters, and in their half of the inning they began their climb toward victory.

It was a strange, exciting, hilarious game.

Phil had never played in such fast company before or faced such a murderous array of bats. He was in hot water half a dozen times, but he never lost the healing gift of laughter.

And the team played as if baseball came under the head of pleasure.

Samboy said to Risler, who sat beside him on the bench in the eighth:

"Whether we win or lose, this is the answer. We're going to build a new idea and a new style of play around that southpaw. You watch our smoke for the next three years, Rissy."

"Just my luck, Ken. In about fifteen minutes I'm through with college baseball forever."

"Well, don't you ever regret what you did today. I can't officially approve it, but—there goes Phil fanning again."

Samboy now addressed the departing warriors.

"All right, boys—last frame and two to the good. All you have to do is hold 'em."

Now it appeared that Phil had been saving the finest joke of all for the end. The season was over, and he could take liberties with his arm. He dug his warts and bumps and calluses into the horsehide and proceeded to retire the side with three straight strike-outs, nine rowdy laughs, two informal dances, and an incredible noise that was a hideous parody on song.

But it was an altered and sobered Phil who found his old coach after the game and received his fervent congratulations.

"Were you worried, Phil?" Mr. Huckley asked.

"Yes, but I was glad they let me play. I had so much fun I forgot my trouble."

"What trouble, Phil?"

"Well, I got a letter from Father this morning, and my Dolly is terribly sick. Seems she got hold of an old paint can some place. Cows like to lick paint, you know, and it's deadly poison. They don't think Dolly will live. Maybe I left a can of paint somewhere myself. That's what bothers me."

"Listen, Phil. I was supposed to tell you, but you got away too quick. Your father telephoned me this morning. Dolly's out of danger. She's doing fine."

"Oh, boy!" cried Phil and his eyes shone with tears.

Down in the field the Sparta students, led by the band, were circling the stadium in that parade of victory which must follow every triumph over Athens.

"There'll be plenty more ball games," said Phil, "but there'll never be another cow like Dolly."

HERE IS a thorough job of reporting on a difficult topic.

Mid-Career Tragedies

BILL BRYSON

BETWEEN-SEASON DEATHS and crippling accidents or illnesses have wrenched the hearts and hopes of many ball clubs, just as Roy Campanella's critical injury saddened the Dodgers and crimped their playing plans for the first year in their new Los Angeles home.

At least 21 established big-leaguers died, most of them still in their prime, at a time when they figured strongly in the designs of their employers for the season ahead. Between-season deaths also have cut down a dozen or more rookies before they had a chance really to prove themselves.

Many spring-training sessions have been blighted by the death of players or, in one case, of the manager. Pat Moran, who had masterminded pennants for the Phils in 1915 and for the Reds in 1919, was stricken by Bright's disease at the Cincinnati camp in 1924 and, after only a four-day illness, died on March 7.

Charles (Chick) Stahl, the Red Sox' talented center fielder, had resigned as manager only a few days before he killed himself by swallowing carbolic acid at the training camp in West Baden, Ind., March 28, 1907.

Addie Joss, one of the eminent pitchers of his era, died while the Cleveland Indians were homeward bound on the exhibition trail in 1911.

Gallant but pathetic efforts in spring training brought the shocking disclosure of illnesses that forced the retirement of Ross Young, Urban Shocker, Bill DeLancey, Lou Gehrig and Bill Sarni.

Off-season accidents to big-league regulars have ranged from the mangling of Catcher Charlie Bennett's legs by a train in 1893 to the hunting mishaps of the 1930s that cost Pitcher Monty Stratton a leg and damaged Charlie Gelbert's foot so badly that the Cardinal shortstop missed two seasons and never regained top-notch form.

Some between-seasons ailments and accidents have had only temporary ill effects, though mighty damaging to each player's club in the year it happened:

Johnny Evers' nervous breakdown before the Cubs' 1911 season; the eye trouble that benched George Sisler throughout 1923, the year after he hit .420 for the Browns; Babe Ruth's monumental bellyache on a 1925 exhibition junket, a major item in the Yankees' seventh-place finish; the sinus infection that forced Chick Hafey to leave the Reds early in the 1935 season and miss all of 1936, and the beaning of the Giants' Hank Leiber by Bob Feller in a 1937 exhibition game.

Then, of course, there have been the more routine injuries, such as twisted knees, broken legs, bumped heads and tortured arms that have marked spring training down through the years. Occasionally there's a less commonplace injury, like the one that both hurt and embarrassed Joe DiMaggio one year. This was one instance in which Joe, who usually skipped the early drills, showed up on time for training. But the Yankee Clipper promptly was incapacitated because an overzealous trainer left a heat lamp on his foot too long.

Campanella's broken neck, suffered when his car careened off the road and turned over, cast a pall on baseball's recent off-season gatherings. The stumpy, skillful catcher was luckier, however, than two big-leaguers of the '20s who were involved in auto accidents.

Tony Boeckel, the Braves' regular third baseman, had finished his seventh and best big-league season with a .298 average in 1923. Driving his car on Feb. 15, 1924, Boeckel had a collision with a truck. He died the next day at the age of 29.

Walter Lerian was only an innocent bystander when he was killed Oct. 22, 1929. A truck leaped the curb of a Baltimore street and pinned Lerian against a building. Walter, 26, was one of the promising catchers of the era.

He had hit .246 in 201 games two previous seasons with the Phils.

Another catcher killed in an automobile accident was Alvin Montgomery, 21, who had hit .192 in 42 games for the Braves in 1941. His fatal wreck occurred in West Virginia, April 26, 1942, when he was on his way from spring training to open the season with Hartford of the Eastern League.

Several players have escaped from wintertime auto wrecks with no permanent impairments. Lee (Jeep) Handley, a Pittsburgh infielder the previous five years, emerged miraculously from a fearsome smashup after the 1941 season. The only damage was to his throwing arm. This kept him from holding his job at third base for the Pirates, but he was able to drop down a notch and play first for Toronto in 69 games. After another year of recuperation in the minors, he came back to play three seasons for the Bucs and one for the Phils.

Even Bobo Newsom himself can chuckle now over the bad breaks that beset his preparations for a 1932 trial with the Cubs, earned by a 16-14 record at Little Rock.

Bobo's car skidded off a high embankment that winter. Newsom says the auto dropped 225 feet and, giving the impression this would have killed an ordinary mortal, admits he suffered a broken leg.

While convalescing, Bobo wrote long, chummy letters to Cub officials, congratulating them upon their shrewdness in buying him and assuring them he was rapidly rounding into shape to win the pennant for Chicago.

A few days after Newsom was discharged from the hospital, he attended a mule sale. One of the critters on display kicked him on the freshly healed leg and broke it all over again. Bobo limped through spring training and had to put in two more seasons in the minors before he reached the big leagues for a lively 20-year stay marked but not stopped by such injuries as another broken leg, a fractured kneecap, a skull fracture, a broken jaw and assorted other fractures.

Besides the two automobile fatalities in the '20s, there was one in an airplane accident. Marvin Goodwin, a part-time major-league pitcher for several years, had become manager of Houston in the Texas League in 1925. Then the Reds bought him for a fresh trial. Goodwin, 33, died in the crash of a plane he was piloting, Oct. 22.

Red Sox ranks, dismayed by Stahl's suicide on the eve of the 1907 season, were shocked by murder while the club was getting ready for the 1932 campaign. Ironically, Pitcher Ed Morris was killed at a party in his honor, a send-off for spring training, on February 29. Friends arranged a fish fry at Century, Fla., and there Ed became embroiled in a fight with Joe White, a service-station operator. Morris was stabbed twice and died three days later. He was 32.

There is no more poignant memory in baseball than the recollection of Ironman Lou Gehrig's pathetic efforts to swing a bat with his old authority in the Yankee camp of 1939. Already Lou was in the grip of the wasting disease that was to bring his death two years later. Gallantly, he even began the season, played the first eight games to bring his remarkable durability record to 2,130 consecutive contests.

But when, in that eighth game, teammates gathered around and congratulated him after he had scooped an ordinary ground ball and thrown to Pitcher Johnny Murphy for an out at first, Gehrig knew he was through. "They meant it to be kind," Lou said later, "but it hurt worse than any bawling out I ever got in baseball."

Before the next game, Gehrig went to Manager Joe McCarthy and said: "You'd better put Babe (Dahlgren) on first. I'm not doing the club any good out there."

Addie Joss courageously forced himself through Cleveland's 1911 training grind until he fainted at Chattanooga, where the Indians were playing an exhibition game. He was taken to a hospital but rejoined his teammates that night with apologies for his "baby trick." Not until the club reached Cincinnati would Addie admit he was really sick. At a hospital there, it was discovered he had tubercular meningitis. He died a week later, on April 14, only 31.

Joss had a victory range of 20-27 from 1905 through 1908. His 1909 effectiveness shrank to 14-13 and the onset of his fatal illness might have been suspected the next year when he was able to appear in only 13 games for a 5-5 record.

On the other hand, Urban Shocker had one of his best seasons, 18 victories against only six defeats, before he was stricken in 1928. Shocker appeared in one game before heart disease compelled him to retire. Urban went to live in Denver, there fell victim to pneumonia and died Sept. 9 at the age of 38.

Ross Young, too, bowed out courageously on a high note. The Texan, one of Manager John McGraw's favorites, had dropped to .264 in 1925 after seven seasons in which he ranged from .302 to .355.

McGraw received his first inkling that Young had a serious stomach ailment during spring training in 1926. But Ross kept bearing down, never complaining, admitting only that "my stomach bothers me a little" and "I don't have the pep I had when I was a young squirt."

When the season began, Young was examined by a physician almost every day the Giants were home. When they went on the road, a male nurse accompanied Ross. He played most of the time, but now and then the nurse would advise McGraw that Young should miss a game. And McGraw would say: "All right. Take good care of him."

Young played in 95 games and whacked out an average that was the envy of many healthy men—.306. But it was literally a dying effort. Ross couldn't play at all in 1927 and, at 30, died that Oct. 22.

Tuberculosis sidelined Bill DeLancey after he thrust himself into the ranks of the top catchers with bright freshman-sophomore years for the champion Cardinals of 1934 and their runners-up of 1935. A comeback in 1940 lasted only 15 games and Bill died in 1946.

Bill Sarni's case, happily, was diagnosed early enough for the Giant catcher to take the precautionary measure of quitting active play last year. He had heart trouble, but not bad enough to keep him from serving as a coach. The Giants also created a coaching job for Davey Williams when a back ailment brought his retirement as a player in the spring of 1956.

Among players who died between seasons while still on active rosters, the most prominent not already mentioned were Leonard (King) Cole, Jake Daubert and Benny Frey.

Pitcher Cole's first two years with the Cubs netted 20-4 and 18-7 records in 1910-11. He slipped out of the majors a year later, but was rescued in 1914 by the Yankees, for whom he won eleven, lost nine. He was able to appear in only ten games with a 2-3 mark in 1915 and died the following January at 29.

Daubert was an old war horse when he died, Oct. 9, 1924. At 39, he had just finished his fifteenth big-league season. Still, he had been able to play 102 games at first base for the Reds and his .281 average wasn't too far from his lifetime clip of .303. Not even a postseason operation to remove appendix and gallstones was expected to keep Jake from another year or two as a player. But complications followed the surgery and Daubert died a week after the operation.

Frey was a Cincinnati pitcher whose eight-year big-league career ended in 1936 after his best won-lost mark (10-8). His illness led to death on Nov. 1, 1937.

Double tragedy struck the Washington Senators before their 1906 campaign, while the Cardinals' 1922 season was bracketed by player deaths.

At 23, Joe Cassidy had been Washington's full-time shortstop for two years when he died March 25, 1906. The other Senator victim was Charles (Punch) Knoll, a 24-year-old outfielder who had played in 79 games the year before.

Sorrow began for the Cardinals in 1922 when William (Pickles) Dillhoefer, veteran second-string catcher, died on Feb. 22 when 27. Late that season, Outfielder Austin McHenry, also 27, suddenly began to have trouble following the flight of fly balls. Unsuspecting fans jeered the hesitation waltz of McHenry when drives came his way, but Manager Branch Rickey knew something was physically amiss. He sent Austin to a doctor and a brain tumor was discovered. An operation was unsuccessful and, on Nov. 27, death came to the outfielder who had hit .350 in 1921 and .303 in his fatal year.

Other established regulars whose between-seasons deaths shocked baseball followers included:

1884—Charles F. Householder, 28, Oct. 10; had hit .240 in 80 games as a rookie with Chicago and Pittsburgh of the Union Association that year.

1891—Edward M. Daily, 29, Oct. 21; 64-72 as a pitcher and .250 as an outfielder in six seasons for Louisville, Washington and other teams.

1892—John F. O'Brien, 24, March 11; 17-13 pitching mark for Boston of the American Association in 1891 and a four-year total of 57-65.

1893—Sy Sutcliffe, 29, Feb. 13; seven-year big-league batting average of .273, two under his figures as Baltimore's first baseman in 66 games the previous season.

1894—Edgar (Texas) McNabb, 29, Feb. 28; 8-9 in 17 games as a promising rookie for Baltimore of the National League in 1893.

1901—Thomas F. O'Brien, 27, Feb. 4; .284 for four seasons as outfielder and first baseman, including .305 in 152 games for the 1899 Giants; .294 in 94 games for Pittsburgh in 1900.

1903—George (Win) Mercer, 28, Jan. 13; 15-18 for Tigers in 1902, his ninth big-league season.

1907—Patrick (Cozy) Dolan, 34, Jan. 1; ten-year veteran as pitcher, first baseman and outfielder; .248 in 152 games for 1906 Braves, compared to career average of .271.

1901—Alan Storke, 25, March 18; outfielder and shortstop who hit .270 in 80 games for Pittsburgh and the Cardinals in 1909, his fourth season.

1912—James Francis Doyle, 30, Feb, 1; .282 in 127 games as Cubs' third baseman previous season.

1915—Marcus Hall, 27, Feb. 24; 14-25 pitching record in three years, including 4-6 for 1914 Pirates.

Among the rookies or part-timers who died between seasons in the past 30 years, one was victim of a heart attack during spring training. Pitcher Roy Meeker, 28, had put in one full season (5-12 with the 1924 Athletics) and parts of two others in the majors. He was receiving a new chance with the Reds when he was stricken, March 25, 1929.

Others included Outfielder Denny Williams of the Braves, competitor in 119 big-league games over four seasons, who died March 24, 1929, and Clyde Hatter, Detroit pitcher, owner of a 1-0 record for 11 appearances in 1935 and 1937. He died Oct. 16, 1937.

A number of players have died, of course, while the season was in progress—none more dramatically than Ray Chapman, the clever Cleveland shortstop whose fatality was the only one resulting from major-league competition. Chapman, 29, died Aug. 17, 1920, after being struck in the head by a pitch from Carl Mays of the Yankees.

Violent death has claimed four other players in off-field mishaps during the schedule. Ed Delahanty, one of the greatest of all hitters, either fell or jumped from a train crossing a bridge near Niagara Falls, July 2, 1903. Delahanty, 35, owned a .338 average for 43 games that season with Washington.

Len Koenecke, young Brooklyn outfielder, was killed in a fight with a two-man crew of an airplane he had chartered. Death came as the plane wobbled dangerously high above a race track at Toronto, Sept. 17, 1935. Both the pilot and co-pilot were exonerated on grounds of self-defense. Koenecke had hit .283 in 100 games for the Dodgers that year, his third in the majors, but had been given his unconditional release by Casey Stengel, then the Dodger manager, just before his ill-fated flight.

Tom Gastall, 23-year-old catcher who received $40,000 to sign with Baltimore in 1955, was killed Sept. 20, 1956, when the small plane he was piloting crashed into Chesapeake Bay.

Willard Hershberger, 29-year-old reserve catcher of the Reds, killed himself in a Boston hotel room, Aug. 3, 1940, at a time Cincinnati was on its way to a second straight pennant.

Regulars of comparatively recent years who died of natural causes during the season included Pitcher Hal Carlson of the Cubs, May 28, 1930; Infielder Cornelius (Mickey) Finn of the Phillies, July 7, 1953, and pitcher Tiny Bonham, former Yankee stalwart who had gone to the Pirates, Sept. 15, 1949.

Harry Agannis, former all-American quarterback at Boston U. and a bonus player with the Red Sox, had got off to a promising start in 1955, his second with the Boston club. Harry owned a .313 average for 25 games when he came down with pneumonia. One recovery was followed by another attack of pneumonia. The 25-year-old first baseman appeared to be regaining his health when he was suddenly stricken by a massive pulmonary embolism and died on June 27.

Miller Huggins was a manager who died with a race still in progress—one of the few in which he failed to lead his Yankees to the top.

The bantam-size leader had relinquished his field command to go to the hospital less than a week before he died, Sept. 25, 1929. A combination of influenza and erysipelas was fatal to the 50-year old manager.

Here comes Pogo.

WALT KELLY

WHIRLED SERIES

HOW'D YOU LIKE TO STEP OUTSIDE?

THERE'S A QUIET GROUND SWELL OF OPINION, DAZZLER, THAT YOUR PITCHIN' COULD BE DISPENSED WITH.

PHOO! IT'S THIS *JACK RABBIT* BALL--- BESIDES I ISN'T GITTIN' NO SUPPORT FROM YOU MENS.

NO SUPPORT? WE BRUNG BACK THE BALL FROM ALL 72 HOME RUNS.

YES, **BUT,** MR. MANAGER, SIR--- WHAT INNING IS IT?

FIRST HALF OF THE **FIRST** AND YOU ISN'T GOT NOBODY OUT YET!

HA! *AND WHAT,* PRAY TELL, IS THE SCORE?

THE UPSTATE RETURNS AREN'T IN SO FAR---BUT IT LOOKS LIKE 149 TO *NOTHIN':*

SEE!? **SOME SUPPORT**---MY OWN TEAM ISN'T GOT ME ONE **MEASLE RUN YET!**

I'LL PITCH FOR A WHILE--- MAYBE I CAN PROTECT *THEIR* LEAD OF 149 TO NOTHIN' AND GET THE FIRST HALF OF THE FIRST INNING OVER--- -- YOU PLAY LEFT FIELD.

INGRATE

CRACK

I GOT IT! I GOT IT! **I GOT IT!**

I GOT IT I GOT IT I GOT IT I GOT IT I G..

GAME'S OVER, POGO--- WE LOST THE BALL.

I THOUGHT HE GOT IT!?

OH, HE **GOT** IT, ALLRIGHT!

THE DAY baseball's color barrier fell, told by a fine sports writer.

1947:
Brooklyn Dodgers 5,
Boston Braves 3

JIMMY CANNON

SOMEONE such as Norman Corwin should sit down at a typewriter and intelligently explain to the people beyond the Hudson what happened in Ebbets Field yesterday as the Dodgers opened their season by beating the Braves, 5-3. It would be small compensation for the abuse the people of Brooklyn have taken from the incompetent and unfunny liars who describe them as Metropolitan hillbillys. There were 25,623 of them in the joint and they behaved with dignity and compassion. Their wit was clean and good-humored as they pulled for Jackie Robinson as he struggled through a hitless day. They had opportunities to chastise him and no one could have quarreled with their peevishness because he hit into a double play and seemed tight and unnatural as he played first base. They convinced him they were going to be square with him and that cooled off some of the heat that burns around him constantly because he is the first Negro ever to come up in what even in the reign of Happy Chandler is still our national sport.

After the ball game Robinson sat off from the other players with Eddie Tolan, the old Olympic sprinter, and the misery of his impotence at the plate dissipated as soon as he spoke about what has happened to him since coming to Brooklyn.

"The help I've had on the ball club," he said. "It's really something."

Someone asked him how he liked playing first base because he came up as a shortstop, was switched to second and now is trying to learn the mechanics of another strange position.

"It's a tough play for me," he said. "A man on first and a left-handed hitter. I don't know when to jump off the bag. It will backfire in a tough spot if I don't learn."

I asked him what impressed him most on his first day as a big-leaguer. He made a gesture as though he were throwing a ball, letting his wrist flop limply as he completed the motion.

"The way Johnny Sain threw the fast ball and the curve in the same motion," Robinson answered.

"Is Sain the best pitcher you ever hit against?" Tolan asked.

"I hit against Bob Feller on the exhibition tour," Robinson said.

"Sain is a hell of a pitcher," a guy said.

"If Sain doesn't give me more trouble than any other pitcher I'm going to face," Robinson said, and then paused to laugh, "it's going to be a very rough season."

The sports journalist said the crowd didn't get on him and they wanted to see him stick.

"I know the crowd was pulling for me," Jackie said. "I could hear them at first base. They're sure with me. I hope I can keep them with me by playing some baseball for them."

"You will," a guy said. "After a while the pressure will lift."

"When the game starts I don't give that a thought," Robinson said. "My only hope is I can be of some service to the Dodgers."

"How do you feel, Jackie?" said a sports writer who had just walked in.

"Great," he said. "You always feel great when you win."

THE GRAND OLD MEN

International News

Vide World

Here, in characteristic poses,

Connie Mack, complete with collar and score-card,

Commissioner Kenesaw Mountain Landis, chin on rail.

WHAT?!?!

In a Jeff Keate cartoon in the first *Fireside Book of Baseball,* an umpire holds up a decision on a close play while he wonders, "I wonder what the pictures will show?" Here, we can see for ourselves, in three action views of World Series games.

First sequence *(above),* 1948 Series, Lou Boudreau, Indians' shortstop-manager, takes pickoff throw from Bob Feller in attempt to catch Boston Braves' runner Phil Masi off second. Look carefully at the second photo in the sequence. Photos 3 and 4 tell the rest of the story better than words.

Next shot *(opposite page, top)* comes from the 1952 World Series. The umpire calls base runner Johnny Sain out at first.

Next shot *(opposite, bottom)* shows Henry Aaron catching (so said the umpire) a Gil McDougald fly in the 1957 World Series. Hard to tell here. What do you think?

Meanwhile, back at the umpires' school.

THE INCLUSION of this piece is in part an experiment by the editor—
I want to learn whether it is true that if an anthologist uses a piece by
Bennett Cerf the book blows up. In large measure, though, "Two-Top"
is here because it has become a standard routine rivaling "Who's on
First?" Very funny stuff. Mr. Cerf leaves out one thing: Two-Top
was in love with Simone Simon.

Two-Top Gruskin

BENNETT CERF

THE WONDERFUL SAGA of Two-Top Gruskin, the two-headed pitcher, is the brain child of Ed Gardner, the incomparable Archie of Duffy's Tavern radio program. It goes something like this:

Duffy's Irish Yankees have mechanical perfection, but no color. "This guy, Athos and Porthos McGinnes, may be your dish," says Dugan, the shortstop, to the disconsolate Duffy. "They call him Two-Top Gruskin for short, I guess, on account of him having two heads."

"A pitcher with two heads?" says Duffy dubiously. "You think it'd be a novelty?"

"What if it ain't?" points out Dugan. "Who else could watch first and third base at the same time? Besides, he's a great guy to pitch double-headers."

So Two-Top is summoned from his home (Walla Walla, of course) and arrives to sign his contract in a dress suit. "What are all you guys staring at?" he asks sourly. "Ain't none of you seen a tuxedo before?"

"Two-Top," says Duffy, "I'm a man of few words. Report tomorrow. There's a uniform and two caps waiting for you. Waiter, bring my new pitcher two beers."

Two-Top wins a masquerade that very night by disguising himself as a pair of book ends with a copy of My Son, My Son between the two heads. The next afternoon Duffy introduces him to his catcher, Gorilla Hogan, who measures 6 foot 14 inches and squats standing up. "Most people," says Duffy proudly, "calls Gorilla a monstrosity, and I agree with them—a swell guy." Gorilla soon gets into trouble with Two-Top, however. He signals for a high fast one. Two-Top nods "yes" with one head, but shakes the other one "no." Confused and mortified, Gorilla hurls off his mask and yells to Duffy, "Duffy, you such-and-such, I am sick and tired of two-headed pitchers around this place."

"Take it easy," soothes Duffy. "Talk it over with the guy. After all, three heads is better than one."

But the Gorilla says, "It's no use, Duffy. I got a feeling that the guy ain't normal. Besides, you notice how he's always got those two heads together? Maybe he's cooking up a strike around here. No, sir, one of us will have to go, Duffy—and don't forget who owns the baseball."

Well, that's the end of Two-Top Gruskin's baseball career. For a while he watches tennis matches for the News of the Day. Then the Army gets him. The doctor takes his chart to the colonel. "Lemme see," says the colonel. "Eyes—blue and brown. Hair, blond and brunette. Mustache: yes and no. This guy sounds as if he's got two heads." "He has," says the doc. "Oh," says the colonel.

Two-Top will be a big success in the Army as soon as he can make up his mind which head to salute.

HERE is the final chapter from *Baseball Joe of the Silver Stars*, first of the Baseball Joe books, which were quite possibly the longest continuous series of boys' books ever done—in point of time, that is; the first Baseball Joe book came out in 1912, the last in 1926. The reason: popular demand. Why is it they don't write like this any more?

The Winning Throw—Conclusion

━━━━ LESTER CHADWICK ━━━━

FOR A MOMENT Tom stood there a bit embarrassed, for he saw that something unusual had happened.

"I—I hope I'm not intruding," he stammered. "I didn't think—I came right in as I always do. Has anything—"

"It's all right!" exclaimed Joe quickly. "We just got word that Dad has lost his patent case."

"Gee! That's too bad!" exclaimed Tom, who knew something of the affair. "What are you going to do?"

"I'm going to pitch against the Resolutes, the first thing I do!" cried Joe. "After that I'll decide what's next. But is my glove mended, Clara? Come on, Tom, we mustn't be late. We're going to wallop them—just as you said."

"I hope you do!" burst out Clara.

"Play a good game and—and—don't worry," whispered Mrs. Matson to her son as he kissed her good-bye.

The team and substitutes were to go to Rocky Ford in two big stages, in time to get in some practice on the grounds that were none too familiar to them. A crowd of Silver Star "rooters" were to follow on the trolley. The captain and managers of the rival teams watched their opponents practice with sharp eyes.

"They're snappier than when they beat us before," was Darrell's conclusion.

"They've got a heap sight better pitcher in Joe than Sam Morton ever was," concluded Captain Hen Littell of the Resolutes, who twirled for his team. "I shouldn't wonder but what we'd have a mighty close game."

The last practice was over. The scattered balls had been collected, the batting list made

out and final details arranged. Once more came the thrilling cry of the umpire:

"Play ball!"

The Resolutes were to bat last, and Seth Potter went up to bat first for the Stars.

"Swat it," pleaded the crowd, and Seth smiled. But he fanned the air successively as well as successfully and soon went back to the bench. Then came Fred Newton's turn and he knocked a little pop fly that was easily caught before he reached first. Captain Rankin himself was up next and managed to get to first on a swift grounder that got past the shortstop. But he died on second, for the next man up fanned. No runs for the Stars.

The Resolutes were jubilant, thinking this argued well for them, but they looked a little blank when Joe retired their first two men hitless. For Joe had started off in good form. With the first ball he delivered he knew that he was master of the horsehide—at least for a time.

"But oh! I hope I don't slump!" and he almost found himself praying that such a thing would not happen.

He was in an agony of fear when he heard the crack of the bat on the ball when the third man came up. The spheroid went shooting off in center field, but by a magnificent stop Percy Parnell gathered it in and the side was retired runless. Things were not so bad for the Stars.

For the next two innings neither side got a run, though there were some scattered hits. Again was there talk of a pitchers' battle, though in the strict sense of the word this was not so, as both Joe and Hen Littell were hit occasionally, and for what would have been runs only for the efficient fielding on both sides.

"See if we can't do something this inning!"

pleaded Rankin when his side came up in their half of the fourth. The lads all tried hard and Joe knocked a pretty one that was muffed by the second baseman. However, he quickly picked it up and hurled it to first. Joe got there about the same time as the ball did, and to many he seemed safe, but he was called out.

"Aw, that's rotten!" cried Tom Davis.

"Let it go!" said Darrell sharply, and Tom subsided.

The Stars got another goose egg—four straight—and in their half of the fourth the Resolutes got their first run. The crowd went wild and Joe found himself clenching his hands, for the run came in because he had given a man his base on balls. The runner had successively stolen second and third, and went home on a nice fly.

"I hope I'm not going to slump!" thought Joe and there was a lump in his throat. For an instant he found himself thinking of his father's troubles, and then he firmly dismissed them from his mind. "I've got to pitch!" he told himself fiercely.

"We've got him going!" chanted the Resolute "rooters." Joe shut his teeth grimly and struck out the next man. Then he nipped the runner stealing second and threw him out with lightning speed. That somewhat silenced the jubilant cries and when Joe managed to retire one of the Resolutes' heaviest hitters without even a bunt a big crowd rose up and cheered him.

"They're only one ahead," said Rankin as his lads came in to bat. "Let's double it now."

And double it they did, the Star boys playing like mad and getting enough hits off Littell to make two runs.

"That's the way to wallop 'em!" sang someone in the visiting crowd and the song composed for the occasion was rendered with vim.

Desperately as the Resolutes tried in their half of the fifth to catch up to their rivals, they could not do it. Joe was at his best and in that half inning did not allow a hit. He had almost perfect control, and his speed was good. Only once or twice did he pitch at all wild and then it did no harm as there was no one on base.

The sixth inning saw a run chalked up for each team, making the score three to two in favor of the Stars.

"Oh, if we can only keep this up!" exclaimed Darrell, "we'll have them. Can you do it, Joe?"

"I guess so—yes, I can!" he said with conviction.

Then came the lucky seventh, in which the Stars pounded out three runs, setting the big

crowd wild with joy, and casting corresponding gloom over the cohorts of the Resolutes. The Stars now had six runs and their rivals were desperate. They even adopted unfair tactics, and several decisions of the umpire were manifestly in their favor. The crowd hooted and yelled, but the young fellow who was calling strikes and balls held to his opinion, and the Resolutes closed their half of the seventh with two runs.

"Six to four in our favor," murmured the Stars' manager. "If we can only keep this lead the game is ours."

"That word 'if' is a big one for only two letters," spoke Captain Rankin grimly. "But maybe we can."

Neither side scored in the eighth and then came the final trial of the Stars unless there should be a tie, which would necessitate ten innings.

Joe was to the bat in this inning, and oh! how hard he tried for a run! He knocked a two-bagger and stole third. There was one out when Bart Ferguson came up, and Bart was a heavy hitter. But somehow he did not make good this time. He managed to connect with the ball, however, and as soon as Joe heard the crack he started for home.

But there was brilliant playing on the part of the Resolutes. With a quick throw to home the shortstop nipped Joe at the plate, and then the catcher, hurling the ball to first, got the horsehide into the baseman's hands before Bart arrived. It was a pretty double play and retired the Stars with a goose egg.

Still they had a lead of two runs and they might be able to hold their rivals down. It was a critical point in the game. As Joe took his place and faced the batter he felt his heart wildly throbbing. He knew he must hold himself well in hand or he would go to pieces. The crowd of Resolute sympathizers was hooting and yelling at him. Darrell saw how things might go and ran out to the pitcher.

"Hold hard!" he whispered. "Just take it easy. Pitch a few balls to Bart and your nerve will come back. We've *got* to win."

"And we will!" exclaimed Joe. The delivery of a few balls, while the batter stepped away from the plate, showed Joe that he still had his speed and control. He was going to be wary what kind of curves he delivered.

He struck out the first man up with an ease that at first caused him wild elation, and then he calmed himself.

"There are two more," he reasoned. "I've got to get two more—two more."

He was almost in despair when he was hit for a two-bagger by the next player, and he was in a nervous perspiration about the man stealing to third. Then Darrell signaled him to play for the batter, and Joe did, getting him out with an easy fly.

Then there was a mix-up when the next man hit, and by an error of the left fielder the man on second, who had stolen to third, went home with a run, while the man who had brought him in got to the last bag.

"That's the stuff!" yelled the crowd. "Now one more to make it a tie and another to win!"

"Steady, boys! Steady!" called Darrell, as he saw his team on the verge of a breakdown. "We can beat 'em!"

There were now two out, one run was in, a man was on third and a heavy batter was up—one of the best of the Resolutes.

"Swat it, Armstrong! Swat it!" cried the crowd, and the big left fielder smiled confidently.

"Ball one!" cried the umpire, after Joe's first delivery.

There was a gasp of protest from Bart behind the plate, for the sphere had come over cleanly. Darrell signaled to the catcher to make no protest. Joe felt a wave of anger, but he endeavored to keep cool. But when the second ball was called on him he wanted to run up and thrash the umpire. The latter was grinning derisively.

"Here's a strike!" cried Joe in desperation and he was gratified when Armstrong struck at it and missed.

"Why didn't you call that a ball?" asked Bart of the umpire. The latter did not answer.

Another ball was called and then a strike. Now came the supreme moment. Two men out, a man on third waiting to rush in with the tying run, a heavy hitter at bat and three balls and two strikes called on him. No wonder Joe's hand trembled a little.

"Easy, old man!" called Darrell to him. "You can make him fan."

Joe thought rapidly. He had studied the batter and he thought that by delivering a swift inshoot he could fool Armstrong. It was his last chance, for another ball meant that the batter would walk, and there was even a better stickman to follow.

Joe wound up, and sent in a swift one. His heart was fluttering, he could hardly see, there was a roaring in his ears. And then he dimly saw Armstrong strike at the ball desperately. Almost at the same moment Joe knew he would miss it.

The ball landed in the center of Bart's big glove with a resounding whack. He held it exactly where he had caught it. Joe had delivered the winning throw.

"Strike three—batter's out!" howled the umpire, and then his voice was drowned in a yell of joy from the sympathizers of the Stars.

For their team had won! The Resolutes were retired with but one run in the ninth and the final score was five to six in favor of our friends. They had beaten their old rivals on their own grounds and they had won the county championship!

"Great work, old man! Great!" yelled Darrell in Joe's ear. "You saved the day for us."

"Nonsense!" exclaimed Joe modestly.

"Three cheers for Baseball Joe!" yelled Tom Davis, and how those cheers did ring out.

"Three cheers for the Stars—they beat us fair and square!" called Captain Littell, and this was quite a different ending than that which had marked the previous game.

Some wanted to carry Joe around on their shoulders but he slipped away, and got off his uniform. Soon the team was on its way back to Riverside.

"You ought to be in a bigger team," Darrell told Joe. "You've got the making of a great pitcher in you."

"Well, I guess I'll have to stick around here for a while yet," replied our hero, as he thought of the fallen finances of his father. Never in all his life had he so longed for the chance to go to boarding school, and thence to college. But he knew it could not be, chiefly through the treachery of Benjamin and Holdney. Joe felt a wave of resentment against them sweep over him, and his thoughts were black and bitter.

Tom walked as far as Joe's street with him. He had a silent sympathy that spoke more than mere words could have done.

"So long," he said softly as they parted. "It was a great game, Joe, and I'm almost glad you've got to stay with the Stars."

"Well, did you win?" asked his mother, as Joe entered the house—entered it more listlessly than winning a big game would seem to warrant. "Did you beat the Resolutes, Joe?"

"Yes, we did—why, Mother, what's the matter?" cried the young pitcher, for there was a look of joy and happiness on her face, a look entirely different than when he had left her after the bad news. "Has anything—anything good happened?" he asked.

"Yes!" she exclaimed, "there has. I just had another telegram from your father. Everything is all right. He gets back his patents."

"No!" cried Joe, as if unable to believe the news.

"But I tell you yes!" repeated Mrs. Matson, and there was joy in her voice. "At first your father believed that all was lost, just as he wired us. Then, most unexpectedly he tells me, they were able to obtain some evidence from outside parties which they had long tried for in vain.

"It seems that a witness for Mr. Benjamin and his side, on whom they very much depended, deserted them, and went over to your father and his lawyer, and—"

"Hurray for that witness, whoever he was!" cried Joe.

"Be quiet," begged Clara, "and let Mother tell."

"There isn't much to tell," went on Mrs. Matson. "With the unexpected evidence of this witness your father's lawyer won the case, almost at the last moment. In fact your father had given up, and was about ready to leave the court when the man sent in word that he would testify for them. That was after your father sent the telegram that came just before you went off to the game, Joe."

"Oh, I'm so glad!" cried Clara.

"Now it's your turn to be quiet and listen," admonished Joe, with a smile at his sister.

"I have just about finished," went on their mother. "The judge decided in your father's favor, and he doesn't even have to share the profits of the invention with the harvester company or with Mr. Rufus Holdney, as he at one time thought he would, for they have violated their contract. So we won't be poor, after all, children. Aren't you glad?"

"You bet!" exploded Joe, throwing his arms around his mother's neck.

"And we won't have to leave this nice house," added Clara, looking around the comfortable abode.

"Then I can go to boarding school—and pitch on the school nine; can't I, Mother?" cried Joe, throwing his arms around her.

"Oh, yes; I suppose so," she answered, with half a sigh. "But I do wish you'd do something else besides play baseball."

"Something else besides baseball, Mother! Why, there's nothing to be compared to it. Hurray! I'm going to boarding school! I'm going to boarding school!" and Joe, catching Clara around the waist, waltzed her around the room. Then he caught his mother on his other arm—the arm that won the victory for the Stars that day—and her, too, he whirled about until she cried for mercy.

"Oh, but this is great!" Joe cried when he stopped for breath. "Simply great! I must go and tell Tom. Maybe he can go to boarding school with me."

And whether Tom did or not, and what were our hero's further fortunes on the diamond, will be related in the next volume, to be called: "Baseball Joe on the School Nine; or, Pitching for the Blue Banner."

There was an impromptu feast that night for the victorious Silver Stars and Joe was the hero of the occasion. He was toasted again and again, and called upon to make some remarks, which he did in great confusion. But his chums thought it the best speech they had ever heard.

"Three cheers for Baseball Joe!" called Tom Davis, and the room rang with them, while Joe tried to hide his blushes by drinking glass after glass of lemonade.

And now, for a time, we will take leave of him, crying as his chums did after the great victory on the diamond: "Hurrah for Baseball Joe!"

FOR the greatest news event to hit New York since Lindbergh's parade
up Broadway, we take you now to the matchless Bill Corum—here
spot-reporting not only the story, but the story's story!

1948: Leo Changes Jobs

BILL CORUM

ON SUNDAY EVENING July 4th the writer drove out to Long Beach for dinner. Coming home around 1 A.M., he found a telephone message that read:

"At whatever hour you come in call Leo Durocher at this number."

I called and Durocher said he must see me at once on a matter of vital importance. Asked if he had gone to bed, he said he had.

"How about tomorrow morning?" I asked him.

After a moment's hesitation, he replied: "So far as I know I'm supposed to catch a nine o'clock train for a double-header in Philadelphia. It's a helluva time to ask a fellow to get up so you can tell him your troubles, but could I see you at seven?"

So we agreed that he should meet me in my room at the Park Lane Hotel at that time. I left a call for seven and he was at the door by the time I'd ordered toast and coffee and hung up the phone.

That was when I found out that on the previous afternoon during the ball game with the Giants at Ebbets Field, Secretary Harold Parrott of the Dodgers had come to Durocher in his office in the Brooklyn dressing room and said:

"I hate to tell you this, Leo, but the boss (Branch Rickey) wants you to resign." Durocher was in the clubhouse because he had been chased by an umpire.

But before we go any further with that, let me point out again that Durocher wasn't coming to me with the idea of giving me the story. What he wanted was to seek advice on what to say, if anything, to the press when the story broke.

There was no doubt in his mind that it was only a matter of days, maybe hours, until he would be ousted. In fact he half expected to find that news waiting for him when he reached Shibe Park.

So it was thoughtful, and typical of the few contacts of this kind that the writer has had with him, for him to say:

"The things that I am going to tell you are not in confidence. You use your own judgment. Write any part of this today, or whenever you like."

Even had I been so minded, I couldn't have put it in the paper that day, however. There were no afternoon papers on July 5th. Besides, I wasn't thinking along the lines of the story at the moment. Not, at any rate, any more than a reporter always is thinking about a story, or column, in the back of his mind.

It was my feeling that since Durocher had come to me as a friend, it was my duty to treat what he had to tell me as between us. For the time being, at any rate. And to give him the best advice I could muster, whether it would be good or bad.

It's hardly necessary to tell you that when Parrott brought him the message from the Mahatma behind the strawstack on his Maryland farm, Leo hit the ceiling.

He wanted to know what he had done this time. Parrott told him "nothing at all," according to Rickey. But that Branch had said the team had collapsed completely "and that not even a miracle man could win with it." (This is the same team, incidentally, that now has won 9 of its last 10 games—8 victories and 1 defeat under Durocher and 1 victory under Burt Shotton.)

Which reminds me, to digress just once more, that the column thinks it has a great battle cry for Uncle Burt and the Brooks. How about, "He Did It Before and He Can Do It Again."

So right now in the Brooklyn clubhouse under the stands, while his team is driving a sell-out crowd nuts by coming from behind again to win, 13 to 12, against a team that he is to be managing in less than two weeks, Durocher is tearing the telephone from its mooring and bellowing:

"Hell, no, I won't resign. He's going to have to fire me and he's going to have to do it, man to man. Get him on here and let's have him do it like a man!"

By now, however, it would appear that Brother Branch had crawled completely under the hayrick and pulled it in after him. Suddenly, he, Rickey, had vanished into the bright blue yonder.

That I know because many times that afternoon and evening I tried to reach him by phone before I finally sat down and wrote a column called "Frenzy in Flatbush" in which I made it plain that Durocher's days as manager of the Dodgers were numbered.

They finally did get young Rickey on the phone. All he wanted to do was wash his own hands of the matter. He did ask Parrott: "Did he quit?"

"Not yet," Harold told him. "Well, then, as far as I can see," said Rickey, Jr., "he's still the manager."

But was he? Durocher didn't know. In fact, he was to go on and win 5 games out of 6 and manage the N. L. All Stars and make a scouting trip to Montreal before he finally found out yesterday morning that he was "out" in Flatbush and "in" in Harlem in the most sensational managerial shakeup baseball has ever known.

Getting back to my conversation with Durocher on the morning of the 5th, we talked for almost two hours.

"If you want to stay, how about your contract?" I asked him. "I haven't got one," he replied, surprisingly. "I mean my wife discovered when I brought it home after signing it without looking, as I always have with contracts, that there was a typewritten line at the top which reads: 'This contract can be terminated on immediate notice by either of the contracting parties.'"

So he was right, that being true. It actually was no contract.

Durocher told me, among other things, his side of the Eddie Stanky story. A far different story than the cracks you've heard about a-knife-in-the-back, etc.

Maybe I'll write it some day. All there's room to say now is that I doubt if ever a manager fought harder to keep a player on a ball team than Leo fought to keep Eddie in Brooklyn.

I told Durocher to sit tight. Wrote a column to try to smoke out the whole story. Phoned Mike Gaven in Philly. The Dodgers are Mike's beat. He does a top job with 'em. What I had, I wanted him to have, except my source. Told Max Kase the same and asked if it was okay to play along with the story and work it out my way.

Rickey finally emerged from his deep freeze to ask Parrott, about Durocher: "What's he going to do, gimme both barrels?" Then added, "Tell him to keep winning."

"Keep winning!" barked Leo, when he heard it. "Nobody knows better than Rickey that if I knew he was going to fire me in the third inning I'd be trying to make ten runs in the second."

By now Rickey and Leo hadn't spoken in two weeks. Didn't until the All-Star game. I'd known for a long time that Stoneham had his eye on Durocher if that grandest of little guys, Mel Ott, couldn't make it this year.

Sunday at the P. G. Pat Lynch told me that Ott might well be out during the St. Louis soiree. Now I was cooking on both sides of the stove. It was getting warm. Rickey invited me to lunch, said: "Maybe you know some things I don't know. But I have no story for you. Just want to talk this over."

I didn't go. I didn't want my hands tied. That's why I wouldn't call Frick, Stoneham, Schumacher. Never talked to any of 'em at any time. Or even Toots Shor, by golly. What do you know, Pal?

Night before last night I learned there'd been a conference between Rickey, Frick, Stoneham. Yesterday morning I called a fellow, and said I was "going" with the story. He laughed and said, "Fools'll be fools." But he laughed. So I knew. Later Durocher phoned and said the *Journal-American* had called him.

"Why not, Mr. Giant?" I asked. He gulped and laughed, too. The story already was in type. A tabloid said it got 1,752 calls between 10 and 6 on the shakeup. I hear we sold some papers. Hope so.

THE "meaning" of the All-Star Game each year? Try this.

Stars in Their Eyes

ROBERT CREAMER

IT IS EASY to forget, now that psychiatric research has taken over a substantial portion of baseball reporting, that the essence of the professional game in the United States of America is a small boy looking with absolute rapture at a grown man.

This is the basic appeal of the annual All-Star Game. The small boy does not know that the best third baseman in baseball is human: that he fights with his wife, worries about bills and occasionally swears at the bat boy. All the small boy knows is that the third baseman is a hero, and a hero always does the right thing. It would be sinful to disillusion him, to tell him that Babe Ruth was a glutton, that Enos Slaughter has had five wives.

President Hoover's epitaphic statement on baseball (which the Cincinnati Redlegs' management thought highly enough of to reproduce on Crosley Field's right-field wall) seems naïve, if you read it while pondering a baseball player's domestic difficulties and the personal reasons causing them. But if you read it again, and think of yourself as a boy playing the game and watching it, and realize that the abiding affection you have for baseball comes *despite* the frailties of those who play it professionally and *because* of real values you yourself have gained from it, you come to understand that Hoover's statement is not at all naïve, and very possibly profound. Perfection is an ideal always to be sought; because it cannot actually be attained does not mean it should be cast aside. The Cobb-Durocher influence ("Stick it in his ear, Charlie; cut him in half!") is strong in baseball, but the George Sisler-Gil Hodges (or Old-Fashioned Sportsman) school carries on. And the boy openly and the man inwardly admire the sportsman (John Landy stopping in the middle of a race to pick up a fallen opponent; Joe Louis stepping back from a momentarily defenseless challenger) even more than they do a winner.

Baseball is undeniably sordid at times. The current hearings in Washington have shown clearly the heavy overlay of rank commercialism. The distressing comedy of errors surrounding the public vote for starting players for this year's All-Star Game reveals an astonishing ineptness at baseball's highest executive level.

But if the man is aware of baseball's feet of clay, the boy is not. The boy leans over the stadium wall to ask George Zuverink for his autograph. Zuverink? If the man may not be quite sure just who George Zuverink is, the boy has no doubts. George Zuverink is a great man: he's Baltimore's relief pitcher, isn't he?

As a human storehouse for sheer and wonderful baseball anecdotage, Pulitzer Prize-winning Arthur Daley probably is without peer in the writing craft today. Here are some examples.

Baseball's Human Comedy

ARTHUR DALEY

According to the record books, Jimmy Dykes became the manager of the Chicago White Sox on May 9, 1934, a post he was to hold for a dozen years. But the record books don't tell the entire story. This is one of baseball's most bizarre tales. If it needs a title, it would almost have to be called "When Is a Manager Not a Manager?"

The White Sox had gone nowhere under Lew Fonseca in 1933, and they were heading precipitously in the same general direction at the start of the 1934 season. Alarmed by the zealous fashion in which the Pale Hose were solidifying their iron grip on last place, owner J. Louis Comiskey accompanied the team on an Eastern trip. His dissatisfaction grew with each passing day. By the evening of May 7, he had made up his mind. Fonseca would have to go.

After the ball game, Comiskey summoned to his room James Joseph Dykes, a third baseman and a private in the ranks. "Jimmy," said the ponderous owner of the White Sox, "how would you like to be a big-league manager?"

Jimmy puffed contemplatively on his cigar while his agile brain raced and his heart did flip flops. "Every ballplayer wants to be a manager some day," he said slowly, sparring for time and evading a direct reply. "Why do you put me on a spot? You already have a manager and I'm his third baseman. I'm satisfied where I am."

"You're just being loyal to Fonseca," persisted Comiskey. "But I've decided to change managers and I'd like you to take the job. If you don't, I'll just have to ask someone else. Will you take it?"

"Yes," snapped Jimmy, his reluctance vanishing instantly. They shook hands on the deal and Comiskey reached for the phone to break the news to Fonseca. There was no answer. The Chicago owner left a message for the ex-manager to phone him back, waited two hours, then departed. While he was gone, the return call came through and it was too late to call back.

Comiskey phoned again the first thing in the morning. Fonseca was out for breakfast. He gave the owner a ring while Comiskey was having breakfast. Fonseca was out checking on a ballplayer when Comiskey returned the call. It was a monstrous comedy of errors. . . .

Blithely unaware of the fact that he had been deposed as manager, Fonseca went out to the ball park. Dykes went there, too, walking on clouds figuratively but traveling by taxi actually, Jimmy being never one to overexert himself. Breezily, Dykes stepped into the clubhouse, ready to take over the helm. Then his jaw dropped. The first person he saw was his predecessor, acting as if nothing had happened. Quick on the trigger, Jimmy immediately sensed that something had gone wrong. Slowly and silently, he strode over to his locker. If manager Dykes had to play third base for ex-manager Fonseca, he would do so.

Just before the game began, Fonseca assembled his heroes for a meeting. "I know that we've been going lousy, fellows," he began. "But I'm not asking you to hustle for me as much as I am asking you to hustle for yourselves. A club that's going as bad as this one is has to have a shake-up. The players who are giving their best are sure to stay. The others are on their way out."

He paused and glanced around the room. "Who'll be the first to go?" he asked. He shrugged his shoulders and continued with more significance than he ever suspected, "Who knows? Maybe I'll be the first one out myself."

Only James Joseph Dykes, nervously studying his shoe tops in embarrassment, knew how right Fonseca was.

* * *

The more deeply you penetrate baseball's surface, the more frequently you learn how fickle a miss is Lady Luck. The game is filled with all sorts of ironies, some cruel, some gentle, some that affect the destinies of an entire team, and some that are strictly personal.

This is a story of a home run, not an ordinary home run but an extra special one. It is the tale of Hank Greenberg's 250th major-league homer, a notable milestone in the career of any ballplayer and one that a comparative few are permitted to reach.

What made it all the more poignant was that Hammering Henry had almost five years to think about it because the story of No. 250 on his Hit Parade revolves around his farewell game before he enlisted in the Army. Since it is such a completely personal yarn and since he tells it so well, we'll just turn the use of the hall over to the large Mr. Greenberg and let him tell a story that is freighted with the most peculiar sort of drama. Take it away, Hank:

"My final game before I went into the service was on May 6, 1941, and it was against the Yankees in Detroit. It was no secret that this was to be my farewell. The newspapers were filled with the news of my imminent departure and everyone was rooting hard for me to go off to war with some sort of flourish.

"In my first time at bat, I leaned and darned if I didn't hit a homer. The next time up, I hit another—both off Tiny Bonham.

"You know what they say about ballplayers—that all of them have their batting averages practically written on their cuffs and that they can rattle off every statistic at any given moment. Well, I was standing in the outfield and I started to do a little figuring.

"I told myself that I held some sort of record for hitting two home runs in a game over the course of a season. Yet I never had been able to punch out three homers in a game. Suddenly, I realized that I'd just walloped the 248th and 249th of my major-league career. I couldn't help but also think how dramatic my farewell would be for me to wind up with three homers in one game for the first time, especially since the third would be No. 250.

"All of a sudden, I was intensely interested in hammering one into the stands. That's a funny thing about baseball. In my first two times at bat, I'd never even given it a thought, just taking my cut without consciously trying for that home run. Yet I'd connected both times.

"As I stepped up to bat in the last half of the eighth, we had the game won and everyone in the park was pulling for me to finish up with a homer—myself included. Atley Donald was pitching for the Yankees by that time, and the bases were full. What a perfect spot that was! Frank Merriwell himself couldn't have picked a nicer way to leave baseball before going off to war.

"Donald didn't have a thing but he was wild enough to toss up three balls. I didn't want to walk and I was both surprised and amused to discover that even Bill Dickey was rooting for me. He kept pleading with his pitcher to whip in a fast one, letter high.

"The next pitch came in as big as a balloon. I swung violently and missed it. The next pitch was even bigger. I missed that one too. Then came the final pitch, the payoff for my home-run ambitions. I really took a belt at that one. A home run? No. A triple? No. A doub—oh, why string it out? I struck out magnificently."

Hank grinned sheepishly as he concluded his story. He carried with him all over the world the memory of the 250th homer-that-might-have-been-and-never-was.

But that isn't the real ending, which comes almost as a postscript, full of dramatic connotations. On July 1, 1945, four years and 55 days after he had made homer No. 249, Captain Hank Greenberg exchanged his Army uniform for that of the Detroit Tigers. By way of celebrating his return, he hit a home run, a homer which was to head the Bengals toward a pennant and a world championship. It was a long time coming, but he finally did get that No. 250.

* * *

There are richly sentimental overtones to that story, almost romantic ones. But for genuine romance, well, how about a look at this one?

About a quarter of a century ago, Joe Engel was beating his way through the bushes for Clark Griffith and the Washington Senators. In the course of his travels, he wandered out to Kansas City and watched a fellow who must have been the worst-looking shortstop any scout ever saw.

He was a 150-pound six-footer with a pugnacious jaw, an 18-year-old kid from San Francisco named Joe Cronin. The Pittsburgh Pirates had given him a tryout, subconsciously compared him to their own flawless Glenn Wright, and shuddered. So Cronin drifted down to Kansas City. Only his hustle and tireless ambition to improve himself kept him in the lineup. His fielding was erratic and he was hitting approximately .220.

But there was something about the kid that struck the fancy of the Washington scout. To this day, Engel can't explain why he bought Cronin for the Senators. It was perverse Fate, operating in one of her most capricious moods, that attracted one to the other. In fact Fate kicked the Cronin gong around considerably at this particular time.

Engel wired Griffith that he'd bought the kid shortstop. Then he sat in the telegraph office in a cold sweat, suddenly aware of the monumental crime he'd committed. Spending Griff's money is always a hazardous undertaking, and here he was, paying twice as much for Cronin as the kid was worth. Griff would scream as though stabbed.

But the deed was done beyond recall. So the veteran scout decided to write a letter. He sent it to Mildred Robertson, Griff's niece, who also was the owner's adopted daughter. She worked in the Washington front office and Engel enjoyed kidding her whenever he got the chance.

"I'm bringing you a young sweetie," he wrote with heavy-handed humor.

Eventually, he returned to Washington with Cronin in tow. He strode into the office with the tall, shy, gangling youngster.

"Hello, Mildred," boomed Engel, indicating his companion. "I've brought you a husband. Meet Joe Cronin."

The boy and the girl stared at each other in an embarrassed silence. But Griff's greeting was even more frosty. He was mad clean through. He already had a shortstop, Bobby Reeves, who the Washington owner was positive would some day be a star. That was why he resented Cronin so much—that and the fancy price tag on him.

Nor did his annoyance grow any less when manager Bucky Harris, quickly perceiving that the square-jawed young Irishman had the makings of a far greater ballplayer, persisted in giving Cronin the call over Reeves. Crustily, Griff wired Harris during a Western swing, "Reeves will never become great if you don't use him more."

Tartly, Bucky wired back, "Neither will Cronin."

Harris was right, of course. Cronin grew in stature as a ballplayer, and he also grew in the esteem of Griff. Cronin remained in Washington more and more, where he also grew in the affections of another member of the Griffith family, the adopted daughter, Mildred.

Engel had called the turn with uncanny exactitude at the very beginning. He had delivered to Griff a wonderful shortstop. He had also delivered to Mildred a wonderful husband.

Yep. Joe Cronin married Mildred Robertson. And, in true storybook fashion, they proceeded to live happily ever after.

*　　*　　*

Cronin is the lad, you know, who once lined into as extraordinary a triple play as was ever engineered. With the bases full and none out (naturally) the slugging shortstop rifled a drive that had two-base hit marked on the ball from the moment it left his bat. The ball went screaming down the third-base line, shoulder-high. It came so fast at third baseman Sammy Hale that he was helpless. He couldn't even get up his glove in time. All three base runners were on the move. The ball rocketed at Hale, struck him on the forehead, and caromed gently off on the fly into the glove of shortstop Billy Knickerbocker for one out. Around the horn the ball was whipped for the second and third outs.

The fourth out of the inning wasn't scored in the book. It belonged to Hale, who also was out—out cold.

*　　*　　*

There is a certain amount of fascination to the big-league debut of any athlete. Sometimes they are incredible successes. Sometimes they are frenetic failures. Sometimes they are tinted with comedy, tragedy, pathos or—well, sometimes there is a debut like Al Schacht's.

The nicest part about this story is that it comes with the sound track already supplied. The Clown Prince of Baseball is his own narrator and he is strictly nonstop once he gets under way. There is no sense in beginning with his preliminaries because he rambles indefinitely. So I'll set it up for him. . . .

Although Schacht doesn't claim to be the first white child ever born at Yankee Stadium, he at least was born where the Stadium now stands. But from that day in 1910 when ambition first hit him, he dreamed of his big-league debut. The dream grew when he hustled peanuts at the Polo Grounds as a boy just so he could sneak looks at his idols.

Eventually, he won the First World War. "All I know about it was that we were losing the war when I enlisted, and by the time I was discharged, we'd won it," he says. He began pitching for Jersey City but no major-leaguer was paying any attention. So the wily Schacht began bombarding Clark Griffith with letters.

"That guy Schacht is going great. Why don't you grab him?" would be one missive. "Schacht is a comer," would say the next. "Grab Schacht. He's ready now," would be a third. So he would not be accused of immodesty, Al thoughtfully signed each letter: "Just a fan."

Finally, Griff got curious enough to scout him personally and Schacht impressed the Old Fox sufficiently to have his contract purchased from Jersey City.

Without waiting for further station identification, the next voice you hear will be that of Al Schacht:

"Here it is, that moment I've been waiting for since 1910. I report to Griff in Detroit. 'I'm your new pitcher, Schacht,' I tell him, gulping hard. 'Are you ready to pitch?' he asked. I gulp again and admit I am although I've been watching those Detroit hitters in batting practice and I don't like what I see. Even the infielders are hitting about .360 and Ty Cobb is over .400. But he ain't the best. Harry Heilmann's leading the league at .412.

"So I whisper to George McBride, the captain, 'How does a guy know when he's gonna pitch?' He nods toward the ball bag. 'Watch the ball bag,' he says. 'Twenty minutes before the game, Griff will reach in there, take out a ball, and toss it to the pitcher.' So I watch. Griff grabs a ball and tosses it past my nose— and that's a long throw, brother—to a guy named Courtney. So I relax. This won't be the day I've been waiting for since 1910.

"We go into the ninth inning with a 2-1 lead. Boom! Things begin to happen. One guy singles, another triples, and the score is tied. The winning run is on third and Heilmann is the hitter. Then I notice Griff looking up and down the bench. I run for the water cooler because my throat is suddenly awfully dry.

"But it's no use. Griff is hollering, 'Where's that new pitcher?' I know then that he means me. But I'm hardly in the bull pen before Courtney has three balls on Heilmann and I hear a blood-curdling whistle.

"This is the moment I've been waiting for since 1910.

"As I'm strolling across the field, I look at Heilmann. I don't like his looks. All of a sudden, those fences start moving closer to the plate. I'm getting crowded. He gazes fondly at me as if to say, 'Gosh, kid, you look cute. I wonder if you can cook.'

"I step onto the mound and Gharrity, the catcher, meets me.

" 'You're in a helluva spot, kid,' he says. 'You got the winning run on third and three balls on the batter.'

" 'I got?' I scream. 'It was all there when I come in.'

" 'Howya feel, kid?' he asks.

"So I tell him, 'Not hot, not cold—just mediocre.'

" 'All you have to do, kid,' he says, 'is get the ball over the plate.'

" 'Is that all?' I says, kind of sarcastic.

"So he leaves me alone out there. I feel terribly alone because Heilmann looks bigger than ever and the fences look closer. I suddenly realize that here is the moment I've been waiting for since 1910. I throw the ball and—"

Schacht always ends his story there. As an afterthought, he usually adds that he wrote the end of the story in his book, *My Particular Kind of Screwball,* and any listener interested in the outcome can go out and buy a copy.

But come closer while I whisper. The moment Al Schacht had been waiting for since 1910 ended when Heilmann doubled to left, almost killing the third baseman in the process.

JOE DiMAGGIO was sidelined for nearly half the 1949 season because of a heel injury, and when he finally did get to see action—two weeks ahead of the date suggested by his doctor—there was considerable question whether he would be of any value to the Yankees. Such question did not long go unresolved.

1949: DiMag Returns to the Lineup

DANIEL M. DANIEL

JOE DiMAGGIO did it again for the third consecutive day, in Boston. The still convalescent and as yet unconditioned outfielder tore the Red Sox apart with his home-run power. Once more Joe's flaming spirit, his flair for coming through against odds, his penchant for dramatic achievement and consummate showmanship, were stressed as he drove the ball over the left-field wall for three runs, and won for the Yankees by 6 to 3.

Thus the Bombers gained a three-game sweep over the Red Sox in the Fens. It was recollected that in 1939 the Yankees tore into the Hub and won three out of four from a Boston club which, up to then, had nurtured pennant hopes. When the New York team last took three in a row in Boston not even the oldest historians could recollect.

If there had been any doubt among some of the Yankees that they could win the pennant despite April's almost unanimous expert opinion to the contrary, that thrilling sweep in Boston dissipated it.

If there had been any doubt that DiMaggio was worth the $100,000 salary for which he signed last winter it was smashed by the all-conquering blow he administered to Mel Parnell, left-handed star of Joe McCarthy's Red Sox pitching staff, in the wake of Joe's two homers for four runs in Wednesday's 9-7 success, and his circuit drive with a man on base in his long-delayed pennant debut in Tuesday night's 5-4 battle.

DiMaggio emerged from his first series of the year with nine runs driven in, four homers and a single, and an average of .455.

"How much healthier and better conditioned does this man have to be to perform at his best?" wailed Boston, as it dug out of the wreckage and began to entertain serious doubts that its Red Sox could overhaul the DiMaggio-sparked Yankees.

"This was the greatest series of my career," exulted DiMaggio. "I've had some fair days in the World Series. I have had thrills in All-Star games, and in pennant competition. But those three straight days in Boston, two weeks ahead of my schedule, gave me the kick of kicks.

"I wish I were in better shape. I wish my legs were ready. Haven't the drive in them that I need in the field."

Joe was digging out of a mass of telegrams and letters. "Many are from friends," he explained. "Most of them are from fans I don't know."

Boston fans were gracious to Joe last October when he went limping off the field with a charley horse and swollen knees. They could afford to be kind to Giuseppe that afternoon because they had seen the Yankees kicked out of the race.

Yesterday the customers in the Fens shouted themselves hoarse for the pro. A Yankee acclaimed in the Hub, and the Red Sox bleeding.

DiMaggio liked yesterday's homer best of the four he exploded over Fenway's left-field wall.

It was the consummate achievement because McCarthy had turned cautious and wasn't letting Parnell pitch to the Clipper.

The Clipper's seventh-round drive against the lighting tower some 80 feet above the field came off a three-and-two pitch.

With one gone, Snuffy Stirnweiss singled. So did Tommy Henrich. Yankees on first and third, with New York in front by 3 to 2.

Up came a fast ball after the full count, and once again Joe swung for a ball game.

A Letter to Edward B. Talcott

JAMES WHYTE DAVIS

Mr. Edward B. Talcott:

My good friend,

Referring to our lately conversation on Baseball I now comply with your request to write you a letter on the subject then proposed by me and which you so readily and kindly offered to take charge of, after my death, namely, to procure subscriptions to place a Headstone on my grave.

My wish is that Baseball players be invited to subscribe Ten Cents each and no matter how small a sum is collected, it will be sufficient to place an oak board with an inscription on my resting place, but whatever it may be, I would like it as durable as possible without any ornamentation—simply something that "he who runs may read."

The Knickerbocker Baseball Club was formed in 1845. I joined in Sept. 1850. At that time it was the only organized club in the United States. I was a member for thirty years and the only one claiming so long a membership. My excellent friend Mr. Samuel H. Kissam being next in duration of membership, and who would gladly assist you in your undertaking.

The cognomens of "Father of Baseball," "Poor old Davis" and "Too Late," as applied to me, are well known to the Baseball fraternity.

All relations and immediate friends are well informed that I desire to be buried in my baseball suit, and wrapped in the original flag of the old Knickerbockers 1845, now festooned over my bureau and for the past eighteen years and interred with the least possible cost.

I suggest the following inscription in wood or stone:

Wrapped in the Original Flag
of the
Knickerbocker Base Ball Club of N.Y.
Here Lies the Body of
JAMES WHYTE DAVIS
a member for thirty years
He was not "Too Late"
Reaching the "Home Plate"
Born March 2, 1826
Died

I should be pleased to show you my Glass Case containing the trophies of my Silver Wedding with the Old Knickerbockers in 1875 and which I intend to bequeath to you, should you so desire as a mark of appreciation of the kindly act which you have undertaken to perform. Kindly acknowledge receipt of this.

And I am Yours sincerely and thankfully,

James Whyte Davis.

Duane Decker's Blue Sox books are among the most popular in all boys' baseball fiction. Each book has a different hero. Each hero plays a different position on the Blue Sox. Here is a chapter from *Mister Shortstop*, which, though not overlong, shows Decker at his game-describing best.

From *Mister Shortstop*

DUANE DECKER

After Stookey left the kid stranded, with a long fly to deep center, the game settled down. Going into the seventh, those three runs were all the Sox had, but they looked like a couple more than they actually needed. Lasky was pouring his best stuff in. He had given up four scattered singles and no walks, and not a man had reached third base against him.

There was real sparkle in quite a few plays that Hammill made—the easy, careless kind that hit a crowd harder than the tough, precision-made ones do. In the third inning he made a leaping stab of a real bullet to his left and merely had to step on second for an unassisted double play. Spectacular, yes. Tough, no. One of those you-do-or-you-don't balls, in Andy's book.

He plucked one deep from the hole to his right, with a pretty, skidding stop, and nailed the runner at first. But he would not have nailed a fast runner on it, because he had not put on the brakes at the exact moment he gloved the ball and so had lost at least a full second, perhaps two, in getting it over to first. It had been the pitcher who hit it and he was no reindeer going down the base line. But it had been a beautiful play just the same. Only, Andy was thinking, it did not have that last ounce of perfection with which, time and time again, a shortstop wins or loses a ball game for the team. He did not expect the stands to see such a thing. But he had an idea it did not pass Jug by, unnoticed.

Then Slick made a nice pivot on a double play started by Bud Walker, getting rid of the ball without the instant of hesitation that would have let the sliding runner take him out

or upset the aim on the throw. This was all very good, but none of these feats were done under pressure, because Lasky never let himself get in trouble.

In three times up the kid had singled and doubled. The double had been especially eye-catching, because it had crashed the right-field barrier looking like a triple but had caromed just right for the fielder, and Slick had had to dive back to the safety of second after rounding the bag.

But sitting on the bench making a microscopic study of him, Andy reminded himself that both those hits had come with the bases empty. On his third trip to the plate, with Sox runners on first and second, one out, and a second big inning in view, he looked positively feeble. Overeager, he bit on a bad first pitch. It was a low sinker ball designed to produce exactly the result that it did—a skimming grounder to the second baseman with more than enough speed to turn it into the Grays' double-play retort.

"Too bad, kid!" they yelled from the stands. "Can't do it every time!"

True enough. Nobody could do it every time. But the teams that won pennants had the ball-players who did it when it counted, no matter what their batting average showed. Andy knew some .250 hitters around this league who frightened a pitcher more, in the old clutch spot, than several guys listed every morning in the paper among the top five.

This was just one ball game, of course. But if it was a preview of Slick Hammill's competitive pattern, it was not as impressive to Andy as it seemed to be to the stands. Those things had a way of coming to general light in the big leagues. Managers were paid very good money to find them out.

Anyway, a bench rider can dream, can't he, Andy thought.

In the seventh inning he became more convinced than ever that he was up against less than an all-star shortstop. In that seventh the first threat of danger to Lasky arose. The game suddenly stopped being a cakewalk and became grim.

Lasky took the loser's end of a questionable 3-2 call by the plate umpire, on the first man up. After a wide-open forum discussion of the call by a group consisting of the umpire, Lasky, Gibbs, Madigan, Jug Slavin, and—inevitably—Slick Hammill, a Gray nested on first with nobody out.

Three runs behind, they were not going for a run—they were going for the big inning. Lasky was angry and showed it. An angry pitcher is always an untalented pitcher, no matter how great his natural talents are. Lasky demonstrated the truth of this axiom by breaking off a curve that hung like a Japanese lantern at a garden party, and the ball promptly whistled back between his legs and into center field. Hammill gave it the hopeless chase of a whippet after a dog-track bunny and even after he saw it was gone, he dove. It was a dive that would have looked great in Technicolor, but a more mature shortstop would not have expended that much wasted body risk. Anyway, Grays now resided in comfort on first and second, Lasky still looked angry, and the serene ball game had suddenly taken on Pearl Harbor aspects.

To the plate strode Count Blassingame. The Count was sometimes referred to as Track Meet and always as the swiftest base runner in the league. You could not dawdle a single instant, if you were an infielder, on a ground ball hit by the Count. This was a fact that had not been established by a poll; it had been established by a stop watch.

Andy was remembering how every time the Count had come to bat he had always kept saying to himself, Get ready, boy. If he bangs one down this way, tear in for it. He knew that Slick Hammill had been thoroughly briefed on the Count.

Figuring that Lasky was still as angry as he looked and that a double play on the Count occurred as often as a snowfall in Atlanta, the Grays let him hit away. He hit the second pitch. The ball traveled, with dreadful slowness, down toward short. But Slick had drawn

himself in a little. He got the jump. He rushed it. In fact, he looked like a man who was doing everything as right as a robot—until he reached the ball.

Then he froze. Andy knew exactly what was going on in his mind, because it had gone on in his own more than once when the Count had knocked a slow one down his way. What went on inside there was a solemn prodding by your nervous system reminding you that no flick of a second could be wasted in getting this ground ball over to your first baseman. Everything counted—especially in a spot like this, with two on, nobody out, and a lead that would be easily wiped out if you did not get old Track Meet. The force at second was a lost cause; the runner had been off with the pitch. Both runners had, so no business could be transacted at third, either. It was first or nothing.

But he froze. He grabbed for the handle, missed it, grabbed again, and got it. It was too late. He straightened, looked, and did not even throw. The bases were now loaded on Lasky and still there was nobody out.

Hammill walked over and handed Lasky the ball. He seemed to be talking freely. Lasky was not. Lasky was glancing around from base to base, as though thinking of asking a recount on the number of Gray inhabitants.

Meanwhile, Jug stalked out of the dugout and reached the mound as Gibbs, mask in hand, also arrived. Later, in the dressing room, Andy heard Gibbs reporting the conversation that ensued. According to Gibbs, it went like this.

Jug: "How you feeling, Eddie? You feeling O.K.?"

Eddie: "Sure, Skip. I feel O.K."

Jug: "Because if you're not feeling O.K., I can get a fellow warmed up in the pen in no time and—"

Slick: "I pulled the rock. He was O.K."

Eddie: "Honest, Jug, I never felt more O.K."

Jug: "Well, if you're sure, then O.K."

Eddie: "Then O.K., Skip. Let's go."

Strangely enough, Lasky came out of it looking like a man who did feel O.K. Going for the seats, but guessing wrong on a let-up pitch, the next Gray connected for an outfield fly to left. It was deep enough to bring the runner on third in after the catch, spoiling Lasky's shutout, and it left first and second occupied. But one man was out now, the Sox still had a two-run lead, and the real terror was over. Lasky's anger was gone. His mind was once more cool and cagey. He struck out the next batter, then induced an easy high hoist to Woodward in center. And the Grays were through scoring for the day.

In the bottom of the eighth Hammill came up with his third hit, a ground-ball single between first and second. It occurred once more with two outs and nobody on, and he died there. His big-league batting average stood at .750 after his first day and he made still another dazzling stop, behind second, with nobody on in the ninth. The crowd milled through the exits, raving about him. His single error was forgotten, because Lasky had rendered it practically harmless, except for the brief moments of fright that it had produced.

His hitting had been unquestionably authentic, but the only time the Grays had got him out had been a spot where the game could have been locked up by a base hit.

Who cared? The kid had proved he could hit big-league pitching. He had proved he could field with a dazzle that did not show up every year. The Blue Sox had beaten the Grays handsomely, and the fact that the Grays were a bunch of pushovers had yet to be ascertained. The further fact that, behind Lasky's superb pitching, the issue had never been in the slightest doubt except for that seventh inning, seemed to be completely inconsequential.

But Andy did not go along with the statistics. As he saw it, the kid had not played the way a shortstop has to play on a team that wants to win a pennant. He was wondering, as he soaped himself thoughtfully under the shower, if Jug Slavin had seen the same things he had in this flashy opening-day performance of Slick Hammill.

JOHN GALLAGHER

Courtesy *Sport* Magazine. ©

WHEN it comes to getting advice from the master, you could do a lot worse than here. Title and by-line will clue you.

How to Play the Outfield

JOE DIMAGGIO

"OUTFIELDERS should pay their way into the park."

This, of course, is baseball's saddest gag.

As an outfielder, I'm not going to defend our right to free admission or claim that we're as busy as a catcher. The statistics show that outfielders average about three chances a game, which is slightly less than the third baseman's daily work. In some games the fans see an outfielder stand around for so many innings with nothing to do that they wonder why he doesn't take a chair out to his position with him.

The fact is that an outfielder who does a real job for his club works as hard as anyone in baseball. He covers a position as extensive as an oversized building lot, a position to which every fly ball hit will drop either as a safe hit or a put-out. In the outfield there is no such thing as a muff and a recovery in time to make the put-out, except in the rare instance of the deliberate trapping of a fly ball to make a force play on a runner already on base.

A muff in the outfield usually is worse even than an infielder's error on a sure double-play ball. A missed ball not only breaks the pitcher's heart because it robs him of an out which he has earned, but frequently goes for extra bases and allows a run or more to score.

And by "muff" I don't mean only the actual mishandling of a ball. An outfielder may play a ball in absolutely errorless fashion, so far as the box score is concerned, but still be guilty of a tremendous flop if he fails to get the jump on a ball that he might have caught and lets it fall safe. A team is far better off with an outfielder who piles up errors trying for hard catches than with one who handles perfectly every ball hit to him but doesn't go after the tough ones.

In addition to his fielding skill, an outfielder must carry his share, or more than his share, of the wood to the plate. An outfielder who can't

hit around .300 should be a Tris Speaker or a Terry Moore defensively if he isn't to be a drag on the club. And the days of the outfielder who's a good hitter but a poor fielder are gone, probably forever.

There used to be outfielders who were heavy hitters but clumsy fielders, fellows who would knock in two runs but kick away three; but you don't see them around any more. To be an outfielder in the majors today a player must be a good, consistent hitter, exceptionally fast if he isn't a long-ball hitter, and a first-rate fly-chaser and thrower. Otherwise he won't be up very long.

The lively ball and the bigger parks have put bigger chores on the outfielders. Since the early 1920s they have had to play deeper and go back farther. And because they have to play deeper, they have to cover far more ground between their normal positions and the infield.

Although he may not handle the ball for innings at a stretch, the outfielder must be on his toes for every play. Because he now plays deep, a runner is much more likely to try to go from first to third on an outfield single, and the fielder must be adept at handling ground balls and throwing to keep the runner from taking the extra base.

Before every play an outfielder must size up all the possibilities. He must know the hitter. He must know the ground conditions—whether the bounce is likely to be hard or soft. He must know what the wind currents will do to a fly ball, how backgrounds, shadows, or haze will distort his vision, how he will play the ball if it is beyond him and against the fence.

The outfielder must try to make every catch in the best possible position from which to throw. Some players like to catch the ball in front of them, with hands outstretched. My own preference is to take fly balls with my hands above my head, with my left foot toward the plate. I've found that from that position I can save time making the throw.

On ground balls an outfielder rarely has any choice; when he catches up with it the ball usually will be hugging the ground. But if it happens to be a bounding ball, he should charge it in order to field it at the top of the hop, leaving him in good throwing position.

In the 1942 World Series, Enos Slaughter, playing right field for the Cardinals, saved the second game for his club when he caught a bounding ball shoulder-high and threw out the Yankees' potential tying run trying to go from first to third on a single in the ninth. Had he fielded the ball at his feet he would never have been able to straighten up and make the throw in time to get the runner.

Pregame fielding practice ought to give the outfielder a fairly accurate idea of ground conditions. If the ground is soft from recent rains, the ball will hug the grass. If the ground is hard, the ball will take hard, fast hops.

If the outfield is bumpy, and sometimes it is, even in big-league parks, the outfielder must try to get in front of the ball to block it with his body if it takes a bad hop. The sight of a ground ball getting away from an outfielder and going for extra bases is extremely painful to the pitcher and everyone else except the batting team and their fans.

In the big parks the wind can be very tricky, shifting from inning to inning, and the fielder should take an occasional look at the flags around the stands to learn which way it's blowing.

The effects of backgrounds and shadows must be learned by experience. Observations during pregame practice aren't of much help, since the conditions change as the sun sets. And crowded stands, with thousands of fans smoking, make game conditions far different from those in the practice period. Before the game the crowd is small, and haze from tobacco smoke is at a minimum. As the game goes on the haze deepens, especially if the day is humid and there is no breeze to carry the smoke from the park.

Backgrounds vary with the seasons. In Yankee Stadium, for instance, the haze is a greater problem in the fall than in spring and summer. Even with sunglasses an outfielder is likely to become confused. My own dodge is to shield my eyes with my hand as the pitch is being delivered. I find that it gives me a better perspective and makes it easier to follow the delivery to the bat.

Because conditions vary not only with the seasons but in every ball park and with the position of the sun, the knack of finding the ball against tricky backgrounds must be cultivated through experience and observation. Eventually the fielder will find himself perfectly at home in his own park regardless of the variations.

Playing a ball as it caroms off a fence is another problem that varies according to ball parks and must be solved by experience. Naturally, the sharper the angle of the ball's path to the fence the wider the bounce should be back onto the field. Mel Ott, in the Polo Grounds, Tommy Henrich, in Yankee Stadium, and Dixie Walker, in Ebbets Field, are three outfielders who had this play down to an exact science in their own parks.

The most important thing about outfielding is getting a jump on the ball. The most common excuse of an outfielder who just does not get up to a fly ball is "I didn't get a jump on it." The most usual explanation of an exceptional outfield catch is "I got a good jump on it."

Getting the jump is merely making a quick start after a fly ball, and the outfielder roaming a wide expanse of ball park to pull down a real blast that seemed sure for extra bases is a sight which thrills fans and fills them with wonder at the outfielder's intuitive power.

After more than ten years a friend of mine still talks about the day he saw Earl Combs, the old Yankee center fielder, make nine put-outs in one game.

"It seemed that every time the pitcher started his delivery Combs started to move," he says. "One ball he'd catch 'way over in right field and the very next one deep in left. It didn't look as if he was running very fast, but he was always there waiting for the ball. It looked like black magic, the way he knew just where to be."

Combs was a wonderful fly catcher. He didn't need black magic to put him under the ball as it descended. He simply knew how to get the jump on it.

A prime necessity in getting the jump on the ball is knowing the hitter, knowing where he is likely to hit certain types of pitches. For instance, ballplayers know that my power is to left, that if I hit an inside curve I am likely to pull it down the left-field foul line, that if I connect with an outside curve it will probably go just to right of center. They know that Johnny Mize pulls inside pitches down the right-field line.

Most major-league fans have seen Connie

Mack standing on the step of the Athletics' dugout waving his score card, motioning to an outfielder to go over a few steps. He was communicating to the outfielder his knowledge of the hitter.

As the pitcher prepares to deliver the ball the outfielder is up on his toes, moving forward, ready to move in any direction the instant the ball is hit. The phrase "off with the crack of the bat," while romantic, is really meaningless, since the outfielder should be in motion long before he hears the sound of the ball meeting the bat. Through experience and practice the outfielder acquires a working knowledge of the probable distance and speed of the hit from the first quick glance he gets at it as it begins its flight.

The sooner the outfielder gets to the spot where the ball is descending the more easily he can make the catch. There are many times, of course, when the fielder must make the catch on the dead run; but when he is standing still it is easier and surer. When there is a runner on third who could score after the catch, the outfielder, after getting the jump on the fly, may slow down in order to take the ball deliberately on the run to increase the force of his throw to the plate.

No outfielder is a real workman unless he can turn his back on the ball, run his legs off, and take the catch over his shoulder. Outfielders should practice this play until they are sure of it. Backpedaling outfielders get nowhere on balls hit behind them. On many such balls the fielder may be able to turn after his run and make the catch facing the infield, but frequently there is no time to turn.

For the fan the diving, or shoestring, catch is one of the most spectacular plays in the outfielder's repertoire. For the player, for his team, it is one of the most speculative. Since it deprives the batter of a sure base hit, it gives a real lift to the pitcher; but it is not routine play.

There are times when it should be attempted, and times when it is far better to play it safe and field the ball on the hop. That means giving the batter a single; but a miss on an attempted diving catch gives him a three-bagger, or maybe a home run if the park is big enough.

The diving catch is a play on which the outfielder has to make his decision in a split second. He must have weighed all the possibilities beforehand—the score, the inning, the men on base. Unless the outfielder is really skillful at this type of catch, he should never gamble on making it unless the conditions are such that a base hit means the ball game to his club. If

there are two out, and such a catch means cutting off a run, he is justified in the gamble only if the run is an important one, such as the winning or tying run. If his club is ahead, he should never attempt the catch if a miss would permit the tying runs to move into scoring position.

There is a story about Yankees' diving catches in the last ball game Babe Ruth ever pitched. It was the last day of the season, and he defeated the Red Sox in Boston. They scored three runs on him because of a timely triple to left center. Dusty Cooke, later a trainer for the Philadelphia Phillies, played center for the Yankees that day. The triple, a low line drive, was hit between Cooke and the left fielder, and Dusty had to come across the path of the ball on a straight line to catch it. He just missed connections.

On the way back to New York, Ruth was kidding Cooke about the ball's getting away from him.

"You know, Dusty," said Babe, "I'd have had a shutout if you'd dived for that ball."

"Well, Babe, I'll tell you," Cooke replied. "I was debating diving for that ball."

Since Cooke had all of four fifths of a second to make up his mind, it must have been the shortest debate on record.

The rule about catching a ball with two hands rather than one whenever possible applies to outfielders as well as infielders. There will be times, however, when an outfielder must take a fly one-handed because he can't reach the ball with both hands. An outfielder can reach as much as two feet farther for a ball with his gloved hand than he can when trying to make the catch with both hands.

It does an outfielder no harm to take an occasional infield workout, since this will sharpen his judgment and his handling of ground balls. Even in the fielding of ground balls, the "jump" is important to an outfielder, because it enables him to field the ball directly in front of him and lessens the chance that it will go through him.

Balls which a right-hander hits to right or right-center field have a tendency to slice toward the foul line, and balls to left and left center tend to hook toward the left-field foul line. Outfield hits by a left-hander act just the reverse. There isn't much slice or hook to balls hit directly to center, but the center fielder must make allowances for slices and hooks on balls hit to either side of him.

The better the right and left fielders can protect the foul lines the stronger the team's defense. In parks with short foul lines this isn't so important, but in larger parks a ball which is hit down the foul line and which isn't fielded always spells extra bases. Experience will teach right and left fielders just how far in they can play and still cover balls hit between themselves and the foul line.

In playing the hitter, the outfielder should insist on getting the signs from the shortstop so that he will know in which direction to break. Curve balls are more likely to be pulled than fast balls. An outfielder should watch how the infielders are playing a hitter and govern himself accordingly.

With a man on base, the outfielder must have his mind made up in advance on where he will throw, but he should react instantly to any change in circumstances. The safest rule to follow is: always throw ahead of the runner. Suppose, for instance, there is a man on second, and the outfielder, who is set for a throw to the plate in the event a single is hit to his territory, fumbles the ball. Now he must decide whether he has any chance to catch the runner with a throw to the plate or whether he should throw to second to prevent the batter from moving into scoring position on a useless throw home.

An outfielder's throws must always be governed by the score. If his team has a two-run lead, it is far more important for him to keep the tying run from reaching second base, and thus getting into scoring position, than it is for him to attempt to throw a runner out at the plate. He may miss the play at the plate, and the important tying run will be allowed to advance an extra base on the throw.

On throws to all bases, including home, a throw on one hop is preferable to a throw on the fly. A bounding throw is more accurate and far easier for the infielder to handle, particularly if a situation develops which gives him an opportunity to make a cutoff play. And bounce throws are far less likely to get away from the man making the catch.

I can always remember a throw I made in my first year with the Yankees, a throw which was spectacular and pleased the fans but left my manager, Joe McCarthy, unimpressed.

It was in the ninth inning of a September game against Detroit. The Tigers had men on first and third in the ninth with one out, and we had a 6 to 5 lead. Charlie Gehringer was the hitter and he drove a long fly to me. I cut loose with the peg home to stop Pete Fox from scoring with the tying run. The ball carried all the way to Bill Dickey on a line, and he tagged Fox to end the game. I got a terrific hand from the stands; when I reached the clubhouse all I got from McCarthy was a look.

"What are you trying to do, Joe?" he asked quietly. "Show me how strong you are?"

There was no use in telling him that I had honestly intended to get the ball to Dickey on the bounce but had miscalculated the distance. It would have sounded like an alibi, and no manager wants to hear alibis.

A story which Al Moore tells about just such a throw makes me know how lightly I got off. Moore played the outfield with the Cardinals and the Giants. One day when he was a rookie with the Giants he was sent to left field to replace Irish Meusel, a fine hitter but a weak thrower. A runner was on second. The batter singled to left. Moore threw all the way to the plate on the fly, nailing the runner and ending the inning.

Moore trotted happily to the bench, expecting to hear words of praise from Manager McGraw. What he heard was this: "Moore, I thought I explained to you that I always wanted throws from the outfield to take one hop, in case a cutoff is necessary. You probably think you've made a fine throw. You've heard those fans cheering you and you think you're big stuff. I'll show you how big you are in relation to the team.

"Suppose I put a sign up which says, 'Tomorrow afternoon there will be a throwing exhibition by Al Moore at the Polo Grounds.' How many fans do you think it would attract? You wouldn't get fifty. I could and should fine you fifty, but I won't. In the future, just remember that the fans came here to see the Giants play, not to see Al Moore exercise his arm."

There is, however, an exception to the bounce-throw rule when the field is soft as the result of overnight rains or a drizzle during the game. Then, if the outfielder is close enough to reach his base without a bounce, he would throw the ball all the way. If the ball hits a soft spot on a wet field it doesn't "take off," it merely dribbles toward the target.

On a relay the outfielder should remember his throw, the first throw, must be the long one. An infielder who goes out to take a relay should not roam so far that his throw is a long one, unless, of course, he has a weak-throwing outfielder, and there aren't many of those in the big leagues.

Ever since Tris Speaker played for the Red Sox and Cleveland—and Tris started his career before I was born—there has been a red-hot debate about the advantages and disadvantages of an outfielder's playing short, or "shallow," as the ballplayers call it. I don't think it is possible to play a shallow outfield in these days of the lively ball.

An outfielder who can play short is invaluable to his ball club. He can catch many damaging Texas-league flies which ordinarily would fall for singles. In fact, Speaker, twice in one season, made unassisted double plays at second base because of his ability to catch these bloopers just over the infield.

The hardest thing for an outfielder to do is to go back on a fly ball. Apparently Speaker could do this better than anybody else, and because of this rare ability he could afford to play shallow. But Speaker was a genius, at least one of the greatest outfielders who ever lived. I advise the average outfielder to play deep, rather than shallow, because it is comparatively easy for him to come in for a fly ball. An occasional ball which might drop between an outfielder and the infield can't cause nearly as much harm as a ball hit over his head which he could have caught if he had been playing normally deep.

There are times when an outfielder must play shallow. Such a time is when his team is in the field in the last half of the ninth inning, and the other club has the winning run on third and less than two out. In such a setup, a long fly ball wins the game anyway, so it doesn't matter whether the outfielder catches it or not. And by playing shallow he has a chance to catch a Texas-league single and an even chance to throw out the runner on any fly ball he catches. This is an exception, a case which won't come up more than two or three times in any one season.

All outfielders should wear sunglasses. This may sound like gratuitous advice in this era of night games, but baseball has to come into the sunshine occasionally, and then the fielder, even if not playing the sun field, must have his glasses.

The sun field is so tough to play that it requires almost a special instinct in an outfielder. There will be occasions when every outfielder has to take a ball against the sun, but this is a handicap under which the sun-fielder works all the time. The only suggestion for sun-fielders is to try to gauge the ball by getting a sidewise glimpse and shielding his eyes with his glove. Never look directly into the sun. Even with sunglasses, no fielder can take a ball coming out of the sun.

Outfielders should always be quick to back up defensive plays, in the infield as well as in the outfield. The center fielder should be moving forward on all plays at second base, the right fielder on plays to first base, and the left fielder on plays to third. The center fielder comes directly in to protect overthrows or other errors at second base, but the left and right fielders should, in most cases, advance at an angle to the foul line. This is because an overthrow of those bases is likely to hit the stands and carom off.

It is, of course, essential for outfielders to back each other up whenever possible. Sometimes even the most experienced of outfielders will "lose" a ball for any of a number of reasons, and the other fielder, if he is alert, can make the saving catch. And, of course, an extra base can be prevented when one outfielder backs up another on base hits.

Outfielders should remember at all times when they are chasing a fly ball that another outfielder, and sometimes an infielder, may be chasing the same ball. All three will be running with their heads back, watching only the ball. The only way to avoid a collision is for the outfielder to yell that he has the ball under control, and to keep his ears open for the shouts of the other players.

Once the outfielder hears another player calling "I have it!" he should immediately take his eyes off the ball and locate the other player. Sometimes it will be necessary for one outfielder to throw himself to the ground to avoid a crash. Whatever the way out, take it; for a collision means not only that one or more players may be injured, but that the fly ball won't be caught at all.

On fly balls hit between infield and outfield (Texas leaguers) the outfielder should call for the ball and make the catch whenever he can reach it, for he has the play in front of him and will be in a better throwing position. On balls to the outfield, the outfielder who can make the catch in the best throwing position should get the right of way.

Some outfielders, notably Tommy Henrich of the Yanks, are particularly good at coming in for short flies and, with a man on first, trapping the ball and getting a force-out at second. This is a dangerous play and should be attempted only by the experts. In the first place, the chances of a double play on such a trap are almost nonexistent, unless the batter fails to run out his hit; and the only advantage, a slight one, is that the fielder may force a fast runner at second, leaving a slow runner on first.

Henrich could confuse the opposition with runners on first and second because of his adroitness at trapping the ball. When he first bluffed a catch and then trapped the ball under these conditions, he usually had both runners moving in opposite directions. I repeat, however, this is no maneuver for the novice. I once saw one of our Yankee outfielders, not Tommy, attempt this play and he wound up throwing the ball into the Red Sox dugout at Fenway Park.

There are times, of course, when the skillful outfielder can bluff the runner on first so that he comes too far down, in which case the outfielder can catch the fly and double him at first. Plays like this, however, demand perfect coordination and a world of experience.

One simple defense play which the outfielder should perfect is the bluff catch on Texas leaguers. This is simply charging the ball with arms outstretched, giving the impression that it can be caught. This naturally causes the base runners to hold up and often paves the way for a force-out. At least it prevents the runner from taking too long a lead and thus getting an extra base on the Texas leaguer.

On all flies which the outfielder catches near the infield, flies so short that a runner couldn't possibly score from third after the catch, the fielder should get the ball back to the infield as quickly as possible, without resorting to bluff throws. On flies of this type, the runner on third will make a bluff run to the plate to draw a throw, in the hope that the outfielder will throw hurriedly and wildly. Under these circumstances, the smartest thing for the outfielder to do is get the ball to the nearest infielder, thus throttling any sneak run for the plate and eliminating entirely the possibility of a bad throw from the greater distance.

There is one outfielding assignment that no baseball guidebook describes. That's the detail of playing straight man to the patter of the fans. It's part of the job. The outfielders, especially the right and left fielders, are the players whose positions bring them nearest to the stands and place them most readily in range of the yelling of the fans.

The people in the stands are as much a part of professional baseball as the players on the field. Sometimes they sandpaper an outfielder down to a thin finish. No man in his right mind enjoys being called "bum," "punk," "palooka," or worse, or having his personal affairs described to a park full of people by a voice that could call close-order drill for a whole army corps. But any man who plays professional baseball must be as ready to accept a going

over as he is to receive a burst of applause for a nice catch or a timely hit.

Just as the player's tools are his bat and glove, the fan's equipment is his lungs, and the fan has as much right to holler as a player has to take his turn at bat or to jockey an opponent. Moreover, the crowd noise usually balances itself—a good play will bring as much appreciation as a boner brings abuse.

No matter how partial a crowd may be to its home team, it usually gives the visitor a sporting break and polices itself to see that its sportsmanship is not violated. Mel Ott tells a perfect story of this.

It was a Sunday game in St. Louis, in the middle of a pennant fight between the Giants and the Cards, with Carl Hubbell and Dizzy Dean pitching before an overflow crowd parked behind ropes all around the outfield.

"The fans were on me all day, principally because Hub was outpitching Diz, and also because I was the nearest Giant player to them," Mel tells it. "Hub was really great, on a day when almost any ordinary fly would fall into the crowd for a ground-rule double.

"The Cards not only didn't get a ground-rule double, but not one of them hit a fly to our outfielders until about the sixth, when I caught a soft fly in right. Just as I caught this ball I was hit in the middle of the back with a pop bottle.

"I got rid of the ball and looked around, and there was almost a riot among the fans parked behind me. They found the guy who threw the bottle and worked him over, and for the rest of the game everything they yelled at me was friendly and encouraging."

Jockeys in the stands are like jockeys on the bench. Some of them are sharp, and some just noisy. Some can make a point out of any situation. Old-timers still tell of a crack that was made when the late Fatty Fothergill, a hard-hitting American League outfielder, knocked himself out in a White Sox exhibition game in Roanoke, Virginia, when he chased a fly ball and crashed into the fence. The crash splintered the fence.

An announcer (this was before the days of the public address system) rushed onto the field with a megaphone and shouted, "Is there a doctor in the stands?"

From right above the spot where Fothergill had fallen, a fan yelled back, "Is there a carpenter in the stands?"

From the next section came another call: "Is there an outfielder in the stands?"

WAS there ever a day in baseball when everything went right like this one? For Cardinal fans, that is. Here's the Gas House Gang, featuring Dizzy Dean, Pepper Martin, Leo Durocher, Ducky Medwick, and—unscheduled—the ol' judge himself, Commissioner Landis. At one point in this game Dean, with the team ahead 9 to 0, inclined to clown a mite on the mound. Manager Frank Frisch came over from second base. "Listen," he said, "this is the World Series. Behave yourself or I'll get a new pitcher." "No you won't," Dean said. Frisch pondered this for a stretch of time. Then he went back to second base.

1934:
St. Louis Cardinals 11,
Detroit Tigers 0

JOHN DREBINGER

AMID THE MOST riotous scenes in the history of modern World Series play, Frankie Frisch's ripsnorting band of Cardinals today brought an amazing and crushing finish to the seven-game struggle for the world's baseball championship.

The intervention of Commissioner K. M. Landis was made necessary before the Cardinals, who already had achieved unprecedented deeds this year by coming from nowhere to gain a pennant in the final leap to the tape, won the crown.

With their inimitable Dizzy Dean back on the firing line once more to give a final display of his matchless pitching skill, the National League champions fairly annihilated the Tigers, led by their wounded but doughty Mickey Cochrane. The score of the seventh and deciding game was 11 to 0.

Figuratively and literally this most astonishing ball club of modern times tore the game apart. In a whirlwind sweep they blasted seven runs across the plate in the third inning, the first three riding home on a two-bagger by the indomitable Frisch himself. They routed Elden Auker, Schoolboy Rowe, only a short time ago the pride of all Detroit, and two other pitchers.

For a finish, one of their cast, Jersey Joe

Medwick, touched off the spark that sent part of the crowd into a raging demonstration that interrupted the game for twenty minutes and for a time threatened to end the battle without further play. Commissioner Landis then took a hand and quelled the disturbance by ordering the Cardinal outfielder from the field.

The uproar had its inception during the upper half of the sixth inning. Medwick bounced a triple off the right-field bleachers and finished his dash around the bases with a slide into third while the disconsolate gathering looked sullenly on.

Just what provoked Medwick could not be seen as he crashed into the bag in a cloud of dust, with Marvin Owen, the Tiger third baseman, standing over him. Suddenly the St. Louis player was seen to lift his left foot and strike out with his spikes toward Owen's chest.

Medwick missed his mark, but the flare-up was sufficient to arouse the hostile feeling between the rival teams that had been brewing for several days, and players of both sides rushed to the spot. However, the four umpires quickly stepped in between the irate players. When Bill Klem, dean of the National League staff and the arbiter at that base, decided to take no action, the uproar subsided.

It looked like the end of the disturbance, but it proved to be only the beginning.

With the end of the Cardinal inning, Medwick started out for left field and was greeted by rounds of boos from the 17,000 fans packed solidly in the huge wooden bleachers. Pop bottles, oranges, apples and anything else that came ready to hand were hurled out on the field and the Cardinal player beat a retreat toward the infield while the umpires called time.

Attendants rushed out to clear away the debris and Medwick returned to his post. The din now increased twofold, more bottles and fruit were showered on the field, and once more the umpire had to call time. Four times the performance was repeated and each time the anger of the fans increased in its intensity. In vain an announcer implored the fans to desist and allow the game to continue. These Detroit fans were boiling mad and doubtless would have continued the demonstration until the end of time.

Finally, after another deluge of refuse on the playing field, Commissioner Landis rose in his box and waved the umpires to come to him. He ordered Umpire Klem, the two players, Owen and Medwick, and the rival managers, Frisch and Cochrane, to stand before him, and there, out in full view, he held an open court.

The hearing lasted not more than a minute and the upshot of it was that Landis ordered Medwick to remove himself quickly and quietly from the field. The fiery Frisch attempted to protest, but Landis, with an angry gesture, motioned the St. Louis leader to get out on the field and resume play without further delay. Chick Fullis, utility outfielder, took Medwick's place in left and the crowd, very much appeased, actually cheered this unassuming St. Louis player as he came trotting out.

Later Commissioner Landis, in explaining his action, stated he primaily ordered Medwick off the field as the only means of continuing the game in the face of the crowd's hostile demonstration.

"Before the series," said baseball's czar, "the umpires are instructed not to put any player off the field unless the provocation is very extreme. I saw as well as everybody what Medwick did, but when Umpire Klem took no action and the players quieted down I hoped the matter was ended. But when it became apparent that the demonstration of the crowd would never terminate I decided to take action.

"I asked Owen whether he knew of any reason why Medwick should have made such an attack on him. He said he did not, and with that I ordered Medwick off the field. I do not intend to take any further action."

The uproar, of course, quite overshadowed all else that happened on the field, even taking the play away from the marvelous Dizzy Dean, who was out to revenge himself for the beating he had taken in the fifth game in St. Louis last Sunday. Although he had only one day of rest, the elder Dean was in marvelous form as he shut out the Tigers on six hits, to round out the fourth and final victory of the celebrated Dean family. Paul, his twenty-year-old brother, had won the third and sixth game of the series. He himself had won the first game.

Now Dizzy was back to display his complete mastery with the only shutout of the entire series. With his brother he had pitched the Cardinals into a pennant when the entire nation deemed the feat impossible. Together the pair had brought to St. Louis its third world championship since 1926.

The paid attendance was 40,902 and the receipts were $138,063, bringing the total for the seven games up to $1,031,341. The total attendance was 281,510.

Against the sort of pitching the older and greater Dean turned on, the Tigers simply had nothing to offer. They strove valiantly, however, to rally around their leader, the stouthearted Cochrane. Despite the fact that he had spent the night in a hospital nursing a spike wound in his left leg received yesterday, Mickey insisted on playing behind the bat.

When in that torrid third inning the Tiger pitchers crumbled before the fury of the aroused St. Louis host the entire bottom fell out of the game. In all, Cochrane tossed six hurlers into the fray.

All the Detroit pitchers who had appeared previously in the series passed in review. But there was no restraining this remarkable St. Louis team. Shortly after Labor Day these same Cardinals had trailed the New York Giants by eight games in the National League pennant race, only to rout last year's world champions out of the picture on the final two days.

The crowd was still coming through the gates as the rival forces squared off. Auker, after pitching three straight balls to Martin, fanned the overanxious Pepper. Jack Rothrock rammed a double in deep left center, but Auker retired Frisch on a pop fly to Rogell and Medwick on a foul to Owen.

In the second the Cards clipped Auker for two more hits but wound up the inning without out a run or a man left on base. After Collins singled, De Lancey grounded into a double play, snappily executed by Owen, Gehringer and Greenberg. Orsatti, after sending a hit into right, was thrown out on an attempted steal.

The Tigers themselves were able to make no headway whatsoever against Dean in those first two innings, only one of their cast reaching first base. He got on only because Collins dropped a low throw by Durocher after Leo had made quite a dashing pickup of Rogell's awkward bounder in the infield.

Then the first explosion came. It came without warning after Durocher opened the third inning by lifting a high fly to White in center. Still nothing threatened as Dizzy strode to the plate.

Dean hit a high foul behind the plate and right there, had the usually alert Cochrane been himself, a lot of subsequent disaster might have been avoided. The ball dropped just inside the front row of boxes. Cochrane, had he made a try for it, doubtless could have easily caught it.

The next moment the singular Dean person shot a double to left. Martin outsprinted an infield hit to Greenberg, Dean going to third. A moment later Martin stole second. Then the charge was on.

Auker passed Rothrock, filling the bases, and Frisch came up. He ran the count to two and two. Then he hammered a double down the right-field foul line, and all the three Cardinals on the bases crossed the plate.

Frisch's blow finished Auker, and Rowe was called to the mound but didn't stay there long. Schoolboy pitched to three batters and his day's work was done. He got Medwick on a grounder, but then Collins' sharp single to left chased Frisch across the plate. De Lancey connected for a long two-bagger to right, Collins was in with the fifth run, and Rowe was out.

Elon Hogsett was Cochrane's next selection and the left-hander, too, had a short stay in the box. Orsatti, the first man to face him, walked. Durocher, making his second appearance at the plate during the inning, singled to right and again the bases were filled. Dean scratched a hit along the third-base line and De Lancey came in, leaving the bags still filled.

Martin drew a walk on four straight balls, forcing Orsatti over the plate for the seventh St. Louis run. Now Tommy Bridges, victor over Dizzy Dean in last Sunday's game, relieved Hogsett and managed to bring the inning to a close, Rothrock grounding to Gehringer to force Martin at second for the third out.

Bridges stopped the scoring until the sixth. Martin opened that frame with a drive to left and raced to second when Goslin handled the ball poorly. Pepper was held at second while Goslin gathered in Rothrock's fly. Frisch then flied to center, bringing Medwick up, and Jersey Joe walloped the triple which brought on his entanglement with Owen after he slid into the base, Martin scoring. Collins lashed a single to center, where White fumbled the ball. Medwick came home with the second run of the inning and the ninth of the battle.

There followed the twenty-minute uproar that preceded Medwick's final retirement from the game under orders from Landis. Dizzy Dean, wearing a bright Cardinal windbreaker, stood around the infield while the demonstration was going on in full blast, utterly unmindful of what was happening. When play was finally resumed for the last of the sixth the wonder pitcher of the day returned to his task of mowing down the Tigers.

Whenever the Tigers threatened, Dizzy merely turned on the heat and poured his blazing fast ball and sharp-breaking curve right down the middle. One could scarcely imagine that this man in the final week of the National League pennant race had pitched his team to victory in three successive starts, that he was making his third appearance in the series and with only forty-eight hours intervening since his last game.

It was superhuman. Three days before he had entered a game as a pinch runner and had received a belt on the head with a thrown ball that might have slain most any other man. But nothing perturbs Dizzy, except when he is in a fit of anger. Then he may tear up uniforms and do all sorts of things. But nothing disturbed his equanimity today. He smiled and joked through it all.

In the seventh the Cards scored two more. Leo Durocher tripled. Gehringer fumbled Martin's grounder and Leo counted. Martin stole his second base of the day. Then came a long double to left center by Rothrock and the Wild Horse of the Osage thundered over the plate.

Fred Marberry pitched the eighth and fell for a hit, but escaped without a score against him. Alvin Crowder, who had started that ill-fated first game when the Tiger infield exploded five errors all around him, pitched the ninth and retired three Cards in a row.

The Tigers had only two scoring chances in the entire battle. They had runners on second and third with only one out in the fifth. They also had runners on first and second with one out in the ninth. Whereupon Dizzy fanned Greenberg for the third time, turning around even before the third strike reached the plate, and Owen ended the battle with a grounder to Durocher.

And so Detroit, faithful to its Tigers to the last, is still seeking its first world championship. It won three pennants in a row in the days of Ty Cobb and the immortal Hughie Jennings from 1907 to 1909, but lost all three World Series clashes. It waited twenty-five years for another chance. But an amazing ball club, with two of the most remarkable pitchers baseball ever has seen grow up in one family, blocked the path.

Less than a month ago these Cardinals did not appear to have one chance in a thousand of reaching their present goal. But they edged Bill Terry and his Giants right off the baseball map and today they crushed the Tigers.

HARRY LYONS

Courtesy *Sport* Magazine. ©

"Excellent, Hobbs, excellent . . . we'll have a well-trained little team by opening day."

Mr. Dooley on Baseball

FINLEY PETER DUNNE

"D'YE IVER go to a baseball game?" asked Mr. Hennessy.

"Not now," said Mr. Dooley. "I haven't got th' intellick f'r it. Whin I was a young fellow nathin' plazed me betther thin to go out to th' ball grounds, get a good cosy seat in th' sun, take off me collar an' coat an' buy a bottle iv pop, not so much, mind ye, f'r th' refrishment, because I niver was much on pop, as to have something handy to reprove th' empire with whin he give an eeronyous decision. Not only that, me boy, but I was a fine amachure ball-player mesilf. I was first baseman iv th' Prairie Wolves whin we beat th' nine iv Injine Company Five be a scoor iv four hundherd an' eight to three hundherd an' twinty-five. It was very close. Th' game started just afther low mass on a Sundah mornin' an' was called on account iv darkness at th' end iv th' fourth inning. I knocked th' ball over th' fence into Donovan's coal yard no less thin twelve times. All this talk about this here young fellow Baker makes me smile. Whin I was his age I wudden't count annything but home-runs. If it wasn't a home-run I'd say: 'Don't mark it down' an' go back an' have another belt at th' ball. Thim were th' days.

"We usen't to think base-ball was a science. No man was very good at it that was good at annything else. A young fellow that had a clear eye in his head an' a sthrong pair iv legs undher him an' that was onaisy in th' close atmosphere iv th' school room, an' didn't like th' profissyon iv plumbing was like as not to join a ball team. He come home in th' fall with a dimon in his shirt front an' a pair iv hands on him that looked like th' boughs iv a three that's been sthruck be lightenin' and he was th' hero in th' neighborhood till his dimon melted an' he took to drivin' a thruck. But 'tis far different nowadays. To be a ball-player a man has to have a joynt intilleck. Inside base-ball, th' pa-apers calls it, is so deep that it'd give brain fever to a pro-fissor iv asthronomy to thry to figure it out. Each wan iv these here mathy-matical janiuses has to carry a thousand mys-teeryous signals in his head an' they're changed ivry day an' sometimes in the middle iv th' game. I'm so sorry f'r th' poor fellows. In th' old days whin they were through with th' game they'd maybe sthray over to th' Dutch-man's f'r a pint iv beer. Now they hurry home to their study an' spind th' avnin' poorin' over books iv allgibera an' thrigynomethry.

"How do I know? Hogan was in here last night with an article on th' 'Mysthries iv Base-ball.' It's be a larned man. Here it is: Th' ordi-nary observer or lunk-head who knows nawthin' about base-ball excipt what he learned be playin' it, has no idee that th' game as played to-day is wan iv th' most inthricate sciences known to mankind. In th' first place th' player must have an absolute masthry iv th' theery iv ballistic motion. This is especially true iv th' pitcher. A most exact knowledge in mathy-matics is required f'r th' position. What is vul-garly known as th' spit-ball on account iv th' homely way in which th' op'rator procures his effects is in fact a solution iv wan iv th' most inthricate problems in mechanics. Th' purpose iv th' pitcher is to project th' projectile so that at a pint between his position an' th' batsman th' tindincy to pr-ceed on its way will be coun-theracted be an impulse to return whence it come. Th' purpose iv th' batsman is, afther judgin' be scientific methods th' probable coorse or thrajecthry iv th' missile, to oppose it with sufficyent foorce at th' proper moment an' at th' most efficient point, first to retard its for-ward movement, thin to correct th' osseylations an' fin'ly to propel it in a direction approxi-mately opposite fr'm its original progress. This, I am informed, is technically known as 'bustin' th' ball on th' nose (or bugle).' In a gr-reat num-ber iv cases which I observed th' experiment iv th' batsman failed an' th' empire was obliged so to declare, th' ball havin' actually crossed th' plate but eluded th' (intended) blow. In other cases where no blow was attimpted or aven meditated I noted that th' empire erred an' in gin'ral I must deplore an astonishin' lack in thrained scientific observation on th' part iv this officyal. He made a number iv grievous blundhers an' I was not surprised to larn fr'm a gintleman who set next to me that he (th' empire) had spint th' arly part iv his life as a fish in the Mammoth Cave iv Kentucky. I thried me best to show me disapproval iv his unscientific an' infamous methods be hittin' him over th' head with me umbrella as he left th' grounds. At th' request iv th' iditor iv th' magazine I intherviewed Misther Bugs Mulligan th' pitcher iv th' Kangaroos afther th' game. I found th' cillybrated expert in th' rotundy iv th' Grand Palace Hotel where he was settin' with other players polishin' his finger nails. I r-read him my notes on th' game an' he expressed his approval addin' with a show at laste iv enthusyasm: 'Bo, ye have a head like a dhrum.' I requested him to sign th' foregoin' statement but he declined remarkin' that th' last time he wrote his name he sprained his wrist an' was out iv the game f'r a week.

"What'd I be doin' at th' likes iv a game like that? I'd come away with a narvous headache. No, sir, whin I take a day off, I take a day off. I'm not goin' to a base-ball game. I'm goin' to take a bag iv peanuts an' spind an afthernoon at th' chimical labrytory down at th' colledge where there's something goin' on I can undherstand."

"Oh, sure," said Mr. Hennessy, "if 'twas as mysteryous as all that how cud Tom Donahue's boy Petie larn it that was fired fr'm th' Brothers School because he cuddn't add? . . ."

"Annyhow 'tis a gr-rand game, Hinnissy, whether 'tis played th' way th' pro-fissor thinks or th' way Petie larned to play it in th' backyard an' I shuddn't wondher if it's th' way he's still playin'. Th' two gr-reat American spoorts are a good deal alike—polyticks an' baseball. They're both played be pro-fissyonals, th' teams ar-re r-run be fellows that cuddn't throw a base-ball or stuff a ballot box to save their lives an' ar-re on'y intherested in countin' up th' gate receipts, an' here ar-re we settin' out in the sun on th' bleachin' boords, payin' our good money f'r th' spoort, hot an' uncomfortable but happy, injying ivry good play, hottin' ivry bad wan, knowin' nathin' about th' inside play an' not carin', but all jinin' in th' cry iv 'Kill th' empire.' They're both grand games."

"Speakin' iv polyticks," said Mr. Hennessy, "who d'ye think'll be ilicted?"

"Afther lookin' th' candydates over," said Mr. Dooley, "an' studyin' their qualifications carefully I can't thruthfully say that I see a prisidintial possibility in sight."

REMEMBER the outlaw Mexican League just after World War II, and the continuing howl about baseball as a "monopoly" that has been going on ever since? This article, which appeared in 1949, is a remarkably good review of the whole business—and states, you may well agree, a remarkably reasonable point of view.

Of course, it may scare you. It was written by a lawyer and appeared in a *Law Review* (The University of Chicago's) and is replete with formidable citations, so you probably don't want to read it at all.

Before you turn the page, though, check footnote 1 and then footnote 2. Betting is you won't turn the page at all after that. You stand in danger of being entertained here, as well as instructed. Know the history of the player contract? Know what a reserve clause really is? It's all here.

Bear in mind when this article was written; there have been changes since, of course. The Lanier and Martin suits, for example, were dropped. The Gardella suit was settled out of court. But the facts of the case remain unchanged.

Baseball–Sport or Commerce?

JOHN ECKLER, ESQ.

FEW BUSINESS efforts receive the public attention accorded baseball. Every rhubarb[1] is given nationwide consideration; the calcium deposit on the heel of a quasi-peon[2] becomes the object of universal concern. The country's greatest metropolitan dailies and its smallest bi-weekly newspapers invariably contain sport pages which dedicate themselves to the reporting of the minutest detail of every game, trade, or development in the sport of baseball. It is familiar scheduling for radio stations to provide fifteen minutes for news of the world, followed by an equal period of baseball news. As a result of such coverage, almost everyone has a fairly intimate knowledge of baseball.

In significant contrast to this familiarity with the play of the game is the lack of familiarity with "baseball law," the self-imposed body of regulations under which "organized baseball"[3] regulates its activity. The Agreement of the National Association of Professional Baseball Leagues,[4] adopted in 1901 "to perpetuate baseball as the national game of America, and to surround it with such safeguards as will warrant absolute public confidence in its integrity and methods,"[5] together with the Major League Agreement,[6] the Major-Minor League Agreement,[7] and the rules promulgated thereunder, comprise "baseball law." Because of faithful adherence to the dictates of its own rules, "or-

---

[1] A term used by sports writers to describe an altercation, more or less intense in nature, between participants on a baseball field.

[2] A term used by the Court of Appeals for the Second Circuit to describe a young athlete who receives a base pay ranging from $5,000 to $100,000 for each baseball-playing season of five and one-half months. Gardella v. Chandler, 172 F. 2d 402, 410 (1949).

[3] "Organized baseball" connotes the integrated system of baseball comprised of the two major leagues and the so-called minor leagues described more fully later in this paper. The players are "professional" in that they are paid salaries. Many other teams and leagues, often called "semiprofessional," are composed of players some or all of whom are paid and, therefore, are in reality "professional."

[4] The Baseball Blue Book 701 et seq. (1948).

[5] National Association Agreement § 2.01 (a), The Baseball Blue Book 701 (1948).

[6] The Baseball Blue Book 501 (1948).

[7] Ibid., at 601.

ganized baseball" has had few excursions into the courts, and reported decisions are practically devoid of any reference to baseball.[8] This tranquillity, however, has been abruptly interrupted. The entire framework of the law of "organized baseball" has been challenged twice recently as illegal under the Sherman and Clayton Acts,[9] and that challenge has been given a substantial "assist" by the Court of Appeals for the Second Circuit in its remarkable decision in *Gardella v. Chandler*.[10]

I. GARDELLA, MARTIN, AND LANIER

In the spring of 1946 the owners of baseball interests in Mexico undertook to hire for their teams certain players who were under contract to play for teams operating within the framework of "organized baseball." Among the players who responded to the enticing offers to go south were Daniel Gardella, an outfielder with the New York Giants, and Fred Martin and Max Lanier, pitchers with the St. Louis Cardinals. Those three players, along with several others who also "jumped" their contracts to play in Mexico, were immediately placed on a so-called "ineligible list" by Commissioner Chandler and barred for a period of five years from participation in "organized baseball" in accordance with the express provision of the Major League Rules[11] which had been specifically incorporated in each player's contract.[12] The attraction of Mexican baseball apparently proved to be more illusory than real, for most

of the players who "jumped" to Mexico have not returned to that country. Gardella, Martin, and Lanier, plaintiffs in the pending actions against certain officials and teams in "organized baseball,"[13] following their abortive careers in Mexico, have returned to the United States. Since their return they have engaged in professional baseball,[14] but, because of their suspensions, they were for a time denied an opportunity to play on a team associated with "organized baseball." Recently,[15] "to temper justice with mercy," Commissioner Chandler "lifted" the suspension, and Gardella, Martin, and Lanier, as well as all the other players who went to Mexico, have been given permission to return to "organized baseball." The Commissioner's action does not affect any possible rights of the plaintiffs that may have accrued prior to the lifting of the suspensions, and their counsel have announced that the reinstatement will have no effect on the pending cases.

None of the players denies that in "jumping" to Mexico he breached the express terms of his contract with his club, the penalty for which was suspension from "organized baseball." They premise their action upon the allegation that the contracts are illegal because they serve to effect an illegal restraint of trade or commerce and to promote an illegal monopoly over trade or commerce in contravention of Sections 1, 2, and 3 of the Sherman Act and of Section 4 of the Clayton Act. To the extent that these sections are relevant to the pending actions, they are set out in the footnotes.[16]

[8] Baseball has from time to time received the attention of legal periodicals: Topkis, Monopoly in Professional Sports, 58 Yale L.J. 691 (1949); Neville, Baseball and the Antitrust Laws, 16 Fordham L. Rev. 208 (1947); Baseball and the Law—Yesterday and Today, 32 Va. L. Rev. 1164 (1946); Organized Baseball and the Law, 19 Notre Dame Lawyer 262 (1944); Johnson, Baseball Law, 73 U.S.L. Rev. 252 (1939); Organized Baseball and the Law, 46 Yale L.J. 1386 (1937).
[9] 26 Stat. 209 (1890), 15 U.S.C.A. § 1 et seq. (1941).
[10] 172 F. 2d 402 (C.A. 2d, 1949).
[11] Rule 15, Major League Agreement, The Baseball Blue Book 530 (1948).
[12] Uniform Players Contract ¶ 9(a): "The Club and the Player agree to accept, abide by and comply with all provisions of the Major and Major-Minor League Rules which concern player conduct and player-club relationships and with all decisions of the Commissioner and the President of the Club's League, pursuant thereto."
[13] Gardella has filed suit against Chandler, Commissioner; Frick and Harridge, Presidents of the National and American Leagues, respectively; Trautman, President of the National Association (minor leagues); and the New York Giants Club. Martin and Lanier are more ambitious. They have sued the same individuals, and, in addition, all sixteen clubs of the major leagues.
[14] Supporting affidavits filed by Martin and Lanier with their complaint. Martin and Lanier are playing this year, the 1949 season, with the Quebec Professional League. Martin is with the Sherbrooke Club and Lanier is with the Drummondville Club earning a reported $10,000 for season's play. The Sporting News, p. 32, col. 2 (June 1, 1949). Now that their suspension has been lifted, they are back in "organized baseball."
[15] June 5, 1949.
[16] Sherman Act: "Section 1. . . . Every contract, combination in the form of trust or otherwise, or conspiracy, in restraint of trade or commerce among the several States, or with foreign nations, is hereby declared to be illegal. . . .

"Section 2. . . . Every person who shall monopolize, or attempt to monopolize, or combine or conspire

A DAY IN THE LIFE OF MICKEY MANTLE

Marvin Newman

The Yankees' great fence-buster, here seen in consecutive photographs,

chews bubble gum,

hits,

runs,

Marvin Newman

fields,

Marvin Newman

Marvin Newman

checks with a certain fan,

Wide World

108C

and chews bubble gum.

United Press

The particular provision of the player's contract considered most offensive and directly calculated to effect the alleged monopoly is the so-called "reserve clause."[17] Under this provision each player gives his present club or its assignee an option for his services for the succeeding year. Although, as Gardella quite frankly admits in his complaint, "the ultimate objective of this clause was to equalize the opportunities for each team representing a particular city or part thereof to win the pennant and thus to keep alive the interest of its supporters,"[18] it is nevertheless maintained that the universal use of contracts containing this reservation empowers "organized baseball" to control playing talent in violation of the federal mandate against restraints of trade and commerce. The plaintiffs allege that the asserted conspiracy of "organized baseball" to restrain trade and commerce among the states and its concerted action to monopolize the baseball profession has resulted in their personal damage. Martin and Lanier have stated their treble damages as being $1,000,000 and $1,500,000, respectively; Gardella places his at $300,000.

To be sure, the complaints of the plaintiffs have not been confined to a mere recital of the players' contracts and the reserve clause therein, but in considerable detail have discussed numerous provisions of the agreements comprising "baseball law," the apparent arbitrary power reposing in the Commissioner of Baseball to enforce discipline thereunder, the mechanical operations by which baseball teams move from city to city to meet their scheduled games, and particularly the more recent practice of broadcasting and televising games. The rationale of the plaintiffs' cases remains, however, that these players, because of their violation of provisions of their contracts,[19] have, under the rules of "baseball law," been deprived of an opportunity to practice their profession in "organized baseball," and that the concerted effort of "organized baseball" in the creation and enforcement of those rules is a "conspiracy in restraint of trade or commerce among the several States."[20]

II. The Federal Case

The *Gardella* case and the *Martin and Lanier* case, although not yet disposed of, have been the object of considerable judicial attention. The defendants filed a motion to dismiss the *Gardella* action on the ground that the plaintiff had failed to state a cause of action. The district court agreed[21] and granted the defendants' motion on the grounds that *Federal Baseball Club of Baltimore v. National League of Professional Baseball Clubs*[22] was still the law, and that the federal antitrust laws were not applicable to the operation of "organized baseball."

The *Federal Baseball Club* decision[23] was handed down in a case which presented the only other serious challenge to the legality of the pattern established over the years by "organized baseball." There a similar raid had been made in 1914 on players under contract with clubs operating in "organized baseball" by interests in this country who were intent on creating a "third major league." When that ef-

---

with any other person or persons, to monopolize any part of the trade or commerce among the several States, or with foreign nations, shall be deemed guilty of a misdemeanor. . . .

"Section 3. . . . Every contract, combination in form of trust or otherwise, or conspiracy, in restraint of trade or commerce in any Territory of the United States or of the District of Columbia, or in restraint of trade or commerce between any such Territory and another, or between any such Territory or Territories and any State or States or the District of Columbia, or with foreign nations, or between the District of Columbia and any State or States or foreign nations, is declared illegal." 26 Stat. 209 (1890), 15 U.S.C.A. §§ 1-3 (1941).

Clayton Act: "Section 4. . . . Any person who shall be injured in his business or property by reason of anything forbidden in the anti-trust laws may sue therefor in any district court of the United States in the district in which the defendant resides or is found or has an agent, without respect to the amount in controversy, and shall recover three fold the damages by him sustained, and the cost of suit, including a reasonable attorney's fee." 38 Stat. 731 (1941), 15 U.S.C.A. § 15 (1941).

[17] Uniform Player's Contract ¶ 10(a).

[18] Gardella complaint ¶ 53.

[19] Gardella had not signed his 1946 contract, but went off to Mexico in violation of the "reserve clause" in his 1945 contract—that he would play with the Giants or their assignee in 1946. Martin and Lanier had signed their 1946 contracts, and were playing and drawing pay thereunder. They left for Mexico on May 26, 1946, when Lanier had the enviable pitching record of five victories against no defeats.

[20] Sherman Act § 1, 26 Stat. 209 (1890), 15 U.S.C.A. § I (1941).

[21] Gardella v. Chandler, 79 F. Supp. 260 (N.Y., 1948).

[22] 259 U.S. 200 (1922).

[23] Ibid.

fort proved unsuccessful, the Baltimore club of the short-lived Federal League claimed damages which it asserted were experienced because "organized baseball" had conspired to monopolize the baseball business in violation of the Sherman Act. The Court of Appeals for the District of Columbia held for the defendants.[24] The United States Supreme Court affirmed that decision. Justice Holmes, speaking for a unanimous Court, concluded that the business involved was that of giving exhibitions of baseball, "which are purely state affairs."[25] In addition, the decision held that baseball was not "commerce." The Court acknowledged that the teams played in different states and that men and equipment necessarily had to cross state lines, but said: "That to which it [interstate transportation] is incident, the exhibition, although made for money, would not be called trade or commerce in the commonly accepted use of those words. As it is put by the defendant, personal effort, not related to production, is not a subject of commerce. That which, in its consummation, is not commerce, does not become commerce among the States because the transportation that we have mentioned takes place."[26] In the twenty-seven years since that decision, the details of "baseball law" have been the subject of constant revision, but the game remains identical in all its major aspects —three strikes are still an "out," the Brooklyn Dodgers still travel to St. Louis to play the Cardinals, the clubs still carry balls and bats over state lines, and peanuts are still sold in the stands.

III. Gardella v. Chandler

It has been the general consensus of opinion of persons both in and out of baseball that the Federal case disposed of the issue with respect to the character of the game, and that, since baseball was deemed not to be "interstate trade or commerce," it did not come within the ambit of the Sherman and Clayton Acts. The Court of Appeals for the Second Circuit, as recently as 1947, expressly followed the Federal case, but now it would seem as if "organized baseball" is to be regarded as having changed its "spots."[27] Two judges concluded that the judgment of the district court should be reversed and the cause remanded for trial on the complaint; one decided the district court's judgment should be affirmed. Each judge wrote a separate opinion.

Judge Chase reached the decision that the judgment below should be affirmed upon the grounds that (1) the Federal case was controlling and (2) that, even if that decision could be distinguished, Gardella had not stated a cause of action.[28] The judge found that the Holmes decision had never been reversed, that subsequent decisions had not overruled it by implication, and that the facts now before the court were indistinguishable from those considered by the Court in the Federal case. Commenting on the plaintiff's allegation that baseball games are now broadcast and televised, a development since the Federal case which proved so persuasive to the other two members of the court, Judge Chase observed that the record of the Federal case revealed that at the time of that decision "play-by-play" was sent over telegraph wires, and that now the same "information is sent through the air by impulses which are transformed either into words or pictures. So far as I can perceive, the difference in the method of transmission is without significance."[29]

As a second ground for his decision, Judge Chase concluded that, irrespective of the binding effect of the Federal case, personal services and skills are not subjects of trade or commerce within the antitrust laws. Therefore, Gardella's allegation that the alleged conspiracy had deprived him of a right to work shoots wide of the mark.[30] The Sherman Act, this opinion holds, has never been applied unless "there was some form of restraint upon commercial competition in the marketing of goods and services

24 National League of Professional Baseball Clubs v. Federal Baseball Club of Baltimore, 269 Fed. 681 (1920).

25 Federal Baseball Club of Baltimore v. National League of Professional Baseball Clubs, 259 U.S. 200, 208 (1922).

26 Ibid., at 209.

27 Conley v. San Carlo Opera Co., 163 F. 2d 310 (C.C.A. 2d, 1947); Gardella v. Chandler, 172 F. 2d 310 (C.A. 2d, 1949).

28 Gardella v. Chandler, 172 F. 2d 402, 404 (C.A. 2d, 1949).

29 Ibid.

30 Ibid., at 407. In this connection it may be noted that the Supreme Court has made distinctions between restraints upon interstate commerce transactions and restraints imposed in the course of interstate labor disputes. See United States v. Frankfort Distilleries, 324 U.S. 293, 297 (1945), and, at a lower court level, United Brick & Clay Workers of America v. Robinson Clay Products Co., 64 F. Supp. 872 (Ohio, 1946).

in interstate commerce. . . ."[31] In that connection, Judge Chase quoted from the opinion of Justice Stone in *Apex Hosiery Co. v. Leader:*

In the cases considered by this Court since the *Standard Oil* case in 1911 some form of restraint of commercial competition has been the *sine qua non* to the condemnation of contracts, combinations or conspiracies under the Sherman Act, and in general restraints upon competition have been condemned only when their purpose or effect was to raise or fix the market price. It is in this sense that it is said that the restraints, actual or intended, prohibited by the Sherman Act, are only those which are so substantial as to affect market prices.[32]

Judge Learned Hand took what might be considered an intermediate position between that of Judge Chase and Judge Frank. Because the complaint alleged that the sale of radio and television rights had indelibly impressed upon the sport of baseball a characteristic substantially different from that which was before the Supreme Court in the *Federal* case, Judge Hand decided that the plaintiff should have an opportunity to prove his assertions at a trial.

It may be asserted unequivocally that Judge Frank, in his opinion, did not take an intermediate position. In his first sentence he branded the Holmes decision in *Federal Baseball Club v. National League*[33] as an "impotent zombi,"[34] but concluded that nevertheless it was a decision with which the court must reckon. Thereupon, in a statement which is commendable for its candor but which, nonetheless, reflects on the judicial temperament, he stated that the *Gardella* case should be distinguished, if possible, from the *Federal* decision. The reason ascribed for this eager search for a means of placing the brand of illegality on "organized baseball" was that "we have here a monopoly which, in its effect on ballplayers like the plaintiff, possesses characteristics shockingly repugnant to moral principles that, at

least since the War Between the States, have been basic in America, as shown by the Thirteenth Amendment to the Constitution, condemning 'involuntary servitude,' and by subsequent Congressional enactments on that subject."[35]

The *Federal* case had decided that the playing of a ball game was intrastate activity. For that reason, then, the players' contracts, good or bad, related to intrastate activity. The Frank opinion proceeds on the theory that if the game can be found to be interstate, then the players' contracts relate to interstate activity, and if bad (and Judge Frank has no question in his mind on that score) they violate the Sherman Act.

The ingredient grasped upon by Judge Frank to prove the present interstate aspect of "organized baseball" in contradistinction to the situation which existed at the time of the *Federal* case was the frequent broadcast of baseball games by radio and television. Because of this activity, the decision says, the games "are, so to speak, played interstate as well as intrastate."[36] It was conceded that the question was one of degree, but to resolve that difficult issue it was said: "However, to the question whether the difference between a difference of kind and difference of degree is itself a difference of degree or of kind, the sage answer has been given that it is a difference of degree, but a 'violent' one."[37] In final testimony to the difficulties of this tail-wags-the-dog point of view —that the sport of baseball, as it has operated for more than fifty years, is illegal because recently its games have been broadcast—stands what seems to be the fairly strained assumption upon which Judge Frank based his decision: "I think we must, for purposes of deciding the applicability of the Sherman Act, consider this case as if the only audiences for whom the games are played consist of those persons who, in other states, see, hear, or hear about, the games via television and radio."[38]

---

[31] Gardella v. Chandler, 172 F. 2d 402, 406 (1949).
[32] 310 U.S. 469, 500 (1940).
[33] 259 U.S. 200 (1922).
[34] 172 F. 2d 402, 409 (1949). Because of the adjective "impotent" used by the Judge we can assume he employed "zombi" to mean "the walking dead" rather than the alcoholic beverage by the same name.
[35] Ibid. Now it would seem that the "national pastime" is "un-American."
[36] Ibid., at 411.
[37] Ibid., at 412.
[38] Ibid., at 414. The thoroughness and zeal with which Judge Frank has pursued his mission is indicated by his footnote number 9a. Ibid., at 415. There he suggests an accounting technique to be used by plaintiff in the trial of his case. The "broadcast theory" will, of course, be met with the argument that while the sale of radio and television rights is a valuable asset, it in no sense controls or determines any aspect of the baseball undertaking. In anticipating that argument, the footnote seems to admit the argument's validity by calling income from that source "velvet." Nonetheless, Judge Frank would have that income compared to net profits rather than gross profits in order that it may be shown to be more than "trifling." This pro-

IV. MARTIN AND LANIER V. CHANDLER

On June 2d of this year, the Court of Appeals for the Second Circuit, speaking through Judge Learned Hand, filed an opinion in a proceeding which it denominated a "sequel" to its decision in the *Gardella* case.[39] Motions had been filed in both the *Gardella* and *Martin and Lanier* cases for injunctions *pendente lite* to compel the defendants to remove the plaintiffs' suspensions and to reinstate them to the "eligible" list. The motions were denied by the judge of the district court on three grounds. "First, he held that the injunction would 'disturb the status quo by restoring the plaintiffs to positions which they had voluntarily resigned three years before'; second, he held that their rights depended upon disputed questions of fact and law; third, he held that they had an adequate remedy of law in the recovery of damages."[40]

In affirming the decision of the district court, Judge Learned Hand wrote a short but significantly unanimous opinion. Of the three grounds, the court found it necessary to consider only the second ground, that the plaintiff's rights depended on disputed questions of fact and law. While briefly analyzing the courts' opinion in the *Gardella* case, Judge Hand amplified his own position and, on the intrastate vs. interstate issue, said: "It seemed to me that it was [in the *Federal* case] a question of the proportion of the interstate activities to the whole business and that the new activities of radio broadcasting and television should be added to the earlier interstate activities and the sum should be compared with the business as a

whole."[41] The court had before it the controversial "reserve clause" (which is set out in full later in this article) and in reference to it said: "Apart from the question of jurisdiction, we are not prepared to say, on the record now before us, the 'reserve clause' violates the Anti-Trust Acts. Such a determination may involve consideration, among other things, of the needs and conduct of the business as a whole."[42] Judge Frank did not dissent.[43]

As has been indicated, at the time of this writing neither the *Gardella* case nor the *Martin and Lanier* case has been tried on the facts. Irrespective of the outcome of those trials, it seems likely that at least the *Gardella* case will finally be argued before the United States Supreme Court unless, of course, legislation makes moot the issues.[44] In light of the encouragement he has received from the Court of Appeals for the Second Circuit, the plaintiff is not likely to yield; "organized baseball" has at stake its entire structure.

V. TRADE OR COMMERCE?

Gardella, Martin, and Lanier seek damages under the antitrust laws. In order to bring "organized baseball" within the purview of those laws, two fundamental questions must be answered in the affirmative. (1) Is baseball an interstate activity? (2) Is baseball trade or commerce?

The new element which the plaintiff asserts has been added since the *Federal* case, the broadcast of the play of the games,[45] goes only to the answer to question number one: whether or not "organized baseball" is an intrastate or

cedure seems to be not only bad accounting, but inconsistent with the theory of his decision. If, because of radio and television, baseball has become interstate, then certainly income from that source must be lumped with and considered in relation to income from baseball's intrastate activity. Compare Judge Hand's opinion in Martin and Lanier v. Chandler, 174 F. 2d 917 (C.A. 2d, 1949).

[39] Martin and Lanier v. Chandler, 174 F. 2d 917 (C.A. 2d, 1949).

[40] Ibid., at 918.

[41] Ibid., at 918.

[42] Ibid., at 918.

[43] The court did not file a separate opinion in Gardella's action for an injunction *pendente lite* but affirmed the district court's denial of the injunction by a per curiam opinion citing as authority its discussion in the Martin and Lanier case. Gardella v. Chandler, 174 F. 2d 919 (C.A. 2d, 1949).

[44] Two identical bills have been introduced in the 81st Congress: H.R. 4018 and H.R. 4019, which provide: "That section 313 of the Communications Act of 1934, as amended, is amended by inserting "(a)" after "313." And by adding at the end of such section the following new subsection:

"(b) No organized professional sports enterprise shall by reason of radio or television broadcasts of sports exhibitions, or by reason of other activities related to the conduct of such enterprise, be held to be engaged in trade or commerce among the several States, Territories, and the District of Columbia, or with foreign nations, or in activities affecting such trade or commerce, within the meaning of any law of the United States relating to unlawful restraints and monopolies or to combination, contracts, or agreements, in restraint of trade or commerce."

It seems unlikely that these, or bills designed to have the same effect, will be pressed for action until the pending cases have reached final decision.

[45] Gardella Complaint, ¶ 30, 31, 33, 34, 35, 36. Martin and Lanier Complaint, ¶ 32.

interstate activity.[46] The Supreme Court, indeed, did hold in the *Federal* case that the business of baseball was giving exhibitions, a "purely state affair,"[47] but assuming *arguendo* that it is found that selling the right to broadcast does in some way place an interstate aspect on the game, the second fundamental question still remains—is baseball "trade or commerce"?

To state the question thus simply compels a negative answer. "Trade or commerce" inexorably connotes activities of the market place—the buying or selling of a commodity. In answer to those who would conspire to restrain the flow of goods to the market place or who would attempt to monopolize the supply of such goods, with the objective in both instances to fix or raise the price to the consumer, Congress passed the Sherman Act. The meaning of the words "trade or commerce" and the abuse at which the antitrust laws are directed have been analyzed and stated by the Supreme Court in *Apex Hosiery Co. v. Leader:* "Restraints in competition or on the course of trade in the merchandising of articles moving in interstate commerce is not enough, unless the restraint is shown to have or is intended to have *an effect upon prices in the market or otherwise to deprive purchasers or consumers of the advantages which they derive from free competition.*"[48] (Italics added.) As Judge Chase put it, dissenting in the *Gardella* case, "The Supreme Court has never, so far as I know, applied the Sherman Act in any case unless it was of the opinion that there was some form of restraint upon commercial competition in the marketing of goods and services in interstate commerce. . . ."[49]

By no standard, however elastic, can baseball be considered such "trade or commerce." On the contrary, baseball is a sport, an athletic contest. The function and purpose of "organized baseball" as such, is to provide for, regulate, maintain and discipline such sporting events. The essence of baseball is the game; the essence of the game is the personal, physical efforts of the players in that game. "Trade or commerce" is not involved. There is no production of goods or services which have any effect on either intrastate or interstate commerce. As the appellees in the *Federal* case argued: "Playing baseball, whether for money or not, is a striking instance of human skill exerted for its own sake and with no relation to production. In the case of an exhibition of athletic skill, as in the case of dramatic performance, the onlookers derive nothing but enjoyment."[50]

The rationale of the *Federal* case is that baseball is not trade or commerce, and it is submitted that the court's decision would have been quite the same had the facts shown that every ball park was located on a state line and the players had to pass from one state to another as they ran from first to second base. Justice Holmes said that "the decision of the court of appeals went to the root of the case."[51] The lower court had said that "the game effects no exchange of things according to the meaning of 'trade or commerce' as defined above."[52]

It is believed that only two other decisions have determined specifically the question as to whether or not baseball is "trade or commerce." One of them, *American Baseball Club of Chicago v. Chase,*[53] contains little language to cheer the officials of "organized baseball," and a large portion of it was found by Judge Frank to be useful in support of his quasi-peon theory of ballplayer servitude.[54] When called upon, however, to resolve the argument that "organized baseball" was subject to the Sherman Act because it was "trade or commerce," the court there said:

---

[46] In a recent Sherman Act case, Mandeville Island Farms v. American Crystal Sugar Co., 334 U.S. 219 (1948), the Court seems to have established a new intrastate frontier for the antitrust laws. There refiners of sugar purchased sugar beets, raised and delivered in refiners' state. Because the ultimate act, the sale of the refined sugar, was admittedly an interstate transaction, the Court ruled the whole process was given an interstate character and the Sherman Act covered the preliminary step, the purchase of sugar beets. The reverse situation is presented by baseball, where the ultimate act, production of the ball game, is an intrastate activity, and the preliminary or ancillary activity is alleged to be interstate.

[47] Federal Baseball Club of Baltimore v. National League of Professional Baseball Clubs, 259 U.S. 200, 208 (1922).

[48] 310 U.S. 469, 500 (1940).

[49] 172 F. 2d 402, 406 (C.A. 2d, 1949).

[50] Brief of Defendants in Error, Federal case, p. 47.

[51] Federal Baseball Club of Baltimore v. National League of Professional Baseball Clubs, 259 U.S. 200, 208 (1922).

[52] National League of Professional Baseball Clubs v. Federal Baseball Club of Baltimore, 269 Fed. 681, 685 (1920).

[53] 86 N.Y. Misc. 441, 149 N.Y. Supp. 6 (1914).

[54] Gardella v. Chandler, 172 F. 2d 402, 410 (C.A. 2d, 1949).

. . . I cannot agree to the proposition that the business of baseball for profits is interstate trade or commerce, and therefore subject to the provisions of the Sherman Act. An examination of the cases cited by the defendant confirms rather than changes my conclusion. Commerce is defined by the Century Dictionary as an "interchange of goods, merchandise or property of any kind; trade, traffic; used more especially of trade on a large scale carried on by transportation of merchandise between different countries, or between different parts of the same country, distinguished as foreign commerce and internal commerce."

The defendant urges that under the National Agreement baseball players are bought and sold and dealt in among the several States, and are thus reduced and commercialized into commodities. A commodity is defined as: "That which is useful; anything that is useful or serviceable; particularly an article of merchandise; anything moveable that is a subject of trade or of acquisition."

We are not dealing with the bodies of the players as commodities or articles of merchandise, but with their services as retained or transferred by contract. The foundation of the National Agreement is the game of baseball conducted as a profitable business, and if this game were a commodity or an article of merchandise and transported from State to State, then the argument of the defendant's counsel might be applicable. . . .

Baseball is an amusement, a sport, a game that comes clearly within the civil and criminal law of the State, and is not a commodity or an article of merchandise subject to the regulation of Congress on the theory that it is interstate commerce.[55]

More recently, the court in *American League Baseball Club of New York v. Pasquel*[56] was confronted with the question of whether or not baseball was trade in relation to a New York statute. There the court said: "Organized baseball has been in existence for many decades. The plaintiff's activities involve the rendition of services. Even if organized baseball, as claimed by defendants, be a monopoly, it would seem that it is not a combination in restraint of trade, either under the provision of Section 340 of the General Business Law, known as the Donnelly Act, or at common law."[57]

Although, in this era of pragmatic thinking, considerations of legislative intent,[58] like the principle of *stare decisis*[59] and the issue of federal constitutionality,[60] have lost much of their weight as precepts for judicial construction, to the extent that the will of the citizens of the country expressed through the acts of their elected representatives is controlling, it settles this issue. Twenty-seven years ago the Supreme Court ruled that baseball was not "trade or commerce." Since that time both major political parties have at different times had incontestable control of both houses of the national legislature, yet no effort has been made by legislative fiat to bring baseball under the Sherman Act.[61]

On the issues presented by the pending cases it can be affirmatively stated that Congress has, in fact, expressed itself. The rationale of the plaintiff's cases is not that "organized baseball" is in the television business and that they are damaged because the defendants refuse to show their pictures, but rather that they are baseball players and are being deprived of an opportunity of exercising their efforts in the play of the game. The finding of fact upon which Congress premised the exemption of unions from the antitrust laws is that "the labor of a human being is not a commodity or article of commerce."[62] To be sure the pending actions do not involve any issues of labor unions and the Sherman Act, but the finding by Congress that the ability to work is not a subject of trade or commerce is pertinent.[63] Manifestly, if baseball is not "trade or commerce" under Section 1 of the Sherman Act,[64] it is not trade or commerce which is subject to a monopoly condemned by Section 2.[65]

[55] 86 N.Y. Misc. 441, 149 N.Y. Supp. 6 (1914).
[56] 187 N.Y. Misc. 230, 63 N.Y.S. 2d 537 (1946).
[57] Ibid., at 540. See American League Baseball Club of New York v. Pasquel, 188 N.Y. Misc. 106, 66 N.Y.S. 2d 743 (1946).
[58] United States v. South Eastern Underwriters Ass'n, 322 U.S. 533 (1944), where the Court, divided four and four, extended the Sherman Act to cover insurance in spite of "overwhelming" evidence of congressional intent to the contrary. See dissenting opinion of Justice Frankfurter. Ibid., at 583.
[59] Comm'r of Internal Revenue v. Church, 335 U.S. 632 (1949); Spiegel v. Comm'r of Internal Revenue, 335 U.S. 701 (1949).
[60] Compare Helvering v. Davis, 301 U.S. 619, 640 (1937).
[61] And the President gives the game executive sanction by continuing the practice of throwing out the first ball at the season's start—with either his right or his left hand.
[62] Clayton Act § 6, 38 Stat. 731 (1914), 15 U.S.C.A. § 17 (1941).
[63] Gardella v. Chandler, 172 F. 2d 402, 406 (C.A. 2d, 1949).
[64] 26 Stat. 209 (1890), 15 U.S.C.A. § 1 (1941).
[65] 26 Stat. 209 (1890), 15 U.S.C.A. § 2 (1941).

VI. BASEBALL LAW: REASONABLE OR UNREASONABLE?

Of considerable significance in the disposal of the pending cases will be the question as to whether or not the restraint alleged by the plaintiffs is, in fact, unreasonable. That "organized baseball" has imposed restraints upon itself and all associated with it cannot be gainsaid—that is the very essence of "baseball law." To be condemned, however, those restraints must be unreasonable. Justice Brandeis stated the rule of law in *Chicago Board of Trade v. United States:*

. . . But the legality of an agreement or regulation cannot be determined by so simple a test, as whether it restrains competition. Every agreement concerning trade, every regulation of trade, restrains. To bind, to restrain, is of their very essence. The true test of legality is whether the restraint imposed is such as merely regulates and perhaps thereby promotes competition or whether it is such as may suppress or even destroy competition. To determine that question the court must ordinarily consider the facts peculiar to the business to which the restraint is applied; its condition before and after the restraint was imposed; the nature of the restraint and its effect, actual or probable. The history of the restraint, the evil believed to exist, the reason for adopting the particular remedy, the purpose or end sought to be attained, are all relevant facts. This is not because a good intention will save an otherwise objectionable regulation or the reverse; but because knowledge of intent may help the court to interpret facts and to predict consequences. . . .[66]

"Organized baseball" is composed of two major leagues, the National and American, both nonprofit, unincorporated associations composed of eight teams each. The corporations operating the teams are organized for profit under the laws of the several states. In addition to the major leagues are the so-called minor leagues, composed of clubs in various classifications designated as AAA, AA, A, B, C, and D. These classifications are based upon the aggregate population of the cities composing the league[67] and determine, for instance, the number of players a team in a given classification may carry[68] and the monthly salary limit for each club as a whole.[69]

The leagues and the teams which compose them have entered into various agreements to regulate the conduct of "organized baseball" and the play during each league's championship season and any postseason competitions such as the "World Series." These agreements, three in number, compose "baseball law."

The "Major League Agreement"[70] executed by the two major leagues and their sixteen constituent clubs, and the rules promulgated thereunder, relate specifically to the conduct of the major leagues. That agreement creates the office of Commissioner, and gives the Commissioner broad powers to investigate, determine, and discipline conduct found to be "detrimental to the best interests of the national game of baseball."[71] Such discipline may be by way of fine, suspension, or "such other steps as he [the Commissioner] may deem necessary and proper in the interest of the morale of the players and the honor of the game."[72]

Other business communities have never ceased to be amazed at the degree of unbridled power those representing baseball interests have voluntarily surrendered to the Commissioner. The explanation lies in the long history of the game. The very nature of a sports enterprise requires submission by those competing to the "rules of the game." That has been the characteristic pattern of baseball since its inception. The need of self-discipline and regulatory control of those within the framework of "organized baseball" was underlined in 1919 when certain interests entirely independent of "organized baseball" aproached players in an effort to "influence" the outcome of the World Series of that year. Baseball itself discovered and revealed what has been popularly known as the "Black Sox Scandal."

Regular avenues of law enforcement had proved inadequate to protect the integrity of the game. "Organized baseball" concluded that it could and would keep its own house in order so that it might properly command the respect of a sports-loving nation. It was then that the office of Commissioner was created. A federal judge, Kenesaw Mountain Landis, whose courage and integrity were exemplary, stepped down from the bench to assume that office. Following his death, a United States Senator,

---

[66] 246 U.S. 231 (1917).
[67] National Association Agreement § 10.02(a), The Baseball Blue Book 710 (1948).
[68] National Association Agreement § 17.02, The Baseball Blue Book 728 (1948).
[69] National Association Agreement § 180.04, The Baseball Blue Book 730 (1948).
[70] The Baseball Blue Book 501 (1948).
[71] Major League Agreement Art. I, § 2(a), The Baseball Blue Book 507 (1948).
[72] Major League Agreement Art. I, § 4, The Baseball Blue Book 502 (1948).

Albert B. Chandler, resigned that public trust to assume the responsibilities of the office of Commissioner. The power the Commissioner exercises over ownership and players alike is, in many respects, absolute, but the sports community of the country knows and appreciates that "organized baseball" is entitled to command its unquestioned confidence and respect.

In addition to establishing the office of Commissioner, the Major League Agreement and Rules provide in meticulous detail the regulations under which the major leagues operate. A player limit of twenty-five is established; prohibitions against the signing of high-school and American Legion Junior players are provided; rules for selection of players in order that a capable player will not be held in the minor leagues, and waiver rules which prevent a player being transferred from a major to a minor league, are stated; a minimum salary for players of $5,000 is established; the right to own stock in a competing club is denied; rules against misconduct which prohibit and penalize the throwing of games, gifts to umpires and gambling are included; and regulations affecting the World Series are defined.[73] These are a very few of the detailed provisions of the Agreement and Rules.

Under the Major-Minor League Agreement and Rules thereunder,[74] the minor leagues agree to submit to the jurisdiction of the Commissioner, and in the agreement the major and minor leagues defined the rules for the conduct of those leagues.

The third agreement, rounding out "baseball law," is the National Association Agreement.[75] This document creates the office of President of the National Association, now occupied by George M. Trautman, and gives to that office many of the powers of discipline over minor leagues reposed in the Commissioner over the majors. This agreement establishes rules for the conduct of the minor leagues.

Rule 3A of the Major-Minor League Rules provides:

To preserve morale and to produce the similarity of conditions necessary to keen competition, the contracts between all clubs and their players in the Major League shall be in a single form which shall be prescribed by the Major League Executive Council; and the contract between all clubs and players in the Minor Leagues shall be in a single form which shall be prescribed by the President of the National Association. No club shall make a contract different from the uniform contract, and no club shall make a contract containing a non-reserve clause except permission be first secured from the Major League Executive Council in case of a Major League player, or from the President of the National Association in case of a Minor League player. The making of any agreement between a club and a player not embodied in the contract shall subject both parties to discipline; and no such agreement, whether written or verbal, shall be recognized or enforced.[76]

Rule 3(a) of the Major League Rules[77] and Section 15.01 of the National Association Agreement[78] contain similar language.

Each such "uniform contract" incorporates, by reference, the Major-Minor League Agreement and Rules and either the National Association Agreement or Major League Agreement, as the case may be,[79] and requires the signatories' assent to all decisions of the Commissioner of Baseball. Thus, the Uniform Player's Contract becomes the instrumentality by which the players assent to and become regulated by "baseball law."

The court of appeals in the *Gardella* case did not attempt to analyze the player's contract as such. Although Judge Frank made some fairly harsh observations about the contracts, the court did not have before it the text of the contract and the rules incorporated therein, or any evidence as to the purpose, operation and effect of the contract and rules as bearing upon the reasonableness of the restraints contained in them.[80] It is likely, however, that considerable attention will be given to its terms and provisions in the trial of the case. Of particular interest will be the "reserve clause" and the power of the club to assign a player's contract.

VII. The Reserve Clause

The paragraph providing for renewal, or the "reserve clause," in the current major-league Uniform Player's Contract provides:

---

[73] Major League Rules 2(a) and (b), 3(i), 3(j), 5(a)-(f), 10, 17(d), 20(a)-(e), 21, 33-50. The Baseball Blue Book 508, 512-14, 531-34, 539 (1948).
[74] The Baseball Blue Book 601 et seq. (1948).
[75] Ibid., at 701 et seq.
[76] Ibid., at 609.
[77] Ibid., at 508.
[78] Ibid., at 719.
[79] Minor League Contract § 7a; Major League Contract § 9a.
[80] Compare the same court's comments in Martin and Lanier v. Chandler, 174 F. 2d 917 (C.A. 2d, 1949).

10. (a) On or before February 1st (or if a Sunday, then the next preceding business day) of the year next following the last playing season covered by this contract, the Club may tender to the Player a contract for the term of that year by mailing the same to the Player at his address following his signature hereto, or if none be given, then at his last address of record with the Club. If prior to the March 1 next succeeding said February 1, the Player and the Club have not agreed upon the terms of such contract, then on or before 10 days after said March 1, the Club shall have the right by written notice to the Player at said address to renew this contract for the period of one year on the same terms, except that the amount payable to the player shall be such as the Club shall fix in said notice; provided, however, that said amount, if fixed by a Major League Club, shall be an amount payable at a rate not less than 75% of the rate stipulated for the preceding year.

(b) The Club's right to renew this contract, as provided in subparagraph (a) of this paragraph 10, and the promise of the Player not to play otherwise than with the Club have been taken into consideration in determining the amount payable under paragraph 2 hereof.

It is the use of the clause just quoted that Judge Frank found "virtual slavery";[81] yet in that clause lies the secret of baseball's successful operation year after year. Upon the proposition that the "reserve clause" is absolutely necessary to baseball, the officials, owners and players are in total agreement. In their brief the defendants in the *Gardella* case said: "The restraint of which the plaintiff here complains, namely, the reserve clause and the Commissioner's disciplinary power, are the very heart of the system of self-regulation by which baseball has preserved the competition and integrity which are the public's principal concern."[82]

The players in whose contracts the "reserve clause" appears are even more positive. The Committee on Labor and Industries of the Massachusetts Legislature recently held hearings on a bill[83] to outlaw the "reserve clause" in baseball player contracts. John Murphy, a pitcher for the New York Yankees, who had been elected by the players on the eight teams in the American League as their spokesman, and Dixie Walker, an outfielder for the Pittsburgh Pirates, similarly elected as spokesman for the players in the National League, appeared at the hearing. Murphy advised the Committee of a meeting held to discuss the "reserve clause" by representatives of the players from each team in the American League. His testimony was:

We knew what it [the reserve clause] meant. It simply means that at the end of the year, or the following spring the ball club owners have the right to resume their option on our services. We spoke as informally as that in our meeting, and we said that is the only way baseball can continue; that if our livelihood is to continue, we have to have that in our contract, as an integral part of the contract, because without that clause if a ball player were free to sign up with anybody whom he pleases at the end of that year or the next spring, why, the whole structure of the game would be destroyed. . . .[84]

Dixie Walker reported that he had been a player in "organized baseball" for twenty years and had "never heard any of the ballplayers who have said that they were anxious to have that [reserve] clause stricken out." Walker affirmed John Murphy's testimony, adding that "the ballplayers felt that it [the reserve clause] should be left as it was, because it was the very backbone of the game."[85]

The minor leagues, as well as the majors, benefit from and are dependent on the "reserve clause." A substantial percentage of the teams in the minors have direct identity with major-league teams either by ownership or "working agreements" under the "farm system." That system gives an associated team the benefit of the financial stability of its parent club, the advantage of its scouting system and, most important, the use of its personnel in training and developing young players. The accomplished result has been more teams in the minors, hence, more communities with baseball, more players gainfully employed and more quickly trained for participation in the major leagues. Without the "reserve clause" and the attendant right to claim a player's services as he is thus trained, no major-league team would undertake the considerable expense required to operate a farm system.

The "reserve clause" is designed to prevent raids by wealthy clubs upon the players of

[81] Gardella v. Chandler, 172 F. 2d 402, 410 (1949).
[82] Appellee's Brief, p. 30.
[83] Massachusetts Legislature, House Bill No. 1636 (1948).
[84] Hearing, Committee on Labor and Industries, Massachusetts Legislature, January 22, 1948.
[85] Ibid. George "Birdie" Tebbetts of the Boston Red Sox appeared, as well, and told the committee, "I am a baseball player and I have no connection with management, and I have no sympathy with them. . . . However, there is no reason that I can see why this bill [outlawing the "reserve clause"] should go through, because if it does it will absolutely ruin the baseball players. It will deprive fellows like me of a tremendous earning power in baseball."

poorer members of the league, thereby preserving more equal competition from year to year and maintaining more stable identity of players with clubs and the baseball fans of their communities. As the Court of Appeals in the *Federal* case said, ". . . [I]f the reserve clause did not exist, the highly skillful players would be absorbed by the more wealthy clubs, and thus some clubs in the league would so far outstrip others in playing ability that the contest between the superior and inferior clubs could be uninteresting, and the public would refuse to patronize them."[86]

Theoretically, except for the seventy-five per cent proviso, the "reserve clause" gives the player no alternative to a grossly inadequate salary. In practice that has never been the case. Efforts to produce "awful examples of the operation of the reserve clause" during the trial of the *Federal* case were unavailing.[87] It is unlikely that any will be produced at the trial of the pending actions. The average age of the players in the National League at the beginning of the 1949 playing season was 27.31 years,[88] the average salary for the five and one-half months' season was approximately $12,000.

The reason for lack of abuse of the "reserve clause" lies in the nature of the game more than in the "benevolent" aspects of the baseball "dictatorship."[89] There is always a shortage of capable players; the threat of voluntary retirement is efficacious. More than that, *esprit de corps*, possible only with salary-satisfied players, is essential to a winning team. As some evidence of the success of baseball's "collective bargaining" stands the fact that at the commencement of the 1949 season there were no "holdouts" among the more than 600 major-league players, a situation which is more the rule than the exception. Dictates of competition on the playing field prohibit abuse of the "reserve clause."

VIII. POWER TO TRADE

The second feature of the player's contract which will be given attention upon the trial of the pending cases is the right given the club to assign a player's contract. In order, in fact, to prohibit a monopoly such as the pending cases allege, each club in the major leagues is restricted to a player roster of twenty-five men. Because of this limit, however, it is necessary to the game and to the welfare of the players that the clubs have the right, by assignment, to exchange players skilled in the play of one position, but not needed or being used, for other players needed to strengthen the team. The right of assignment is a valuable and necessary right in management. The players agree:

That is another way of keeping competition in baseball. One club will think they have too many pitchers, and another club has too many infielders, and the only way to maintain a balance is for one club to trade a pitcher for two infielders, or vice versa. It is the structure of baseball. The fans love it and the players love it. In most cases of trades of players, I would say nine out of ten times the player receives an increase in salary when he is transferred from one club to another, because the new owner wants a satisfied ballplayer. . . . We knew that was part of our business of baseball as much as balls and strikes, and we went right along with it.[90]

"Baseball law" surrounds the right of assignment with specific protections in the players' interests. Under the "waiver system" it is impossible to assign a player to a classification lower than he holds unless all other teams of

[86] National League of Professional Baseball Clubs v. Federal Baseball Club of Baltimore, 269 Fed. 681, 687 (1920).

[87] Brief on Behalf of Defendants in Error, p. 14.

[88] NATIONAL LEAGUE AVERAGE AGES AS OF MARCH 1, 1949

	Catchers	Infielders	Outfielders	Pitchers	Team
1. Brooklyn	26.45	26.23	26.15	26.22	26.22
2. Philadelphia	27.17	27.61	24.77	27.06	26.77
3. New York	29.90	28.38	26.41	26.15	27.25
4. Chicago	24.86	26.52	26.37	28.75	27.28
5. Boston	29.90	28.31	28.97	25.78	27.31
6. Cincinnati	26.40	27.56	27.52	27.51	27.35
7. St. Louis	27.99	27.03	27.03	27.65	27.40
8. Pittsburgh	27.51	28.46	28.67	29.58	28.93
League	27.35	27.49	27.01	27.35	27.31

[89] Compare Gardella v. Chandler, 172 F. 2d 402, 415 (C.A. 2d, 1949).

[90] John Murphy's testimony before Committee on Labor and Industries, Massachusetts Legislature, January 22, 1948.

that classification claim no interest in his services. Similarly the "selection system" allows a team of higher classification to force the assignment of a player's contract against the will of his club, thereby assuring that a capable player will not get lost in the minor leagues.

The assignment of rights to personal services often presents troublesome aspects. The Uniform Player's Contract anticipates and provides for that right.[91] Williston in his work on Contracts says, "Rights which would not otherwise be capable of assignment because too personal in their character, and duties, the performance of which for a similar reason could not be delegated, may be assigned or delegated if the contract so provides. . . ." And the author continues in the footnote: "Thus the contracts of professional ball players often contain provisions enabling a club which has employed a player to assign to another club the right to his services. See Griffin v. Brooklyn Ball Club, 68 App. D. 566, 73 N.Y.S. 864, aff'd., 174 N.Y. 536; Baseball Players' Fraternity v. Boston, etc., Club, 166 App. D. 484, 151 N.Y.S. 557."[92]

Were the "reserve clause" and the right to assign players' contracts abolished, there would

immediately be introduced incentives tending to destroy the loyalty of players to their team, an element so important to the integrity of the game. For instance, if a player knew he would be a "free agent" at the end of a season he might be tempted to shop around for next season's job and to relax his efforts if he thought he had made an arrangement with another team. In the case of assignments, if the player had the right to stipulate as to where and when he would be assigned, there would be an incentive for a player to endeavor to make a deal for himself during the season and to have divided loyalties which would inevitably affect the quality of his play. There can be no doubt that the integrity of the game and the public confidence in it would be adversely affected if players became free to move from club to club at their own choice.

"Baseball law" and the Uniform Player's Contract, for which it provides, are designed solely for the production of baseball games and to preserve all aspects of the game's integrity. For the plaintiffs, Gardella, Martin and Lanier, to prevail, it will be necessary for the court to find such an arrangement unreasonable.[93]

[91] The Uniform Player's Contract provides:

"6. (a) The Player agrees that this contract may be assigned by the Club (and reassigned by any assignee Club) to any other club in accordance with the Major and Major-Minor League Rules.

"(b) The amount stated in paragraph 2 hereof which is payable to the Player for the period stated in paragraph 1 hereof shall not be diminished by any such assignment, except for failure to report as provided in the next sub-paragraph (c).

"(c) The Player shall report to the assignee Club promptly (as provided in the Regulations) upon receipt of written notice from the Club of the assignment of this contract. If the Player fails so to report, he shall not be entitled to any payment for the period from the date he receives written notice of assignment until he reports to the assignee Club.

"(d) Upon and after such assignment, all rights and obligations of the Assignor Club hereunder shall become the rights and obligations of the assignee Club; provided, however, that

(1) The assignee Club shall be liable to the Player for payments accruing only from the date of assignment and shall not be liable (but the assignor Club shall remain liable) for payments accrued prior to that date.

(2) If at any time the assignee is a Major League Club, it shall be liable to pay the Player at the full rate stipulated in paragraph 2 hereof for the remainder of the period stated in paragraph 1 hereof and all prior assignors and assignees shall be relieved of liability for any payment for such period.

(3) Unless the assignor and assignee clubs agree otherwise, if the assignee Club is a Minor League Club, the assignee Club shall be liable only to pay the Player at the rate usually paid by said assignee Club to other players of similar skill and ability in its classification and the assignor Club shall be liable to pay the difference for the remainder of the period stated in paragraph 1 hereof between an amount computed at the rate stipulated in paragraph 2 hereof and the amount so payable by the assignee Club.

"(e) In the event this contract is assigned by a Major League Club during the playing season, the assignor Club shall pay the Player his reasonable and actual moving expenses resulting from such assignment up to the sum of $500.

"(f) All references in other paragraphs of this contract to "the Club" shall be deemed to mean and include any assignee of this contract."

[92] 2 Williston, Contracts § 423 (1936).

[93] In his complaint Gardella alleged:

"72. That the defendants are utilizing the 'reserve clause,' the standard Minor League contract, the Major League Agreement, the Major League Rules, the Major-Minor League Agreement and the Minor League Rules, contrary to the settled principles of equity and common law, and to monopolize or attempt to monopolize trade or commerce among the several states and with foreign nations contrary to Section

IX. AND NOT BASEBALL ALONE

It may be obvious without comment that "organized baseball" is not alone on the execution block. All professional sports, because of the problems common to all, have adopted systems similar to that under which "organized baseball" operates. Another observation, which may be categorized as a *reductio ad absurdum* but which nonetheless is compelled by consideration of this subject, is the effect on college football of a final decision that baseball does violate the antitrust laws. The production of football, at least by the larger universities, is strikingly similar to that of "organized baseball." Teams cross state lines, they carry paraphernalia with them, admissions are charged the spectators, the games result in profit for the sponsoring universities, "scholarships" make participation "attractive" for the players, and the games are broadcast and televised by interstate facilities. More than that, practically every university in the country, to prevent "jumping" and "raids on its players," enforces the "one-year rule" under which a player, having played for a university, is deprived of the opportunity of playing football the succeeding year if he transfers to another university. Percentagewise his loss of one of three years is strikingly similar to Gardella's loss of five years out of an expected playing life of fifteen years. Can it be said that the application of the "one-year rule" has not "deprived such a player of his occupation?" Is every university president whose institution subscribes to and enforces the "one-year rule" guilty of a misdemeanor and liable, under the Sherman Act, to a fine of $5,000 and one year's imprisonment?

A decision by the United States Supreme Court reversing its ruling in the *Federal* case and finding that "organized baseball" is "interstate trade or commerce," its restraints unreasonable, and therefore in conflict with the Sherman and Clayton Acts, would have a profound effect upon organized sports in this country. It is a fairly standard technique for each industry when first charged with violating the antitrust laws to respond with the cry that only ruin to that industry lies in an application of the antitrust laws to its particular restraints. The frequent use of that assertion, however, does not deny its validity respecting any particular set of facts. It is the serious judgment of both management and players that a finding that the operation of "organized baseball" violates the antitrust laws would mean the end of baseball as we know it. Such a consequence will not be taken lightly by any court.

It is difficult to conceive a rationale upon which a decision compelling that result might be based. Overruling the Federal case would assuredly not serve the ends of social justice. In opposition to the interests of three young men who consciously breached their contracts and deliberately and knowingly subjected themselves to the prescribed penalty for such action are the interests of those representing the ownership of baseball, the thousands of players who each year realize a substantial and often extraordinary income from their playing efforts, and, of paramount importance, the interest of a sports-loving public which has through its emotional and monetary support made baseball the "National Game."

2 of the Sherman Anti-Trust Act (15 U.S.C.A., Sec. 2) and to Section 13 of the Clayton Act (15 U.S.C.A., Sec. 13)." In answer the American League replied, in part:

"Further answering paragraph 72, defendant alleges: The form of the player contract, the Major League Agreement, the Major League Rules, the Major-Minor League Agreement and the Minor League Rules have evolved naturally and progressively to meet the unique conditions necessarily inherent in a sport in which contests can only be played between independent competing teams. The form of said contract provisions, agreements and rules has evolved and has been determined by what was reasonable and necessary from time to time, to promote the highest degree of competition between teams and to safeguard and preserve the integrity of the game and the conditions under which it is played. The overall objects and purposes of the contract provisions, agreements and rules are, and have been, to perpetuate baseball as the national game of the United States, to surround it with the safeguards necessary to warrant the highest public confidence in its integrity and in the manner in which the game is played and to provide uniform rules and regulations for umpiring, scoring and other matters involved in the playing of the game. These objectives were and are beneficial to, and necessary for the protection of, the proper interests of the players, the Clubs and the public in the game. The contract provisions, agreements and rules are both reasonable and essential to protect and preserve the respective interests of the players, the Clubs and the Public in the game and to preserve the existence of the game itself. Experience has demonstrated that such contracts, agreements, rules and regulations operate, and have operated, with great benefit to the public interest in the national game of baseball and that their prohibition would not only unjustifiably injure the interests of players and Clubs but also would irreparably injure the public."

THE FOLLOWING, which appeared in the Boston *Record* in 1944, is tough stuff. Much of what the late Dave Egan wrote was tough stuff. But, as you will see, there was sympathy too and great honesty.

The Barrymore of Baseball

DAVE EGAN

ROGERS HORNSBY, a member of baseball's Hall of Fame and a connoisseur of the superior mudder, has accepted a position as manager of the Vera Cruz team in the Mexican League, and the righteous brethren who operate major-league baseball should hang their heads in shame.

There would be fierce resentment, I feel sure, if Man o' War were put to work pulling a vegetable wagon through his declining years, and the Society for the Prevention of Cruelty to Animals would take an immediate interest in the affair. But the baseball brethren will derive smug satisfaction from the fact that one of their immortals will play in the patched-roof circuit, and one of their idols will gather the dust of sleepy Mexican towns. He sinned against their narrow code, and as a sinner should, he now gets his comeuppance.

His sin was that he was a robust horseplayer, and did not care who knew it. So he was ridden on a rail out of the major leagues, not because he wagered on the steeds but because he had the common honesty to admit it and ask, in a cold voice, whose business it was.

I could name you a highly respected umpire who in the privacy of his hotel room wears thick-lensed glasses, the better to study the past performances in the racing sheets.

I could name you a prominent major-leaguer who, under a convenient alias, owns and races a string of thoroughbreds.

I could name you squads and platoons and regiments of big-leaguers, from general managers down to substitute right fielders, who wager on the relative speed of the dobbins. But Hornsby, with his ruthless honesty, did not conceal it and would not deny it. So you may believe me when I tell you that hypocrisy pays

large dividends in our national pastime, and that ordinary candor winds you up in Vera Cruz.

Your correspondent lately has been reading the life story of John Barrymore, by the brilliant Gene Fowler, and it strikes me that Hornsby is the Barrymore of baseball; that these two men, so diametrically different, are strangely alike. No more turbulent figures ever took such twisted routes to their individual halls of fame, and no two gentlemen ever got more action wherever they went.

The big guy with the ice-water eyes and the disarming dimple was appointed playing manager of the Cardinals in the midst of the 1925 season. In 1926, he led them to the first National League championship they ever had won. He parlayed that into a stirring victory over the Yankees in the World Series. So he asked for a boodle of money and the Cardinals, out of sheer gratitude for their first championship, promptly traded him to the Giants, in a pleasant little display of sportsmanship that led the customers to boycott the team.

The horses, however, had been running to form in the good year 1926, and Hornsby had the forethought to purchase more than 1000 shares of stock in the Cardinals at $45 the share. Now the momentous question arose, could a player on the Giants hold stock in the Cardinals? The answer, of course, was an emphatic no. So Hornsby hung on the neck of the Cardinals like unto an albatross until he sold them back the stock. Not, however, at $45 the share, but at $116 the share, to make a net profit of more than $75,000 from the tidy little deal.

He played in New York for one season, which seems to have been par for his particular course. Mr. Stoneham, president of the club, asked him one day whether or not it was true that he wagered on horses. His answer offended Mr. Stoneham deeply, with the result that he was traded to the Braves in return for Frank Hogan and Jimmy Welsh. The ordinary athlete, traded to the Braves, usually slips into obscurity and is forgotten by everybody except his next of kin, but Hornsby, somehow or other, succeeded only in stepping from the frying pan into the fire.

Here in Boston, he became manager as successor to the popular Jack Slattery and immediately was hailed on all sides as a *Ku Kluxer*. The truth was that he had married a Catholic girl, and was bringing up his children in the Catholic faith, but it made no difference then, and it makes little difference now. He was born to be a target, and brought up to be a stormy petrel, as one of the lads at the gym always puts it.

So he moved on to Chicago, and naturally became manager of the Cubs. There a genteel shakedown ensued, and Hornsby refused to be shaken. So a bloodthirsty bookmaker, in a laudable effort to ruin his career, sued him for something like $60,000. The case was thrown out of court, but Hornsby also was thrown out of Chicago, with the result that he found himself back in St. Louis as manager of the Browns.

The rest of the column could be written with ditto marks, if I were as lazy as some folks, mentioning no names and present company naturally excepted. Mr. Donald Barnes, owner of the club, one day asked him the usual question about betting on horses. The Rajah made the usual answer, and appended the usual so-what-if-I-do. So he was fired forthwith —fired out of the American League, fired out of the National League, fired out of the life he had known for a quarter of a century because he had not been a hypocrite, and had not played it smart, and had not told smooth lies.

This is not the usual picture of a baseball immortal, but it is the right picture of Hornsby, a great ballplayer and a great manager who did not drink and did not smoke and could not lie even when his career depended upon a successful lie. So now he is in Vera Cruz, which is a long way from Cooperstown as the crow flies, yet, somehow or other, he is of taller stature and greater dignity than the righteous brethren who now rejoice that the mighty have fallen.

Of all the baseball stories I have had published, this one, which appeared in the old *Bluebook* magazine, remains my own favorite.

The Sleeper

CHARLES EINSTEIN

In my time, I have roomed with a lot of crazy rookies, a situation that probably was more my fault than theirs. They got thrown in with me because I was kind of the elder statesman on the Barons; and whenever you have a big-league baseball team that has a coach who's been around a long time, you almost always room some wild busher with him. The idea is it is a restraining influence. It calms the kid down.

So I have had Bernhardt, a nineteen-year-old who slept with his catcher's mask on, and Vorhees, who liked to walk on his hands, and Halloway, a young third baseman who used to like to read aloud from the telephone directory.

But those three were nothing. They were a pleasure compared to Groves.

Groves came up to the Barons one season when we didn't have an eccentric on the club. He had a great record in the Association the season before, and he could hit like crazy. Nottingham, the manager, figured with Groves in left field maybe the Barons had a shot at taking it all, so he roomed Groves with me.

"Just to make sure nothing goes wrong," Nottingham says to me.

"But this one's normal," I said.

"Try to put up with him anyway," Nottingham says.

Well, it's a delight. We're down in Florida at the start of spring training, and this kid Groves is always in bed by nine-thirty P.M. and doesn't shine the light in your eyes or anything. After what I'd been through in other years, in a week's time I wanted to adopt him.

Until the night before our schedule of exhibition games was supposed to begin. Nottingham was going to start Groves in left against the Phillies the next day, and I figured maybe the kid would be nervous. But he goes off to sleep as calm and composed as you ever saw. Me, I read for a while and then I fell off too.

But sometime in the middle of the night—it must have been about four A.M.—something wakes me up. I sit up in bed, and there's Groves, standing in the middle of the room and holding his hands like there's a baseball bat in them.

"Hey, Glen," I said to him—that was his name, Glen Groves—"what's the matter?"

He doesn't say a word. Just stands there, sort of peering into the bathroom like there's a pitcher in there going to throw to him. All of a sudden, he looks behind him, like there's a catcher there, and starts to laugh like crazy.

"Is that all he's got?" he says, and laughs some more.

I said, "Hey, Glen, what's up?"

But he didn't say a thing. Just stood there going through a phantom batting practice for about ten minutes. Then he throws the non-existent bat away and went and got into bed.

"Listen," I said to him in the morning, "what the hell were you up to in the middle of the night?"

"What do you mean?" he says.

"You were up at bat in the middle of the room."

"In my pajamas?"

"I know it sounds sort of silly," I said, "but . . ."

"It sure does," Groves says. "I'll tell you, though, I had some dream. I dreamed I was batting against the Phillies and I come up twice against Roberts."

"How'd you do?"

"Walked once, flied out to center the next time."

"Yes, sir," I said, and I went down to breakfast without waiting for him.

Sure enough, in the game that afternoon Roberts pitched the first four against us. First time against Groves, he walks him. Next time, Groves flies out to center.

I got Nottingham in a corner and said, "Listen, I think maybe there's some trouble around here. This Groves, he knows what he's going to do before he does it."

"Yeah?" Nottingham said.

"Yeah," I said. "He told me this morning."

"How did he find out?"

"He bats in his sleep."

"You mean he walks in his sleep?"

"He doesn't do a hell of a lot of walking. He just gets up to bat."

"Stay out of the sun," Nottingham says to me.

I had trouble getting to sleep that night. It didn't take much to wake me. And when I did sit up in bed, along around four A.M., there's Groves hitting in the middle of the room again and talking and laughing to beat the band. This time he turned his face toward me, and I could see his eyes were open. What's more, he recognized me.

"Hit or take?" he says.

"Hit away," I said, and watched. He took a good cut, laughed again, and got back in bed.

"Went four for three last night," he told me in the morning. "Brought a man around with a double."

"Okay," I said, and got out of there. At the ball park, before the game, I got ahold of Nottingham and said, "You think I'm crazy, hah?"

"I didn't say that," Nottingham said. "You know how it is."

"Watch Groves," I told him. "He gets three hits."

Groves got three hits. Actually he was up five times, and he didn't bring any runners around, but he gets his three hits, and one of them's a double.

After the game, Nottingham says to me, "What's going on between you two?"

"I'm telling you," I said. "He hits in his sleep. You're the guy that put him in to room with me."

"I don't believe it," Nottingham said. "Don't press me too far or I might see if I can't trade you to Pittsburgh."

"We been friends a long time," I said to him.

"Yeah," Nottingham said.

Next morning, after the same sleep-hitting routine in the middle of the night, Groves awakes, fresh as a flower, and says, "By Hector, I'm finding the range now. Hit two over the wall last night."

He hit a pair of home runs that afternoon, and that convinced Nottingham. "Look," he says to me, "let's make an arrangement. You say he actually talks to you while he's doing this?"

"Hell, yes," I said. "Last night he told me to

get a new ball in there because they were throwing a spitter."

"All right," Nottingham said. "Tonight when he's asleep, I'll come in the room to watch. You let me in when I knock. Don't you fall asleep."

"I haven't slept since last Friday," I said.

Well, a little after midnight Nottingham taps on the door and I go and let him in. He sits down in a chair and I get back in bed, and we wait for nearly three hours, and then all of a sudden Glen Groves sits up in bed, goes to the night table, selects a bat, and marches up to the plate in the middle of the room. He stood so that Nottingham was sitting right back of his elbow—about where the catcher would be if Groves was really up at bat. I went and stood behind Nottingham's chair so I could see what was going on.

Well, Groves takes his stance and flexes, and here comes the pitch. He lets it go through. Then he turns and looks at me. "What was it?"

"Ball," I said.

"It looked all right to me," Nottingham says.

"You keep out of this," I said to him. "Play ball."

We went that way for twenty minutes. Then Groves throws away his bat and goes back to bed and begins to snore.

Next day the phone rings at seven A.M. It's Nottingham.

"How'd he do?"

"He had a perfect night," I said. "Three hits and a sacrifice."

"How does he feel?"

"He says he feels great."

"I'm a wreck," Nottingham said.

The manager put up with it for four more days. Two more nights he had to come to our room to see for himself. Then he said to me, "Listen, there's a Dr. Fleischmann at the Institute in Miami. Let's you and me have a talk with him."

We went to see Dr. Fleischmann. He was a little European guy with a mustache. We told him the story.

"Ah," he said, and his eyes lit up. "I would never have believed it."

"Believe what?" Nottingham says.

"Transcendency in wish fulfillment," Dr. Fleischmann said. "Steckel speaks of it. It is very rare."

"I'll bet," Nottingham said. "What does it mean?"

"We all," Dr. Fleischmann says, "dream of things which in one way or another we wish to come true. Your young friend wishes to hit a baseball."

"Why does he get out of bed to do it?"

"He can't hit lying down," Dr. Fleischmann said. "Can you?"

"No," Nottingham said. "No, I can't. But if it's what you say it is, how come he ever makes out? Why don't he hit safely every time up? The other night Porterfield struck him out twice."

"What is he hitting now?" Dr. Fleischmann said.

".624," Nottingham says.

"Why are you complaining?"

"I ain't complaining."

"Then just leave him alone," Dr. Fleischmann says. "And make sure he doesn't have to take an upper berth when you travel."

"Just tell me one thing," Nottingham says. "You think this . . . this . . . "

"Transcendency in wish fulfillment," the doctor says.

"That's it," Nottingham says. "Hitting in his sleep. You think it gives him confidence?"

"Of course," Dr. Fleischmann says. "That's what makes this such a rare case. Your dreams and mine seldom come true. This young man hits a home run because he dreamed he could. A great rarity. You ought to win the pennant by seven games."

"If I don't die from loss of sleep meanwhile," Nottingham says.

So the club traveled north, and after a while I reached the point where I wouldn't even ask Groves how he did during the night. It was too much fun the other way, trying to guess in advance and then watching him whale the cover off the ball. You never saw such a kid. He got eight hits in the first three games, once the season got under way, and against good pitching, too. By Decoration Day he was hitting .454, and he was the talk of the baseball world.

Then we hit west, and for some reason Groves began to fall off. By the time we got to Chicago, he couldn't buy a base hit.

"Is he still hitting at night?" Nottingham asks me.

"Hell, yes," I said.

"How does he say he's going to do?"

"I'm afraid to ask him."

"Listen," Nottingham said. "We better do something."

That night Nottingham hides out in the room again, and when Groves gets up to do his hitting, Nottingham and I are both sitting there, cheering him on.

"You can do it, boy!" Nottingham calls. "All-away in there, boy! Little base hit, baby! Alla time in the world, boy! Only need one, boy! Straighten it out, baby, let's go!"

In the morning, Nottingham gets me on the house phone.

"How'd he do?"

"Fanned four straight times," I said. "He feels terrible about it."

"What do you suppose is the matter?"

"How the hell do I know?"

"What was the name of that doctor in Miami?"

"Fleischmann," I said.

"Let's get him up here."

We flew Dr. Fleischmann in from Miami and told him the whole story. He twirled his mustache for a while and looked wise. Finally he shrugged his shoulders.

"I know what it is," he said, "but I can't think what to do with it."

"What do you mean?" Nottingham says. "What is it? What's he done?"

"He hasn't done anything," the doctor said. "It's the time of year that's doing it to him." And he nodded gravely and packed his little bag and left.

Long after we benched Groves because of his bad hitting, long after he had been shipped back to the minors, it came to me what he was talking about. It had been June when Glen Groves's slump occurred—the month when the hot weather sets in and the pitchers start to come around.

Like nine rookies out of ten, Groves couldn't hit a curve.

HERE is a thought from Dr. Bergen Evans, the genial fellow who always has the last word on television except when Groucho Marx is on the program.

From *A Dictionary of Contemporary American Usage*

BERGEN EVANS *and* CORNELIA EVANS

pinch-hitter, as a term for a substitute, is a cliché. Except when used of baseball, the term is often misused. When a manager sends out a pinch-hitter, he assumes that the pinch-hitter will do better than the man at bat. But in other activities, when sickness or some other circumstances makes it impossible for the principal to appear and a substitute or understudy is rushed in to fill the place, he is not expected to do better than the principal would have done. It is a triumph if he or she does what is required in any acceptable fashion.

FROM his splendid book *My Baseball Diary,* one of America's great writers talks about a great ballplayer.

"He Got a Raw Deal"

JAMES T. FARRELL

SHORTLY AFTER NOON on a day in January, 1956, a slender man of 64 years of age was walking along West 71st Street on the South Side of Chicago, on his way to see an income tax consultant. He began to crumble and clutched a picket fence. A passing motorist saw the stricken man, stopped his automobile and rushed to give what aid he could. But before he could be reached, the old man dropped to the sidewalk. A small crowd collected. The police were called. The body was taken to a hospital and there it was said that the man had died of natural causes.

The next day, the obituary page of *The New York Times* carried, over a seven-paragraph story, the following head:

*Buck Weaver of 1919 'Black Sox' Dead;
3rd Baseman One of 8 Barred
from Game*

For years, Buck Weaver had been a baseball legend. Now and then, I would ask a baseball fan:

"Do you remember Buck Weaver?"

Generally, I would be answered:

"Do I remember Buck Weaver? He was one of the greatest third basemen who ever lived. He got a raw deal."

Fans in American League towns, and especially in Chicago where he played with the White Sox from 1912 to 1920, thought of him with sympathy and affection. As is well known, Weaver was one of the eight White Sox players suspended by the late Charles A. Comiskey, White Sox owner, late in the 1920 season on the grounds that they had allegedly thrown the 1919 World Series to the Cincinnati Reds.

The evidence against Weaver has always been vague and unclear. It was charged that he had been approached by Eddie Cicotte, pitcher, and one of the eight "Black Sox," and

asked to participate in the Series fix. Also, it was alleged that he had been present when the conspiracy was discussed by the involved players, and, hence, he knew of the plot but did not talk.

Since Weaver's death, Chick Gandil, White Sox first baseman in the 1919 Series, granted an interview in which he declared that Weaver attended a meeting of the guilty players. Gandil further asserted that Weaver wanted to collect the money from the gamblers immediately. But Weaver is dead now and cannot speak any more.

There were also other rumors and stories. One is that Buck refused to take a lie detector test. Another is that Weaver, after the 1919 Series, is supposed to have gone hunting with a teammate of previous years. Buck seemed troubled and not at all himself. Finally, he is rumored to have broken down and told the story of the "fix" but, also, to have insisted that he had done nothing himself to throw the games.

If this story is true, then Buck had what is termed "guilty knowledge." But his distress while hunting is easily understandable. His knowledge, then, could only have left him in a moral quandary, faced with the risk of being a squealer, and possibly, a goat. For had he told on his teammates, he could not have been certain that he would have been believed.

During Buck's playing days, it seems that there was considerable talk of thrown games among players and in baseball circles. In *Mc-Graw of the Giants,* Frank Graham writes that Hal Chase's manager in Cincinnati, Christy Mathewson, charged Chase with not having given his best efforts to the club in 1918. Graham declares that Mathewson meant throwing games.

Chase was tried, but Mathewson was in

France, and ignored cables requesting a deposition. The testimony of other players was inconclusive, and Chase was exonerated. But there are other stories about the Mathewson-Chase incident which, to my mind, have not been printed. Mathewson is reported to have been advised by a baseball writer that if charges of crookedness were made against Chase and not proven, Chase could sue and collect heavy damages.

For this reason, it is believed that Chase was exonerated. In 1919, Chase was first baseman for John McGraw's New York Giants, and Mathewson, returned from France, signed up as a coach. Frank Graham comments on this strange coincidence: "Chase grinned inscrutably when he heard" that Mathewson was to be a coach. Toward the end of the 1919 season, Chase dropped away from the Giants. So did Heinie Zimmerman, the third baseman. When the Black Sox scandal broke, Chase never denied allegations of crookedness made against him, but Heinie Zimmerman did. At all events, both players were let out of baseball in such a manner that they could not sue. And Mathewson did not press the charges against Hal Chase to the point where he was out on a limb.

Buck Weaver knew only baseball. The code by which he grew up cast scorn and opprobrium on a squealer. He must have heard tales and rumors of other thrown games prior to 1919. These, if there was such—as seems to have been the case—were not reported. What should a player like Weaver have done? And had he told of the "fix," could he have felt safe in his own career? There could have been the word of seven against one.

With Buck dead after having suffered for years because of his disbarment from organized baseball, I most certainly do not want to accuse him. But there was a cloud over him and the evidence suggests that he probably knew. Withal, his failure to report this "guilty knowledge" is more than understandable. And he well could not have known what to do.

Up to his death, Weaver consistently maintained his innocence. He and the other players were indicted by a Cook County Grand Jury in the early Twenties. As I have suggested, the legal evidence against Buck was so insubstantial that the judge* wanted to dismiss the indictment against him. Lawyers for the other indicted players feared that if this were done, the defense of their clients would be damaged. Weaver agreed, therefore, to stand trial. The

judge consented to this, but also declared that, were Weaver to be found guilty by the jury, he would overrule the verdict. All of the defendants were acquitted. Weaver periodically applied for reinstatement in organized baseball, but his efforts all were in vain. Two baseball Commissioners, the late Judge Kenesaw Landis and Governor Happy Chandler, rejected his appeals for the clearing of his name and his reinstatement in organized baseball. He had wanted to do this before he died. Many fans supported him in this effort.

One Chicago sports writer remarked to me while Buck was still living:

"The two players I have sympathy for are Weaver and Joe Jackson. They were brought up in an environment where you were not supposed to squeal. What could they have done? Jackson once talked to me about it. He said: 'I was just a dope!' And Weaver—I'd like to see him clear himself. If baseball would clear him, it wouldn't hurt baseball."

And an old-time ballplayer and teammate of Buck's remarked:

"I'm in Buck's corner."

In the fall of 1954, I went to Chicago to interview Buck Weaver and to get him to tell his story in his own words. After some difficulty, I located him through his old and loyal friend, Marty Bleeker, a tavern keeper on the South Side of Chicago who is a familiar and popular figure among Chicago's baseball old-timers. Buck came to see me in my room at the Morrison Hotel.

He was a thin, pale, gray man in his sixties. He dressed on the sporty side, and there were small red blotches on his face. He smiled easily and readily. During his playing days, he was always smiling and kidding on the field. Buck's smile as well as his great playing ability made him one of the most popular White Sox players of his time at Comiskey Park.

In answer to the contention that he should have talked about the alleged conspiracy, he told me:

"Landis wanted me to tell him something that I didn't know. I can't accuse you and it comes back on you and I am . . . a goof. That makes sense to me. I didn't have any evidence."

He went on to say:

"All I did in that Series was fielded 1.000 and I hit something like .336. (EDITOR's NOTE: *He hit .334, with five of his 11 hits in 34 times at bat being for extra bases, one triple and four doubles.*) I'd have hit .600 if I had any luck.

* *Judge Hugo Friend.*

There wasn't a game that they didn't spear one or two line drives. But that's the breaks. In the court session, it lasted a month . . . all I can say is the only thing we got left in the world is our judges and our jurors. I was acquitted in court."

He spoke of his visits to the office of the late Judge Landis.

"He was a funny man. I'd come in. He'd say, 'Sit down, sit down!' He had that big box on his desk full of tobacco. He knew I chewed tobacco, too. He'd give me a chew of tobacco. I appealed I don't know how many times, maybe a half a dozen times. But he never did tell me to my face. He said he'd send me a letter."

According to the *Chicago Daily Tribune*, Landis, in his decision rejecting Weaver's appeal, wrote:

"I regret that it was not possible for me to arrive at any other conclusion than that set forth in the previous decision that your own admissions and actions in the circumstances forbid your reinstatement.

"You testify that preceding the World Series, Cicotte, your team's leading pitcher that season, asked you if you wanted 'to get in on something—fix the World Series,' and you replied: 'You are crazy; that can't be done.'"

When Weaver was disbarred, he had one more year to play on a three-year contract. He filed suit for breach of contract. The case was finally settled out of court.

"I sent a letter to Frick (present Commissioner Ford Frick). I says Mr. Comiskey settled for my 1921 contract. That shows that they're wrong and I'm right. But still they paid it and I can't do nothin' about it."

He was disappointed that he received no answer from Frick.

"I never threw a ball game in my life," he said with passion and a ring of sincerity. "All I knew was win. That's all I know."

And several times, he repeated:

"I can't do nothin' about it."

Weaver believed that if he were to have had his name cleared, he might have become a scout, or else helped kids to learn the game. He prided himself on having discovered Nick Etten who played on one Yankee world's championship team. Following his disbarment, he played semipro ball with the Duffy Florals in Chicago and was rarely seen at social events where sports people gather. Almost every day, during the off-racing season, he went to a saloon near Sixty-third Street and Cottage Grove Avenue and in the back room he played pinochle with some cronies. He did not drink.

He had no children of his own, but raised two children of relatives. In recent years, his wife was ailing and he took care of her and was usually home with her almost every evening. All he wanted from life was to support and care for Mrs. Weaver, see his cronies and clear his name. About the latter, he was pessimistic and at times, when he talked to me, bitterness came into his voice.

But about the game of baseball itself, he felt love, not bitterness. He talked of baseball enthusiastically and with a sharp and clear baseball intelligence. Baseball was a way of life to him as well as a profession. He lived the game and thought of it on and off the field. And because of his feeling for the game, the mark against him hurt.

"A murderer," he said, "even serves his sentence and is let out. I got life."

Speaking of the game, he said:

"What are the qualifications you have got to have to be a ballplayer? You got to run. You got to throw. You got to hit. You got to field. You got to think. If you can't meet all of these qualifications you ain't a 100 per cent ballplayer."

He was not only a fans' player but he was also something of a ballplayer's player. And many who saw Weaver play between 1912 and 1920 would readily agree that he met all of these qualifications. In his last few years especially, he had developed into a highly polished big-leaguer. Lean and of medium height, he almost invariably had the dirtiest uniform of any player on the team. When he broke in with the White Sox in 1912, he was an erratic shortstop. He would throw many balls away. Fans even spoke of his daily error and for a while, some of them nicknamed him "Error-a-Day Weaver." Buck said that he couldn't explain why this was so. Once he was shifted to third, he rarely made a wild throw. When he broke into the American League, he was a weak hitter. In his first year, he batted .224 in 147 games. But when he became a switch hitter, his average picked up and in his last season, 1920, he hit .333 in 151 games.

"I couldn't hit 'em high. I couldn't hit 'em low. I couldn't hit," he said, speaking of his early years in the American League.

During one off season he was visiting Oscar Vitt, the Detroit Tiger third baseman, at the latter's cabin in California. Buck was chopping wood. He noticed that when he chopped left-handed, he always hit the groove in the wood; when he swung the ax right-handed, he missed the groove. This led to his decision to bat left-handed.

"But I didn't start swinging right away," Buck explained. "First I just stood up at the plate like this." He illustrated his stance with his feet close together. "I let them pitch to me. Then, I practiced taking one step forward like this. Then I practiced my swing like this. I didn't try to hit the ball. I just wanted to get my swing and my confidence. Then, I practiced getting away, runnin'. I got my confidence that way. And then I knew I could hit anything. I'd have the ball always comin' in to me. If a left-hander was pitching, I'd bat right-handed where my power was. The ball would still be comin' in to me. All of them pitches would be comin' in."

Fans may still remember how Buck often played a shorter third base than most of his contemporaries.

"I didn't know nothin' about the National League. I didn't play in it. But I knew the American League. You take this situation. There's a man on first. There's a man on second. There's a man on third. I'm playing third, right on the line with the base. I know the speed of each of them runners. I know how fast the batter can run. I know the speed of the ball. So I get the ball. I know what to do just like that. If I played back a few feet, I'd be licked on a dragging bunt. And I could get the hard ones, too, where I played."

Buck stood up and showed me how he could pick up a bunt with both hands and without bending his knees.

Following his death, the Associated Press reported comments of Ty Cobb on Weaver as a third baseman. Calling him "the greatest third baseman I ever saw," Cobb also remarked:

"Weaver was one third baseman I didn't try to bunt against. I was supposed to be a fast man getting to first base but I knew better than to lay one down in Weaver's direction. There was no chance of beating out a bunt to him. He'd throw you out every time.

"Buck just wasn't the type to be in a crooked deal like that and certainly there wasn't anything wrong with the way he played in the 1919 Series."

"One year," Buck also said in our interview, "a baseball writer asked me why I played shortstop in 15 feet closer than he thought I ought to. I explained it to him this way. 'I'll play where I stand. You play 15 feet behind me. I won't make more than one or two errors than you make. And I'll have a chance to get runners out. You see it in the assists.'"

Speaking of players of the past and the present, he asked:

"Who's a shortstop today?"

"Phil Rizzuto was."

"I'll give you that. But in our day, who was the shortstop for the Red Sox? Everett Scott. And who did the Yankees have? Roger Peckinpaugh. And the Tigers had Donie Bush. Who did Cleveland have? Ray Chapman. Who did the Athletics have? Jack Barry. Do you have shortstops like that now?"

He spoke of the salaries today as compared with salaries in his day. Perhaps there was a touch of bitterness here. He began with the White Sox for $1,800 and in 1920 his salary was $7,200.

He recalled some of his rival stars. "I was playing in a game in St. Louis in 1917. George Sisler hit one along the ground. I run in and scoop it up. But I don't throw this ball. I hold it. There were ten perforations in it, one, two, three, four, ten perforations. I ran to the umpire and said he had better look at Sisler's bat. He had driven nails in it and filed them down."

And Ty Cobb.

"That was a fellow, that Cobb. And they say he was a dirty player. That base line belongs to the runner. Take Baker. He was a little bit slow. A man is coming in. He jumps high for the ball and comes down on that line and it belongs to the runner. So what happens? He gets spiked. When I went up for one and came down, I spread my legs and I didn't get spiked. To me Cobb was not dirty.

"And I used to hit the ball with nothin' and two on me. Some batters need three strikes to hit. I could hit with one. Here's why I do it. When the pitcher has nothing and two on you, you know he's going to waste one. The infielders know it. So what do they do? They relax. So I have nothin' and two on me and the infielders are relaxed. They throw it outside or inside, but what difference does it make? I'd hit it and be off and the infielders were relaxed. They'd ask me how come I done a thing like that. I'd say, 'I don't know why I done it. I must have been a goof.'"

Weaver was born in Pennsylvania in 1890. His father was a laborer in the iron works. Back in 1909, he was playing semipro ball. A team of barnstorming major-leaguers, managed by Charlie Dooin, then manager of the Philadelphia Phillies, played against Buck's team. And a scout named Kennedy came to watch the games.

"I didn't know nothin' from nothin'. Kennedy, the scout from Philadelphia, saw me and he asked me to sign a contract for $125 a month. *$125 a month!* Why, I never seen that much money."

During the winter, Kennedy shifted from Philadelphia to Cleveland and hence Weaver signed a Cleveland contract. But he heard nothing about his contract and the 1910 season opened. Two or three weeks went by and he had not received word. He wrote a letter to the National Commission and was mailed a check for $62.50.

"Boy was that money!"

He was sent to play at Northampton, Mass. Suddenly he discovered that when a batted ball was two feet away from him, he would lose sight of it. He told his manager about this, and he was never able to understand how this happened to him. His manager told him he was through. He thought that he was through. He was released and went to Philadelphia to see Dooin. He saw a game on a Saturday afternoon, the first big-league game he ever saw.

"When I seen them fellows hit and run, I said, 'Hell, I can't play.' "

He spoke with Dooin and then was offered a contract to play with Park, Pa., for $175 a month. He played in the outfield and ran in on line drives. The fans hollered for him to be put in the infield. Dooin had the choice of taking Weaver or a pitcher and he passed up Buck. But Ted Sullivan, White Sox scout, bought Weaver for $750. In 1911, he was sent to play with San Francisco in the Pacific Coast League.

"I didn't get nowhere in spring practice. They had Oscar Vitt playing third base. I'm a goof. I didn't know nothin' from nothin'. Oscar was sick. He would field a few balls and call it a day. So I practiced. I didn't know they considered Vitt the best third baseman in the league. I said to myself, 'Brother, I can take your job.'

"I sat on the bench for about three weeks. One day the center fielder got hurt. The manager says to me, 'Georgie, can you play the outfield?' I told him, 'I can play any place.'

"A ball was hit just over the infield. I run. I keep running and make the catch right here off the ground." Buck stood up and illustrated. "And then I come to bat and swing. The ball sails and hits the fence. I make a two-base hit. The next time I bat, I hit the fence again. See, I got the breaks. But after that, I told myself, 'Georgie, my boy, now you're in.' "

He reported to the White Sox at Waco the next spring.

"When I joined the Sox, I didn't know Kid Gleason from the man in the moon. That's how green I was."

Gleason hit grounders to him. He missed one and chased it and called to Gleason to hit them harder. Gleason slammed the ball at him and every time he missed, he called for Gleason to hit the grounders still harder. In later years, he and Gleason laughed over this incident.

He spoke warmly and admiringly of Gleason as a man who was for the ballplayers. He remembered other players of his day with affection and friendliness.

"We had a kid on our team," he also said, "a third baseman named Fred McMullin. He comes to me one day and says to me, 'Buck, can't you get sick for a couple of days?' He was dying to get into a ball game. So I made myself indisposed for a couple of days to let him play. Then I went back in there myself."

At the end of a long interview, he flashed at me his own winning smile. But there was something wounded and sad in Buck's smile. Buck wanted his reinstatement but he felt that nothing could be done about it.

When we rode down in the hotel elevator, I suggested seeing him again for dinner, but he refused, saying that he always spent the evening with his wife.

"You know," he added, "she was a good hairpin."

Ironically, there was an Old-Timers' dinner held in Chicago on the evening of that same day when Weaver died in the street.

Two of his old White Sox teammates, Red Faber and Ray Schalk, were present. According to David Condon, Chicago sports writer, both were visibly shaken. Faber said:

"I played baseball with Weaver, and I played cards with him, and I found him as honest as could be. No one can ever be certain about 1919, I guess. Weaver was a wonderful competitor, a fellow who played baseball because he loved it. Buck Weaver and Lena Blackburne were two I knew who never wanted to leave the field, not even in practice."

And Ray Schalk, who generally refuses to talk about the thrown World Series, remarked, as he often has done on other occasions:

"That incident caused Weaver the tortures of hell."

And an old-time baseball fan, who, like myself, used to see Buck play when we were boys, wrote me a few days later:

"Last Thursday evening on my way home from work I stopped at 79th Street and Emerald Avenue at the undertaker's chapel where Buck Weaver was laid out. It was about 6:00

P.M. No one was there at the time except the undertaker's assistant. Though Buck was not a Catholic and the chapel is used mostly by non-Catholics, nevertheless they had kneelers by the coffin. I knelt down and said a few prayers for him. Contrary to some places it did not seem cold to me. He looked, outside of thining gray hair and that is all, like he could get right up and don a uniform and play third base for the Sox again. I don't think he was more than five pounds heavier than when he was playing ball. It sure was a shame to see him go from this world without getting his name cleared."

Many baseball fans had similar feelings when he passed away.

Like many others who saw him spear hot ones at third with graceful ease, who cheered and watched him, this writer also considers himself as one of those who was in Buck Weaver's corner. And now, on reflection, I have a hunch that when Buck said to me, "Landis wanted me to tell him something that I didn't know. I can't accuse you and it comes back on you and I am . . . a goof. That makes sense to me. I didn't have any evidence," he was telling his real story. I suspect that he did not know what to do. And because of a moral dilemma he suffered a life-long torment. Could he have accused? And had he, would he have been a "goof"?

Now, it is all over and long ago. But Buck Weaver was a great ballplayer and very likable. He was caught in a net of circumstances as are many characters in tragic novels. For to him, baseball was a way of life, and his disbarment was a supreme defeat.

"Those fellows suffered hell," Ray Schalk often says.

Buck did.

HERE is one of the most delightful chapters from Robert Fontaine's well-known book, *The Happy Time.*

God Hit a Home Run

ROBERT FONTAINE

LONG AGO when I was very young my mother and father and I moved to Canada, to the lovely city of Ottawa.

We settled down in one half of a double house, next door to my several unusual uncles, my grandfather, and my aunt Felice, all of whom spoke, as we did ourselves, a strange language. It was a mixture of corrupt French, literally translated idioms, and, in time, the salt of French-Canadian patois.

There are but few memories of the first years in Ottawa. They are only bright fragments, like the little pieces of colored glass in the small hallway window at the stair landing.

The time, however, that God hit a home run is very clear.

My father played the violin and conducted an orchestra for a two-a-day vaudeville theater, so he had little time for diversion. In what spare moments he had, he turned to baseball. In spite of his sensitive, debonair temperament, he loved the game. It refreshed him, perhaps, because it was so far from his métier.

I remember well how many times he begged my mother to go with him to the twilight games at Strathcona Park. There was just time for him to see a game between the end of the matinée and the beginning of the evening performance.

My mother seemed always too busy.

"I must get the dinner, you know," she would say, with the faint, calm, resigned, Presbyterian air she often assumed.

"Dinner!" my father would exclaim. "We will stuff our pockets with apples and cheese."

"What about the Boy?" my mother would ask.

My father would look at me.

"The Boy is already too fat. Regard him!"

"It is only," my mother would smile, "because he has his cheeks full of shortbreads."

If it was not dinner she had to cook, it was socks she had to darn or blouses she had to make for me, or the kitchen floor she felt the need of shining.

All this made my father quite sad, even though, at each invitation, my mother promised to accompany him "some other time." Still, he never abandoned the hope that he would, in time, have the warm joy of explaining the principles of the intricate game to her. I suppose he knew that she was proud of his artistic talents and he wanted her to be pleased with his athletic knowledge, too.

One warm Sunday in the summer, when I was five or six (who can remember precisely those early times of coming-to-life when every week is as a year?), my mind was occupied with the American funny papers and the eccentric doings of one Happy Hooligan, he of the ragged, patched coat and the small tin can on the side of his head.

My father came into the room where my mother was dusting the china on the mantel and shining the golden letters on the sign that proclaimed: *Jesus Christ Is the Unseen Guest in This House.*

There was, by the way, nothing else to do in Ottawa on a Sunday in those days but to dust religious signs and plates on the mantel or to read the papers. All stores were closed. All theaters were closed. There was prohibition, too, as I recall, so there was not even a bar where one could sit and dream. True, one could go across the Inter-Provincial Bridge to Hull, in Quebec province, and return with a secret bottle of wine, but it could not be served in public.

No, Sunday was the Sad Day in Ottawa.

But to return to my father. He spoke to my mother with some hesitation: "The Boy and I . . . we . . . we go to a game of baseball."

My mother turned from the plates and regarded my father coldly.

"On Sunday?" she inquired.

My father ran his finger the length of his nose, a gesture which always indicated an attempt at restraint. Then he removed the band from his cigar as nonchalantly as possible.

"But naturally," he replied. "Do I have some other time to go?"

"You can go, as usual, to the twilight games."

My father bit off the end of his cigar.

"Bah!" he exclaimed. "Baseball for seven innings only is like dinner without cognac at the end. It is like kissing the woman you love good night by blowing it from your fingers. No. Baseball in the shadows, when the stars are appearing, is not in the true spirit of the game. One must have the bright sun and the green grass."

My mother looked at my eager, shining face and then looked back at my father.

"What is wrong," she asked, smiling faintly, "with kissing a woman you love good night by blowing it from your fingers?"

My father put his arm around her and laughed.

"The same thing that is wrong," he said, "with making from sour cherries an apple pie."

"You can't make an apple pie from sour cherries."

"*Eh bien*, you can't kiss a woman good night this way . . . you can only kiss your fingers."

He touched his lips to the back of my mother's neck.

I coughed impatiently at this dallying. My mind was fastened firmly on baseball.

"Papa," I said anxiously, "we go now? Yes?"

"You come with us," my father said to my mother. "Eh? We will stuff our pockets with apples and cheese and make a picnic. Red wine, too, perhaps."

"And an onion," I said, loving onions.

"Some other time," my mother said hastily. "Certainly not on Sunday."

"Ah!" my father cried. "Always some other time. Do you promise some time soon?"

"Yes," my mother replied without much conviction. I suppose the thought of sitting on a hard bench for hours, watching that of which she knew nothing, frightened her. I felt, though, that in time my father's plaintive eagerness would win her over.

"Why," she questioned, as if to soften the blow, "do you not ask Uncle Louis or Uncle Felix?"

"Uncle Louis will be full and will chase butterflies across the diamond. Uncle Felix will wish to measure the speed at which the baseball arrives at the catcher. Besides, they are gone up the Gatineau to bring back the Boy's grandfather."

"Grandpa is coming?" I asked happily.

"Yes. He will stay next door as usual and sleep here."

I laughed. "Why is it that Grandpa stays next door and sleeps here?"

My father shrugged.

"When you are old you sleep where you wish."

My mother was at the window, fixing the small jars of ivy that stood there.

"It looks like a thunderstorm coming," she said. "Grandpa and the uncles will get wet. You and the Boy, too, should not go out in a thunderstorm."

Our entire family was frightened to death of thunderstorms. At the first deep roll in the Laurentian Hills or up the Gatineau we huddled together in one room until the sun broke through, or the stars.

My father spoke bravely, though, on this occasion: "It will probably follow the river."

He did not mention the fact that there were three or four rivers it might follow, all of which came, in the end, almost to our back yard.

"Look!" my mother exclaimed, as a white flash lit the horizon's dark clouds.

"Bah!" my father said nervously. "Heat lightning."

"To me," my mother countered solemnly, "it looks like chain lightning."

"Chain lightning . . . heat lightning . . . it is miles away, *n'est-ce pas*? It is not here, is it?"

"*Maman*," I begged, "let us go please, before the storm begins."

"*Voilà*, a smart boy!" my father said proudly, patting me on the head.

My mother sighed and adjusted the tiebacks of the curtains.

"Very well," she said sadly, "but you know what Louis says—he pays too dear a price for honey who licks it off thorns!"

"Honey . . . thorns," my father repeated, rolling his eyes unhappily. "It is baseball of which we speak now."

"All right," my mother said. "All right. Only, just be careful. Don't stand under trees or near cows."

"No," my father agreed, "no cows and no trees."

He kissed my mother gently on the lips, and I naturally understood there would be no further discussion. I put on my best straw sailor, a white hat with the brim curled up and with a black elastic under the chin to keep the bonnet from the fury of any possible gales.

My mother regarded me with sadness, tucking in the string of my blouse. It was as if I were soon to be guillotined.

"It just doesn't seem right," she said slowly, "on Sunday."

My father lit his cigar impatiently.

"We must be going," he announced hastily. "The game will commence before we arrive."

My father took me by the hand. My mother put her arms around me and hugged and kissed me. It was as if I was going away forever to become a monk.

"Be careful," she said.

"Yes, *Maman*," I said dutifully.

"And pull up your stockings," she added.

*　　*　　*

On the trolley car going up Rideau Street I was happy. The wind blew through the open, summer seats and the sun was not too warm.

It is true I should have been in Sunday school at my mother's Presbyterian church, learning about the Red Sea turning back. Instead, I was on my way to the very brink of hell. For Hull, where my father whispered confidentially we were going, was well known to be a place of sinful living, and the sulphur that drifted daily from the match factories was enough to convince me of the truth of the report.

"Papa," I asked, "is it true Hull is wicked?"

"Not in the part where they play baseball," my father assured me.

A faint flash of lightning startled me a little.

"Papa. I have fear Uncle Louis and Uncle Felix and Grandpa will be struck by lightning."

My father smiled.

"Louis and Felix are too fast for the lightning."

"And Grandpa?" I plucked nervously at the tight elastic under my warm chin.

"Grandpa is too close a friend of the Lord to suffer from such things."

I felt better after this. I reasoned that if the Lord was a friend of Grandpa, then Grandpa would no doubt see that nothing happened to Papa and me.

We changed cars presently and were soon crossing the bridge into Hull and the province of Quebec.

I looked down the dirty, roaring falls that ran the factories.

"No sulphur," I observed.

"Not on Sunday," my father said.

This pleased me a great deal. On the one hand, Grandpa and the Lord were good friends. On the other, the Devil did not work on Sunday. I was in a splendid strategic position to deal with Evil.

We descended from the trolley on the main street of Hull.

"We can walk from here," my father informed me. "At the theater, they say it is not far out on this street."

Soon we found ourselves in the midst of hundreds of jabbering French-Canadians, all speaking so quickly and with such laughter and mockery that I could not follow them. The patois, too, was beyond my young understanding. What is more, every other building on the main street of Hull was one of swinging doors from which came the strong smell of ale, making my head dizzy.

"What do they say, Papa? What do they all say so fast?"

My father laughed.

"They say that Hull will beat Ottawa like a hot knife enters the butter! The pitcher of Hull will fan every batter of Ottawa. The batters of Hull will strike the ball every time into the Lachine Rapids, which is many, many miles away. In the end, they say, everybody will become full as a barrel of ale except the people from Ottawa. They will return home crying and drink lime juice and go to bed ashamed."

I clapped my hands happily at this foolishness which sounded like a fairy tale—the white balls flying by the hundreds, like birds, up the Lachine Rapids.

A man reeled by from a bar as I was pondering the flight of the baseballs. He began to shout loudly. "Hooray for Ottawa! Hull is full of pea soups. Down with Hull and the pea soups!"

The crowd picked him up and tossed him on high from group to group, laughing all the while, until, at last, he admitted Hull was the fairest city in all Canada and pea soup the most delicious dish.

I laughed joyfully. "It will be a good game, no?" I asked happily.

"*Mais oui*," my father chuckled. "With the Hull and the Ottawa it is like with David and Goliath."

*　　*　　*

It had become quite cloudy and dark when we made our way through the grounds to the ancient wooden stand. In the gray distance the lightning continued to dance.

My father patted my head gently. "Heat lightning," he said uneasily.

"I know," I said. In spite of the fact that I knew Grandpa was a friend of the Lord and that the Devil had taken the day off, I nevertheless felt a little nervous. After all, I *had* skipped Sunday school for the first time. And we *were* so far from home!

My attention turned from the storm for a time as the Hull team began field practice amid great roars of approval that drowned out the rumbling thunder. The crowd began to chatter happily and proudly like many birds screaming in our back yard.

"All the world," I said, "speaks French here."

"*Mais oui*," my father agreed. "In Hull all the world is French. In Ottawa it is mostly English. That is why there is so much desire to fight with each other."

"And we," I asked curiously, "what do we speak, you and me?"

"Ha!" my father exclaimed, patting my knee, "that is a problem for the French Academy!"

Since I did not know what the French Academy was, I placed my small chin in my hands and watched the Ottawa team as it came out on the field.

Groans and jeers now filled the air. Bottles, legs of chairs, programs, and bad fruit were thrown on the field like confetti at a wedding.

Two umpires and several groundkeepers cleared away the debris. One of the umpires announced through a megaphone:

"*Mesdames et messieurs*, we are the hosts. They are the guests. They are from Ottawa, but that is not a sin. We cannot always help where we live. It is requested not to throw bottles while the game proceeds as this is not the fair way we shall win. I am born in Hull and also my wife and four children and I am proud of it. But I do my honest duty to make a fair game. God save the King! *Play ball!*"

The game went on evenly and colorlessly for five or six innings. The darkness of the afternoon turned a sulphur yellow and the air became filled with tension.

The rumble of thunder grew louder.

In the seventh inning the Ottawa pitcher singled and stood proudly on first base. The bat boy ran out with a sweater. This is, of course, the custom in the big leagues, so that the pitcher will not expose his arm to possible chills.

To Hull, however, it was a fine opportunity to start something.

"Sissy!" someone shouted.

"Si . . . sssssyyyyyyyy!" The crowd made one long sound as if the wind were moaning. Most of them probably did not know what the word meant, but it had a pleasant sound of derision.

The pitcher, O'Ryan, stepped far off first base in an attempt to taunt the Hull pitcher to throw, which he did.

O'Ryan darted back safely, stood arrogantly on the white bag, and carefully thumbed his nose.

The crowd jeered.

O'Ryan removed his cap and bowed from the waist in sarcasm.

Once more bottles, legs of chairs, programs, and overripe fruit came down on the field like hailstones.

Again the umpire picked up his megaphone and spoke.

"*Mes amis*," he begged, "they are the guests . . . we are the hosts."

A tomato glanced off the side of his head; a cushion landed in his face. He shrugged his shoulders, brushed himself off, and ordered wearily: "Play ball!"

The next pitch was hit and it was accompanied by a violent peal of thunder which almost coincided with the crack of the bat.

O'Ryan started for second base and was forced to slide when the Hull second baseman attempted to force him out. The second baseman, with his spiked shoes, jumped on O'Ryan's hand.

The Ottawa pitcher was safe by many seconds, but the crowd shouted insistently: "Out! *Out!*" with such anger that the umpire hesitated but a moment and then waved the astonished and stunned Irishman off the field.

Two thousand French-Canadian noses were instantly thumbed.

O'Ryan stood up dazedly and regarded his maimed hand. He brushed the dust from his uniform and strode quietly to the Ottawa bench. There he picked up several bats, swung them together for a while, and selected his favorite.

He pulled down his cap firmly, walked calmly to second base, and, with only a slight motion, brought the bat down solidly on the head of the Hull second baseman.

This was the signal for a riot. Spectators, umpire, players, peanut vendors—all swarmed across the field in one great pitched battle. In the increasing darkness from the oncoming storm they were as a great swarm of hornets, moving around the diamond.

My father and I, alone, remained seated. We did not speak for a long time.

I began to wish I had gone to Sunday school to have the Red Sea divided, or that I had stayed home with *Maman* and Happy Hooligan. I was coming to believe that Grandpa was not so good a friend of the Lord as he pretended and that if the Devil did not work on Sunday he had assistants who *did*.

My father spoke, at length, with the hollow sound of sin: "Poor *Maman* would be angry if she knew, eh?"

"*Mais oui,*" I mumbled, fearfully watching the lightning tear the sky.

Papa tried to be calm and to talk lightly.

"Ah, well," he remarked, "it is not always so simple, eh, to tell the heat lightning from the chain lightning?"

"*Mais non,*" I muttered.

"Also, in this case, one can see the storm did not follow the river."

"It followed *us*," I replied nervously, almost to myself.

"Well, we are safe here, no? We are, thank the good Lord, not in the melee. Here we are safe. When the fight is ended we will go home. Meanwhile we are safe. *N'est-ce pas?*"

"And the storm, Papa?" I queried, pulling my sailor hat down over my head as far as it would go.

"The storm," my father announced, as thunder sounded so loudly it shook the flimsy stand, "is mostly wind. It will blow itself away in no time."

I sighed. I will pray, I told myself. I will ask to be forgiven for going to the city of the Devil on Sunday. I will pray the good Lord forgive me, in the name of my grandfather, for forgetting to attend the opening of the Red Sea, also.

I had but managed to mutter: "Dear Lord . . ." when the sky, like the Red Sea, divided in two and there was hurled at us a great fiery ball, as if someone in heaven had knocked it our way.

Before I could get my breath, the dry, wooden stand was in flames.

"Dear Lord," I began again, breathlessly and hastily, "we are not so bad as all this . . . we only . . ." But my father had me by the hand and was dragging me swiftly onto the field.

By this time, the rioters had stopped banging heads and were wistfully watching their beloved stand disappear with the flames.

* * *

By the time we arrived home the storm was over and even the rain had stopped. We had been at a restaurant to eat and rest and had recovered a little when we faced *Maman*.

In fact *I* did not feel bad at all. I reasoned that the Lord had not been after my destruction but after the rioters who profaned his Sabbath with fighting. For if the Lord had been after me, He could, in His infinite wisdom, have made the ball come even closer.

"I told you we would have a thunderstorm," my mother said angrily.

"To me," my father replied meekly, "it looked like heat lightning."

"You know I don't like the Boy out in thunderstorms!"

"Ah, well, he is safe now. Eh, *bibi?* And Louis and Felix and Papa?"

"They are here."

"Good."

"A baseball game on Sunday is just not right," my mother went on, refusing to be deflected from the subject. "Look how pale and sick-looking you both are!"

My father coughed uneasily.

"Let us call down Grandpa and have some wine and shortbreads. Let us forget the rest. No?" He kissed my mother. She turned to me, relented a bit, and smiled.

"Was it a good game?"

I clapped my hands together excitedly. "It was wonderful, *Maman!* Everything happened!"

"Wine and shortbreads," Papa interrupted nervously.

"What do you mean, everything happened?" my mother asked, glancing sidelong at Papa.

"I must go up and see my poor father," said Papa. "It is now many months . . ."

"One moment," my mother cautioned. She turned and motioned for me to sit on her knee. My father sank wearily into a chair.

"Well?" my mother urged.

It was too wonderful and exciting to keep!

"*Maman,*" I exclaimed, "God hit a home run!"

My father groaned. My mother's eyes widened.

"He what?" she asked, pale.

The words came rushing out: "He hit a home run and He struck the grandstand with His powerful lightning and then the grandstand burned to very small pieces, all of a sudden, and this was because everybody was fighting on the Sabbath and . . ."

My mother let me down slowly from her knee.

"Is this true?" she said to my father.

My father shrugged and waved his delicate hands helplessly.

"A small fire. The stand in Hull is made of . . ."

My mother jumped to her feet.

"*Where?*"

My father lowered his eyes.

"Hull," he admitted slowly. "After all, they do not permit baseball on Sunday in Ottawa. If they permit you to breathe it is something. All the world knows that."

"Hull!" my mother whispered, as if it were a dreadful name. "Hull! No wonder! To take the Boy from Sunday school to Hull! And on Sunday! Hull!"

"*Maman*," I said, tears coming into my eyes, "I will speak to the Lord . . ."

"Go," said my mother, and she sounded like a voice from the heavens, "and wash your dirty face."

"*Ma chère*," my father said, trying to be pleasant, "does one always know where a storm will travel?"

"You," my mother ordered, "go wipe your shoes. Look at the mud you have tracked in!"

As Papa and I went our respective ways, heads bowed, we heard her whisper once more: "Hull!"

I knew then that she would never go to a baseball game with Papa. The memory of the Lord's home run which so barely missed us would remain, I thought, forever in her mind. She would know one of the places the Lord was going to strike and she would know now that His aim was very good, if not perfect.

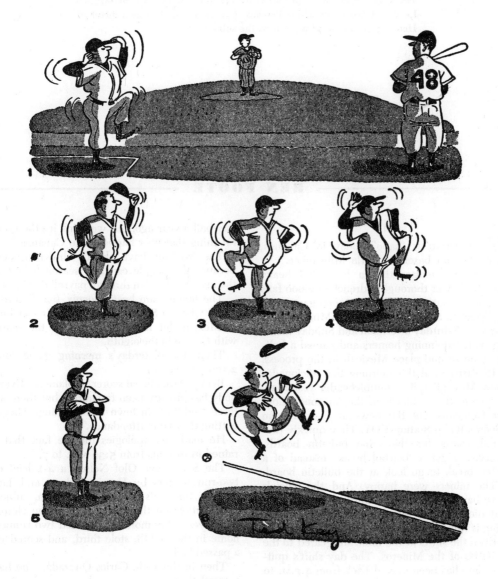

THIRD-BASE COACH

THE PIECE by Jim Bishop earlier in these pages showed that, in Phoenix, all that takes place in a baseball setting is not always baseball. The same applied a handful of years ago to the whole Arizona-Mexico League (Class C) of which Phoenix (now in Triple A) was a member. Here are both parts of a series on the subject.

The Road to Cananea

BEN FOOTE

1

EVERYTHING IS "sapo" today in Cananea, Mexican baseball's little Milwaukee.

It doesn't matter that a loud and heavy thundershower thoroughly drenched 2,000 fans and rained out yesterday's afternoon game with the Phoenix Stars. After all, the Mineros beat the Stars Saturday afternoon and Sunday morning with late-inning homers and gained a half-game on second-place Mexicali in the process.

It wasn't until this morning that aficionados knew Mexicali split a doubleheader yesterday.

Two or three officials of the Anaconda Copper Company got the news at 6 A.M. from Phoenix Radio Station KOY. They quickly prepared charts for the mine bulletin boards. Everybody got a "beisbol break" instead of a coffee break to go look at the bulletin board.

The miners were happy. And the officials were happy, because this town of 20,000 lives and dies with its Mineros. That's why everything is "sapo."

Even the shifts at the mine are geared to the activities of the Mineros. The day shift's quitting time has been moved back from 4 P.M. to 3:30 to permit the men to attend the game.

If the wives of the American company officials have a bridge game scheduled, that's knocked out, too.

"My friends used to laugh at me last year when I said I couldn't play bridge," says Mrs. Buck Eckstein, wife of the club business manager who doubles as assistant purchasing agent of the mine. "Now they wouldn't possibly think of scheduling a card game the same day as the baseball game."

Says her husband, "Frankly we didn't think much of the idea of sponsoring professional baseball a year ago, but we think it's the greatest thing that ever happened to Cananea."

The Mineros have already drawn 125,000 because the people can buy season tickets on the installment plan through payroll deductions.

The home team beat Phoenix, 6-4, Saturday when Claudio Solano, a magazine "cover boy" in Mexico, hit his 26th homer of the season with two on in the eighth.

Then, for yesterday's morning game "only 2,100" showed up.

Benny Rios, official scorer, explained, "Everybody has already been to church, but there are three weddings in town this morning. They're cutting down our attendance."

He made no apologies for the fact that it rained in torrents from 5:30 A.M. to 7.

The Stars gave Olof Nelson a 4-1 lead on two-run homers by Howie Padgett and Jack Spence, but Luis Miguel Casablanca, subject of an article on the sports page of the church paper yesterday morning, doubled two runners home in the eighth, stole third, and scored on a passed ball.

Then in the 10th, Carlos Quezada, who had entered the game as a pinch runner, homered to take it all for Cananea.

The Stars were ahead 4-0 in the afternoon game when the next heavy shower came.

2

A 47-mile trip from Cananea to Naco on the Arizona border is by unanimous agreement among the Phoenix Stars the most arduous journey in organized baseball.

The twisting, rutted, dirt "camino" is bad enough when it is fairly dry. It was that way early Saturday morning when the Stars went

GREAT MOMENTS

Al Gionfriddo's "impossible" catch off Joe DiMaggio in the 1947 World Series . . .

United Press

The last strike of the game gets away from Mickey Owen in the 1941 World Series . . .

International News

. . . and old Pete Alexander strikes out Tony Lazzeri with the bases loaded and two out in the 1926 Series.

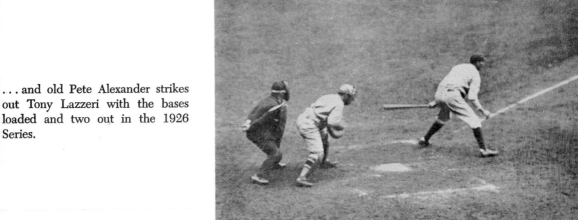

International News

PISTOL PETE

The W. C. Heinz story on page 190 reports that Pistol Pete Reiser had two characteristic poses on the ball field—one to be snapped when he was stealing home,

and the other—well . . .

HELLO AND GOODBYE!

The Yankees' Elston Howard tries vainly for a Vic Power home run.

Wide World

DON LARSEN PITCHING

These two pictures tell their own story. The date: October 8, 1956. The scoreboard in the background tells everything you need to know. For the outcome of the pitch, turn the page.

United Press

Wide Wo

into Cananea. When it's wet and many mountain streams are using it as their private channels, as they were Sunday night, it's worse.

With Chico, the smiling, dampened, tattered driver for the Mexican bus line, the trip either way is diabolical.

Chico and his mechanical-age relic were pressed into service because the Phoenix company which ordinarily takes the Stars on their junkets lost its transmission system on the last trip to Cananea and wouldn't cross the border.

He made his first appearance about 7 A.M. Saturday morning in the old bus which had at one time been painted red and white. He pulled up beside the almost sleek-looking American model with a screeching of brakes, grinding of gears, and a rattling noise like an entire field of racing jalopies coming to a stop.

When he wasn't bouncing the Stars over the road, Chico would stop and pour a little water in the radiator, or maybe some brake fluid in the brake system. If a bus-driving friend happened by, Chico stopped, and the two passed the time of day as though nobody cared when or why he got anywhere.

Mañana was obviously the favorite word in his vocabulary.

For the return trip, Manager Jerry Gardner had trouble locating Chico and his mount. He was finally found, but he obviously didn't want to make the run into the menacing black thunderheads in the general direction of Naco.

After three false starts, Gardner found through Third Baseman Ralph Wilcox, the club's only Spanish-speaking player, that Chico wanted his money first.

The transaction was completed, and Chico, the bus, and Stars rattled into the mud and blackness.

Occasionally the gear shift stuck. Chico would draw his arm back like a boxer and then accompany a lightning jab at the knob with a kick to the rod.

The bus rolled on to the first arroyo. Cars and trucks were stopped on either side, one in the middle. Chico stopped as the car in the water slowly extricated itself. Gardner got out and threw a rock toward the middle to test the depth. He suggested Chico proceed. Then he commanded.

On the other side, another car was stalled. Trying to help, Chico pushed it into a bank with the bus. The Stars pulled it out.

The bus's brakes failed and Chico went out with a screw driver and small wrench and tied two lines together to stop leaking fluid.

There were more arroyos and more stops. Earl Smith got out and waded into one to look for holes.

Later another bus appeared from the opposite direction. The road was too narrow for the buses to pass, and after much backing and conversation each was headed in the right direction. Chico and his bus-driving colleague chatted an instant in the pouring rain. That time four of the huskiest Stars carried him back into the driver's seat and angrily ordered him to go ahead.

The radiator was watered a few more times. Once, Chico ripped the border off a grimy towel to tie the hood down.

Four hours and 45 minutes from Cananea the Stars finished the 47-mile trip to Naco. They taunted Chico as they hurried to the waiting Phoenix bus.

"Let's go, bussy," they shouted happily. But they still weren't fated to get to Bisbee and a hot supper immediately.

That seemingly ultramodern bus had stalled in the rain.

HERE, right from the pitcher's mouth—star left-hander Whitey Ford of the New York Yankees, telling his tale in 1957—is evidence of a strange nether world in baseball where Macy's makes sure to tell Gimbel's.

The Great American Pitchers' Union

WHITEY FORD
as told to EDWARD LINN

WHEN I FIRST came to the Yankees in July 1950, everybody was running around trying to find a way to stop the Bostons' Walt Dropo. Big Walt hadn't even been with the Red Sox at the start of the season, but by July he was outhitting Ted Williams, Vern Stephens and the rest of that powerful Boston crew. He was, in fact, leading the whole league in batting and runs batted in, and he was right up there in home runs. The first time I ever saw him swing, to give you an idea of how he was going, he hit a grand-slam home run off Tommy Byrne.

Faced with this threat, the pitchers from the other seven American League teams started comparing notes on their experiences with Dropo, and exchanging tips on how to handle the big guy. By September the "book" on Dropo had been pretty well set, and he was no longer feared. Dropo, we pitchers had discovered, could hit any kind of pitch that was inside the strike zone. But—one pitcher quickly told another—he would chase balls that were just a little off the plate; high, low, inside, outside. Some power hitters, such as Yogi Berra, hit that kind of pitch very well. Dropo, went the whisper, couldn't.

So, armed with this information, we all started throwing the "book" at Big Walt. Immediately he stopped hitting—although he had been so hot up to then that he was still able to tie for the league leadership in runs batted in and had well over 30 home runs.

This was my introduction to the pitchers' grapevine. As soon as one of us learns anything about someone as hot as Dropo, everybody else knows it almost overnight. The way this game is going—with hopped-up balls, pulled-in fences and lighter and livelier bats—we major-league pitchers have got to stick together at least to that extent.

Sometimes it seems as if we have more in common with each other than with the non-pitchers on our own club.

If that statement shocks you, it was meant to. It's about time that baseball fans put aside their childhood ideas about how their home-town players hate all their opponents, and want nothing more than to spike them or bean them or club them over the head with a Louisville Slugger. For the past 30 years every change in baseball has been designed to develop more home-run hitters, and pitching has been getting to be a rougher and rougher task. In the old days, any good pitcher hung around the league for 10 or 15 years. Now they're calling you an old man after five or six seasons—and you are. So we all feel that we've gotten something of a raw deal, and we're fighting back in every way we know how.

Of course, since baseball is played by human beings, there have always been isolated instances of one pitcher exchanging information with another. But it's only become widespread in recent years. And the pitchers' grapevine has always been kept pretty quiet. I know that when I first joined the Yankees it came as a complete surprise to me.

Now, when I'm talking about how all pitchers are good buddies, I'm not trying to say that anybody ever went out on the mound and did less than his best, because that certainly isn't true. It's just that once we get out of uniform, the only secrets between us pitchers are those involving the business of our own team and players. We'll teach each other how to throw pitches, how to cure sore arms, how to handle the tough hitters in the league—anything that will help another pitcher to stay in business. Remember that the next time you hear some baseball announcer talking about a "bitter rivalry" between opposing pitchers, because it just isn't so. We've got to stick together to survive, and we know it. There is no other arrangement like this in all of baseball. Catchers don't compare notes; shortstops exchange no confidences; certainly managers don't ask each other's advice in the course of a season. Only pitchers have a "union"—and it's a strong one.

After we figured out how to pitch to Walt Dropo, he changed from "the new Babe Ruth" into little more than a fair hitter who can hurt you every now and then. (Especially me. I'll tell you a story about that a little later.) Doesn't Walt know how we're pitching him? Of course he does. He has played under Steve O'Neill, Lou Boudreau, Fred Hutchinson and Marty Marion, and each of them, I'm sure, kept telling him he could be a great hitter if he'd just lay off the bad pitches.

Dropo, at least, stayed in the lineup. You may have wondered what happened to a couple of other players who got off to great starts and then disappeared completely. Two summers ago, Bob Speake of the Cubs seemed to be hitting a home run every other day. Then the word got around among the National League pitchers that he couldn't do a thing with a fast ball in across the letters—and that was the end of him. I see, though, that he's getting another shot with Chicago this year after a pretty good season out on the Coast. Maybe he learned to hit that pitch out there—or maybe the Coast pitchers just couldn't hit the right spot often enough. It should only take a couple of weeks after the season starts for the pitchers to find out.

In our league, at almost the same time, Norm Zauchin of the Red Sox was off on an even longer streak. For a few weeks he stayed right up with the home-run leaders. Then some pitcher discovered that Zauchin had a lot of trouble with the change-up, and the word soon spread to the rest of the pitchers in the league. At first, we didn't think we'd learned anything very sensational, as an inability to hit the change-up wouldn't be enough to knock a solid fast-ball hitter out of the lineup.

Up to then, Zauchin had been murdering the fast ball, but he began to worry so much about all the slow stuff we were mixing in with the fast balls, that he stopped hitting anything. It got so that you could switch him either way.

You could use the fast ball to set up the change one time, and use the change to set up the fast ball the next. Before long, Zauchin's timing got so fouled up that he'd have streaks where he was striking out three or four times a game. The Red Sox finally had to give up on him and make a deal for Mickey Vernon.

Luke Easter (who, by coincidence, had taken Vernon's job away at Cleveland) was supposed to be the coming great hitter in the game when the Indians brought him up. But the first word to be spread around about him was that he was pretty weak against a left-hander's curve (which I always like to hear) and not too tough on the high fast ball. The funny thing about Luke was that although he hung on as a regular for three full seasons, he seemed to get a little weaker on those pitches every year. And yet we pitchers would probably be giving ourselves the best of it if we said *we* stopped him. Easter was supposed to be under 30 when he first came up, but I'd have to say he was considerably older than that. If he'd come up five or six years earlier he might very well have been able to straighten himself out; as it was, he was probably already over the hill, and we just speeded up the process.

With lesser hitters, the word does not always spread that quickly; you usually have to go looking for information about them. Last year, for instance, the Yankees had as much trouble with Chicago's little shortstop, Luis Aparicio, as with anybody in the league. A 22-year-old Venezuelan with only two years in the low minors behind him, Aparicio had come up with the reputation of being a great fielder but a weak hitter. Nobody else in the league had any trouble with him: against us he was a solid .300 hitter. Against me—and I started against the White Sox eight times—he hit closer to .400.

Aparicio doesn't hit a long enough ball to kill you but, believe me, there is nothing more aggravating than to get past the good hitters and then have a weak hitter come up and push across a couple of runs. Since it's axiomatic that young players can hit the fast ball but have to learn to hit the curve, I tested him with breaking stuff to every conceivable part of the plate. And every time I faced him, he seemed to hit me a little better.

As the Yankees were leaving New York toward the end of the year, we found ourselves on the same train as another eastern club, a situation that comes up two or three times during a season. I made it my business to visit one of their pitchers. "Listen," I said. "What about this kid Aparicio?"

"Yeah," he said, grinning, "he hits the curve pretty good, doesn't he? I just try to overpower him."

As you may have guessed all along, Aparicio happens to be the exception to that rule about young hitters. He hits the breaking stuff better than the fast ball. We had one last game left in Chicago, and I had pretty good luck setting him up for the fast ball. I don't think Luis Aparicio is going to be a .300 hitter against the Yankees again this year.

It is not as easy as you might imagine for pitchers to get together to exchange information. One pitcher can't just walk up to another on the field and start talking, because there is an anti-fraternization rule in the majors. (Incidentally, no other professional sport has such a ridiculous rule. Its only purpose is to support the somewhat simple-minded belief that no professional ballplayer would think of making a friendly comment to a player from a rival team. As the *Official Baseball Rules* puts it: "The basic reason for baseball's hold upon its patrons is the competitive nature of the game; the traditional assurance that when a baseball game is played, the teams forget all else except to win in a sportsmanlike manner. Any mingling with spectators or fraternization by opposing players tends to destroy this conviction." Well, maybe I'm destroying organized baseball by writing this article, but I sure don't think so. I hope that someday baseball's brass hats will agree with me, and erase this foolish rule from the books.)

Anyway, they're still trying to enforce the anti-fraternization rule. If you happen to get to the ball park early, look behind the home-team dugout—about three or four rows up—and you will probably see one of the umpires keeping a close watch. One good story I heard about this was told by a sportswriter who happened to be in the Red Sox dugout before their opening game with Washington a couple of years ago. We had opened the season against Chuck Stobbs, the Washington lefty, two days before, and Mel Parnell, the Boston lefty who was going to pitch against us in the Stadium before the week was over, wanted to talk to Stobbs in the worst way.

"I got to find out," he kept saying, "about those two new righties, Skowron and Cerv."

Lou Boudreau, who was then managing Boston, said: "Go ahead. Things get confused out there on opening days. Nobody will be looking."

"Who's up there?" Parnell asked Billy Consolo.

Consolo backed up out of the dugout, looked into the box seats and said: "McGowan."

"Oh, gee," Parnell said. "He doesn't miss a thing. It will cost me $25 sure."

Boudreau kept needling him. "Go ahead," he said. "We'll pass the hat for you. I'll put in $10 myself."

But Parnell wouldn't take a chance. Not with McGowan watching. But from what I know about how pitchers get together, I'm sure that Parnell found some way to talk to Stobbs before the Senators left town.

Although it's pretty risky to try exchanging information on the field, there are plenty of opportunities for rival pitchers to get together. On trains, in restaurants or hotel lobbies, or right in their own homes. The barnstorming tours that have sprung up in the past few years offer an excellent opportunity, as these teams are made up of players from all over both leagues, and when you put a half-dozen pitchers together it isn't long before they're talking shop. I've only been on one of these tours myself, but other guys have told me how useful they are.

And we're not only talking about other hitters. One guy will tell another how to throw a knuckler or a palm ball, while another pitcher will be holding forth on how he cured that sore flipper. If a pitcher's got any information that might help all pitchers, he spreads it around. None of us want to see pitchers degenerate into throwing machines that are out there just to get the ball up to where the hitters can get at it. And the way that rabbit ball has been leaping out of parks the last few years, we know we've got to pull everything we can to keep from becoming as extinct as the dodo.

I guess the best opportunity for us pitchers to exchange information comes at the All-Star game. In the first place, you get a real gathering of the pros there, the very best in the business; in the second place, you're all living together as members of the same team. And, perhaps most important of all, it comes right in the middle of the season—after you've all had a chance to look over the talent.

At the All-Star game in Washington last year, for instance, there was a lot of talk about Charlie Maxwell, who had suddenly caught fire with Detroit after being bounced around by Boston for years. I had pitched against him in the Piedmont League and the Eastern League, and I had always considered him a real good hitter. In fact, when Detroit picked him up on waivers at the beginning of the season, I kept telling the guys in our locker room that he'd do the Tigers a lot of good if they'd put him out there and let him play regularly for a change. He sure did. At the All-Star break he was hitting .360.

I told the other pitchers there that in the minors you could sometimes get Charlie with a curve-curve-high fast ball pattern, but that he seemed to be hitting the fast ball very well now and doing a good job with the curve, too.

"He's got to die," one of the other pitchers kept saying. "A .220 hitter doesn't become a .360 hitter this late in life. Wait and see—he'll find his level over the rest of the year and end up around .270."

Well, he didn't. Charlie finished at .326, behind only Mantle, Williams and Kuenn. There is no reason why he shouldn't be a solid .300 hitter for Detroit for three or four years to come. The good hitters are going to hit no matter how much the pitchers talk them over.

Over on the National League side last year, pitchers huddled together in Washington to talk about Dale Long. And they must have had a lot more information than we did because Long, who had been going wild over there, did skid right back to his level thereafter.

At the previous year's All-Star game, the talk had been mostly about Al Kaline, whose case could not have been more completely different than Maxwell's. In his first year, as a bonus boy, Al had gone pretty much as you might expect. Like most kids, he had been strictly a fast-ball hitter. With two strikes on him, you could sometimes even get him to chase the curve all the way into the dirt.

In 1955, as any fan knows, he started murdering everybody. I've read about the weight he put on and all that, but it was really just a case of Al's suddenly learning how to hit that curve, the way a good young hitter will. We still talk about Kaline, and if he gets in a slump it's not long before all of us know what pitch he's having the most trouble with, but no amount of talk is going to run a hitter like that out of the league.

It may seem to you that this pitchers' grapevine completely wipes out team lines, but that isn't precisely true. There are definite areas in which communication breaks down completely. No pitcher would think of asking another pitcher about one of his own teammates, for instance, and there's a limit to the information you'll give each other about yourselves.

I think I had better say before we go too much further that this game would be a lot simpler if the "book" were infallible in all cases. (And let me say, too, that the book is a purely mental catalogue, consisting of the sum total of knowledge learned by all the pitchers in the league and contributed to the common pool. I have never heard of anybody actually writing all this stuff down.) But after all the information has been collected, each pitcher still has to go with his own stuff. What works for most pitchers will not necessarily work for me. Until the end of last season, for instance, I had never faced Jim Lemon, a long-ball-hitting outfielder who had been around with Cleveland and Washington for a few years. Last year, he finally won a starting job with the Senators and by the end of the year he had hit 27 home runs. He had also set an all-time major-league record in strike-outs.

Now, this is the kind of hitter you really want information about. Anybody who strikes out that much can obviously be pitched to. Anybody who hits that many home runs can just as obviously hurt you.

By huddling with several other pitchers from teams that had just played Washington, I found there was general agreement that (1) you could curve him with a lot of success; (2) you could get him on the high fast ball. The first time I faced Lemon, President Eisenhower was in the stands. After I'd got through pitching by the book, Ike must have left the park thinking Jim Lemon was one of the great hitters of all time. The first time he came up, I threw him the curve. He hit it out of the park. The second time, I gave him the curve again. He hit it out of the park again. By this time, I had somehow got the impression that he could hit my curve pretty good, so when he came up again I threw him the high hard one. He hit that farther than he had hit the curves. By the next time he came up, I was out of the game.

Even when the advice of other pitchers does work for you, you can't just keep throwing to the batter's indicated weakness. Any hitter seeing the same pitch over and over is eventually going to learn how to hit it. Larry Doby is a spectacular example of that. After Doby had been in the league a couple of weeks, our grapevine sent around word that he was weak on high pitches. Normally, he'd have been thrown a certain amount of low pitches to set up the high pitches, but it seemed that every time you threw him a low pitch he set a new long-distance record. For years, any new pitcher coming into the league was told to keep the ball high on him and to make sure that any waste pitches were thrown all the way down into the dirt.

And then a funny thing happened. All of us

pitchers suddenly realized that Doby was beginning to hit the high ball about as well as anybody in the league. (There are very few good high-ball hitters. The best I ever saw was Dale Mitchell.) We began to test him again—after all those seasons—on the low ball. We discovered that he had seen so few of them over the years that, far from setting any long-distance records any more, he was actually pretty weak against them. So the book on Doby has turned completely around.

Hitters—especially young ones—are adaptable. So the wise pitcher has to be adaptable too. Take Jimmy Piersall. Piersall came to the Red Sox as a straightaway swinger who hit the ball almost exclusively between left center and right center. That kind of a hitter wants the ball outside, so you make life as difficult as possible for him by keeping it inside. For three years Jimmy was a .280 hitter of no particular power, a combination which isn't awfully frightening in an outfielder.

And then last year, after a particularly slow start, Jimmy suddenly began to win game after game with extra-base hits. All hitters get hot sometimes during the season, and yet the power of Piersall's blows had to make you suspicious that he had suddenly learned how to pull that inside pitch. It wasn't long before all of the members in good standing of the Great American Pitchers' Union (American League Local) were aware of the fact that Piersall had, indeed, overcome his major weakness. From then on we couldn't rely on the inside stuff, and there was nothing that all the interpitcher conferences in the world could do to stop him from hitting. Jimmy went on to lead the league in doubles by a wide margin, and over the last half of the season he must have hit something like .350.

Sometimes you can have a lot of luck against a good hitter that way, and then all at once he'll catch on to what you're doing and begin to out-guess *you* on those switches. Nellie Fox, for instance, has always been tough for me. Among the left-handers, only Ted Williams is rougher. Since Nellie can spray the ball to all fields, the other pitchers have always advised me to keep the ball fast and inside on him and try to make him pull. Two years ago, I had great success by throwing him change-ups when he was expecting the fast ball. Nellie would swing out in front of the ball and hit harmless little grounders down to first or second.

Then last year, pitching him exactly the same way, I got murdered. Fox would wait on the pitch and either slap it right back through the box or line it into left.

This year, maybe I'll go back to the book. Pitchers tell me it hasn't changed. Maybe I'll try something altogether new on him. Maybe. But you have to remember that Fox is figuring that I'll be trying something new too. So maybe, Nellie, I just won't switch at all.

If you are coming to the conclusion that baseball is primarily a guessing game between the pitcher and the batter you are, for the most part, absolutely correct. The toughest hitters for me are the ones, like Harvey Kuenn, who *don't* guess. Kuenn hits anything and everything. I've thrown high inside pitches to him and seen him, in some magical way, line the ball to the *opposite* field. There's just no book at all for that kind of a batter.

Of course, even when you think you have a batter perfectly set up for a certain pitch, he can always cross you up. I said I had another story about Walt Dropo. Here it is:

In our pennant-clinching game against Chicago last year, Billy Pierce and I went into the last of the eighth tied up 1-1. I threw Dropo two slow curves, both low. He took one and fouled off the other, so I had a count of one ball, one strike. Then I threw him a fast ball, low and away. He swung and missed, so the count went to one ball, two strikes. At this point, I figured I'd throw him another slow curve, low and away. If he swung, fine. If he didn't, I was still ahead of him and, after four consecutive low pitches, I could switch to a high inside fast ball just on the corner. The subsequent events can be chronicled in three parts:

(1) He took the curve.

(2) I put the fast ball exactly where I wanted it.

(3) He belted it out of the park.

It can work the other way too. You can do everything wrong and still get out of an inning through blind luck. By coincidence, the best example I can cite goes back to the pennant-clinching game of the previous year. It was in the last of the eighth again, and we were leading Boston by one run. But the Red Sox had the bases loaded with one out and Ted Williams at bat. The count went to three balls and one strike, which meant I had to get the ball in there or force across the tying run. So I just threw the ball as hard as I could, hoping to get it somewhere within the strike zone. The ball went right down the middle of the plate. Right down the middle. And Ted hit the most perfect double-play ball you ever saw down to second base.

Now, don't get the idea that I immediately went out and advised the other pitchers around the league to throw Williams fast balls down the middle! All I'm saying is that you can make bad mistakes, as far as the book is concerned, and still not get hurt. I have to laugh when I read something like: "Ford made only one bad pitch and it cost him the game." In an average game, I'll make about *ten* bad pitches. Sometimes one of them will hurt me, sometimes none at all. There are seven men out there behind me and they are perfectly entitled to catch the ball whether it's been hit off a bad pitch or not.

There are a lot of times, too, when you *deliberately throw the ball right into the batter's strength.* You would be amazed how many important outs you can get by working the count down to where the hitter is sure you're going to throw to his weakness, and then throw to his power instead.

Duke Snider, for instance, wears out fast balls but can have trouble with curves, especially a left-hand pitcher's curve. In the second game of this past World Series, if you remember, Tommy Byrne made a fast ball too good and Duke hit it a mile to tie up a game we thought we had won. The reports on the game were pretty unanimous in stating that we wouldn't give Duke a pitch like *that* again.

The very next game, I struck out Snider twice in the early innings with curve balls. In the eighth, I started him off with a curve and got a strike. Then I wasted a fast ball. The routine thing to do now would have been to throw another curve or, possibly, a change-up. Instead, I threw another fast ball. Swinging late, Snider fouled it off. At this point, Snider's thoughts should have been going like this: *Damn it, he crossed me up with the fast ball. . . . I should have belted it right out of here. Now he's got me where he can try to pick off the outside corner with a couple of curves. If he gets me again, it will be three strike-outs this game . . . I've got to protect the outside of the plate.*

So I threw him a fast ball inside and caught him flat-footed. That's a pitch I wouldn't dare throw to Snider unless I was sure he was looking for something else. The beauty of it is that once you get a guy pressing like that you can really keep switching on him. Yogi kept outguessing him on the fast ball throughout the rest of the Series, and when you've stopped Snider you've put a big dent in the Brooklyn offense.

There are other little things we pitchers do to give ourselves an edge in the never-ending war with the hitters. You can learn a lot just by watching the other team take its batting practice. Since batting-practice pitches come right over the plate at medium speed, you can get a wonderful line on each batter's basic swing. If you see him hitting straightaway or to the opposite field, you know he likes the ball outside. So naturally you give it to him inside. If he pulls everything, you know he likes it inside. So you do your best to keep it outside.

We all help ourselves, too, by studying the box scores every morning to keep track of who's hitting and who isn't.

But we need more than just the box scores, because one guy might be hitting in tough luck and another guy might be having a run of cheap hits. Here again, you can learn a lot if you can go over a series with a pitcher from another club. My buddy happens to be Tom Gorman of the Athletics, who lives fairly close to me on Long Island during the winter and is godfather to my son Eddie. When I'm in Kansas City, I'll probably go over to the Gormans for dinner, and Tom and I will run over each series pretty thoroughly. I remember once last year when we came in right after Boston and he told me: "Jensen got only one hit but he hit eight line drives that were caught. Williams got his base hits all right but he wasn't hitting the ball like he can. I don't think his timing is real sharp."

(Don't think, incidentally, that hitters don't do the same thing with pitchers. If I've pitched a good game, the hitters will spread the word in the next city.)

I don't think it would be inaccurate to say that the rabbit ball has forced pitchers to become better craftsmen. I've heard Joe DiMaggio say that when he first came up, batting was just a matter of getting himself into a groove where he was ready for either the fast ball or the curve. After the war, though, pitchers began to develop knucklers and change-ups and screwballs and sinkers and palm balls and sliders. Even more than that, almost all of the pitchers tried to keep the batters off stride by throwing at three or four different speeds.

The great new pitch of modern baseball has been the slider, which is thrown with the same motion as a fast ball, looks like a fast ball until it gets right up to the plate, and then gives a quick little swerve. Nobody seems to know exactly where the pitch originated. Lefty Grove apparently used it in his day, and maybe one or two others used it as their curve. But it wasn't until Freddie Hutchinson in the American League and Larry Jansen in the National

League both started to throw it with great success just after the war that it began to catch on. One pitcher taught it to another and pretty soon everybody who felt he needed another pitch was using it. The idea is to throw it like the fast ball, but to put the same kind of side spin on it that you'd put on your curve.

Frankly, I'm a little ashamed to talk about the slider. The reason it has been such a success is that most pitchers seem to be able to pick it up overnight and—more important—to control it very easily. And yet, I have never been able to get the hang of it at all. When my curve left me at the end of last year, I decided to give it a final try. I threw it once against the Red Sox, hurt my elbow and was out for a week. I think I had just better forget about it.

You hear a lot of talk about another pitch—the spitball. I haven't listed it because I can honestly say that I don't know anybody in the American League who throws it. Just before the World Series I was on a TV program where they ran off some pictures of Sal Maglie pitching his no-hitter. I was asked, specifically, for my opinion as to whether he was throwing a spitter. From what I could see, Sal was touching two fingers to his tongue all right, but he was then bringing his hand down to his pants' leg and wiping the fingers off. I'll tell you something: I do exactly the same thing and nobody has ever accused me of throwing a spitter. Every once in a while an umpire will say, "Be sure you wipe those fingers off, Whitey," but that's about all. It's just a nervous habit.

I don't think Maglie throws a spitter, but I'm sure he's just as happy to let the batters think he does. It gives them just one more thing to worry about. And by now, you should have got the idea that we pitchers are out to battle the hitters with every weapon—mental or physical—that we can find. We do it by trying to improve ourselves, yes, but we also do it by looking for information about the hitters from whatever source it can be found. If it surprises you that pitchers from opposing clubs are the greatest source of all, then let me ask you this question: Can you think of anybody else who would *have* that kind of information?

A SUPERLATIVE television fiasco took place in 1956, when it was announced that, to cap a baseball "spectacular," Billy Pierce of the
Chicago White Sox would throw a curve ball at the camera. Curve?
What he threw I could have hit. The other several hundred thousand
pitches he has thrown, I can not hit. Neither can you. Details, from
this early-1958 story:

Billy Pierce

———— BILL FURLONG ————

IN HIS OWN muted and low-decibel way, Billy
Pierce of the Chicago White Sox has finally
won the recognition that hung, like a tantaliz-
ing sunbeam, always just out of reach.

He is the best left-handed pitcher in the
American League—and perhaps in the major
leagues. His toughest competition—Herb Score
of the Cleveland Indians and Whitey Ford of
the New York Yankees—encountered enough
vagaries of fate in 1957 to surrender the su-
premacy to Pierce. Score's eye was injured by a
ball smashed off the bat of Gil McDougald of
the Yankees early in the season, while Ford
managed to settle into a more routine rut with
the aid of an on-again, off-again sore arm.

Pierce combines the best assets of both pitchers. Like Score, he's led the American League
in strike-outs. Like Ford, he's led it in earned
run averages. He's won 20 games a year twice
and in 1953 he hurled almost 40 consecutive
shutout innings—a record for southpaws that
falls just short of Carl Hubbell's memorable
46⅓ shutout frames. And he did this against the
toughest competition in the league.

For many years the White Sox employed
Billy specifically to lick the Yanks and the Indians. He was their "stopper."

"If he wasn't spotted against the tough teams
—if he came up against some of the second-
division clubs more often—he'd have won his
20 games a year long ago," says Sherman Lollar, the White Sox catcher.

This is a paradox of Pierce—that while he
was long recognized as one of the top pitchers
in the game, he was long delayed in winning 20
games, the payoff point for a pitcher. For years

he swirled around in the good-but-not-good-
enough orbit—going 12-16 one year, 15-14 the
next, 15-12 the next, and so on. Even today,
his over-all won-lost record is not staggering
for its brilliance—134 wins and 110 losses.

There were many good reasons for this.

Part of it was that he was going up against
the rough teams. Part of it was luck. In 1954,
for instance, when his record was 15-10, he
lost six games (four 1-0 games and two 3-2
games) by one run.

Part of it was stamina. Though he's always
been a fast-ball pitcher, Pierce has also been
somewhat small. He weighed only 130 pounds
when he broke into organized ball. Now he
weighs around 160. He always seemed to do
his best in the early season, sag a bit in the
middle months, then revive in September.

The White Sox tried to solve this problem by
giving Pierce four or five days rest—instead of
the more customary three days—between starts.
This seemed to have one notable effect: it prevented him from getting in enough games to
become a 20-game winner. Once he started
taking a regular every-fourth-day turn in 1956,
he lost nothing in effectiveness and gained
much in the win column. He went up from a
14-game-a-year winner—his average for 1951-
55—to a 20-game-a-year winner.

Through all this, Pierce was slowly maturing
as a pitcher, developing and exploiting his
natural talents.

With Pierce, the natural talent was impressive. His fast ball is not one of the big cannonball shots that zoom straight past the batter
like an armor-piercing charge. "Actually, Billy

throws a 'light,' ball," says Phil Masi, once a catcher on the Sox. "It doesn't crash into your mitt; it just sort of lands there." Pierce's speed is augmented by a tormenting liveliness—a tendency to "take off" in highly unpredictable ways as it speeds past the batter, like a balloon with the air escaping, flitting wildly about a room.

All this talent demanded was discipline—control, self-restraint, variety.

The control came slowly and with it came success. Pierce has always been high up on the strike-out lists, leading the league on two occasions. But like many other southpaws, he started out like a wild man, walking as many as 137 batters in a year. Since 1950, he's managed to get his lively fast ball under control, until now he usually walks only about 70 or 80 batters a year. And as his wildness disappeared, his wins increased.

Part of this is due to subtle changes in technique and temperament. But some of it was due to a simple change in handling the ball.

"I used to hold the ball with my fingers across the seams," says Billy, "to get more liveliness. Now I hold it with my fingers between the seams sometimes. That gives me better control." The shift from liveliness to control is not a radical one—but it is just enough to give Billy a preference, and confidence, in tight situations.

Another flaw which Billy had to learn to tame was his working habits. He's a fast pitcher, wasting little time or motion on the mound. Once he gets the ball, he likes to pitch it. This is gratifying in an era of torturously long ball games but it can lead a pitcher to swift oblivion. For batters have a tendency to pick up the rhythm of a pitcher—and in picking up his rhythm they manage to pick off his best pitches, no matter how much "stuff" they may have on them. At times, they fell as easily into the fast working rhythm of Pierce as Pierce did—and at times, they profited immensely.

So Paul Richards, who was manager of the White Sox in the days of Billy's deliverance, worked long and hard to slow down his delivery and to give it—not only the pitch—a change of pace. "When you see Sherm Lollar walking out to the mound," says Billy, "he isn't trying to calm me down so much as to get me to slow down on my delivery, to break up my rhythm."

He was also perilously unimaginative in his choice of pitches. "He didn't want to throw anything but fast balls in the old days," Paul Richards has said. "He laughed at the change

of pace and the slider, so most of the strong right-hand hitters were laying back for him, waiting for a fast ball down the middle."

One day Richards persuaded him to try a slider against the Yanks. Pierce got Mantle to bounce out and Bauer to tap an easy one-bouncer back to the mound. His confidence in the slider grew so much that soon he was throwing nothing but sliders. Then Richards had to pry him loose from that tendency and teach him the change of pace and its effectiveness as an alternative to a fast ball.

"Even now," Richards went on, "he'll pitch a whole ball game and almost never throw anything but fast balls. But only on certain days."

There were always other less dangerous flaws that had to be overcome. He had a tendency to tip off the opposition when he was going to throw a curve. "The Yankees always knew when he was going to throw a curve," said Richards. He also had a tendency to windmill in his windup which makes a fast ball spin too much and takes the life out of it.

Learning these things was not always easy for a man of Pierce's temperament. Richards believes that Billy might well be the most stubborn man alive. "It took Billy extra long to learn some of these things because he had his own way of pitching and he wanted to stick to it."

Billy listens carefully to advice—but he always measures to see its inherent value, to see whether it's good or bad advice. "You better be right when you tell him to do something," Richards said, "because the first time you tell him wrong, he'll never listen to you again."

What Pierce's temperament lacks in bombast, it makes up in thoughtfulness. The shades of temperament were outlined by him one day during a streak when he was pitching well. "I wasn't pitching any better," he said. "At least not any better than I'd been pitching all along. But on some days you feel like an offensive pitcher and other days you're a defensive pitcher. The days when you feel like an offensive pitcher are good ones, no matter how much 'stuff' you lack."

Though he's usually a quiet and serious young man, Pierce possesses a furtive humor that emerges in unlikely moments.

One day during the 1950 campaign, when the Sox were coming out of a long retirement to challenge the Yankees, Pierce found himself in continual trouble. Only the acrobatics of Jim Busby in center field—then on his first tour of duty with the White Sox—prevented the shelling from becoming disastrous. Richards loped out of the dugout to the mound.

"How do you feel?" he asked Pierce.

"Don't ask me, ask Busby," said Pierce. "If he's strong enough, I'll finish the game."

At 30, Billy Pierce is a heavy-bearded young man with the piping voice and earnest innocence of a teen-ager. Though he's developing a bald spot on his skull, and filling out in his frame a bit, he still lends the impression of youth personified.

But in matters regarding baseball he shows an astounding maturity—as White Sox vice-president Chuck Comiskey has discovered at contract-signing time. Pierce is a man with a well-developed, if well-concealed, sense of his own importance to the club. As a result, he's been able to wheedle more than $30,000 a year out of the Comiskey bursars—more than any other Sox pitcher in history.

Pierce has had this subdued sense of determined destiny since he was 13 and went out to pitch for his local club in a Detroit recreation league after the team's regular pitcher deserted to join a rival club with prettier uniforms. By the time he was 17, Billy was the top high-school pitcher in the country, giving up only two earned runs in his final season as a prep pitcher. He hurled in a high-school all-star game in New York, helped rack up a five-hit 6-0 shutout, won a four-year scholarship to the college of his choice—and ignored the opportunity. For the Detroit Tigers came along, offered him a $15,000 bonus and shuffled him off to their minor-league affiliate in Buffalo.

For three years, Pierce hurled for Buffalo—for the most part under the tutelage of Paul Richards. He came up to the Tigers in 1948, turned in an unspectacular record of three wins and no losses, and was promptly traded off to the White Sox, along with $10,000 in cash, for Catcher Aaron Robinson—then a .252 hitter. It was the first trade negotiated by Frank Lane as a major-league general manager. It was, quite possibly, his best.

This was not immediately apparent. Pierce won only seven and lost 15 for the White Sox in 1949 and the next year he was still below the .500 mark with a 12-15 record. But he was firmly established as one of the most skillful southpaws in the big leagues—and gradually the honors accumulated enough to sustain the view.

In 1953 he led the league in strike-outs with 186. He did it again in 1956 with 196 strike-outs. In 1955, he led the league—both leagues, in fact—in earned-run average with 1.97, the only man in either league to hold his rivals to less than two runs a game. In 1956 he became the first left-hander to win 20 games since Mel Parnell did it for Boston back in 1953. No White Sox pitcher had scaled the 20-game heights since Thornton Lee did it in 1941.

His recognition was a trifle parochial. The public knew comparatively little about him—but the big-leaguers harbored a profound respect for his ability. Three times in four years—in 1953, 1955, and 1956—he was selected to start the All-Star game for the American League. Last year he was in on relief, when the National League exploded in the ninth inning.

Still, trouble occurred and reoccurred during this advance towards fame. One year he suffered a torn fingernail; that kept him from putting pressure on the ball. Another year, 1954, his performance slipped, largely because of a sore arm. The extraction of a few infected teeth solved that problem. And sometimes he's been the victim of the subtle mental letdown that follows an outstanding effort. The puzzling year of 1953 serves as an example.

By mid-August of 1953, Pierce had won 17 games and weaved together that string of almost 40 consecutive scoreless innings. He seemed certain to win 20 games and perhaps lead the league. But he went to the mound five times in the next month without winning a game. He didn't take his 18th win until the last week of the season—and then he was pushed to 11 innings before claiming it.

"Perhaps there was an unconscious mental letdown after my scoreless streak was snapped," Pierce suggested later. "On August 14, I went into a game against the St. Louis Browns with 34⅔ scoreless innings and with three straight shutouts behind me. Then somebody told me I needed only 12 more scoreless innings to beat Carl Hubbell's record for a left-hander and 22 more to beat Walter Johnson's all-time mark.

"I shut out the Browns for 5⅓ innings but an error gave them two unearned runs in the sixth and I finally lost the game in the 10th. That was a big disappointment to me—and it might have weighed on my mind a little."

The normal Pierce method to escape such problems is to go to the movies—in which he allegedly holds the club record—or to watch television. He's also the most avid candy consumer on the club.

During the off season, Billy occasionally

gives his father a hand in his drugstore. But now most of his spare time is devoted to his family. His wife, Gloria, was a friend of his in grade school and his high-school "steady" in Highland Park, Michigan, a suburb of Detroit where the Pierces still make their home. An avid baseball fan, Gloria married Billy in October, 1949—just a few weeks before he was

traded to the White Sox. They now have two children—Billy, now four (born July 7, 1953), and Patricia, two (born October 6, 1955). Billy runs his family with the same quiet determination that he runs his career. With a little more bombast, Billy Pierce might have won his place as the league's best left-hander sooner—but not any more certainly.

JOHN GALLAGHER

Courtesy *Sport* Magazine. ©

"This guy murders a fast ball, wears No-wrink shorts, eats Poppos with bananas and cream, shaves with new and improved Swoosh blades, smokes El Ropos, prefers zesty Choco-drink, and is a sucker for an inside curve."

IN the maze of the many and authentic accounts of the great wit and clownsmanship of Vernon (Lefty) Gomez, the fact sometimes gets buried that this was one whale of a pitcher. Here is his own tale of the biggest thrill of his career.

1932:

New York Yankees 5, Chicago Cubs 2

LEFTY GOMEZ
as told to JOHN DROHAN

To TELL THE TRUTH, in relating my biggest baseball day, I'm torn between two loves. I'm something like the Old Soak who never knew whether his wife told him to take one drink and come home at 12, or take 12 and come home at one. Of course, there have been complaints? I've been a pitcher. On the other hand, there was a hot day last August in Washington—and can it get hot there—when I got four for five, as they say down at the clubhouse.

I'd like to dwell a bit on that, because those days have been rare in my career. But inasmuch as I've drawn my best salary checks for pitching, rather than hitting, I'll have to pass it up, much as I dislike to. However, the fact I got four for five might have had something to do with Bucky Harris resigning his job a few weeks later.

Searching the old cerebellum, I think my biggest thrill in baseball was my first World Series game. It was against the Chicago Cubs in the second game of the 1932 series.

Red Ruffing had won the first game, 12-6, from Guy Bush at the Yankee Stadium and I was to work the second against Lon Warneke, the Arkansas Humming Bird.

Joe McCarthy had us hopped up to pour it on the Cubs and lick 'em quick. He'd got the old heave-ho from the Cubs only two years before, and was anxious to get back at them. He figured he hadn't got such a good shake in Chi-

cago and often said he'd like to get even. This was his chance.

Revenge couldn't be as sweet to him as if Rogers Hornsby had stayed as manager of the Cubs. Hornsby had succeeded McCarthy as manager of the Cubs in 1931 and then had been given the old heave-ho in his turn in August, '32. That had brought in Charley Grimm as Cub manager, and the club has turned it on hot to come down the stretch whooping and hollering and kicking everybody out of their way to grab the flag in one of baseball's best stretch drives.

The Yanks under Huggins had swept the World Series four straight from the Pirates in '27 and again from the Cards in '28, and McCarthy naturally wanted to do what Miller had done. We figured we could do it, for while Grimm had Jurges, Herman, Koenig and English with him on the infield, Cuyler Stephenson and Demaree in the outfield, Hartnett catching and Warneke, Root, Malone, Bush, Grimes and Jakie May pitching, we had what we thought was a much stronger club, with Dickey catching, Gehrig on first, Crosetti at short, Lazzeri at second, Sewell at third, Babe Ruth, Sam Chapman and Earle Combs in the outfield and Red Ruffing, Wilcy Moore, Johnny Allen, George Pipgras and myself.

There was a lot of talk, as the second game came up, about the kid-competition between Lon Warneke and me—two beanpoles. Both of us were sophomores; he was 23, I was 21; he had won 22 that summer for the Cubs, I had managed to get by with 24 for the Yankees.

Babe Ruth was 37 and beginning to slow down in the field, but he could still flatten the ball and had hit 41 homers that year.

I remember how Ed Barrow, our general manager, kept after me all my first and second years to put on weight. It scared him when he looked at me, for I weighed only 152, which was thin enough for my height, over 6 feet. Barrow figured I couldn't last.

At the end of the first season he told me, "About 25 years ago we had a pitcher around here named Jack Chesbro, the first pitcher ever to win 16 straight games in the American League. If you'd only put on more weight you could make the fans forget Chesbro."

I wasn't any fatter my second year, '32, but I could fire the ball through a two-inch plank. Barrow, however, kept after me, and I knew during the series that I'd have to spend the winter at a health resort in California Barrow had picked out—a sort of old ladies' home where I was to fatten up.

Incidentally, I did come back to start the '33 season 20 pounds fatter and they put me to rooming with Pat Malone, whom McCarthy had bought from the Cubs, and who was a fat man.

That '33 season I won only 16 and lost 10 and instead of making the fans forget Chesbro I was making 'em forget Gomez, so that winter of '33-35 I took off so much weight I showed up in '34 spring training thinner than Bill Powell —and won 26 games and lost five for an .839 percentage, the best I ever hung up. Anyway, on Sept. 29, 1932, when I went against Lon Warneke and the Cubs, I was thin and felt good.

I had a break, for Warneke showed up wild and kept putting men on for us to bat around, while I found I could get the ball where I wanted and where the Cubs didn't. That afternoon I fanned eight and walked only one. Guy Bush had been wild in the first game of the series and in these first two games we got ten walks which turned into nine runs.

As I remember it, the Cubs didn't even threaten mildly after tying the score in the third, for we went ahead with a couple more in our half and wound up winning 5-2.

It wasn't any closeness of score or suspense that made it my biggest baseball day; it was simply that it was my first World Series game and I won it.

I remember Gabby Hartnett hitting one down the left-field line and Ben Chapman, the fastest man in the American League, scooping up the ball and firing it to second in time for Crosetti to be waiting with it when the old "Milford Freight" came steaming into the bag.

When the rest of the Yanks got through slapping ol' Lon around about all he had left was his chaw of terbacker. And even that was pretty well used up. But if I didn't hit Lon he didn't hit me. So I guess we're even in that respect.

That one game was my only chance in the '32 series. The Babe fixed the third one up for us in Chicago by pointing to the bleachers in center field and then whacking one of Charley Root's pitches in there. Pipgras pitched us to a 7-5 win, and the next day Wilcy Moore beat Bush, Warneke, Jakie May, Bud Tinning and a great many other gentlemen whose names escape me, 13-6.

The whole series was pretty enjoyable for me. I was going with June O'Dea, prima donna of the Broadway show, *Of Thee I Sing*, at the time and, hanging around the theater, saw the show so often I felt I could act myself. So when bookers came to me after the series I signed up without a quiver for vaudeville monologues on a 12-week booking. I lasted three weeks, but the audiences didn't.

I knew so little about show business that one afternoon at Loew's State in New York, when the manager said, "There won't be anybody here for the supper show," I started to skip that show as a matter of course. He caught me as I was leaving for the Rodeo over at Madison Square Garden and drove me back into my dressing room, where I put on my Yankee uniform and went out and gave my monologue to three stews, two of whom were asleep when I started and the third soon was.

The year 1932 I am safe in saying saw an end to my career in the theater.

THIS piece appeared in 1957. Since then, of course, The Man has become more so. Just one example: he's now in the 3,000-hit bracket.

The Man

———— **DICK GORDON** ————

STANLEY FRANK MUSIAL may qualify as the closest embodiment of all-around perfection baseball has ever seen.

That extreme and all-embracing statement takes into consideration his actions off the field as well as on. It includes such intangibles as character, personality and leadership in addition to these more basic factors:

His average has never slipped below .300 in 15 big-league seasons.

He has won six batting championships and three Most Valuable awards.

He has now played in more than 823 consecutive games at first base and the outfield—he's equally adept at both spots—and has smashed Gus Suhr's National League record of 822, set in 1931-37.

He has more than 2,800 hits and is moving inevitably into that select "3,000" society.

Other greats, past and present, may equal or even pass Musial's many diamond achievements.

But Babe Ruth, an overgrown boy almost until his death, was fined more than once when he strayed from the straight and narrow.

Ty Cobb, whose home life was never a model, was involved in brawls with teammates and opponents.

Joe DiMaggio was moody, Rog Hornsby irascible, Bill Terry was never known for his sunny disposition and Ted Williams, of course, is known for his lack of it.

Ted makes the headlines for his spitting almost as much as his hitting. And then, by contrast, there's Musial.

Stan just happens to be one of the most charmingly gracious fellows in any line of endeavor. He is a devoted family man to his wife and three children, with a sense of humor that appreciates good jokes, including those on himself.

It was he who told the story about how son Dickie greeted him at the door, following his record Sunday output of five homers a few years ago: "Gee, Dad, they must have been giving you fat pitches."

Eddie Stanky once said, "When it comes to team value, to playing when hurt, to trying for that extra base, Stan is in a class by himself." All his other Cardinal managers, Billy Southworth, Eddie Dyer, Marty Marion, Harry Walker and now Fred Hutchinson, share that viewpoint.

His St. Louis teammates obviously do, too, for they recently gave him a plaque which said, among other things: "He's a gentleman in every respect, the perfect answer to a manager's prayer."

His is something of a rags-to-riches story, since Stan, the current 100-grand man, is the son of a Polish immigrant who toted wire bundles in suburban Pittsburgh and a New York-born Czechoslovakian mother who sorted nails in a lumber mill.

And from those simple beginnings to his current place on Easy Street those who know him best note only two changes:

"He has more polish," says Lillian, the high-school sweetheart whom Stan married when he was still playing for peanuts in the bush leagues. "The only difference is he hits the ball farther," says Red Schoendienst, his former Card roommate.

The Musial who year in, year out murders opposing pitchers is the same one who has NEVER been ejected by a National League umpire and who once waited two hours in the winter cold of St. Louis to keep an autographing date with an out-of-town high-school band.

The fact that he diligently answers 15,000 postcards and letters a year is just another case in point.

All this fame might not have been forthcoming had it not been for his father and Burt Shotton, the old Philly-Dodger pilot.

Lukasz Musial was determined his boy should have something better in life than his own lot around smog-filled Donora, Pa. He believed one of several athletic scholarships offered to the football-able Stan provided the best means.

His eldest son had other ideas. He wanted to try professional baseball after once leaving the bat-boy ranks at 15 to pitch for the Zinc Workers town team and fan 13 rival semipros.

The father remained firm until Stan's actual tears made him relent. He signed with the St. Louis chain for $65 a month.

That was step No. 1 in the career of one of baseball's all-time hitters. No. 2 came after Stan, the pitcher, had won 18 games for Daytona Beach in 1940. His throwing arm was injured in a tumble and his future hung in the balance.

But the keen eye of Shotton, the manager of the Cards' Rochester farm in the International League, took cognizance of the manner in which Musial crouched at the plate—Ted Lyons used to say, "like a kid peeking around a corner"—and got his bat on opposing pitches.

Shotton said, "I'm going to recommend to (Branch) Rickey that you give up pitching and become an outfielder."

"I don't think I'd ever have made it as a pitcher, regardless of the injury," says Stan. But in batting there never was much doubt about the man with the hula-hip warmup and the striding swing.

In his first year as a full-time outfielder he batted .379 for Springfield, Mo., .326 for Rochester and then .426 in a late-season trial with the Cards.

From then on the course was clear, and sure to be onward and upward. His .310 average last season was the lowest of his N.L. career.

He has scored more than 100 runs eleven times, has made more than 150 hits thirteen straight seasons and his total bases have exceeded 300 twelve times in a row. He has driven in more than 100 runs nine seasons and has topped 20 homers nine times, too.

This season, nearing 37, the usually slow-starting Musial was winging away at a mighty .370 clip after two months of play.

From his $65-a-month start, he now earns close to $125,000 a year from his salary, endorsements, a restaurant partnership in St. Louis and his office of bank director.

Brooklyn fans, always rabid but appreciative of a great opponent, named the Cards' No. 6 "The Man" a long time ago. And no one has seen fit to change the alias.

As Tommy Henrich said when the two appeared on the same program in Minneapolis:

"That's just what he is. The Man."

THIS chapter from Frank Graham's exceptional book *The New York Yankees* marks the beginning of an unparalleled era in baseball history. From 1936 through 1951, the Yankees, with DiMaggio, won eleven pennants and ten World Series. Only two of those ten Series (interestingly enough, both vs. the Giants) went as far as six games. It might have been even worse. Three of the five seasons in which they failed to win pennants during the DiMaggio era were the war and immediate postwar years of 1944, '45 and '46, when for part or all of the time Dimag and others were in service.

The Window Breakers

FRANK GRAHAM

1

MEANWHILE, IN San Francisco, a young Italian by the name of Joseph Paul Di-Maggio had set fire to the Pacific Coast League. His father and an older brother, Tom, were fishermen. But Joe and another brother, Vince —and a very little brother named Dominick— wanted to be ballplayers; and every time they could get away from the boats or the fish wharves, they played in Golden Gate Park or on the neighborhood playgrounds. Vince and Joe played with amateur and professional teams, and in 1932 Vince was signed as an outfielder by the San Francisco club and farmed out to Tucson in the Arizona-Texas League. Recalled by the Seals late in the season, he arranged for a trial for Joe, who was then an infielder. Joe played in three games, made a couple of hits, and at the end of the season was ordered to report in the spring.

Later, Lefty Gomez said in the Yankee clubhouse one day in Joe's presence:

"Nice boy, this DiMaggio. His brother gets him a trial with the Seals—and he beats his brother out of his job."

"I didn't," Joe said.

"No," Gomez said. "I guess not. You were together on the club in the spring of 1933, weren't you?"

"Yes."

"Vince was a regular in the outfield, wasn't he?"

"Yes."

"And after a while you were a regular?"

"Yes."

"And whose place did you take?"

"Well, but . . ."

"But what?"

"I don't know."

"You don't know! What happened to Vince?"

"Hollywood bought him."

Gomez howled.

"How do you like that! 'Hollywood bought him!' You mean the Seals sold him to Hollywood to make room for you."

Turning to his amused listeners he said: "You see? He is nothing but an ungrateful bum who beat his brother out of a job."

Seriously, by the spring of 1934, Joe Di-Maggio was the most talked-of player in the Coast League or, for that matter, in any minor league. Major-league scouts looked at him, were entranced with what they saw, and promptly wired to their employers, urging them to buy him. He had hit safely in sixty-one consecutive games while rolling up an average of .340 in 1933. Now he was hitting .360 or better. The major-league clubs began to bid for him. Charles Graham, owner of the Seals, was in no hurry to sell him. The longer he waited, the more hits Joe got, the higher the bids would go. Up they went—$50,000, $60,000, $75,000.

One day the Seals were playing in Seattle where Dutch Ruether was managing the club. Before the game, the Seattle trainer said to Joe:

"Dutch wants to know if you ever had any trouble with your left leg."

"No," Joe said. "Why?"

"He says you drag it a little when you run."

"Tell him he's nuts," Joe said. "I never hurt it, and I don't drag it."

The trainer returned to the Seattle dugout. In a few minutes he was back.

"Dutch says he ain't nuts," he said.

Joe looked across to where the veteran sat, peering at him.

"I still say you're nuts!" he yelled.

The Dutchman shrugged.

A week later the Seals were at home.

"I had a date for dinner at my sister's house," Joe recalled, a couple of years later, "and the game dragged, so I was in a hurry to get there. As my cab pulled up at her door, I jumped out —and my left knee popped like a pistol. I swear you could have heard it down the block."

They heard it in New York . . . in Boston . . . in Chicago . . . in Cleveland . . . in all the towns whence the bids on him had come. They wanted no part of him now. The great young ballplayer had a trick knee that popped like a pistol.

He had to be helped into his sister's house, and from there to a hospital. It was a couple of weeks before he returned to the line-up. When he did, he was playing for Sweeney, so far as the scouts were concerned. All, that is, save one.

Bill Essick watched him closely, saw that his speed was unimpaired, that he ran not only as swiftly but as easily as before, that he pivoted smoothly at the plate.

"Don't give up on DiMaggio," he said to Barrow over the telephone one night. "Everybody out here thinks I'm crazy, but I'm not. I still think he's all right. Let me watch him for a couple of weeks more, and I'll have the final answer on him."

Barrow had great faith in the scout.

"All right, Bill," he said, "stick with him."

About two weeks later, Essick called him again.

"Buy DiMaggio," he said. "I think you can get him cheap. They're all laughing at me, but I know I'm right."

Barrow called Graham.

"How much do you want for DiMaggio?" he asked.

"Forty thousand dollars."

"I'll give you twenty."

"Not a chance," Graham said.

They went on from there. Graham knew that no other major-league club was willing to take a chance on the boy. He also knew that Barrow knew it. He put up a battle as long as he could for $40,000, but finally settled for

$25,000. It was the greatest buy in the history of modern baseball.

In consenting to sell the player, Graham made one proviso to which Barrow readily assented. This was that DiMaggio was to remain with the Seals through 1935 and report to the Yankees in the spring of 1936.

Joe hit .341 in 1934, and in 1935 he fairly roared through the league. He hit .398, and included in his 270 blows were 48 doubles, 18 triples, and 34 home runs. His name was in the headlines not only in the towns up and down the Coast but all over the country. Barrow had hung up another score. He not only had given the boy another year of minor-league baseball to fit him for the majors, but had reaped nationwide publicity for this fledgling Yankee.

One night in Detroit during the World Series in 1935, a Seattle newspaperman looked up one of the baseball writers from New York.

"Dutch Ruether told me to see you," he said. "He told me that you are a good friend of his and that he wanted you to have the right steer on DiMaggio. He said to tell you not to be afraid to go out on a limb for this fellow, because he is a great ballplayer.

" 'Tell him,' he said, 'that DiMaggio is more than just a great hitter. Everybody talks about his hitting, but he is the best center fielder since Tris Speaker and can throw better than Speaker could the best day he ever saw.' "

2

But back to New York, and the spring of 1935, and the Yankees moving into a pennant fight without Babe Ruth for the first time since 1920.

McCarthy was easier in mind than he had been at any time since he had taken command of the Yankees. Now—and only now, with Ruth out of the way—could he make this ball club his club. Smart enough to know from the beginning that as long as the Babe was at the Stadium he would be the dominant figure, and much too smart to tangle with him in the open, Joe had waged a silent war of attrition with the Babe. At long last he had won.

Now, however, he had to prove that the Yankees could win without the Babe. The indications were that they could. The Tigers had suffered a terrific loss of prestige in the 1934 World Series with the Cardinals. No one seemed to remember the great fight they had made to win the pennant. All anyone seemed to recall clearly was that they had folded miserably before the charge of the Cardinals, losing the final game 11 to 0, and reeling from the field almost deafened by the booing of their own fans. If that was the only team the Yankees had to beat to win the flag, the odds seemed in their favor. And, as it turned out, that was the only team.

Through the first couple of weeks of the season, the Yanks bobbed up and down, but with the coming of May they were straightened out and by the end of the month they had knocked out the front-running Indians and White Sox and were in the lead. If Gehrig had been hitting and if Gomez had been pitching with his usual effectiveness, it would have looked like a breeze. But Lou was lagging, and Gomez was in and out.

McCarthy was scowling, Barrow was grumbling, and Ruppert was fretful. Both Lou and Lefty had made a trip around the world, setting out with the Babe, campaigning through the Orient with him and then separating, each following his own route in his own time from Yokohama around to New York. The popular verdict, in which McCarthy, Barrow, and Ruppert shared—perhaps, even, inspired—was that the young men had had too much baseball and too much touring and were tired when they reached the training camp. Gehrig tended to smash that theory by quickening his pace at the bat—there never had been anything wrong with his fielding—as the season advanced. But it might have fitted Lefty's case, at that. He never did catch up.

Anyway, that was the way they were as they headed into June. Selkirk, Chapman, and Combs in the outfield. Gehrig at first base. Lazzeri playing most of the time at second but giving over now and then to Heffner or Saltzgaver. Rolfe at third. Crosetti at shortstop. Dickey doing almost all the catching, with Arndt Jorgens or Joe Glenn to relieve him. Gomez, Ruffing, Allen, DeShong, Murphy, Johnny Broaca, and Vito Tamulis cutting up the heavy duty in the box.

But now the Tigers were on the loose again. The Yankees held on through June and most of July, but as July faded the Yanks faded with it, and before the month was out the Tigers were on top. Combs had recovered from his injuries of the year before, but he was playing his twelfth season in the big show, and he was wearing out fast. McCarthy benched him and switched Chapman to center field, using Hoag or the speedy Jesse Hill in left. Crosetti floundered at shortstop, and McCarthy called up Nolen Richardson and Blondy Ryan (the latter famous for his "We can't lose, I'm on my way" telegram to Bill Terry on rejoining the Giants

in 1933) to help out, but neither was an improvement on Crosetti. Pat Malone, who had been the mainstay of McCarthy's pitching staff when he won the pennant with the Cubs in 1929, also responded to a call for aid but was unable to contribute much. Van Atta had failed and was released to the Browns.

The rest of the clubs practically were nowhere as the Yankees pursued the Tigers through August and September. McCarthy drove his players hard. Ruppert stamped an impatient foot. Barrow was restless in his mezzanine box seat when the team was at home, restless in his office when it was on the road. The players gave all they had to the chase. But they didn't have enough. When the final returns were in, the Tigers had won by three games.

The figures on the Yankees that year, broken down a little bit, show that Gomez, who had won twenty-five games while losing only six in 1934, had won only twelve and lost fifteen in 1935. Ruffing topped the pitchers, yet he won only sixteen games. Gehrig, in spite of his belated rush, slipped thirty-four points in his batting average and fell off by nineteen in his production of home runs.

Spotty pitching, an attack that lacked sustained power, and fielding that was frequently ragged—these had held the Yankees back through the last two months of the season. It galled McCarthy to know that although the Tigers had fallen off, too—winning eight less and losing five more than they had in 1934—he had been unable to beat them. It was easy for him, looking back, to see how easily the Yankees might have won four or five of the games they had lost and so have won the pennant.

They were dark days for him. It was no consolation to him to know that in five seasons in New York he had not finished worse than second, and that he had won one pennant. That pennant was beginning to look a little tattered to him by now. All he could think of was that four times he had finished second—he who didn't like to finish second.

Could he have looked ahead, around the bend of winter, to another season, he would have been happy as he sat before his fireplace on Gates Circle in Buffalo, for in 1936 he was to launch an era brighter and more amazing than any major-league manager ever had known—or ever has known, up to now.

3

To begin with there was the long-awaited arrival of Joe DiMaggio at the training camp in the spring of 1936. He had made the trip across from San Francisco to St. Petersburg in a car with Lazzeri and Crosetti. That was Tony's idea. Tony didn't know Joe very well. Since Joe was only eleven years old when Tony joined the Yankees, Tony never had seen him play, but he had adopted him because he was another Italian kid off the sandlots of San Francisco, just as he had adopted Crosetti for the same reason, three years before.

It also was Tony's idea that the three of them should share the driving chore on the transcontinental haul. He took the wheel when they set out and drove steadily for four or five hours and then moved over to make room for Crosetti in the driver's seat. After Frankie had piloted the car for four or five hours, Tony motioned to Joe.

"All right," he said. "It's your turn."

"I'm sorry," Joe said. "I can't drive."

Lazzeri and Crosetti looked at each other.

"Let's throw the bum out and leave him here," Tony said.

DiMaggio settled himself more comfortably in the rear seat.

"Get going," he said, with a laugh. "I got a date with the Yankees."

It isn't likely there was much conversation on the trip. None of the three even remotely resembles a chatterbox. One day that summer Jack Mahon, International News sports writer, reported a scene featuring them in the lobby of the Hotel Chase, where the Yankees stop in St. Louis.

"I came down in the elevator," he said, "and the three of them were sitting there, watching the guests coming and going. I bought a paper and sat down near them, and after a while became aware of the fact that none of them had a word to say to the others. Just for fun, I timed them to see how long they would maintain their silence. Believe it or not, they didn't speak for an hour and twenty minutes. At the end of that time DiMaggio cleared his throat. Crosetti looked at him and said:

" 'What did you say?'

"And Lazzeri said: 'Shut up. He didn't say nothing.'

"They lapsed into silence and at the end of ten more minutes I got up and left. I couldn't stand it any more."

When they reached the clubhouse at Huggins Field the other players looked curiously at DiMaggio as Tony took him around and introduced him. DiMaggio was pleasant but silent, merely smiling as he shook hands with his new teammates. The only one who said anything to

him beyond "Pleased to meet you" was Ruffing. Charlie looked at him quizzically, grinned, and said:

"So you're the great DiMaggio!"

Joe gulped, Tony glared at Ruffing, and the pair went down the line of players. McCarthy, in his office at one end of the clubhouse, also looked at Joe with interest. Lazzeri left DiMaggio there, and player and manager had a brief conversation.

When DiMaggio came out, the newspapermen were there to meet him, and Tony again took over the introductions.

"What did McCarthy say to you?" the newspapermen wanted to know.

"Not much."

"Did he tell you where you would play?"

"No."

"Did you express any preference?"

"No. Wherever he wants me to play is all right with me."

"Left field is the sunfield at the Stadium. Did you ever play the sunfield?"

"No."

"Ruth never would play it."

Joe shrugged. "I'll play it if Mr. McCarthy wants me to."

"More likely he'll play you in center field."

"That's all right with me."

Once in uniform, DiMaggio convinced McCarthy, the players, and the newspapermen that the stories of his skill and power had not been exaggerated. Of course, he was hitting only batting-practice pitching and catching fungoes hit to the outfield, but the stamp of the major-league ballplayer was unmistakable.

Unmistakably, too, he was the number-one man in the camp. Gehrig, who had walked so long in the shadow of Ruth, now walked in the shadow of DiMaggio. It was, however, without envy on Gehrig's part that he saw DiMaggio usurp the place he had held so briefly since the departure of Ruth. DiMaggio moved into it without a swagger.

In good condition when he reached the camp, DiMaggio had only to take a few days of batting practice to adjust his swing and to lope around the park or shag flies to limber up his leg muscles, and he was ready for the exhibition games that the Yankees had scheduled. He had played in four of them—one with the Reds, one with the Braves, and two with the Cardinals— when he injured his left foot.

Earle Painter, the Yankee trainer, examined the injury.

"A couple of days of rest and a little diathermy will fix that up," he said.

The second day, as Joe sat with the foot under a lamp, something went wrong with a gadget. Before he realized it and before Painter was aware of what had happened, the foot was burned. A doctor was called, who shook his head after the examination.

"This man will not be able to play for two or three weeks at the least," he said.

The Yankees were about to break camp.

"You may as well go on to New York," McCarthy said to DiMaggio. "There would be no sense in taking you on the tour with us."

And so the great DiMaggio, a day or two later, limped into New York, his burned foot encased in a carpet slipper, as his teammates hammered their way up along the exhibition trail.

4

The day the Yankees opened the season at the Stadium—they had already played in Washington—there was a fellow seated back of first base who yelled, all through the game:

"Where's Joe DiMaggio?"

No one took the trouble to tell him, but Joe was at the office of the Yankees' physician, having his burned foot treated.

Babe Ruth, in his familiar fawn-colored overcoat, with cap to match, sat in a field box near the dugout, looking on at a Yankee opening for the first time. It was a dismal day, atmospherically and otherwise. The sky was gray, a cold wind swept the stands, and the Yankees couldn't hit Lefty Grove, who was pitching for the Red Sox. They couldn't field, either; and Ruffing, opposed to Grove, never had a chance to win.

There was little reason to believe, that day, that the Yankees could beat out the Tigers, finally accepted as real champions after their defeat of the Cubs in the 1935 World Series. There even was some doubt at the time that they could beat out the Red Sox, strengthened by the presence of Jimmy Foxx on first base. And yet, three weeks later, they were in first place. Almost overnight they had clicked. They were a smash hit. They were terrific.

DiMaggio was in the line-up now. He had never seen major-league pitching before, but he was hitting it as though he had been looking at it for years and had reeled off a string of sixteen consecutive games in which he made one or more safe drives. He had never played a sunfield before, but he was playing the difficult sunfield at the Stadium as though he had grown up in it, Combs definitely having retired as an active player to become a coach with the

team and McCarthy having kept Chapman in center with Selkirk in right. This gave the Yankees the best outfield they had had since Ruth, Combs, and Meusel were at the peak—and yet McCarthy was looking curiously at the temperamental Chapman and, perhaps, even then framing in his mind a deal for a replacement for him.

Gehrig, of course, was at first base. Lazzeri at second base and Crosetti at shortstop, were in top form once more. Rolfe, a sounder and steadier player than he had been the year before, was doing a grand job at third base. Dickey never had been quite as good and was pounding the ball. Bump Hadley and Monte Pearson, newcomers on the pitching staff, were winning consistently. So were Ruffing, Gomez, Broaca, and Brown. Murphy and the veteran Malone were solid relief men.

The Yankees mauled the Red Sox, the only threat in the East, then went West and mopped up the Tigers and the Indians. As they hurtled through June, there was no doubt that they were going to win the pennant. The baseball writers called them the new Murderers' Row. They hammered the ball against the fences and over the fences. They drove enemy pitchers to cover and frightened the infielders.

Eddie Brannick, secretary of the Giants, saw them play one day, and when somebody asked him what he thought of them he summed them up in two words.

"Window breakers," he said.

DiMaggio's popularity was tremendous. As they had done when Lazzeri had first worn a Yankee uniform nine years before, Italian fans poured into the ball parks all over the circuit to see the new hero. Dinners and parties were given in his honor. Gifts awaited him everywhere he went. One day Barrow, fearing his head might be turned by the clamor, called him to his office and gave him some excellent advice.

"Don't take the applause too seriously, Joe," he said, "and don't become overanxious in your efforts to hold to the pace you have struck."

"Don't worry about me, Mr. Barrow," Joe said. "I never get excited."

Not only his words but his tone convinced Barrow that he needn't go any further.

In June McCarthy traded Chapman to Washington for Jake Powell. On the face of it, it wasn't an even trade, and McCarthy was criticized for it. But he knew what he was doing. Chapman, for all his natural ability, was not McCarthy's type of ballplayer—and Powell was. Ben was hotheaded, quarrelsome, and at times would sulk. Powell was tough and hard-talking, but he played earnestly every time he walked on the field and never got into jams with his teammates. He took orders unquestioningly and slipped easily into the spot McCarthy had prepared for him. This was left field, DiMaggio being moved to center because he covered a wider range of territory than Jake.

By August the other clubs in the league had folded under the impact of the Yankees' continued assaults. And on September 9 the Yanks clinched the pennant, thereby setting an American League record, for never before had a club settled the issue as early as that. Smashing on, they finished the season nineteen and a half games in front of the second-place Tigers.

Dickey led the team in batting with an average of .362. Gehrig hit .354, DiMaggio .323, Rolfe .319, Selkirk .308. Only three regulars failed to hit .300—and Powell missed by only one point, while Crosetti's average was .288 and Lazzeri's .287. The home-run yield was startling. Gehrig accounted for forty-nine, DiMaggio for twenty-nine, Dickey for twenty-two, Selkirk for eighteen, Crosetti for fifteen, Lazzeri for fourteen, Rolfe for ten, and Powell for eight. Besides, DiMaggio and Rolfe each collected fifteen triples.

Ruffing won twenty games and Pearson won nineteen. Hadley won fourteen, and Gomez thirteen. Brown and the somewhat ancient Malone each came up with twelve. Murphy tagged along with twelve, but he had saved a number of games that didn't appear in his won-and-lost totals.

5

That year there was a revival of the World Series on the subway. The Giants had crashed through in the National League. Thirteen years had elapsed since the Yankees and Giants last had clashed with the title hanging on the line, and the town was ready for their meeting. A new generation of fans had grown up at the Stadium and the Polo Grounds, and the excitement was as great, or almost as great, as it had been back in 1921, when the first series between the teams had been played.

This series opened at the Polo Grounds, with Ruffing pitching against Carl Hubbell. It was a miserable day for a game. Rain fell intermittently as the afternoon wore on, but Hubbell pitched so magnificently through the rain and mud that the Yankees never had a real chance to beat him. For seven innings Ruffing pitched well, too, so that going into the eighth the score was 2 to 1 in the Giants' favor. But there Ruff-

ing weakened, and the Giants, aided by errors by Crosetti and Dickey, rushed four runs over the plate to win by a score of 6 to 1.

Hubbell's screwball magic had throttled the Yankee power, and in the second game Bill Terry sent Hal Schumacher to the mound, hoping that Hal's fast ball would be equally effective. But it wasn't. President Franklin Delano Roosevelt was in the stands that day, seated in a box near the Giants' dugout, and the Yankees put on a breathtaking show for him, hammering Schumacher, Coffman, Gabler, and Gumbert for seventeen hits, including home runs by Dickey and Lazzeri—Tony's came with the bases filled in the ninth inning—and winning by a score of 18 to 4. Gomez, who pitched for the Yankees, had such a soft time of it that once he actually ignored the hitter and, stepping out of the box, calmly watched a transport plane flying over the grounds.

Ten World Series records for a single game were broken or tied in this engagement. Lazzeri was the second player to hit a home run with the bases filled, Elmer Smith of Cleveland having achieved that feat in the 1920 series with the Dodgers. Lazzeri and Dickey, each driving in five runs, beat the record held by nine players, one being Lazzeri himself. Crosetti equaled a mark jointly held by Ruth and Combs by scoring four runs. DiMaggio tied Ott of the Giants and Orsatti of the Cardinals by making three put-outs in one inning. No team ever had made as many as eighteen runs, thirteen having been the record. No two teams had ever made a total of twenty-two runs. Every player on the Yankees made a hit and scored a run. The teams gathered a total of sixteen bases on balls. Leiber, with eight, had the most chances accepted by a center fielder. And, which wasn't at all surprising, it was the longest series game ever played, dragging through two hours and forty-nine minutes.

The scene was shifted to the Stadium the following day, and there Fred Fitzsimmons, pitching for the Giants, lost a heartbreaker. Fitz hooked up with Hadley, and the pair of them went to the eighth inning with the score tied at 1-1, Gehrig having hit a homer in the second inning and Jimmy Ripple of the Giants having hit one in the fifth. Then, in the eighth, Selkirk opened with a single to right, Powell walked, and Lazzeri moved them along with a sacrifice. Ruffing was sent up to hit for Hadley and slapped weakly to Fitzsimmons, who threw Selkirk out at the plate. Now came the break. Crosetti hit a high bounder just to the right of the box; and, as Fitz was perhaps the best fielding pitcher in baseball at the time, it seemed an easy chance for him. But the ball glanced off his glove for a scratch hit, and Powell raced home with what proved to be the winning run. Fitz, tears of rage in his eyes, got rid of Rolfe to close out the inning; but Malone, who pitched the ninth inning for the Yankees, turned the Giants back scoreless.

After the game a reporter who covered the Yankees regularly said to McCarthy in the clubhouse:

"I was rooting for you, as you know. But I felt sorry for Fitz."

Joe nodded. "To tell you the truth," he said, "I did, too."

Hubbell came back to pitch the fourth game, drawing Pearson as his opponent, but this time he could not foil the Yankees. A home run by Gehrig, jammed into a third-inning attack that yielded three runs, really sewed up the game, the Yankees winning, 5 to 2.

The Giants struck back in the fifth game, winning 5 to 4 in ten innings as Schumacher, pitching doggedly all the way, took a decision over Ruffing and Malone. Selkirk hit a home run in this game, but it didn't matter. A double by Joe Moore, a sacrifice by Bartell, and a long fly by Terry decided the game in the tenth.

But that was the end of the Giants' resist-ance, and the series ended in the sixth game, played at the Polo Grounds. For eight innings this combat was a thriller, with Gomez and Murphy tussling against Fitzsimmons and Castleman in the box, but Castleman was removed for a pinch hitter in the eighth and, with Coffman pitching for the Giants in the ninth, there was a sudden outbreak of Yankee power, and seven runs clattered over the plate as the Giants were counted out, 13 to 5.

It was a triumph for McCarthy in more ways than one. Not only had the Yankees established themselves once more at the top of the heap; but Powell, lightly regarded by some of the critics right up to the time of the series, played a whale of a game in the outfield—and hit .455. Rolfe hit .400, and DiMaggio .346. Seven home runs had splattered into the stands, Gehrig and Selkirk getting two each, and Powell, Lazzeri, and Dickey one.

Ruppert was happier than he had been since 1932. Barrow no longer was restless. At his desk in the office on Forty-second Street he hummed an old-time tune as he cleaned up his correspondence preparatory to a hunting trip with Paul Krichell. In the newspapers McCarthy was being hailed as the greatest manager in baseball.

THE appearance of the story "The Redheaded Outfield" in the first *Fireside Book of Baseball* brought an occasional gasp from readers who thought that its author, Zane Grey, was all Wild West. Of course, he wasn't. He was a pro ballplayer in his own right for a time, and loved the game. Here's another of his famous diamond stories—one of the few, we think, ever written with a fan as the central character. This is a real old-time story. You can see this to be true from the fact that in those days the home team came to bat first—let alone that you could get into the ball park for a quarter.

Old Well-Well

ZANE GREY

HE BOUGHT a ticket at the 25-cent window, and, edging his huge bulk through the turnstile, laboriously followed the noisy crowd toward the bleachers. I could not have been mistaken. He was Old Well-Well, famous from Boston to Baltimore as the greatest baseball fan in the East. His singular yell had pealed into the ears of five hundred thousand worshipers of the national game and would never be forgotten.

At sight of him I recalled a friend's baseball talk. "You remember Old Well-Well? He's all in—dying, poor old fellow! It seems young Burt, whom the Phillies are trying out this spring, is Old Well-Well's nephew and protégé. Used to play on the Murray Hill team—a speedy youngster. When the Philadelphia team was here last, Manager Crestline announced his intention to play Burt in center field. Old Well-Well was too ill to see the lad get his tryout. He was heartbroken and said, 'If I could only see one more game!'"

The recollection of this random baseball gossip and the fact that Philadelphia was scheduled to play New York that very day gave me a sudden desire to see the game with Old Well-Well. I did not know him, but where on earth were introductions as superfluous as on the bleachers? It was a very easy matter to catch up with him. He walked slowly, leaning hard on a cane, and his wide shoulders sagged as he puffed along. I was about to make some pleasant remark concerning the prospects of a fine game, when the sight of his face shocked

me and I drew back. If ever I had seen shadow of pain and shade of death they hovered darkly around Old Well-Well.

No one accompanied him; no one seemed to recognize him. The majority of that merry crowd of boys and men would have jumped up wild with pleasure to hear his well-remembered yell. Not much longer than a year before, I had seen ten thousand fans rise as one man and roar a greeting to him that shook the stands. So I was confronted by a situation strikingly calculated to rouse my curiosity and sympathy.

He found an end seat on a row at about the middle of the right-field bleachers and I chose one across the aisle and somewhat behind him. No players were yet in sight. The stands were filling up and streams of men were filing into the aisles of the bleachers and piling over the benches. Old Well-Well settled himself comfortably in his seat and gazed about him with animation. There had come a change to his massive features. The hard lines had softened; the patches of gray were no longer visible; his cheeks were ruddy; something akin to a smile shone on his face as he looked around, missing no detail of the familiar scene.

During the practice of the home team Old Well-Well sat still with his big hands on his knees; but when the gong rang for the Phillies, he grew restless, squirming in his seat and half rose several times. I divined the importuning of his old habit to greet his team with the yell that had made him famous. I expected him to get up; I waited for it. Gradually, however, he became quiet as a man governed by severe self-restraint and directed his attention to the Philadelphia center fielder.

At a glance I saw that the player was new to me and answered the newspaper description of young Burt. What a lively-looking athlete! He was tall, lithe, yet sturdy. He did not need to chase more than two fly balls to win me. His graceful, fast style reminded me of the great Curt Welch. Old Well-Well's face wore a rapt expression. I discovered myself hoping Burt would make good; wishing he would rip the boards off the fence; praying he would break up the game.

It was Saturday, and by the time the gong sounded for the game to begin the grandstand and bleachers were packed. The scene was glittering, colorful, a delight to the eye. Around the circle of bright faces rippled a low, merry murmur. The umpire, grotesquely padded in front by his chest protector, announced the batteries, dusted the plate, and, throwing out a white ball, sang the open-sesame of the game: "Play!"

Then Old Well-Well arose as if pushed from his seat by some strong propelling force. It had been his wont always when play was ordered or in a moment of silent suspense, or a lull in the applause, or a dramatic pause when hearts beat high and lips were mute, to bawl out over the listening, waiting multitude his terrific blast: "Well-Well-Well!"

Twice he opened his mouth, gurgled and choked, and then resumed his seat with a very red, agitated face; something had deterred him from his purpose, or he had been physically incapable of yelling.

The game opened with White's sharp bounder to the infield. Wesley had three strikes called on him, and Kelly fouled out to third base. The Phillies did no better, being retired in one, two, three order. The second inning was short and no tallies were chalked up. Brain hit safely in the third and went to second on a sacrifice. The bleachers began to stamp and cheer. He reached third on an infield hit that the Philadelphia shortstop knocked down but could not cover in time to catch either runner. The cheer in the grandstand was drowned by the roar in the bleachers. Brain scored on a fly ball to left. A double along the right foul line brought the second runner home. Following that the next batter went out on strikes.

In the Philadelphia half of the inning young Burt was the first man up. He stood left-handed at the plate and looked formidable. Duveen, the wary old pitcher for New York, to whom this new player was an unknown quantity, eyed his easy position as if reckoning on a possible weakness. Then he took his swing and threw the ball. Burt never moved a muscle and the umpire called strike. The next was a ball, the next a strike; still Burt had not moved.

"Somebody wake him up!" yelled a wag in the bleachers. "He's from Slumbertown, all right, all right!" shouted another.

Duveen sent up another ball, high and swift. Burt hit straight over the first baseman, a line drive that struck the front of the right-field bleachers.

"Peacherino!" howled a fan.

Here the promise of Burt's speed was fulfilled. Run! He was fleet as a deer. He cut through first like the wind, settled to a driving stride, rounded second, and by a good, long slide beat the throw in to third. The crowd, who went to games to see long hits and daring runs, gave him a generous hand-clapping.

Old Well-Well appeared on the verge of apoplexy. His ruddy face turned purple, then black; he rose in his seat; he gave vent to smothered gasps; then he straightened up and clutched his hands into his knees.

Burt scored his run on a hit to deep short, an infielder's choice, with the chances against retiring a runner at the plate. Philadelphia could not tally again that inning. New York blanked in the first of the next. For their opponents, an error, a close decision at second favoring the runner, and a single to right tied the score. Bell of New York got a clean hit in the opening of the fifth. With no one out and chances for a run, the impatient fans let loose. Four subway trains in collision would not have equaled the yell and stamp in the bleachers. Maloney was next to bat and he essayed a bunt. This the fans derided with hoots and hisses. No team work, no inside ball for them.

"Hit it out!" yelled a hundred in unison.

"Home run!" screamed a worshiper of long hits.

As if actuated by the sentiments of his admirers, Maloney lined the ball over short. It looked good for a double; it certainly would advance Bell to third, maybe home. But no one calculated on Burt. His fleetness enabled him to head the bounding ball. He picked it up cleanly and checking his headlong run, threw toward third base. Bell was halfway there. The ball shot straight and low with terrific force and beat the runner to the bag.

"What a great arm!" I exclaimed, deep in my throat. "It's the lad's day! He can't be stopped."

The keen newsboy sitting below us broke the amazed silence in the bleachers.

"Wot d'ye tink o' that?"

Old Well-Well writhed in his seat. To him it was a one-man game, as it had come to be for me. I thrilled with him; I gloried in the making good of his protégé; it got to be an effort on my part to look at the old man, so keenly did his emotion communicate itself to me.

The game went on, a close, exciting, brilliantly fought battle. Both pitchers were at their best. The batters batted out long flies, low liners, and sharp grounders; the fielders fielded these difficult chances without misplay. Opportunities came for runs, but no runs were scored for several innings. Hopes were raised to the highest pitch only to be dashed astonishingly away. The crowd in the grandstand swayed to every pitched ball; the bleachers tossed like surf in a storm.

To start the eighth, Stranathan of New York tripled along the left foul line. Thunder burst from the fans and rolled swellingly around the field. Before the hoarse yelling, the shrill hooting, the hollow stamping had ceased, Stranathan made home on an infield hit. Then bedlam broke loose. It calmed down quickly, for the fans sensed trouble between Binghamton, who had been thrown out in the play, and the umpire, who was waving him back to the bench.

"You dizzy-eyed old woman, you can't see straight!" called Binghamton.

The umpire's reply was lost, but it was evident that the offending player had been ordered out of the grounds.

Binghamton swaggered along the bleachers while the umpire slowly returned to his post. The fans took exception to the player's objection and were not slow in expressing it. Various witty encomiums, not to be misunderstood, attested to the bleachers' love of fair play and their disgust at a player's getting himself put out of the game at a critical stage.

The game proceeded. A second batter had been thrown out. Then two hits in succession looked good for another run. White, the next batter, sent a single over second base. Burt scooped the ball on the first bounce and let drive for the plate. It was another extraordinary throw. Whether ball or runner reached home base first was most difficult to decide. The umpire made his sweeping wave of hand and the breathless crowd caught his decision.

"Out!"

In action and sound the circle of bleachers resembled a long curved beach with a mounting breaker thundering turbulently high.

"Rob-b-ber-r!" bawled the outraged fans, betraying their marvelous inconsistency.

Old Well-Well breathed hard. Again the wrestling of his body signified an inward strife. I began to feel sure that the man was in a mingled torment of joy and pain, that he fought the maddening desire to yell because he knew he had not the strength to stand it. Surely, in all the years of his long following of baseball he had never had the incentive to express himself in his peculiar way that rioted him now. Surely, before the game ended he would split the winds with his wonderful yell.

Duveen's only base on balls, with the help of a bunt, a steal, and a scratch hit, resulted in a run for Philadelphia, again tying the score. How the fans raged at Fuller for failing to field the lucky scratch.

"We had the game on ice!" one cried.

"Get him a basket!"

New York men got on bases in the ninth and made strenuous efforts to cross the plate, but it was not to be. Philadelphia opened up with two scorching hits and then a double steal. Burt came up with runners on second and third. Half the crowd cheered in fair appreciation of the way fate was starring the ambitious young outfielder; the other half, dyed-in-the-wool home-team fans, bent forward in a waiting silent gloom of fear. Burt knocked the dirt out of his spikes and faced Duveen. The second ball pitched he met fairly and it rang like a bell.

No one in the stands saw where it went. But they heard the crack, saw the New York shortstop stagger and then pounce forward to pick up the ball and speed it toward the plate. The catcher was quick to tag the incoming runner, and then snap the ball to first base, completing a double play.

When the crowd fully grasped this, which was after an instant of bewilderment, a hoarse crashing roar rolled out across the field to bellow back in loud echo from Coogan's Bluff. The grandstand resembled a colored cornfield waving in a violent wind; the bleachers lost all semblance of anything. Frenzied, flinging action—wild chaos, shrieking cries—manifested sheer insanity of joy.

When the noise subsided, one fan, evidently a little longer-winded than his comrades, cried out hysterically, "O-h! I don't care what becomes of me—now-w!"

Score tied, three to three, game must go ten innings—that was the shibboleth; that was the overmastering truth. The game did go ten innings—eleven—twelve, every one marked by masterly pitching, full of magnificent catches, stops and throws, replete with reckless base-running and slides like flashes in the dust. But they were unproductive of runs. Three to three! Thirteen innings!

"Unlucky thirteenth," wailed a superstitous fan.

I had got down to plugging, and, for the first time, not for my home team. I wanted Philadelphia to win, because Burt was on the team. With Old Well-Well sitting there so rigid in his seat, so obsessed by the playing of the lad, I turned traitor to New York.

White cut a high twisting bounder inside the third base, and before the ball could be returned he stood safely on second. The fans howled with what husky voice they had left. The second hitter batted a tremendously high fly toward center field. Burt wheeled with the crack of the ball and raced for the ropes. Onward the ball soared like a sailing swallow; the fleet fielder ran with his back to the stands. What an age that ball stayed in the air! Then it lost its speed, gracefully curved and began to fall. Burt lunged forward and upward; the ball lit in his hands and stuck there as he plunged over the ropes into the crowd. White had leisurely trotted halfway to third; he saw the catch, ran back to touch second and then easily made third on the throw-in. The applause that greeted Burt proved the splendid spirit of the game. Bell placed a safe little hit over short, scoring White. Heaving, bobbing bleachers— wild, broken, roar on roar!

Score four to three—only one half inning left for Philadelphia to play—how the fans rooted for another run! A swift double play, however, ended the inning.

Philadelphia's first hitter had three strikes called on him.

"Asleep at the switch!" yelled a delighted fan.

The next batter went out on a weak pop-up fly to second.

"Nothin' to it!"

"Oh, I hate to take this money!"

"All-l o-over!"

Two men at least of all that vast assemblage had not given up victory for Philadelphia. I had not dared to look at Old Well-Well for a long while. I dreaded the next portentous moment. I felt deep within me something like clairvoyant force, an intangible belief fostered by hope.

Magoon, the slugger of the Phillies, slugged one against the left field bleachers, but, being heavy and slow, he could not get beyond second base. Cless swung with all his might at the first pitched ball, and instead of hitting it a mile as he had tried, he scratched a mean, slow, teasing grounder down the third-base line. It was as safe as if it had been shot out of a cannon. Magoon went to third.

The crowd suddenly awoke to ominous possibilities; sharp commands came from the players' bench. The Philadelphia team were howling and hopping on the sidelines and had to be put down by the umpire.

An inbreathing silence fell upon stands and field, quiet, like a lull before a storm.

When I saw young Burt start for the plate and realized it was his turn at bat, I jumped as if I had been shot. Putting my hand on Old Well-Well's shoulder, I whispered, "Burt's at bat. He'll break up this game! I know he's going to lose one!"

The old fellow did not feel my touch; he did not hear my voice; he was gazing toward the field with an expression on his face to which no human speech could render justice. He knew what was coming. It could not be denied him in that moment.

How confidently young Burt stood up to the plate! None except a natural hitter could have had his position. He might have been Wagner for all he showed of the tight suspense of that crisis. Yet there was a tense alert poise to his head and shoulders which proved he was alive to his opportunity.

Duveen plainly showed he was tired. Twice he shook his head to his catcher, as if he did not want to pitch a certain kind of ball. He had to use extra motion to get his old speed, and he delivered a high straight ball that Burt fouled over the grandstand. The second ball met a similar fate. All the time the crowd maintained that strange waiting silence. The umpire threw out a glistening white ball, which Duveen rubbed in the dust and spat upon. Then he wound himself up into a knot, slowly unwound, and, swinging with effort, threw for the plate.

Burt's lithe shoulders swung powerfully. The meeting of ball and bat fairly cracked. The low driving hit lined over second a rising, glittering streak and went far beyond the center fielder.

Bleachers and stands uttered one short cry, almost a groan, and then stared at the speeding runners. For an instant, approaching doom could not have been more dreaded. Magoon scored. Cless was rounding second when the ball lit. If Burt was running swiftly when he turned first he had only got started, for then his long sprinter's stride lengthened and quickened. At second he was flying; beyond second he seemed to merge into a gray flitting shadow.

I gripped my seat strangling the uproar within me. Where was the applause? The fans were silent, choked as I was, but from a different cause. Cless crossed the plate with the score that defeated New York; still the tension never laxed until Burt beat the ball home in as beautiful a run as ever thrilled an audience.

In the bleak dead pause of amazed disappointment Old Well-Well lifted his hulking figure and loomed, towered over the bleachers. His wide shoulders spread, his broad chest expanded, his breath whistled as he drew it in. One fleeting instant his transfigured face shone with a glorious light. Then, as he threw back his head and opened his lips, his face turned purple, the muscles of his cheeks and jaw rippled and strung, the veins on his forehead swelled into bulging ridges. Even the back of his neck grew red.

"Well! Well! Well!"

Ear-splitting stentorian blast! For a moment I was deafened. But I heard the echo ringing from the cliff, a pealing clarion call, beautiful and wonderful, winding away in hollow reverberation, then breaking out anew from building to building in clear concatenation.

A sea of faces whirled in the direction of that long-unheard yell. Burt had stopped statuelike as if stricken in his tracks; then he came running, darting among the spectators who had leaped the fence.

Old Well-Well stood a moment with slow glance lingering on the tumult of emptying bleachers, on the moving mingling colors in the grandstand, across the green field to the gray-clad players. He staggered forward and fell.

Before I could move, a noisy crowd swarmed about him, some solicitous, many facetious. Young Burt leaped the fence and forced his way into the circle. Then they were carrying the old man down to the field and toward the clubhouse.

I waited until the bleachers and field were empty. When I finally went out there was a crowd at the gate surrounding an ambulance. I caught a glimpse of Old Well-Well. He lay white and still, but his eyes were open, smiling intently. Young Burt hung over him with a pale and agitated face. Then a bell clanged and the ambulance clattered away.

HERE is a great (and prize-winning) piece of baseball journalism. I venture to suspect you will read it, and it will stay with you, and you will read it many times again. It says a lot—not only about baseball or a baseball player.

The Long Ride Home

MILTON GROSS

IT IS ONLY 35 miles and 70 minutes between Ebbets Field and Colonia, N. J., but for Don Newcombe it was a lifetime. This was his longest voyage home and he wept all the way.

He drove his Ford station wagon with his right hand and with his left he held a handkerchief to his face. Sometimes he put it to his mouth, sometimes to his eyes and sometimes he dropped it on the seat between his legs. He balled it into his fist or he rolled it between his fingers and always he stared straight ahead, almost unseeing, because there was a mist before his eyes and memories he cannot erase.

Only Newcombe knew the gnawing pain within him, the doubts, the anger, the confusion and frustration of the pitcher who was reached for two home runs by Yogi Berra and one by Elston Howard, which beat the Dodgers yesterday.

But it was more than the game and the Series that went with it, more than being KO'd by the Yankees twice within a week and five times in a career. It was so much more than the conviction that he had good stuff and threw hard and courageously. It was a man being torn apart worse inwardly than he was on the field by forces beyond his control. It was a giant of a man, who needed the comforting of a child.

"It's tough, Newk," said a guy standing in the parking lot as we came to Don's car, "but you can't win them all."

Last week Newcombe hit a man who needled him as he entered his car, but this time the words didn't seem to touch him.

"I'm sorry, pop," Don mumbled as we drove away.

His voice was so low, his father couldn't hear. "What?" he asked.

"I'm sorry," Don repeated.

"What have you got to be sorry for?" James Newcombe said to his son.

What, indeed? What could Newcombe say or what could his father say? And what are they all saying today? That he doesn't win the big ones . . . that he chokes when it's tough . . . that he showered hurriedly and left the field as quickly as he could after being replaced in the fourth and left his teammates to their despair.

It was all there in the car as we drove along Washington, Flatbush and Atlantic Avenues, over the Manhattan Bridge, through the Holland Tunnel and along the Pulaski Skyway. It was all unsaid and hanging heavy in the air like the load that's within Don.

"How do I get rid of it?" he seemed to be thinking. "How do I get it out of my mind? How do I stop them from thinking that?"

As a newspaperman I was intruding in a time that should have been private, but I wanted to help. I didn't have the answers, but I had compassion.

"You won 27," I said. "You know there were some big ones among them."

"Remember that," Don's father said.

"I don't want to talk," Don said. "I don't want to say anything."

So we drove along in silence, a father and a son and an outsider, who had left a World Series game before it was done for the first time in 20 years.

"Don't you want to turn the game on the radio?" I asked Don.

"Not now," he said. "Not yet."

We were at Mulberry and Broome Sts. in Manhattan when Newcombe turned on the radio. Announcer Bob Wolf's voice was saying: "After six innings it's Yanks 5, Dodgers 0.

Roger Craig now takes over the mound."

Newcombe listened, but seemed not to be listening. Twice he had to apply his brakes swiftly when his car came up on another too suddenly.

As we entered the Holland Tunnel, Billy Martin was at bat for the Yankees in the seventh, with one ball called.

The radio died under the river. "Why didn't you change your shirt and go back into the dugout?" I asked Newk because Manager Walter Alston instituted a rule last year after the Yankees KO'd Don in the opening game of the World Series that players must not leave the park before a game's completion.

"I don't know," he said. "I don't know a lot of things."

Approaching the New Jersey side, Newcombe compressed his lips. "I felt good," he said. "I was throwing hard, real hard."

The radio came alive again as we left the tunnel and Mickey Mantle walked in the seventh. "This brings up Yogi Berra with no out," Wolf said. "He has had two two-run homers and there's two aboard." There was a wild pitch, Martin going to third and Mantle to second.

"They're putting Berra on intentionally," the radio voice said, and his was the only sound in the car.

Bill Skowron was at bat. The cars whizzed by on the Pulaski Skyway. The Jersey meadows were barren and wind whipped the bulrushes when Skowron smashed his home run.

"It can happen to somebody else, too," Mr. Newcombe said, and Don merely nodded his head.

When Ed Roebuck came in and the announcer said he was Brooklyn's fourth pitcher, Don still seemed impassive. The fingers of his left hand rubbed the handkerchief he held and what was in his mind he didn't say until we left the skyway.

"In the second," he said, "after I had two and oh on (Johnny) Kucks, Jackie (Robinson) came over and asked if I was aiming the ball. I said I didn't think so."

Again we rode along in silence before I started to ask a question.

"I was getting the ball where I wanted it to go," Don said. "Except the first one Yogi hit.

"The first one," Newk said. "I tried to brush him back, but I didn't get it inside enough. When I came up in the third inning after Yogi hit the second one, he said to me: 'I hit a perfect pitch. It was perfect—low outside fast ball and I hit the hell out of it.' Mantle may hit

more, but I respect Berra more. You can strike Mantle out, but I don't know where you can throw the ball to get Berra out."

"What about our hitters?" Mr. Newcombe said. "No hits the other day, two hits yesterday and what have they got today?"

"How do you figure that Stengel?" Newk asked. "Today against me he throws in all right-handers. The way Collins hits me, too. I don't understand it. I don't know about Slaughter, but why did he take Collins out the way he hits me?"

We were outside Linden then. "Drop me off at the house," Mr. Newcombe said, and Don nodded.

Norman, the youngest of Don's four brothers, answered the ring. "Too bad, Don," he said.

In the little parlor, the TV set was still on the game, but Newk's mother was in the kitchen. "Get it over with," she said. "It's over and done."

"I'm sorry, Ma," Newk said.

"What's to be sorry," she answered.

"A couple of guys I'll have to handle tomorrow," Norman said.

Newk went to the refrigerator for two quarts of beer and poured a glass for his dad, himself and me. "Drink up," he said. "I want to call my wife."

It was the ninth inning.

"You going to work tomorrow?" Newcombe's mother asked her husband.

"I don't think so," he said.

"Why worry about it. If it happened, it happened," she said.

"No hits. No hits at all," Don's brother said. "All of a sudden nobody hits. I'm biting my nails. Look at them."

Newk came back from his phone call. "Freddy was ironing and watching the game," he said. "She said it's all right. She asked when I was coming home."

When we were on the way, I asked Newk what he had been thinking about during the entire ride.

"I was thinking about what I do wrong," he said, "but I can't put my finger on why I do it. It always happens to me in the first two innings or the last."

For a moment Newk sat silent again. "I was running in the outfield at the Stadium the other day and a guy called me a yellow-bellied slob. How do you take things like that?" Newk said, with anguish.

"Today," Newk said, "before the game, Pee Wee (Reese) said: 'I don't care what you do today. We wouldn't be here without you.'"

"And other people say I choke up," Newk said, in a voice hoarse with emotion. "I think it's rubbed off in the clubhouse."

Ahead, I could see the Pennsylvania Railroad. I had told Newcombe I'd go home with him.

"I got to pass the railroad," he said.

I sensed he didn't want me coming with him all the way, at least not this day.

"How did you sleep last night?" I asked.

"Terrible," he said. "I was up four times. I took a pill but I couldn't sleep. I told my wife what's the use keeping you awake. She said for me to go in the other room, but I tossed and turned. It wasn't today's game. It was this

other business I wanted to beat, but dammit, I can't get away from it."

We were at East Milton and Fulton in Rahway when I got out of the car. My sympathy was with this tormented man, who would give his soul to prove the big ones are like the little ones. There were five boys on the corner—four Negro and one white—and they recognized Newcombe as he drove off.

"That Newk?" one asked.

"How'd he get here so soon?" another said. "The game just ended."

"He left early," I said, and the white boy giggled.

"Don't laugh," one of the Negro boys said. "Just don't laugh."

WALT DITZEN

Courtesy National Newspaper Syndicate © 1957 by Walt Ditzen

FAN FARE

How to Pitch to Ted Williams

PAT HARMON

BIRDIE TEBBETTS tells it. "When I was catching with Detroit," recalls the Cincinnati manager, "we were never able to get Ted Williams out. Finally we hit on the idea of letting him call the pitch. Figured he hit whatever we called, so why not let him get in the act?

"His first time up, I explained our new plan to him. He thought it was a gag, but he said, 'Fast ball.'

"So I called for a fast ball, right over the plate. Ted let it go by. He wasn't sure we meant it.

"I asked him what he wanted for the next pitch, and he said 'Fast ball' again.

"So I called for the same thing. This time Ted swung. But he wasn't sure we weren't fooling him this time, so he hesitated, and he swung too late.

"That went on all day. Williams didn't get a hit in five times up. And the reason was he wasn't concentrating on the ball like he usually does. He was concentrating on what we told him, and whether we were kidding him, or were on the level."

BROTHER ACT

Four famous sets of baseball brothers. In order,

Wide World

The DiMaggios,

Wide World

The Waners, Lloyd and Paul;

Wide World

The Coopers, Walker and Mort;

Wide World

The Deans, Daffy and Dizzy.

172A

LADIES DAY

The late Babe Didrickson pitching for Cleveland in an exhibition game against New Orleans in 1934.

Jackie Mitchell, who at the age of 17 held a contract as a pitcher for the Chattanooga Lookouts of the Southern Association in 1931.

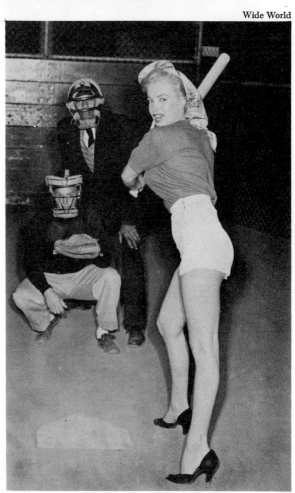

Marilyn Monroe: The Stance.

Is this pitch a floater or a sinker? Who knows? If you think this is a shot of a girls' baseball game underwater, you're right.

HERE is a chapter from Mark Harris' fine baseball novel, *Bang the Drum Slowly*. The narrator is Henry (Author) Wiggen, pitching hero of Harris' earlier novel, *The Southpaw* (*q.v.* in the first *Fireside Book of Baseball*). In the sequel—specifically, in the chapter reprinted here —Wiggen has not yet come to terms with the ball club on his season's contract. It is spring-training time. Wiggen alone knows that a teammate, Bruce Pearson, is dying of an incurable disease. The doctors have made Wiggen promise to stay close to Pearson at all times. With this background material, here is the chapter. Do you agree that the third paragraph from the last is one of the truly memorable speeches of our time?

From *Bang the Drum Slowly*

MARK HARRIS

THE TALK of the camp last spring was a kid name of Piney Woods, a wild and crazy catcher out of a place called Good Hope, Georgia, that the writers all called "Dutch's good hope from Good Hope" until it become obvious that he could not last. Back he went to QC in April, and we went into the year with the same 3 catchers we finished 54 with, Goose and Bruce and Jonah Brooks. Jonah come up from QC when Red split his finger in St. Paul, Minnesota, that time, a fine boy, just fine, always singing. 13 runs behind and he will still be singing, calling "Wing her through, Author, wing her through," and then after a good pitch singing, "Author wung her through, he wung her through," except when now and then he thought the call was wrong, and then sung, "Oh-o-o-o Lord my big black ass," his jaw always going and his mind always working, his eye everywhere, a natural catcher if ever I seen one, except he could not hit.

For a time it looked like Piney Woods might be the answer. He can hit. But he is no natural. He is too wild and crazy. He drives in motorcycle races in the winter. Dutch was looking for a combination of a natural catcher like Jonah and a hitter like Piney, and still is. I guess there is only one Red Traphagen in a lifetime.

The first few days me and Lucky Judkins sat in the stands watching the drill and lying about money, telling each other how much we were holding out for. I don't know why you lie about money. I guess you figure people figure you are lying, so you might as well. One morning Ugly Jones clumb up from the field and said, "Author, leave me give you one piece of advice. Do not hang in the park because your eye gleams and your hand itches. You are becoming anxious to play ball, and this will cost you money," which was true. I mean it was true I was becoming gleamy, I guess. Ugly is a wild old hand, veteran of many a holdout, and I went back to the house, and we swum and laid on the beach and played badminton and waited for the telephone to ring, and every time it rung I said, "This is Old Man Moors meeting my price," but it never was, and to myself I thought, "This is Bruce. The attack come." But it never was Bruce neither. It was writers, or one of the boys, or Joe Jaros wishing to play Tegwar [a card game played by members of the team—ED.]. The boys phoned a lot, or dropped by, and I kept in touch. My weight kept going up something awful.

The real bomb-burst was Lucky getting swapped to Cincinnati for F. D. R. Caselli, a right-hand pitcher and a good boy, a cousin by marriage of Gussie Petronio, the Mammoth catcher before Red, leaving me the last and only holdout. I might of went out of my mind a little if there been any left-hand pitching in camp, but there was none, 90 boys that threw with their left hand maybe, but none that threw very hard or very smart, and I sat tight.

The boys were all with me, down to the last penny.

It all dragged on so long I said to Holly ["Author's" wife—Ed.], "Am I a baseball player or only a man living on the beach at Aqua Clara?" and she said, "What difference?" Everything you said to her any more she said, "What difference?" meaning lay in the sun and enjoy life. She was happy. I never seen her so still before. She is usually always running around doing 77 things at once, hanging with the wives, reading books, studying taxes, cleaning the house, gassing on the phone, but now she done nothing only laid on the beach and looked at the waves. Now and then she took a dip and flipped over and left the waves wash her in, and then she laid on the sand again and browned up, and nights she got all dressed for Bruce.

He come down every night after work. You could see him from far off, walking along and looking at the waves and whistling "Come Josephine in My Flying Machine," which the boys all sung in honor of Piney and his stupid motorcycle. Piney himself sung it every time you asked him, closing his eyes, not laughing, thinking you loved hearing it for the singing, when the reason you loved it was he took it so serious, singing—

Come Josephine in my flying machine,
Going up she goes, up she goes.
Balance yourself like a bird on the beam,
In the air she goes, there she goes.
Up, up, a little bit higher,
Oh my, the moon is on fire.
Come Josephine in my flying machine,
Going up, goodbye, all on, goodbye.

He always dragged a stick in the sand behind him. He parked it by the door and come in and ate, salads for me mostly, and lean meat and no bread and butter and this disgusting skim milk, my weight at 209 by now and climbing a mile a minute, and when we was done we sat out back, out of the ocean breeze, until along about 10 he went around the house for his stick, and I drove him back to the Silver Palms.

In the hotel we shoved his bed around near the phone, and I wrote my number on a piece of paper and tacked it on the wall, and he said, "I hope if it happens it will not happen at a bad hour," and I said, "It might or might not probably never happen. I have no faith in those cockeyed doctors up there. But if it happens do not stop and check the time, just call me," and he said he would.

I begin selling policies to kill the time. ["Author" has a sideline as an insurance salesman.—Ed.] I drove down to St. Pete every couple days, and Tampa and Clearwater, and over to Lakeland once, never pushing, only chatting with the various boys and leaving it sell itself, which it does once you put the idea in their mind. All spring they see too many old-time ballplayers floating from camp to camp and putting the touch on old friends, maybe giving a pointer to a kid and then saying, "By the way, could you advance me 5 until the first of the month?" which kids often do, probably writing home, "Oh boy, I just had the privilege of loaning 5 to So-and-so," until after they loaned out enough 5's it did not seem so much like a privilege any more.

I drove Lucky down to Tampa the day he was traded. Lucky was the second person I ever sold an annuity to, and he said, "Well, Author, one day we will all be done working. We will just fish and look in the box once a month for the checks, me and you and Bruce and all the rest," and I almost told him, for it was getting hard to carry it around. But I smothered it back. Once you told somebody everybody would know, and once Dutch knew it would of been "Goodby, Bruce." "It is hard picturing you in a Cincinnati suit," I said. In the lobby of The Floridian I got to gassing with Brick Brickell, the manager of Cincinnati. "You are holding out serious," he said. "For what?"

"$27,500," I said.

"You will never get it," he said. Then he looked around to see if anybody was listening. "*We* would pay it," he said.

"I doubt that," I said.

"Try me," he said. "Hold out long enough and we will buy you, and I give you my verbal word we will pay you 25,000 at the least. I been trying to buy you already."

"What are they asking?" I said.

"A quarter of a million dollars and players," he said.

"What will they take?" I said.

"150,000 and players," he said.

"What will you give?" said I.

"Now, Author," he said, "I cannot reveal a thing of that sort. The trouble is that they want Sam Mott. Dutch is worried about his catching."

"Does he not worry about his left-hand pitching?" I said.

"Brooklyn will sell him Scudder," he said, "but only if you are gone, not wishing to cut their own throat."

I drove F. D. R. Caselli back with me, jabbering all the way, him I mean, and all the time he jabbered I kept making up these little conversations where Old Man Moors called me on the phone, pleading with me, "Come on and sign. I will meet your price," until I was just about ready to call him myself. But then again I told myself, "No! Do not sell yourself short!" F. D. R. had blisters on his hands, and he kept asking me what was good for them, and I told him something or other. I forget what.

* * *

All spring the wives kept pumping Holly full of miserable stories about babies born with this or that missing, and mothers suffering, which if she ever believed any of it she would of went wild. But she never believes what people say, and all that happened I kept getting as fat as a pig until what we done we bought a badminton set and played badminton all day, deductible, for my weight is a matter of business. By the middle of March I was probably the world's champion heavyweight left-hand badminton player, and still no call from the boss.

One day the club said it was definitely closing a deal with Cleveland for Rob McKenna, saying this on a Friday night for the Saturday paper and leaving no chance for anybody to deny it on Sunday, for they have no Sunday paper in Aqua Clara, and putting all the writers a little bit on the spot since they hated calling Cleveland all the way out in Arizona to check on the truth of what they already probably knew was the bunk. This scared me, though, and I went to the phone, and the instant I touched it it rung, and a voice said, "Do not touch that phone!" It was Ugly Jones. "Author," he said, "you are doing fine."

"I am fatter than a pig," I said.

"Good," he said. "That is the way to convince them, for it worries them more than it worries you. It might not even be a bad idea to show yourself around. Leave the brass see how fat you are."

What we done we went out the park the following Wednesday and sat in the stands behind first. There was about 6 left-handers warming, a few wearing QC suits that been up the spring before, the rest wearing Mammoth shirts, one kid wearing my number, 44, kids, all kids, and all full of hope.

Old Man Moors and Patricia and some automobile people up from Miami strolled in and sat down, Bradley Lord joining them soon after. Patricia said "Hello" and asked Holly how she was. Her and Holly gassed awhile, and then she went back. Old Man Moors glanced up my way, pretending he was looking over the paint job on the park, and I called for peanuts, which fat you up about a pound for a dime, and I begun munching away.

The first left-hander set George and Perry down 1-2, and the peanuts went dry in my mouth a little. Pasquale then took 2 strikes and belted one out amongst the palms, and I give a little look down at the Moorses and scarcely had time to look back when Sid hit one that fell not 4 feet from where Pasquale's went, back-to-back homers from the power factory, always a nice sight, and Canada shot a single into left, and Piney one into right. Dutch shouted, "I seen enough of that one," waving the left-hander out of there and bringing on a new one, a tall, thin kid with a dizzy habit of wearing his glove with 3 fingers out. He walked Vincent and Ugly and hit Herb Macy on the butt until when he finally found the plate George blasted one back at him that bounced off his knee and blooped out over second base, and the poor kid was lugged off on a stretcher. Another one went out the same way the same day.

Once Dutch looked up at me, and I waved. He did not wave back. He takes it as a personal insult. Behind your back he tells you, "Sure, sock it to them for every nickel you are worth," but when you do he does not like it, though he himself was a holdout more than once in his playing days, and anyhow he was quite busy waving one left-hander out and a new one in, about 5 of them before a kid come on in the sixth and struck Sid and Canada out. The Moorses begun shaking their head "Yes" between themself, Bradley Lord shaking his, too, as soon as he seen it was safe, The World's Only Living Human Spineless Skunk. This newest kid was rather fast, but no curve whatsoever, and I said to Holly, "The boys see that he has no curve by now," which they did all right. Piney and Vincent singled. Ugly stepped in, looking up my way and giving me a kind of a wink and taking a couple and then lacing a drive down the line in right that the whole park busted out laughing over because it slammed up against the fence and stuck there, this old rat-trap fence made of boards, the drive getting jammed in between 2 boards. The right fielder went over and tried to wedge it out. But it was in tight, and Ugly trotted around the bases laughing, and even Dutch was laughing, and by then the Moorses and the people from Miami were laughing, and Bradley Lord, too, seeing all the rest, and about one minute later Lindon bounced one off the same fence that knocked the first ball through, and Mr. Left-Hander Number 6 went to the shower. You really had to laugh. I mean, when a ball slams up against a fence your eye is back out on the field, looking for the rebounce, and then when it don't you think the whole world has went flooey or something, like when you drop a shoe you hear it clunk, and if no clunk comes you quick dial the madhouse. Every so often I begun to laugh, and Holly, too, and Old Man Moors turned around and give me a look, and me and Holly got up about then and yawned and stretched and bought a couple more peanuts and went home and waited for the phone to ring.

* * *

After supper it rung, and I sat beside it and left it ring 12 or 13 times until I picked it up and said in my most boring voice, "Fishing pier. Hookworms for sale," only it wasn't Old Man Moors a-tall but Joe Jaros, and he said, "Author, how about a hand of Tegwar or 2?"

I already turned him down a number of times, not wishing to hang in the hotel and look anxious, but I was in the mood now, and I said, "We will be right down."

"Who do you mean by 'we'?" he said, and I said I meant me and Bruce. "Me and Bruce been playing quite a bit all winter," I said. "He is pretty good by now," though this was not true, for he was not.

"I will stay here," said Bruce, and that settled it, at least for now, and he stood with Holly. When I got there Joe had things set up in the lobby, a table for 3, one chair for me and one for him and one empty and waiting for the slaughter. He had a pocket full of change and little bills. Next to the empty chair he stood a lamp all lit and bright, and at the empty place a clean and shining ash tray. The empty chair stood just a little sideways so a cluck could slide in easy.

He shuffled, shuffling over and over again but never dealing, just waiting for the cluck to wander in sight. Joe knew. He can spot one a block away, or walk through a dining car and spot one, or pick one out in a crowd. He been at it 30 years, and I said, "Joe, when my wife goes home Bruce must play with us."

"Sure," he said, not thinking, but then it hit home, and he said, "Now, Author, Bruce is not the type. He is too damn dumb. Anyhow, the way Piney Woods been hitting Bruce might not last the year."

"You must promise me," I said, and he prom-

ised, for right about then he seen his party and would of promised you could hang him in the morning. He got all excited. "That looks like it," he said, and we begun to deal, and in through the lobby come a big chap wearing sun glasses, though he was indoors, and though it was night, his arms all red the way a fellow gets when he never sees the sun except a couple a weeks on vacation, a big button in his coat in the shape of a fish saying FEARED IN THE DEEP that the local people hand out by the bushel to every cluck that don't actually faint dead away at the sight of the ocean. He bought a magazine and sat down in an easy chair and begun to read, soon wondering why he could not see, and then shoving his glasses up on his head, every so often peeking at us over the top of his magazine, me and Joe dealing fast and furious now, really working, too, because I will swear if you concentrate hard enough you can bring the cluck up out of his chair and over, which we soon done, for he closed his magazine and worked up his energy and hauled himself up, his sun glasses falling back down over his eyes. Over he come, sticking his magazine in his coat and leaning his hands down on the back of the empty chair and finally saying, "Would you mind if I watch?"

We never spoke nor looked up. We played Casino, your 8 takes a 5 and a 3, your 10 takes a 6 and a 4, like that, pictures taking pictures, and when the hand was done Joe flipped his wrist around and said, "A quarter of 8."

"No," said Mr. Feared In The Deep, "I said would you mind if I watch."

"Oh," said Joe, "I thought you asked me if I had a watch," not saying another word, only dealing again, straight Casino again except with a little switch here and there, maybe a 7 taking in a 5 and a 9, or a deuce an ace and a 3, Casino, only doubled, so there was still some sort of a system to it, though not too much system to the cash sliding back and forth, the cluck watching and studying, taking off his glasses and twirling them, 2 or 3 times starting to say something but then not saying it, only saying once, "It looks like Casino," neither me nor Joe answering him nor even hearing him for all he knew until after the hand I said, "Did you speak?"

"I only said it looks like Casino," he said.

"Casino?" said Joe.

"Like the card game called Casino," said Feared In The Deep.

"You mean the game they play in boarding schools for girls?" said Joe.

"I did not know it was played there," said the cluck. "I personally played Casino myself from time to time."

"We only play men's games," said Joe.

We dealed again. "Would you mind if I sat down?" said the cluck. Nobody said "No," and he sat, and he slapped his pants where his money was and looked at his watch and sort of inched his chair around until he was finally forward over the table, his eye going from my hand to Joe's, the game becoming a little more complicated now, Joe calling once, "Goddam it, fence-board!" and slapping down his hand and showing how he fence-boarded, me laughing and gathering in the money, Joe saying, "I never fence-boarded before since one time against Babe Ruth in St. Pete," the cluck really quite confused about now and ready to go back and look at his magazine.

Right about then I was paged, and Joe went red. "Hang around," he said. "Never mind it. Hang around."

"It is the boss," I said.

"So you are Henry Wiggen," said the cluck. "I seen you was left-handed but did not know who. It is quite an honor."

"I must go, Joe," I said.

"Damn it, Author. Stick around." He was boiling inside, for Tegwar is serious business to him, the great laugh of his life. He will laugh for days after a good night of Tegwar. He will tell you Tegwar stories going back 30 years, of clucks on trains and clucks in hotels, and of great Tegwar partners he had, ballplayers now long since faded from the scene, remembering clubs not half so much by what they done but how they rode with the gag, how they gathered, like the boys even at that moment were gathering for a glimpse of the big fish on the line. It is the gathering of the boys that Joe loves, for without the watching of the crowd the laugh would be hollow. It would be like playing ball to empty stands, and the page come by, saying, "Mr. Wiggen, Mr. Wiggen," and Joe said, "Scram!" and the page scrammed.

But it was no good, and the boys knew it and Joe knew it and I knew it. It takes time. The cluck has got to lay his money on the table and leave it there awhile. He has got to think about it. It has got to be the cluck's own choice every minute of the way, and he has got to hang himself, not be hung by others. It must never be hurried. Yet with the page calling we could not play it slow, though we tried.

Then soon the boys all stepped aside, and Dutch come through and said, "I been trying for days to get some sleep and finally was just drifting off when I am told you are playing cards and too busy to talk contract. Do not push things too far, Author."

"It was my fault," said Joe. "I would not leave him go," and Dutch seen the cluck there and felt sorry for Joe, or as sorry as he can ever feel, and he said so. "What good is being sorry?" said Joe, and he slammed down the cards, and he swore, and Mr. Feared In The Deep begun back-watering as fast as he could, hearing both laughing and swearing but not understanding a word, and I went on up to the Moorses sweet, feeling sorry for Joe and yet also laughing.

Nobody else was laughing but me when I got there. I said, "Leave us not waste time talking contract unless you are willing to talk contract. I was taught in school where slavery went out when Lincoln was shot."

"I know," said Old Man Moors, "for you wrote it across the top of your contract."

"Not across *my* contract," I said. "Maybe across the contract of a turnstile turner."

"Author," said Patricia, "leave us all calm down." She was very beautiful that night, and I said so, and she thanked me. Her nose was quite sunburned. "You are looking over your weight," she said. "It will no doubt take you many weeks to get in shape."

"He looks 10 pounds over his weight at least," said Bradley Lord.

"*Mr.* Bradley Lord," said I, whipping out my loose cash. "I have $200 here which says I am no more than 2 and ⅝ pounds over my weight if you would care to go and fetch the bathroom scale."

"What do you consider your absolute minimum figure?" said Mr. Moors.

"19,000," I said.

"In that case," said he, "we can simply never do business, and I suppose I must be put to the trouble of scouring up another left-hand pitcher."

"That should not be hard," said I, "for I seen several promising boys out there this afternoon. Any one of them will win 4 or 5 games if God drops everything else."

"They are top-flight boys," said Mr. Moors. "Dutch thinks extremely high of at least 3 of them. I will tell you what I will do, Wiggen. I will jack up my absolute maximum figure to 13,500 and not a penny more, and if you have a good year we will make it back to you in 56."

"And when I have a good year in 56 you will make it back to me in 57," I said, "and I will go on being paid for the year before. This shorts me out of a year in the long run."

"We heard this one before," said Bradley Lord.

"Every time Bradley Lord opens his mouth I am raising my absolute minimum figure," I said.

"Bradley," said Patricia, "go get some drinks."

"You feel very confident about this year," said Mr. Moors, "and I will tell you what I will do." He turned my contract over and begun scratching down figures. "For the 20th victory you win this year I will pay you a bonus of 2,500, and for every game over 20 I will pay you 2,000 more, and then to show you where my heart is I will jack up my absolute maximum figure to 14,000."

"We are coming closer together," said Patricia.

"I believe we are just about there," said Old Man Moors.

Bradley come back with 3 cokes, giving one to Old Man Moors and one to Patricia and keeping one for himself.

"As a starter," said I, "I like the look of the arrangement. But instead of 20 victories you must write in 15."

"If I write in 15 I must lower the amount," he said. "You are so damn-fire sure you are going to have such a top-flight year I would think you would jump at the arrangement."

"I am sure about the year I am going to have," said I, "but I am deep in the hole, owing money left and right and Holly pregnant and the high cost of Coca-Cola. I am tired living like a sharecropper."

"Bradley," said Patricia, "go get Author a coke."

Old Man Moors was sketching out the new bonus arrangement on the back of my contract, but he looked up now. "How much do you still owe the goddam Government?" he said.

"$421.89," I said.

He wrote this down on a separate sheet. "I will throw this in," he said, "plus pay you a bonus of $1,500 for the 15th victory you win this year, and 1,000 for every victory over 15. You are better off than you were under the first arrangement."

"Not if I win 25 games," I said.

"If you win 25 games I will round out Bonus Plan Number 2 to equal Number One," said he. "But you know you are not libel to win 25 games. I do not see why you are trying to heckle me. If you win 25 games I will be so

goddam pleased I will pay you a flat 5,000 bonus if I do not drop dead from surprise."

"I won 26 in 52," said I.

"Yes," said he, "but never come near it since." He mentioned my Won-and-Lost for 53 and 54, which everybody knows, so no need to repeat. Bradley Lord come back with my coke, and Old Man Moors shoved him the separate sheet, saying, "Make out a check in this amount and send it to the United States Bureau of Internal Revenue in the name of Wiggen. Very well, Henry, your base pay will be 14,000 plus Bonus Plan Number 2. I think that is fair. I know that you are going to have a grand year," and he reached out his hand. He was calling me "Henry" now, all smiles, which he had a right to be, I guess, for I believe he was ready to go much higher on his absolute maximum. But I did not push him, for the main job was yet ahead, and I did not take his hand, saying, "Sir, there is one clause yet to go in my contract."

"Shoot," said he.

"There must be a clause," said I, "saying that me and Bruce Pearson will stay with the club together, or else go together. Whatever happens to one must happen to the other, traded or sold or whatever. We must be tied in a package on any deal under the sun."

"No deals are on the fire," said he.

"I never heard of such a thing," said Bradley Lord.

Patricia was powdering her nose out of a little compact. She snapped the lid shut, and it was the only sound, and she said, "It is not a matter of whether anybody ever heard of such a thing before or not, and it is not a matter whether any deals are on the fire or not. It is a thing we could never do for many reasons, the first reason being that Dutch would never hear of it, and all the rest of the reasons second."

"Boys and girls," said Old Man Moors, "leave us be calm. Wiggen, I will give you my verbal word instead of writing it in."

"It must be wrote in," said I.

"Bradley," said Patricia, "call Dutch."

"He is asleep," said Bradley.

"He been trying for days to get some sleep," said I.

"Call him," she said.

Bradley called him, and it rung a long time, and when you heard his voice you could hear it all over the room, like he was there, and Bradley held the phone away from his ear, and then he said, "Mr. Moors wishes to see you," and after awhile he come down in his slippers and robe, pajama pants but no top. "I been trying for days to get some sleep," he said, still not awake. "Go get me a coke."

"Tell him your clause," said Patricia.

He looked at me with his eyes shut. "So it is you with a special clause, Author? I will bet it is a dilly." His voice was low and full of sleep, and he kept scrounging in his eyes with his hands, trying to wake up. "Bradley, run get me a wet rag," he said. He took a swig of his coke. "Sterling must be shot for hay fever with a special shot. Vincent Carucci must have contact lenses. Gonzalez must have a buddy along to speak Spanish with, and Goldman must go home on Passover. What do you wish, Author, the Chinese New Year off or Dick Tracy's birthday?"

"I wish a clause," said I, "tying me in a package with Pearson."

"Does he owe you money?" said Old Man Moors.

Bradley brung him the rag, and Dutch squeezed it out on the floor. "Jesus, Bradley, you ain't got much strength in your hand," he said. "How do you mean tied in a package?"

"If he is sold I must be sold," I said. "Or if he is traded I must be traded the same place. Wherever he goes I must go."

His face was covered with the rag, and when he took it away the color was gone, drained away down in his chest. I will swear the hair of his chest was red, and then slowly it drained back up again, and he said, "This is telling me who I must keep and who not, which nobody ever told me before, Author, and nobody will ever tell me again as long as I am upright. If it is money talk money, and good luck. Talking money is one thing. But talking business is another, and I will as soon trade the whole club for a tin of beans as leave anybody tell me who stays and who gets cut loose."

"I am sorry to hear it," said I, "because without that clause there will be no contract."

"Then there will be no contract," said Dutch, "and I must suffer along the best I can."

"Several of those left-handers looked good to me," said Old Man Moors.

"Good for what?" said Dutch.

"Will you go sell insurance?" said Bradley Lord. "You do not know a soul on earth to sell insurance to outside of ballplayers. Will you sell insurance to other insurance agents? Where will you run up against people with money with the language you speak? I never seen you wear a necktie."

"Shut up," said Dutch.

"I am ignoring him," said I. "I am only lay-ing it out straight, all my cards up. I do not wish to sell insurance. Insurance is for later. I rather play baseball than anything else. I do it best. I like the trains. I like the hotels. I like the boys. I like the hours and the money. I like the fame and the glory. I like to think of 50,000 people getting up in the morning and squashing themself to death in the subway to come and see me play ball."

"That is how I feel," said Dutch.

"I am dead serious," said I.

"What is up between you 2? A roomie is a roomie, Author, not a Siamese twin brother fastened at the hip. I do not understand this a-tall, and I will investigate it. I will run it down to the end of the earth. Are you a couple fairies, Author? That can not be. It been a long time since I run across fairies in baseball, not since Will Miller and another lad that I forget his name, a shortstop, that for Christ sake when they split they went and found another friend. This is all too much for me."

"You will understand it sometime," I said.

"When?"

"No telling," I said. "Maybe soon, maybe not for 15 years."

"I am 62," said Dutch. "I will certainly be hanging by my thumb until I hear. Christ Almighty, I seen you on days when you hated Pearson, when you ate him out as bad as I myself ever ate him out. I seen you about to kill him for his stupidity. I seen you once get up from the table and walk away."

"Because he laughed without knowing why," I said.

"Such a thing can be not only hate but also love," said Patricia.

"It is not love," said I.

"I do not mean fairy love," she said.

"He laughs because he wishes to be one of the boys all the time," said Dutch. "Must this clause go on forever?" He closed his eyes again, not sleeping but thinking. "I have 4 catchers," he said. "I have a catcher that is old and another that can not hit and another that is wild and crazy and another that is just plum dumb." He opened his eyes and begun checking them off on his fingers. "I would give both my eyes for Sam Mott of Cincinnati, but they want Author, and I cannot give Author, or if I give you I must have Scudder off Brooklyn which the son of a bitches will not give me except for all my right-hand power. I could spare my right-hand power if I could swing a deal with Pittsburgh, but Pittsburgh wants Author and I have already give you to Cincinnati on paper for Sam Mott.

So I must play my old catcher on days when he feels young, and my catcher that can not hit on days the power is on, and my wild and crazy catcher on days he ever comes to his senses, which so far he has give me no sign of really having any. I will ship him back to QC and see if Mike can talk him off his motorcycle. We must never have another motorcycle in camp. I been trying for days to get some sleep. When you really stop and think about it I am libel to wind up using my catcher that is just plum dumb more and more." He finished off his coke and belched a loud belch and scratched the hair on his chest.

"Some day you will understand," I said.

"No," said he. "That is too much to ask. Forget it. I will agree to this clause. I never done such a thing before and would not do it now except there is a look in your eye that tells me that I must." He looked in my eye a long time. "Yes," he said, "there is a look which tells me that I must," and that was all he said but went back out and up to bed, and Bradley Lord drew up the contract and we all signed.

JOHN GALLAGHER

Courtesy *Sport* Magazine. ©

"Kill the ump!"

For sheer dramatics, it's hard to beat this one in all baseball annals.
Old Pete Alexander coming in to pitch to Lazzeri . . . bases loaded
. . . two out . . . Remember?

1926:
St. Louis Cardinals 3,
New York Yankees 2

JAMES R. HARRISON

THE CARDINALS WON. The baseball drama had a happy ending after all, for as the last reel faded out the sentimental favorites were holding the championship. They beat the Yankees and the Yankees beat themselves, and between the two the greatest game of the series went to St. Louis, 3 to 2.

The old story can be written again. The breaks of the game decided it. To baseball history can be added one more chapter where the seventh game of the big series was decided, not by skill or courage, but by fate.

After millions of words had been scribbled and tons of white paper covered with expert calculations, the World Series worked itself down to four short words: Koenig's fumble, Meusel's muff.

If Mark Koenig, the Yankee shortstop, had gripped his fingers around the grounder in the fourth inning; if the veteran Bob Meusel had caught an easy fly that bobbed out of his hands in the same round, the Yanks would have won and would have been world champions this morning.

If the Cardinals had not scored three unearned runs on those two devastating errors, Waite Hoyt would not have been robbed for the second time in his career of the glory of a shutout in the final game of the World Series. Babe Ruth would not today be mourning the fact that his home run in the third did not bring the championship to New York singlehandedly and unaided.

And St. Louis last night and through the early hours of the morning would not have

been celebrating the happy ending to its wait of thirty-eight years.

Everything was incidental to those two errors. It was incidental that Herb Pennock came back to pitch in a hopeless cause. It was incidental, even though highly dramatic, that in the seventh inning, with the bases full and two out, Alexander the Great came out of the shadows of the bull pen to strike out Tony Lazzeri and throttle the Yankees' last great rally. It was incidental, too, that Tommy Thevenow, Cardinal shortstop, drove in the winning runs with a single in the fourth.

Alexander wrote finis to the hopes of the surging Yanks with an old hand but a steady one. To his already superb work in the series he added this one climax. His pitching in the series was probably the greatest since the days of Matty and Babe Adams, but if Meusel and Koenig had held on to the ball, Alex would have been merely a gallant old pitcher on a losing ball team.

Fate made a hero of Alexander and a victim of Hoyt. Fate was the scene shifter who set the stage in the seventh, out upon which Alexander shuffled. His cap was perched on one side of his head and he was slowly chewing a quid of tobacco. He was a quaint, almost humorous, figure with his jaunty cap, his old man's gait and his quizzical face, but when he wound up his arm and threw, the Yanks had reached the end of the trail.

There was nothing more left for them. They had battled through six games and now had

181

the championship at the ends of their fingers when suddenly they came face to face with Alex. While 40,000 went wild with delight at Yankee Stadium, he stood across the path and the Yanks took a detour to second-place money in the greatest money series of all time.

In the third, Babe Ruth hit his fourth homer, setting a new record for a single series. With Hoyt pitching the game of a lifetime, this run looked enough to win. But in the fourth Koenig fumbled and Meusel muffed, and the Yanks found themselves two runs behind.

Miller Huggins reorganized his scattered battalion and the Yanks charged on. They swirled at Jesse Haines in the sixth and luck was with them this time, for Chick Hafey played a line drive rashly and Dugan scored with the second run.

Only one to go now, and Haines, his pitching hand bruised, was weakening. In the seventh, Combs opened with a single. The Yanks were coming again. Koenig sacrificed Combs to second and Ruth was walked intentionally.

Meusel, the unfortunate lad with the feeble fingers of an earlier inning, had his chance to wipe the slate clean, but his grounder to Bell was turned into a force-out of Ruth at second while Combs dashed on to third.

Gehrig was now at bat. His single had won one game and his double helped to win another. Haines faltered after he had thrown two strikes on the native-born New Yorker. Something suddenly went wrong with the Haines right arm. He floated three bad balls up to the plate, and another high one sent Gehrig to first and filled the bases.

Rogers Hornsby called his men into a huddle. Hornsby, O'Farrell, Haines, Bottomley, Bell, Thevenow—they were all there. When the conference broke up, Haines took off his glove and walked to the bench.

The Cardinals were going to try a new pitcher. Forty thousand pairs of eyes peered anxiously through the gray mist toward the bull pen out in deep left. There was a breathless pause, and then around the corner of the stand came a tall figure in a Cardinal sweater. His cap rode rakishly on the corner of his head. He walked like a man who was going nowhere in particular and was in no hurry to get there. He was a trifle knock-kneed and his gait was not a model of grace and rhythm.

Any baseball fan would have known him a mile away. It was Grover Cleveland Alexander. Alexander the Great was coming in to pull the Cardinal machine out of the mudhole. The ancient twirler, who had gone nine full innings the day before, was shuffling in where younger men feared to tread.

On any other day he would have been sitting contentedly on the bench, chewing his quid and ruminating on life. This time he was plucked out from the bull pen and thrust into the limelight as the last hope of the Cardinals.

He warmed up in that leisurely, methodical way of his, and as he faced Tony Lazzeri, fresh young slugger from the Coast, he was outwardly as unconcerned as if it were a spring exhibition game. Throughout the park there came a silence. The fans slid forward to the edge of their seats. Hardly a mother's son of them seemed to be moving a muscle, but, although the crowd was rigid with the thrill of the moment, old Alex was undisturbed.

He had been through all that before. Apparently there wasn't a nerve in his body. Ball one to Lazzeri was low and the crowd stirred, but Alex calmly carved the outside corner with a strike, like a butcher slicing ham.

Another one outside and Lazzeri fouled it into the stand. The Yankee was now in the hole. "This lad is in a tighter fix than I am," thought Alex, and so he essayed a low curve that one of the Singer midgets couldn't have hit. Lazzeri swung and missed. The deed was done. Alex took off his glove and shuffled again to the bench. The Cardinals, young and impetuous, pounded his back and hugged him madly, but old Alex took it with placid good humor—not the shadow of a smile on his face.

Only once did he turn his head and send a half-smile toward the stand and we suspect that that was his only gesture of triumph.

In the eighth the Yanks went out one, two, three. The old arm of Alexander was now rising and falling with a steady beat, tolling off the last minutes of the World Series. Against him was Pennock, but Alex had a one-run lead and there was nothing in his mellow past which made anyone believe that Alexander would lose a one-run lead in the ninth inning of the last World Series game.

Combs and Koenig were child's play for him, as the Yankees' final turn began. Combs grounded to Bell and was out. Koenig gave the same fielder an easy roller.

And now the drama was almost done. There was only one more scene. Ruth was at bat—the Yankees' last hope. Would Alexander pitch to him as he had to lesser men?

It would have been the last great story of the

series if Alex had fanned him. But Alex was not concerned with great stories, drama, climaxes, headlines or anything else of the sort. He pitched carefully and deliberately to Ruth. He brought the count to three and two, but Alex just missed the corner of the plate on the next one and the Babe walked.

Meusel rather than Ruth was on the program, but before Meusel could settle the issue Ruth did it for him by breaking for second base. O'Farrell whipped a fast throw to Hornsby and the series was over.

Now Rogers Hornsby can go back to Texas, where his mother lies dead, and Alexander the Great can go back to his easy chair, his slippers and a winter fireplace and dwell pleasantly on the October afternoon when Tony Lazzeri swung at a low ball which a Singer midget could not have hit. If Alex wants to chuckle, he is clearly entitled to it.

He can look back to the series which saw him winning two masterful victories and helping to win a third. The man who was fired by Joe McCarthy, manager of the Cubs, in midsummer, came back in October to fashion one of the greatest World Series pitching achievements.

Matty, Babe Adams, Combs and Coveleskie twirled three victories in other baseball classics, but they were all young men and full of strength. Alex was not only old but he was a baseball discard, tossed onto the scrap heap as an antique without worth.

Rogers Hornsby can go back to Texas with the comforting thought that he "stayed with the team" and won. The young man who caught the imagination and sympathy of the country as only Walter Johnson before him had done is undoubtedly glad the series is over. Not for him any triumphant celebrations; he has discharged one duty only to take on another.

The series set nineteen playing records and was the greatest ever in total receipts and attendance. Although yesterday's crowd was a miserable disappointment, with only 38,093 paid, it was enough to send the attendance up to 328,051, and the receipts to $1,207,864. When 63,600 paid to see the second game in the stadium, all marks for a single day's attendance were also passed. The total of winning and losing players' share was bigger than anything before.

The weather man is being blamed for yesterday's financial slump. Showers and an overcast sky in the morning made it certain that the crowd would be small.

Hoyt pitched fine ball all the way through. For a short spell he was again the Hoyt of 1921, when his work against the Giants earned him the brief sobriquet, a "second Matty." His fast ball was a work of art and his curve the best he has shown in five years—both wonderfully controlled and hopping through like the wind.

Hoyt came through in magnificent style, but it was again his misfortune to be beaten by the breaks of the game. His mind must have wandered back to 1921. In the last ill-fated game of that series Roger Peckinpaugh booted a ball away and Hoyt lost, 1 to 0. Once again fate came along to kick him on the shins.

Ruth had hit his homer, and when the fourth opened Hoyt was in front of Hornsby's easy grounder. Bottomley singled to left. Hoyt forced Bell to ground to Koenig, who had an easy double play in sight.

But the kid shortstop played the ball to one side, and in his eagerness to kill two birds with one stone fumbled the roller. One bad break for Hoyt followed another. With two strikes and no balls against Hafey, the left fielder lifted a weak fly which fell in left between the scurrying figures of Koenig and Meusel.

The bases were full and only one out, and fate was saving its best prank for the last. O'Farrell raised a fly to left center. Meusel, having a stronger arm than Combs, waved the Kentuckian away so that he could make the throw to the plate. There was only an outside chance of keeping Bottomley from scoring, but Meusel did not even catch the ball.

The white pill hit his outstretched hands and popped out again, like a rabbit from the magician's hat. For a minute there was a stunned silence. Even the Cardinals were so taken aback that they hardly knew what to do. Bottomley, of course, was lighting out for the plate, and the others finally got into action and ran for the next base.

There is only one explanation for the Meusel muff. He tried to throw the ball before he got it, and thereby made himself the greatest World Series goat since Fred Snodgrass of Giant fame.

With the score tied and bases still full, Hoyt settled gamely down, but the "breaks" had beaten him. He laid two strikes over on Thevenow and was pitching stanchly when the boy shortstop happened to tap the ball with the end of his bat and loop a safe hit to right center, which scored two more runs.

Hoyt, pitching like Matty of old, was beaten nevertheless. He was beaten like Matty of 1912, when Snodgrass muffed an easy fly. You have heard of the famous "$100,000 muff." You know about the time Hank Gowdy tripped over his mask and lost the deciding game of the 1924 series. You know about Peckinpaugh of last October, but they were as nothing compared to the fumble of Koenig and the muff of Meusel.

For this was the biggest money series of all, with the spoils bigger and the stake greater. There has never been a 7-game World Series without the seventh game producing its Meusels and Snodgrasses and Gowdys. Hoyt now joins the unhappy ranks with Mathewson, Virgil Barnes and Walter Johnson.

John McGraw can sympathize with Miller Huggins, for it happened to him twice.

There has also never been a full-limit series which ended satisfactorily—never a seventh game decided strictly on its merits. Invariably the breaks have decided it. For three straight years this has happened, and in each case the winner was the winner because on that afternoon the run of the cards was with him.

To Ruth as well as to Hoyt should go the heartfelt condolences of Yankee rooters. The playboy of baseball might have heard his name go ringing down the corridors of baseball as a man who won a series game with a home run.

It was the only earned run of the game. In the third Haines was going along nicely until he met Ruth. Jess fell back to his slow ball. Ruth fouled the first one into the stand, but the next one was too low and was a ball. The third was slow and inside.

The Babe's timing was perfect and the swish of his bat terrific. Remember that it was a slow ball and hard to knock for any distance. Ruth had to supply the momentum himself, yet he whaled that ball clear over the outfielders' heads and into the bleachers off right center.

Barely hurdling the fence, the ball passed directly over the words "World's Champions" in the razor ad. "A happy omen," yelled the Yankee rooters. It was a good omen until Koenig

and Meusel ruined it, for with that blow Ruth would have made world champions of the Yankees.

A crowd lukewarm toward the Yanks rose to its feet and acclaimed the king as he has not been acclaimed in years. The furor and the din were earsplitting.

It was Ruth's second great moment in the series, the first being when he hit three homers in the fourth game at St. Louis. His total for the series was four, setting a record, and his total for all series is eight, two above the previous high-water mark.

George Herman started the winning rally in one game with a single, carried the flag in another with three homers, and would have won the last but for the mistakes of his teammates. In this series Ruth and Pennock were nine-tenths of the Yanks.

It was Ruth who also made the most sensational play of the closing game when he sprinted at top speed back almost to the running track and enfolded O'Farrell's terrific line drive in his glove. For this he got another tornado of cheers from the multitude. Ruth was carrying the crowd by storm. In another inning his apathetic subjects were actually rooting for the Yankees—the greatest tribute possible to the colorful personality of King George.

The series is over. The Yanks were outbatted and outfielded, but their superior experience and balance carried them along. Even those assets were failing them until Ruth completely turned the tide with his St. Louis homers. Those three pitched balls almost cost the Cardinals the title.

Ruth is still the Yankee team. The Cards made great talk about pitching to him, but in the deciding game they walked him four out of five times.

It was a series of great crowds and busy turnstiles, but not much action compared to many another series. Not a well-played series and not a thrilling one, except in spots. The breaks were evenly divided. The new champions earned what they got and old Alex earned a quiet winter in his rocking chair.

HERE is Gabby Hartnett's own story of one of baseball's truly great moments—his "home run in the gloaming" in 1938. The fabulous scene as Gabby crossed home plate is recorded in picture in the first *Fireside Book of Baseball.*

1938:
Chicago Cubs 6,
Pittsburgh Pirates 5

GABBY HARTNETT
as told to HAL TOTTEN

Do you know how you feel when you're real scared, or something BIG is going to happen? Well, that's the way I felt for one terrific minute of my biggest day in baseball—and I don't believe you'll have to guess very much as to just which day that was.

It was in 1938, Sept. 28, the day of "the home run in the dark." But as a matter of fact, that day—that one big moment—was the climax of a series of things that had gone on for a week or more. And every one of those incidents helped to make it the biggest day in all my years in the major leagues.

The week before—on Sunday—you'll remember we had played a double-header in Brooklyn. We lost the first game 4 to 3, and we were leading the second game by two runs along about the fifth inning. It was muddy and raining and was getting dark fast. Then big Fred Sington came up with a man on base and hit a home run to tie the score.

It was too dark to play any more, so they called the game and it ended in a tie. Now—every game meant a lot to us just then. We were three and a half games behind. Winning was the only way we could hope to catch the Pirates. And we were scheduled in Philadelphia the next day. So we couldn't play the game off then.

But MacPhail wanted to play it. We had an open date for travel at the end of the series in Philly, and he wanted us to go back to Brooklyn and play off the tie. The boys wanted to play it, too. They figured we could win it and gain on the Pirates.

Well, I couldn't make up my mind right away, so I asked MacPhail to give me 24 hours to decide. He said he would. But I'd been figuring—you see, we had to win all three games in the series with Pittsburgh if we were to win the pennant. And I had to think of my pitchers. I had to argue with the whole ball club—they wanted to play.

But I stuck my neck out and turned it down. I'll admit that I didn't feel any too easy about it. But I had to make the decision. And I felt that we might lose that game just as easy as we could win it. So I took that chance.

Well, we sat for three days in Philly and watched it rain. Of course, Pittsburgh wasn't able to play in Brooklyn, either. And they were three and a half games in front of us. On Thursday we played the Phils twice and beat 'em both times, 4 to 0 and 2 to 1. Lee won his 20th game of the season in that first one—and his fourth straight shutout. Clay Bryant was the pitcher in the second. But Pittsburgh beat Brooklyn twice, so we were still three and a half back.

The next day we won two again—and we had

to come from behind to do it. Rip Collins put the second one on ice by doubling in the ninth with the bases full to drive in three runs just as they posted the score showing that Cincinnati had beaten the Pirates. That put us within two games of the leaders. We were really rollin'.

Then we came home and on Saturday we played the Cardinals—and beat 'em 9 to 3. But the Pirates won, too. On Sunday it was the same thing—we both won. Monday Pittsburgh wasn't scheduled, so the Pirates were in the stands at Wrigley Field as we played the final of the series with St. Louis. Bill Lee was scored on for the first time in five games, but we won 6 to 3. And then came the big series—with the lead cut to a game and a half.

I stuck my neck out in the very first game of the series. Several times, in fact. I started Dizzy Dean on the mound. He hadn't pitched since Sept. 13 and hadn't started a game since Aug. 13. But how he pitched! Just a slow ball, control, and a world of heart.

We got him out in front in the third when Collins tripled and Jurges drove him in with a single. For five innings Dean was superb. Then he seemed to tire. Not due to anything that happened on the field.

Lloyd Waner grounded out in that inning, and Paul Waner fouled out. Rizzo singled, but Vaughan popped to Herman. Still, I noticed that he didn't have as much on the ball.

Probably I was the only one to notice it—except maybe Diz himself. I began to worry a bit. And I made up my mind right then and there that no matter how anything else was going, the minute Dean got in trouble, I was going to get him out of there. We got another run the last half of that inning. And Diz got through the seventh and eighth, although it took a great play by Dean himself to cut down a run at the plate in the eighth.

When the ninth came around I decided to play safe and started Lee warming up in the bull pen. Bill wasn't usually a good relief pitcher, but he was the best pitcher in the league, and that was a spot for the best we had.

Dean hit Vaughan to start the ninth and I was plenty uneasy. But Suhr popped out, and Jensen batted for Young and forced Arky at second. Then came little "Jeep" Handley and he hit one clear to the wall in left center for a double. That put the tying runs on second and third, and that was my cue.

Todd was up. He always hit Dean pretty good, even when Diz had his stuff—and Diz

didn't have a thing then. Not only that, but Todd never hit Lee very well. So even though Lee hadn't been a steady relief pitcher, I called him in. My neck was out again. What if Todd hit one? What if Lee had trouble getting started—after all, he'd been working day after day. But—well, when it gets to the place where it means a ball game, you've got to make a change, even if the hitter socks one into the bleachers.

I'll say this for Dean—he never complained about that. He walked right in and said I'd done the right thing—that he'd lost his stuff and his arm didn't feel so good. So Lee came in. The first pitch was a strike. Todd fouled the next one off. Then Lee cut loose with as wild a pitch as I ever saw and Jensen scored. Handley went to third with the tying run. My hunch didn't look so good. But Lee wound up again; he pitched; and Todd swung and struck out. We'd won the game and were only a half game out of first place.

That brings us up to the big day. We scored in the second inning on a couple of errors. But Pittsburgh went ahead with three in the sixth. We tied it up in our half. But the Pirates got two in the eighth and led, 5 to 3. In our half Collins opened with a single and Jurges walked.

Lazzeri batted for Lee, who had gone in again that day, and doubled, scoring Rip. They walked Hack. Then Herman drove in Jurges to tie it up again, but Joe Marty—who had run for Tony—was thrown out at the plate by Paul Waner. A double play ended that round.

It was very dark by then. But the umpires decided to let us go one more. Charlie Root got through the first half of the ninth all right. In our half Cavarretta hit one a country mile to center, but Lloyd Waner pulled it down. Reynolds grounded out. And it was my turn.

Well—I swung once—and missed; I swung again, and got a piece of it, but that was all. A foul and strike two. I had one more chance. Mace Brown wound up and let fly; I swung with everything I had and then I got that feeling I was talking about—the kind of feeling you get when the blood rushes out of your head and you get dizzy.

A lot of people have told me they didn't know the ball was in the bleachers. Well, I did —maybe I was the only one in the park who did. I knew it the minute I hit it. When I got to second base I couldn't see third for the players and fans there. I don't think I walked a step to the plate—I was carried in. But when I got there I saw George Barr taking a good look—he was going to make sure I touched that platter.

That was the shot that did it. We went into first place. And while we still had the pennant to win, we couldn't be headed. We won again the next day for Bill Lee, easy—10 to 1. The heart was gone out of Pittsburgh. And we clinched the pennant down in St. Louis the next Saturday when we won and Pittsburgh lost to Cincinnati.

DAVE HIRSCH

"Fastest outfielder in the league."

ERNIE HARWELL, who broadcasts the Baltimore Oriole games, is not only an incurable fan but an enthusiastic collector of all sorts of base-ball curios and customs. From his collection have come the Davis and Anson letters you will find elsewhere in this volume, and here, under his own by-line as it appeared in *True* magazine, is as odditious an oddity as you are liable to encounter.

Baseball among the Headhunters

ERNIE HARWELL

THE DIAMOND RING symbolizes romance to modern Americans, but the baseball diamond at one time was the most influential factor in the courtship of young Filipinos.

When ex-President William Howard Taft was governor of the Philippines in the early 1900s he was dismayed by the prevalence of head-hunting among some of the natives. So, with the help of soldiers, sailors and marines serving in the islands, he introduced baseball to the aborigines hoping it would sublimate their savagery.

Tribes in the mountain sections of the Philippines maintained an ancient custom that before a young Filipino could marry the girl of his choice he must hang on the wall of his hut the scalp of his most bitter enemy. However, once the brown-skinned athletes learned the finer points of baseball they changed their custom to one of sportsmanship.

Under the new diamond tradition it was decreed that before the young suitor could marry his "best," he must hit a home run. Native "Ladies' Days" attracted the belles to the contests to see their beaux—performing in uniforms comprised solely of a healthy smile and a loincloth.

Americans, acting as muscle-bound cupids, often played simple grounders and easy outs into home runs so their Filipino friends could escape bachelorhood.

But the ones who profited most by the switch in tradition were the suitors' enemies. Under the new custom they managed to keep their heads while yelling "Kill the umpire."

"He's nervous as a cat. His baby sitter's in the stands."

FOR combination of story, subject, and writer, you would look far to beat this one. Mr. Reiser was—I say "was"; I was almost tempted to classify this piece under "history"—a great ballplayer. He busted more fences than busted him—though the margin wasn't very big.

The Rocky Road of Pistol Pete

W. C. HEINZ

OUT IN Los Angeles," says Garry Schumacher, who was a New York baseball writer for 30 years and is now assistant to Horace Stoneham, president of the San Francisco Giants, "they think Duke Snider is the best center fielder they ever had. They forget Pete Reiser. The Yankees think Mickey Mantle is something new. They forget Reiser, too."

Maybe Pete Reiser was the purest ballplayer of all time. I don't know. There is no exact way of measuring such a thing, but when a man of incomparable skills, with full knowledge of what he is doing, destroys those skills and puts his life on the line in the pursuit of his endeavor as no other man in his game ever has, perhaps he is the truest of them all.

"Is Pete Reiser there?" I said on the phone.

This was last season, in Kokomo. Kokomo has a population of about 50,000 and a ball club, now affiliated with Los Angeles and called the Dodgers, in the Class D Midwest League. Class D is the bottom of the barrel of organized baseball, and this was the second season that Pete Reiser had managed Kokomo.

"He's not here right now," the woman's voice on the phone said. "The team played a doubleheader yesterday in Dubuque, and they didn't get in on the bus until 4:30 this morning. Pete just got up a few minutes ago and he had to go to the doctor's."

"Oh?" I said. "What has he done now?"

In two and a half years in the minors, three seasons of Army ball and ten years in the majors, Pete Reiser was carried off the field 11 times. Nine times he regained consciousness either in the clubhouse or in hospitals. He broke a bone in his right elbow, throwing. He broke both ankles, tore a cartilage in his left knee, ripped the muscles in his left leg, sliding. Seven times he crashed into outfield walls, dislocating his left shoulder, breaking his right collarbone and, five times, ending up in an unconscious heap on the ground. Twice he was beaned, and the few who remember still wonder today how great he might have been.

"I didn't see the old-timers," Bob Cooke, who is sports editor of the New York Herald Tribune, was saying recently, "but Pete Reiser was the best ballplayer I ever saw."

"We don't know what's wrong with him," the woman's voice on the phone said now. "He has a pain in his chest and he feels tired all the time, so we sent him to the doctor. There's a game tonight, so he'll be at the ball park about 5 o'clock."

Pete Reiser is 39 years old now. The Cardinals signed him out of the St. Louis Municipal League when he was 15. For two years, because he was so young, he chauffeured for Charley Barrett, who was scouting the Midwest. They had a Cardinal uniform in the car for Pete, and he used to work out with the Class C and D clubs, and one day Branch Rickey, who was general manager of the Cardinals then, called Pete into his office in Sportsman's Park.

"Young man," he said, "you're the greatest young ballplayer I've ever seen, but there is one thing you must remember. Now that you're a professional ballplayer you're in show business. You will perform on the biggest stage in the world, the baseball diamond. Like the actors on Broadway, you'll be expected to put on a great performance every day, no matter how you feel, no matter whether it's too hot or too cold. Never forget that."

Rickey didn't know it at the time, but this was like telling Horatius that, as a professional soldier, he'd be expected someday to stand his ground. Three times Pete sneaked out of hospitals to play. Once he went back into the lineup after doctors warned him that any blow on the head would kill him. For four years he swung the bat and made the throws when it was painful for him just to shave and to comb his hair. In the 1947 World Series he stood on a broken ankle to pinch hit, and it ended with Rickey, then president of the Dodgers, begging him not to play and guaranteeing Pete his 1948 salary if he would just sit that season out.

"That might be the one mistake I made," Pete says now. "Maybe I should have rested that year."

"Pete Reiser?" Leo Durocher, who managed Pete at Brooklyn, was saying recently. "What's he doing now?"

"He's managing Kokomo," Lindsey Nelson, the TV sportscaster, said.

"Kokomo?" Leo said.

"That's right," Lindsey said. "He's riding the buses to places like Lafayette and Michigan City and Mattoon."

"On the buses," Leo said, shaking his head and then smiling at the thought of Pete.

"And some people say," Lindsey said, "that he was the greatest young ballplayer they ever saw."

"No doubt about it," Leo said. "He was the best I ever had, with the possible exception of Mays. At that, he was even faster than Willie." He paused. "So now he's on the buses."

The first time that Leo ever saw Pete on a ball field was in Clearwater that spring of '39. Pete had played one year of Class D in the Cardinal chain and one season of Class D for Brooklyn. Judge Kenesaw Mountain Landis, who was then Baseball Commissioner, had sprung Pete and 72 others from what they called the "Cardinal Chain Gang," and Pete had signed with Brooklyn for $100.

"I didn't care about money then," Pete says. "I just wanted to play."

Pete had never been in a major-league camp before, and he didn't know that at batting practice you hit in rotation. At Clearwater he was grabbing any bat that was handy and cutting in ahead of Ernie Koy or Dolph Camilli or one of the others, and Leo liked that.

One day Leo had a chest cold, so he told Pete to start at shortstop. His first time up he hit a homer off the Cards' Ken Raffensberger, and that was the beginning. He was on base his first 12 times at bat that spring, with three homers, five singles and four walks. His first time against Detroit he homered off Tommy Bridges. His first time against the Yankees he put one over the fence off Lefty Gomez.

Durocher played Pete at shortstop in 33 games that spring. The Dodgers barnstormed North with the Yankees, and one night Joe McCarthy, who was managing the Yankees, sat down next to Pete on the train.

"Reiser," he said, "you're going to play for me."

"How can I play for you?" Pete said. "I'm with the Dodgers."

"We'll get you," McCarthy said. "I'll tell Ed Barrow, and you'll be a Yankee."

The Yankees offered $100,000 and five ballplayers for Pete. The Dodgers turned it down, and the day the season opened at Ebbets Field, Larry MacPhail, who was running things in Brooklyn, called Pete on the clubhouse phone and told him to report to Elmira.

"It was an hour before game time," Pete says, "and I started to take off my uniform and I was shaking all over. Leo came in and said: 'What's the matter? You scared?' I said: 'No. MacPhail is sending me to Elmira.' Leo got on the phone and they had a hell of a fight. Leo said he'd quit, and MacPhail said he'd fire him —and I went to Elmira.

"One day I'm making a throw and I heard something pop. Every day my arm got weaker and they sent me to Johns Hopkins and took X rays. Dr. George Bennett told me: 'Your arm's broken.' When I came to after the operation, my throat was sore and there was an ice pack on it. I said: 'What happened? Your knife slip?' They said: 'We took your tonsils out while we were operating on your arm.'"

Pete's arm was in a cast from the first of May until the end of July. His first two weeks out of the cast he still couldn't straighten the arm, but a month later he played ten games as a left-handed outfielder until Dr. Bennett stopped him.

"But I can't straighten my right arm," Pete said.

"Take up bowling," the doctor said.

When he bowled, though, Pete used first one arm and then the other. Every day that the weather allowed he went out into the back yard and practiced throwing a rubber ball left-handed against a wall. Then he went to Fairgrounds Park and worked on the long throw, left-handed, with a baseball.

"At Clearwater that next spring," he says, "Leo saw me in the outfield throwing left-handed, and he said: 'What do you think you're doin'?' I said: 'Hell, I had to be ready. Now I can throw as good with my left arm as I could with my right.' He said: 'You can do more things as a right-handed ballplayer. I can bring you into the infield. Go out there and cut loose with that right arm.' I did and it was okay, but I had that insurance."

*　*　*

So at 5 o'clock I took a cab from the hotel in Kokomo to the ball park on the edge of town. It seats about 2,200, 1,500 of them in the white-painted fairgrounds grandstand along the first base line, and the rest in chairs behind the screen and in bleachers along the other line.

I watched them take batting practice; trim, strong young kids with their dreams, I knew, of someday getting up there where Pete once was, and I listened to their kidding. I watched the groundskeeper open the concession booth and clean out the electric popcorn machine. I read the signs on the outfield walls, advertising the Mid-West Towel and Linen Service, Basil's Nite Club, The Hoosier Iron Works, UAW Local 292 and the Around the Clock Pizza Café. I watched the Dubuque kids climbing out of their bus, carrying their uniforms on wire coat hangers.

"Here comes Pete now," I heard the old guy setting up the ticket box at the gate say.

When Pete came through the gate he was walking like an old man. In 1941 the Dodgers trained in Havana, and one day they clocked him, in his baseball uniform and regular spikes, at 9.8 for 100 yards. Five years later the Cleveland Indians were bragging about George Case and the Washington Senators had Gil Coan. The Dodgers offered to bet $1,000 that Reiser was the fastest man in baseball, and now it was taking him forever to walk to me, his shoulders stooped, his whole body heavier now, and Pete just slowly moving one foot ahead of the other.

"Hello," he said, shaking hands but his face solemn. "How are you?"

"Fine," I said, "but what's the matter with you?"

"I guess it's my heart," he said.

"When did you first notice this?"

"About eleven days ago. I guess I was working out too hard. All of a sudden I felt this pain in my chest and I got weak. I went into the clubhouse and lay down on the bench, but I've had the same pain and I'm weak ever since."

"What did the doctor say?"

"He says it's lucky I stopped that day when I did. He says I should be in a hospital right now, because if I exert myself or even make a quick motion I might go—just like that."

He snapped his fingers. "He scared me," he said. "I'll admit it. I'm scared."

"What are you planning to do?"

"I'm going home to St. Louis. My wife works for a doctor there, and he'll know a good heart specialist."

"When will you leave?"

"Well, I can't just leave the ball club. I called Brooklyn, and they're sending a replacement for me, but he won't be here until tomorrow."

"How will you get to St. Louis?"

"It's about 300 miles," Pete says. "The doctor says I shouldn't fly or go by train, because if anything happens to me they can't stop and help me. I guess I'll have to drive."

"I'll drive you," I said.

Trying to get to sleep in the hotel that night I was thinking that maybe, standing there in that little ball park, Pete Reiser had admitted out loud for the first time in his life that he was scared. I was thinking of 1941, his first full year with the Dodgers. He was beaned twice and crashed his first wall and still hit .343 to be the first rookie and the youngest ballplayer to win the National League batting title. He tied Johnny Mize with 39 doubles, led in triples, runs scored, total bases and slugging average, and they were writing on the sports pages that he might be the new Ty Cobb.

"Dodgers Win On Reiser HR," the headlines used to say. "Reiser Stars As Brooklyn Lengthens Lead."

"Any manager in the National League," Arthur Patterson wrote one day in the New York *Herald Tribune,* "would give up his best man to obtain Pete Reiser. On every bench they're talking about him. Rival players watch him take his cuts during batting practice, announce when he's going to make a throw to the plate or third base during outfield drill. They just whistle their amazement when he scoots down the first base line on an infield dribbler or a well-placed bunt."

He was beaned the first time at Ebbets Field five days after the season started. A sidearm fast ball got away from Ike Pearson of the Phillies, and Pete came to at 11:30 that night in Peck Memorial Hospital.

"I was lying in bed with my uniform on," he told me once, "and I couldn't figure it out. The room was dark, with just a little night light, and then I saw a mirror and I walked over to it and lit the light and I had a black eye and a black streak down the side of my nose.

I said to myself: 'What happened to me?' Then I remembered.

"I took a shower and walked around the room, and the next morning the doctor came in. He looked me over, and he said: 'We'll keep you here for five or six more days under observation.' I said: 'Why?' He said: 'You've had a serious head injury. If you tried to get out of bed right now, you'd fall down.' I said: 'If I can get up and walk around this room, can I get out?' The doc said: 'All right, but you won't be able to do it.'"

Pete got out of bed, the doctor standing ready to catch him. He walked around the room. "I've been walkin' the floor all night," Pete said.

The doctor made Pete promise that he wouldn't play ball for a week, but Pete went right to the ball park. He got a seat behind the Brooklyn dugout, and Durocher spotted him.

"How do you feel?" Leo said.

"Not bad," Pete said.

"Get your uniform on," Leo said.

"I'm not supposed to play," Pete said.

"I'm not gonna play you," Leo said. "Just sit on the bench. It'll make our guys feel better to see that you're not hurt."

Pete suited up and went out and sat on the bench. In the eighth inning it was tied, 7-7. The Dodgers had the bases loaded, and there was Ike Pearson again, coming in to relieve.

"Pistol," Leo said to Pete, "get the bat."

In the press box the baseball writers watched Pete. They wanted to see if he'd stand right in there. After a beaning they are all entitled to shy, and many of them do. Pete hit the first pitch into the center-field stands, and Brooklyn won, 11 to 7.

"I could just barely trot around the bases," Pete said when I asked him about it. "I was sure dizzy."

Two weeks later they were playing the Cardinals, and Enos Slaughter hit one and Pete turned in center field and started to run. He made the catch, but he hit his head and his tail bone on that corner near the exit gate.

His head was cut, and when he came back to the bench they also saw blood coming through the seat of his pants. They took him into the clubhouse and pulled his pants down and the doctor put a metal clamp on the cut.

"Just don't slide," he told Pete. "You can get it sewed up after the game."

In August of that year big Paul Erickson was pitching for the Cubs and Pete took another one. Again he woke up in a hospital. The Dodgers were having some pretty good bean-ball contests with the Cubs that season, and Judge Landis came to see Pete the next day.

"Do you think that man tried to bean you?" he asked Pete.

"No sir," Pete said. "I lost the pitch."

"I was there," Landis said, "and I heard them holler: 'Stick it in his ear.'"

"That was just bench talk," Pete said. "I lost the pitch."

He left the hospital the next morning. The Dodgers were going to St. Louis after the game, and Pete didn't want to be left in Chicago.

Pete always says that the next year, 1942, was the year of his downfall, and the worst of it happened on one play. It was early July and Pete and the Dodgers were tearing the league apart. In a four-game series in Cincinnati he got 19 for 21. In a Sunday doubleheader in Chicago he went 5 for 5 in the first game, walked three times in the second game and got a hit the one time they pitched to him. He was hitting .381, and they were writing in the papers that he might end up hitting .400.

When they came into St. Louis the Dodgers were leading by ten and a half games. When they took off for Pittsburgh they left three games of that lead and Pete Reiser behind them.

"We were in the twelfth inning, no score, two outs and Slaughter hit it off Whit Wyatt," Pete says. "It was over my head and I took off. I caught it and missed that flagpole by two inches and hit the wall and dropped the ball. I had the instinct to throw it to Peewee Reese, and we just missed gettin' Slaughter at the plate, and they won, 1-0.

"I made one step to start off the field and I woke up the next morning in St. John's Hospital. My head was bandaged, and I had an awful headache."

Dr. Robert Hyland, who was Pete's personal physician, announced to the newspapers that Pete would be out for the rest of the season. "Look, Pete," Hyland told him. "I'm your personal friend. I'm advising you not to play any more baseball this year."

"I don't like hospitals, though," Pete was telling me once, "so after two days I took the bandage off and got up. The room started to spin, but I got dressed and I took off. I snuck out, and I took a train to Pittsburgh and I went to the park.

"Leo saw me and he said: 'Go get your uniform on, Pistol.' I said: 'Not tonight, Skipper.'

Leo said: 'Aw, I'm not gonna let you hit. I want these guys to see you. It'll give 'em that little spark they need. Besides, it'll change the pitching plans on that other bench when they see you sittin' here in uniform.' "

In the fourteenth inning the Dodgers had a runner on second and Ken Heintzelman, the left-hander, came in for the Pirates. He walked Johnny Rizzo, and Durocher had run out of pinch hitters.

"Damn," Leo was saying, walking up and down. "I want to win this one. Who can I use? Anybody here who can hit?"

Pete walked up to the bat rack. He pulled out his stick. "You got yourself a hitter," he said to Leo.

He walked up there and hit a line drive over the second baseman's head that was good for three bases. The two runs scored, and Pete rounded first base and collapsed.

"When I woke up I was in a hospital again," he says. "I could just make out that somebody was standin' there and then I saw it was Leo. He said: 'You awake?' I said: 'Yep.' He said: 'By God, we beat 'em! How do you feel?' I said: 'How do you think I feel?' He said: 'Aw, you're better with one leg, and one eye than anybody else I've got.' I said: 'Yeah, and that's the way I'll end up—on one leg and with one eye.'

"I'd say I lost the pennant for us that year," Pete says now, although he still hit .310 for the season. "I was dizzy most of the time and I couldn't see fly balls. I mean balls I could have put in my pocket, I couldn't get near. Once in Brooklyn when Mort Cooper was pitching for the Cards I was seeing two baseballs coming up there. Babe Pinelli was umpiring behind the plate, and a couple of times he stopped the game and asked me if I was all right. So the Cards beat us out the last two days of the season."

* * *

The business office of the Kokomo ball club is the dining room of a man named Jim Deets, who sells insurance and is also the business manager of the club. His wife, in addition to keeping house, mothering six small kids, boarding Pete, an outfielder from Venezuela and a shortstop from the Dominican Republic, is also the club secretary.

"How do you feel this morning?" I asked Pete. He was sitting at the dining-room table, in a sweat shirt and a pair of light-brown slacks,

typing the game report of the night before to send it to Brooklyn.

"A little better," he said.

Pete has a worn, green 1950 Chevy, and it took us eight and a half hours to get to St. Louis. I'd ask him how the pain in his chest was and he'd say that it wasn't bad or it wasn't so good, and I'd get him to talking again about Durocher or about his time in the Army. Pete played under five managers at Brooklyn, Boston, Pittsburgh and Cleveland, and Durocher is his favorite.

"He has a great mind, and not just for baseball," Pete said. "Once he sat down to play gin with Jack Benny, and after they'd played four cards Leo read Benny's whole hand to him. Benny said: 'How can you do that?' Leo said: 'If you're playin' your cards right, and I give you credit for that, you have to be holding those others.' Benny said: 'I don't want to play with this guy.'

"One spring at Clearwater there was a pool table in a room off the lobby. One night Hugh Casey and a couple of other guys and I were talking with Leo. We said: 'Gee, there's a guy in there and we've been playin' pool with him for a couple of nights, but last night he had a real hot streak.' Leo said: 'How much he take you for?' We figured it out and it was $2,000. Leo said: 'Point him out to me.'

"We went in and pointed the guy out and Leo walked up to him and said: 'Put all your money on the table. We're gonna shoot for it.' The guy said: 'I never play like that.' Leo said: 'You will tonight. Pick your own game.' Leo took him for $4,000, and then he threw him out. Then he paid us back what we'd gone for, and he said: 'Now, let that be a lesson. That guy is a hustler from New York. The next time it happens I won't bail you out.' Leo hadn't had a cue in his hands for years."

It was amazing that they took Pete into the Army. He had wanted to enlist in the Navy, but the doctors looked him over and told him none of the services could accept him. Then his draft board sent him to Jefferson Barracks in the winter of 1943, and the doctors there turned him down.

"I'm sittin' on a bench with the other guys who've been rejected," he was telling me, "and a captain comes in and says: 'Which one of you is Reiser?' I stood up and I said: 'I am.' In front of everybody he said: 'So you're trying to pull a fast one, are you? At a time like this, with a war going on, you came in here under a false name. What do you mean, giving your name as Harold Patrick Reiser? Your name's Pete Reiser, and you're the ballplayer, aren't you?' I said: 'I'm the ballplayer and they call me Pete, but my right name is Harold Patrick Reiser.' The captain says: 'I apologize. Sergeant, fingerprint him. This man is in.'"

They sent him to Fort Riley, Kansas. It was early April and raining and they were on bivouac, and Pete woke up in a hospital. "What happened?" he said.

"You've got pneumonia," the doctor said. "You've been a pretty sick boy for six days. You'll be all right, but we've been looking you over. How did you ever get into this Army?"

"When I get out of the hospital," Pete was telling me, "I'm on the board for a discharge and I'm waitin' around for about a week, and still nobody there knows who I am. All of a sudden one morning a voice comes over the bitch box in the barracks. It says: 'Private Reiser, report to headquarters immediately.' I think: 'Well, I'm out now.'

"I go over there and the colonel wants to see me. I walk in and give my good salute and he says: 'Sit down, Harold.' I sit down and he says: 'Your name really isn't Harold, is it?' I say: 'Yes, it is, sir.' He says: 'But that isn't what they call you where you're well known, is it? You're Pete Reiser the ballplayer, aren't you?' I say: 'Yes, sir.' He says: 'I thought so. Now, I've got your discharge papers right there, but we've got a pretty good ball club and we'd like you on it. We'll make a deal. You say nothing, and you won't have to do anything but play ball. How about it?' I said: 'Suppose I don't want to stay in?'

"He picked my papers up off his desk," Pete was saying, "and he tore 'em right up in my face. I can still hear that 'zip' when he tore 'em. He said: 'You see, you have no choice.'

"Then he picked up the phone and said something and in a minute a general came in. I jumped up and the colonel said: 'Don't bother to salute, Pete.' Then he said to the general: 'Major, this is Pete Reiser, the great Dodger ballplayer. He was up for a medical discharge, but he's decided to stay here and play ball for us.'

"So, the general says: 'My, what a patriotic thing for you to do, young man. That's wonderful. Wonderful.' I'm sittin' there, and when the general goes out the colonel says: 'That major, he's all right.' I said: 'But he's a general. How come you call him a major?' The colonel says: 'Well, in the regular Army he's a major and I'm a full colonel. The only reason I don't

outrank him now is that I've got heart trouble. He knows it, but I never let him forget it. I always call him major.' I thought: 'What kind of an Army am I in?'"

Joe Gantenbein, the Athletics' outfielder, and George Scharein, the Phillies' infielder, were on that team with Pete, and they won the state and national semipro titles. By the time the season was over, however, the order came down to hold up all discharges.

The next season there were 17 major-league ballplayers on the Fort Riley club, and they played four nights a week for the war workers in Wichita. Pete hit a couple of walls, and the team made such a joke of the national semipro tournament that an order came down from Washington to break up the club.

"Considering what a lot of guys did in the war," Pete says, "I had no complaints, but five times I was up for discharge, and each time something happened. From Riley they sent me to Camp Livingston. From there they sent me to New York Special Services for twelve hours and I end up in Camp Lee, Virginia, in May of 1945.

"The first one I meet there is the general. He says: 'Reiser, I saw you on the list and I just couldn't pass you up.' I said: 'What about my discharge?' He says: 'That will have to wait. I have a lot of celebrities down here, but I want a good baseball team.'"

Johnny Lindell, of the Yankees, and Dave Philley, of the White Sox, were on the club and Pete played left field. Near the end of the season he went after a foul fly for the third out of the last inning, and he went right through a temporary wooden fence and rolled down a 25-foot embankment.

"I came to in the hospital, with a dislocated right shoulder," he says, "and the general came over to see me and he said: 'That was one of the greatest displays of courage I've ever seen, to ignore your future in baseball just to win a ball game for Camp Lee.' I said: 'Thanks.'

"Now it's November and the war is over, but they're still shippin' guys out, and I'm on the list to go. I report to the overseas major, and he looks at my papers and says: 'I can't send you overseas. With everything that's wrong with you, you shouldn't even be in this Army. I'll have you out in three hours.' In three hours, sure enough, I've got those papers in my hand, stamped, and I'm startin' out the door. Runnin' up to me comes a Red Cross guy. He says: 'I can get you some pretty good pension benefits for the physical and mental injuries you've sustained.' I said: 'You can?' He said: 'Yes, you're entitled to them.' I said: 'Good. You get 'em. You keep 'em. I'm goin' home.'"

* * *

When we got to St. Louis that night I drove Pete to his house and the next morning I picked him up and drove him to see the heart specialist. He was in there for two hours, and when he came out he was walking slower than ever.

"No good," he said. "I have to go to the hospital for five days for observation."

"What does he think?"

"He says I'm done puttin' on that uniform. I'll have to get a desk job."

Riding to the hospital I wondered if that heart specialist knew who he was tying to that desk job. In 1946, the year he came out of the Army, Pete led the league when he stole 34 bases, 13 more than the runner-up Johnny Hopp of the Braves. He also set a major-league record that still stands, when he stole home eight times.

"Nine times," he said once. "In Chicago I stole home and Magerkurth hollered: 'You're out!' Then he dropped his voice and he said: '————, I missed it.' He'd already had his thumb in the air. I had nine out of nine."

I suppose somebody will beat that some day, but he'll never top the way Pete did it. That was the year he knocked himself out again trying for a diving catch, dislocated his left shoulder, ripped the muscles in his left leg and broke his left ankle.

"Whitey Kurowski hit one in the seventh inning at Ebbets Field," he was telling me. "I dove for it and woke up in the clubhouse. I was in Peck Memorial for four days. It really didn't take much to knock me out in those days. I was comin' apart all over. When I dislocated my shoulder they popped it back in, and Leo said: 'Hell, you'll be all right. You don't throw with it anyway.'"

That was the year the Dodgers tied with the Cardinals for the pennant and dropped the play-off. Pete wasn't there for those two games. He was in Peck Memorial again.

"I'd pulled a Charley horse in my left leg," Pete was saying. "It's the last two weeks of the season, and I'm out for four days. We've got the winning run on third, two outs in the ninth and Leo sends me up. He says: 'If you don't hit it good, don't run and hurt your leg.'

"The first pitch was a knockdown and, when I ducked, the ball hit the bat and went down

the third base line, as beautiful a bunt as you've ever seen. Well, Ebbets Field is jammed. Leo has said: 'Don't run.' But this is a big game. I take off for first, and we win and I've ripped the muscles from my ankle to my hip. Leo says: 'You shouldn't have done it.'

"Now it's the last three days of the season and we're a game ahead of the Cards and we're playin' the Phillies in Brooklyn. Leo says to me: 'It's now or never. I don't think we can win it without you.' The first two up are outs and I single to right. There's Charley Dressen, coachin' on third, with the steal sign. I start to get my lead, and a pitcher named Charley Schanz is workin' and he throws an ordinary lob over to first. My leg is stiff and I slide and my heel spike catches the bag and I hear it snap.

"Leo comes runnin' out. He says: 'Come on. You're all right.' I said: 'I think it's broken.' He says: 'It ain't stickin' out.' They took me to Peck Memorial, and it was broken."

We went to St. Luke's Hospital in St. Louis. In the main office they told Pete to go over to a desk where a gray-haired, semistout woman was sitting at a typewriter. She started to book Pete in, typing his answer on the form. "What is your occupation, Mr. Reiser?" she said.

"Baseball," Pete said.

"Have you ever been hospitalized before?"

"Yes," Pete said.

* * *

In 1946 the Dodgers played an exhibition game in Springfield, Missouri. When the players got off the train there was a young radio announcer there, and he was grabbing them one at a time and asking them where they thought they'd finish that year.

"In first place," Reese and Casey and Dixie Walker and the rest were saying. "On top" . . . "We'll win it."

"And here comes Pistol Pete Reiser!" the announcer said. "Where do you think you'll finish this season, Pete?"

"In Peck Memorial Hospital," Pete said.

After the 1946 season Brooklyn changed the walls at Ebbets Field. They added boxes, cutting 40 feet off left field and dropping center field from 420 to 390 feet. Pete had made a real good start that season in center, and on June 5 the Dodgers were leading the Pirates by three runs in the sixth inning when Culley Rikard hit one.

"I made my turn and ran," Pete says, "and,

where I thought I still had that thirty feet, I didn't."

"The crowd," Al Laney wrote the next day in the New York *Herald Tribune*, "which watched silently while Reiser was being carried away, did not know that he had held onto the ball . . . Rikard circled the bases, but Butch Henline, the umpire, who ran to Reiser, found the ball still in Reiser's glove. . . . Two outs were posted on the scoreboard after play was resumed. Then the crowd let out a tremendous roar."

In the Brooklyn clubhouse the doctor called for a priest, and the Last Rites of the Church were administered to Pete. He came to, but lapsed into unconsciousness again and woke up at 3 A.M. in Peck Memorial.

For eight days he couldn't move. After three weeks they let him out, and he made that next western trip with the Dodgers. In Pittsburgh he was working out in the outfield before the game when Clyde King, chasing a fungo, ran into him and Pete woke up in the clubhouse.

"I went back to the Hotel Schenley and lay down," he says. "After the game I got up and had dinner with Peewee. We were sittin' on the porch, and I scratched my head and I felt a lump there about as big as half a golf ball. I told Peewee to feel it and he said: 'Gosh!' I said: 'I don't think that's supposed to be like that.' He said: 'Hell, no.'"

Pete went up to Rickey's room and Rickey called his pilot and had Pete flown to Johns Hopkins in Baltimore. They operated on him for a blood clot.

"You're lucky," the doctor told him. "If it had moved just a little more you'd have been gone."

Pete was unable to hold even a pencil. He had double vision and, when he tried to take a single step, he became dizzy. He stayed for three weeks and then went home for almost a month.

"It was August," he says, "and Brooklyn was fightin' for another pennant. I thought if I could play the last two months it might make the difference, so I went back to Johns Hopkins. The doctor said: 'You've made a remarkable recovery.' I said: 'I want to play.' He said: 'I can't okay that. The slightest blow on the head can kill you.'"

Pete played. He worked out for four days, pinch hit a couple of times and then, in the Polo Grounds, made a diving catch in left field. They carried him off, and in the clubhouse he was unable to recognize anyone.

Pete was still having dizzy spells when the Dodgers went into the 1947 Series against the Yankees. In the third game he walked in the first inning, got the steal sign and, when he went into second, felt his right ankle snap. At the hospital they found it was broken.

"Just tape it, will you?" Pete said.

"I want to put a cast on it," the doctor said.

"If you do," Pete said, "they'll give me a dollar-a-year contract next season."

The next day he was back on the bench. Bill Bevens was pitching for the Yankees and, with two out in ninth, it looked like he was going to pitch the first no-hitter in World Series history.

"Aren't you going to volunteer to hit?" Burt Shotton, who was managing Brooklyn, said to Pete.

Al Gionfriddo was on first and Bucky Harris, who was managing the Yankees, ordered Pete walked. Eddie Miksis ran for him, and when Cookie Lavagetto hit that double, the two runs scored and Brooklyn won, 3-2.

"The next day," Pete says, "the sports writers were second-guessing Harris for putting me on when I represented the winning run. Can you imagine what they'd have said if they knew I had a broken ankle?"

At the end of that season Rickey had the outfield walls at Ebbets Field padded with one-inch foam rubber for Pete, but he never hit them again. He had headaches most of the time and played little. Then he was traded to Boston, and in two seasons there he hit the wall a couple of times. Twice his left shoulder came out while he was making diving catches. Pittsburgh picked Pete up in 1951, and the next year he played into July with Cleveland and that was the end of it.

Between January and September of 1953, Pete dropped $40,000 in the used-car business in St. Louis, and then he got a job in a lumber mill for $100 a week. In the winter of 1955 he wrote Brooklyn asking for a part-time job as a scout, and on March 1, Buzzy Bavasi, the Dodger vice-president, called him on the phone.

"How would you like a manager's job?" Buzzy said.

"I'll take it," Pete said.

"I haven't even told you where it is. It's Thomasville, Georgia, in Class D."

"I don't care," Pete said. "I'll take it."

At Vero Beach that spring, Mike Gaven wrote a piece about Pete in the New York *Journal American*.

"Even in the worn gray uniform of the Class

D Thomasville, Georgia, club," Mike wrote, "Pete Reiser looks, acts and talks like a big leaguer. The Dodgers pitied Pete when they saw him starting his comeback effort after not having handled a ball for two and a half years. They lowered their heads when they saw him in a chow line with a lot of other bushers, but the old Pistol held his head high. . . ."

The next spring, Sid Friedlander, of the New York *Post,* saw Pete at Vero and wrote a column about him managing Kokomo. The last thing I saw about him in the New York papers was a small item out of Tipton, Indiana, saying that the bus carrying the Kokomo team had collided with a car and Pete was in a hospital in Kokomo with a back injury.

* * *

"Managing," Pete was saying in that St. Louis hospital, "you try to find out how your players are thinking. At Thomasville one night one of my kids made a bad throw. After the game I said to him: 'What were you thinking while that ball was coming to you?' He said: 'I was saying to myself that I hoped I could make a good throw.' I said: 'Sit down.' I tried to explain to him the way you have to think. You know how I used to think?"

"Yes," I said, "but you tell me."

"I was always sayin': 'Hit it to me. Just hit it to me. I'll make the catch. I'll make the throw.' When I was on base I was always lookin' over and sayin': 'Give me the steal sign. Give me the sign. Let me go.' That's the way you have to think."

"Pete," I said, "now that it's all over, do you ever think that if you hadn't played it as hard as you did, there's no telling how great you might have been or how much money you might have made?"

"Never," Pete said. "It was my way of playin'. If I hadn't played that way I wouldn't even have been whatever I was. God gave me those legs and the speed, and when they took me into the walls that's the way it had to be. I couldn't play any other way."

A technician came in with an electrocardiograph. She was a thin, dark-haired woman and she set it up by the bed and attached one of the round metal disks to Pete's left wrist and started to attach another to his left ankle.

"Aren't you kind of young to be having pains in your chest?" she said.

"I've led a fast life," Pete said.

On the way back to New York I kept thinking how right Pete was. To tell a man who is this true that there is another way for him to do it is to speak a lie. You cannot ask him to change his way of going, because it makes him what he is.

Three days after I got home I had a message to call St. Louis. I heard the phone ring at the other end and Pete answered. "I'm out!" he said.

"Did they let you out, or did you sneak out again?" I said.

"They let me out," he said. "It's just a strained heart muscle, I guess. My heart itself is all right."

"That's wonderful."

"I can manage again. In a couple of days I can go back to Kokomo."

If his voice had been higher he would have sounded like a kid at Christmas.

"What else did they say?" I said.

"Well, they say I have to take it easy."

"Do me a favor," I said.

"What?"

"Take their advice. This time, please take it easy."

"I will," he said. "I'll take it easy."

If he does it will be the first time.

THE excerpt from Jimmy Piersall's autobiography in the first *Fireside Book of Baseball* acts as a memorable backdrop for this true aftermath.

Jimmy Piersall's Greatest Day

──────────────── **AL HIRSHBERG** ────────────────

JIMMY PIERSALL, the Boston Red Sox outfielder whose dramatically successful return to major-league baseball from the depths of mental illness was immortalized in story and on film, has enjoyed dozens of great days during his colorful career. He has known the thrill of being mobbed by teammates after saving a game with a miraculous catch or winning one with a clutch home run. His ears have tingled to the music of ten thousand cheers, and his eyes have smarted from the joyful popping of photographers' flash bulbs.

But Jimmy Piersall's greatest day came, not on the ball field, but in the dimly lit room of a child—a child so disturbed that he teetered on the threshold of permanent oblivion; a child so depressed that life had lost its meaning; a child so impervious to therapy that his parents and his doctor had reached the end of mortal resource and were resorting to prayer alone to break him out of his shell of lethargy.

For nearly all of his eleven years, the boy, born and brought up in New York City, had lived in a world of petty tumult. His parents, mismated from the outset, disliked each other so intensely that not a day passed without an argument between them. Each quarrel left its searing imprint on the mind of their high-strung son. He was growing up nervous, irritable, sickly and afraid of his own shadow. He was so jumpy that the slightest sound gave him a start, and whenever his parents smothered each other in noisy invective, he retreated to the sanctuary of his bedroom, where he cowered in terror.

The terror never abated; in fact, it grew more acute as time went by. The parental arguments increased in intensity, and perpetual turmoil swirled about the boy's head. The child was fast becoming a nervous wreck, and needed only a slight push to get beyond the edge of reason.

The push came suddenly one sultry evening in August of 1955. The baseball season was at its height, and the boy was devouring everything he could find about Jimmy Piersall, who was his special hero. On that night, Piersall's life story was to be shown on a coast-to-coast television network. The child wanted to see the show, and his parents permitted him to stay up for it.

As a boy, Piersall was forced into an unnatural concentration on baseball by a well-meaning but too ambitious father who demanded absolute perfection. Jimmy tried hard to please him, and learned to become an outstanding ballplayer, but, instead of winning praise for what he did right, all he ever heard was criticism for what he did wrong. He grew up in fear of a man whom he loved but could never satisfy. He lived in an atmosphere of tension which grew constantly worse. By the time he was a high-school sophomore, Piersall was on the verge of a breakdown. He could neither eat nor sleep properly. He suffered chronic headaches. Just before he graduated, his father, a house painter, suffered a heart attack, putting new burdens on Jimmy's already heavily weighted shoulders.

Despite the tensions which plagued him, Jimmy became a great ballplayer. He was a Red Sox star at the age of 22. By then, married and a father, he had additional responsibilities. Deeply aware of the necessity for making enough money to support everyone dependent on him, Jimmy drove himself too hard. In the middle of the 1952 baseball season, he was committed to a mental institution. Later, thanks to shock treatments, a sympathetic doctor and a devoted wife, Jimmy began a comeback which was successfully completed when he returned to the Red Sox fully cured and a better ballplayer than ever.

Piersall's full story was depicted on television. It was hardly a show for a high-strung child. As the boy sat and watched the events of Jimmy's troubled life unfold in a rapid buildup to the actual breakdown, his own tight nerves stretched beyond the danger point. Putting himself in the ballplayer's shoes, he suffered all the pangs that Piersall suffered. And as the character on the screen lost his sense of reason, the boy in the Manhattan living room lost his, too. When the program reached its exciting climax, the youngster went completely berserk. He fell to the floor screaming, and, even after they turned the program off, his frightened parents could not quiet him down. Before the night was over, the boy, raving and incoherent, was placed under a doctor's care.

"He was in very bad shape at first," the doctor later said. "He had been under such terrific tension for so long that something had to give. The television show happened to be the instrument that set him off, but if it hadn't been that, it would have been something else."

The doctor spent hours both with the boy and his parents. When he learned the whole story, he told the parents that their son would never be normal until they either patched up their differences or separated. Realizing that they could not live together in harmony, they decided to separate, leaving the boy in the care of the mother.

After the first acute stage of his illness was past, the child began to show signs of recovery. He quieted down to a point where he could talk lucidly and, after a while, he was able to understand that there would be no more fights between his parents. But he was indifferent to his surroundings. It was virtually impossible to get him out of the house and, in fact, he spent most of his time in his room.

"This sort of thing often occurs in these cases," the doctor explained. "Once the acute stage is over, you level off on a plateau of serenity. If you're not pulled out of that plateau, you stay there, and if you're there too long, you may never come out of it. This boy hit that plateau very early after his initial breakdown. But we worked with him for weeks after that, and no matter what we did, it failed to have an appreciable effect on him."

One day the doctor, who had often talked baseball with the boy and was well aware of his affection for Piersall, hit upon the idea of asking the ballplayer to help. Piersall agreed to see the boy the next time the Red Sox were in New York. The doctor kept the impending visit a secret from the boy, but he brought up the subject of Piersall more and more often. While the child's face always lit up momentarily, his interest flagged quickly, and in a few moments, his eyes reflected only indifference.

Then one morning, the doctor asked, "Would you know Jimmy Piersall if he walked into this room?"

The child's eyes widened.

"Would I know him?" he exclaimed. "Sure, I'd know him. Only—"

His voice trailed off, and he looked away.

"Only—what?" the doctor asked, gently.

"Only Jimmy Piersall isn't walking into this room," the boy said, dully. "Jimmy Piersall doesn't even know I'm alive."

"Yes, he does, son."

A strange voice cut across the room like an electric current. The boy started, then stared. There was no doubt about it. The man standing at the door was Jimmy Piersall.

The boy and the ballplayer held each other's eyes for long seconds, then Piersall, grinning, balled his right hand into a fist and playfully grazed the youngster's jaw. The child smiled back. It was the first time the boy had smiled since his breakdown.

Piersall sat beside the child and began talking. He told him of his own troubles, how he had once been so sick and despondent, so unhappy and discouraged that he thought he'd never pull out of it. He pointed out that having a mental breakdown was just like breaking a leg—it wasn't very much fun while it lasted, but once it was cured, it was cured for good. He told the boy to stop feeling sorry for himself and stop moping around the house.

Over and over, Piersall insisted that, while the boy's doctor and parents could help him, no one could do as much as he could do himself. He told the child to get outdoors, where he could enjoy himself playing ball and having fun. And he told the boy to have faith in God. "He'll help you as He helped me," said Piersall. "But He didn't do it alone. I had to do my share. You do yours."

Later, they talked baseball until Piersall had to leave for the ball park.

"The boy's cure really dated from that morning," the doctor said, later. "After Piersall left, he told me he was going to try to get well the way Jimmy did. He went outdoors that afternoon for the first time since his breakdown.

After a week or so, he was able to go back to school again.

"Piersall's visit jolted him off that plateau—there isn't any question about it. It was the best medicine the child could have had."

Today, the boy is a healthy, happy, normal thirteen-year-old. He never thinks about his illness. But every once in a while, he talks about his friend Jimmy Piersall, who once came to his home and talked to him, man to man. That was his greatest day.

It was Piersall's, too.

MARTY LOWE

*"How do you like that!—I was fined
$50 for not running out a fly ball!"*

JIMMY FOXX was a ballplayer's ballplayer—one who, as many people forget, could and did play every position on the team. He's best remembered for his prowess as a home-run hitter. The following will remind you why.

Double X

BOB HOLBROOK

JIMMY Foxx came along before the days of the tape-measure home runs.

And maybe it was just as well, for they didn't make tapes long enough to measure some of the rocketlike homers he bashed during his 17 years in the majors.

Where was Foxx's longest home run . . . Cleveland? . . . Chicago? . . . Boston?

"No," he grinned recently, "it was in Tokyo." Tokyo?

"Yes, in Meiji Stadium to be exact," he added. "It was a mighty big stadium, too, seated something like 50,000 people. The distance to the left-field stands was 400 feet. Now there were an awful lot of rows between the base of the stands and the top.

"Well, I got hold of one. It was a high, towering one that hit right on the top of the back wall behind all those fans and skipped right out of the ball park. How far did it go? It must have gone 600 feet, they told me.

"We didn't think of measuring home runs. You hit one out of the park and you said, 'I hit that pretty good.' You didn't measure them."

His longest home run in the American League?

"I guess it was the one I hit in Chicago," said Double X. "That ball went over the roof in left field, cleared 34th Place, and went over a parking lot and landed in a tennis court.

"I know where it landed because a few years ago I was walking down that same street when this fellow says to me, 'You're Foxx, aren't you?' I said yes and he said, 'Do you remember the ball you hit over the roof? Well, I was over in the tennis courts playing tennis and that ball came down and hit me on the foot. I've still got the ball.'

"I tried to talk him out of the ball, but the feller says he might send it to the Hall of Fame."

People talk about the sluggers of today. Listen to Foxx:

"I thought I was having a very bad year unless I hit at least .330.

"Runs batted in? Heck, one year I knocked in 165 runs and the next 168, and I didn't come close to leading the league. I knocked in at least 115 runs for 13 straight seasons."

Foxx's top pay was $32,000.

What is the matter with the modern-day hitter?

"They're all trying too hard to hit the ball out of the park," Foxx declared.

"Hitting is not as hard as they make it seem. I say this: Get the right bat and keep your eye on the ball.

"Some of these players are swinging so hard they can't see the ball. If you keep your eye on the ball it's impossible to swing too hard.

"Never in my career did I swing so hard that I knocked myself off my feet."

Did he try for home runs?

"No," Foxx said. "Once I did that I was licked. A proper bat, a good swing and meet the ball squarely was my method. If you have enough power and meet the ball right it's going to go out of the park anyway. There is no difference between a ball hit 400 feet and one hit 500 feet. They're both homers."

The toughest pitcher for Jimmy?

"Simple. Johnny Allen. I never figured out that guy and I still haven't. I couldn't pick up the ball when he threw. I had one good day against him . . . four for four. But if you put all four hits together they wouldn't have measured into one healthy line drive.

"Bobo Newsom gave me trouble when he

first came up with all those different motions," Foxx smiled. "I figured him out. I waited flat-footed until he threw the ball and then I was okay."

Did Bob Feller's vicious fast balls bother Foxx?

"No," he answered, "Feller never bothered me. I always hit his curve ball. He couldn't get one out of three of his fast balls over, so I never offered at them, only the curve."

Foxx still chuckles when he recalls a day in Yankee Stadium batting against Lefty Gomez.

"The count was two and two," Foxx reminisced. "Bill Dickey was catching and he called for every sign he ever knew. Gomez didn't throw the ball.

"Finally, Dickey went to the mound. 'What in h--- do you want to throw, Gomez?' he barked.

"Lefty says, 'Nothing. Maybe he'll get tired and walk away.'

"The next pitch I hit into the third deck in left field. The next day Gomez was late getting into the dressing room. Somebody asked him where he'd been and Lefty said:

" 'I walked out to where Foxx hit that ball yesterday, and it took me exactly one hour and a half to make the round trip.' "

Talk about right-handed sluggers! You can start with James Emory Foxx and work down.

ACCORDING to the table of contents in the front of this book, this is a story about mountain climbing. It is also a story of getting to the Los Angeles Coliseum for an early Dodger game in 1958.

The two matters, according to the following piece, are interchangeable.

Mike Jackson's column appeared in the Laguna Beach (Calif.) *Post*, and we are proud to reprint this one here—and to suggest that here may be one of the authentic humorists in American journalism today. Not to lessen the point, but to use less flowery words, this one cracked me up. Incidentally, Jackson now writes a column for the Los Angeles *Examiner*.

Take Me Out to the Ball Game (I Can Get Home by Myself)

MIKE JACKSON

IT WAS WELL AFTER MIDNIGHT and we were the only group in the mahogany-paneled room when Manners set a tray of savories and Kleenex before us and asked, "Will that be all, gentlemen?" I dismissed him with a gesture. None of us wanted to break the spell that permeated the atmosphere. Col. B.V.D. "Spiv" Smythe-Bitters, DC-AC, had been persuaded to relate the mystery-shrouded events of his safari into the San Fernando out-back and the ill-fated but glorious attempt to reach the headwaters of the Los Angeles River.

In the lambent glow of the dying embers we reflected upon that adventure which has become a fable in every bazaar from Sadi-el to Malibu. We were four—"Spiv" Smythe-Bitters, whose collection of *National Geographics* was the envy of every dentist east of Suez; Kent Manoshewitz, who had made a packet in copra and robbers; Zsa-Zsa, the native girl who followed me everywhere since I had found her wandering on the Sunset Strip after the monsoon of '58. She knew only a few simple words—Cartier, Saks, Valentina—and, childlike, delighted in repeating them.

I completed the group. It was good to be among old friends and for a blessed moment out of the spotlight. It's deucedly awkward, this public-hero business. The cheering throngs following me about, the press fellows begging

for interviews, and a rajah's ransom in free Wheaties all mine, if only I'll endorse it. It's a ruddy bore, the whole show. In point of fact, I'm inclined to think I might be happier today if I had never tried it. But it's something that gets into a man's bones. "Why did you do it?" they all ask.

Why indeed? You climb it because it's there.

"Spiv" Smythe-Bitters sipped his sherry, then turned those keen blue eyes on us. "See here, chaps. I've been going on like a ghat of amahs at suttee." He placed a friendly hand on my shoulder. "What we all want is your own story of the whole astounding triumph. The first man to see a baseball game from the top of the Coliseum."

"Hear, hear," cried the others.

I protested, "Any man-jack among you would've done the same, I dare say. Ain't nobody wants to hear about li'l ole no-count me."

My modesty only goaded them on. They began to chant, "Speech. Speech. Speech."

"Mink stole!" cried Zsa-Zsa.

I own that there were tears in my eyes. I had trouble making out my notes. "It was a team victory," I said, and proposed a moment of silence for those who were not with us. For Erik, who collapsed at Costa Mesa; for Derek, who faltered at the Freeway; for Nigel, who fell victim to an Abominable Snowjob and sold

SLUGGERS!

In order,

ck Wilson,

International News

Rogers Hornsby,

United Press

Ott,

United Press

International News

Jimmy Foxx. Do not think the picture of Foxx is a trick shot. This is precisely what he looked like to pitchers.

FIGHT!!

And here they go. The fellows in most of these pictures are—you'll have to take our word for it—

First picture *(below)* Stanky of Brooklyn, Merullo of Chicago.

Second picture *(bottom right)* we have the Cincinnati Reds. The hatless fellow is Don Hoak. Prospective opponent seems to be somebody from Brooklyn.

(Top right) Brooklyn is involved again. No. 41 is Eddie Mathews of Milwaukee. We think he is about to belt Don Drysdale.

The center photo is easy for identification. Matter of fact, there was no fight at all. Joe Adcock *(bottom)* of the Braves chased the Giants' Ruben Gomez, but never caught him.

United Press

Wide World

Wide World

International News

Groundskeepers mop up after a healthy riot at an old-time ball park, possibly the old High-landers Park in New York . . .

. . . And Enos Slaughter of the Yankees heads for the clubhouse (where the umpires sent him and four others) following a free-for-all with the White Sox.

his ticket. I did not mention those who had showed the White Feather by pretending that they were needed at home.

"Spiv" Smythe-Bitters broke the string on a package. "Here's a little something I've been saving just for this." It was a rare old 78 of Nelson Eddy singing "Stout-Hearted Men." We stood while he crashed it into the fireplace.

"Now," they beseeched me, "the story!"

"My story begins with the dream of a boy," I began. I do not know precisely when I first gazed out over the horizon and beheld that eminence, so cold, so threatening, yet so alluring. It seated 100,000, so the legend ran, and on the lower plains the Big Ten invaders annually slaughtered the local youths. Some day, one part of me knew, I would climb to the top of it.

My plan was simple but audacious. After tiffin at Knott's Berry Farm, we followed the Great Circle route, gradually acclimatizing ourselves to the traffic. Breathing became laborious in the smog area. Zsa-Zsa was the first to drop out. She quit at I. Magnin's. As we neared the dangerous downtown area, swarms of excited natives waved pennants inscribed "LA Dodgers."

"Don't worry," I told our tense group. "They're friendly."

They surged past us in endless caravans—Kiwanis, Rotary, Lions, Business Mens Association, Jr. Chamber of Commerce. I walked up to a native, slapped him on the back, saw from his lapel button that he was Charlie, a chiropodist. "Charlie," I said, "I've got my own little column. I live in the fastest-growing little town in the U.S.A. I've shot three eggheads."

Charlie gave me a slice of his mom's apple pie. He slapped me on the back, and I motioned to our group that it was safe to move on. At the confluence of Vermont and Pico we traded our watches for a parking space. Then, mile after mile, we trudged on. We began to throw out all unnecessary equipment. We rested at the base of the North Wall and looked up. We had trained by climbing the Hollywood Bowl and the Beverly-Hilton. But nothing had prepared us for this.

I put on my crampons, adjusted the oxygen, sipped two cc.'s of Geritol. At the fiftieth row, my Sherpa guide was through. We were at an altitude where no hot-dog vendor had ever trod. "Me pooped," he gasped. "You go. Take this." He gave me his Diner's Club card. I never saw him again.

I climbed on. Then, when it seemed I must give up, that no mortal could ever conquer this mass of stone and steel, I was in K-5, the fabled unreserved section. There were only twenty-seven more rows to go. They passed in a blur.

What can I say of my moment of triumph? I could not absorb its true import. Because sound travels more slowly than sight, I could hear the faint cheers left over from the USC-UCLA game. Due to the curvature of the earth, it was not possible to see the Dodger ball game itself. However, I did sight two girls in Oxnard playing Jacks. One was on her fivesies. We hope to bring you a full report of that contest in the very near future.

OF COURSE, the small type in the title here is on purpose. This is from Miss Jackson's marvelous book *Raising Demons*.

braves 10, giants 9

SHIRLEY JACKSON

BEFORE THE CHILDREN were able to start counting days till school was out, and before Laurie had learned to play more than a simple scale on the trumpet, and even before my husband's portable radio had gone in for its annual checkup so it could broadcast the Brooklyn games all summer, we found ourselves deeply involved in the Little League. The Little League was new in our town that year. One day all the kids were playing baseball in vacant lots and without any noticeable good sportsmanship, and the next day, almost, we were standing around the grocery and the post office wondering what kind of a manager young Johnny Cole was going to make, and whether the Weaver boy—the one with the strong arm— was going to be twelve this August, or only eleven as his mother said, and Bill Cummings had donated his bulldozer to level off the top of Sugar Hill, where the kids used to go sledding, and we were all sporting stickers on our cars reading "We have contributed" and the fund-raising campaign was over the top in forty-eight hours. There are a thousand people in our town, and it turned out, astonishingly, that about sixty of them were boys of Little League age. Laurie thought he'd try out for pitcher and his friend Billy went out for catcher. Dinner-time all over town got shifted to eight-thirty in the evening, when nightly baseball practice was over. By the time our family had become accustomed to the fact that no single problem in our house could be allowed to interfere in any way with the tempering of Laurie's right arm, the uniforms had been ordered, and four teams had been chosen and named, and Laurie and Billy were together on the Little League Braves. My friend Dot, Billy's mother, was learning to keep a box score. I announced in family assembly that there would be no more oiling of baseball gloves in the kitchen sink.

We lived only a block or so from the base-ball field, and it became the amiable custom of the ballplayers to drop in for a snack on their way to the practice sessions. There was to be a double-header on Memorial Day, to open the season. The Braves would play the Giants; the Red Sox would play the Dodgers. After one silent, apoplectic moment my husband agreed, gasping, to come to the ball games and root against the Dodgers. A rumor got around town that the Red Sox were the team to watch, with Butch Weaver's strong arm, and several mothers believed absolutely that the various managers were putting their own sons into all the best positions, although everyone told everyone else that it didn't matter, really, *what* position the boys held so long as they got a chance to play ball, and show they were good sports about it. As a matter of fact, the night before the double-header which was to open the Little League, I distinctly recall that I told Laurie it was only a game. "It's only a game, fella," I said. "Don't *try* to go to sleep; read or something if you're nervous. Would you like an aspirin?"

"I forgot to tell you," Laurie said, yawning. "He's pitching Georgie tomorrow. Not me."

"*What?*" I thought, and then said heartily, "I mean, he's the manager, after all. I know you'll play your best in *any* position."

"I could go to sleep now if you'd just turn out the light," Laurie said patiently. "I'm really quite tired."

I called Dot later, about twelve o'clock, because I was pretty sure she'd still be awake, and of course she was, although Billy had gone right off about nine o'clock. She said she wasn't the least bit nervous, because of course it didn't really matter except for the kids' sake, and she hoped the best team would win. I said that that was just what I had been telling my husband, and she said *her* husband had suggested that perhaps she had better not go to the game at all because if the Braves lost she ought to be home with a hot bath ready for Billy and perhaps a steak dinner or something. I said that even if Laurie wasn't pitching I was sure the Braves would win, and of course I wasn't one of those people who always wanted their own children right out in the center of things all the time but if the Braves lost it would be my opinion that their lineup ought to be revised and Georgie put back into right field where he belonged. She said *she* thought Laurie was a better pitcher, and I suggested that she and her husband and Billy come over for lunch and we could all go to the game together.

I spent all morning taking movies of the Memorial Day parade, particularly the Starlight 4-H Club, because Jannie was marching with them, and I used up almost a whole film magazine on Sally and Barry, standing at the curb, wide-eyed and rapt, waving flags. Laurie missed the parade because he slept until nearly twelve, and then came downstairs and made himself an enormous platter of bacon and eggs and toast, which he took out to the hammock and ate lying down.

"How do you feel?" I asked him, coming out to feel his forehead. "Did you sleep all right? How's your arm?"

"Sure," he said.

We cooked lunch outdoors, and Laurie finished his breakfast in time to eat three hamburgers. Dot had only a cup of coffee, and I took a little salad. Every now and then she would ask Billy if he wanted to lie down for a little while before the game, and I would ask Laurie how he felt. The game was not until two o'clock, so there was time for Jannie and Sally and Barry to roast marshmallows. Laurie and Billy went into the barn to warm up with a game of ping-pong, and Billy's father remarked that the boys certainly took this Little League setup seriously, and my husband said that it was the best thing in the world for the kids. When the boys came out of the barn after playing three games of ping-pong I asked Billy if he was feeling all right and Dot said she thought Laurie ought to lie down for a while before the game. The boys said no, they had to meet the other guys at the school at one-thirty and they were going to get into their uniforms now. I said please to be careful, and Dot said if they needed any help dressing just call down and we would come up, and both boys turned and looked at us curiously for a minute before they went indoors.

"My goodness," I said to Dot, "I hope they're not nervous."

"Well, they take it so seriously," she said.

I sent the younger children in to wash the marshmallow off their faces, and while our husbands settled down to read over the Little League rule book, Dot and I cleared away the paper plates and gave the leftover hamburgers to the dog. Suddenly Dot said, "Oh," in a weak voice and I turned around and Laurie and Billy were coming through the door in their uniforms. "They look so—so—*tall*," Dot said, and I said, "Laurie?" uncertainly. The boys laughed, and looked at each other.

"Pretty neat," Laurie said, looking at Billy.

"Some get-up," Billy said, regarding Laurie.

Both fathers came over and began turning the boys around and around, and Jannie and Sally came out onto the porch and stared worshipfully. Barry, to whom Laurie and his friends have always seemed incredibly tall and efficient, gave them a critical glance and observed that this was truly a baseball.

It turned out that there was a good deal of advice the fathers still needed to give the ballplayers, so they elected to walk over to the school with Billy and Laurie and then on to the ball park, where they would find Dot and me later. We watched them walk down the street; not far away they were joined by another boy in uniform and then a couple more. After that, for about half an hour, there were boys in uniform wandering by twos and threes toward the baseball field and the school, all alike in a kind of unexpected dignity and new tallness, all walking with self-conscious pride. Jannie and Sally stood on the front porch watching, careful to greet by name all the ballplayers going by.

A few minutes before two, Dot and I put the younger children in her car and drove over to the field. Assuming that perhaps seventy-five of the people in our town were actively engaged in the baseball game, there should have been about nine hundred and twenty-five people in the audience, but there seemed to be more than that already; Dot and I both remarked that it was the first town affair we had ever attended where there were more strange faces than familiar ones.

Although the field itself was completely finished, there was only one set of bleachers up, and that was filled, so Dot and I took the car robe and settled ourselves on top of the little hill over the third-base line, where we had a splendid view of the whole field. We talked about how it was at the top of this hill the kids used to start their sleds, coasting right down past third base and on into center field, where the ground flattened out and the sleds would stop. From the little hill we could see the roofs of the houses in the town below, half hidden in the trees, and far on to the hills in the distance. We both remarked that there was still snow on the high mountain.

Barry stayed near us, deeply engaged with a little dump truck. Jannie and Sally accepted twenty-five cents each, and melted into the crowd in the general direction of the refreshment stand. Dot got out her pencil and box score, and I put a new magazine of film in the movie camera. We could see our husbands standing around in back of the Braves' dugout, along with the fathers of all the other Braves players. They were all in a group, chatting with great humorous informality with the manager and the two coaches of the Braves. The fathers of the boys on the Giant team were down by the Giant dugout, standing around the manager and the coaches of the Giants.

Marian, a friend of Dot's and mine whose boy Artie was first baseman for the Giants, came hurrying past looking for a seat, and we offered her part of our car robe. She sat down, breathless, and said she had mislaid her husband and her younger son, so we showed her where her husband was down by the Giant dugout with the other fathers, and her younger son turned up almost at once to say that Sally had a popsicle and so could he have one, too, and a hot dog and maybe some popcorn?

Suddenly, from far down the block, we could hear the high-school band playing "The Stars and Stripes Forever," and coming closer. Everyone stood up to watch and then the band turned the corner and came through the archway with the official Little League insignia and up to the entrance of the field. All the ballplayers were marching behind the band. I thought foolishly of Laurie when he was Barry's age, and something of the sort must have crossed Dot's mind, because she reached out and put her hand on Barry's head. "There's Laurie and Billy," Barry said softly. The boys ran out onto the field and lined up along the base lines, and then I discovered that we were all cheering, with Barry jumping up and down and shouting, "Baseball! Baseball!"

"If you cry I'll tell Laurie," Dot said to me out of the corner of her mouth.

"Same to you," I said, blinking.

The sky was blue and the sun was bright and the boys stood lined up soberly in their clean new uniforms holding their caps while the band played "The Star-Spangled Banner" and the flag was raised. From Laurie and Billy, who were among the tallest, down to the littlest boys

in uniform, there was a straight row of still, expectant faces.

I said, inadequately, "It must be hot out there."

"They're all chewing gum," Dot said.

Then the straight lines broke and the Red Sox, who had red caps, and the Dodgers, who had blue caps, went off into the bleachers and the Giants, who had green caps, went into their dugout, and at last the Braves, who had black caps, trotted out onto the field. It was announced over the public-address system that the Braves were the home team, and when it was announced that Georgie was going to pitch for the Braves I told Marian that I was positively relieved, since Laurie had been so nervous anyway over the game that I was sure pitching would have been a harrowing experience for him, and she said that Artie had been perfectly willing to sit out the game as a substitute, or a pinch hitter, or something, but that his manager had insisted upon putting him at first base because he was so reliable.

"You know," she added with a little laugh, "I don't know one position from another, but of course Artie is glad to play anywhere."

"I'm sure he'll do very nicely," I said, trying to put some enthusiasm into my voice.

Laurie was on second base for the Braves, and Billy at first. Marian leaned past me to tell Dot that first base was a *very* responsible position, and Dot said oh, was it? Because of course Billy just wanted to do the best he could for the team, and on the *Braves* it was the *manager* who assigned the positions. Marian smiled in what I thought was a nasty kind of way and said she hoped the best team would win. Dot and I both smiled back and said we hoped so, too.

When the umpire shouted, "Play Ball!" people all over the park began to call out to the players, and I raised my voice slightly and said, "Hurray for the Braves." That encouraged Dot and *she* called out, "Hurray for the Braves," but Marian, of course, had to say, "Hurray for the Giants."

The first Giant batter hit a triple, although, as my husband explained later, it would actually have been an infield fly if the shortstop had been looking and an easy out if he had thrown it anywhere near Billy at first. By the time Billy got the ball back into the infield the batter—Jimmie Hill, who had once borrowed Laurie's bike and brought it back with a flat tire—was on third. I could see Laurie out on second base banging his hands together and he looked so pale I was worried. Marian leaned around me and said to Dot, "That was a nice try Billy made. I don't think even *Artie* could have caught that ball."

"He looks *furious*," Dot said to me. "He just *hates* doing things wrong."

"They're all terribly nervous," I assured her. "They'll settle down as soon as they really get playing." I raised my voice a little. "Hurray for the Braves," I said.

The Giants made six runs in the first inning, and each time a run came in Marian looked sympathetic and told us that really, the boys were being quite good sports about it, weren't they? When Laurie bobbled an easy fly right at second and missed the out, she said to me that Artie had told her that Laurie was really quite a good little ballplayer and I mustn't blame him for an occasional error.

By the time little Jerry Hart finally struck out to retire the Giants, Dot and I were sitting listening with polite smiles. I had stopped saying "Hurray for the Braves." Marian had told everyone sitting near us that it was her boy who had slid home for the sixth run, and she had explained with great kindness that Dot and I had sons on the other team, one of them the first baseman who missed that long throw and the other one the second baseman who dropped the fly ball. The Giants took the field and Marian pointed out Artie standing on first base slapping his glove and showing off.

Then little Ernie Harrow, who was the Braves' right fielder and lunched frequently at our house, hit the first pitched ball for a fast grounder which went right through the legs of the Giant center fielder, and when Ernie came dancing onto second Dot leaned around to remark to Marian that if Artie had been playing closer to first the way Billy did he might have been ready for the throw if the Giant center fielder had managed to stop the ball. Billy came up and smashed a long fly over the left fielder's head and I put a hand on Marian's shoulder to hoist myself up. Dot and I stood there howling, "Run run run," Billy came home, and two runs were in. Little Andy placed a surprise bunt down the first-base line, Artie never even saw it, and I leaned over to tell Marian that clearly Artie did not understand all the refinements of playing first base. Then Laurie got a nice hit and slid into second. The Giants took out their pitcher and put in Buddy Williams, whom Laurie once beat up on the way to school. The score was tied with two out and Dot and I were both yelling. Then lit-

tle Ernie Harrow came up for the second time and hit a home run, right over the fence where they put the sign advertising his father's sand and gravel. We were leading eight to six when the inning ended.

Little League games are six innings, so we had five more innings to go. Dot went down to the refreshment stand to get some hot dogs and soda; she offered very politely to bring something for Marian, but Marian said thank you, no; she would get her own. The second inning tightened up considerably as the boys began to get over their stage fright and play baseball the way they did in the vacant lots. By the middle of the fifth inning the Braves were leading nine to eight, and then in the bottom of the fifth Artie missed a throw at first base and the Braves scored another run. Neither Dot nor I said a single word, but Marian got up in a disagreeable manner, excused herself, and went to sit on the other side of the field.

"Marian looks very poorly these days," I remarked to Dot as we watched her go.

"She's at *least* five years older than *I* am," Dot said.

"More than that," I said. "She's gotten very touchy, don't you think?"

"Poor little Artie," Dot said. "You remember when he used to have temper tantrums in nursery school?"

In the top of the sixth the Braves were winning ten to eight, but then Georgie, who had been pitching accurately and well, began to tire, and he walked the first two batters. The third boy hit a little fly which fell in short center field, and one run came in to make it ten to nine. Then Georgie, who was by now visibly rattled, walked the next batter and filled the bases.

"Three more outs and the Braves can win it," some man in the crowd behind us said. "I don't *think*," and he laughed.

"Oh, *lord*," Dot said, and I stood up and began to wail, "No, no." The manager was gesturing at Laurie and Billy. "No, no," I said to Dot, and Dot said, "He can't do it, don't let him." "It's too much to ask of the children," I said. "What a terrible thing to do to such little kids," Dot said.

"New pitcher," the man in the crowd said. "He better be good," and he laughed.

While Laurie was warming up and Billy was getting into his catcher's equipment, I suddenly heard my husband's voice for the first time. This was the only baseball game my husband had ever attended outside of Ebbets

Field. "Put it in his ear, Laurie," my husband was yelling, "put it in his ear."

Laurie was chewing gum and throwing slowly and carefully. Barry took a minute off from the little truck he was placidly filling with sand and emptying again to ask me if the big boys were still playing baseball. I stood there, feeling Dot's shoulder shaking against mine, and I tried to get my camera open to check the magazine of film but my fingers kept slipping and jumping against the little knob. I said to Dot that I guessed I would just enjoy the game for a while and not take pictures, and she said earnestly that Billy had had a little touch of fever that morning and the manager was taking his life in his hands putting Billy up there in all that catcher's equipment in that hot shade. I wondered if Laurie could see that I was nervous.

"*He* doesn't look very nervous," I said to Dot, but then my voice failed, and I finished, "does he?" in a sort of gasp.

The batter was Jimmie Hill, who had already had three hits that afternoon. Laurie's first pitch hit the dust at Billy's feet and Billy sprawled full length to stop it. The man in the crowd behind us laughed. The boy on third hesitated, unsure whether Billy had the ball; he started for home and then, with his mother just outside the third-base line yelling, "Go back, go back," he retreated to third again. Laurie's second pitch sent Billy rocking backward and he fell; "Only way he can stop it is fall on it," the man in the crowd said, and laughed.

Dot stiffened, and then she turned around slowly. For a minute she stared and then she said, in the evilest voice I have ever heard her use, "Sir, that catcher is my son."

"I beg your pardon, ma'am, I'm sure," the man said.

"Picking on little boys," Dot said.

The umpire called Laurie's next pitch ball three, although it was clearly a strike, and I was yelling, "You're blind, you're blind." I could hear my husband shouting to throw the bum out.

"Going to see a new pitcher pretty soon," said the man in the crowd, and I clenched my fist, and turned around and said in a voice that made Dot's sound cordial, "Sir, that pitcher is *my* son. If you have any more personal remarks to make about any member of my family—"

"Or mine," Dot added.

"I will immediately call Mr. Tillotson, our local constable, and see personally that you are put out of this ball park. People who go around attacking ladies and innocent children—"

"Strike," the umpire said.

I turned around once more and shook my fist at the man in the crowd, and he announced quietly and with some humility that he hoped both teams would win, and subsided into absolute silence.

Laurie then pitched two more strikes, his nice fast ball, and I thought suddenly of how at lunch he and Billy had been tossing hamburger rolls and Dot and I had made them stop. At about this point, Dot and I abandoned our spot up on the hill and got down against the fence with our faces pressed against the wire. "Come on, Billy boy," Dot was saying over and over, "come on, Billy boy," and I found that I was telling Laurie, "Come on now, only two more outs to go, only two more, come on, Laurie, come on. . . ." I could see my husband now but there was too much noise to hear him; he was pounding his hands against the fence. Dot's husband had *his* hands over his face and his back turned to the ball field. "He can't hit it, Laurie," Dot yelled, "this guy can't hit," which I thought with dismay was not true; the batter was Butch Weaver and he was standing there swinging his bat and sneering. "Laurie, Laurie, Laurie," screeched a small voice; I looked down and it was Sally, bouncing happily beside me. "Can I have another nickel?" she asked. "Laurie, Laurie."

"Strike," the umpire said and I leaned my forehead against the cool wire and said in a voice that suddenly had no power at all, "Just two strikes, Laurie, just two more strikes."

Laurie looked at Billy, shook his head, and looked again. He grinned and when I glanced down at Billy I could see that behind the mask he was grinning too. Laurie pitched, and the batter swung wildly. "Laurie, Laurie," Sally shrieked. "Strike two," the umpire said. Dot and I grabbed at each other's hands and Laurie threw the good fast ball for strike three.

One out to go, and Laurie, Billy, and the shortstop stood together on the mound for a minute. They talked very soberly, but Billy was grinning again as he came back to the plate. Since I was incapable of making any sound, I hung onto the wire and promised myself that if Laurie struck out this last batter I would never never say another word to him about the mess in his room, I would not make him paint the lawn chairs, I would not even mention clipping the hedge. . . . "Ball one," the umpire said, and I found that I had my voice back. "Crook," I yelled, "blind crook."

Laurie pitched, the batter swung, and hit a high foul ball back of the plate; Billy threw off his mask and tottered, staring up. The batter, the boys on the field, and the umpire, waited, and Dot suddenly spoke.

"William," she said imperatively, *"you catch that ball."*

Then everyone was shouting wildly; I looked at Dot and said, "Golly." Laurie and Billy were slapping and hugging each other, and then the rest of the team came around them and the manager was there. I distinctly saw my husband, who is not a lively man, vault the fence to run into the wild group and slap Laurie on the shoulder with one hand and Billy with the other. The Giants gathered around their manager and gave a cheer for the Braves, and the Braves gathered around *their* manager and gave a cheer for the Giants, and Laurie and Billy came pacing together toward the dugout, past Dot and me. I said, "Laurie?" and Dot said, "Billy?" They stared at us, without recognition for a minute, both of them lost in another world, and then they smiled and Billy said, "Hi, Ma," and Laurie said, "You see the game?"

I realized that my hair was over my eyes and I had broken two fingernails. Dot had a smudge on her nose and had torn a button off her sweater. We helped each other up the hill again and found that Barry was asleep on the car robe. Without speaking any more than was absolutely necessary, Dot and I decided that we could not stay for the second game of the double-header. I carried Barry asleep and Dot brought his dump truck and the car robe and my camera and the box score which she had not

kept past the first Giant run, and we headed wearily for the car.

We passed Artie in his green Giant cap and we said it had been a fine game, he had played wonderfully well, and he laughed and said tolerantly, "Can't win 'em all, you know." When we got back to our house I put Barry into his bed while Dot put on the kettle for a nice cup of tea. We washed our faces and took off our shoes, and finally Dot said hesitantly that she certainly hoped that Marian wasn't really offended with us.

"Well, of course she takes this kind of thing terribly hard," I said.

"I was just thinking," Dot said after a minute, "we ought to plan a kind of victory party for the Braves at the end of the season."

"A hot-dog roast, maybe?" I suggested.

"Well," Dot said, "I *did* hear the boys talking one day. They said they were going to take some time this summer and clean out your barn, and set up a record player in there and put in a stock of records and have some dances."

"You mean . . ." I faltered. "With *girls?*"

Dot nodded.

"Oh," I said.

When our husbands came home two hours later we were talking about old high-school dances and the time we went out with those boys from Princeton. Our husbands reported that the Red Sox had beaten the Dodgers in the second game and were tied for first place with the Braves. Jannie and Sally came idling home, and finally Laurie and Billy stopped in, briefly, to change their clothes. There was a pickup game down in Murphy's lot, they explained, and they were going to play some baseball.

Stuffy and the Error

HAROLD KAESE

BACK IN 1921, John (Stuffy) McInnis, Red Sox first baseman, made but one error in 152 games, which is still the big-league record. The error was given him by Gus Rooney, the official scorer. Both are still living and remember the incident well, although it happened 36 years ago.

In the eighth inning of the afternoon game at Boston's Fenway Park, Al Walters, 145-pound Boston catcher, picked Jimmie Dykes of the Athletics off first base—but McInnis dropped the ball.

Errors were not flashed on the scoreboard then, but Rooney gave his fellow writers in the press box the familiar "O" sign with his thumb and forefinger.

Nobody protested. It was just another error.

But McInnis was not to make another miscue until June 2 of the next season—after 163 errorless games—when he was playing for Cleveland.

The error looked bigger and bigger as the season advanced, and finally, in late September, according to Rooney, McInnis said to him, "Gus, how about taking away that error you gave me. It's kind of tough getting my only error in my home town."

"It's too late, John," answered Rooney. "I couldn't change it even if I wanted to—which I wouldn't."

And that's the way it stayed, without the fast friendship between player and writer being fractured or even shaken.

A story started later that McInnis had socked the official scorer—identified as the late Paul Shannon of the Boston *Post*—for giving him the error.

This was a fable. Rooney was the scorer, not Shannon. McInnis socked Shannon for something else.

Shannon had written stories McInnis did not like. One quoted him on the injustice of the 1918 Red Sox—who had struck briefly before the final game—not getting World Series rings.

"We're leaving Fort Worth on a train the next spring when Shannon came up to McInnis and an argument started. McInnis finally whacked him," explained Rooney. "I was sitting with Stuffy at the time, and still remember Paul carrying a magazine. He was always reading, even during games.

"After the scrap I went to Ed Barrow, but he only said, 'Sometimes those things are justified.'

"But it bothered some of us, and later, on Easter Sunday at Dallas, Dave Shean, our second baseman, and I got Stuffy to apologize and Shannon to accept. Stuffy was in his uniform in the hotel lobby at the time and he was carrying a bat.

"'Why the bat?' I asked. 'You going to take care of Shannon?'

"'Oh, no,' he laughed. 'I don't need a bat for that. I'm taking it to the park to use this afternoon.'"

Rooney recalls McInnis, a right-handed first baseman, as such a good fielder that Billy Evans once said, "He's the best ever on low throws, better than Sisler or Chance."

Although he had a chronic Charley horse that handicapped his running, McInnis stayed in the lineup and batted averages respectable even in those days.

One spring he was a holdout until one hour before the opening game at Washington. Signed just as he was about to catch a train home, he played the game and despite having missed all of spring training, played in every one of the Red Sox' games that year and batted .315 for the season. His lifetime average (1909-27) was .308.

"Don't forget to hold the label toward you."

AT the time this piece appeared—in *The American Scholar*, of all places—Mr. Kahn observed this was the first chance he'd had "to write seriously about the most remarkable aspect of baseball—its popularity."

Intellectuals and Ballplayers

ROGER KAHN

THE ROMANCE between intellectuals and the game of baseball is, for the most part, one-sided to the point of absurdity. A large percentage of intelligent Americans evaluate the four hundred men who play major baseball as awesomely gifted demigods. A large percentage of the muscular four hundred rate intellectuals several notches below umpires.

Neither point of view is necessarily conscious, of course, but the unconscious, as they say in the trade, will out. Occasionally intellectuals considering baseball retreat behind cultivated cynicism which ranges in phrase from the stock remark about bread and circuses to more dignified indictments of false values and commercialism. Similarly, some ballplayers, whose closest contact with printed matter occurs when they run their hands across the photographs in *Playboy*, swiftly protest, "I know all about that reading stuff." Both these false fronts are wholly transparent to the practiced eye.

During a five-year term I served covering major-league baseball for a newspaper in New York, both my eyes were given plenty of practice. As social evenings wore on, the guest who had first pointedly skirted a discussion of Mickey Mantle's swing to analyze the late Beethoven quartets ("so vague, so illusory, yet so magnificent") would usually come a complete cycle, and ask at midnight, "How does Mickey do it? I mean is it in his wrists or is it just plain brawn?" Far more common and far more enjoyable was the unaffected egghead who avoided the whole complexity of a façade. Simply and directly, he would begin, "What's Leo Durocher really like?" or "How do you hold a slider?" or "Is there any chance of the old bent-leg slide coming back?"

Bright ladies generally steer clear of such technical discussions, but that is not to say they give baseball much berth. One woman who applied herself brilliantly to interpreting Wallace Stevens and somewhat less successfully to illustrating his work in nonrepresentational painting, returned from her first baseball game in many years with a series of representational sketches of Stan Musial, a graceful man with sloping shoulders who has been among the game's outstanding batters for fifteen years.

"What's this?" someone remarked in surprise when he was shown the Musial sketches. "The last time we talked you said you were going to paint the poem about the blackbird."

"I know," the lady said, "but I had to try my hand at sketching this man. He moves so beautifully."

Ballplayers generally are negative about painting, but written words and men who write, they agree, are things to be approached carefully, like land mines. Better still, they are not approached at all. This situation is entirely logical.

The ballplayer's first postschool contact with the printed word ordinarily comes through the sports columns of a newspaper. All is well when the player is successful, but as soon as he makes an important error or strikes out at a critical time, there is a headline, an article, a box score and possibly a feature story documenting and publicizing his failure. Even assuming a thoroughly happy school experience with books, something rather rare among athletes who can easily find greater success outside the classroom, sports-page reading in itself can be traumatic. Baseball writers and baseball players have a relationship which resembles that of teacher and pupil, or surgeon and patient, or Ben Gurion and Nasser.

One veteran baseball writer on the New York *Times* suffered a painful back injury while covering the Yankees twenty-five years ago and still remembers what happened after he limped into the trainer's room in the clubhouse deep underneath the grandstands at Yankee Stadium. No less a figure than Lou Gehrig walked in as the trainer was laboring over the reporter.

"Writer?" Gehrig asked, pointing to the tortured figure.

"Uh huh," said the trainer. "Yup."

"Good," Gehrig said, quite seriously.

It is not really a long jump for a ballplayer to go from a *Times* reporter to Tolstoy, Yeats or Marcus Aurelius. They all write, don't they, or they all wrote? Well, wouldn't it be just as well if all their backs were broken so they'd stop taking all those swipes at ballplayers? Joe Trimble of the New York *Daily News*, who wrote of an awkward Yankee first baseman named Nick Etten when he signed an $18,500 contract, "the $500 is for his fielding," was chased through a train by Etten and escaped only by locking himself inside a ladies' rest room which, fortunately, was unoccupied for the moment. Try telling Etten that Tolstoy and Trimble are different kinds of writers and you would be pushed headlong over your nuance.

One ballplayer, Peewee Reese of the Brooklyn Dodgers, enjoys reading so that he wisely ignores the sports pages whenever the Dodgers lose. "If I don't see what they write about us when we get beat," he says, "I figure I'm that much ahead." As a result, Reese has few unpleasant associations with the act of reading.

Another Dodger, a pitcher named Carl Erskine, is well versed in Kipling and Robert W. Service. He even eased a trying descent through fog one night by reciting the entire "Cremation of Sam McGee" loudly and clearly over the rumbling and creaking of what I then believed to be a doomed DC-4.

Still another pitcher, Mal Mallette, who had unsuccessful trials with both the Dodgers and the Yankees, became spellbound during the summer he played for Asheville by the lore and legend which surround Thomas Wolfe. The next winter Mallette began to write a bit himself; and soon afterward, when his pitching arm went bad, he switched to journalism. Mallette is now a successful sports editor, fittingly enough, in Asheville.

These instances, sadly, are exceptional. I have it on excellent authority that the first book Mickey Mantle ever finished reading was his own ghosted autobiography. "Not started," my source carefully explains, "just finished."

Perhaps the entire case of baseball men *vs.* the written word comes down to a single incident involving Charlie Dressen, the sincere, ineloquent former manager of the Washington Senators. Gesturing at a copy of *Crime and Punishment* a young sportswriter had accidentally carried into the dugout, Dressen asked immediately, "What's that?"

"Huh?" the reporter said. "Oh, that—that's a book."

"I know," Dressen said. "But what kind of a book?"

"A novel. A tragic kind of a novel."

Dressen, who was then over fifty, nodded, dropped his guard and said almost regretfully, "You know I never read a book in my whole life."

"You ought to," the reporter said too eagerly. "It would help you make speeches and things like that."

"Nah," Dressen said, closing the discussion, "I've got by pretty good up to now without books. I ain't gonna start making changes."

From the grandstand or, more significantly, on a twenty-one-inch television screen, the attitude of a baseball player toward a book and the whole process of thought it implies is undetectable. Nor is it even germane. How does he move? Does the curve ball bother him? Can he throw? These are the only relevant questions. Any sensitive intellectual moved by the majesty of a Ted Williams home run is bound to be disturbed that the Williams he meets is not a man to match the deed, but an egocentric emotionalist who seems most of all to need a good spanking.

But Williams' personality has no more to do with his home runs than Wagner's personal habits had to do with Siegfried. From even the best box seat, the petulance and ignorance that Ring Lardner noted inside dugouts subside to less than sound and fury. If it were possible they would also signify less than nothing. I don't think the intellectual spectator should be troubled by the private attitudes of ballplayers, and fortunately I don't believe that he is.

But the lure is not a negative thing. The attractiveness of baseball is not measured by things overlooked any more than its existence has come to pass by accident. The appeal was dampened for me only slightly by five years of covering games from March to October. If Williams was a pill and Jackie Robinson had never heard of Alan Paton when that estimable author unexpectedly arrived for an interview, then there was one massive consolation. There is severe classic tragedy within major-league baseball; tragedy which catches and manipulates the life of every athlete as surely as forces beyond the heaths manipulated Hardy's simple Wessex folk into creatures of imposing stature.

Major-league baseball is an insecure society: it pays lavish salaries to athletes and then, when the men reach thirty-five or so, it abruptly stops paying them anything. But the tragedy goes considerably deeper than that. Briefly, it is the tragedy of fulfillment.

Each major-leaguer, like his friends, wanted desperately to become a major-leaguer years ago. Whenever there was trouble at home or in school or with a girl, there was the sure escape of baseball; not the stumbling, ungainly escape of the ordinary ballplayer, but a sudden, wondrous metamorphosis into the role of hero. For each major-leaguer was a star in his neighborhood or in his town years ago, and each lived with the unending solace that there was one thing he could always do with grace and skill and poise. Somehow, he believed once with the most profound faith he possessed, if he ever did make the major leagues, everything would then become ideal.

A major-league baseball team is a collection of twenty-five youngish men who have made the major leagues and discovered that in spite of it, life remains distressingly short of ideal. A bad knee still throbs before a rainstorm. Too much beer still makes for an unpleasant fullness. Girls still insist on tiresome preliminaries. And now there is a wife who gets headaches or a baby who has colic. No, despite the autograph hunters, things are a long way from ideal. In retrospect, they may have been better years ago, when the dream was happily simple and vague. Among the twenty-five youngish men of a ball club who individually shared a common dream which now has come to be fulfilled, cynicism and disillusion are common as grass. So Willie Mays angrily announces that he will henceforth charge $500 to be interviewed, and Duke Snider shifts his dream site from a ball park to an avocado farm that looks over the Pacific, and Peewee Reese tries to fight off a momentary depression by saying: "Sure I dreamt about baseball when I was a kid, but not the night games. No sir. I did not dream about the lights."

For most men the business of shifting and reworking dreams comes late in life, when there are older children upon whose unwilling shoulders the tired dreams may be deposited. It is a harsh, jarring thing to have to shift dreams at thirty, and if there is ever to be a major novel written about baseball, I think it will have to come to grips with this theme.

The imaginative intellectual whose legs go bad when he is twenty-two is obviously more fortunate than he knows. His dream, the one in which he strikes out Williams, Mantle and the boss on nine pitches, employing the secret backspin slider that breaks two ways before reaching the catcher, is good for the rest of his life. If it dims at any time he has only to visit a ball park for a recharge.

By its nature, the watching of baseball appeals most strongly to imaginative people. The average major-league game lasts approximately two hours and forty-five minutes. There is action for perhaps fifteen minutes of that time. The rest is either inaction or suspense, depending on imagination and point of view.

The pitcher throws, the batter looks, the umpire says, "Strike," and the game is on. The batter steps quickly out of the batter's box, knocks his bat against his shoe spikes to loosen what little dirt has become lodged there. From a good seat, or on a large screen, it is possible to see his lips move as he mutters something toward the umpire. What did he say? Possibly, "One-thirty is a helluvan early time to start a game, ain't it, Charley?" The umpire shakes his head. "Hell, I wish I had your money," he says. "I wouldn't complain about nothing." Then it is time for another pitch, but if the imaginative chooses to believe so, there is already a small feud flaring between the umpire and the batter. Didn't the batter mutter? Didn't the umpire shake his head? "Come on," our imaginative man demands of the umpire, "call them right."

By the time the eighth inning arrives, the visiting team is one run ahead, but the home club starts an interesting rally. The lead-off man lines a clean single to right, the next man doubles off the center-field wall, sending the runner to third, and now the home club's toughest man marches up to bat. The catcher flashes a sign, and the pitcher shakes his head violently. The catcher tries another sign. Again the pitcher shakes his head. When it happens a third time, the imaginative spectator remembers an anecdote from the vast store of baseball stories he has read.

"He doesn't want to pitch to him," the spectator remarks. "It's like the time in '37 when Lefty Gomez was pitching to Jimmy Foxx and the catcher ran through every sign he had and still Gomez was shaking his head. So the catcher charged out to the mound and Gomez said, 'Hell, I just don't want to throw this guy *anything.*' "

The imaginative man has had time to tell this anecdote, which, with other names, may date from either the early Bill Stern or late Abner Doubleday era, because the game itself now comes to a new standstill. The visiting manager has called time out so that he can walk to the pitcher's mound and discuss matters with the pitcher, catcher, plus an unwanted fourth hand, the veteran shortstop who, to the manager's continuing annoyance, invariably seems to have managerial theories of his own. Before leaving the dugout, the manager probably placed his right hand to his left ear lobe, a signal which directly ordered the pitcher to "Shake him off for a while so we can give the relief pitcher more time to warm up." This signal was given too quickly to be noticed by anyone but the pitcher. Consequently it did not interfere with the Gomez anecdote.

As the four worried men talk intensely, the imaginative fan again can only guess at the dialogue. Actually, the manager opens with sarcasm: "Well, that was a great nothing ball you just threw."

"You come all the way out here to tell me that?" the pitcher says.

"Is he tired?" the manager asks the catcher.

The pitcher glares at the catcher, who then shrugs.

"He's tired," says the shortstop. "Didn't you see the way he . . ."

"I didn't ask you," the manager says. "Is he tired?"

"He threw that last guy a nothing ball," the catcher says, cautiously.

"Okay," says the manager. "Stick a fork in him. He's done." The manager waves to the bull pen, and a new pitcher begins a long walk into the game.

Ten minutes later, when the game resumes, the imaginative fan has thought of two further anecdotes and, in addition, has come to a personal conclusion. "If I'd had someone like that manager to give me pitching tips," he thinks, "I might have been out there myself."

The batter hits the relief pitcher's third pitch into the left-field grandstand, and the imaginative fan, once again identifying with the home team, jumps triumphanly to his feet, slaps a stranger on the back, and glows until dinner, when his wife asks why he had not taken her and the baby or, better yet, devoted some time to doing what his family wants for a change and gone rowing in the park. The imaginative man can offer no good answer. If he is wise, he does not try.

Football is violence and cold weather and sex and college rye. Horse racing is animated roulette. Boxing is smoky halls and kidneys battered until they bleed. Tennis and golf are best played, not watched. Basketball, hockey and track meets are action heaped upon action, climax upon climax, until the onlooker's responses become deadened.

Baseball is for the leisurely afternoons of summer and for the unchanging dreams. I do not suggest that major-league baseball can take the place of the late Beethoven quartets, merely that the two frequently coexist in harmony within the thoughts of the American intellectual. I think this is in no way incongruous. The one came out of a life that was like thunder; the other cost four hundred men their dreams.

WHAT would "Dr." Katzander say if he saw them pull the hidden-ball trick?

Case History of Joey J., Baseball Player

HOWARD L. KATZANDER

THIS PATIENT is a professional athlete who earns his living in the national sport, called baseball. He is physically sound and shows few signs of the discomfort of which he complains except for a nervous habit of plucking at the waistband of his trousers, even when they do not seem to be falling down, a behaviorism that might have significance. He seems to be suffering from a sense of inadequacy and a feeling of rejection by society. He tells me that he has recently found himself unable to cope with the ordinary demands of his work, at which he previously was quite proficient. One gathers that his present emotional discomfort stems mainly from a feeling that he has roused the displeasure of his playing mates.

He describes himself as a "pitcher" (with the implication in his tone that he has gone too often "to the well"). Although he shows no outward signs of psychosis, he speaks of frequently losing control and of being hit often, apparently by the playing mates whose displeasure he has aroused. (It is interesting to note that he makes no connection in his own mind between his own loss of control and the punishment that results.) He also speaks of being "knocked out of the box regularly," the box presumably being the structure in which the game is played. If so, this could account for his sense of rejection.

From this first interview it is immediately apparent that I will have to do as I did in the case of the girl from Nyirogyhaza, when I spent a day learning the movements involved in candling eggs in order to help her overcome her infantile hostilities (Case of Giza T., age 17). I shall learn baseball. As a prospective American citizen, newly arrived from Budapest, I must learn all I can about the mores and pleasures of this new society. I shall keep careful notes for my journal and for my colleagues in Vienna, Budapest and Berlin.

* * *

Tonight I have attended my first baseball game. It is played in an amphitheater called the Polo Grounds, although there is no indication that the field is used for this sport. I would know, because I have seen polo on the American screen. Nor was there any sign of anything resembling a box. I shall have to ask Joey J. what he meant by that expression.

The game had many aspects of interest from a psychoanalyst's point of view. It centers around a father figure, who stands on a raised mound of earth. All around him is lush, green grass. Only the earth on which the father walks is bare. (Is this mound the burial place of his ancestors or only a symbolic burial ground? I will have to ask Joey J.)

From this eminence the father figure looks about him in lordly fashion at his minions, who are divided into an inner circle and an outer circle. His glance seems to have in it an element of reproof that makes his minions, particularly those of the inner circle who should be the more secure, extremely nervous. They shift about from foot to foot under his gaze, pound their fists in a gesture of despair into ill-fitting leather gloves they wear on one hand, or pluck nervously at their belts in the manner I have previously noted in Joey J. Perhaps there is a ritual of beating with the belts which would account for this gesture.

There are four men in the inner circle around the father figure. Three serve as guardians of one of the talismans of the sport, soft white pillows (marriage-bed symbols, perhaps) fixed to the ground at approximately regular intervals, forming with the hearthstone (see below) an approximate diamond.

The pillows seem to confer an immunity on those close to them. The men of the inner circle frequently touch the pillow they guard with a toe and stride a short distance away. Reluctance is evident in their departure in the many backward longing looks they cast toward this talisman. The fourth member of the inner circle seems to be a neophyte who has not yet reached sufficient stature (age, experience) to become guardian of a pillow.

The outer circle consists of three men. Far from the center attraction (the father figure), they are probably serving an apprenticeship that will lead them ultimately into the inner circle. (Perhaps the fourth member of the inner circle is a recent initiate from the group outside.) The apprenticeship of the outer circle is an ordeal quite possibly capable of causing the kind of emotional discomfort from which Joey J. suffers. It seems to be a lonely life, and the performance of these men is watched closely and critically by the crowd. From the description Joey J. gave of his role, I am inclined to believe, however, that he is a member of the inner circle, perhaps the father figure himself, although I gather that he has been deposed from his role—"benched," he called it.

The father figure is custodian of the principal talisman (or fetish) of the game. This is a sphere which he caresses lovingly, raising it toward his lips cradled in a soft leather glove, rubbing it with great tenderness against his thigh. Obviously this is the female symbol. He has one other talisman whose significance is somewhat obscure. This is what seems to be a small white sack that lies on the bare earth behind him. From time to time he reaches down, lifts it from the earth with his bare hand and quickly drops it as though there was something repulsive about the feel of it.

During the course of the evening four father figures performed. Each carried out the movements of an important ritual dance, no doubt a love dance, centering on the female symbol. There were variations which probably reflect differences in cultural (or tribal) backgrounds, but the essential movements were retained by each. I made close observation of this dance and took careful notes, which follow:

The father figure receives the sphere from a figure in a cage (of whom more later). He holds the sphere in his gloved hand, either raised against his breast or close to his thigh. Then he turns and casts a piercing glance at the first

baseman (the epithet here is part of the jargon of the sport). This creature obviously is unsure of his status, for he cringes, bowing from the waist with his hands on his knees in an abject attitude of supplication. Having exacted this obeisance, the father figure similarly turns his gaze toward the second baseman and third baseman, not neglecting the neophyte (called "shortstop," a reference probably to the transitory nature of his stay in that role), who give identical responses.

Then father figure turns his gaze toward the figure in the cage. This character is somewhat confusing in its identity. From the padding worn across breast, stomach and legs one has the impression it characterizes (or caricatures) fecundity, or the mother figure. But over the face is worn a screen of heavy metal, like the bars of a cage, suggesting that if this is a female representation it is a harem figure. She wears her little cap backward (a sign in some cultures of mourning).

Behind the caged woman stands a man in somber black. He wears a similar cage over his head, and padding, but only on the chest and concealed by his black coat. He is a complex personality, guardian of the caged woman, protector of the hearth and keeper of the spheres. His talisman is a small broom with which he periodically dusts off the hearth symbol, a flat white stone called "home." In doing so, he avoids turning his back to the caged woman, but bends over with his buttocks toward the father figure in an old gesture of contempt.

Toward the hearthstone now comes the hero, a member of the opposing *équipe*. He makes an impressive figure, wearing a shiny helmet that distinguishes him from his fellows. He strides forward and chooses his weapon, the last of the talismans of the game—a long, tapering article of wood thickening from a slender hand grip at one end to a club at the other—from a number lying in a rack. Occasionally a hero selected two of these symbols and swung them about ferociously, as though boasting of his prowess. But this was just for show. In all cases they approached the hearthstone with only one.

A few feet from the hearth the hero does his dance. This also had variety, as among heroes, but all followed this pattern: Hero approaches, swinging his wooden club with both hands. Nearing the hearth he stops, looks back over his shoulder to his playing mates, who are encouraging him with small cries. Then he does a quick shuffle toward the hearthstone, dancing forward with one foot, then the other. As he moves each foot he taps it with his weapon, obviously a charm favoring fleetness of foot.

Now he is at the hearth. He faces it, his profile to the father figure. He ignores the figure in the cage and its guardian. He rests his club on one shoulder, swings it back and forth, drops the end to the hearth, then raises it again. Now he sets his feet wide, flexes his knees and turns a defiant gaze toward the father figure. Behind him the caged figure squats. On one hand she wears a huge, pillowy glove. She pounds its center with her small fist, forming an indentation. Then she raises her hand, gloved palm outward toward the father figure, awaiting the blow. Behind her the guardian leans forward, hands clasped behind his back, the anguished parent behind the door of the bridal room.

Now attention focuses on the father figure. Languidly he stretches his arms forward in a long, lazy movement. He glances once to his left, and first baseman tenses slightly. He turns then toward the hero, who is menacingly waving his weapon. He drops his arms, studies the adversary, advances one foot, sphere couched in his soft glove. He hitches at his trousers, rubs the sphere against his thigh, and wags his head as in a catatonic trance. Then he stretches his arms wide, and from that position begins a circling movement, with his free arms holding the sphere in his bare hand. In an intricate striding motion he lunges forward and releases the sphere with a shocking suddenness in the direction of the waiting glove. The hero figure tries to fend it off, swinging his club wildly. He misses. The sphere strikes the waiting glove with a resounding thump. "Strike," the guardian calls, raising his right hand. The first effort has succeeded. Twice more this is repeated. With the third "strike," the guardian motions the hero disdainfully away. The hero hurls his club violently to the ground. It has failed him. Then he slumps disconsolately back to what is known as the "dugout." Here he seeks refuge deep in its inner recesses, shielded from harm as in the womb.

Another hero takes his place. He goes through much the same ritual, except that the second time the sphere approaches, his club sends it flying high into the air toward the middle ground of the outer circle. The minion there tries to capture it in flight. For a moment it seems he has succeeded, but it falls through his fingers to the ground. There is a confusing roar from the crowd, cries of "go, go, go" (into

banishment?). The hero runs swiftly to the first white pillow, touches it with a foot in passing and hurries to the next. Approaching it, he hurls himself headlong, stretching his hand to the pillow. The man with the sphere meanwhile has retrieved it and thrown it to the guardian of the second pillow. There is apparently some significance here as to whether the hero or the sphere reaches the pillow first, the sphere apparently nullifying whatever immunity the pillow confers on those who touch it.

The purpose of these maneuvers now began to be perfectly plain. The hero figures must, if they are able, prevent the sphere from passing beyond the hearthstone into the soft glove of the caged figure. Should they succeed in doing so, they must round the diamond-shaped area, touching each pillow in passing. Their objective is the hearth, but to regain it they may not cross the burial ground; this terrain is sacred to the father figure. Each time a hero figure accomplishes this, his *équipe* is credited with a "run." If one of the opposing *équipe* drops the sphere or throws it inaccurately he is guilty of error. I must ask Joey J. whether there is a ritual of absolution for such error or whether the offender must carry his guilt for all time. The team that scores the most runs is the victor. (Some of these facts I gleaned from a handbook on the sport, sold at the Polo Grounds, which unaccountably ignores all the obviously psychological and anthropological factors of the game.)

An interesting aspect of baseball is that at regular intervals (called "innings," which are marked in a confusing fashion by "outings"), the two *équipes* exchange positions—and personalities. The heroes slough off that role and adopt the status of their opponents (father figure, woman caged, inner circle, outer circle). And in doing so they assume all the psychological attitudes of those roles, losing in the very act of exchanging positions the psychological postures they have thus far maintained. The converse is equally true. Even the lowliest member of the outer circle, no matter how he may be looked down upon by his colleagues, assumes the swaggering, masterful air that goes with the hero role, once he is called upon to approach the hearth with the hero's weapon in his hands.

Here I think I may have hit upon one of the roots of Joey J.'s troubles. It is a well-known fact that such a violent shift in personality as an essential in meeting the daily requirements of life can lead to a complete loss of identity. After a time a participant in this sport must inevitably become confused as to whether he is a hero or a minion, a father figure or a woman caged, a confusion that could lead to a variety of complications in his life away from the sporting field.

The crowd, too, seemed to suffer from a certain confusion. At one moment it would cheer a hero figure and harass the father figure, at another moment it was cheering the father and harassing the hero. The hero, under this harassment, has a sole recourse. He may not go among the crowd, laying about him with his weapon, but he may drive the sphere into the crowd, in that way seeking his revenge.

Tomorrow Joey J. is coming for another interview. I have many questions to ask him. I look forward to his astonishment when he sees how complete is my grasp of his way of life and my understanding of the finer nuances of baseball.

JOE TRECENO

Courtesy *Sport* Magazine. ©

"Don't let it worry you, Joe, anyone can make 22 errors in one inning."

THOSE who have read and treasured John Lardner's delightful profile of Babe Herman in the first *Fireside Book of Baseball* will understand that his offering reprinted here from *True* Magazine follows as the night the day.

The One and Only Bobo

JOHN LARDNER

ONCE THERE WAS a ballplayer named Louis Norman Newsom, who called himself and everyone else Bobo. He was born in 1906, 1907, 1908, or 1909, depending on which way he told it. Early in life, he gave out the news that he was the greatest pitcher in baseball. Partly on the strength of this report—but mainly because of certain supporting evidence—he was hired 17 times by big-league ball clubs in the next 20 years. He was fired or sold just as often as he was hired, and seldom with much delay. But, in the end, no one in baseball could have said for sure that Bobo hadn't been right about himself all along.

This doubt—and the legend of Newsom—linger on. They still see him now and then. He casts his portly shadow over baseball gatherings at All-Star Games and World Series, looking like a Dixie senator, or rather, like one Dixie senator standing on another senator's shoulders. And they wonder, was this indeed the most valuable slab of baseball meat in the last quarter-century? Will it turn out that the big fellow's gifts—apart from a nerve of brass, and lungs of leather—were unique in the brittle modern game? Was he a throwback to ancient times? They know what L. N. Newsom would say if they asked him.

"Bobo," Newsom sometimes tells a hard-pressed manager nowadays, in a hotel lobby, backing him up against a potted palm, "you could surely use Bobo now. But where ya gonna find a guy like Bobo? They don't grow in bunches like bananas, son."

Among pitchers, this is an age of sore arms and neuroses. With these boys, the inferiority complex has become as common as freckles. Stalked by fear and insecurity, they rotate between the whirlpool bath and the halls of Johns

Hopkins, where they throw their elbow chips into the pot and hear the world's wisest healers say glumly that pitching is fundamentally unnatural. Thanks in part to a ball that takes off from a bat like a skyrocket, the average talented pitcher of today has six or eight years of life as a starter, plus two or three years in the bull pen, living on cunning alone.

Since the birth of the lively, or firecracker, ball, Newsom has been the only pitcher to last 20 years in the major leagues. Twice, he pitched both ends of a double-header. Several times, he started one game of a double-header and relieved in the other.

Once, his knee was broken by a line drive in an early stage of a game. He went on to pitch the distance.

Once, in the third inning of a game, his jaw was broken in two places by an infielder's throw. He finished out the game.

Once, a line drive from the bat of a pitcher named Oscar Judd hit Newsom on the skull and bounced 400 feet into center field. The target remarked later—after completing the game without difficulty—that occasionally, during the later innings, he heard strains of music ringing pleasantly through his brain. After the game, in a hotel, a sports writer introduced Newsom to his wife. Newsom made a courtly bow. "A pleasure, madam," he said gallantly. "Would you like to feel the bump on my head?"

When Bobo retired from baseball for life, in 1953 (after telling Connie Mack, his last manager, "You can't afford my wages, Bobo," which was true), two things had been clearly established about his anatomy (of which there was between 210 and 230 pounds, measuring six feet three in length). You couldn't hurt Newsom in the head. And, while a leg or a jawbone might chip, his right arm was foolproof and painproof. It was a genuine rubber arm—in our time, an anachronism. With it, the owner could work three or four times a week and relieve in between. In the World Series of 1940, he started three games within a week and nearly won all three of them.

That is why present-day managers tend to water at the mouth when they see Newsom at baseball reunions. Then they think it over; and most of them, as one kind of memory leads to another, tremble with relief at the thought that Bobo today, at 50 or so, is too old to tempt them into the kind of trouble that always came to those who tried to harness this erratic natural force.

The late Connie Mack once enlisted a bodyguard, coach Earle Brucker, to keep him from rehiring Newsom, who had worked for Mack and the Philadelphia Athletics once before. Mack was making a trip to Orlando, Florida, near Newsom's home in Winter Park. Newsom was temporarily unemployed. "I know he'll meet me at the train," Connie told Brucker, "and I know that if you don't stick by me every minute, I'll weaken and sign him up." The strategy worked. However—showing the insidious strength of the Newsom habit—Mack did rehire Bobo a year later. In another year, Clark Griffith, owner of Washington, said: "Newsom will never again wear a Washington uniform." He re-employed Bobo the same year.

The explanation of this split or schizoid attitude toward Newsom is that no player in baseball history could fluctuate so swiftly from the sublime to the unspeakable. After winning the pennant and almost winning the World Series for Detroit in 1940, Bobo was rewarded by the highest pitcher's salary in the game, $35,000. The following spring, he drove into training camp in an automobile one block long, which carried a sign that spelled "Bobo" in neon lights, and a horn that played the first four notes of "Tiger Rag." During the season, he kept a table reserved in a Detroit hotel, where quail and champagne were served to Newsom and guests, while the other Tiger players got along on steak and milk. That year, Bobo lost 20 games.

Another thing that upset employers was Newsom's effect on managers. Once, while working for Brooklyn, he inspired a mutiny that drove manager Leo Durocher to tears. As soon as Leo had dried his eyes, Bobo was sold as far out of town as possible (namely, St. Louis). Once, while working for the Boston Red Sox, Bobo got into trouble on the mound, and manager Joe Cronin came in from shortstop with words of advice. "Listen, Bobo," said Bobo. "You play shortstop, and I'll do the pitching." At the end of that season, Newsom was sold as far out of town as possible (namely, St. Louis).

Bobo's crunching impact on managers went back almost as far as his baseball childhood. In 1928, his first season in organized ball, Newsom served a hitch in Greenville, N. C., where Hal Weafer, later a Brooklyn scout, was the manager. Newsom and his young wife lived at Weafer's house when the team was at home. After supper, Bobo and Weafer invariably repaired to the front porch to sit, swat flies, and converse. Invariably, before the evening was over, a fight broke out between them—brought on, perhaps, by the fact that Weafer was charging the Newsoms rent, though the meals were free. Once, Mrs. Weafer and Mrs. Newsom arranged a special reconciliation supper, to make their husbands love each other better. That night, the fight began earlier than usual, at the table.

On the field one day, while pitching for batting practice, Newsom aimed a tangential pitch at the head of Weafer, who was standing on the sidelines. Weafer ducked and chased Bobo twice around the field with a bat in his hand, before peace was restored. They fought again that night after supper.

Temperament was native to Bobo—temperament, a strong imagination, and a tongue that vibrated like a hummingbird. He was born in Hartsville, S. C., the son of a farmer named Henry Quillan Buffkin Newsom. The day was August 11; the year, as noted above, came to depend on Bobo's free-wheeling autobiographical instinct, which never produced the same date twice in a row. The same instinct created three or four stories of how he came by the name Bobo. Once, Bobo said that he had been nicknamed Buck, as a child, by his uncle Jake (J. R. Newsom); he couldn't pronounce Buck, and called himself Bobo instead. Another time, Newsom said that he adopted the name Bobo himself, from a character in a book he'd been reading. These versions of history, and many others, were recited by Bobo tirelessly for the next 40 years, in a high, plaintive voice that came strangely out of his huge body and big, round, blue-jowled face.

Bobo played home-town baseball as a boy. He also developed a gift for preparing food that later won him work as supervisor-of-barbecue in southern eating places, including a café in Hartsville co-managed by his Uncle

Jake and himself. This double life became useful to Newsom, when big-league owners hesitated to pay him the princely salaries he thought he deserved. "If you try to starve me up no'th," Bobo would say, "I'll stay home in my kitchen all summer and eat off the fat of the land."

After demoralizing a few minor-league managers like Weafer, and serving a short youthful hitch in Brooklyn, under the late Uncle Wilbert Robinson, who liked big pitchers ("But this fella's head is *too* big," said Uncle Robbie), Newsom signed with the Chicago Cubs early in 1932. He started for training camp in his car and was several miles from home before he drove off the edge of a 200-foot cliff, smashing the car and breaking his leg. Bobo spent the rest of the spring writing bulletins about his health to P. K. Wrigley, Cub owner, and assuring Wrigley that he would win the pennant for him as soon as he got out of bed. When he got out of bed, he went to a mule sale, where a mule kicked him in the same leg and broke it again. What with one thing and another, Newsom played his next baseball for Los Angeles, in 1933. He burned up the Coast League. The record says he won 30 and lost 11. Newsom says he won 32 (if not 33) and lost 10.

"Who ya gonna believe, Bobo," he says, "the record book, or the guy that done it?"

The St. Louis Browns bought the new young star for use in 1934. With this abysmal ball club, Newsom one day pitched a "no-hitter." That is, according to the records, he pitched nine innings of no-hit ball against Boston. In the 10th inning, two bases on balls followed by a bad-hop single beat Bobo 2-1. Records or no records, this feat has always been an official no-hitter in Newsom's book.

"How many no-hit games did you pitch in the big leagues, Bobo?" someone asked him recently.

"Just the one," Bobo said. "They don't grow in bunches like bananas, son."

Newsom had a purpose in pitching well against the Red Sox; he wanted to be sold to Boston, where salaries were big. Instead, the Browns sold him for $45,000 to Washington, where salaries were small. In this way, Bobo found a lifetime home-away-from-home—he was to work for the Senators five different times—and Clark Griffith launched a new career, buying Bobo to get some well-pitched games and selling Bobo to recover expenses (he usually sold him for twice his salary). Between sales, Bobo became Griff's favorite pinochle partner. This alone, some critics have said, was enough

to persuade the magnate to buy Newsom again whenever he felt lonely.

In 1937, the rich Red Sox bought Newsom from Griffith in self-defense—twice in the previous season he had beaten the great Lefty Grove in crucial games. As it turned out, wealth did not make Bobo happy, and Bobo did not make Joe Cronin happy. For company's sake, Newsom installed a hutch of rabbits in his hotel room in Boston. Then he forgot them. The rabbits ate their way steadily through the room, missing no bets. They had begun to go to work on the curtains when the hotel management discovered them, dispossessed them, and presented Cronin with a bill for the damages. As noted, Newsom was sold to the Browns soon afterward.

If there was no mistaking Bobo's shortcomings, there was no mistaking his gifts, either. He could work all day, and his arm was as strong and supple as a buggy whip. He threw his vivid fast ball and his sharp curve from all levels, sidearm, overhand, three-quarters. His 1938 season with St. Louis was one of his greatest; the team finished seventh, with a total of 55 wins, and 20 of those wins were Newsom's. Before the season began, the owner, Don Barnes, told Bobo that he would give him a new suit of clothes if he won the opener. Bobo won it. That night, Barnes pressed a roll of money into his hand and told him to buy the suit.

"Keep the sugar, Bobo," Bobo said, handing it back. "Bobo bought the suit before the game. The bill is on your desk."

Big winner though he was that year, Newsom was far from businesslike in all his moves on the mound. Showmanship was vital to him, especially when he worked for losing ball clubs which he felt needed his special sales flair. To the intense distaste of manager Gabby Street of the Browns, Bobo indulged in triple windups. He alternated between right-hand and left-hand batting at the plate. He threw the "ephus" pitch, which sailed high into the air and sometimes—but not often—dropped into the strike zone. After watching an ephus pitch one day, Mr. Barnes decided to entertain a proposition from the Yankees to trade Newsom for Lefty Gomez. Then he thought again. Gomez was getting $20,000 a year. Newsom was getting $10,000. Mr. Barnes canceled the deal.

Newsom, however, did not propose to struggle along forever on $10,000. The Browns were training in San Antonio, Texas, in the spring of 1939. When they refused him a raise in pay, their star pitcher walked out of the hotel in a huff. "Bobo is going home," he said, "to live off the fat of the land." He went as far as a motel on the edge of San Antonio. While living there, he dictated statements and manifestos to the public stenographer at the Browns' hotel, which he then distributed to the press. After several manifestos, Barnes raised Bobo's pay. This move sealed Newsom's fate with the Browns. He had to be sold, to atone for his salary. It also changed his luck, for the better. He was sold in 1940, to Detroit. If Detroit was not the best team in the league, Bobo soon made it so. He also, in his first full season with the Tigers, made pitching history.

In 1940, Newsom had his third straight 20-wins-or-better season, with a record of 21 and 5. He struck out 164 batters. His earned-run average was 2.83. He put together a string of 13 straight wins. While engaged in this streak, he came up against the All-Star Game, in his old home in Washington. Newsom was a member of manager Joe McCarthy's All-Star pitching staff—but when he heard that McCarthy was planning to start Red Ruffing for the American League, he resigned from the squad.

"If I don't start, I don't pitch," Bobo said. "Bobo follows nobody."

It was pointed out to him by friends that McCarthy's plan called for a sequence of Ruffing, Newsom, and Bob Feller. In other words, Bobo would take precedence over Feller, the greatest pitcher in baseball. This thought mollified Bobo, and he rejoined the squad.

"But," he told McCarthy, the smartest man in the game, "if you had the brains of a motherless shoat, Bo, you would pitch Bobo all the way."

It might have been better that way. The National League, in winning the game, 4-0, got three runs off Ruffing, one off Feller, and none at all off Newsom in the three middle innings.

The Tigers had a series with Washington scheduled to follow the All-Star Game. Meeting his old pinochle partner, Griffith, at the ball park, Newsom told him that he was mortally certain to beat Griff's team in his next start, on a Saturday, and that the Washington team stood to make several thousand dollars extra at the box office if it advertised this boast in the newspapers. Griffith said he would think it over.

A day or so before the Saturday game, a Washington sports column carried the news that Bobo had been seen molesting or brow-beating a guest in a Washington hotel lobby. The author of the column was Robert Ruark (later a novelist of considerable stamina). His words annoyed Bobo greatly. Newsom and Ruark came face to face at the ball park the same day. Newsom, who was sucking on a bottle of yellow pop, stopped drinking long enough to call the columnist an unchaste name. Ruark drew back his right arm to take a punch at Bobo. Bobo, always nonchalant in action, held Ruark off with one hand while continuing to swill from the pop bottle. In the course of this savage contest, Bobo happened to score a brush knockdown when Ruark fell backward over a bench. The incident created a certain amount of high feeling among Washington fans—and Griffith decided to take Newsom's tip and advertise Bobo's boast that he would infallibly whip the Nats in his next start.

It was a situation made to Bobo's order. Publicity was mother's milk to him. With a splendid crowd in the stands on Saturday, howling now and then, in a brooding way, for his blood, he shut out the Senators with two hits and thumbed his nose grandly at the audience as he walked off the field at the end of the day.

As it happened, this was the 13th win in Newsom's string of winning games. In his next start, in Boston, Bobo jammed and broke his thumb against Ted Williams' ribs in a tag play at first base in an early inning. The thumb went into a cast. When it came out again, a few days later, Newsom pitched and lost a close game in Philadelphia which ended his streak. The thing to be noticed here is that, broken thumb and all, he was out of action no more than a week. With all his childish moods, his bombast and his pettiness, the big man had an oddly heroic quality of mind and body that led him to defy and challenge pain, and to pretend that none of the ills of heaven and earth were a match for a Newsom of South Carolina. Bobo had begun resisting nature long before 1940.

Take the case of a game in 1935, when Newsom was pitching for Washington against Cleveland. He had two strikes on Earl Averill, the fiercest of Cleveland batsmen. He shouted brashly to Averill: "Now, Bobo, I'm gonna whiff you with an outside pitch!" Averill's lips tightened. He clubbed the outside pitch on a low, vicious line that caught Newsom in the knee with a crack that could have been heard in Baltimore. Somehow, Bobo threw his man out at first. Then he stamped around the box in agony for a minute or so. Then he resumed pitching, and kept pitching till the game was over.

225

"I got a piece of news for you, Mike," he told the trainer in the dressing room afterward. "Bobo thinks his laig is broke." It was. It was in a cast for five weeks.

Take the case of Opening Day, 1936, with President Roosevelt watching from a box seat, and Newsom and Washington facing the Yankees. In the third inning, Ben Chapman, New York's swiftest runner, laid down a bunt toward third. It was a good bunt, and a tough play, and Ossie Bluege, the Nats' third baseman, threw the ball blindly and with all his might toward first. It didn't get to first. Newsom, squarely in the line of fire, was observing the play with detached admiration. The ball hit him in the rear of the jaw, and bounced high into the air. Clasping his face, Bobo reeled in circles like a drunken moose. The players of both teams went to the mound to inspect the victim. "Come on, call it a day," said manager Bucky Harris to Newsom. "We'll put some ice on it." "Naw," mumbled Bobo. "Naw. Ole FDR came out to see me, and he's gonna get me all the way." And that's what the President got—Newsom all the way, and a 1-0 win for Washington.

It turned out later that Bobo's jaw had been broken in two places. For the next few days, he talked only half as much as usual. Which, as manager Harris said at the time, was still more than was strictly necessary.

The 1940 World Series, Detroit against Cincinnati, found Newsom at the height of his glory, clearly—for that year, at least—the most effective pitcher in baseball, and his team's best hope for the Series. What's more, he was behaving like a normal man, as baseball understands normality—no tricks, no ephus balls, no showboating, nothing but efficiency and will to win. And the Goddess of Chance, in her cockeyed way, chose this time of the great man's utmost sanity to strike him a blow that made his first World Series twice as hard, and twice as memorable.

The entire Newsom family—Bobo's father, H.Q.B. Newsom, his stepmother, his sisters and his wife—had come up to Cincinnati from Hartsville. Bobo, naturally, pitched the opening game. In a strong, steady effort, he beat Paul Derringer and the Reds, 7-2. Early the next morning, his father died of a heart attack in his hotel room. Bobo was broken up. But, when the rest of the family went back to Carolina, to bury the old farmer at home, he elected to stay on and pitch out the Series. He had a thought in mind, a kind and richly senti-

mental thought that appealed to the depths of his sentimental soul. On the day of the fifth game, in Detroit, with tears streaming down the big, round, dark-bearded face, Bobo announced that he was "dedicating" this one to his dead father. It turned out to be quite a tribute—a three-hit shutout, in which no Red reached third base, and seven of them went down swinging at Bobo's dancing fast ball.

Two days later, Newsom sat in the clubhouse waiting to pitch the seventh and deciding game of the Series on one day's rest. There was a soft, faraway look in his eyes. His thoughts, as he absently oiled his glove, seemed to be a thousand miles from the ball park in space and time. A reporter, touched and curious, stopped in front of him.

"Will you try to win this one for your daddy, too?" the reporter asked.

Bobo looked up. "Why, no," he said, considering the point carefully. "No. I think I'll win this one for Bobo."

If he had won it, he would have been the first pitcher since the dawn of the lively baseball in 1920 (when the Series was the best five games out of nine) to score three wins in one World Series. And Bobo came very close, indeed. He had the Reds blanked, 1-0, in the seventh inning, when Frank McCormick hit to left field for two bases. Jim Ripple, the next Cincinnati hitter, lifted a deep, high fly to right. It was questionable whether the ball would scrape the fence or be caught; so McCormick held up between second and third, waiting to see. The ball struck the top of the fence, dropped onto the field, and was thrown in quickly to the infield; but Dick Bartell, Detroit shortstop, who took the throw, stood with the ball in his hands and his back to the plate for a moment, assuming that the run would score, and so McCormick was able to lope home. When Ripple scored from third a few minutes later, on a fly ball, the score became 2-1. It stayed that way to the end.

Three-game winner or not, Bobo was the greatest man in baseball. He liked to think so, at any rate, and so did his owner, Walter O. Briggs. When the report got out that Feller of Cleveland, at $30,000, would be as highly paid as Newsom in 1941, Briggs decided to raise Bobo an additional $5,000, as a matter of institutional pride. He sent for Newsom to tell him so. Spike Briggs, the late owner's son, had a desk just outside his father's office in those days. He remembers looking up one day and seeing Bobo looming before him, ablaze with great expectations and brand-new haberdashery. "Step aside, Little Bo," said Newsom expansively. "Big Bobo wants to see me." He moved on into the boss's office, and there signed the contract that made him the game's richest and most contented pitcher.

Exactly a year later, as previously noted, contentment, quail, and champagne had set in so deeply that Newsom was a 20-game loser. We find him back in the Tigers' office, prepared to defy to the death a pay cut of about 60 per cent, to $12,500. His opponent was Jack Zeller, the Detroit general manager. Zeller had a surpassingly bald head and recent spiritual flesh wounds, which had been caused when Commissioner Landis liberated 90 Tiger farmhands and declared them free agents. Newsom and Zeller argued Newsom's pay cut with passion. Bobo said he would not stand for it. He screamed that his feelings had been deeply and fatally wounded. "But, listen, Bobo," Zeller expostulated, "you lost 20 games." "Hell, Curly," said Bobo, with a withering glance at Zeller's nude scalp, "you lost 90 of Briggs' ball players last year, and I don't see you taking no cut."

This line of reasoning, cogent though it was, got Newsom nowhere. He continued to hold out and was shortly afterward sold back to his old home-away-from-home on the Potomac River for the season of 1942.

Not that Bobo stayed the whole season in Washington. Griffith, after extracting a certain number of wins and a certain number of pinochle hands from his favorite chattel, scored a most ingenious coup, by selling him to Brooklyn for the sum of about two years' salaries. The purchase was made by Larry MacPhail. Newsom promptly sent manager Durocher of the Dodgers a telegram reading: "Wish to congratulate you on buying pennant insurance."

Things did not quite work out that way. In the following winter, MacPhail was replaced in the front office by Branch Rickey, who liked nearly everything he found in Brooklyn except Bobo. The Dodgers trained in the wartime spring of 1943 in Bear Mountain, N. Y. Newsom, who hated cold weather, held out at home in South Carolina. "B'Judas Priest," said Rickey to Durocher, "this is a wonderful excuse to get rid of the fellow!"

"But I need him," cried Durocher. He was later to eat those words and wash them down with his own tears.

By July of 1943, Newsom was Brooklyn's biggest winner, with nine games in the book. He had also taken full management of himself out of Durocher's hands and, Durocher suspected, was secretly trying to manage the rest of the team as well. One day, in a game against Pittsburgh, Bobo delivered an oddly erratic pitch that got away from Bob Bragan, the young Dodger catcher. Durocher and some of the other Dodgers on the bench thought that it looked like a spitball. A Pittsburgh runner scored from third on the passed ball. Newsom put his hands on his hips, stamped about, and otherwise showed his scorn and disgust with Bragan; when the inning ended, he threw his glove in the air. After the game, which he failed to finish, Bobo heard Durocher and some of the players discussing the so-called "spitter." He broke in on the talk to deny the charge with righteous anger—the pitch had been a good fast ball, Bobo said. Durocher replied by bawling him out for "showing up" Bragan in front of the crowd, and for other shortcomings. Bobo countered with a long, strong oration on managerial incompetence in the National League. Durocher suspended his leading pitcher on the spot, without pay.

The stormy one-day revolution which followed has since taken its place as a milestone in Brooklyn baseball history. It had many dark and twisting ramifications, which we won't follow in detail here, except to claim for Bobo his rightful place at the root of it all. The day after Newsom's suspension, Arkie Vaughan, Dodger infielder, because of a version of the story he had heard, turned in his uniform to Durocher and said he would not play. The mutiny spread quickly, guided by friends of Vaughan's like Dixie Walker. In the end, Durocher, weeping freely as he spoke to the assembled team, won Walker and nearly all the others back. Everyone played that day except Vaughan and Newsom, and Brooklyn beat Pittsburgh by the emotional score of 23-6.

"Do you still want this anarchist on your staff, my dear boy?" said Rickey, speaking of Bobo, to Durocher.

"No, no," said Durocher, almost breaking down again. "How far away can you send him?"

"I can send him to the St. Louis American League club for two competent left-handers," said Rickey complacently, and the deal went more or less as advertised, except that the two left-handers turned out to be worthless, while Bobo, now 35 or more, still had a few volts of genius and 10 years of baseball left in his system. For the moment, after a short stay in St. Louis, he reverted to Washington again, as naturally as a homing squab, and finished out the season as he had begun the previous one, playing pinochle with Griffith.

During the war years, Newsom met and left his mark on the late Connie Mack. Nothing in his seven decades of baseball had prepared this wise and gentle old man for the likes of Bobo. Connie acquired Newsom early in 1944, and Bobo came to Mack's Philadelphia office to discuss salary. He took over Mack's chair, at Mack's desk, while Connie politely sat hugging his knees on a settee.

There was a telephone call for Newsom, which he took outside the office. Mack regained his chair and desk for a few minutes. Then Newsom returned, and Mack went back to the settee. They struck a bargain, and Mack told the press about it, adding the news that, because of wartime restrictions, the team would train that spring in Frederick, Maryland. "Ah, yes," interrupted Newsom. "All the team except me. I will train at home in Hartsville, and will see you all next April. Ain't that right, Bobo?" he said to Mack. "Why—uh—yes, I guess that's right," said Connie, who had never heard of the plan before. Newsom trained at home for the next two springs, on a Philadelphia expense account.

There was not only some baseball left in Newsom's system as he neared 40, there was one more pennant, and one more World Series. In midseason of 1947, Griffith, having briefly repossessed Bobo, sold him at the usual smart profit to the Yankees, who were struggling toward the flag. Newsom won seven games from there on in. He was instrumental in the push that won the pennant. But Bobo, though he often pined from a distance for service with rich teams, was always stifled by the atmosphere of wealth when he reached it. The Yanks were too stuffy for him. He was too gay and uncouth for the Yanks. In one game with Chicago, batting against a pitcher named Joe Haynes, Newsom tapped the ball back to the box. He refused to run to first base. Haynes refused to throw the ball to first. Bobo went back to the dugout, as though to take a drink from the water cooler. From there, he made a sudden, sneaky, elephantine dash toward the base. It was almost successful, because Rudy York, the first baseman, had wandered off the bag, and Haynes had to wait till York got back there to throw Newsom out. The fans giggled. The Yankees looked down their noses. "Fun in

the bush, hey?" Bobo heard one of them, who shall be nameless, say to another. The remark mortified him, for he had been pitching in that league when the speaker was, as Bobo pointed out, chin-high to a hog.

He was not surprised when the Yanks voted him only three quarters of a share of the players' World Series pool. At the jeweler's, ordering his Series ring, he said: "Just make it three-quarter size, Bobo. That's my measure in this town." In two Series appearances against Brooklyn, one as a starter, one in relief, Bobo failed to last as much as three quarters of a game. But, by the most likely of the many estimates of his age, he was more than 40 years old by then. He could still win a pennant for a good team, but he could no longer follow it up by dominating the World Series too. Some of the spring was gone from the tall, steamboat-captain's figure and from the buggy-whip arm.

This was the period during which Connie Mack carried a bodyguard to keep him from signing Newsom again. Once, also, around this time, Bobo approached Bucky Harris in spring training for another chance with the Washington team. Harris decided to give him a tryout. In batting practice, Bobo's first pitch broke a finger on the meat hand of Mickey Grasso, the Nats' best catcher. Harris, looking on, reached for a bat. Newsom observed the gesture from a corner of one eye. He dropped his glove where he stood and began to make for a gate in the fence at a fast walk. He was running by the time he reached the gate, and he kept running till he found a cab that took him out of town.

Yet Bobo still had a few big-league wins left in the arm. He won a game here and a game there for the Nats and the Athletics (they could not resist him—and they knew him better than most) in 1952, and a couple for Mr. Mack again in 1953.

There is this to be said. Perhaps there was never a time in his life, old or young, with the kind of arm he had, and the big, loose, easy body, and the whimsical but cunning baseball brain, when Louis Norman Newsom of Hartsville, S. C., could not have pitched and won a ball game at the highest baseball level.

As they used to say, he was a throwback. He was at least 45, probably, when he stopped pitching. And when Bobo stopped pitching, it was by his own choice. Late in the season of 1953, he worked a game for the A's and Mr. Mack against Detroit. He went all the way and won. There was a reason for his stopping right there. It was his 200th victory in the American League. If you add his record with Brooklyn, Bobo won 211 big-league games in all. But the American League was the real big league to him, his home and his favorite stage as an actor, and when he reached the total of 200 there, he was satisfied.

"I guess that's all, Bo," he told Connie. "Besides, you can't afford to pay Bobo no more."

"Maybe not, Newsom," said Mack, who had nearly reached the end of his own span by then. "By the way, you told me you had that Detroit shortstop's weakness figured out, and I noticed he got a couple of two-base hits. What's his weakness?"

"Two-base hits, Bobo," said Newsom.

In the few years since then, Bobo has served as a counselor on barbecue in a Florida eating house, and as a baseball broadcaster in Baltimore. Those were always his specialties: food, baseball, and the human voice.

QUICK, now—who's the craziest ballplayer Ring Lardner ever wrote
about? And the greatest hitter? And the only man who had better
alibis than Alibi Ike? "My Roomy," that's who.

My Roomy

RING LARDNER

I

No—I AIN'T SIGNED for next year; but there
won't be no trouble about that. The
dough part of it is all fixed up. John and me
talked it over and I'll sign as soon as they send
me a contract. All I told him was that he'd
have to let me pick my own roommate after
this and not sic no wild man on to me.

You know I didn't hit much the last two
months o' the season. Some o' the boys, I notice,
wrote some stuff about me gettin' old and losin'
my battin' eye. That's all bunk! The reason I
didn't hit was because I wasn't gettin' enough
sleep. And the reason for that was Mr. Elliott.

He wasn't with us after the last part o' May,
but I roomed with him long enough to get the
insomny. I was the only guy in the club game
enough to stand for him; but I was sorry afterward that I done it, because it sure did put a
crimp in my little old average.

And do you know where he is now? I got a
letter today and I'll read it to you. No—I guess
I better tell you somethin' about him first. You
fellers never got acquainted with him and you
ought to hear the dope to understand the letter.
I'll make it as short as I can.

He didn't play in no league last year. He was
with some semipros over in Michigan and somebody writes John about him. So John sends
Needham over to look at him. Tom stayed
there Saturday and Sunday, and seen him work
twice. He was playin' the outfield, but as luck
would have it they wasn't a fly ball hit in his
direction in both games. A base hit was made
out his way and he booted it, and that's the
only report Tom could get on his fieldin'. But
he wallops two over the wall in one day and
they catch two line drives off him. The next day
he gets four blows and two o' them is triples.

So Tom comes back and tells John the guy is

a whale of a hitter and fast as Cobb, but he
don't know nothin' about his fieldin'. Then John
signs him to a contract—twelve hundred or
somethin' like that. We'd been in Tampa a
week before he showed up. Then he comes to
the hotel and just sits round all day, without
tellin' nobody who he was. Finally the bellhops
was going to chase him out and he says he's
one o' the ballplayers. Then the clerk gets John
to go over and talk to him. He tells John his
name and says he hasn't had nothin' to eat for
three days, because he was broke. John told me
afterward that he'd drew about three hundred
in advance—last winter sometime. Well, they
took him in the dinin' room and they tell me he
inhaled about four meals at once. That night
they roomed him with Heine.

Next mornin' Heine and me walks out to the
grounds together and Heine tells me about him.
He says:

"Don't never call me a bug again. They got
me roomin' with the champion o' the world."

"Who is he?" I says.

"I don't know and I don't want to know,"
says Heine; "but if they stick him in there with
me again I'll jump to the Federals. To start
with, he ain't got no baggage. I ast him where
his trunk was and he says he didn't have none.
Then I ast him if he didn't have no suitcase,
and he says: 'No. What do you care?' I was
goin' to lend him some pajamas, but he put on
the shirt o' the uniform John give him last
night and slept in that. He was asleep when I
got up this mornin'. I seen his collar layin' on
the dresser and it looked like he had wore it
in Pittsburgh every day for a year. So I threwed
it out the window and he comes down to breakfast with no collar. I ast him what size collar
he wore and he says he didn't want none, because he wasn't goin' out nowheres. After

breakfast he beat it up to the room again and put on his uniform. When I got up there he was lookin' in the glass at himself, and he done it all the time I was dressin'."

When we got out to the park I got my first look at him. Pretty good-lookin' guy, too, in his unie—big shoulders and well put together; built somethin' like Heine himself. He was talkin' to John when I come up.

"What position do you play?" John was askin' him.

"I play anywheres," says Elliott.

"You're the kind I'm lookin' for," says John. Then he says: "You was an outfielder up there in Michigan, wasn't you?"

"I don't care where I play," says Elliott.

John sends him to the outfield and forgets all about him for a while. Pretty soon Miller comes in and says:

"I ain't goin' to shag for no bush outfielder!"

John ast him what was the matter, and Miller tells him that Elliott ain't doin' nothin' but just standin' out there; that he ain't makin' no attemp' to catch the fungoes, and that he won't even chase 'em. Then John starts watchin' him, and it was just like Miller said. Larry hit one pretty near in his lap and he stepped out o' the way. John calls him in and ast him:

"Why don't you go after them fly balls?"

"Because I don't want 'em," says Elliott.

John gets sarcastic and says:

"What do you want? Of course we'll see that you get anythin' you want!"

"Give me a ticket back home," says Elliott.

"Don't you want to stick with the club?" says John, and the busher tells him, no, he certainly did not. Then John tells him he'll have to pay his own fare home and Elliott don't get sore at all. He just says:

"Well, I'll have to stick, then—because I'm broke."

We was havin' battin' practice and John tells him to go up and hit a few. And you ought to of seen him bust 'em!

Lavender was in there workin' and he'd been pitchin' a little all winter, so he was in pretty good shape. He lobbed one up to Elliott, and he hit it 'way up in some trees outside the fence—about a mile, I guess. Then John tells Jimmy to put somethin' on the ball. Jim comes through with one of his fast ones and the kid slams it agin the right-field wall on a line.

"Give him your spitter!" yells John, and Jim handed him one. He pulled it over first base so fast that Bert, who was standin' down there, couldn't hardly duck in time. If it'd hit him it'd killed him.

Well, he kep' on hittin' everythin' Jim give him—and Jim had somethin' too. Finally John gets Pierce warmed up and sends him out to pitch, tellin' him to hand Elliott a flock o' curve balls. He wanted to see if lefthanders was goin' to bother him. But he slammed 'em right along, and I don't b'lieve he hit more'n two the whole mornin' that wouldn't of been base hits in a game.

They sent him out to the outfield again in the afternoon, and after a lot o' coaxin' Leach got him to go after fly balls; but that's all he did do—just go after 'em. One hit him on the bean and another on the shoulder. He run back after the short ones and 'way in after the ones that went over his head. He catched just one— a line drive that he couldn't get out o' the way of; and then he acted like it hurt his hands.

I come back to the hotel with John. He ast me what I thought of Elliott.

"Well," I says, "he'd be the greatest ballplayer in the world if he could just play ball. He sure can bust 'em."

John says he was afraid he couldn't never make an outfielder out o' him. He says:

"I'll try him on the infield tomorrow. They must be some place he can play. I never seen a lefthand hitter that looked so good agin lefthand pitchin'—and he's got a great arm; but he acts like he'd never saw a fly ball."

Well, he was just as bad on the infield. They put him at short and he was like a sieve. You could of drove a hearse between him and second base without him gettin' near it. He'd stoop over for a ground ball about the time it was bouncin' up agin the fence; and when he'd try to cover the bag on a peg he'd trip over it.

They tried him at first base and sometimes he'd run 'way over in the coachers' box and sometimes out in right field lookin' for the bag. Once Heine shot one acrost at him on a line and he never touched it with his hands. It went bam! right in the pit of his stomach—and the lunch he'd ate didn't do him no good.

Finally John just give up and says he'd have to keep him on the bench and let him earn his pay by bustin' 'em a couple o' times a week or so. We all agreed with John that this bird would be a whale of a pinch hitter—and we was right too. He was hittin' 'way over five hundred when the blowoff come, along about the last o' May.

II

Before the trainin' trip was over, Elliott had roomed with pretty near everybody in the club. Heine raised an awful holler after the second night down there and John put the bug in with Needham. Tom stood him for three nights. Then he doubled up with Archer, and Schulte, and Miller, and Leach, and Saier—and the whole bunch in turn, averagin' about two nights with each one before they put up a kick. Then John tried him with some o' the youngsters, but they wouldn't stand for him no more'n the others. They all said he was crazy and they was afraid he'd get violent some night and stick a knife in 'em.

He always insisted on havin' the water run in the bathtub all night, because he said it reminded him of the sound of the dam near his home. The fellers might get up four or five times a night and shut off the faucet, but he'd get right up after 'em and turn it on again. Carter, a big bush pitcher from Georgia, started a fight with him about it one night, and Elliott pretty near killed him. So the rest o' the bunch, when they'd saw Carter's map next mornin', didn't have the nerve to do nothin' when it come their turn.

Another o' his habits was the thing that scared 'em, though. He'd brought a razor with him—in his pocket, I guess—and he used to do his shavin' in the middle o' the night. Instead o' doin' it in the bathroom he'd lather his face and then come out and stand in front o' the lookin'-glass on the dresser. Of course he'd have all the lights turned on, and that was bad enough when a feller wanted to sleep; but the worst of it was that he'd stop shavin' every little while and turn round and stare at the guy who was makin' a failure o' tryin' to sleep. Then he'd wave his razor round in the air and laugh, and begin shavin' agin. You can imagine how comf'table his roomies felt!

John had bought him a suitcase and some clothes and things, and charged 'em up to him. He'd drew so much dough in advance that he didn't have nothin' comin' till about June. He never thanked John and he'd wear one shirt and one collar till someone throwed 'em away.

Well, we finally gets to Indianapolis, and we was goin' from there to Cincy to open. The last day in Indianapolis John come and ast me how I'd like to change roomies. I says I was perfectly satisfied with Larry. Then John says: "I wisht you'd try Elliott. The other boys all kicks on him, but he seems to hang round you a lot and I b'lieve you could get along all right."

"Why don't you room him alone?" I ast.

"The boss or the hotels won't stand for us roomin' alone," says John. "You go ahead and try it, and see how you make out. If he's too much for you let me know; but he likes you and I think he'll be diff'rent with a guy who can talk to him like you can."

So I says I'd tackle it, because I didn't want to throw John down. When we got to Cincy they stuck Elliott and me in one room, and we was together till he quit us.

III

I went to the room early that night, because we was goin' to open next day and I wanted to feel like somethin'. First thing I done when I got undressed was turn on both faucets in the bathtub. They was makin' an awful racket when Elliott finally come in about midnight. I was layin' awake and I opened right up on him. I says:

"Don't shut off that water, because I like to hear it run."

Then I turned over and pretended to be asleep. The bug got his clothes off, and then what did he do but go in the bathroom and shut off the water! Then he come back in the room and says:

"I guess no one's goin' to tell me what to do in here."

But I kep' right on pretendin' to sleep and didn't pay no attention. When he'd got into his bed I jumped out o' mine and turned on all the lights and begun stroppin' my razor. He says:

"What's comin' off?"

"Some o' my whiskers," I says. "I always shave along about this time."

"No, you don't!" he says. "I was in your room one mornin' down in Louisville and I seen you shavin' then."

"Well," I says, "the boys tell me you shave in the middle o' the night; and I thought if I done all the things you do mebbe I'd get so's I could hit like you."

"You must be superstitious!" he says. And I told him I was. "I'm a good hitter," he says, "and I'd be a good hitter if I never shaved at all. That don't make no diff'rence."

"Yes, it does," I says. "You prob'ly hit good because you shave at night; but you'd be a better fielder if you shaved in the mornin'."

You see, I was tryin' to be just as crazy as him—though that wasn't hardly possible.

"If that's right," says he, "I'll do my shavin' in the mornin'—because I seen in the papers where the boys says that if I could play the outfield like I can hit I'd be as good as Cobb. They tell me Cobb gets twenty thousand a year."

"No," I says; "he don't get that much—but he gets about ten times as much as you do."

"Well," he says, "I'm goin' to be as good as him, because I need the money."

"What do you want with money?" I says.

He just laughed and didn't say nothin'; but from that time on the water didn't run in the bathtub nights and he done his shavin' after breakfast. I didn't notice, though, that he looked any better in fieldin' practice.

IV

It rained one day in Cincy and they trimmed us two out o' the other three; but it wasn't Elliott's fault.

They had Larry beat four to one in the ninth innin' o' the first game. Archer gets on with two out, and John sends my roomy up to hit—though Benton, a lefthander, is workin' for them. The first thing Benton serves up there Elliott cracks it a mile over Hobby's head. It would of been good for three easy—only Archer—playin' safe, o' course—pulls up at third base. Tommy couldn't do nothin' and we was licked.

The next day he hits one out o' the park off the Indian; but we was 'way behind and they was nobody on at the time. We copped the last one without usin' no pinch hitters.

I didn't have no trouble with him nights durin' the whole series. He come to bed pretty late while we was there and I told him he'd better not let John catch him at it.

"What would he do?" he says.

"Fine you fifty," I says.

"He can't fine me a dime," he says, "because I ain't got it."

Then I told him he'd be fined all he had comin' if he didn't get in the hotel before midnight; but he just laughed and says he didn't think John had a kick comin' so long as he kep' bustin' the ball.

"Some day you'll go up there and you won't bust it," I says.

"That'll be an accident," he says.

That stopped me and I didn't say nothin'. What could you say to a guy who hated himself like that?

The "accident" happened in St. Louis the first day. We needed two runs in the eighth and Saier and Brid was on, with two out. John tells Elliott to go up in Pierce's place. The bug goes up and Griner gives him two bad balls—'way outside. I thought they was goin' to walk him—and it looked like good judgment, because they'd heard what he done in Cincy. But no! Griner comes back with a fast one right over and Elliott pulls it down the right foul line, about two foot foul. He hit it so hard you'd of thought they'd sure walk him then; but Griner

gives him another fast one. He slammed it again just as hard, but foul. Then Griner gives him one 'way outside and it's two and three. John says, on the bench:

"If they don't walk him now he'll bust that fence down."

I thought the same and I was sure Griner wouldn't give him nothin' to hit; but he come with a curve and Rigler calls Elliott out. From where we sat the last one looked low, and I thought Elliott'd make a kick. He come back to the bench smilin'.

John starts for his position, but stopped and ast the bug what was the matter with that one. Any busher I ever knowed would of said, "It was too low," or "It was outside," or "It was inside." Elliott says:

"Nothin' at all. It was right over the middle."

"Why didn't you bust it, then?" says John.

"I was afraid I'd kill somebody," says Elliott, and laughed like a big boob.

John was pretty near chokin'.

"What are you laughin' at?" he says.

"I was thinkin' of a nickel show I seen in Cincinnati," says the bug.

"Well," says John, so mad he couldn't hardly see, "that show and that laugh'll cost you fifty."

We got beat, and I wouldn't of blamed John if he'd fined him his whole season's pay.

Up 'n the room that night I told him he'd better cut out that laughin' stuff when we was gettin' trimmed or he never would have no pay day. Then he got confidential.

"Pay day wouldn't do me no good," he says. "When I'm all squared up with the club and begin to have a pay day I'll only get a hundred bucks at a time, and I'll owe that to some o' you fellers. I wisht we could win the pennant and get in on that World's Series dough. Then I'd get a bunch at once."

"What would you do with a bunch o' dough?" I ast him.

"Don't tell nobody, sport," he says; "but if I ever get five hundred at once I'm goin' to get married."

"Oh!" I says. "And who's the lucky girl?"

"She's a girl up in Muskegon," says Elliott; "and you're right when you call her lucky."

"You don't like yourself much, do you?" I says.

"I got reason to like myself," says he. "You'd like yourself, too, if you could hit 'em like me."

"Well," I says, "you didn't show me no hittin' today."

"I couldn't hit because I was laughin' too hard," says Elliott.

"What was it you was laughin' at?" I says.

"I was laughin' at that pitcher," he says. "He thought he had somethin' and he didn't have nothin'."

"He had enough to whiff you with," I says.

"He didn't have nothin'!" says he again. "I was afraid if I busted one off him they'd can him, and then I couldn't never hit agin him no more."

Naturally I didn't have no comeback to that. I just sort o' gasped and got ready to go to sleep; but he wasn't through.

"I wisht you could see this bird!" he says.

"What bird?" I says.

"This dame that's nuts about me," he says.

"Good-looker?" I ast.

"No," he says; "she ain't no bear for looks. They ain't nothin' about her for a guy to rave over till you hear her sing. She sure can holler some."

"What kind o' voice has she got?" I ast.

"A bear," says he.

"No," I says; "I mean is she a barytone or an air?"

"I don't know," he says; "but she's got the loudest voice I ever hear on a woman. She's pretty near got me beat."

"Can you sing?" I says; and I was sorry right afterward that I ast him that question.

I guess it must of been bad enough to have the water runnin' night after night and to have him wavin' that razor round; but that couldn't of been nothin' to his singin'. Just as soon as I'd pulled that boner he says, "Listen to me!" and starts in on "Silver Threads Among the Gold." Mind you, it was after midnight and they was guests all round us tryin' to sleep!

They used to be noise enough in our club when we had Hofman and Sheckard and Richie harmonizin'; but this bug's voice was louder'n all o' theirn combined. We once had a pitcher named Martin Walsh—brother o' Big Ed's—and I thought he could drownd out the Subway; but this guy made a boiler factory sound like Dummy Taylor. If the whole hotel wasn't awake when he'd howled the first line it's a pipe they was when he cut loose, which he done when he come to "Always young and fair to me." Them words could of been heard easy in East St. Louis.

He didn't get no encore from me, but he goes right through it again—or starts to. I knowed somethin' was goin' to happen before he finished—and somethin' did. The night clerk and the house detective come bangin' at the door. I let 'em in and they had plenty to say. If we made another sound the whole club'd be canned out o' the hotel. I tried to salve 'em, and I says:

"He won't sing no more."

But Elliott swelled up like a poisoned pup. "Won't I?" he says. "I'll sing all I want to."

"You won't sing in here," says the clerk.

"They ain't room for my voice in here anyways," he says. "I'll go outdoors and sing."

And he puts his clothes on and ducks out. I didn't make no attemp' to stop him. I heard him bellowin' "Silver Threads" down the corridor and down the stairs, with the clerk and the dick chasin' him all the way and tellin' him to shut up.

Well, the guests make a holler the next mornin'; and the hotel people tells Charlie Williams that he'll either have to let Elliott stay somewheres else or the whole club'll have to move. Charlie tells John, and John was thinkin' o' settlin' the question by releasin' Elliott.

I guess he'd about made up his mind to do it; but that afternoon they had us three to one in the ninth, and we got the bases full, with two down and Larry's turn to hit. Elliott had been sittin' on the bench sayin' nothin'.

"Do you think you can hit one today?" says John.

"I can hit one any day," says Elliott.

"Go up and hit that lefthander, then," says John, "and remember there's nothin' to laugh at."

Sallee was workin'—and workin' good; but that didn't bother the bug. He cut into one, and it went between Oakes and Whitted like a shot. He come into third standin' up and we was a run to the good. Sallee was so sore he kind o' forgot himself and took pretty near his full wind-up pitchin' to Tommy. And what did Elliott do but steal home and get away with it clean!

Well, you couldn't can him after that, could you? Charlie gets him a room somewheres and I was relieved of his company that night. The next evenin' we beat it for Chi to play about two weeks at home. He didn't tell nobody where he roomed there and I didn't see nothin' of him, 'cep' out to the park. I ast him what he did with himself nights and he says:

"Same as I do on the road—borrow some dough some place and go to the nickel shows."

"You must be stuck on 'em," I says.

"Yes," he says; "I like the ones where they kill people—because I want to learn how to do it. I may have that job some day."

"Don't pick on me," I says.

"Oh," says the bug, "you never can tell who I'll pick on."

It seemed as if he just couldn't learn nothin' about fieldin', and finally John told him to keep out o' the practice.

"A ball might hit him in the temple and croak him," says John.

But he busted up a couple o' games for us at home, beatin' Pittsburgh once and Cincy once.

V

They give me a great big room at the hotel in Pittsburgh; so the fellers picked it out for the poker game. We was playin' along about ten o'clock one night when in come Elliott—the earliest he'd showed up since we'd been roomin' together. They was only five of us playin' and Tom ast him to sit in.

"I'm busted," he says.

"Can you play poker?" I ast him.

"They's nothin' I can't do!" he says. "Slip me a couple o' bucks and I'll show you."

So I slipped him a couple o' bucks and honestly hoped he'd win, because I knowed he never had no dough. Well, Tom dealt him a hand and he picks it up and says:

"I only got five cards."

"How many do you want?" I says.

"Oh," he says, "if that's all I get I'll try to make 'em do."

The pot was cracked and raised, and he stood the raise. I says to myself: "There goes my two bucks!" But no—he comes out with three queens and won the dough. It was only about seven bucks; but you'd of thought it was a million to see him grab it. He laughed like a kid.

"Guess I can't play this game!" he says; and he had me fooled for a minute—I thought he must of been kiddin' when he complained of only havin' five cards.

He copped another pot right afterward and was sittin' there with about eleven bucks in front of him when Jim opens a roodle pot for a buck. I stays and so does Elliott. Him and Jim both drawed one card and I took three. I had kings or queens—I forget which. I didn't help 'em none; so when Jim bets a buck I throws my hand away.

"How much can I bet?" says the bug.

"You can raise Jim a buck if you want to," I says.

So he bets two dollars. Jim comes back at him. He comes right back at Jim. Jim raises him again and he tilts Jim right back. Well, when he'd boosted Jim with the last buck he had, Jim says:

"I'm ready to call. I guess you got me beat. What have you got?"

"I know what I've got, all right," says Elliott. "I've got a straight." And he throws his hand down. Sure enough, it was a straight, eight high. Jim pretty near fainted and so did I.

The bug had started pullin' in the dough when Jim stops him.

"Here! Wait a minute!" says Jim. "I thought you had somethin'. I filled up." Then Jim lays down his nine full.

"You beat me, I guess," says Elliott, and he looked like he'd lost his last friend.

"Beat you?" says Jim. "Of course I beat you! What did you think I had?"

"Well," says the bug, "I thought you might have a small flush or somethin'."

When I regained consciousness he was beggin' for two more bucks.

"What for?" I says. "To play poker with? You're barred from the game for life!"

"Well," he says, "if I can't play no more I want to go to sleep, and you fellers will have to get out o' this room."

Did you ever hear o' nerve like that? This was the first night he'd came in before twelve and he orders the bunch out so's he can sleep! We politely suggested to him to go to Brooklyn.

Without sayin' a word he starts in on his "Silver Threads"; and it wasn't two minutes till the game was busted up and the bunch—all but me—was out o' there. I'd of beat it too, only he stopped yellin' as soon as they'd went.

"You're some buster!" I says. "You bust up ball games in the afternoon and poker games at night."

"Yes," he says; "that's my business—bustin' things."

And before I knowed what he was about he picked up the pitcher of ice-water that was on the floor and throwed it out the window—through the glass and all.

Right then I give him a plain talkin' to. I tells him how near he come to gettin' canned down in St. Louis because he raised so much Cain singin' in the hotel.

"But I had to keep my voice in shape," he says. "If I ever get dough enough to get married the girl and me'll go out singin' together."

"Out where?" I ast.

"Out on the vaudeville circuit," says Elliott.

"Well," I says, "if her voice is like yours you'll be wastin' money if you travel round. Just stay up in Muskegon and we'll hear you, all right!"

I told him he wouldn't never get no dough if

he didn't behave himself. That, even if we got in the World's Series, he wouldn't be with us—unless he cut out the foolishness.

"We ain't goin' to get in no World's Series," he says, "and I won't never get a bunch o' money at once; so it looks like I couldn't get married this fall."

Then I told him we played a city series every fall. He'd never thought o' that and it tickled him to death. I told him the losers always got about five hundred apiece and that we were about due to win it and get about eight hundred. "But," I says, "we still got a good chance for the old pennant; and if I was you I wouldn't give up hope o' that yet—not where John can hear you, anyway."

"No," he says, "we won't win no pennant, because he won't let me play reg'lar; but I don't care so long as we're sure o' that city-series dough."

"You ain't sure of it if you don't behave," I says.

"Well," says he, very serious, "I guess I'll behave." And he did—till we made our first Eastern trip.

VI

We went to Boston first, and that crazy bunch goes out and piles up a three-run lead on us in seven innin's the first day. It was the pitcher's turn to lead off in the eighth, so up goes Elliott to bat for him. He kisses the first thing they hands him for three bases; and we says, on the bench: "Now we'll get 'em!"—because, you know, a three-run lead wasn't nothin' in Boston.

"Stay right on that bag!" John hollers to Elliott.

Mebbe if John hadn't said nothin' to him everythin' would of been all right; but when Perdue starts to pitch the first ball to Tommy, Elliott starts to steal home. He's out as far as from here to Seattle.

If I'd been carryin' a gun I'd of shot him right through the heart. As it was, I thought John'd kill him with a bat, because he was standin' there with a couple of 'em, waitin' for his turn; but I guess John was too stunned to move. He didn't even seem to see Elliott when he went to the bench. After I'd cooled off a little I says:

"Beat it and get into your clothes before John comes in. Then go to the hotel and keep out o' sight."

When I got up in the room afterward, there was Elliott, lookin' as innocent and happy as though he'd won fifty bucks with a pair o' treys.

"I thought you might of killed yourself," I says.

"What for?" he says.

"For that swell play you made," says I.

"What was the matter with the play?" ast Elliott, surprised. "It was all right when I done it in St. Louis."

"Yes," I says; "but they was two out in St. Louis and we wasn't no three runs behind."

"Well," he says, "if it was all right in St. Louis I don't see why it was wrong here."

"It's a diff'rent climate here," I says, too disgusted to argue with him.

"I wonder if they'd let me sing in this climate?" says Elliott.

"No," I says. "Don't sing in this hotel, because we don't want to get fired out o' here—the eats is too good."

"All right," he says. "I won't sing." But when I starts down to supper he says: "I'm li'ble to do somethin' worse'n sing."

He didn't show up in the dinin' room and John went to the boxin' show after supper; so it looked like him and Elliott wouldn't run into each other till the murder had left John's heart. I was glad o' that—because a Mass'chusetts jury might not consider it justifiable hommercide if one guy croaked another for givin' the Boston club a game.

I went down to the corner and had a couple o' beers; and then I come straight back, intendin' to hit the hay. The elevator boy had went for a drink or somethin', and they was two old ladies already waitin' in the car when I stepped in. Right along after me comes Elliott.

"Where's the boy that's supposed to run this car?" he says. I told him the boy'd be right back; but he says: "I can't wait. I'm much too sleepy."

And before I could stop him he'd slammed the door and him and I and the poor old ladies was shootin' up.

"Let us off at the third floor, please!" says one o' the ladies, her voice kind o' shakin'.

"Sorry, madam," says the bug; "but this is a express and we don't stop at no third floor."

I grabbed his arm and tried to get him away from the machinery; but he was as strong as a ox and he throwed me agin the side o' the car like I was a baby. We went to the top faster'n I ever rode in an elevator before. And then we shot down to the bottom, hittin' the bumper down there so hard I thought we'd be smashed to splinters.

The ladies was too scared to make a sound durin' the first trip; but while we was goin' up and down the second time—even faster'n the first—they begun to scream. I was hollerin' my

Pete Gray, the one-armed outfielder of World War II;

International News

Left, Bob Nieman, following his record major-league debut of home runs on his second and third times at bat. Consulting with him is Max Patkin, the comedian hired by the team to be a first-base coach.

United Press

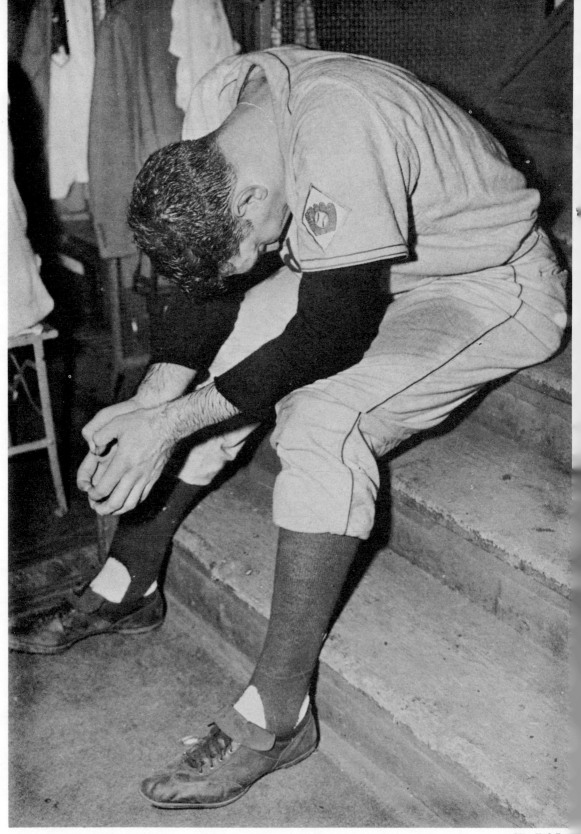

AFTER THE BALL WAS OVER

This is Barney Stein's famous picture of Ralph Branca taken moments after the Brooklyn Dodger right-hander had thrown the pitch that Bobby Thomson hit for "the home run heard round the world" in 1951. You can't see the number on Branca's back, but it's 13.

236B

**THE
SHORTSTOP
FLIES
HIGH**

But did any
ever fly
higher
than

by MacMillan?

International News

United Press   or Phil Rizzuto?

PAY DAY FOR THE BABE

Here is one of Babe Ruth's salary checks—covering half a month's pay in 1922, when he was making $52,000. Also the endorsement. That $200 deduction is for when the Babe threw dirt in the umpire's face, and, upon being ejected from the game, chased into the stands after a heckler. According to Ernie Harwell, from whose private collection this check was contributed to this book, the heckler left so fast when he saw Ruth coming that his shoes remained where they were.

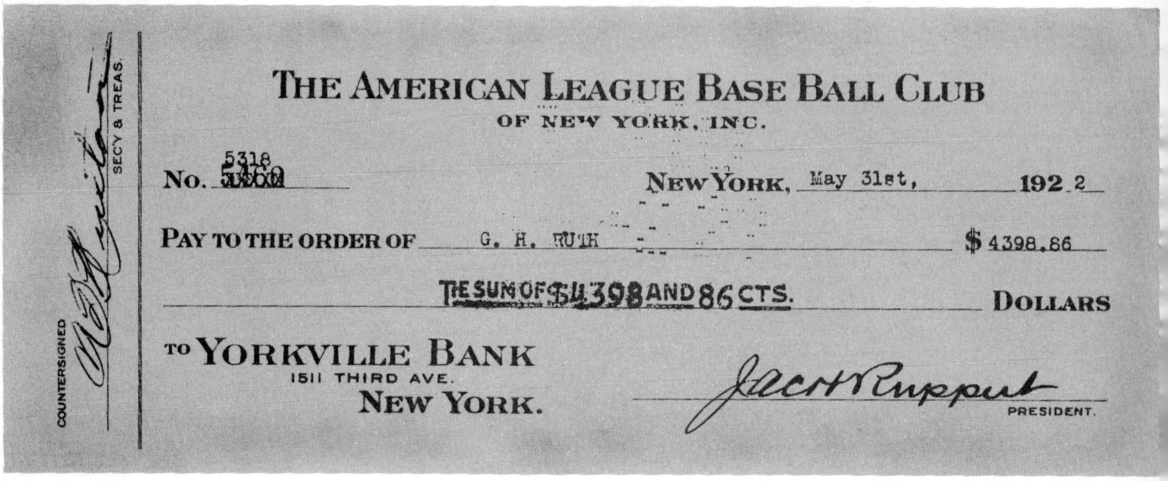

THE AMERICAN LEAGUE BASE BALL CLUB
OF NEW YORK, INC.

No. 5318

NEW YORK, May 31st, 192 2

PAY TO THE ORDER OF _____ G. H. RUTH _____ $ 4398.86

THE SUM OF $4398 AND 86 CTS. _____ DOLLARS

TO YORKVILLE BANK
1511 THIRD AVE.
NEW YORK.

PRESIDENT.

SECY & TREAS
COUNTERSIGNED

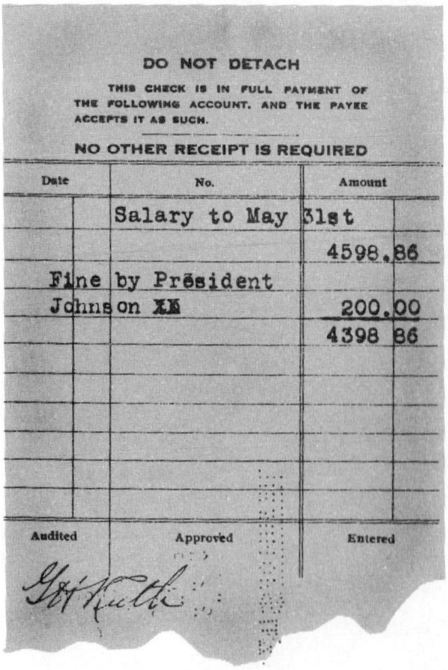

DO NOT DETACH

THIS CHECK IS IN FULL PAYMENT OF
THE FOLLOWING ACCOUNT, AND THE PAYEE
ACCEPTS IT AS SUCH.

NO OTHER RECEIPT IS REQUIRED

Date	No.	Amount
	Salary to May 31st	
		4598.86
	Fine by President	
	Johnson	200.00
		4398.86

Audited	Approved	Entered

head off at him to quit and he was makin' more noise than the three of us—pretendin' he was the locomotive and the whole crew o' the train.

Don't never ast me how many times we went up and down! The women fainted on the third trip and I guess I was about as near it as I'll ever get. The elevator boy and the bellhops and the waiters and the night clerk and everybody was jumpin' round the lobby screamin'; but no one seemed to know how to stop us.

Finally—on about the tenth trip, I guess—he slowed down and stopped at the fifth floor, where we was roomin'. He opened the door and beat it for the room, while I, though I was tremblin' like a leaf, run the car down to the bottom.

The night clerk knowed me pretty well and knowed I wouldn't do nothin' like that; so him and I didn't argue, but just got to work together to bring the old women to. While we was doin' that Elliott must of run down the stairs and slipped out o' the hotel, because when they sent the officers up to the room after him he'd blowed.

They was goin' to fire the club out; but Charlie had a good stand-in with Amos, the proprietor, and he fixed it up to let us stay—providin' Elliott kep' away. The bug didn't show up at the ball park next day and we didn't see no more of him till we got on the rattler for New York. Charlie and John both bawled him, but they give him a berth—an upper—and we pulled into the Grand Central Station without him havin' made no effort to wreck the train.

VII

I'd studied the thing pretty careful, but hadn't come to no conclusion. I was sure he wasn't no stew, because none o' the boys had ever saw him even take a glass o' beer, and I couldn't never detect the odor o' booze on him. And if he'd been a dope I'd of knew about it—roomin' with him.

There wouldn't of been no mystery about it if he'd been a lefthand pitcher—but he wasn't. He wasn't nothin' but a whale of a hitter and he throwed with his right arm. He hit lefthanded, o' course; but so did Saier and Brid and Schulte and me, and John himself; and none of us was violent. I guessed he must of been just a plain nut and li'ble to break out any time.

They was a letter waitin' for him at New York, and I took it, intendin' to give it to him at the park, because I didn't think they'd let him room at the hotel; but after breakfast he come up to the room, with his suitcase. It seems he'd promised John and Charlie to be good, and made it so strong they b'lieved him.

I give him his letter, which was addressed in a girl's writin' and come from Muskegon.

"From the girl?" I says.

"Yes," he says; and, without openin' it, he tore it up and throwed it out the window.

"Had a quarrel?" I ast.

"No, no," he says; "but she can't tell me nothin' I don't know already. Girls always writes the same junk. I got one from her in Pittsburgh, but I didn't read it."

"I guess you ain't so stuck on her," I says.

He swells up and says:

"Of course I'm stuck on her! If I wasn't, do you think I'd be goin' round with this bunch and gettin' insulted all the time? I'm stickin' here because o' that series dough, so's I can get hooked."

"Do you think you'd settle down if you was married?" I ast him.

"Settle down?" he says. "Sure, I'd settle down. I'd be so happy that I wouldn't have to look for no excitement."

Nothin' special happened that night 'cep' that he come in the room about one o'clock and woke me up by pickin' up the foot o' the bed and droppin' it on the floor, sudden-like.

"Give me a key to the room," he says.

"You must of had a key," I says, "or you couldn't of got in."

"That's right!" he says, and beat it to bed.

One o' the reporters must of told Elliott that John had ast for waivers on him and New York had refused to waive, because next mornin' he come to me with that dope.

"New York's goin' to win this pennant!" he says.

"Well," I says, "they will if someone else don't. But what of it?"

"I'm goin' to play with New York," he says, "so's I can get the World's Series dough."

"How you goin' to get away from this club?" I ast.

"Just watch me!" he says. "I'll be with New York before this series is over."

Well, the way he goes after the job was original, anyway. Rube'd had one of his good days the day before and we'd got a trimmin'; but this second day the score was tied up at two runs apiece in the tenth, and Big Jeff'd been wobblin' for two or three innin's.

Well, he walks Saier and me, with one out, and Mac sends for Matty, who was warmed up and ready. John sticks Elliott in in Brid's place and the bug pulls one into the right-field stand.

It's a cinch McGraw thinks well of him then,

and might of went after him if he hadn't went crazy the next afternoon. We're tied up in the ninth and Matty's workin'. John sends Elliott up with the bases choked; but he doesn't go right up to the plate. He walks over to their bench and calls McGraw out. Mac tells us about it afterward.

"I can bust up this game right here!" says Elliott.

"Go ahead," says Mac; "but be careful he don't whiff you."

Then the bug pulls it.

"If I whiff," he says, "will you get me on your club?"

"Sure!" says Mac, just as anybody would.

By this time Bill Koem was hollerin' about the delay; so up goes Elliott and gives the worst burlesque on tryin' to hit that you ever see. Matty throws one a mile outside and high, and the bug swings like it was right over the heart. Then Matty throws one at him and he ducks out o' the way—but swings just the same. Matty must of been wise by this time, for he pitches one so far outside that the Chief almost has to go to the coachers' box after it. Elliott takes his third healthy and runs through the field down to the clubhouse.

We got beat in the eleventh; and when we went in to dress he has his street clothes on. Soon as he seen John comin' he says:"I got to see McGraw!" And he beat it.

John was goin' to the fights that night; but before he leaves the hotel he had waivers on Elliott from everybody and had sold him to Atlanta.

"And," says John, "I don't care if they pay for him or not."

My roomy blows in about nine and got the letter from John out of his box. He was goin' to tear it up, but I told him they was news in it. He opens it and reads where he's sold. I was still sore at him; so I says:

"Thought you was goin' to get on the New York club?"

"No," he says. "I got turned down cold. McGraw says he wouldn't have me in his club. He says he'd had Charlie Faust—and that was enough for him."

He had a kind o' crazy look in his eyes; so when he starts up to the room I follows him.

"What are you goin' to do now?" I says.

"I'm goin' to sell this ticket to Atlanta," he says, "and go back to Muskegon, where I belong."

"I'll help you pack," I says.

"No," says the bug. "I come into this league with this suit o' clothes and a collar. They can

have the rest of it." Then he sits down on the bed and begins to cry like a baby. "No series dough for me," he blubbers, "and no weddin' bells! My girl'll die when she hears about it!"

Of course that made me feel kind o' rotten, and I says:

"Brace up, boy! The best thing you can do is go to Atlanta and try hard. You'll be up here again next year."

"You can't tell me where to go!" he says, and he wasn't cryin' no more. "I'll go where I please—and I'm li'ble to take you with me."

I didn't want no argument, so I kep' still. Pretty soon he goes up to the lookin'-glass and stares at himself for five minutes. Then, all of a sudden, he hauls off and takes a wallop at his reflection in the glass. Naturally he smashed the glass all to pieces and he cut his hand somethin' awful.

Without lookin' at it he come over to me and says: "Well, good-by, sport!"—and holds out his other hand to shake. When I starts to shake with him he smears his bloody hand all over my map. Then he laughed like a wild man and run out o' the room and out o' the hotel.

VIII

Well, boys, my sleep was broke up for the rest o' the season. It might of been because I was used to sleepin' in all kinds o' racket and excitement, and couldn't stand for the quiet after he'd went—or it might of been because I kep' thinkin' about him and feelin' sorry for him.

I of'en wondered if he'd settle down and be somethin' if he could get married; and finally I got to b'lievin' he would. So when we was dividin' the city series dough I was thinkin' of him and the girl. Our share o' the money—the losers', as usual—was twelve thousand seven hundred sixty bucks or somethin' like that. They was twenty-one of us and that meant six hundred seven bucks apiece. We was just goin' to cut it up that way when I says:

"Why not give a divvy to poor old Elliott?"

About fifteen of 'em at once told me that I was crazy. You see, when he got canned he owed everybody in the club. I guess he'd stuck me for the most—about seventy bucks—but I didn't care nothin' about that. I knowed he hadn't never reported to Atlanta, and I thought he was prob'ly busted and a bunch o' money might make things all right for him and the other songbird.

I made quite a speech to the fellers, tellin' 'em how he'd cried when he left us and how his heart'd been set on gettin' married on the series dough. I made it so strong that they finally fell for it. Our shares was cut to five hundred eighty apiece, and John sent him a check for a full share.

For a while I was kind o' worried about what I'd did. I didn't know if I was doin' right by the girl to give him the chance to marry her.

He'd told me she was stuck on him, and that's the only excuse I had for tryin' to fix it up between 'em; but, b'lieve me, if she was my sister or a friend o' mine I'd just as soon of had her manage the Cincinnati Club as marry that bird. I thought to myself:

"If she's all right she'll take acid in a month—and it'll be my fault; but if she's really stuck on him they must be somethin' wrong with her too, so what's the diff'rence?"

Then along comes this letter that I told you about. It's from some friend of hisn up there—and they's a note from him. I'll read 'em to you and then I got to beat it for the station:

DEAR SIR:

They have got poor Elliott locked up and they are goin' to take him to the asylum at Kalamazoo. He thanks you for the check, and we will use the money to see that he is made comf'table.

When the poor boy come back here he found that his girl was married to Joe Bishop, who runs a soda fountain. She had wrote to him about it, but he did not read her letters. The news drove him crazy—poor boy—and he went to the place where they was livin' with a baseball bat and very near killed 'em both. Then he marched down the street singin' "Silver Threads Among the Gold" at the top of his voice. They was goin' to send him to prison for assault with intent to kill, but the jury decided he was crazy.

He wants to thank you again for the money.

Yours truly,
JIM——

I can't make out his last name—but it don't make no diff'rence. Now I'll read you his note:

OLD ROOMY:

I was at bat twice and made two hits; but I guess I did not meet 'em square. They tell me they are both alive yet, which I did not mean 'em to be. I hope they got good curve-ball pitchers where I am goin'. I sure can bust them curves—can't I, sport?

Yours,
B. ELLIOTT.

P. S.—The B stands for Buster.

That's all of it, fellers; and you can see I had some excuse for not hittin'. You can also see why I ain't never goin' to room with no bug again—not for John or nobody else!

HERE, from the typewriter of the late Lloyd Lewis, a brilliant journalist, is a story different as night from day from the one on page 271. Here is how Home Run Baker got his name.

1911:
Philadelphia Athletics 4,
New York Giants 2

LLOYD LEWIS

WHEN THE bleacher gates at Shibe Park in Philadelphia were thrown open on the morning of Oct. 24, 1911, I was in the mob that went whooping toward the front seats. I got one, partly because the right-field crowd was smaller than the one in left, partly because most Philadelphians wanted to sit close to their worshiped Athletics, for the World Series at that moment stood two games to one for Connie Mack against John McGraw, and Philadelphia was loud and passionate in the confidence that now they would get revenge for the bitter dose—four games to one, three shutouts—the Giants had given them six years before.

Me, I wanted to get as close to the Giants as possible, and found a place at the rail close to the empty chairs which would that afternoon become the Giants' bull pen. My whole adolescence had been devoted, so far as baseball went —and it went a long way to an Indiana farm boy—to the Giants and to their kingly pitcher, "Big Six," the great, the incomparable Christy Mathewson. I hadn't had the courage to cut classes in the nearby college and go to the first game of the series at Shibe Park. But today I had. Things were desperate. Up in New York's Polo Grounds to start this, the World Series, Mathewson had won—2 to 1—giving but five hits and demonstrating that with 12 years of herculean toil behind him he was practically as invincible as when in 1905 he had shut out these same Athletics three times.

It had looked like 1905 over again; then, in the second game, the A's long, lean yokel third baseman J. Franklin Baker had suddenly and incredibly knocked a home run off Rube Marquard, the Giants' amazing young pitcher. Baker, who had hit only nine homers all season, had tagged the 22-year-old Giant and two runs had come in—and the final had stood 3 to 1.

The papers which I read, as the morning wore on, were still full of that home run and its aftermath.

From the start of the series the newspapers had been publishing syndicated articles signed by Giant and Athletic stars—the real start of the "ghost writers" whose spurious trade flourished so long but which the better papers in time eliminated. And in the article signed by Mathewson the day after Marquard's disaster it had been said that Rube had lost the game by failing to obey orders. The article rebuked the boy for throwing Baker the high outside pitch he liked, instead of the low fast one he didn't like and which McGraw had ordered.

The rebuke had been a sensation which grew in the third game when Baker had hit another homer off Mathewson himself, and had been the main wrecker of the great man's long sway over the A's. Up in the ninth inning of that third game Matty had kept command. Always when the Athletics had got men on bases he had turned on his magic. As he went to the bench at the end of the eighth, New York had risen and given him a tremendous ovation, for in 44 innings of World Series play, 1905 and 1911, he had allowed the Mack-men exactly one run—and the A's were hitters, indeed. Their season's average for 1911 had been .297.

Then in the ninth, Eddie Collins had gone

out, and only two men had stood between Matty and his fifth series victory over his victims. Up had come Baker with the American League fans begging him to do to Matty what he had done to Marquard—and, incredible as it seemed, he had done this.

As home runs go, it hadn't been much more than a long fly that sailed into the convenient right-field stand at the Polo Grounds, but it had gone far enough to tie the score and give Baker a nickname for life—"Home Run" Baker.

Snodgrass, the Giants' center fielder, one of the smartest and greatest of base runners, had ripped Baker's trousers almost off him, sliding into third in the first of the 10th inning. With McGraw snarling, railing, jeering from the coaching line, the Giants made no secret of their hatred of Baker. To them he was merely a lucky lout, a greenhorn who had by sheer accident homered off the two top pitchers of the season.

But Baker had hit again, a scratch single in the 11th, which had been part of the making of the run which had won, and Marquard in his "ghosted" article had quipped at Mathewson's advice.

All that was in everybody's mind—and mine—as on Oct. 24 the fourth game came up. The papers had had time to chew the sensation over and over, for it had rained for a week after the third game and now, with seven days' rest, Mathewson was to try again—this time in Shibe Park.

The long delay hadn't cooled excitement. The press box was still as crowded as at the opening game. This was the first World Series to be handled in the modern publicity fashion —the first to have as many as 50 telegraphers on the job—the first to wire the game by play-by-play to points as distant as Havana, Cuba—the first to which newspapers in the Far West and South sent their own writers. And though the A's now had a lead of two games to one, the threat of the Giants was still great enough to keep fever high.

It was a little after one o'clock when my long vigil ended. Onto the field came the Giants with their immemorial swagger, chips still on their shoulders—the cocky, ornery, defiant men of Muggsy McGraw—the rip-roaring demons who had that season of 1911 set a record of 347 stolen bases—a record which would stand for another 31 years without any other club ever coming nearer to it than the Senators' 288 in 1913.

And here at long last they were! I knew them from their pictures as, clad in dangerous black,

they came strutting across toward their dugout. McGraw had dressed his men in black, back in 1905 when he had humbled the Athletics, and he was playing hunches now.

Muggsy was first—stocky, hard-eyed. Behind him came slim, handsome Snodgrass, striding as became a genius at getting hit by pitched balls and in scaring infielders with his flashing spikes. Then came swart, ominous Larry Doyle; lantern-jawed Art Fletcher; Buck Herzog, whose nose curved like a scimitar; lithe little Josh Devore; burly Otis Crandall; flat-faced, mahogany-colored Chief Meyers, the full-blooded Indian; Fred Merkle, all muscles even in his jaws, a lion-heart living down the most awful bonehead blunder ever made in baseball.

Then came Marquard, 6 feet 3, his sharp face and slitlike eyes smiling—his head tilting to the left at the top of a long wry neck—Marquard the meteoric! At 19 years of age he had been bought at a record price from Indianapolis and had immediately flopped two straight years for McGraw, becoming the nationally goatish "$11,000 lemon." Then, this 1911, he had flamed out, won 24 games, and become the "$11,000 beauty."

As the Giants began to toss the ball around, I couldn't see my hero, the Mathewson whom I had come to see, the great one who from the time I was nine I had pretended I was, playing ball in the Indiana cow pasture, throwing his famous "fadeaway" which, for me, never came off. Then, suddenly, there he was, warming up and growling "Who am I working for, the Giants or the photographers," as the cameramen, not 20 feet from my popeyed head, begged him for poses.

I was let down for a minute. He didn't speak like a demigod but as I stared, he looked it, all the same. He held his head high, and his eye with slow, lordly contempt swept the Athletics as they warmed up across the field. He was 31, all bone and muscle and princely poise. Surely he would get those Athletics today and put the Giants back in the running. Surely his unique "fadeaway," the curve that broke backward, his speed, his snapping curve, his fabulous brain, couldn't be stopped. It had been luck that had beaten him in the last game. Now he'd get them.

My eye never left him till the bell rang and he strode, hard but easy, with the swing of the aristocrat, into the dugout and little Josh Devore went up to hit.

Josh singled, Doyle tripled, Snodgrass scored Larry with a long fly. Black figures were flying everywhere. The big copper-colored Chief

Bender on Mack's mound was wobbling, and when the side was finally out he practically ran for the dugout. Later, we learned, he had run in to cut off bandages from his ribs, tape from a recent injury. After that he was to be unbeatable.

Up came the Athletics. Matty, as though in princely disdain, fanned the first two men. The third man, Eddie Collins, singled. Here came Baker, his sun-tanned face tense, his bat flailing —the air thick with one word from 25,000 throats, "Homer! Homer!"

Matty studied him as a scientist contemplates a beetle, then struck him out! What I yelled I don't know. All I remember is standing there bellowing and paying no heed to the wadded newspapers the Athletic fans around me threw. It was wonderful.

In the fourth, Baker came up to start it and doubled. Dannie Murphy doubled. Harry Davis doubled. Ira Thomas hit a sacrifice fly— three runs. It couldn't be. Up came Baker again in the fifth with Collins on first and another double boomed across the diamond. I saw Snodgrass eventually stop it, but he didn't really have it in his glove at all. It had stuck in my gullet.

Right in front of me an unthinkable thing happened. Hooks Wiltse, the southpaw, began warming up for the Giants. Was Matty knocked out? Another figure rose from the bull pen. Rube Marquard. He didn't warm up, he only strolled up and down, a great sardonic grin on his face. The fans around me were screaming at him, "You're even with Matty now, Rube! He won't tell you what to pitch any more!" etc., etc. Rube smirked at them.

Matty got by without more scores, but in the seventh with a man on third Christy walked Baker on four intentional balls, and Shibe Park's walls waved in a cyclone of boos. I wished I were dead.

The eighth. A pinch hitter went up for Mathewson. I was sorry I hadn't died in the seventh.

Finally it was all over.

I walked out through 25,000 of the most loathsome individuals ever created—all jeering at Mathewson, all howling Baker's virtues. I dragged my feet this way and that trying to escape the currents of fans. At the end of a dolorous mile I stopped at a saloon. I had never had a drink. Now was the time.

"Beer," I said, in the voice of Poe's raven.

"You ain't 21," the bartender rasped. Then he took a second look, saw that I was 100 years old, and splashed a great stein in front of me.

I took one swallow. It was bitter, just as bitter as everything else in the world. I laid down a nickel and walked out. Every step of the way downtown I kept telling myself that in my coffin, some day, there'd be only room for one thing besides myself—my hatred of the Athletics.

But what I started out to tell was about my greatest day in baseball. That came three years later, Oct. 9, 1914, when the lowly, despised Boston Braves wallowed, humbled, trampled, laughed at the lofty Athletics to the tune of 7 to 1. Hoarse and happy, I came out of Shibe Park, spent hours hunting that same saloon, but I couldn't find it. It had to be that one. What I wanted to do was to walk in all alone— find nobody else in there—order two beers, and when the bartender looked inquiringly at the extra one, say to him in a condescending voice, "Oh, that? That's for Mathewson."

WHEN *The Natural* was published, *The New York Times* called it "a brilliant and unusual book" and Alfred Kazin wrote, "Malamud has raised the whole passion and craziness of baseball . . . to its ordained place. He takes up from where Ring Lardner's stories left off."

In the chapter from *The Natural* that is used here, Roy Hobbs, the hero, makes good in the major leagues—with Wonderboy, the bat he made himself, and under instructions to "knock the cover off the ball."

From *The Natural*

BERNARD MALAMUD

AT THE CLUBHOUSE the next morning the unshaven Knights were glum and redeyed. They moved around listlessly and cursed each step. Angry fist fights broke out among them. They were sore at themselves and the world, yet when Roy came in and headed for his locker they looked up and watched with interest. He opened the door and found his new uniform knotted up dripping wet on a hook. His sanitary socks and woolen stockings were slashed to shreds and all the other things were smeared black with shoe polish. He located his jock, with two red apples in it, swinging from a cord attached to the light globe, and both his shoes were nailed to the ceiling. The boys let out a bellow of laughter. Bump just about doubled up howling, but Roy yanked the wet pants off the hook and caught him with it smack in the face. The players let out another yowl.

Bump comically dried himself with a bath towel, digging deep into his ears, wiping under the arms, and shimmying as he rubbed it across his fat behind.

"Fast guesswork, buster, and to show you there's no hard feelings, how's about a Camel?"

Roy wanted nothing from the bastard but took the cigarette because everyone was looking on. When he lit it, someone in the rear yelled, "Fire!" and ducked as it burst in Roy's face. Bump had disappeared. The players fell into each other's arms. Tears streamed down their cheeks. Some of them could not unbend and limped around from laughing so.

Roy flipped the ragged butt away and began to mop up his wet locker.

Allie Stubbs, the second baseman, danced around the room in imitation of a naked nature dancer. He pretended to discover a trombone at the foot of a tree and marched around blowing oompah, oompah, oompah.

Roy then realized the bassoon case was missing. It startled him that he hadn't thought of it before.

"Who's got it, boys?"—but no one answered. Allie now made out like he was flinging handfuls of rose petals into the trainer's office.

Going in there, Roy saw that Bump had broken open the bassoon case and was about to attack Wonderboy with a hacksaw.

"Lay off that, you goon."

Bump turned and stepped back with the bat raised. Roy grabbed it and with a quick twist tore it out of his sweaty hands, turning him around as he did and booting him hard with his knee. Bump grunted and swung but Roy ducked. The team crowded into the trainer's office, roaring with delight.

But Doc Casey pushed his way through them and stepped between Roy and Bump. "That'll do, boys. We want no trouble here. Go on outside or Pop will have your hides."

Bump was sweaty and sore. "You're a lousy sport, alfalfa."

"I don't like the scummy tricks you play on people you have asked for a favor," Roy said.

"I hear you had a swell time, wonderboy."

Again they grappled for each other, but Doc,

shouting for help, kept them apart until the players pinned Roy's arms and held on to Bump.

"Lemme at him," Bump roared, "and I will skin the skunk."

Held back by the team, they glared at one another over the trainer's head.

"What's going on in there?" Pop's shrill blast came from inside the locker room. Earl Wilson poked his grayhaired, sunburned head in and quickly called, "All out, men, on the double." The players scurried past Pop and through the tunnel. They felt better.

Dizzy hustled up a makeshift rig for Roy. He dressed and polished his bat, a little sorry he had lost his temper, because he had wanted to speak quietly to the guy and find out whether he was expecting the redhead in his room last night.

Thinking about her made him uneasy. He reported to Pop in the dugout.

"What was that trouble in there between Bump and you?" Pop asked.

Roy didn't say and Pop got annoyed. "I won't stand for any ructions between players so cut it out or you will find yourself chopping wood back in the sticks. Now report to Red."

Roy went over to where Red was catching Chet Schultz, today's pitcher, and Red said to wait his turn at the batting cage.

The field was overrun with droopy players. Half a dozen were bunched near the gate of the cage, waiting to be pitched to by Al Fowler, whom Pop had ordered to throw batting practice for not bearing down in the clutches yesterday. Some of the men were at the sidelines, throwing catch. A few were shagging flies in the field, a group was playing pepper. On the line between home and first Earl Wilson was hacking out grounders to Allie Stubbs, Cal Baker at short, Hank Benz, the third baseman, and Emil Lajong, who played first. At the edge of the outfield, Hinkle and Hill, two of the regular starters, and McGee, the reliefer, were doing a weak walk-run-walk routine. No one seemed to be thoroughly awake, but when Roy went into the batting cage they came to life and observed him.

Fowler, a southpaw, was in a nasty mood. He didn't like having his ears burned by Pop, called a showboat in front of the other men, and then shoved into batting practice the day after he had pitched. Fowler was twenty-three but looked thirty. He was built rangy, with very light hair and eyelashes, and small blue eyes. As a pitcher he had the stuff and knew it, but all season long he had been erratic, and did

a great amount of griping. He was palsy with Bump, who as a rule had no friends.

When Roy came up with Wonderboy, he hugged the plate too close to suit Fowler, who was in there anyway only to help the batters find their timing. In annoyance Fowler pitched the ball at Roy's head. Roy hit the dirt.

Pop shrieked, "Cut that out, you blasted fool." Fowler mumbled something about the ball slipping. Yet he wanted to make Roy look silly and burned the next one in. Roy swung and the ball sailed over the right-field fence. Red-faced, Fowler tried a hard, sharp-breaking curve. Roy caught it at the end of his bat and pulled it into the left-field stands.

"Try this one, grandpa." Fowler flung a stiff-wrist knuckler that hung in the air without spin before it took a sudden dip, but Roy scooped it up with the stick and lifted it twenty rows up into the center-field stands. Then he quit. Fowler was scowling at his feet. Everybody else stared at Roy.

Pop called out, "Lemme see that bat, son."

Both he and Red examined it, hefting it and rubbing along the grain with their fingers.

"Where'd you get it?" Pop asked.

Roy cleared his throat. He said he had made it himself.

"Did you brand this name Wonderboy on it?"

"That's right."

"What's it mean?"

"I made it long ago," Roy said, "when I was a kid. I wanted it to be a very good bat and that's why I gave it that name."

"A bat's cheap to buy," Red said.

"I know it but this tree near the river where I lived was split by lightning. I liked the wood inside of it so I cut me out a bat. Hadn't used it much until I played semipro ball, but I always kept it oiled with sweet oil and boned it so it wouldn't chip."

"Sure is white. Did you bleach the wood?"

"No, that's the true color."

"How long ago d'you make it?" Pop asked.

"A long time—I don't remember."

"Whyn't you get into the game then?"

Roy couldn't answer for a minute. "I sorta got sidetracked."

But Pop was all smiles. "Red'll measure and weigh it. If there's no filler and it meets specifications you'll be allowed to use it."

"There's nothing in it but wood."

Red clapped him on the back. "I feel it in my bones that you will have luck with it." He said to Pop, "Maybe we can start Roy in the line-up soon?"

Pop said they would see how it worked out.

But he sent Roy out to left field and Earl hit fungos to him all over the lot. Roy ran them down well. He took one shot over his shoulder and two caroming off the wall below the stands. His throwing was quick, strong, and bull's eye.

When Bump got around to his turn in the cage, though he did not as a rule exert himself in practice, he now whammed five of Fowler's fast pitches into the stands. Then he trotted out to his regular spot in the sun field and Earl hit him some long flies, all of which he ran for and caught with gusto, even those that went close to the wall, which was unusual for him because he didn't like to go too near it.

Practice picked up. The men worked faster and harder than they had in a long time. Pop suddenly felt so good, tears came to his eyes and he had to blow his nose.

* * *

In the clubhouse about an hour and a half before game time, the boys were sitting around in their underwear after showers. They were bulling, working crossword puzzles, shaving and writing letters. Two were playing checkers, surrounded by a circle of others, and the rest were drinking soda, looking at the *Sporting News* or just resting their eyes. Though they tried to hide it they were all nervous, always glancing up whenever someone came into the room. Roy couldn't make sense of it.

Red took him around to meet some of the boys and Roy spoke a few words to Dave Olson, the squat catcher, also to the shy Mexican center fielder, Juan Flores, and to Gabby Laslow, who patrolled right field. They sidestepped Bump, sitting in front of his locker with a bath towel around his rump, as he worked a red thread across the yellowed foot of a sanitary sock.

"Changes that thread from sock to sock every day," Red said in a low voice. "Claims it keeps him hitting."

As the players began to get into clean uniforms, Pop, wearing half-moon specs, stepped out of his office. He read aloud the batting order, then flipping through his dog-eared, yellow-paged notebook he read the names of the players opposing them and reminded them how the pitchers were to pitch and the fielders field them. This information was scribbled all over the book and Pop had to thumb around a lot before he had covered everybody. Roy then expected him to lay on with a blistering mustard plaster for all, but he only glanced anxiously at the door and urged them all to be on their toes and for gosh sakes get some runs.

Just as Pop finished his pep talk the door squeaked open and a short and tubby man in a green suit peeked in. Seeing they were ready, he straightened up and entered briskly, carrying a briefcase in his hand. He beamed at the players and without a word from anybody they moved chairs and benches and arranged themselves in rows before him. Roy joined the rest, expecting to hear some kind of talk. Only Pop and the coaches sat behind the man, and Dizzy lounged, half openmouthed, at the door leading to the hall.

"What's the act?" Roy asked Olson.

"It's Doc Knobb." The catcher looked sleepy.

"What's he do?"

"Pacifies us."

The players were attentive, sitting as if they were going to have their pictures snapped. The nervousness Roy had sensed among them was all but gone. They looked like men whose worries had been lifted, and even Bump gave forth a soft grunt of contentment. The doctor removed his coat and rolled up his shirt sleeves. "Got to hurry today," he told Pop, "got a polo team to cheer up in Brooklyn."

He smiled at the men and then spoke so softly, at first they couldn't hear him. When he raised his voice it exuded calm.

"Now, men," he purred, "all of you relax and let me have your complete attention. Don't think of a thing but me." He laughed, brushed a spot off his pants, and continued. "You know what my purpose is. You're familiar with that. It's to help you get rid of the fears and personal inferiorities that tie you into knots and keep you from being aces in this game. Who are the Pirates? Not supermen, only mortals. What have they got that you haven't got? I can't think of a thing, absolutely not one. It's the attitude that's licking you—your own, not the Pirates'. What do you mean to yourselves? Are you a flock of bats flying around in a coffin, or the sun shining calmly on a blue lake? Are you sardines being swallowed up in the sea, or the whale that does the swallowing? That's why I'm here, to help you answer that question in the affirmative, to help you by mesmerism and autosuggestion, meaning you do the suggesting, not I. I only assist by making you receptive to your own basic thoughts. If you think you are winners, you will be. If you don't, you won't. That's psychology. That's the way the world works. Give me your whole attention and look straight into my eyes. What do you see there? You see sleep. That's right, sleep. So relax, sleep, relax . . ."

His voice was soft, lulling, peaceful. He had

raised his pudgy arms and with stubby fingers was making ripples on a vast calm sea. Already Olson was gently snoring. Flores, with the tip of his tongue protuding, Bump, and some of the other players were fast asleep. Pop looked on, absorbed.

Staring at the light gleaming on Pop's bald bean, Roy felt himself going off . . . way way down, drifting through the tides into golden water as he searched for this lady fish, or mermaid, or whatever you called her. His eyes grew big in the seeking, first fish eyes, then bulbous frog eyes. Sailing lower into the pale-green sea, he sought everywhere for the reddish glint of her scales, until the water became dense and dark green and then everything gradually got so black he lost all sight of where he was. When he tried to rise up into the light he couldn't find it. He darted in all directions, and though there were times he saw flashes of her green tail, it was dark everywhere. He threshed up a storm of luminous bubbles but they gave out little light and he did not know where in all the glass to go.

Roy ripped open his lids and sprang up. He shoved his way out from between the benches.

The doctor was startled but made no attempt to stop him. Pop called out, "Hey, where do you think you're going?"

"Out."

"Sit down, dammit, you're on the team."

"I might be on the team but no medicine man is going to hypnotize me."

"You signed a contract to obey orders," Pop snapped shrilly.

"Yes, but not to let anybody monkey around in my mind."

As he headed into the tunnel he heard Pop swear by his eight-foot uncle that nobody by the name of Roy Hobbs would ever play ball for him as long as he lived.

* * *

He had waited before . . . and he waited now, on a spike-scuffed bench in the dugout, hidden from sky, wind and weather, from all but the dust that blew up from Knights Field and lodged dry in the throat, as the grass grew browner. And from time ticking off balls and strikes, batters up and out, halves and full innings, games won and (mostly) lost, days and nights, and the endless train miles from Philly, with in-between stops, along the arc to St. Louis, and circling back by way of Chi, Boston, Brooklyn . . . still waiting.

"C'mon, Roy," Red had urged, "apologize to Pop, then the next time Knobb comes around, join the boys and everything will be okay."

"Nix on that," said Roy. "I don't need a shyster quack to shoot me full of confidence juice. I want to go through on my own steam."

"He only wants everybody to relax and be able to do their best."

Roy shook his head. "I been a long time getting here and now that I am, I want to do it by myself, not with that kind of bunk."

"Do what?" Red asked.

"What I have to do."

Red shrugged and gave him up as too stubborn. Roy sat around, and though it said on his chest he was one of the team, he sat among them alone; at the train window, gazing at the moving trees, in front of his locker, absorbed in an untied shoe lace, in the dugout, squinting at the great glare of the game. He traveled in their company and dressed where they did but he joined them in nothing, except maybe batting practice, entering the cage with the lumber on his shoulder glistening like a leg bone in the sun and taking his chops at the pill. Almost always he hammered the swift, often murderous throws (the practice pitchers dumped their bag of tricks on him) deep into the stands, as the players watched and muttered at the swift flight of the balls, then forgot him when the game started. But there were days when the waiting got him. He could feel the strength draining from his bones, weakening him so he could hardly lift Wonderboy. He was unwilling to move then, for fear he would fall over on his puss and have to crawl away on all fours. Nobody noticed he did not bat when he felt this way except Pop; and Bump, seeing how white his face was, squirted contemptuous tobacco juice in the dust. Then when Roy's strength ebbed back, he would once again go into the batters' cage and do all sorts of marvelous things that made them watch in wonder.

He watched *them* and bad as he felt he had to laugh. They were a nutty bunch to begin with but when they were losing they were impossible. It was like some kind of sickness. They threw to the wrong bases, bumped heads together in the outfield, passed each other on the baselines, sometimes batted out of order, throwing both Pop and the ump into fits, and cussed everybody else for their mistakes. It was not uncommon to see them pile three men on a bag, or behold a catcher on the opposing team, in a single skip and jump, lay the tag on two of them as they came thundering together into home plate. Or watch Gabby Laslow, in a tight spot, freeze onto the ball, or Allie Stubbs get socked with it in the jaw, thrown by Olson on a steal as Allie admired a lady in the stands. Doc Knobb's hypnotism cut down their jitters but it didn't much help their co-ordination, yet when they were left unhypnotized for a few days, they were afflicted with more than the usual number of hexes and whammies and practiced all sorts of magic to undo them. To a man they crossed their fingers over spilled salt, or coffee or tea, or at the sight of a hearse. Emil Lajong did a backward flip whenever he located a cross-eyed fan in the stands. Olson hated a woman who wore the same drab brown-feathered hat every time she showed up. He spat through two fingers whenever he spotted her in the crowd. Bump went through his ritual with the colored threads in his socks and shorts. Pop sometimes stroked a rabbit's foot. Red Blow never changed his clothes during a "winning streak," and Flores secretly touched his genitals whenever a bird flew over his head.

They were not much different from the fans in the patched and peeling stands. On weekdays the stadium usually looked like a haunted house but over the weekend crowds developed. The place often resembled a zoo full of odd-balls, including gamblers, bums, drunks, and some ugly crackpots. Many of them came just to get a laugh out of the bonehead plays. Some, when the boys were losing, cursed and jeered, showering them—whenever they came close enough—with rotten cabbages, tomatoes, blackened bananas and occasionally an egg-plant. Yet let the umpire call a close play against the Knights and he became a target for pop bottles, beer cans, old shoes or anything that happened to be lying around loose. Surprisingly, however, a few players were chosen for affection and even admiration by their fans. Sadie Sutter, a girl of sixty-plus, who wore large flowered hats, bobby sox, and short skirts, showed her undying love for Dave Olson every time he came up to the plate by banging with all her might on a Chinese gong she dragged into the stadium every day. A Hungarian cook, a hearty man with a hard yellow straw hat jammed tight on his skull, hopped up on his seat and crowed like a rooster whenever Emil Lajong originated a double play. And there was a girl named Gloria from Mississippi, a washed-out flower of the vestibules, who between innings when her eyes were not on the game, lined up a customer or two for a quickie later. She gave her heart to Gabby, yelling, "Get a

move on, mo-lasses," to set him in motion after a fly ball. Besides these, there had appeared early in the present season a pompous Otto P. Zipp, whose peevish loudspeaker could be heard all over the park, his self-chosen mission to rout the critics of Bump Baily, most of whom razzed the big boy for short legging on the other fielders. The dwarf honked a loud horn at the end of a two-foot walking stick, and it sounded as if a flock of geese had been let loose at the offenders, driving them—his purple curses ringing in their ears—to seek shelter in some hidden hole in the stands or altogether out of the ball park. Zipp was present at every home game, sitting at the rail in short left field, and Bump made it his much publicized business, as he trotted out to his position at the start of the game, to greet him with a loud kiss on the forehead, leaving Otto in a state of creamy bliss.

Roy got to know them all as he waited, all one if you looked long enough through the haze of cigarette smoke, except one . . . Memo Paris, Pop's redheaded niece, sad, spurned lady, who sat without wifehood in the wives' box behind third base. He could, if she would let him, find her with his eyes shut, with his hands alone as he had in the dark. Always in the act of love she lived in his mind, the only way he knew her, because she would not otherwise suffer his approach. *He* was to blame, she had wept one bitter midnight, so she hated his putrid guts. Since the team's return to the city (the phone banged in his ear and she ripped up his letters when they were delivered) whenever he got up from his seat in the hotel lobby as she stepped out of the elevator, to say how sorry he was for beginning at the wrong end, she tugged at her summer furpiece and breezed past him in green-eyed scorn, withering in the process Bump at the cigar stand, who had laughed aloud at Roy's rout. ("Honeybunch," he had explained, "it was out of the pity of my heart that I took that shmo into my room, because they didn't have one for him and I was intending to pass the night at the apartment of my he cousin from Mobile. How'd I know you'd go in there when you said you weren't speaking to me?" He swore it hadn't been a gag—had he ever pulled one on her?—but Memo punished him in silence, punishing herself, and he knew it because she still came every day to see him play.) She walked out of the lobby, with her silver bracelets tinkling, swaying a little on her high heels, as if she had not too long ago learned to walk on them, and went with her beautiful body away, for which Roy everlastingly fried Bump Baily in the deep fat of his abomination.

It was for her he waited.

❈   ❈   ❈

On the morning of the twenty-first of June Pop told Roy that as of tomorrow he was being shipped to a Class B team in the Great Lakes Association. Roy said he was quitting baseball anyway, but that same day, in answer to an angry question of Pop's as to why the team continued to flop, Doc Knobb said that the manager's hysterical behavior was undoing all the good he had done, and he offered to hypnotize Pop along with the others without hiking his fee. Pop shrilly told the psychologist he was too old for such bamboozlement, and Knobb retorted that his attitude was not only ridiculous but stupid. Pop got redfaced and told him to go to perdition with his hocus pocus and as of right then the doctor was canned.

That afternoon the Knights began a series with the second-place Phils. Instead of falling into a swoon when they learned there was to be no further hypnosis, the team played its best ball in weeks. Against superior pitching, in the sixth they bunched three singles for a run, and though Schultz had already given up five hits to the Phils, they were scattered and came to nothing. The Phils couldn't score till the top of the eighth, when with two out Schultz weakened, walking one man and handing the next a good enough throw to hit for a sharp single, so that there were now men on first and third. Up came Rogers, the Phils' slugger, and hit a fast curve for what looked like no more than a long fly ball, a routine catch, to left center. Now it happened that Bump was nearer to the ball than Flores, who was shifted to the right, but he was feeling horny in the sun and casting about in his mind for who to invite to his bed tonight, when he looked up and noticed this ball coming. He still had time to get under it but then saw Flores going for it like a galloping horse, and the anguished look on the Mexican's face, his black eyes popping, neck like a thick rope, and mouth haunted, fascinated Bump so, he decided to let him have it if he wanted it that bad. At the last minute he tried to take it away from the Mex, risking a head-on collision, but the wind whipped the ball closer to the wall than he had bargained for, so Bump fell back to cover Flores in case he misplayed it.

The ball fell between them, good for a double, and scoring two of the Phils. Pop tore at what was left of his gray hair but couldn't

grip it with his oily, bandaged fingers so he pulled at his ears till they were lit like red lamps. Luckily the next Phil smothered the fire by rolling to first, which kept the score at 2-1. When Bump returned to the dugout Pop cursed him from the cradle to the grave and for once Bump had no sassy answers. When it came his time to go out on deck, Pop snarled for him to stay where he was. Flores found a ripe one and landed on first but Pop stuck to his guns and looked down the line past Bump. His eye lit on Roy at the far end of the bench, and he called his name to go out there and hit. Bump turned purple. He grabbed a bat and headed for Roy but half the team jumped on him. Roy just sat there without moving and it looked to everyone like he wouldn't get up. The umpire roared in for a batter to come out, and after a while, as the players fidgeted and Pop fumed, Roy sighed and picked up Wonderboy. He slowly walked up the steps.

"Knock the cover off of it," Pop yelled.

"Attention, please," the P.A. man announced. "Roy Hobbs, number forty-five, batting for Baily."

A groan rose from the stands and turned into a roar of protest.

Otto Zipp jumped up and down on his seat, shaking his furious little fist at home plate.

"Throw him to the dogs," he shouted, and filled the air with his piercing curses.

Glancing at the wives' box, Roy saw that Memo had her head turned away. He set his jaw and advanced to the plate. His impulse was to knock the dirt out of his cleats but he refrained because he did not want to harm his bat in any way. Waiting for the pitcher to get set, Roy wiped his palms on his pants and twitched his cap. He lifted Wonderboy and waited rock-like for the throw.

He couldn't tell the color of the pitch that came at him. All he could think of was that he was sick to death of waiting, and tongue-out thirsty to begin. The ball was now a dewdrop staring him in the eye so he stepped back and swung from the toes.

Wonderboy flashed in the sun. It caught the sphere where it was biggest. A noise like a twenty-one gun salute cracked the sky. There was a straining, ripping sound and a few drops of rain spattered to the ground. The ball screamed toward the pitcher and seemed suddenly to dive down at his feet. He grabbed it to throw to first and realized to his horror that he held only the cover. The rest of it, unraveling cotton thread as it rode, was headed into the outfield.

Roy was rounding first when the ball plummeted like a dead bird into center field. Attempting to retrieve and throw, the Philly fielder got tangled in thread. The second baseman rushed up, bit the cord and heaved the ball to the catcher but Roy had passed third and made home, standing. The umpire called him safe and immediately a rhubarb boiled. The Phils' manager and his players charged out of the dugout and were joined by the nine men on the field. At the same time, Pop, shouting in defense of the ump, rushed forth with all the Knights but Bump. The umpire, caught between both teams, had a troublesome time of it and was shoved this way and that. He tossed out two men on each side but by then came to the decision that the hit was a ground-rules double. Flores had scored and the game was tied up. Roy was ordered back to second, and Pop announced he was finishing the game under protest. Somebody then shouted it was raining cats and dogs. The stands emptied like a yawn and the players piled into the dugouts. By the time Roy got in from second he was wading in water ankle deep. Pop sent him into the clubhouse for a change of uniform but he could have saved himself the trouble because it rained steadily for three days. The game was recorded as a 2-2 tie, to be replayed later in the season.

In the locker room Pop asked Roy to explain why he thought the cover had come off the ball.

"That's what you said to do, wasn't it?"

"That's right," said Pop, scratching his bean.

The next day he told Roy he was withdrawing his release and would hereafter use him as a pinch hitter and substitute fielder.

The rain had washed out the Phils' series but the Knights were starting another with the seventh-place Redbirds. In batting practice, Roy, who was exciting some curiosity for his freak hit of yesterday, looked tremendous but so did Bump. For the first time in a long while Roy went out to left field to limber up. Bump was out there too and Earl swatted fungos to both.

As they were changing into clean uniforms before the start of the game, Bump warned Roy in front of everybody, "Stay out of my way, busher, or you will get your head bashed."

Roy squirted spit on the floor.

When Pop later handed the batting order to Stuffy Briggs, the plate umpire, it had Bump's name scribbled on it as usual in the fourth slot, but Pop had already warned him that if he didn't hustle his behind when a ball was hit out to his field, he would rest it a long time on the bench.

Bump made no reply but it was obvious that he took Pop's words to heart, because he was a bang-up fielder that day. He accepted eight chances, twice chasing into center field to take them from Flores. He caught them to his left and right, dove for and came up with a breathtaking shoestringer and, running as if on fire, speared a fantastic catch over his shoulder. Still not satisfied, he pounded like a bull after his ninth try, again in Flores' territory, a smoking ball that sailed up high, headed for the wall. As Bump ran for it he could feel fear leaking through his stomach, and his legs unwillingly slowed down, but then he had this vision of himself as the league's best outfielder, acknowledged so by fans and players alike, even Pop, whom he'd be nothing less than forever respectful to, and in love with and married to Memo. Thinking this way he ran harder, though Zipp's geese honked madly at his back, and, with a magnificent twisting jump, he trapped the ball in his iron fingers. Yet the wall continued to advance, and though the redheaded lady of his choice was on her feet shrieking, Bump bumped it with a skull-breaking bang, and the wall embraced his broken body.

*   *   *

Though Bump was on the critical list in the hospital, many newspapers continued to speculate about that ball whose cover Roy had knocked off. It was explained as everything from an optical illusion (neither the ball nor the cover was ever found, the remnant caught by the catcher disappeared, and it was thought some fan had snatched the cover) to a feat of prodigious strength. Baseball records and newspaper files were combed but no one could find any evidence that it had happened before, although some of the older scribes swore it had. Then it leaked out that Pop had ordered Roy to skin the ball and Roy had obliged, but no one took that very seriously. One of the sports writers suggested that a hard downward chop could shear off the outer covering. He had tried it in his cellar and had split the horsehide. Another pointed out that such a blow would have produced an infield grounder, therefore maybe a tremendous upward slash? The first man proved that would have uncorked a sure pop fly whereas the ball, as everyone knew, had sailed straight out over the pitcher's head. So it had probably resulted from a very very forceful sock. But many a hitter had plastered the ball forcefully before, still another argued, and his idea was that it was defective to begin with, a fact the company that manufactured the ball vigorously denied. Max Mercy had his own theory. He wrote in his column, "My Eye in the Knot Hole" (the year he'd done the Broadway stint for his paper his eye was in the key hole), that Roy's bat was a suspicious one and hinted it might be filled with something a helluva lot stronger than wood. Red Blow publicly denied this. He said the bat had been examined by league authorities and was found to be less than forty-two inches long, less than two and three-quarter inches thick at its fattest part, and in weight less than two pounds, which made it a legal weapon. Mercy then demanded that the wood be X-rayed but Roy turned thumbs down on that proposition and kept Wonderboy hidden away when the sports columnist was nosing around in the clubhouse.

On the day after the accident Pop soberly gave Roy the nod to play in Bump's place. As Roy trotted out to left, Otto Zipp was in his usual seat but looking worn and aged. His face, tilted to the warming rays of the sun, was like a pancake with a cherry nose, and tears were streaming through slits where the eyes would be. He seemed to be waiting for his pregame kiss on the brow but Roy passed without looking at him.

The long rain had turned the grass green and Roy romped in it like a happy calf in its pasture. The Redbirds, probing his armor, belted the ball to him whenever they could, which was often, because Hill was not too happy on the mound, but Roy took everything they aimed at him. He seemed to know the soft, hard, and bumpy places in the field and just how high a ball would bounce on them. From the flags on the stadium roof he noted the way the wind would blow the ball, and he was quick at fishing it out of the tricky undercurrents on the ground. Not sun, shadow, nor smoke haze bothered him, and when a ball was knocked against the wall he estimated the angle of rebound and speared it as if its course had been plotted on a chart. He was good at gauging slices and knew when to charge the pill to save time on the throw. Once he put his head down and ran ahead of a shot going into the concrete. Though the crowd rose with a thunderous warning, he caught it with his back to the wall and did a little jig to show he was alive. Every-

one laughed in relief, and they liked his long-legged loping and that he resembled an acrobat the way he tumbled and came up with the ball in his glove. For his performance that day there was much whistling and applause, except where he would have liked to hear it, an empty seat in the wives' box.

His batting was no less successful. He stood at the plate lean and loose, right-handed with an open stance, knees relaxed and shoulders squared. The bat he held in a curious position, lifted slightly above his head as if prepared to beat a rattlesnake to death, but it didn't harm his smooth stride into the pitch, nor the easy way he met the ball and slashed it out with a flick of the wrists. The pitchers tried something different every time he came up, sliders, sinkers, knucklers, but he swung and connected, spraying them to all fields. He was, Red Blow said to Pop, a natural, though somewhat less than perfect because he sometimes hit at bad ones, which caused Pop to frown.

"I mistrust a bad-ball hitter."

"There are all kinds of hitters," Red answered. "Some are bucket foots, and some go for bad throws but none of them bother me as long as they naturally connect with anything that gets in their way."

Pop spat up over the dugout steps. "They sometimes make some harmful mistakes."

"Who don't?" Red asked.

Pop then muttered something about this bad-ball hitter he knew who had reached for a lemon and cracked his spine.

But the only thing Roy cracked that day was the record for the number of triples hit in a major-league debut and also the one for chances accepted in the outfield. Everybody agreed that in him the Knights had uncovered something special. One reporter wrote, "He can catch everything in creation," and Roy just about proved it. It happened that a woman who lived on the sixth floor of an apartment house overlooking the stadium was cleaning out her bird cage, near the end of the game, which the Knights took handily, when her canary flew out of the window and darted down across the field. Roy, who was waiting for the last out, saw something coming at him in the low rays of the sun, and leaping high, bagged it in his glove.

He got rid of the bloody mess in the clubhouse can.

Following are six cartoons by six nationally famous editorial-page artists—Russell, Dowling, Herblock, Talburt, Manning, Jenkins—that show how easily, and indicate how frequently, baseball lends itself to artistic comment on the world and national scenes. The cartoons are all self-explanatory: Mr. Jenkins' drawing of MacArthur came in April 1948, when the Hearst press was booming the general for president. In Jenkins' title "Time for a Real Pinch-Hitter!" maybe it is actually too late for a pinch-hitter. Check the scoreboard over Stalin's left shoulder. 26-0. Hmm.

REGINALD MANNING

Russian "Baseball"

Courtesy McNaught Syndicate, Inc. ©

H. M. TALBURT

Reproduced by permission © 1957 by
Scripps-Howard Newspapers

Time for a Real Pinch-Hitter!

*"That Ain't My Style," Said Casey . . .
And the Umpire Said, "Strike Two!"*

Home Plate
in Freedom's World Series

We've Got to Do Something
About Second Base

253

HERE is a game whose great individual feature, as Mr. McGowen wrote at the time, now twenty years ago, probably never will be duplicated. Interesting: what made the game so memorable was not the thing that drew a record crowd to see it.

1938:
Cincinnati Reds 6,
Brooklyn Dodgers 0

ROSCOE McGOWEN

LAST NIGHT they turned on the greatest existing battery of baseball lights at Ebbets Field for the inaugural night major-league game in the metropolitan area. A record throng for the season there, 40,000, of whom 38,748 paid, came to see the fanfare and the show that preceded the contest between the Reds and the Dodgers.

The game, before it was played, was partly incidental; the novelty of night baseball was the major attraction.

But Johnny Vander Meer, tall, handsome twenty-two-year-old Cincinnati southpaw pitcher, stole the entire show by hurling his second successive no-hit, no-run game, both coming within five days, and making baseball history that probably never will be duplicated. His previous no-hitter was pitched in daylight at Cincinnati last Saturday against the Bees [Braves], the Reds winning, 3 to 0. Last night the score was 6 to 0.

The records reveal only seven pitchers credited with two no-hitters in their careers and none who achieved the feat in one season.

More drama was crowded into the final inning than a baseball crowd has felt in many a moon. Until that frame only one Dodger had got as far as second base, Lavagetto reaching there when Johnny issued passes to Cookie and Dolf Camilli in the seventh. Vandy pitched out of that easily enough and the vast crowd was pulling for him to come through to the end.

Johnny mowed down Woody English, batting for Luke Hamlin; Kiki Cuyler and Johnny

Hudson in the eighth, fanning the first and third men. When Vito Tamulis, fourth Brooklyn hurler, treated the Reds likewise in the ninth, Vandy came out for the crucial inning.

He started easily, taking Buddy Hassett's bounder and tagging him out. Then his terrific speed got out of control and, while the fans sat forward tense and almost silent, he walked Babe Phelps, Lavagetto and Camilli to fill the bases.

All nerves were taut as Vandy pitched to Ernie Koy. With the count one and one, Ernie sent a bounder to Lew Riggs, who was so careful in making the throw to Ernie Lombardi that a double play wasn't possible.

Leo Durocher, so many times a hitter in the pinches, was the last hurdle for Vander Meer, and the crowd groaned as he swung viciously, to line a foul high into the right-field stands. But a moment later Leo swung again, the ball arched lazily toward short center field and Harry Craft camped under it for the put-out that brought unique distinction to the young hurler.

It brought, also, a horde of admiring fans onto the field, with Vandy's teammates ahead of them to hug and slap Johnny on the back and then to protect him from the mob as they struggled toward the Red dugout.

The fans couldn't get Johnny, but a few moments later they got his father and mother, who had accompanied a group of 500 citizens from Vandy's home town of Midland Park, N. J. The elder Vander Meers were completely surrounded and it required nearly fifteen minutes before they could escape.

The feat ran the youngster's remarkable pitching record to 18⅓ hitless and scoreless innings and a string of 26 scoreless frames. This includes a game against the Giants, his no-hitter against the Bees and last night's game. Vander Meer struck out 7 Dodgers, getting pinch hitters twice, and of the 8 passes he issued two came in the seventh and three in the tense ninth.

Added to his speed was a sharp-breaking curve that seldom failed to break over the plate and at which the Dodger batsmen swung as vainly as at his fireball.

On the offense, well-nigh forgotten as the spectacle of Vander Meer's no-hitter unfolded, the Reds made victory certain as early as the third frame, when they scored four times and drove Max Butcher away.

Frank McCormick hit a home run into the left-field stands with Wally Berger and Ival Goodman aboard, while a pass to Lombardi and singles by Craft and Riggs added the fourth run.

Craft's third straight single scored Goodman in the seventh, the latter's blow off Tot Pressnell's right kneecap knocking the knuckleballer out and causing him to be carried off on a stretcher. Berger tripled off Luke Hamlin in the eighth to score Vander Meer with the last run.

DON TOBIN

Courtesy *Sport* Magazine. ©

"He's a sucker for a fast-breaking knuckle ball over the outside corner shoulder-high. Have you got one?"

LEGITIMATE inquiry might be made whether "iron man" here refers to subject or author. Could go either way. It is an offhand belief of mine —I haven't checked it, but wouldn't mind—that Tom Meany has written more baseball books than anybody else. Add this to his newspaper and magazine output over the years, and coming down to a choice of one piece for an anthology is unhappy business. Result, though, is inevitably happy. Included here, by the way, is a fine account of the famous Merkle incident.

The Real Man of Iron

TOM MEANY

THE ELECTRIC EYES of the ornamental owls in the grill-room walls of Atlanta's Ansley Hotel blinked solemnly down on the diners that early April evening in 1926. And just as solemnly as the wooden owls themselves, Iron Man Joe McGinnity was telling a couple of baseball reporters what was wrong with the pitching staff of the Brooklyn Dodgers.

That something was wrong with the staff was patent even to the most inexperienced of the writers. Brooklyn was barnstorming north with the Yankees, the same Yankees who had finished a dismal seventh in the American League the year before, a club which was supposed to be washed up.

Not only were the Dodgers unable to win a game from the Yankees all spring—nor were they to win any on the way home—but their pitchers were getting really clobbered at each stop.

"Our pitchers are trying to throw the ball by the Yankees, that's the trouble," declared old Joe seriously. "What they should do is slow up on them, pull the string. That would upset their timing and then, maybe, you might be able to fast-ball 'em."

The reporters listened seriously to McGinnity, who had been hired that spring as coach by Manager Uncle Wilbert Robinson, who had been a teammate of Joe's on the legendary Baltimore Orioles. His remarks made sense. Whether change-ups and slow curves would fool the Yankees remained to be seen, but it was obvious that fast-balling them was ridiculously ineffective. Only that day, Babe Ruth

had unloaded a home run against Dazzy Vance which had cleared a string of boxcars atop the right-field embankment at Ponce de Leon Field. And the day before, at Rickwood Field in Birmingham, Rube Ehrhardt had been belabored for eight hits, two of them homers and two of them triples, in the first inning.

McGinnity's reasoning made such sense to one of the writers that an hour later he was telling Bob McGraw, a young right-hander, of the Iron Man's theory.

"He says the Yankees can be stopped with slow stuff," advised the writer.

"Slow, slow!" snorted McGraw. "Listen, if you were to go out there and throw the kind of slow curves McGinnity's talking about to the Yankees, it would be suicide! Why, Ruth, Gehrig, Meusel and those guys would throw away their bats, fold up their fists and *punch* it over the fences!"

Whether McGinnity's theory was practical never will be known. The Dodgers never put it to a test and didn't win a game of the entire exhibition series, either through Dixie or at Yankee Stadium, where they concluded with a pair of weekend games. Apparently nobody in the American League tried it, either, for the Yankees won 91 games and the pennant.

As a Dodger coach, McGinnity suffered the common fate of being an anachronism. He hadn't pitched in the majors since 1908, eighteen years earlier, and the players he was trying to instruct simply couldn't believe that the fat old guy had ever been a star pitcher.

This happens often in baseball. The current

players pay little attention to the records of the preceding generation. John McGraw once spoke sharply to a Giant rookie who had hit into a double play, asking him why he had not tried to hit behind the runner.

"I suppose you could have done it," snapped the exasperated rookie.

For once McGraw was silent. He told friends later, "I suppose the kid thought I never played ball," said the man who practically invented the hit-and-run.

Casey Stengel had a similar experience in the spring of 1951 when his Yankees were playing an exhibition game at Ebbets Field. It was the first time his prize rookie, young Mickey Mantle, ever had played the outfield in a park with concrete walls and Casey was telling him how to play the rebounds.

"You won't have too much trouble, kid," said Stengel kindly. "After all, I played that wall for eight years and never had any trouble."

"The hell you did!" replied the astonished Mantle.

"I guess," said Casey, in relating the story, "he thinks I was born at the age of 60 and began managing immediately."

It was unfortunate that McGinnity's last baseball connection had not been a happy one. As a pitching instructor, Joe knew his business, but on the coaching lines he was something else again.

In those days, players wore sweaters instead of the windbreakers fashionable today, and McGinnity on the first-base coaching lines was something to see. He comfortably crossed one leg over the other and plunged his fists deep into his sweater pockets with the result that the season wasn't a month old before the sweater was below Joe's knees. When he got a sign from the bench, he'd spring alive, uncrossing his legs and bending forward, a hand on each knee.

"Every time I give Joe a sign, it's like ringing a fire alarm," grumbled Uncle Robbie. "I don't know if my players are getting the signs but I know everybody in the park is, including the guys selling peanuts in the stands."

*   *   *

If McGinnity wasn't cut out to be a coach, he certainly was made to be a pitcher, one of the best and one of the most durable. His major-league career is remarkable for many things, among them the fact that in ten years he was able to win 248 games, an average of almost 25 per season! And he never was under .500 in the big leagues.

McGinnity is in the Hall of Fame at Cooperstown on the strength of his iron-man pitching in 1903, when he pitched both ends of double-headers three times in the month of August. Most of Joe's other records are forgotten and there is a tendency to regard him as something of a freak, as though those three double victories in one month were his sole contribution to baseball history.

Actually, Joe holds several major-league marks, all of which are tributes to his great stamina. He pitched and won more double-headers than any other pitcher—three—and twice pitched double-headers in which he split the decisons, giving him the record of pitching no fewer than five double-headers. He holds the National League record for the most number of innings pitched in a single season, 434 in 1903, and for the most batsmen faced, 1,658 that same year, and, just to top it all, the National *and* American League records for the most base hits allowed by a pitcher in a single season.

McGinnity, as his record attests, was a strong man. He stood just under six feet and weighed a trifle over 200 pounds. He had a deceptive, almost sidearm pitching motion, a good curve ball and what is known as a "sneaky" fast ball. He also was an exceptional runner and batter for a pitcher.

Joe was born in the heart of the Three-I League country, in Rock Island, Ill., on March 19, 1871. He was making quite a name for himself as a "town ball" pitcher before he went into organized ball with Montgomery, Ala., in the Southern League in 1893 and found town ball so much more profitable than minor-league baseball that he quit after 1894 and devoted himself to it exclusively for three years, returning to professional ball again with Peoria in the Western Association in 1898.

McGinnity landed with the famed Orioles in 1899 and was with Brooklyn the next year when the National League was reduced from 12 clubs to eight and dropped Baltimore. Joe had won 28 games for the Orioles and he went that mark one better with Brooklyn, winning 29, which is still the all-time high-water mark for a Dodger pitcher.

When the American League was formed in 1901, McGinnity jumped to Baltimore to play under John McGraw and jumped again to the Giants and the National League when McGraw, fed up with President Ban Johnson's insistence that umpires must be regarded as human beings, virtually wrecked the Baltimore franchise by staging a wholesale desertion to New York. In addition to McGinnity, McGraw also raided the Orioles for Roger Bresnahan, Dan McGann, Steve Brodie and Jack Cronin.

It was with the Giants in 1903 that McGinnity won the Iron Man title. It was, by and large, a great year for Joe, for he won 31 games that season, one more than his teammate, the great Christy Mathewson. Joe started his string in Boston, Aug. 1, when he beat the Braves, 4-1 and 5-2. His victims were Charley Pittinger and Jack Malarkey. A week later, in the Polo Grounds, Joe took on his ex-club, the Dodgers.

In the first game, McGinnity beat Oscar Jones, 6-1, but he had a squeaker in the second against Harry Schmidt. Joe himself stole home with the first run of the ball game in the third and Schmidt, his pitching rival, raised such a to-do about the decision of Tim Hurst, working under the single-umpire system, that he got the thumb. That brought none other than Jones back on the scene.

It seemed as though Oscar would avenge himself on McGinnity, for Brooklyn picked up two runs on the Iron Man in the fourth, and another in the fifth. Sandow Mertes nailed Jones for the only home run of the game in the sixth.

Brooklyn led going into the ninth, 3-2, but Jones, now pitching his fourteenth inning of the afternoon, couldn't get anybody out. With the score tied and men on first and third, Manager McGraw lifted McGinnity, who already had made two singles, for George Van Haltren. The pinch hitter singled home Billy Gilbert with the winning run and McGinnity had his second double victory within the space of eight days.

On the last day of August, again at the Polo Grounds, Joe twice beat the Phillies, but this time had no trouble. He won a five-hitter, 4-1, over Chick Fraser in the opener and beat Bill Duggleby, 9-2, in the nightcap.

*   *   *

For all of McGinnity's great pitching, he had only one World Series shot, although the stubborn pride of McGraw and the Giants' owner, John T. Brush, deprived him of a shot at the Red Sox in 1904. The first meeting of the American and National Leagues was in 1903, between the Red Sox and Pirates. The next year it seemed as if the New York Highlanders, then in their second season in the American

League, were about to win the pennant, and Brush wanted no part of them. When Boston won on the last day of the season, Brush could hardly reverse his stand, even though the players petitioned to meet the American Leaguers.

McGinnity got his chance against Connie Mack's Philadelphia Athletics in 1905 in what was not only the first formal World Series but one of the most unusual of all Series, in that every game was a shutout. The great Matty blanked the A's in the first, third and fifth games. McGinnity was blanked in the second game by Chief Bender but scored a fine, 1-0 victory over Eddie Plank in the fourth game.

Matty and McGinnity were the big winners for the Giants that year. Joe had 21 victories while Big Six won 31. When the Iron Man faced Bender in the second game, he had little luck. It probably would not have mattered how much luck he had, since the Chippewa was at his best, fanning nine and pitching a four-hit shutout, but damaging errors by Art Devlin and Dan McGann figured in the A's scoring against Joe.

If Joe was unlucky in his first World Series start, luck was riding with him when he beat Eddie Plank, for in an egregious error, Lave Cross, the Philadelphia captain and third baseman, permitted Sandow Mertes to score the only run of the game.

It was ironic that McGinnity, the Iron Man, was the only Giant starter who failed to pitch a complete game. In his game against Bender, he was removed to allow Sammy Strang to bat for him in the eighth, and Leon Ames pitched the ninth.

McGinnity's luck just didn't run in the World Series. He was a member of Ned Hanlon's Brooklyn Superbas in 1900 when they won the National League pennant, but there was no World Series that year because there was no American League. He lost out in 1904 when the Giants won the pennant because of the obduracy of Brush and McGraw already mentioned.

The next time the fates conspired to keep the Iron Man out of a World Series was 1908, his last year in the big time. Joe was slowing up a little now. Accustomed to pitching 300, and even 400, innings a season, he pitched only 184 innings for the Giants that year, showing an 11-7 record at the season's end. Joe's heart was in the right place, as his actions in the famous "Merkle game" showed.

This game, one of the most famous in all baseball, was played at the Polo Grounds on a

Wednesday afternoon, Sept. 23, 1908. There were two weeks still to go in the pennant race and the Giants, Cubs and Pirates were in a hot scramble. In this game the Cubs, with Jack Pfeister pitching against Mathewson, were tied 1-1 in the last half of the ninth. There were two out and the Giants had Al Bridwell at bat, Fred Merkle on first and Moose McCormick on third.

Bridwell hit safely to center field, McCormick trotted home from third and the game was over. Unfortunately for the Giants, it only seemed to be over. Johnny Evers, Chicago second baseman, noted that Merkle, after running halfway to second base, trotted to the center field clubhouse. He ran to second and called frantically for the ball.

Artie Hofman fielded the ball in center field and threw it to Evers but it was an excited throw and it got past not only Evers but Joe Tinker at short. McGinnity, coaching at third for the Giants, took after the ball. So did Floyd Kroh, a third-string Chicago pitcher, who bounded off the Cubs' bench. McGinnity beat Kroh to the ball but before he could do anything with it, Tinker and Kroh were upon him. There was quite a scuffle before Joe could wrestle himself free from the pair to throw the ball as far as he could into the left-field stands.

Somewhere Evers obtained another baseball —some say from the ball bag on the Chicago bench—but at any rate he perched on second base with the ball in his hand and demanded that Umpire Hank O'Day declare Merkle forced out at second. No run, of course, could score when the third out was a force play and when Hank called Fred out, Bridwell's hit was erased.

By now, of course, jubilant Giant fans were swarming over the field, under the impression that the Giants had won a 2-1 victory. There was no possibility of play being resumed and Umpire O'Day called the game a 1-1 tie. The Giants and Cubs were tied for the lead when the season was over and in a replay of the deadlocked game, the Cubs won, 4-2, beating Matty.

"I don't know where Evers got the ball that he used to claim the force-out but it wasn't the ball that Bridwell hit," stoutly maintained McGinnity, "because I flung that one out of sight."

*   *   *

When McGinnity left the majors he was to become sort of a living legend as he wandered through the minors, usually in the role of pitcher and manager. All through as a major-leaguer, Joe went on to win the astounding total of 204 games in the bushes! And he played in a variety of leagues—the International, Eastern, Three-I, Mississippi Valley, Northwestern and something called the Pacific Coast International.

Joe also won a total of 59 games in his first two seasons at Newark while also managing the club and put in three 20-game seasons at Tacoma. Perhaps his most remarkable achievement was with Dubuque in the Mississippi Valley League, where he won 15 games in 1923 at the age of 52!

McGinnity was 54 when he pitched in professional ball for the last time, recording a 6-6 season with Dubuque in 1925. This was the first year of publication of the highly successful weekly, The New Yorker. In one of its early editorials, the magazine reminded its readers that it was being written entirely for the benefit and amusement of New Yorkers and not for outlanders. As a sort of symbol, it specifically mentioned that it wasn't being written for the pleasure of "the old lady of Dubuque."

This caused the late Heywood Broun to write a rather testy column in the New York World, pointing out the achievements of Iron Man Joe McGinnity, whom he referred to as "the old gentleman from Dubuque."

When McGinnity came East the following year to act as coach of the Dodgers, he was more than a little surprised to learn that his name had cropped up prominently in a literary dispute.

"Hell's fire!" said the old chap. "I ain't read anything in years but the box scores. I was just pitching for Dubuque last year because I was part-owner as well as manager. Sorta protectin' my investment, you might say!"

Any investment was pretty well protected when the Iron Man was pitching.

BETTER Mr. Michael's surname began with a Z—so that you'd finish the book before you started in on the following.

Dice Baseball

D. J. MICHAEL

DICE BASEBALL is played with two dice. Especially when refinements are added by the players, it is an astoundingly close replica of actual play, with events occurring on a remarkably similar frequency basis.

Even without the refinements, the basic game is fine as is. It applies the 21 combinations of two dice as follows:

1-1	outfield fly
1-2	ground ball
1-3	walk
1-4	single
1-5	strike-out
1-6	ground ball
2-2	double
2-3	outfield fly
2-4	single
2-5	ground ball
2-6	infield fly
3-3	throw one die again
	if 1, 2, or 3, double
	if 4, 5, or 6, triple
3-4	strike-out
3-5	outfield fly
3-6	ground ball
4-4	error
4-5	infield fly
4-6	outfield fly
5-5	walk
5-6	ground ball
6-6	home run

These eventualities have not been haphazardly set down. Notice, for example, that 1-5 and 3-4 are strike-outs and that 1-3 and 5-5 are walks. Mathematically, the 5-5 combination will occur only half as often as each of the others, so in dice baseball strike-outs occur in the ratio of 4:3 to walks—almost exact major- and fast-minor-league ratio.

Anything that is not a hit, a walk, or an error, is automatically an out in the above schedule.

As we have said, it can be played and enjoyed with no more data than the basic listing above. But the invitation to refine the game further, and to keep individual records, is one the true fan will find hard to ignore.

ADVANCING RUNNERS ON HITS OR FLIES TO THE OUTFIELD

A base runner advances normally one base on a single and two bases on a double. Frequently, however, his coach has him go for an extra base—i.e., from first to third or from second to home on a single, or from first to home on a double. Frequently also runners move up after a long fly is caught. These are discretionary plays depending on the direction and depth of the hits. Therefore, always using *one die*, the following tables are applied:

Advancing a runner from *first base to third base* on a *single* or from *second to third* on an *outfield fly:*

Throw first to see what field ball was hit to (1,4 rf; 2,5 cf; 3,6 lf)
Throw again to determine depth of hit (from 1, very shallow, to 6, very deep)

The player whose team is at bat then applies the following table and decides whether, as "coach," he will wave his runner on to third. If he decides to try for the extra base, he throws once more in accordance with the following table:

Depth of Hit or Fly	If to Right Field	If to Center Field	If to Left Field
1	1–safe; 2,3,4,5,6–out	all out	all out
2	1,2–safe; 3,4,5,6–out	1–safe; 2,3,4,5,6–out	all out
3	1,2,3–safe; 4,5,6–out	1,2–safe; 3,4,5,6–out	1–safe; 2,3,4,5,6–out
4	1,2,3,4,5–safe;6–out	1,2,3–safe; 4,5,6–out	1,2–safe; 3,4,5,6–out
5	all safe	1,2,3,4–safe; 5,6–out	1,2,3–safe; 4,5,6–out
6	all safe	all safe	1,2,3,4,5–safe; 6–out

Advancing a runner from *second to home* on a *single*, from *first to home* on a *double*, or from *third to home* on an *outfield fly*:

Throw to determine depth of hit; direction of hit can be thrown also but is not material. If player whose team is at bat decides to have runner try for home, he throws once more in accordance with the following table:

Depth of Hit or Fly	Play at Home
1	all out
2	1–safe; 2,3,4,5,6–out
3	1,2–safe; 3,4,5,6–out
4	1,2,3–safe; 4,5,6–out
5	1,2,3,4,5–safe; 6–out
6	all safe

Advancing from *first to second* on a *fly* is only possible when the depth of the fly is 5 or 6. If it is 5, then 1–safe; 2,3,4,5,6–out. If it is 6, then 1,2–safe; 3,4,5,6–out.

For instance a ground ball. That means one of the infielders gets it. There are six infielders. There are six numbers on a die. Assign one number to each infielder, throw a single die, and you know who handled the grounder. Now. Suppose you are tied in the seventh with none out and a man on first and you throw a ground ball. Now throw to see whom it went to. If the pitcher, catcher, third baseman or first baseman, surely the likelihood of a bunt can't be ignored. Set up your own possibilities and throw a single die again to establish whether it was a bunt. If it wasn't, or if the ball went to the shortstop or second baseman to begin with, a double play is in prospect. There is not space here to show all the different possibilities, but they will come easily to the established fan— especially if he starts with the basic game and works in his refinements as he goes.

Suppose you want to have a league—your own players with their own averages. After a while, you'll find one shortstop who's gone, say, 40 games without an error. You're on your way to setting up your own individual records in all departments—hitting streaks, home runs, runs batted in, pitching records. In thousands of Dice Baseball games, the author has seen three no-hitters. Two were recorded by the same imagined pitcher in the same season!

The six spots on a die fit the three outfielders too, of course—two numbers for each fielder. Now, let's take a refinement on this, to show how such things can be worked into your game. The whole matter of runners taking extra bases on hits to the outfield or after an outfield fly is caught is assembled on the accompanying chart.

Within a very short period of time, because the table, and all others you will work up, follow progressive arithmetic lines, you will be refining the game with further throws of individual dice swiftly and accurately. The major element that would slow down the enjoyment and the play of the game has been eliminated at the start—individual balls and strikes. They're not needed at all.

One refinement that you should introduce at once—or at least the first one you should use as you continue to play—is the result of a 4-4, which according to the master schedule is an error.

The way we play it, succeeding single dice are thrown as follows.

First, see whether the error was by an outfielder (1, 2) or an infielder (3, 4, 5, 6).

If the error was by an outfielder, chances are it was in fielding a hit rather than a fly ball. Throw to see (1, 2, fly; 3, 4, 5, 6, hit).

Now, if it was a hit, throw to see what kind of a hit (1, 2, 3, 4, single; 5, double; 6, triple).

Now throw to see how many bases the batter got on the error. This applies to infield as well as outfield errors. It goes 1, 2, 3, 4, one base. 5, 6, two bases. In our game we have a refinement for a three-base error, but these are so rare that you need not deal with them, at least while you're doing your own experimenting. Remember that if the error was made on a hit, the number of bases from the error are added to the number of bases from the hit. A one-base error on a double puts the batter on third.

Any runners on base when an error is made move the same number of bases as the batter.

Of course you'll also want to know who made the error. Throw to find out.

Another point for your refinements: the "depth" throws described on the accompanying chart are used in their own way on infield plays too. For example, an infield fly *could* be a line drive, in which case a man already on base *could* be doubled off! You can chart your own possibilities here. In our game, we classify a 5 or a 6 (in the first subsequent throw to an infield fly) as a line drive. If a 5, then a following 6 will double off a runner. If a 6 (harder hit than the 5!), then a following 5 or 6 will do it. Triple plays? Sure, if the setup is there.

You will find missing from this game wild pitches, passed balls, hit batsmen, rundowns, and pickoff plays. Refinements have been worked out for all of these, but our experience has been that they do not add enough to the game, nor actually occur frequently enough, to make it worth the complication. If you want to include them, you can *conclude* them in many instances from actual play. For example, you can classify every third error by a catcher as having been a passed ball. Similarly, on an error by the third baseman, say, you can, if the added realism appeals to you, decide by another throw whether it was on a grounder or a wild throw.

All normal strategy in the hands of an actual manager is in your hands in this game. You can pinch-hit, change pitchers* or other facets of the line-up, decide (as the accompanying chart shows) whether to advance runners. And, of course, steal bases. We use 1, 2, 3 for out at second and 4, 5, 6 for safe. Then we use 5, 6 for safe at third and 1, 2, 3, 4 for out. Then we use 6 for safe at home (though there can be a refinement on that too if you want). On a double steal, we throw first to decide which player the defending team tried to get, then apply the regular steal table to that player.

So—the better you know baseball, the more realistic and enjoyable the game will be. But you do not have to know too much about the game to enjoy Dice Baseball at its fundamental level—that is, the basic 21 combinations by themselves. As the game becomes more familiar, you can't help but add refinements. You will get to the point where you know whether a man struck out on a called pitch or swinging—whether a catch was sensational or routine (one refinement can give you a chance to double up a base runner following a particularly brilliant outfield catch).

* You can also issue an intentional pass to an opposition hitter any time you want, merely by so declaring.

Jim Thorpe Bats 7-for-7

JERRY MITCHELL

THIS WAS in Jim Thorpe, Pa., the day they dedicated a last resting place to the Indian who may have been the greatest athlete of all time.

"Jim loved everything," recalled Al Schacht. "He got a lot out of life in his younger years.

"I remember when I was with Harrisburg," Al went on. "Thorpe joined us and they said he was to room with me. Me, a skinny 130-pound kid with an Indian weighing 200 or so who liked to stay up all night and sometimes used his roommates as exercise bells.

"We played two series in Jersey City an' the fans there got on him somethin' fierce, called him everything. The thing that got him maddest, though, was yelling that he was a sucker for curve-ball pitching.

"The next time we're in Jersey City a bunch of seven guys in a box near our dugout start on him again. They're drinking beer all through the game and yelling and Jim's getting madder an' madder.

"The game ends finally without him jumping into the box an' commiting murder, but I find he's learned where they go after ball games and he grabs me and starts for the place.

"He's got my arm in a grip like a vise and finally he tells me to go in and sneak up to them one at a time and whisper that I'd heard Thorpe was on a rampage and was on his way to the saloon.

"Well, I did as I was told. You would, too, if you were rooming with him. I got my beer and went up to the first guy, took him aside and advised him to leave. I waited a few minutes, then I got hold of the next guy and so forth. Finally there weren't any left, so I went out. There was Jim sitting on a barrel outside grinning. On the ground were the guys from old West Side Park, some of them still stretched out and some sitting up holding their heads.

"Jim looked up and grinned some more. 'How many?' he asked.

" 'Seven,' I said. 'You got 'em all.'

" 'Good,' he said, 'that's pool.' "

In the first *Fireside Book of Baseball*, there was a story about a female impersonator on a ladies' baseball team. If that seems bizarre, try this one here: a ladies' baseball team consisting, as I read it, of six ladies and three men. Therefore the title becomes:

Nine Ladies *vs.* Fate

LYNN MONTROSS

THE PRESIDENT of the Olympic Athletic Goods Co. was in a wide and amiable mood attuned to the May afternoon which smiled back at him from the open windows of his office. He nodded indulgently at Youth across the desk while the languid reporter explained, "And so the *Evening Argus* would like a photo, Mr. Howe, and a personal sketch for the series about state business leaders—how you got started, to what you attribute your success and all that, you know."

Behind octagonal spectacles, Harrison C. Howe's plump face was smooth and youthful, only a slight contour below the chest hinting that he was in his middle forties. He answered dreamily, absent-mindedly, as the reporter jotted down bored and inept notes:

"Born 1889, Teheran, Wis.—pop. 900. Grad. high school. Job groc. store 3 yrs. before came city. Attribs. early suc. to home & mother & hard work, etc., same old bull. Started Olymp. Co. with borrowed $—spread on thick about early struggles, etc. Wife, 3 kids. Belongs all best clubs (be sure look up). Hobby, baseball. Pres. of Twilight b. b. League, etc. *Nuts* about b. b.—"

"Did you ever," said Harrison C. Howe, and his eyes cherished a fondly reminiscent glow, "happen to hear of the Bloomer girls in baseball?"

The cub hadn't, but he nodded. His blank features lighted up with a creditable assumption of interest as he accepted a cigar and settled back in a comfortable armchair.

It was too soon to return to the city room and

he listened drowsily until the mention of legs aroused his attention. . . .

*   *   *

Two blondes (Howe was saying with a mellow air as if talking to himself) led the rest of the Bloomer club on the way up Main Street from the depot. They wore peekaboo waists and slit skirts which showed more silk stocking and green satin petticoat than we were used to seeing in Teheran those days. I was carrying a bag of flour from the store to a buggy outside, but probably I stopped to stare like everybody else. The loafers in front of the pool hall began whistling so the blondes would have to keep step, I remember, and somebody yelled, "Oh, you beautiful doll!"

It was my first summer on the town baseball nine and I felt pretty bashful about playing that afternoon. None of the various traveling ladies' baseball outfits had ever played in Teheran before and we young fellows on the team took a lot of spoofing when the announcements were put up in the store windows.

The wooden grandstand was filled before the game was called, and people sat in buggies or cars behind the base lines. There must have been a crowd of two hundred or so. It was always late when I got off work and changed into uniform; the Bloomers were already in the field practicing, and it sounded funny to hear their shrill voices.

They wore baseball caps pinned on high mounds of hair and their bloomers were cut full and baggy, with blouses to match in gray and red.

Snip Barton, the barber, our catcher and captain, called me to the bench first thing. "Lookit," he said with a grin, "you got to play with the Bloomers. One of their girls quit—took the noon train—and I promised to lend 'em somebody."

My ears felt hot as I crossed over to the Bloomer side, the way I got kidded. "You tell 'em, Harry, I stutter!" "If you can't be good, be careful!" . . . . Things like that.

A slim, dark-haired kid, looking about eighteen, smiled at me and I sat down beside her. "Poor Gus!" she said, pointing out the catcher who was one of the two men on their team. "Gee, he'll have to get another girl right away to take Emma's place, and he's had the most frightful luck with his players, and we've been losing money ever since we started out, and—"

She was still chattering away when the game was called. They put me in at third, a new position for me, and the little, dark-eyed girl started as pitcher. It was a couple of innings before I came to bat for the ladies and there were two on. But I'd played catch with Tommy Leach ever since we were knee-high, and I knew an inshoot was coming when he stuck out his tongue that way. I got set and put my weight behind it: the ball sailed over the creek in left for a round trip. "Gee, you're good!" said the little southpaw when I trotted back to the bench. She was so excited that I was afraid she'd hug me, right in front of everybody. "Hell," she said. "I wish't Gus would keep you."

She must have spoken to him about it, because he was waiting for me after the next inning. "Listen," he said, "how'd you like to fill in for us till I can hire a couple more girls? A week or two, say?"

"Gosh, I couldn't!" I said, feeling scared at the idea. "I'd lose my job and—"

"Huh!" said Gus, looking disgusted. He was a big fellow with hard, blue eyes and a sort of battered face.

By the sixth I was well enough acquainted with the left-handed pitcher to call her Lucy. There was something so young and fresh about her, like sweet peas early in the morning, that I got over my gawky bashfulness. Her brown eyes were wide and serious as she kept on teasing me to play with the Bloomers; and it kept on getting harder for me to refuse. "I don't know what we'll *do!*" she said. "Last week Thelma got sick and left us without a sub. Then, Emma quitting cold today, it might take Gus a week to

hire another girl and—and won't you please and pretty please?"

"All right!" I gulped. I don't know what made me do it—some such reason as the freckles around her snub nose, maybe. But after committing myself I wasn't going to back out. Not for a girl, I wasn't.

The decision left me so weak that I muffed an easy foul and struck out my last time up, but I promised Gus to join the Bloomers that night at the 11:21 train.

Mother was helping out at the Ladies' Aid baked-bean supper, so Dad and I ate leftovers in the kitchen. He looked scared, too, when I finally got up nerve enough to tell him. A hard day at the shoe store had left him more tired and stooped than usual; he kept on shaking his head and muttering, "Harry, I don't know what *she'll* say to this!" He sighed. "Far's I'm concerned, I don't mind. I know you'll act like a gentleman, and I remember I always wanted to travel and see a little of the world before I got married and settled down."

After packing my baseball uniform and new suit I left a note in the dining room where Mother would find it in the morning.

At the grocery store where I worked, Mr. Sipps took a fresh chew of snuff and eyed my suitcase. "H'm," he said. "What you up to now?"

He was a pinched-up little man and I made myself stare at the wart on the side of his nose that I'd always hated. I spoke up, too loudly, "Well, I haven't had a day off in three years and I'd like a two-week vacation—Oscar can take my place."

He thought it over, narrowing his small watery eyes with the pale lashes.

"Well," he said, "just so's you don't expect no pay and get back on time, I'm willing."

That left only Vera Snyder yet to tell, and I had a date with her. She and I had been going steady ever since high school and it was sort of understood we'd be married some day. She looked almost noble under a street lamp that evening—the kind of sweet, sensible girl who'd make a young fellow want to settle down—and I wondered if Lester Crane, the new manual-training teacher, would beat my time while I was gone. It was like pulling teeth to break the news.

"Why, Harry Howe!" she said, starting to cry. "Those women are nothing but *strumpets.*"

Somehow, coming from Vera, the word sounded worse than anything I'd ever heard in the barber shop. I had to beg a long while before she dried her eyes; and I can still remember that wooden sidewalk and the big dark leaves of the catalpas against the sky.

"Oh, all right," she said at last. "I suppose if you must, you must." That was as near as she came to approval, and I felt guilty when I parted from her.

At train time I dodged up a back street to the depot, and waited at the end of the cinder platform, climbing aboard the last coach. Gus scowled at me. He was in a bad temper because Ed, the big pitcher who took Lucy's place in the box after a few innings, had got drunk that night and now lay sprawled over two seats, like a bag of meal. "It's a shame, too," said Lucy solemnly. "He'd be up in the big leagues if he didn't booze so bad."

The local stopped for every milk can, and it was turning gray in the east when we got off at Ozone City. But it gave me a big thrill to straggle along with the sleepy troupe to a rooming house across the depot.

The bashful ordeal of meeting the ladies again at breakfast had me awake and dressing before six. My peg-tops ballooned at the hips and tapered down to three-inch cuffs; the coat came halfway to the knees with a stylish outward flare, and the pockets had pointed flaps which buttoned. With a narrow brimmed hat, lofty collar, bumpty-toed shoes and fire opal stick pin, I felt as nobby as any traveling man. But even new clothes couldn't save me from embarrassment in the dining room and I was glad when Lucy asked me to take her for a walk.

She had the trusting, confiding air of a puppy. As she trotted along beside me in her tight hobble skirt, she told me that she had been raised on an Indiana farm, the tomboy of a large family, and had run away to join a tent show when she was sixteen.

The two gilt blondes were the "Devere sisters," Sadie and Flo, keeping the alluring name after a brief vaudeville tour. During the winter they were in cheap burlesque, which made them feel more sophisticated than the rest of the girls. They laced heroically and were very proud of their fashionable hourglass figures; when Main Street loafers ogled them they were always ready with, "Twenty-three for you!" or "Buy a drum and beat it!" . . . After firing one girl for an all-night date with a traveling man, Gus watched Flo and Sadie suspiciously.

But Mrs. Bensinger, who shared the outfield with them, was a motherly soul. Thirty-six seemed aged to me then, and I was amazed at the nimble way she could beat out a bunt to first.

A Dakota farm wife, she'd learned the game with her three sons; she saved her earnings all summer, doing the club mending for extra pay, and went back to the lonely homestead when the season ended.

The tall, statuesque Miss Simmons, who held down first base as well as any man, was nicknamed "Lady Macbeth." She had played a few such heavy roles in obscure stock companies and never quite recovered. She was a melancholy ash blonde, at least thirty, and used an affected stage voice in speaking of the most ordinary things.

Our best lady player was Bea Swanson at shortstop. I'll always remember her in the hotel parlor threading a pink ribbon through an enormous camisole . . . how she'd blush and hide the garment; she was huge, elephantine, grotesque as anything in a comic strip; and in defense she had become a suffragette. "Ay ban batter man than any man on earth!" she would boast; but her childish eyes were pitiful, pleading, and I understood why Gus had once punched a fellow for mocking her. Yet on the diamond she was amazingly fast, even graceful, and after Gus the best sticker on the team.

Six ladies and three men, without a substitute, we were small pumpkins compared with the other Bloomer teams touring the country. We took what they left, often without a guarantee on a risky percentage. It was Gus's first shaky venture as a promoter on his own hook, and he'd been licked from the start. It rained most of my beginning week with the club and we collected on only three games. A big Sunday date which Gus counted on for payday was stopped by the preachers at the last minute, and the ghost limped in with five dollars apiece.

My second week was no better. At Lark, Illinois, we played to about forty people and next day it had to rain again. The big Fourth of July game at Acropolis, down in the coal-mine country, was our last hope. We hit town with less than ten dollars in the treasury and Gus called us all in the hotel parlor for a conference. He stared at the wire racks of picture post cards and began:

"I guess you know we're busted. All season you nine ladies—"

"Only six," pointed out Sadie Devere.

Gus scowled. "You're a ladies' nine, aren't you? Well! What I started to say was that after all this hard luck—"

"*Fate!*" interrupted Lady Macbeth in a rich, dramatic whisper.

"All right, call it fate if you want to, but we've been versus lots of bad breaks and we're through for the season unless we win tomorrow. These miners are hot sports and I made a deal to play 'em for the gate, winner take all, see? That's our last chance. They got a hired pitcher but if Ed gets going good and Bea hits we got a show for the money."

"I'll pitch league ball," Ed promised. His weak chin and sad, alcoholic eyes meant what he said, too, but he always tumbled off the wagon right when he was needed most. Just one little snort for a bracer, then he was lost.

So it wasn't any surprise when he turned up missing after supper, the night before the game at Acropolis, and Gus sent us out looking for him. Lucy and I went together around the carnival grounds and finally stopped at the outdoor dance pavilion. The band was playing "Everybody's Doing It" and the dancers were swaying to the bear or turkey trot. Suddenly I glanced at Lucy and she was crying! She hurried away from the crowd and I followed.

"That music's so pretty!" she said when she could talk. "And—and I'm so daffy about Gus, I can't bear it if we bust up tomorrow and I lose him!"

I hadn't realized. It was a jolt to me, because I had quite a crush on Lucy myself, but I tried to comfort her with awkward thumps on the shoulder.

Ed was carried up to his room by several miners about four in the morning—probably they'd got him soused on purpose. By game time he was still so bleary and unsteady that the best he could do was play right field without being propped up.

Lucy was our only pitcher and she'd never been strong enough for more than three or four innings. We were first to bat, of course, and Gus was mad enough to sock his own mother when he stepped up to the plate. He slammed the very first pitched ball over the right fielder's head for a three-bagger!

That took some of the confidence out of the hired Acropolis hurler, and the crowd was so silent you could hear it. There must have been twelve or fourteen hundred, the biggest mob I'd ever seen at a ball game then, and they looked tough enough to lynch us if they lost.

Ed was next to bat. Probably he never saw the ball but by some miracle he managed to poke a Texas leaguer over second, fetching Gus home. The girls on the bench were screaming for a hit when I walked up to the platter, and I remember praying myself. The first pitch, a fast one with a wicked hop, showed me that the big semipro had the stuff all right; but my line drive went between short and third for a stinging single.

Big Bea was our "cleanup man." Her little blue eyes danced with rage and I don't think that even Ed Walsh could have fanned her that time. She had a strike and two balls on her— then at the crack of the bat I started running and didn't stop until I slid into home. Bea wound up at second, still muttering at the pitcher.

Mrs. Bensinger laid down a bunt and beat it to first while Bea was held on second. Lady Macbeth let four wide ones go past and filled the bases. . . . But this was too good to last, so near the end of our batting order. One Devere sister struck out, the other fouled to first. Lucy, our weakest hitter, fanned.

The boost to our spirits was worth more than the three runs. We took the field with new pep, not as a team beaten before it started. Gus sent Lucy into the box with an encouraging whack. "Slow-ball 'em to death, kid! These hicks aren't used to southpaw throwing, see?"

She gulped and nodded. Her slow roundhouse curves and the new knuckle ball that Ed had taught her had the mine boys falling all over themselves trying to kill it. They went down in a row on pop flies or soft infield assists.

The next two innings were goose eggs for both sides, even when Acropolis shoved a man as far as third. But in the fourth the miners began to time Lucy better; they connected for two earned runs and with two out filled the bases.

"Steady, girl! Take it easy, honey!" Gus called from behind the plate. Her freckled face, already white with strain, lighted up eagerly.

The batter got under a teaser and arched a high fly to right that any schoolboy could have nabbed. But Ed's bloodshot eyes misjudged the ball and two more scores trickled in.

Acropolis 4, Bloomers 3—with five innings yet to play.

In the last of the fifth they tallied again by smacking Lucy for three straight singles, and we were lucky to get off that easy. It was the same old story in the sixth when another run put them three ahead. Both sessions we went down in a row, eating out of the pitcher's hand.

Somehow Lucy managed to hold them scoreless in the seventh, although she was so tired that the plate must have seemed a mile away. I came up to bat in our half of the eighth and made first on an infield error. Bea stopped glaring at the pitcher long enough to rap out a single, but I was stopped at second until Mrs. Bensinger's weak grounder forced me out at third. Lady Macbeth, looking haughty as ever in spite of the yells from the crowd, lifted one over third to load the bags with only one out.

The hired pitcher bore down and Sadie De-vere whiffed. Then with two out and two strikes on Flo, another miracle saved our necks —the Acropolis shortstop muffed her easy pop-up and threw wild, handing us our fourth score on a silver tray.

Lord, Lord! Two out and three on, with Lucy at bat! It was tough that the big chance had to bring up our poorest hitter, and the head of the batting list just around the corner.

Her shoulders sagging, Lucy let the first one streak past for a called strike. A ball was next. Another ball. And then while I held my breath the pitcher wound up, there was the white flash of his fast one and the sickening impact of hard leather against soft flesh. Lucy dropped her bat, writhing as she clutched her left arm.

It was so perfect that I wasn't sure myself whether it was an accident or not. Anyhow, that umpire had intestines. He motioned Lucy to first and half a dozen constables pushed the bellowing crowd out of the diamond. Bea was forced home for another run while Lucy held up her wrist with a white, sick grin.

Now we were only one behind and Gus would have connected with a cannon ball to drive home those gate receipts! His screaming double put us one run to the good, and with the count seven to six in our favor we were too excited to care when Ed fanned.

But Lucy didn't go back to the mound when she took the field in the last of the eighth. She and Gus went into a huddle at the plate which ended with a call for me. "You got to pitch," he told me. "Lucy's hurt bad and Ed's too shaky— you got to stop 'em two innings or I'll cut your heart out and eat it!"

It was no good protesting . . . I pitched. How I don't know, because all I had was a glove and a prayer. But what a prayer, what a prayer! I prayed that they wouldn't hit or if they did that it wouldn't go to Lucy on second base with her fractured throwing arm. She was doing a good job of pretending but Acropolis knew they had us in a hole.

That inning took years. We retired them at last, after two hits against me, but I was sure my hair was turning gray. We were easy marks at bat in our half of the ninth and it was up to me again. "Them gate receipts, remember!" Gus croaked hoarsely as he shoved me toward the box.

The first man singled. But I knew there was a Santa Claus when the next batter hit into an easy double play. Bea covering second. With two out, just like that, it must have gone to my head—I turned with a sick feeling in the solar plexus and watched my next pitch sail over Mrs. Bensinger's head for a triple. Only her quick relay saved us from a homer and tied game.

While the runner danced off third, the man at the plate swung a club that looked to me like a wagon tongue. He took a mighty swipe and missed. Gus made me kill time till I felt better, and I put everything I had into my one round-house curve. The batter straightened it out into a sizzling grounder between first and second. I tumbled in my wild dive for the ball but Lucy was waiting and took it on the bounce with her gloved hand.

With the man on third tearing for home she hesitated—only a ghastly fraction of a second— before she ran toward first, her left arm hanging limp, to beat the runner to the bag. When she saw it was too late she made a last desperate lunge for momentum and pushed rather than threw with her gloved hand. The ball dropped halfway and rolled to one side, but Lady Macbeth somehow picked it out of the dirt in time.

After it was all over Lucy collapsed in a heap, just where she stood. Gus charged across the diamond without taking off his mask and carried her to the bench.

"How damn dumb of me," she said when she opened her eyes, "not to get hit some other place!"

At the hotel the mining company doctor treated her for a slight green-stick fracture. And when the Acropolis miners heard that Lucy and Gus were to be married, nothing would do but a public ceremony, on the fairgrounds next day after the airplane flight. Of course I had to stay for the wedding even if it did mean getting home a day late for my job.

Gus had phoned a Chicago agency for three new lady players but he invited me with the team as long as I liked. "O. K.," he said when I made my excuses. "But any time you want to try your luck in the city, let me know. I got a pal in the athletic-goods graft, see?"

The train that hauled me back to Teheran didn't realize how I felt or it would have started backing up. On the depot platform Snip Barton spotted me first thing. "Hi, Harry!" he yelled so all the loafers could hear. "The new manual-training teacher has went and beat your time with Vera!"

He didn't muff it. After Mother had lectured me and gone to bed with one of her sick headaches, I found a package addressed in Vera's round, regular hand. She'd sent back my letters and the lavaliere I gave her. . . . And when I reported at the store in the morning, Mr. Sipps fired me in less time than it takes to tell it. Oscar Nelson had my job—in fact, he still has it to this day.

With my girl, my job and my reputation lost, there was only one thing left to do: I wired Gus for help and started for the city. And here I am.

＊　　＊　　＊

The sudden silence in the office was long enough to bridge the gap of years between Teheran, Wis., and the Olympic Athletic Goods Co. The *Argus* reporter still leaned forward, a dead cigar in his clutch. . . . But all at once an annoyed frown crossed the plump features of Harrison C. Howe, as if he felt that he had been doddering. The old brisk decision came back as he glanced at the electric grandfather clock. "Naturally," he said, "these trifling reminiscences are not for publication, and I shall expect to see the proofs. . . . Home training, country environment, early discipline, sticking to the job—I believe I've already sufficiently emphasized those qualities which make for business success. That's all!"

DICK CAVALLI

Courtesy *Sport* Magazine. ©

"Better hit a few long ones, George . . . you know, Mom's watching today."

LIVING in Brooklyn can affect almost anybody. So did the Dodgers affect Miss Marianne Moore, a Brooklyn resident who has won the Pulitzer Prize, the Bollingen Prize, and the gold medal from the National Institute of Arts and Letters, and who has been called by T. S. Eliot "the most accomplished poetess in the English-speaking world today." The following was done at World Series time, 1956.

Hometown Piece for Messrs. Alston and Reese

MARIANNE MOORE

To the tune:
Li'l baby, don't say a word: Mama goin' to buy you a mocking-bird.
Bird don't sing: Mama goin' to sell it and buy a brass ring.

"Millennium, yes; pandemonium!"
Roy Campanella leaps high. Dodgerdom

crowned, had Johnny Podres on the mound.
Buzzie Bavasi and the Press gave ground;

the team slapped, mauled, and asked the Yankees'
match,
"How did you feel when Sandy Amoros made the
catch?"

"I said to myself"—pitcher for all innings—
"as I walked back to the mound I said, 'everything's

getting better and better.' " (Zest, they've zest.
" 'Hope springs eternal in the Brooklyn breast.' "

And would the Dodger Band in 8, row 1, relax
if they saw the Collector of income-tax?

Ready with a tune if that should occur:
"Why not take All of Me—All of Me, Sir?")

Another series. Round-tripper Duke at bat,
"four hundred feet from home-plate"; more like
that.

A neat bunt, please; a cloud-breaker, a drive
like Jim Gilliam's great big one. Hope's alive.

Homered, flied out, Fouled? Our "stylish stout"
so nimble Campanella will have him out.

A-squat in double-headers four hundred times a
day,
he says that in a measure the pleasure is the pay:

catcher to pitcher, a nice easy throw
almost as if he had told it to go.

Willie Mays should be a Dodger. He should—
a lad for Roger Craig and Clem Labine to elude;

but you have an omen, pennant-winning Peewee,
on which we are looking superstitiously

Ralph Branca has Preacher Roe's number; recall?
and there's Don Bessent; he can really fire the ball.

As for Gil Hodges, in custody of first—,
"he'll do it by himself"; already versed

in the reach, he makes that great foul catch far into
the box seats—
gloves the ball, straightens up, and defeats

expectation by a whisker. The modest star,
irked by one misplay, is no hero by a hair;

in a strikeout slaughter when what could matter
more,
he lines a homer to the signboard and has changed
the score.

Then for his nineteenth season, a home run—
with four of six runs batted in—Carl Furillo is big
gun;

almost dehorned the foe—has fans dancing in
delight.
Jake Pitler and his Playground "get a Night"—

Jake, that hearty man, made heartier by a harrier
who can bat as well as field—Don Demeter.

Holding them hitless for nine innings—a hitter
too—
Carl Erskine leaves Cimoli nothing to do.

Take off the goat-horns, Dodgers, that egret
which two very fine base-stealers can offset.

You've got plenty: Jackie Robinson
and Campy and big Newk, and Dodgerdom again
watching everything you do. You won last year.
Come on.

HERE, not only in contrast to Lloyd Lewis' account earlier in these pages but all by itself, is one of the top stories in all baseball history: Christy Mathewson's third shutout of the 1905 World Series.

1905:
New York Giants 2,
Philadelphia Athletics 0

THE NEW YORK TIMES

TWO NEATLY DRESSED, athletic-looking young men, one a giant in contrast to the squattiness of the other, walked along the veranda of the clubhouse at the Polo Grounds about 5 o'clock yesterday afternoon grinning broadly. Below them was a sea of 10,000 faces, wildly emitting a thunderous eruption of enthusiasm. The young men looked down upon the reverberating ocean of humanity for a moment and then walked to a point directly in front of the plaza, where they were in view of all. The ten thousand throats bellowed forth a tribute that would have almost drowned a broadside of twelve-inch guns.

The two smiling athletes stopped; one of them drew forth a roll of yellow paper from under his arm. As the crowd pushed and fought and cheered he unrolled the impromptu banner and let it flutter on the breeze. The multitude pressed forward like a wave to read this inscription:

The Giants,
World's Champions, 1905.

Geological records show that Vesuvius disturbs the earth and that seismic demonstrations are felt by the greater number. But if that doctrine had been promulgated in the vicinity of the Polo Grounds yesterday, as Christy Mathewson and Roger Bresnahan of the New York Baseball Club unfurled their victorious banner, it would have been minimized. For, as volcanoes assert themselves upon the earth's surface, surely must that deafening, reverberating roar have lifted Manhattan's soil from its base.

The Giants, the most intelligent, the quickest, strongest, and grittiest combination of baseball players that ever represented this city in any league, demonstrated beyond quibble paramount superiority over anything extant in diamond life today by winning the fifth and deciding game of the world championship series with the Athletics by the score of 2 to 0.

The victory meant an honor which has not hitherto fallen to the lot of New York through any other team, and the Giants may hold up their heads in the athletic world as being the one collection of peerless ball tossers.

The crowd, in the neighborhood of 27,000 people, saw a battle to cheer the baseball heart and satisfy the rooter's innermost cravings. At no time during the contest were the Giants in danger, and at all times were they masters. It settled the question whether the National or the American League offered the better brand of baseball. The championship decree of yesterday, to be accepted as final, lays at rest all doubt and demonstrates the transcendent superiority of the National brand and the indisputable invulnerability of the Giants.

And be it recorded right here that New York possesses the pitching marvel of the century. Christy Mathewson, the giant slabman who made the world championship possible for his team, may be legitimately designated as the premier pitching wonder of all baseball records. The diamond has known its Clarkson, its Keefe and its Caruthers. Their records radiate. But to Mathewson belongs the palm. His almost superhuman accomplishments during the series which closed yesterday will stand as a mark for all pictures of the future.

Figures show best just what Mathewson accomplished. In the three victories over which he presided he twirled twenty-seven innings. During that series he allowed not a single run; not an Athletic even reached third base. He was touched for a total of only fifteen hits, and by men who are reckoned as the American League's strongest batters. He allowed only one pass to first, hit only a single batsman, and struck out sixteen men. The record is a classic. Baseball New York appreciates this work. That fact was amply demonstrated yesterday, when it gave Mathewson a marvelous vocal panegyric that evoked a half-suppressed smile and bow.

The game yesterday was one of giants—clean, fast, and decisive. Both teams were keyed high, for to the Giants it meant rosy conquest and to the Athletics a saving chance to redeem themselves. But the Giants were not to be repulsed. They went at the ball in the first inning with a we-never-can-lose determination, and there was not a minute during play in which that spirit did not manifest itself. Philadelphia tried its best, but, strive as hard as it did, it was only a shadow reflecting the masterful Mathewson's will. He bestrode the field like a mighty Colossus, and the Athletics peeped about the diamond like pigmies who struggled gallantly for their lives, but in vain.

Bender, the much feared brave from the Carlisle reservation, sought to repeat his scalping bee of Tuesday, but the Spartan McGraw laconically expressed the situation when at the beginning of the game he remarked good-naturedly to the Athletics' pitcher:

"It will be off the warpath for you today, Chief." The phlegmatic copper-colored man only smiled grimly.

"It's uncertain," he replied, "but I did it once, and I'm going to do my best to do it again."

Analyzed to the statistical point, the twirling feature of the game shows little advantage to either side, but when weighed in parts Mathewson had by far the advantage. Five hits were all that the Giants could register off Bender, while the Athletics rang up for a total of six against Mathewson. Mathewson fanned only three to Bender's five, but the Indian gave three passes. Mathewson proved a surprise to his admirers by poorly fielding his position. He made two errors, but they luckily resulted in nothing harmful.

The Giants were well rewarded for their hard work in defeating the Athletics. Each man

today has a check in his wallet for $1,141.41. That is the share of each of the eighteen Giants for the series. The receipts of the first four games, from which the players derive their profit, were $50,750.50.

The crowd which saw yesterday's game was immense. All the stands were filled, while men and women stood in a line ten deep back of the ropes from the right to the left field bleachers. Men hung on the fence and sat on the grandstand roof, and some peered through glasses from distant poles and housetops.

The New York management had a band on the field to enliven things. As McGraw appeared on the diamond he was met with a volley of applause and was obliged to lift his hat in response.

"Clinch it today, Mac," yelled the crowd. "Nothing but the championship will suit us now."

"That's what you'll get," he responded smilingly.

While McGraw was walking across the field the Athletics appeared from the clubhouse with Bender in the lead.

"Back to the tepee for yours," hooted a rooter. "Giants grab heap much wampum," yelled another, giving an imitation Indian yell. Bender looked at his foes in stolid silence but smiled widely as the running fire of comments continued. James J. Corbett walked into the field with the Giants and helped the players to warm up.

Mathewson got a magnificent reception, and the crowd yelled for him to doff his cap. Instead of doing so, however, he walked over to McGinnity, the conqueror yesterday, and ostentatiously removed Joe's headgear. McGinnity returned the compliment.

"Shake 'em up, Matty. Go after 'em," screamed the bleachers. As McGraw went to the plate to bat out in practice the band began to play:

> We'll all get stone blind,
> Johnnie go fill up the bowl.

Time and again during the game Bender was yelled at, to rattle him, but the noise might as well have been directed at a steamboat, for he was impassive and cool at all stages. In one inning he gave two bases on balls in succession and the crowd jumped to its feet in glee. Bender was thunderously informed that he was booked for the soap factory. At another time two bunts were made in succession. Again the crowd rose and expressed the opinion that the chief would surely go to the happy hunting grounds, but he refused to die and stood gamely and quietly to the end.

As the game proceeded the crowd saw that it was to be a magnificent pitching struggle, and both twirlers were cheered. After the fourth, when Bender retired the Giants in one, two, three order, he was heartily applauded. Bender lifted his cap in acknowledgment. Philadelphia had men on bases in the first, second, third, fifth and sixth inning but couldn't get one past the second sack.

New York made its runs in the fifth and eighth. In the fifth inning Mertes got a pass and Dahlen followed suit. With two on bases the crowd roared for Devlin to drive in a run. Devlin, however, had his orders and bunted. He sacrificed the runners to third and second and the crowd nearly yelled itself hoarse.

"Come on, Gilbert, you can do it!" roared the stands. Then came a volley of taunts to Bender, who viewed the situation with absolute imperturbability. Gilbert caught one of Bender's twists on the end of his bat and sent the ball to deep left. Hartzel caught it, but Mertes on third raced home with the first tally of the game. The crowd went wild.

In the eighth, after Gilbert had flied to Lord, Mathewson went to bat amid a storm of yells and walked. Bresnahan stalked to the plate and carefully inspected the business end of his bat.

"Put it in a balloon, Roger, and send it away for good!" screamed the fans. Roger did the next best thing by driving the ball on a straight line to the left field bleachers. Ordinarily it would have counted for a home run, but under the ground rules he was allowed only two bases. Even Matty was enamored of the coup, for as he trotted around to third he paused, under the ground rule allowance, and clapped his hands with satisfaction. Browne, the next up, swung viciously at one of Bender's curves. It went like a shot straight for the Indian. Bender grabbed at the leather, and it struck his right hand, caroming off to Murphy, who retired Browne. Matty, however, jumped across the rubber and registered a second tally.

When the game ended the crowd broke through the police and rushed for the players. The Giants got into the clubhouse before being intercepted. Ten thousand fans surrounded the clubhouse and demanded to see their heroes. One by one the Giants appeared and were cheered. McGraw made a brief speech, in which he said:

"Ladies and Gentlemen: I appreciate the great victory as well as you. I thank you for your patronage, and hope to see you all next spring."

READERS of *The Fireside Books of Baseball* are going to come away convinced that the talented Jack Orr writes about nothing but failure in Philadelphia (see his "Pitchless Wonders" in the first *Fireside,* and now this). Herb Simons of *Baseball Digest* points out that the Cleveland team of the old National League had the record in the pre-1900 era: won 20, lost 134 in 1899.

The Worst Team of All

JACK ORR

Tom Sheehan, the old pitcher who now scouts for the Giants, is making the hegira to California with the team. He was saying good-by to his Philadelphia friends a few weeks ago and boasting that he was on the worst team in the history of modern baseball. The Philadelphia A's of 1916.

"Oh, come now," said a listener, "they couldn't have been worse than the Doc Prothro-Boom Boom Beck Phillies or the Braves of 1935 who won only 38 games or some of those postwar Brownie teams or the Phillies that Fred Fitzsimmons had during the war."

"They were so," Sheehan said. "You could look it up. We lost 117 games, a record. Personally," he said, not without pride, "I had a 1-17 record and my roomie, Johnnie Nabors, won one and lost 20—19 of them in a row."

Study of the records shows that Sheehan had something. Elmer Myers and Bullet Joe Bush, two other pitchers, each lost 24 games. So among four pitchers they lost 85, which some years is almost enough by itself to put you in the cellar. The A's were last by 54½ games.

"You never saw a club like this," Sheehan said. "We lost 20 in a row at one point that summer and I had a haunting feeling we'd never win another.

"We lost 19 straight on the road. In one game our pitchers gave up 18 walks and in another we left 17 men on base, though I don't know how that many guys got on in the first place.

"We had Whitey Witt, an outfielder by trade, at shortstop. He must have made 80 errors that year. [*He made 70—Ed.*] Larry Lajoie was on

second, but he was 41 years old, hit .246 and covered as much ground as the waterbucket. He quit after that year.

"Stuffy McInnis (.295) was the first baseman and he was all right, but the third baseman was new every day. Connie Mack must have recruited them from the stands. Some of them didn't stay around long enough to be introduced. (One of them named Charlie Pick made 41 errors.)

"Wally Schang, the old catcher, was in left field, along with a bunch of others. A kid named Eddie King hit .188 in right. Billy Myer (.232) caught half a season until he got an appendicitis attack in July.

"'Imagine that lucky son-of-a-gun going away for an operation,' we all said.

"After he left, everybody caught. Remember Val Picinich? He was 19, just breaking in. He hit .195. On other days total strangers would catch.

"Once we were playing the Yankees at the Polo Grounds and I'm pitching. Picinich warms me up, but as the first hitter gets in, Val goes back to the bench and takes off the tools.

"Another guy comes out, a guy I've never seen. He comes out to the mound and says, 'My name is Carroll. I'm the catcher. What are your signs?' I tell him not to confuse me and get the heck back there and catch. He stuck around for about a week and nobody ever saw him again. [*The records show a Ralph Carroll caught ten games and hit .091.*]

"We pitchers lost a lot of games, but that collection couldn't have won behind Matty or Grove. Once we go to Boston for a series. I pitch the opener and give up one hit, by Doc Hoblitzel. But it happens to follow a walk and an error by Witt and I lose, 1-0.

"Now Nabors pitches the second game and he is leading, 1-0, going into the ninth. He gets the first man. Witt boots one and the next guy walks. Hooper is up next, I think, and he singles to left and the man on second tries to score.

"Well, Schang has a good arm and he throws one in that has the runner cold by 15 feet. But we have one of those green catchers. (Never forget his name, Mike Murphy.) The ball bounces out of his glove, the run scores, the other runner takes third and it is 1-1.

"Nabors winds up and throws the next pitch 20 feet over the hitter's head into the grandstand, the man on third scores and we lose another, 2-1.

"Later I asked Nabors why he threw that one away.

"'Look,' he said, 'I knew those guys wouldn't get me another run and if you think I'm going to throw nine more innings on a hot day like this, you're crazy.'"

JOHN GALLAGHER

Courtesy *Sport* Magazine. ©

"I hate this sort of thing."

To the innumerable theories as to how baseball originated, it's unique to add this one. Mr. Patchen's idea of how the game began (it appeared in his *Selected Poems,* published by New Directions) might be, as good poetry often is, disquietingly close to the truth.

The Origin of Baseball

KENNETH PATCHEN

Someone had been walking in and out
Of the world without coming
To much decision about anything.
The sun seemed too hot most of the time.
There weren't enough birds around
And the hills had a silly look
When he got on top of one.
The girls in heaven, however, thought
Nothing of asking to see his watch
Like you would want someone to tell
A joke—"Time," they'd say, "what's
That mean—time?," laughing with the edges
Of their white mouths, like a flutter of paper
In a madhouse. And he'd stumble over
General Sherman or Elizabeth B.
Browning, muttering "Can't you keep
Your big wings out of the aisle?" But down
Again, there'd be millions of people without
Enough to eat and men with guns just
Standing there shooting each other.

So he wanted to throw something—
And he picked up a baseball.

As every baseball season nears a close, the fascinating mathematics of the pennant races, in the form of "magic numbers"—how many to clinch the flag if so-and-so etc.—shriek from every sports page. But more than twenty-five years ago, in the pages of the old New York *American,* George Phair said it all in the following four lines:

The Magic Number

GEORGE E. PHAIR

If the Giants win but two of four
And the Dodgers six of ten
The Phillies, as in days of yore,
Will finish last again.

THE title to this piece, done by veteran umpire Pinelli after he retired
following the 1956 season, may be slightly in conflict with the pictures
on pp. 76B, 76C, or for that matter with John Gallagher's cartoon on
p. 180 of this collection. But let's not start arguing with this umpire
at this late date. When he calls it, he means it.

Kill the Umpire? Don't Make Me Laugh!

BABE PINELLI
as told to AL STUMP

IT'S A SAFE BET that if you gave Joe Fan one
question to ask a just-retired, veteran baseball cop like me, he'd say: "Why did you do it?
Why would anyone want to be an umpire?"

Umps, by national agreement, have the
world's lousiest job, in or outside of sports.

Everybody is so convinced of this that it's
become a No. 1 American legend. Fathers all
over the country raise their boys to be big-
leaguers, but they'd probably drown the kid
who wanted a mask and whisk broom for his
birthday.

So much has been written about pop-bottle
blitzkriegs, booing fans, hot-tempered managers
and pop-off players who browbeat the Men
in Blue into cowering patsies, that some people
feel baseball faces a crisis. When a vacancy occurs among the 32 arbiter positions in the two
top leagues, finding a replacement sometimes
involves a long search.

The missing quantity in the game today
seems to be a good young balls-and-strikes man
on his way up.

And all because of a fable that we're down-
trodden dopes and public enemies.

To me that's the bunk. After last October's
World Series, I retired with 22 years behind
me in the National League and I can tell you
that umpires have the best, most secure and
gratifying job in all organized baseball. It's
easy to prove.

Point One: Last summer, my wife, Mabel, sat

among a bunch of ump-baiters at the Polo
Grounds. The names they called me, after I'd
thumbed Willie Mays out on a tight play at
second, were fierce. "Stinking creep" was one
of the milder items.

Just then, Mabel "accidentally" dropped her
official game pass. One of the wolves picked it
up and they all stared in shock at the name on
it: Mrs. Ralph (Babe) Pinelli.

"Go right ahead," she said. "Don't mind me."

The wolves grinned in a sickly way, and for
the next eight innings they couldn't apologize
enough to Mabel—even bought her a sandwich and pop. When she left, one said, "Tell
the old man he's okay." This explodes an old
myth—people don't really mean the insults they
throw, and an umpire doesn't surrender an
ounce of self-respect.

Point Two: There's a theory that we umps are
social pariahs who lead lonely, friendless lives.
Yet here's a letter a Chicago fan sent me last
September:

DR. MR. PINELLI:

Saturday at Wrigley Field I called you a crook,
a beast and a revolving idiot. Thousands of others
were screaming things just as bad.

I've thought it over and I'm ashamed. I know
you treat the Cubs as square as any team. Will you
accept my apology? And please call the enclosed
phone number. My husband and I would like you
over for a special chicken dinner.

I didn't get to sample the lady's southern fried. That same night I was having a wonderful spaghetti feed with some South Side Chicago Italians, who went out of their way to honor the umpire.

It's that way everywhere. In St. Louis, ballplayers stand around before game time, trying to scare up a taxi to the park. The umps ride in style in a de luxe limousine supplied free of charge by a fan named Arthur Donnelly. In Cincinnati, it's fruitcakes and puddings—dozens of them sent us by our devoted public. Fans in Philly presented me with a gold-handled, engraved whisk broom.

Milwaukee's County Stadium draws a lot of elderly grandmother types. One of them called me over to her box after the ninth inning.

"Lean up here, Babe, and let me kiss you," she said, giving me a smacker in front of everyone. "I thought you called a perfect game."

Do I still hear somebody saying an ump is all thumb and no brains, or else he'd take up honest stealing? If so, I'll apply the crusher.

Point Three: Compared to other baseball jobs, mine has been heaven for 22 seasons. More than 50 big-league managers were fired in the past 10 seasons. They ended up with nerves twanging like banjos. Club owners worry about attendance, climbing overhead and pennant flops. Coaches are mere shadows of managers—they come and go. Ballplayers spend short careers fighting slumps, worrying about contract cuts, injuries and old age.

Meanwhile, with a guaranteed pension, umpires go right on until they're 55 or 60, collecting up to $15,000 for 154 games without a real fear in the world. Not only that, they have the best "seat" in the house, plus more executive power than most industrial big shots. If there's anybody in the sport they must kowtow to, I've never met him.

For instance, when I broke in back in the '30s, the story was around that officials trembled and shook and were afraid to call out the great Babe Ruth on strikes. Just not smart box-office tactics, it was said. For rookie umps to set down the Babe was practically suicide.

So in my very first game behind the plate, I twice waved Ruth away on a called third strike. The second time all hell broke loose: he bawled, pawed dirt, threatened to start a riot in the Boston park. "There's forty thousand here know that last one was a ball, tomato-head!" roared Ruth.

"Maybe so," I replied, "but mine is the only opinion that counts."

More than half a century of immovable law was behind me. The big fellow knew better than to press the argument. He walked away.

Still, today, I'm constantly asked how come my ego isn't wrecked from all the abuse I took for so long. I ask, what abuse? In working 3,400 straight games—367 more than Ty Cobb's big-league record for total performances and 1,270 more than Lou Gehrig's consecutive-game mark—I can't recall ever failing to get in the last word in a hassle. Leo Durocher is said to have TKO'd more umps with his tongue than any living man. Let me tell you about Durocher. In his toughest years, he'd approach me to make a complaint with his hands out in a pleading-to-be-heard gesture, ready to back water fast if he saw I was sore.

Taming Durocher was fun. Back in his playing days with the Cardinals, he twice questioned my integrity, and each time I threw him off the field. After the second incident I told his manager, Frankie Frisch, "Keep an extra infielder warmed up all summer."

"Why?" asked Frisch.

"Because I'm bouncing your wisenheimer shortstop every time he opens up. He's going to learn to respect me or else."

Nothing could have been more painful to Durocher than inaction, and later, in his Brooklyn managing days, Leo never came close to getting personal or using profanity around me. He was so tractable that I could get rid of him by merely sniffing the air. "That's lovely toilet water you're wearing, Leo," I'd say, when he was in the middle of a beef. "I hope you'll stay around so I can enjoy it."

Durocher would stalk off in disgust to kick the water cooler.

From the Gas House Gang to the modern Dodgers, I had plenty of other bonuses as an umpire—like all the laughs I got. One time, Billy Raimondi and Charley Schanz had a fight. Each man wore glasses. During the scuffle, both lost their specs and, when the umpires broke it up, each picked up the wrong pair. Raimondi looked vaguely around, then let out a scared yell. "Hey, what has he done to me? I can't see!"

Which reminds me, maybe the most mistaken idea of fans is that no ump would dare wear glasses in public. I've worn mine (which I need *only* for reading) in hotel lobbies, restaurants, railway club cars. Only one person ever risked a wisecrack about them—Eddie Stanky, when he managed the Cardinals in 1954.

One night I was studying the menu in a train diner when Stanky came in. "Well, it's old Horn Rims," he popped off, in a voice the whole car could hear. "I always said you were blind as a potato with a thousand eyes."

Not much later, Stanky's club trailed the Phillies, 8-1, in the top of the fifth inning. The light was failing. To force a postponement before a legal five-inning game could be played, Stanky pulled delay after delay. He complained on every pitch, ran pitchers in and out, had his catcher, Yvars, start a phony fight. Finally, I moved in on him.

While Stanky stood speechless, I told him, "Well, I won't need glasses to read the papers tonight."

I didn't. Headlines read: UMPIRE MAKES RARE RULING; FORFEITS CARDINAL CONTEST BECAUSE OF STANKY STALLING.

It was the first time a big-league game was forfeited short of legal length. Incidentally, Stanky never again mentioned my eyesight.

Here's another fact that may surprise you: In a dangerous spot, the ump's best friend is the ballplayer. Walking past the Pittsburgh stands one day, I didn't see a drunken fan waving a beer bottle and about to leap on my back. Three Pirates rushed up waving bats. "Jump," they told the guy, "and you'll come down with no head." He almost broke a leg getting away from there.

It's true that women can outcuss men in some National League towns. But the gals always gave me more laughs than tears. At Philadelphia, umpires leave the field by way of a narrow exposed alley beneath the stands. You want to step lively and say nothing. Season before last, one of my umpiring partners glanced up at a group of baseball Sadies who were acting as though we were their husbands and were staggering home at 4 A.M. "Please, girls," he said. "I don't think we've been introduced."

One of them reached down and broke her umbrella over his head. "Well, we have now," she replied.

Through my career, I was noted for my few ejections—only about 40 in 22 years. That was because I kept my sense of humor, studied players carefully and discovered that each must be handled in a different way. Some of the greatest actually didn't need any handling at

all. Enos Slaughter never complained about a call in 15 years. But Claude Passeau, a good-hitting pitcher, needed a spanking sometimes. He once shouted after a third strike against him, "Oh, how you missed that one!"

"I wouldn't have if I'd had a bat in my hand," I told him. The bench jockeys took it from there.

You get those embarrassing ejections, though. Not long ago, I kicked out Peewee Reese, of the Dodgers, when he threw his bat in Chicago. Reese took it hard. He moaned it was the first time in 14 years he'd been ousted. Jackie Robinson was next up. "You sure destroyed Peewee's faith," he said. "Just before the game, he took a clubhouse poll to pick the umpire least likely to toss a man out. You won it, Pinelli!"

After the 1952 World Series, I had hundreds of letters from TV fans asking why I broke out laughing after an injury suffered by Duke Snider of the Dodgers. They wrote, "So you hate the Brooklyns, you bum?"

Nothing like it. The facts were that Snider fouled off a pitch. The ball ricocheted off his foot. Duke was hopping about in pain, but Yogi Berra, Yankee catcher, cried, "No foul! No! It's a fair ball!"

Although it was the world's most obvious foul, Berra figured he might steal a decision. "Let's see the scuff mark on his shoe!" he yelled.

What Snider called Yogi as he hopped in agony on one foot was my best moment of the Series.

Not that I needed anything more to convince me that I couldn't have found a more exciting and happy career than umpiring. However, last October, a young fellow named Don Larsen added an amazing final touch.

*   *   *

When you've strung together 3,400 umpiring assignments—my record before I retired from the National League at the age of 61 last October—you don't expect any last-minute fireworks. You figure you've seen and heard it all.

That's where I was wrong. Before I quit, I was to jerk my right arm up, ending the most dramatic ball game ever played—and probably the most agonizing ever umpired.

It had to be on the nervous side to beat some of my past moments under pressure.

Why, I remember a Boston-St. Louis game where a fly ball went up and wouldn't come down. Another time, a hotheaded pitcher chased me with an ice pick. Once, I ran in every direction but up while Art Garibaldi, of the Cardinals, tripled into a double play. There was a 23-inning marathon when players pleaded with me to stop one of history's longest deadlocks, while the fans roared for it to go on. Last summer, a fan caught a long fly that Fred Hutchinson, manager of the Cards, claimed should be ruled a home run. When I disagreed, Hutchinson tried to butt me out of the park with his stomach.

Sounds strenuous? Well, it all happened in the sport I was part of as an official for 22 years, and for 774 games before that as a player. Of the two lines of work, umpiring was by far the best. Umpires are Kings of the Diamond. We last three times as long as managers and athletes. We earn $15,000 salaries. Out there on the field we're the boss.

Only a fool calls an umpire "blind." The average fan sees about 20 per cent of the inside action. I trained myself to split-second reactions. I learned to anticipate the strategy so as to be on top of every play, to miss nothing.

Even then I didn't believe some of the crazy situations that came up.

Take the catcher who made a put-out on a high fly hit to center field. That was the baseball that wouldn't come down.

We were at Braves Field, Boston, in '38. A strong wind was whipping the field. A St. Louis hitter sent a towering fly to Vince DiMaggio in center field. DiMaggio waited, everyone waited. But the ball stayed up there. Suddenly, my cap blew off and the ball was coming back!

It sailed over the infield, past the pitcher's box, over the third-base line and toward the stands. Catcher Al Lopez, dashing backward, made the catch against the Boston dugout. I couldn't believe it. I turned to my umpiring partner, Beans Reardon.

Beans was desperately clutching his pants and coat and 20,000 fans were running for cover. The game was over. A howling hurricane had struck New England.

My tangle with the hot-tempered pitcher could have been fatal. After an exchange of compliments, he caught me coming out of the shower. Stark naked, I ran in circles while he flailed at me with an ice pick until players disarmed him.

When a pennant race gets real hot, that's when an umpire has to stay especially cool. The hysteria just below the surface can break out like an epidemic. If an official doesn't keep his head—while everyone else is losing it—he's in big trouble, might even get a note from League President Warren Giles informing him of a nice opening in the Busted Jitney Bus Class D League of Hayfork, Iowa. Take a Giants-Cardinals game of a while back.

With none out, the Cards had Cotton Pippen on second and Terry Moore at first. Art Garibaldi banged a sure triple off the right-field wall. From second, Pippen raced toward third. But he heard third-base coach Mike Gonzales screaming and saw his arms going like a windmill. Pippen braked. All at once, I was running every direction in pursuit of the action.

Thinking he'd received the "stop—go back" signal, Pippen tried to reverse course. He was run down and tagged out as the outfield throw-in came whistling to third. Moore, piled up behind Pippen, was caught scrambling back to second for the weird double play.

Poor Garibaldi. He lasted only one big-league season, and this was his great moment. But he was robbed of his triple and escaped making the third out only by a frantic diving leap back to first base.

The dust settled on a berserk Garibaldi. Manager Frankie Frisch strewed the field with bats. And Gonzales added the topper. "I don' say 'stop,'" explained Gonzales. "I holler 'don' bother to stop.' Don' nobody know no heengleesh?"

One of the oddest plays I know of came when Max Flack of the Cubs hit a home run out of Wrigley Field and got a complaint from the police. The ball smashed through the window of an across-the-street apartment, almost striking a woman tenant. But Max beat the rap. It turned out the apartment was his own, and the lady was his wife.

Things like that come back when you put on the mask and pad for the last time—for me the 1956 World Series. I felt as blue about it as any man who's retiring. And then in the fourth Series game, something happened that made me feel even worse.

Any umpire feels disgraced when hit by a batted or thrown ball. I'd avoided it for 22 years, but the Yankees' Gil McDougald sliced a drive along the right-field line that curved with me as I ran. It caught me in the pit of the stomach. I was knocked groggy. That night, I moaned to my wife, Mabel, "What a way to wind it up."

Came the fifth game. The first batter was Jim Gilliam, of the Dodgers. The Yankee pitcher—a rawboned youngster named Don Larsen, with a fair season's record of 11 wins, 5 losses—threw Gilliam five pitches. On a two-and-two count, Larsen bent a fast curve over the low inside corner. Gilliam was caught flat-footed. "Out!" I shouted. Then I thought, "Oh-oh, Larsen's got it today."

From then on, I was in the concentrating "trance" of a good plate man. Judging balls and strikes accurately is a matter of fine timing and rhythm, of bobbing and weaving so that the catcher never blocks your view of the ball. Everything else is blotted from your mind. At 90 mph, a baseball is over the plate in ⅟₇₅ of a second—you don't even dare blink. So it wasn't until the sixth inning that I realized something startling was under way. Glancing at the scoreboard, I saw all those goose eggs.

It hit me harder than McDougald's liner that I might be about to umpire the first no-hit, no-walk, no-run game in World Series history.

What a spot to be on. By the eighth inning, with Larsen still showing a perfect shutout, 50,000,000 fans were pulling heart and soul for him. A base on balls called by me now would go down as the Crime of the Century. To bat came big Gil Hodges. "I'll get to this guy," I heard him mutter.

Until then, Larsen's control had been uncanny. But then I had to do it. Two of his first four pitches to Hodges I called balls. Both were only inches off the plate. But to an umpire —no matter what the stakes—a slight miss is as much as a mile. Hodges let me breathe again by lining out to third base.

When the last man in the ninth, pinch hitter Dale Mitchell, stepped up, my blue suit was soaked with sweat. I noticed Commissioner Ford Frick in his box. He was pale as a sheet.

With two out, Larsen was just one man away from immortality. As he prepared to throw, I took a firm grip on my emotions. Everyone else could sympathize with him—but not me. Refusing Larsen anything he didn't earn 100 per cent was the hardest thing I've ever done in baseball.

Larsen's first pitch looked good up to the last instant. Then it broke too high. "Ball," I said. Next, Mitchell took a swinging strike.

Pitch No. 3 was a steaming fast ball a fraction outside. "Ball two," I croaked.

A foul ball followed. The quiet in Yankee Stadium was so deep I could hear the rasp of Larsen's breathing. If he'd heaved the next one into the grandstand, I wouldn't have been surprised.

He let it go (Larsen told me later he didn't remember throwing it). He hid the ball behind his glove so well I didn't pick it up until it was two-thirds in. It was his fast one. To the outside corner. At waist height. It clipped the corner without swerve or dip. Mitchell lunged, but for reasons I'll never know held back. We all stood frozen.

"The third strike," I said, "and out."

The first perfect World Series game was in the books, and the whole country was going crazy.

What did Larsen "have," as I saw it? Great courage. A catcher, Yogi Berra, who directed all 97 of his pitches without a mistake. Plus a radical new no-windup style that speeded up his pitching pace, confusing the Dodgers. Mostly, though, Larsen showed as sharp-breaking a curve as I've ever watched. And he threw it up at varying speeds. That's important. You can have everything else, but you're not a pitcher until you've mastered the change-up curve ball.

No umpire could be in a tighter squeeze than the Perfect Game, of course. I've seen others, though, that weren't larks. Last season, the Cincinnati Reds, driving for the National League pennant, were locked in a 1-1 tie with the Cardinals in the eighth inning. A Card hitter slammed a this-is-it wallop to the left-field wall. Just as Cincy outfielder Frank Robinson leaped for the ball, fans reached down to grab. The ball suddenly disappeared. In my view, it hit the top of the stands, didn't go into them for a home run. "An automatic double," I ruled it.

Charging out, Cardinal manager Fred Hutchinson called me vulgar names. Ejecting managers was always against my philosophy. I closed my ears to what Hutchinson was saying.

His stomach, with 200 pounds behind it, bumped me at this point. We did a backward adagio—bumpety-bump by Hutchinson, bouncety-bounce by Pinelli. Since I was paid to stay in the park, Hutchinson went. I wrote a full report to the league president and Hutchinson drew a three-day suspension.

I'd like to make a parting plea to managers to bear with umpires on such highly confused plays as that. No one has telescopic eyes. Ask those bleacher fans what happened, and you'll get a 50-50 split vote as to where the ball actually went. It's the same problem with the five other most difficult decisions an umpire must make.

I'm not complaining. The whole umpiring trade has gone far forward from the days when you needed a police escort home. The Dodger Sym-Phony Band has orders not to play "Three Blind Mice" before games. The flying pop bottle has almost disappeared. Women fans baked me a cake before I left. Any "enemies" I had on the field wished me good luck. A big-league team, the Cincinnati Redlegs, testified to my eyesight at 61 by hiring me as a West Coast scout. I came away solvent and with my ego all in one piece.

And best of all, there's the story I have to tell my 11 grandchildren: about how I called the Perfect Game.

As the preface to this volume records, Don Larsen pitched his perfect game in the World Series on the day the first *Fireside Book of Baseball* was published. The second and all subsequent printings of that book contain a play-by-play and box score of the Larsen game. However, more than 20,000 copies of the first printing—without the Larsen account—were sold, so if you are one of the 20,000 who bought one you may enjoy the following piece partially on that account. No matter who you are, though, the enjoyment will be there. This is a great baseball lead, written by one of the masters, and that is the chief reason that it is reprinted here. It will not surprise you to learn that it won first prize in the annual *Best Sports Stories* collection for 1956.

1956:
New York Yankees 2,
Brooklyn Dodgers 0

SHIRLEY POVICH

THE MILLION-TO-ONE shot came in. Hell froze over. A month of Sundays hit the calendar. Don Larsen today pitched a no-hit, no-run, no-man-reach-first game in a World Series.

On the mound at Yankee Stadium, the same guy who was knocked out in two innings by the Dodgers on Friday came up today with one for the record books, posting it there in solo grandeur as the only Perfect Game in World Series history.

With it, the Yankee right-hander shattered the Dodgers, 2-0, and beat Sal Maglie, while taking 64,519 suspense-limp fans into his act.

First there was mild speculation, then there was hope, then breaths were held in slackened jaws in the late innings as the big mob wondered if the big Yankee right-hander could bring off for them the most fabulous of all World Series games.

He did it, and the Yanks took the Series lead three games to two, to leave the Dodgers as thunderstruck as Larsen himself appeared to be at the finish of his feat.

Larsen whizzed a third strike past pinch hitter Dale Mitchell in the ninth. That was all. It was over. Automatically, the massive 226-pounder from San Diego started walking from the mound toward the dugout, as pitchers are supposed to do at the finish.

But this time there was a woodenness in his steps and his stride was that of a man in a daze. The spell was broken for Larsen when Yogi Berra ran onto the infield to embrace him.

It was not Larsen jumping for joy. It was the more demonstative Berra. His battery mate leaped full tilt at the big guy. In self-defense, Larsen caught Berra in mid-air* as one would catch a frolicking child, and that's how they made their way toward the Yankee bench, Larsen carrying Berra.

There wasn't a Brooklyn partisan left among the 64,519, it seemed, at the finish. Loyalties to the Dodgers evaporated in sheer enthrallment at the show big Larsen was giving them, for this was a day when the fans could boast that they were there.

So at the finish, Larsen had brought it off,

* See picture, page 140D.

and erected for himself a special throne in baseball's Hall of Fame, with the first Perfect Game pitched in major-league baseball since Charlie Robertson of the White Sox against Detroit 34 years ago.

But this was one more special. This one was in a World Series. Three times, pitchers had almost come through with no-hitters, and there were three one-hitters in the World Series books, but never a no-man-reach-base classic.

The tragic victim of it all, sitting on the Dodger bench, was sad Sal Maglie, himself a five-hit pitcher today in his bid for a second Series victory over the Yankees. He was out of the game, technically, but he was staying to see it out and it must have been in disbelief that he saw himself beaten by another guy's World Series no-hitter.

Mickey Mantle hit a home run today in the fourth inning and that was all the impetus the Yankees needed, but no game-winning home run ever wound up with such emphatic second billing as Mantle's this afternoon.

It was an exciting wallop but in the fourth inning only, because after that Larsen was the story today, and the dumbfounded Dodgers could wonder how this same guy who couldn't last out two innings in the second game could master them so thoroughly today.

He did it with a tremendous assortment of pitches that seemed to have five forward speeds, including a slow one that ought to have been equipped with back-up lights.

Larsen had them in hand all day. He used only 97 pitches, not an abnormally low number because 11 pitches an inning is about normal for a good day's work. But he was the boss from the outset. Only against Peewee Reese in the first inning did he lapse to a three-ball count, and then he struck Reese out. No other Dodger was ever favored with more than two called balls by Umpire Babe Pinelli.

Behind him, his Yankee teammates made three spectacular fielding plays to put Larsen in the Hall of Fame. There was one in the second inning that calls for special description. In the fifth, Mickey Mantle ranged far back into left center to haul in Gil Hodges' long drive with a backhand shoetop grab that was a beaut. In the eighth, the same Hodges made another bid to break it up, but Third Baseman Andy Carey speared his line drive.

Little did Larsen, the Yankees, the Dodgers or anybody among the 64,519 in the stands suspect that when Jackie Robinson was robbed of a line-drive hit in the second inning, the stage was being set for a Perfect Game.

Robinson murdered the ball so hard that Third Baseman Andy Carey barely had time to fling his glove upward in a desperate attempt to get the ball. He could only deflect it. But, luckily, Shortstop Gil McDougald was backing up, and able to grab the ball on one bounce. By a half-step, McDougald got Robinson at first base, and Larsen tonight can be grateful that it was not the younger, fleeter Robinson of a few years back but a heavy-legged, 40-year-old Jackie.

As the game wore on, Larsen lost the edge that gave him five strike-outs in the first four innings, and added only two in the last five. He had opened up by slipping called third strikes past both Gilliam and Reese in the first inning.

Came the sixth, and he got Furillo and Campanella on pops, fanned Maglie. Gilliam, Reese and Snider were easy in the seventh. Robinson tapped out, Hodges lined out and Amoros flied out in the eighth. And now it was the ninth, and the big Scandinavian-American was going for the works with a calm that was exclusive with him.

Furillo gave him a bit of a battle, fouled off four pitches, then flied mildly to Bauer. He got two quick strikes on Campanella, got him on a slow roller to Martin.

Now it was the left-handed Dale Mitchell, pinch hitting for Maglie.

Ball one came in high. Larsen got a called strike.

On the next pitch, Mitchell swung for strike two.

Then the last pitch of the game. Mitchell started to swing, but didn't go through with it.

But it made no difference because Umpire Pinelli was calling it Strike Number Three, and baseball history was being made.

Maglie himself was a magnificent figure out there all day, pitching hitless ball and leaving the Yankees a perplexed gang, until suddenly with two out in the fourth, Mickey Mantle, with two called strikes against him, lashed the next pitch on a line into the right-field seats to give the Yanks a 1-0 lead.

There was doubt about that Mantle homer because the ball was curving and would it stay fair? It did. In their own half of the inning, the Dodgers had no such luck. Duke Snider's drive into the same seats had curved foul by a few feet. The disgusted Snider eventually took a third strike.

The Dodgers were a luckless gang and Larsen a fortunate fellow in the fifth. Like Mantle, Sandy Amoros lined one into the seats in right, and that one was a near thing for the Yankees.

By what seemed only inches, it curved foul, the umpires ruled.

Going into the sixth, Maglie was pitching a one-hitter—Mantle's homer—and being out-pitched. The old guy lost some of his stuff in the sixth, though, and the Yankees came up with their other run.

Carey led off with a single to center, and Larsen sacrificed him to second on a daring third-strike bunt. Hank Bauer got the run in with a single to left. There might have been a close play at the plate had Amoros come up with the ball cleanly, but he didn't and Carey scored unmolested.

Now there were Yanks still on first and third with only one out, but they could get no more. Hodges made a scintillating pickup of Mantle's smash, stepped on first and threw to home for a double play on Bauer, who was trying to score. Bauer was trapped in a rundown and caught despite a low throw by Campanella that caused Robinson to fall into the dirt.

But the Yankees weren't needing any more runs for Larsen today. They didn't even need their second one, because they were getting a pitching job for the books this memorable day in baseball.

SEVERAL pitchers, as baseball editor Joe Reichler of the Associated Press can be found murmuring in the following piece, throw spitballs today, even though the rules prohibit it. When the umpire asks to see the ball, the pitcher, in his confusion, throws it to his third baseman. The third baseman rubs the ball as always, then tosses it to the umpire. The umpire looks. No spit.

Let's Bring Back the Spitball

JOE REICHLER

SOME TEN YEARS AGO, Baseball Commissioner Ford Frick, then president of the National League, scored a hit with pitchers everywhere by stating he favored the return of the spitball. Frick thought it would provide an easy solution to the moundsman's main problem.

This frank statement by an important official excited his conservative, scared-of-a-change confreres. Immediately there arose a howl of indignation.

"It's a foul and unsanitary pitch," they cried. "It would make the game less attractive to the people. It would open the door to all types of cheating. Also, it is a dangerous pitch. With so much night ball today, it would result in beanings."

How silly can they get? Is the spitter, the simple damp one (not the delivery which was loaded with mud, emery, tobacco and rosin) any more unsanitary than the gobs of saliva the hitters use on their hands? Is it any less sanitary than the dirt base runners sometimes eat when they dive into a base?

Frank Shaughnessy, head of the International League and one of the most respected men in baseball, says:

"I really think we would have more interesting baseball if the spitter was allowed. In fact, baseball needs the spitter. It can be a tremendous attraction. It will create a vast amount of publicity. The experts, the players, the public will discuss it."

The question was put before Frank Shellenback, former pitching coach of the Giants and one of the last pitchers officially permitted to use it.

"I don't believe the spitball is at all danger-

ous," he replied. "Certainly not as much as the fast ball in the hands of some of the pitchers we have today."

"Dangerous?" repeated Burleigh Grimes, one of the greatest exponents of the spitter. "It's easier to control than the knuckler. In 19 seasons I hit one batter with it, Mel Ott, and he was leaning over the plate."

When Frick made his saliva pitch, he explained: "Why, with the lively ball, and with everybody swinging, it got so a pitcher's afraid to put the ball in there. The spitter was a great pitch. I spent a great many years in baseball when the spitter was part of the game. Fellows like Burleigh Grimes, Stan Covaleskie, Red Faber and John Quinn used it and lasted 20 years."

The plea for the spitter is made here simply for the purpose of giving the poor harassed pitcher a little more ammunition against streamlined bats and jet-propelled rockets.

Since Babe Ruth popularized the home run in 1919, pitchers have been taking it on the chin from the rules makers. Their troubles have been mounting since the spitter was banished in 1920.

Some 70 years ago, the emphasis was all on pitching. Between 1888 and 1958, the game traveled from one undesirable extreme to another, from overweighted pitching to overemphasized hitting.

Pitching distances were increased from 45 to 50 feet, from 55 in 1892 to 60 a year later and finally to 60½ feet. There was a cry against what was called "pitchers' games." Finally they started cutting the pitcher down to size. Trouble is, it never occurred to them to stop.

The size of the rubber has shrunk; so has the strike zone; balk rules have become more rigid; freak pitches have been outlawed; screens have been taken down and fences have been put up to lessen the playing area; mounds have been shaved to the minimum.

Although the spitter was banned 38 years ago, the spray lingers. Birdie Tebbetts, in his catching days with the Detroit Tigers, was on the receiving end of many a wet one delivered by Tommy Bridges and Schoolboy Rowe, and he insists Lew Burdette, World Series pitching hero, is a constant violator of the spitball rule. Birdie's charges aren't new. They've been accusing Fidgety Lew but they've never been able to catch him. Lew acknowledges he wets his fingers but he refuses to admit he throws the spitter.

Not so bashful was Preacher Roe. The former Brooklyn southpaw confessed he threw the outlawed spitter for seven years and declared the pitch prolonged his life in the big leagues by the same seven years. On the heels of Roe's admission, Joe Page, another famous left-hander, and Red Barrett, who toiled ten years with Boston and St. Louis, joined the "I threw a spitter" club. Subsequently, testimony was given to the effect that such pretty famous pitching names as Claude Passeau, Harry Brecheen, Larry Jansen, George Earnshaw, Fred Frankhouse, Nelson Potter, Ellis Kinder, Johnny Schmitz, Murry Dickson, Steve Gromek, and the aforementioned Rowe and Bridges resorted at times to the spitter.

Only last October, a few months after his release by the Kansas City Athletics, Joe Coleman, a pitcher, declared that he knew of "at least 20 pitchers who are throwing spitters in the big leagues today." He identified only one, however, Lew Burdette. Had he wished to be more informative, he could have added the names of Virgil Trucks, Sal Maglie, Jim Wilson, Marv Grissom, Ray Moore, Bob Lemon, Art Fowler and Raul Sanchez.

Like Burdette, these saliva slingers laugh off any notion that they are depending upon a barred pitch. For an illegal maneuver, the spitter has become the most controversial pitch in diamond history. The writer, conducting his own survey late last season, was surprised to learn that two thirds of the players, managers and coaches were in favor of the spitter's return. The majority of those opposed were infielders and outfielders who would have to throw the batted spitballs, and also hit against them. It was their belief that the public had become used to long balls and that the spitter would cut down the home-run production.

The feeling among the managers and the game's officials was even-Steven. General managers George Weiss of the Yankees and Frank Lane of the Indians were against it but their field managers, Casey Stengel and Bobby Bragan, were for it. Commissioner Frick, as expected, was for it, but the two league presidents, Will Harridge of the American and Warren Giles of the National, were against it.

Of all the arguments against the spitter, Lane's probably is the strongest. "It would definitely be a step backward," he said. "It would be a return toward the dead ball days. The beginning of the Ruth era was the beginning of baseball's tremendous growth in popularity."

One man who doesn't think the pitching fraternity needs sympathy is Fred Haney, manager of the world champion Braves.

"The pitchers don't need any more help," he says. "Look at the batting averages. There is seldom a .350 hitter any more."

The spitter was born in 1902, was killed in 1920, but did not leave the majors until 1934, when Grimes finished up with the New York Yankees.

Elmer Stricklett, who pitched for the Chicago White Sox in 1904, was the first to use it in the major leagues, but another, Frank Corridon, used it two years before him in the minors. The credit for its origin, however, goes not to Stricklett or Corridon, but to George Hildebrand, former American League umpire, who, oddly enough, was not a pitcher but an outfielder.

In 1902, Hildebrand was playing for Providence of the Eastern League. He was warming up alongside of Corridon, who was getting ready to pitch. It had rained that day and the grass was still wet. Hildebrand noticed Corridon's pitches were acting strangely. Suddenly he got an idea. Asking Corridon for the ball, he expectorated heavily on it and threw it to the catcher. The ball took such a peculiar dip that Corridon's eyes popped. A month later, in an exhibition game against the Pirates, Corridon struck out nine batters in five innings with the wet pitch.

Meanwhile, Hildebrand was traded to Sacramento, where another pitcher, Stricklett, was considered over the hill because of a sore arm. Hildebrand told Stricklett about the new pitch and, with the aid of the spitball, Elmer won 11 straight games for Sacramento and earned a trial with the White Sox. In the spring of 1904, Stricklett showed it to Jack Chesbro, New

York's ace right hander, and he won 41 games that year.

With the White Sox, Stricklett was roomed with a rookie pitcher, Ed Walsh. He taught the kid how to throw the spitter and Walsh won 195 games between 1904 and 1917.

The pitch was outlawed because pitchers had found additional ways of doctoring the ball. Instead of sticking to saliva, they began using tobacco juice, pickle brine, emery boards, paraffin, sandpaper, phonograph needles and even razor blades to roughen the edges and cut the seams. When the pitch was banned, 18 major-leaguers were permitted to keep throwing it for the balance of their career. When Grimes took off his uniform for the last time, in 1934, the spitter presumably was gone. Actually, all it did was go underground.

BILL YATES

Courtesy *Sport* Magazine. ©

"How fast can you run?"

The following appeared in the old *Baseball* magazine back in 1908: Grantland Rice telling Theodore Roosevelt to become an umpire when his days as President of the United States were over. Perhaps this marked an end of an era; there is no record that any sports writer, or any one else, has issued similar advice to a President since.

A Tip to Teddy

GRANTLAND RICE

Teddy, when your work is through in the presidential chair
When another takes the shift where you've learned to do and dare,
    You will need another job—one that's a monstrosity
    That will soak up, day by day, all your strenuosity.
It must be a husky job—full of smoke and fire to boot,
And in looking 'round I've found only one I know will suit.
    Only one where your Big Stick will be needed day by day;
    Only one to fit in, Ted, with your rough-and-tumble way;
Only one where in the end you will someday long for rest,
Where your energy will wane and your spirit be depressed.

You will find it different from any nature-faking fuss;
You will find it harder than mauling up the octopus;
    It will be a rougher job than a charge up San Juan Hill,
    Or a battle with the trusts—it will take a stronger will.
Fighting predatory wealth or the kings of high finance,
Calling railroad moguls down will not be a circumstance.

All in all 'twill suit you fine, never having been afraid
Of aught else upon this earth—you should be an umpire, Ted!
That's the only job for you—take your tip now, Theodore;
    Think of how your pulse will leap when you hear the angry roar
    Of the bleacher gods enraged; you will find the action there
Which you've hunted for in vain in the presidential chair.
Chasing mountain lions and such, catching grizzlies will seem tame
Lined up with the jolt you'll get in the thick of some close game.
    Choking angry wolves to death as a sport will stack up raw
    When you see Kid Elberfeld swinging for your jaw.

When you hear Hugh Jennings roar, "Call them strikes—you lump of cheese!"
Or McGraw comes rushing in, kicking at your shins and knees;
    When the bleachers rise and shout, "Robber —Liar—Thief and Dub!"
    You'll be sorry for the gents in your Ananias Club.
You'll find it's a diff'rent thing making peace with old Japan
Than when you have called a strike on O'Connor or McGann.

Holding California down isn't quite the same, I'll state,
As is calling Devlin out on a close-out at the plate.

Though I've hunted far and near, there is nothing else to do

Where you'll get what's coming, Ted—*all* that's coming unto you—
You should be an umpire, Ted, and I'll bet two weeks would be
Quite enough to curb your rash, headlong stren-u-os-i-tee.

BEN THOMPSON

Courtesy *Sport* Magazine. ©

For Polo Grounds fans, this game was, in the language of Broadway, the whole thing together.

1957:
Pittsburgh Pirates 9,
New York Giants 1

MILTON RICHMAN

THEY TORE UP the turf, they tore up the seats, they tore up home plate and if Giant owner Horace Stoneham had been around, they would have torn him up, too.

"We want Stoneham—with a rope around his neck!"

That was the angry chant of a mob which surged against the center-field clubhouse after the San Francisco-bound New York Giants wound up their playing days at the Polo Grounds for all time yesterday by dropping a 9-1 decision to the Pittsburgh Pirates.

Of the 11,606 fans who turned out for the finale, Mrs. John McGraw showed the most emotion.

"I'm not thinking of this as the last game here," said the widow of the Giants' famed manager, dabbing at her eyes with a handkerchief. "I'm just thinking of this as the end of another season."

That wasn't the case, however, with most of the other fans. To the end they held up a sign in the left-field bleachers saying, "Stay Team Stay," and when it became obvious with the final out that all the signs in the world wouldn't help, they swung into action.

First, some of them sawed off parts of grandstand seats to carry home as souvenirs. Then one group made a rush for home plate, digging it up and lugging it away. Other fans took out for the outfield where they scooped up huge chunks of sod.

When it was all over, the Polo Grounds had been picked clean and the tremendous-sized divots in the ground were the kind no self-respecting golfer would ever be guilty of.

Before the crowd departed, it congregated in front of the Giants' clubhouse and pleaded loudly for one last look at Willie Mays. Willie was in the showers at the time, however.

"I was so nervous when I went up to hit in the ninth that my hands were shaking," Mays explained. "Never happened to me before. Not even in the World Series or All-Star games."

To elude the crowd after the final out, the Giant players made a mad dash for the safety of the clubhouse.

"I never saw 'em hustle that much all season," commented one fan, who was almost trampled in the rush.

Many Giant stars of yesteryear were honored in brief pregame ceremonies and most of them came back to the clubhouse for one last nostalgic look after the game was over.

"It doesn't matter where we go," said former southpaw ace Carl Hubbell. "This place will always be home to me."

Hubbell said his most vivid memory of the Polo Grounds was the 18-inning 1-0 victory he pitched over the St. Louis Cardinals in 1933.

Each of the Giants' players, past and present, had his own favorite recollection.

Bobby Thomson, of course, couldn't help but think of the pennant-winning homer he hit at the Polo Grounds in 1951.

"I'd be lying if I said I don't feel kinda

funny in the stomach about leaving this place," he said. "I brought my camera along to the park today. I wanted to take some pictures."

Whitey Lockman recalled how nervous he had been when the Giants first brought him up from the minors 12 years ago.

"A fellow named George Dockins put me at ease, though," he grinned. "He was pitching for the Cardinals and I hit him for a home run my first time up."

Dusty Rhodes tried to make light of the windup by quipping, "Parting is such sweet sorrow," but he didn't fool anybody.

Manager Bill Rigney told how he had come out to the Polo Grounds all by himself the other day.

"I walked around in the park to look around," he said. "First thing you know, I said to myself I had better get out of here. I was starting to feel . . . well, you know."

JOHN GALLAGHER

Courtesy *Sport* Magazine. ©

"Don't break any windows."

BENCH jockeying in baseball is, like sculpture and lyric poetry, one of the fine arts. Elsewhere in this volume, a selection of photographs illustrates that fact.

Stick It in His Ear!

RAY ROBINSON

WHAT'S GOT two arms, two legs and no guts?" The rhetorical question singed Don Newcombe's ears and made his mind an inferno of hostile thoughts and plans.

Wherever he went—in the life of a ballplayer that generally means dugouts, hotel lobbies, restaurants, taxicabs and, in the case of Newcombe, a pitcher, the mound—the hulking Brooklyn Dodger with the prognathic face and choleric disposition was subjected to an unceasing barrage of jockeying, barbering, ribbing, baiting, joshing and verbal lathering.

He had qualified as the pet target of countless vocal rivals because of a single oversight in his pitching past: he had neglected ever to register a victory over the New York Yankees in World Series play, and had tried and been found wanting five times in three different Series.

Now, as he stood staring in at the batter and the big, oversized catcher's mitt of his teammate and occasional chaperon, Roy Campanella, Don heard it again, perhaps for the thousandth time.

Campy heard it, too. He untangled himself from his crouch and trotted out to his friend.

"Don't pay no attention to that stuff. Pitch to me. Just pitch to me," said the catcher, who could demand additional pay from Walter O'Malley for his chore in lay analysis.

"I'll pitch. I'll show 'em what kind of a man I am," said Newcombe.

The jibes continued as Campanella resumed his squat position behind the plate, and as Newcombe unfurled his next pitch, a scorching strike that had the batter missing by the proverbial country mile. Before the afternoon was spent, Newcombe had made good his promise to Campanella. The Cubs, his detractors, had been beaten soundly by a thoroughly competent pitching job, the kind that won him

twenty-seven games in 1956, and recognition as the National League's Most Valuable Player.

Before the current baseball season becomes history, Newcombe will have been called a thousand uncomplimentary and inflammatory names by the slur-salesmen on National League benches. He will smolder, fume, fuss, curse and glare. Sometimes he will return the taunts and abuse with an equally unwholesome estimate of his enemies. But he will meet the challenge every time he takes that inimitable giant stride to the mound, and, unless names can actually hurt him, he will continue to win ball games and make life miserable for the opposition where it hurts most—in the won-and-lost column.

The assault on Don Newcombe's character and eardrums, as distasteful and unfair as it may seem to some, is really nothing new in baseball. Baseball jockeys have been riding herd and hard on each other for years, picking on weaknesses, personal idiosyncrasies, eccentric habits, indiscretions and physical appearance, and sometimes exploiting racial and religious prejudices in a furious fusillade of spleen that might put the late Josef Goebbels or young John Kasper of the White Citizens Councils to shame.

The baseball bench jockey, that verbal herb that sprouts in the spring and increases in spiciness as World Series time approaches, doesn't ride horses. He may, of course, get hoarse riding other players, since he is perpetually jeering, threatening and casting imprecations at the opposition from the relative safety of the sidelines.

Sometimes he is also known as a "barber" (not to be confused with Brooklyn pitcher Sal Maglie). He is a player (more often than not,

an inveterate bench warmer) who has cultivated an acid tongue, which he makes certain
is sufficiently well oiled and garnished with
poison to rattle the enemy with a stream of
malicious and deprecating statements. He flays
and plays on his rivals' well-established frailties,
insults their abilities—or lack of them—and
maintains a steady, repetitious, cacophonic
volley of abuse, often from the start of a game
to the finish.

This behavior, which in polite company
would be frowned on as boorish and indelicate,
is actually encouraged by some big-league
managers. Paul Richards, for instance, insists
that "considerable effectiveness is gained at
times through jockeying." The object, entirely
legitimate in a highly competitive medium like
baseball, is to throw an opponent off balance,
derail his equilibrium, provoke his temper and
thus theoretically rob him of his full efficiency.
In short, it is designed to annoy the hell out of
a man, make him blow his top and pierce even
the thickest rhinoceros hides extant.

The practice is as old as or older than
Frankie Frisch, who, in his day, was one of the
most eloquent practitioners in the trade. When
Frisch managed the rambunctious and high-
spirited St. Louis Cardinals' Gashouse Gang
in the 1934 World Series against the Detroit
Tigers, an edict forbidding freedom of speech
would have canceled out the series. Only the
other day, Frisch, who is still using his voice as
a baseball announcer and sought-after racon-
teur in and around New York, declared:

"If you spot a weakness in the other fellow's
lineup, you're a fool not to go at it. Jockeying
might even win you a game. If a fellow doesn't
like it and shows it, he's going to get it more.
The best thing to do, if you're being jockeyed,
is to keep your mouth shut."

In John McGraw's era it was not unusual for
managers (McGraw, in particular, was reported
to have appropriated money for the practice)
to hire private detectives in order to learn
about the personal vexations of enemy pitchers. McGraw's players would then be encouraged to dwell lovingly and loudly on the afflic-
tions, whatever they might be. On more than
one occasion, hurlers, driven to distraction by
the jockeying, had to be removed from games,
for ineffectiveness or irritability.

Things got so bad in the 1914 World Series—
after George Stallings, manager of the miracle
Boston Braves, had hired Oscar Dugey, a part-
time infielder, to document the temperamental
weaknesses of Connie Mack's Athletics—that the
Braves copped the title in four straight, leaving

Connie such a nervous wreck that he was only
able to live another forty-two years. However,
Mr. Mack was heard to express the opinion at
the time that "the best team didn't win this
Series." Obviously Stallings' strategy—"ignore
'em or insult 'em"—had worked to perfection,
at least when it depended on the "insult 'em"
phase.

Much of the jockeying in the modern game is
benign, rather than below the belt. It is good-
natured and humorous, if unsubtle, and isn't
calculated to start mass riots or decide close
pennant races. It is routine, inoffensive baseball badinage and happens often to be every
bit as enjoyable to the victim as it is to the
villain.

Yogi Berra, who is singularly well endowed
physically, making him a susceptible butt for
jokes about monkeys, apes, and assorted
simians, has always taken the riding in stride
and without any noticeable decline in batting
average. After several seasons of tuning in on
comments like, "How long did it take Frank
Buck to trap you?" "Don't step on his tail" (directed at batters preparing to step up to the
plate with Berra catching), "How does your
wife like living in a tree, Yogi?" Yogi was
moved to remark, in solemn rebuttal, "Aw, nobody wins games with their face."

Two decades ago, when Vernon "Lefty"
Gomez of the Yankees and Jerome "Dizzy"
Dean of the Cardinals were pitching and pun-
ning their way to notoriety, the game was
livelier and richer for the humor provided by
these two affable gentlemen.

Dizzy was a veritable squad of jockeys, all
by himself. He had a favorite routine of discouraging rival batters. As a batter would amble
to the plate to face him, Dizzy would step off
the mound, shuffle the sixty feet down to his
foe, put a patronizing arm around the batter's
shoulder and say, sotto voce, "Listen to the fans
holler, boy. That's just for you 'n me. They
think we're big stars. But in a few seconds one
of us stars is gonna be a terrible bust."

Then the Great Man would return to the
mound and proceed to strike out his deflated
antagonist.

"Well, it sure ain't me!" Diz would holler, as
the frustrated batter moved for the dugout.

Gomez has been credited with any number
of bon mots during his time as a pitcher. But
he demonstrated several years ago at the spring
training camp of the White Sox that the business world had not robbed his tongue of its
light touch.

Lefty eyed the White Sox as they went

through their muscle-toning chores, and he couldn't help noticing that several veterans were on the field at one time. To commemorate the incident, he screeched from the sidelines, "This club is so old they should carry a priest in the bull pen instead of relief pitchers!"

The remark practically broke up the workout, much to the dismay of Marty Marion, who was managing the Chicagoans at the time. But it was innocuous and typical—that is, of Gomez.

However, in recent years there have been some notable instances of rough riding, one of the most flagrant and unwarranted examples being the somewhat despicable greeting Jimmy Piersall received upon his release from a Massachusetts mental institution in 1953.

Piersall, the agile defensive genius of the Boston Red Sox, had spent seven months undergoing treatment for a mental breakdown that followed a period of unbearable tension, anxiety and headaches.

When he emerged in 1953 to resume his baseball career it wasn't easy for him to face people again, whether they happened to be players, managers, coaches, umpires or fans. Piersall has insisted that most of the players were decent and sympathetic.

"I was just a guy who'd been away on a routine winter vacation," Jimmy says.

But that is only part of the truth.

For it seems that Jimmy, the center fielder who reaped his greatest dividends by being farmed out to a mental hospital, would just as soon overlook a few of the savage barbs he was subjected to when he made his comeback with the Red Sox.

"Somebody, somewhere, was bound to start yelling insults at me from the stands," says Jimmy in his book, *Fear Strikes Out*, which has since been made into an effective and successful motion picture.

A loud-mouthed Cleveland fan did exactly that, too, on Piersall's second western trip after his return to baseball.

"Hey, screwball, the man in the white suit is gonna get you!" yelled the fan. The pity is that the bench jockeys picked up the refrain, even after Jimmy took it without flinching and shouted back at the fan, "How would you like to make the dough this screwball is making?"

In any dissection of the bench mores of major leaguers, one inevitably approaches the dossier of Leo Ernest Durocher, who came out of the pool halls of West Springfield, Massachusetts, to deliver some of the most stirring public orations in the game's history.

In his first major-league season with the

Yanks in 1928 (Leo played two well-forgotten games with New York in 1925), Durocher immediately established himself as the flashiest dresser and the loudest mouth in—or out—of baseball.

He had been around only a few weeks when he singled out the ferocious-tempered, all-time-great Ty Cobb for his specialty. One afternoon Leo gave Ty the hip as Cobb scooted around second. Having slowed up the player who still rated as the most fearless base runner of any era, Durocher then threw to third to get his man.

Cobb was enraged by Leo's behavior. He threatened to crush his life out after fracturing Leo's skull. The cocky rookie wouldn't be intimidated. He yelled his defiance from the bench.

"Hit the armchair, you over-aged bum! Next time I'll stuff the ball down your throat," Leo bellowed at the forty-two-year-old veteran.

Delighted with his antics, Leo's fellow Yanks urged the dandy little shortstop on, supplying him with stories about Cobb's penuriousness, his tight hold on a dime. For weeks Cobb—and the Yanks—were forced to listen to his harangues. When Cobb tried to lure Leo under the stands for a fight, the older Yankees intervened. "Whaddaya tryin' to do, hit a kid?" they said.

George Moriarty, manager of the Tigers, became so unsettled by Durocher's repartee that he flung a ball at Leo's head from a distance of approximately twenty-five feet. Durocher proved on the spot why he was so highly regarded as a fielder. He speared the ball in one bare hand and, in the same fluid motion, heaved it right back at the enraged Moriarty, who suffered a wound, not only to his shin, but to his pride, as a result of the incident.

Two years prior to Durocher's contretemps, the Cleveland Cry-Baby Rebellion of 1940 had exposed the lachrymose Indians to a collective tongue-lashing around the American League, that some folks insist cost the Cleveland team a flag.

Oscar Vitt, the Cleveland manager, had a penchant for ridiculing his players and berating them in public. Despite his antics, his team was considered strong enough to win the pennant and did, in fact, lead the league with a healthy margin for a good part of the season. However, in June the Cleveland players, presumably led by such worthies as Mel Harder and Robert William Andrew Feller, petitioned the management for Vitt's release. "Get rid of Vitt and we'll take the pennant. Keep him and we'll probably lose it," was the gist of the peculiar proposal presented to President Alva Bradley.

The result of the demand, which was unique in baseball history, was that Vitt retained his job and the players did exactly what they had promised—lost the pennant in the last few days of the season.

However, long before the pennant was fumbled, the Cleveland players experienced a public humiliation without precedent. The fans got on them in every city in the League, as grocery stores shot their prices sky-high on fruit, eggs and tomatoes, which replaced weapons in the hands of the addicts.

Rival benches were active as beehives and as each day went by new stunts were dreamed up to deprecate the Indians. Baby carriages were wheeled onto the diamond, the top of the Cleveland dugout invariably became the roosting place for diapers, bottles and other infant accessories, and entire teams would line up facing the Indians, their fingers across their throats, in the traditional sign of the "choke-up."

Jimmy Dykes, then manager of the White Sox, has always been reluctant to pass up an opportunity for the needle. He thrived on the cry-baby ordeal. One day he would ask Bob Feller if he could go warm up his bottle. Another afternoon he would make life miserable for Ken Keltner, the third baseman who had deemed his regular baseball pay insufficient for his standard of living and had thereby applied for unemployment insurance during the off season.

"I can remember Keltner walking down to take his position at third," Dykes recalls. "I'd wait for him to take a kick out of the bag. When he did, I'd point to it and yell, 'Look under it, Ken. You might find some loose dough there.' "

But as Dykes himself confesses, that was nothing compared to the day-to-day-needling to which the entire club was exposed.

According to no less an authority than Jackie Robinson, racial and religious jockeying has been decreasing. "Ten years ago, when I first joined the Dodgers, it was much worse than it is now," says the former Brooklyn star, who blazed the way for fifty-five of his fellow Negroes to occupy places today on major-league rosters.

"Most of the Negroes in the majors have great pride in themselves and in their race," adds Robinson. "They would resent below-the-belt jockeying—and so do many white players, who don't like to hear it, especially when their own team has Negroes playing for them."

The abuse Robinson was forced to take in his pioneering months has possibly never been equaled in its intensity or viciousness. He stood it only because he was determined to make good and because he was convinced that others after him would have it easier. The moral support given him by people like Branch Rickey, Peewee Reese, Hank Greenberg and Lee Handley helped him immeasurably, too.

Evidence that the millennium may really be at hand in baseball is contained in one of the last incidents in Robinson's career.

When Jackie thought he heard pitcher Lew Burdette who is also suspected of throwing spitballs at crucial moments, calling him "watermelon," he checked with teammate Gil Hodges for confirmation of his hearing power, then chucked a ball at Burdette's head in the Milwaukee dugout. He also challenged Burdette to a fight. When Burdette turned down the invite, Robinson accused him of being gutless.

The next time Brooklyn met the Braves, Burdette voluntarily approached Robinson and informed him that the "watermelon" remark was directed only at the size of Robinson's waistline. "I don't ride a man about his race. I'm hard in the dugout. But not on things like that," he said.

When asked if Burdette's sincerity could be trusted, Robinson said he thought the man was being "one hundred per cent honest."

The World Series that was renowned above all for the quality of the raillery was the 1934 joust between the Cards and the Tigers. The entire seven games were marked by unmatched beefing, crabbing, barking and name-calling, with Greenberg and Schoolboy Rowe coming in for more than their share of derision. Rowe had the misfortune to have appeared on a radio broadcast right before the Series, in which he slipped in a domestic note ("How'm I doin', Edna") to his wife. The Gashousers never let him forget it.

When Al Schacht, the comedian-restaurateur who was once a big-time hurler, worked out with the Tiger infield of Greenberg, Charlie Gehringer, Bill Rogell and Marv Owen in the minutes before the opening game of the Series, the Cards shouted; "That makes five clowns in the infield."

Strangely, the Tigers' inner quartet *did* behave like harlequins defensively through most of that fall classic, so the jockeying may have had impact.

The Yanks, who have hardly ever had to rely on the uttered, muttered or shouted phrase to win games, have done remarkably well at the pastime when the situation has warranted it. They rode freshman southpaw Cliff Melton of the Giants clear out of the Polo Grounds in the 1937 World Series. Prior to the Series, Melton had dropped some disparaging remarks about the Yanks to the press. The price of his indiscretion was an acid barrage of jockeying that dwelt primarily on the size of Cliff's ears, which were bigger than punching bags.

The Yank jockeys pleaded with the umps to "paint his ears green so we'll have a decent background for our hitters."

Lefty Gomez gazed in horror at Cliff's hearing apparatus and yelled, "Look, a taxi, with both doors wide open!"

Cliff failed in two tries in that Series, and never regained his frosh form. But that may have been strictly coincidental.

Jockeying is such an integral phase of baseball that players sometimes even subject their own mates to a dose of it.

More than fifty years ago the Giants, under McGraw, had a midget pitcher from Kansas named Charlie Faust. An odd ball with practically nothing on the ball, Faust was kept around for laughs, for his gullibility, and because he was a natural butt for his own team's jokes. The Giants would load Charlie's suitcase with bricks, insist he sleep with his pitching arm in a hammock, and send him on false errands.

"Go get the can of striped paint," they howled at Charlie, and the poor guy would do their bidding. Only the kindness and rescue work of Christy Mathewson, a great pitcher as well as a gentleman among hooligans, prevented Faust from being driven half mad by his conscienceless pals.

When little Phil Rizzuto connected for his first home run in the Yankee Stadium some years ago, not a soul was on hand to greet him when he cruised into home plate. Neither was there anyone on the bench. In the trade this form of ostracism is dubbed "the freeze."

After Rizzuto had huddled in a corner of the empty dugout for a couple of minutes, the irrepressible Gomez appeared and remarked, "Well, has anything interesting happened?"

In Casey Stengel's book, Billy Martin is a "fresh kid who's always sassing everybody and getting away with it." In everybody's book,

Martin is a pest, a vicious jockey, and perhaps the damnedest rider of them all.

But when Martin, who is beset with all manner of actual and psychosomatic ailments—including hypertension, anxiety, insomnia and acute melancholia—first arrived with the champs, they rode him unmercifully. Typically, Martin gave it right back. "Some couldn't take it so good, either," he recalls. "After a while they left me alone."

Martin, who saw fit to have his nose remodeled along more aquiline lines, is called "Barrymore" by the bench jockeys—when they choose to call him anything printable.

In any pantheon of modern dugout wolves, Martin's name would have to be listed. So would Jimmy Dykes, now a coach with Birdie Tebbetts' Redlegs.

In a recent sampling of player opinion on the subject, the following men won the nod from their fellow players as the most effective jockeys: Vic Wertz of the Indians; Billy Loes of the Orioles; Martin and Vic Power of the Athletics; Norm Zauchin and Jimmy Piersall of the Red Sox; Clint Courtney of the Senators; Steve Gromek and Frank House of the Tigers; Nellie Fox of the White Sox, and Whitey Ford of the Yanks.

The National League nominations were: Lew Burdette and Red Schoendienst of the Braves; Walker Cooper of the Cardinals; Gale Wade and Clyde McCullough of the Cubs; Don Newcombe and Gil Hodges of the Dodgers; Dusty Rhodes and Danny O'Connell of the Giants; Solly Hemus of the Phillies; Dick Cole of the Pirates (he is now with the Braves), and Joe Nuxhall and Johnny Temple of the Redlegs.

In truth, nobody really would want to legislate bench jockeying out of existence. First, it couldn't be done; and second, even when it gets low-down and dirty, it's a valuable physical release for keyed-up competitors.

After all, as that estimable former jockey, Billy Werber, once stated, "Players burn up more nervous energy during a game than a stoker feeding a furnace."

Multiply that by 400 major-league players, and any number of ulcerated managers and coaches, and you have a quantum of energy that collectively might even win a pennant for the Washington Senators this year.

Los Angeles fans—*attention!*

The Dodger They Don't Boo

BILL ROEDER

As FINAL proof that anything can happen in Brooklyn, it can be stated positively that the fans once booed Gil Hodges in Ebbets Field. There is evidence in the form of newspaper clippings which relate how the strapping Hodges brought a storm on his head by sliding hard into a little Cincinnati second baseman named Bobby Adams. The fans promptly and concertedly let Gil have it. They booed him on the spot, they booed him every time he came to bat for the rest of that game, they booed him every inning as he left the dugout to take the field, and after the game they were still booing him through the frosted clubhouse window.

Of course, this happened in 1948, before Hodges had been around long enough to be appreciated. All the fans knew was that a big guy had crashed into a little guy, and they reacted accordingly. Since then, there has been no recorded instance of a harsh word, syllable or gesture being directed at Hodges, whose fame as a slugging, fancy-fielding first-baseman is almost equaled by his reputation as the Dodger who's never been booed.

Indeed, the fans go out of their way not to boo him. Gil went hitless through seven tortured games of the 1952 World Series. Here was futility of record-breaking proportions, and the Dodgers lost the Series in the bargain, but from the reception Hodges drew you might have thought he was winning every game all by himself.

Every time he stepped up to the plate, the crowd broke out in applause, hand-clapping, cheering, shouts of encouragement that became louder and warmer the longer the streak of helplessness persisted. Nor did it end with the World Series. When the next season opened, Gil was still in his slump and the fans remained faithfully and demonstratively at his side. The season was three weeks old before he hit his first home run. Did the fans give it

the sarcastic, side-of-the-mouth, obviously derisive cheer that traditionally greets the harried hero when he finally does something right? No, sir. They gave it a delighted, full-throated standing ovation.

Such popularity must be deserved, but why? As a general rule, it can probably be said that a ballplayer's crowd appeal is determined in equal measure by his performance and by what the public knows of his personality. In Hodges' case, the accent on his personality is far greater. Basically, he is liked because so many people have heard what a fine fellow he is.

While Hodges has a record to prove that he is one of the most productive hitters of his era— no other current player, for example, drove in 100 or more runs for seven straight years, as Gil did—he never has been regarded as a great hitter by the Brooklyn fans.

For one thing, he has run into too many prolonged slumps. For another, he has usually been overshadowed by one or more teammates. There was Jackie Robinson, one of the outstanding offensive players of all time. There is Duke Snider, who will usually hit more home runs than Hodges and wind up with a better average. Roy Campanella in his best years was a little more consistent than Gil and a lot more spectacular.

Hodges is one of the few players in history who hit four home runs in one game. He did that at Ebbets Field in 1950 against the Boston Braves. And, going into this season, he had hit 11 grand slams, only one short of the National League record shared by Rogers Hornsby and Ralph Kiner. Even so, he has had a history of being bothered by curve balls low and away, and if you asked any Dodger fan for his opinion of Hodges, strictly as a ballplayer, the answer probably would be: "I only wish he could hit more consistently."

This spring he was hitting more consistently;

was leading the league, in fact, through the early season. His explanation, given as usual in a self-deprecating way, was that he was having a little luck poking those outside pitches to right field. The fans would be pleased and surprised if Gil managed to hit that well all season. But if he didn't, they wouldn't stop liking him.

For that matter it has been theorized that to some extent Hodges' hold on the Brooklyn public can be traced to those slumps of his that rouse sympathy by illustrating a lack of perfection. One of the first Flatbush idols, Babe Herman, could hit the long ball with the best of them but, deservedly or not, he was much better known and loved for doing dumb things. Another, Dixie Walker, qualified for endearment partly for his clutch hitting but no less for the fact that he had drifted to the Dodgers as a washed-up, banged-up, taped-up old American Leaguer from whom very little was expected.

Garry Schumacher of the Giant front office covered the Dodgers as a baseball writer for many years and had an unsurpassed grasp of the native emotions. Garry always contended that Joe DiMaggio would never have been taken to those native hearts had he played for Brooklyn. Why? "He's too good."

There is one thing about Hodges that sets him apart from all other Dodgers of the present and the recent past, and it undoubtedly contributes immensely to his store of good will. He lives in Brooklyn all year 'round. He is from Indiana, but he married a Brooklyn girl, bought a house in Flatbush and lives there with his wife and three children. During the winter he usually takes a job selling cars at a downtown Brooklyn automobile agency.

That is important for two reasons. Brooklyn is becoming more and more an unwanted locality, a place that people tend to move out of as soon as they can afford a house in the suburbs. There is an evident bitterness about this in the people who do stay on, a resentfulness that the tide is pulling away from them, and it bolsters their pride when someone as prominent as Hodges, and as well off, settles in their midst.

The second reason is that by being on hand throughout the year, Hodges can't help but let the fans see how likable he is. They run into him out walking with his children, shopping in the neighborhood supermarket, dining with his wife in a local restaurant. The people talk to him whether they know him or not and Gil always has a smile and a pleasant word.

This gets around. You can be in a group on Long Island or in Westchester or Manhattan, talking baseball, and if Hodges is mentioned it's surprising how often somebody will say, "You know, he must be an awfully nice guy. There's a fellow in my office whose father lives in Brooklyn, and the father can't say enough good about Hodges. Says he sees him around and you can kid him or talk to him about anything and he's just wonderful."

And Hodges gets around himself. The Dodgers have a promotion man named Jim Murray who sends ballplayers out to make talks at church suppers and club meetings all over Brooklyn and Long Island, and here is what Mr. Murray says about Hodges: "If we could accommodate one tenth of the people who want him, he'd be too busy to handle even that much. He's No. 1 on our list. Everywhere I go it's 'Can we get Gil out? Can we get Gil?' He's kind of a quiet fellow, not an orator, but when they start asking questions he becomes one of the most graceful and comfortable conversationalists you'd ever want to hear. He's kind and gentle, and no matter how embarrassing the question he has the knack of turning it into a gem."

Every baseball writer welcomes an approachable player like Hodges, and that unquestionably is another source of his popularity. Fans are continually reading or hearing over the air some modest or amusing or gracious quote from Hodges. His admirable personality shines through in these little quotes and the collected weight of them can't help but create a flattering effect.

Once, in a discussion of his batting accomplishments, it was pointed out to Gil that while he wasn't doing badly for a National Leaguer, he certainly couldn't hope to break any of the awesome slugging records set by the late Lou Gehrig. Gil frowned thoughtfully. "I'd like to, of course," he said, "but Gehrig had one terrific advantage."

He paused until somebody picked it up. "What do you mean, one advantage?"

Now Gil smiled. "Gehrig was a better ballplayer," he said.

Traveling with the Dodgers in a plane several years ago, Gil was hungry but when the stewardess brought a steak dinner he turned it down, explaining that as a Roman Catholic he couldn't eat meat on Friday. A teammate, also a Catholic, overheard and advised Gil to accept the steak. "I'm eating mine," said the teammate. "I've heard that there's an automatic dispensation when you're in a plane and they're only serving meat. Go ahead, eat it."

The Chicago White Sox of 1919. Here they're smiling. They became known as the Black Sox when eight of their players were charged with having conspired to throw the World Series to Cincinnati.

This is happiness incarnate—a whole city jumps for joy as the Braves come to Milwaukee . . . first of five franchise shifts in the past decade.

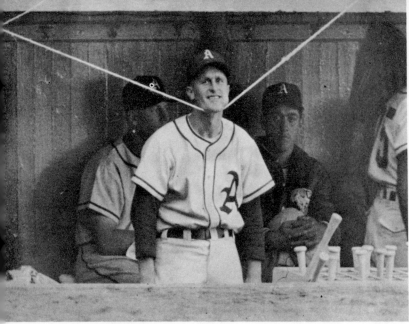

. . . telling the umpire he is a choke-up .

BENCH JOCKEYS   Four different expressions of the art of the razzberry.

. . . breaking into song . . .

International News

. . . greetings en masse . . .

more to tell the umpire. This time it's raining.

United Press

International N

The flamboyant St. Louis Cardinals of 1934—left to right, Dean, Durocher, Orsatti, Delancey, Collins, Medwick, Frisch, Rothrock, Martin.

Spokesmen were Frisch and Durocher, left to right here on either side of that sad-looking fellow with the mask on his face.

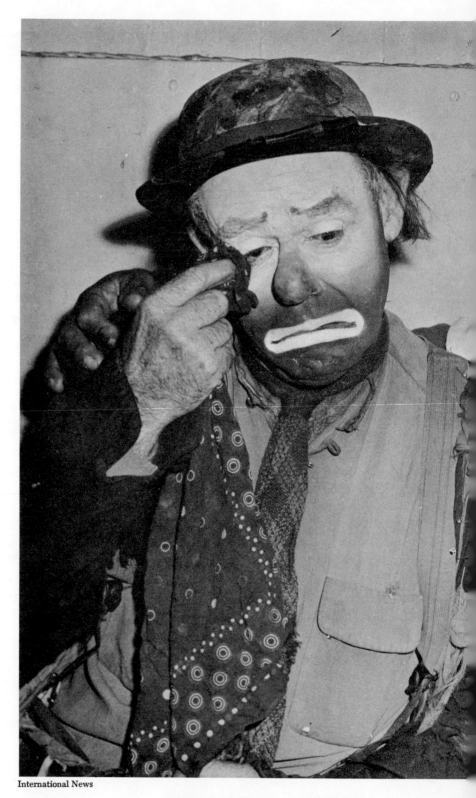

LAST GAME IN BROOKLYN

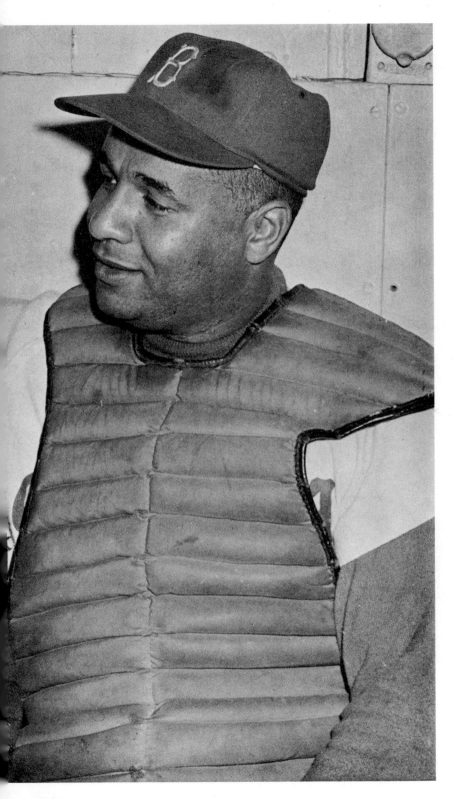

And Emmett Kelly, the great clown, shares the grief of the moment with Roy Campanella, on the bench before the Dodgers' last Ebbets Field appearance. Short months afterward, Campanella encountered the near-fatal automobile accident that ended his career.

"Thou hast eyes to see, and see not!"

300H

Gil turned to the window and peered up at the sky. "Uh, uh," he said. "We're a little too close to headquarters."

He loves to fool around on the ball field, but only in what he considers the proper time and place, such as during batting and infield practice. Just for the fun of it, he'll sometimes swing left-handed in batting practice and he has often hit balls over the right-field fence in Brooklyn. Or he'll work on his pitching. He likes to throw a knuckleball, and there are those who claim that the Hodges knuckler is as tricky as the ones thrown by actual pitchers in the major leagues.

Gil likes to turn almost any situation into an outlet for his deadpan style of needling. One day, waiting his turn to hit in batting practice, he was idly swinging the bat like a golf club, chipping into the dirt at an imaginary ball. A complaint came from Rube Walker, who was inside the cage catching. "Hey, Gil," he said. "You're getting sand in my eyes."

Gil shot him a surprised look. "Of course I am," he said, and went on chipping. "You see, Rube, I've picked out a spot on the green, and you're it. Glad to hear I'm on the target."

As he flicked the bat again, Walker bellowed a protest. Gil adjusted his grip, staring intently at the ground as he got ready to hit still another chip. "Rube," he said patiently, "try not to talk while I'm swinging. You can just let me know when I miss."

Peewee Reese lay on the trainer's table having a foot wound treated. A man sliding into second had spiked him when Peewee took a throw that drew him unavoidably into the runner's path. Hodges clucked disappointedly. "You mean to say that after all your years in the game—probably more years than I've lived—you haven't learned how to make that play without getting hit? That's an interesting weakness, at that. What would you say accounts for it, poor reflexes or lack of intelligence?"

Reese gave him the hard stare. "You were a shortstop in high school, weren't you?" he said. "Why don't you tell me how to make the play?"

Gil looked innocent. "Gee, I only wish I could tell you," he said, "because you obviously need help, but it must have been pure instinct with me. I never got hit and never gave any thought to the mechanics of the play, it came so naturally. Even as a kid I could do it perfectly. And you still have trouble with it, you say?"

The public was a little surprised, but those who knew him weren't, when Hodges turned clown during the Dodgers' tour of Japan last fall. This was just the right theater for his type of funmaking, a place where the games didn't mean anything and where the audience, never having seen anything of the sort, would be sure to get a kick out of it.

Gil was playing left field, and what he did was mimic the styles of the various batters, the deliveries of the pitchers, the action in plays that had just been completed. It was unrehearsed and untutored pantomime, done at first on the spur of the moment. But soon it was being received so enthusiastically and publicized so prominently that Gil turned it into a regular feature.

When the Dodgers returned from Japan, the first thing everyone wanted to know was whether Hodges would stage his comedy in regular season games. His answer was typical. "Not intentionally," he said.

The only side show that Gil permits himself in a serious ball game is his running exchange of kisses with his wife, Joan, whenever he hits a home run at Ebbets Field. This has been going on since a night in 1950 when Gil, taking a tip from his wife to break a slump, brought his feet closer together and got immediate results. He hit a home run and as he crossed the plate he blew a kiss to Joan, who sits in a front-row box. She blew one back and they've been doing it ever since.

Except in fun, Hodges is no braggart but he has made one prediction about himself that has stood up for six years and that still seems as safe as government bonds. It is that he will never be thrown out of a game. Only once, in fact, has he had anything approaching a major dispute with an umpire, and it wasn't a very close approach.

That once was in 1952, when the Dodgers believed they had Eddie Stanky picked off first base and Bill Stewart called him safe. Hodges raised his voice momentarily to object to the decision and Charlie Dressen, managing the Dodgers at the time and constantly pleading with Hodges to tell the umpires off once in a while, was so delighted that he later tried to slip Gil a $10 bill in a handshake. Gil wouldn't take it.

"I suppose arguing should be done," he says. "It won't change many decisions, if any, but maybe it does keep the umpires on their toes. Still, if you're not built that way it's tough to make yourself get on them, and I guess I'm not built that way."

The way Hodges is built discourages fights with other players. He will never be the aggressor and he's a little too big and strong, and for that matter too inoffensive, to be challenged. Any time there's trouble on the field, even in a general commotion as hotheaded as the one that flared up between the Braves and Dodgers at Ebbets Field in July, Gil's role is strictly that of peacemaker.

In 1949, the Dodgers played an exhibition against their farm club at Fort Worth and Dee Fondy, then with Fort Worth, got into a hassle with Peewee Reese. Before any punches could be thrown, Hodges moved in to pull Fondy away and did such a thorough job of it that he lifted the 6-3, 190-pounder clear off the ground. It was an impressive feat as well as a noble one but Gil still doesn't like to talk about it. "Dee is such a nice fellow," he says.

Showing up someone else is not in Gil's nature, but when the laugh is on him he never minds it. Along with everyone else who heard it, he got a chuckle out of a loud, sad-voiced observation that came baying out of the stands in a rich Brooklyn accent at a time when a certain movie was making the rounds. It was also a time when Hodges was advancing to the plate in his hitless World Series.

"Here he comes," said the voice. "Gil Hodges—Da Quiet Man."

Around that same time, Hodges was receiving hundreds of letters, telegrams and packages containing expressions of sympathy, best wishes, good-luck charms and suggestions for breaking his slump from fans who wanted him to know they were pulling for him. There was only one unfavorable letter. "Fellow sounded as if he might have dropped a little money," Gil said.

Even that fellow, if he showed up at the park, kept a civil tongue in his head. No one booed, not then and not the next season when Hodges had so much difficulty getting started, and Gil will be forever grateful for the support he got.

"I'd never have made it if the fans hadn't stuck by me," he says. "They could have booed me out of the park. I've had days since when I deserved to be booed, but they've been good to me."

In the spring of 1953 a Flatbush priest told his parishioners at Sunday mass that it was too warm for a sermon. "Go home, keep the commandments and say a prayer for Gil Hodges," said the priest, who later explained that he had never met Gil but had heard what a decent fellow he was and that he was having his troubles at the plate.

Gil Hodges Night, held at Ebbets Field in July of this year, got rolling through the efforts of Jo Ann Duffy, a 15-year-old schoolgirl from Hewlett, L. I. As president of the Gil Hodges fan club, Jo Ann conceived the idea for a Night and wrote letters to merchants all over Brooklyn, asking support and receiving it in heaping measure. Among the donations: space on 85 billboards in Brooklyn advertising Gil Hodges Night.

The fans like Gil so much they once tried to elect him when he wasn't even running. In 1955 the Brooklyn Junior Chamber of Commerce decided to select an Outstanding Young Man of Brooklyn. A committee was to make the choice, but when baseball writer Dick Young mentioned the award in his column and suggested that it go to Hodges, thousands of readers sent in "votes" for Gil. The civic leader who won the award was eminently entitled to it, but no more so than Hodges in the eyes of his fans. Maybe one of these days they'll make him the Outstanding Young Man of Los Angeles.

HERE, from the smash musical *Damn Yankees,* are the lyrics of one of the numbers written by Richard Adler and the late Jerry Ross. "The Game" is not so well-known perhaps as some other pieces from the show, like "Heart" or "Whatever Lola Wants," but it fills beautifully that delightful plateau between the patter song and the chorus number, and is a favorite among those who have seen the show.

The Game

JERRY ROSS *and* RICHARD ADLER

ROCKY:

No drinking, no women—no late hours, no women. (*Music*)
You got to keep your mind on the game.

(*Sings*)

We've got to think about the game!

ALL:

The game, the game!
We've got to think about the game,
The game, the game!
Booze and broads may be great,
Though they're great they'll have to wait,
While we think about the game!

ROCKY:

There was that waitress back in Kansas City
Built for comfort, dumb but pretty!

ALL:

Yeah? Yeah?

ROCKY:

Man, her perfume sure did smell sweet,
Got her up to my hotel suite!

ALL:

Yeah? Yeah?

ROCKY:

She killed a pint of gin more or less,
The lights were low and she slips off her dress!

ALL:

Yeah? Yeah? Yeah? Yeah?

ROCKY:

But then I thought about the game!

ALL:

The game, the game!

ROCKY:

Oh, yes I thought about the game!

ALL:

The game, the game!

ROCKY:

Though I got the lady high,
I just left her high and dry,
'Cause I thought about the game!

ALL:

He thought about the game!

SMOKEY:

There was the Pullman car that I got lost in,
On a sleeper out of Boston!

ALL:

Yeah? Yeah?

SMOKEY:

Compartment doors all look the same there,
Walked in one and there's this dame there!

ALL:

Yeah? Yeah?

SMOKEY:

Blonde, and stacked, and absolutely bare,
And nothin' separatin' us but air!

ALL:

Yeah? Yeah? Yeah? Yeah?

SMOKEY:

But then I thought about the game!

ALL:

The game, the game!

SMOKEY:

Oh, yes I thought about the game,

ALL:

The game, the game!

SMOKEY:

Though my heart said stay for tea,
All I said was pardon me!
'Cause I thought about the game!

ALL:

He thought about the game!

MICKEY:

When a chick gives you the eye, remember—

ALL:

Abstain!

LOWE:

When you're dyin' for some rye, remember—

ALL:

Refrain!

HENRY:

If you're losin' at crap and the clock says it's
eleven,
And suddenly each roll you roll—"huh"—comes
up a seven,
And you're in the kind of dive where men are
men,

ALL:

Be polite, say good night, you should be in bed
by ten!

SMOKEY:

When your mother bakes you cakes, remember—

ALL:

Stay thin!

ROCKY:

When you're kissin' till it aches, remember—

ALL:

Don't give in!
Every rule we shall obey to be sure,
Cause to win we've gotta stay good and pure,
Good and pure! Mumm.

SMOKEY:

Hey, Rock, remember those twins we took a
ride with,
Operatin' side by side with,

ALL:

Yeah? Yeah?

SMOKEY:

We're out of gas three miles from Philly,

ROCKY:

The night is warm, the sky's a dilly,

ALL:

Yeah? Yeah?

ROCKY:

So I suggest we sleep beneath a tree,

SMOKEY:

No one's there but Rock, the chicks and me.

ALL:

Yeah? Yeah? Yeah? Yeah?

SMOKEY:

So there we are, lyin' side by side under the
tree.

ROCKY:

Four minds with a single thought.

SMOKEY:

I look at my girl.

ROCKY:

I look at mine.

SMOKEY:

Then with one fell swoop—

(*Boys clasp hands over* SMOKEY'S *and* ROCKY'S
mouths.)

ALL:

But then they thought about the game!
The game, the game!

ROCKY *and* SMOKEY:

Oh, yes we thought about the game!

ALL:

The game, the game!
To our women one and all,
We will see you in the fall,
But for now we've got to stall
Every dame!
And think about the game!
Think about the game,
Think about the, think about the, think about
the, think about the,
Think about the game!

(*Blackout*)

Is this a profile of Frank Robinson, of whom you've heard, or of George Poles, of whom you haven't? Well. Whether you ponder "juvenile delinquency" or not, you should get a boot out of this one. It appeared in 1957.

They Gave Him a Bat

JOHN M. ROSS

FRANK ROBINSON might have reached for a zip gun or a switchblade knife. He might have followed the well-worn trail that led from the tough West Side of Oakland, California, to reform school or the penitentiary. Some of the kids he grew up with did take that road.

But young Frank found another one. He followed it to a playground, and someone put a baseball bat in his hands. It was love at first sight. Today, Frank and his bat have followed the road to left field for the Cincinnati Redlegs —a road that may lead, by September, to Cincinnati's first pennant in 17 years.

Last year, when he was only 20, Frank equaled the all-time rookie record by cracking 38 home runs; led the National League in runs scored and game-winning hits; and earned a starting berth in the All-Star game. At the end of the season, sports writers unanimously voted him the league's Rookie of the Year. This was merely confirming what opposing pitchers had been discovering all season.

"That kid's wrists are so strong," Redlegs manager "Birdie" Tebbetts says, "he can take a full cut at the pitch and stop right in the middle of his swing. Ted Williams is the only other hitter I've seen do that regularly."

His overnight triumph has left the boyish, mild-mannered Negro a little breathless, but unaffected. He is quick to credit others.

"Mr. Poles—well, Mr. Poles and Mom— they're the ones who got me this far," Robinson explains. "Mr. Poles started me in baseball at the playground. He taught me most of the things I know about the game. Mom made it possible for me to stay interested in baseball— which was pretty important, too.

"There were 10 of us children at home, and

things were a little rough at times. We didn't have much money, but Mom somehow would scrape up money for a glove or carfare to a game. She didn't know much about baseball, but she knew it kept kids out of mischief."

There is a note of reverence in Frank's voice when he talks about George Poles. A former outfielder for the San Francisco Seals, Poles has lured countless boys off the hectic streets and turned them toward baseball careers. He coaches more than half a dozen sandlot, American Legion and high-school teams.

Robinson was 11 when he wandered into San Francisco's Bushrod Park and crossed Poles's path. By the time he was 13, he was the right fielder on Poles's Bill Erwin Post team— the only club ever to win the American Legion's Little World Series two years in a row. And, still under Poles's wing at McClymonds High, Frank made Oakland's all-scholastic team for three straight years.

A platoon of major-league scouts was in hot pursuit of the stars of the Erwin Post team when Robinson joined the club. The Chicago White Sox landed the team's catcher, J. W. Porter, for a $65,000 bonus. The St. Louis Browns went after the pitcher, Charlie Beamon. In fact, nine of the 16 boys on Poles's 1950 team graduated to the professional ranks. Robinson was the youngest—and the skinniest—but at 14 he had no less than five big-league scouts on his trail. He signed with the Redlegs for a $3,000 bonus when he finished high school.

He had a fine season with Ogden, Utah, and a sizzling campaign with Columbia, South Carolina, before the Redlegs decided to bring him to their 1955 training camp. For two weeks he answered every test. He seemed a cinch to move up to the big time. Suddenly his express train was derailed. He woke up one morning with a sore arm.

"I thought my career was finished right there," Frank recalls. "I went to 12 doctors and each one had a different diagnosis. The Redlegs sent me back to Columbia and the pain was so bad I not only couldn't throw but my batting average dropped to .190."

In desperation he junked all medical advice and took matters into his own hands. Complete rest was his home remedy. He didn't throw a ball for two weeks. The ailment disappeared. In the last month of play, he hit 10 home runs, batted .390, and helped Columbia win 38 of its last 42 games—and the pennant. The next spring he was back with Cincinnati to stay.

Early this season, the mysterious arm ailment made another painful appearance. The alarmists began to mark a large question mark after Robinson's name. But he simply "sat it out" as he had in the minors—and by mid-May he was back in the lineup and among the top 10 hitters in the league. If you believe in omens, remember that pennant in Columbia after his first victory over the ailment.

Frank, 22 next month, already is preparing for the day his baseball career will end. He sends his fat pay check home to his mother. In the off season he studies physical education at Xavier University in Cincinnati. Some day, perhaps, he'll put a bat in some youngster's hands—just as George Poles put one in his.

HERE it is, from *The Babe Ruth Story*—his own account of how things went before he reached the major leagues, as told to his collaborator, the brilliant Bob Considine. The title we use here is the line that starts the story off.

I Was a Bad Kid

———— BABE RUTH *with* BOB CONSIDINE ————

I WAS A BAD KID. I say that without pride, but with a feeling that it is better to say it. Because I live with one great hope in mind: to help kids who now stand where I stood as a boy. If what I have to say here helps even one of them avoid some of my own mistakes or take heart from such triumphs as I have had, this story will serve its purpose.

A lot of wildcat junk has been written about me in my time, along with all the flattering material that has been directed my way by two generations of sports writers. I have often been pictured as a homeless orphan, for one thing. And it has been written that I never had much real interest in baseball, and that it never was hard work for me, because the sport came naturally to me. It has even been written that I never really wanted to be named a big-league manager, because of the responsibilities that go with the job.

In the first place, I was not an orphan. Baseball was, is and always will be to me the best game in the world. I worked hard to learn it, worked even harder to keep playing it after I should have retired. As for the report that I never wanted to be a manager, that's nutty.

My mother, whose maiden name was Schanberg, lived until I was thirteen. My father, George Herman Ruth, lived until my second year in the majors. Few fathers and sons ever looked more alike than my pop and I. My mother was mainly Irish, and was called Kate. My father was of German extraction. It is not true that our family name was Erhardt, as has been repeatedly written. Or Ehrhardt, or Gearhardt.

But I hardly knew my parents. I don't want to make any excuses or place the blame for my shortcomings as a kid completely on persons or places. I might have been hard to handle if I had been born J. Pierpont Morgan V. Yet I probably was a victim of circumstances. I spent most of the first seven years of my life living over my father's saloon at 426 West Camden Street in Baltimore. When I wasn't living over it, I was living in it, studying the rough talk of the longshoremen, merchant sailors, roustabouts and water-front bums. When I wasn't living in it, I was living in the neighborhood streets. I had a rotten start and it took me a long time to get my bearings.

My older brother, John, died before he could be of any help to me. My sister, Mayme, who still lives in Baltimore, never had much control over me. My father and mother, trying to eke out a living for all of us, worked twenty hours a day trying to make a go of the barroom. Whatever I did to bother them was amplified a hundred times by the other cares they had in life.

On June 13, 1902, when I was seven years old, my mother and father placed me in St. Mary's Industrial School in Baltimore. It has since been called an orphanage and a reform school. It was, in fact, a training school for orphans, incorrigibles, delinquents, boys whose homes had been broken by divorce, runaways picked up on the streets of Baltimore and children of poor parents who had no other means of providing an education for them.

I was listed as an incorrigible, and I guess I was. Looking back on my early boyhood, I honestly don't remember being aware of the difference between right and wrong. If my parents had something that I wanted very badly, I took it, but I must have had some dim realization that this was stealing, because it never occurred to me to take the property of anyone besides my immediate family. I chewed tobacco when I was seven, not that I enjoyed it especially, but, from my observations around the saloon, it seemed the normal thing to do.

I was released from St. Mary's in July, 1902, but my parents returned me there in November of the same year. My people moved to a new neighborhood just before Christmas, 1902, and I was released to them again. This time I stayed "out" until 1904, but then they put me back again and I was not released again until 1908. Shortly after my mother died I was returned to St. Mary's once more by my father. He took me back home in 1911 and returned me in 1912. I stayed in the school—learning to be a tailor and shirtmaker—until February 27, 1914. The last item in my "record" at St. Mary's was a single sentence, written in the flowing hand of one of the teachers. It read:

"He is going to join the Balt. Baseball Team."

I believe it is customary for a man whose education was acquired as mine was to look back on those days either with scorn or a wish to conceal the facts. I look back on St. Mary's as one of the most constructive periods of my life. I'm as proud of it as any Harvard man is proud of his school, and, to get crude for a moment, I will be happy to bop anybody on the beezer who speaks ill of it.

It was at St. Mary's that I met and learned to love the greatest man I've ever known. His name was Matthias—Brother Matthias, of the Xaverian Brothers, a Catholic order which concentrates on work among underprivileged boys here and in Europe. The headquarters of the order are in Belgium.

I saw some real he-men in my twenty-two years in organized baseball and in the years since my retirement in 1935. But I never saw one who equaled Brother Matthias. He stood six feet six and weighed about 250. It was all muscle. He seldom raised his voice, a sharp contrast to what I had known at home and in my neighborhood. But when he spoke he meant business. One afternoon at St. Mary's some of the older boys, real hoodlums, started a rough-house in the yard, and for a time it looked like they'd take charge of everything weaker than they were. Brother Matthias was sent for. He was up the road at Mt. St. Joseph's, a fancier place also run by the Xaverians. He leaped in his carriage, laid a whip on the old plug that pulled it and drove very fast to St. Mary's. Then he stood on a piece of high ground in the yard and just looked out over the uprising. A great silence came over the yard, and the trouble stopped immediately. He was that kind of fellow.

It wasn't that we were afraid of Brother Matthias. Some men just have an ability to command respect and love, and Brother Matthias was one of these. He could have been anything he wanted to be in life, for he was good-looking, talented and dynamic. Yet he had taken vows of chastity and poverty and shut himself off from the world. I don't know why, but he singled me out when I first came to St. Mary's. It wasn't that I was his "pet." But he concentrated on me, probably because I needed it. He studied what few gifts I had, and drew these out of me and amplified them. He always built me.

Brother Matthias saw very early that I had some talent for catching and throwing a baseball. He used to back me into a corner of the big yard at St. Mary's and bunt a ball to me by the hour, correcting the mistakes I made with my hands and feet. When I was eight or nine I was playing with the twelve-year-old team. When I was twelve I was with the sixteen-year-olds, and when I was sixteen I played with the best of the many teams we had in school. All because of Brother Matthias.

I think I was born as a hitter the first day I ever saw him hit a baseball. It was during the summer of 1902, my first year at St. Mary's. The baseball of that time was a lump of mush, and by the time St. Mary's got hold of one it was considerably less. But Brother Matthias would stand at the end of the yard, a finger mitt on his left hand and a bat in his right, toss the ball up with his left hand and give it a terrific belt with the bat he held in his right hand. When he felt like it, he could hit it a little harder and make the ball clear the fence in center field. The ball would have to carry at least 350 feet, a terrific knock in those days and a real sock—in view of the fact that it was hit with one hand—even today, when the ball makers are crowding the whole rabbit into each ball.

I would just stand there and watch him, bug-eyed. I had never seen anything like that in my life, nor anyone who was even close to Brother Matthias when it came to manliness, kindness and grace. He became my ideal and I tried, in my feeble way, to do things as he did them. I even learned to walk as he did—with a toeing-in manner which I still have.

Brother Matthias never lost patience with me, no matter what I did. I think he missed me whenever I'd leave St. Mary's, but he'd make a little ceremony out of each "release." He'd tell me that I was on my way, that I'd make a go of things and become a hard-working and industrious part of the community. We'd shake hands and I would head back for the water front. It was the only place I knew. But presently I'd be back again, and though I guess he was disappointed, he never let me know he was. When I'd have trouble with my studies or my tailoring work, he'd help me—though he had a hundred other things to do. He taught me to read and write—and he taught me the difference between right and wrong.

It was Brother Matthias who made me a pitcher. He did it to take me down a notch. I played a lot of baseball at St. Mary's, but I never had any hope of making a career of the game, and I guess I never would have played it professionally if Brother Matthias hadn't put me in my place one day and changed not only my position on the field but the course of my life.

You see, I thought of myself as a pretty good catcher. Brother Matthias and others at the school tried to explain to me that left-handed catchers just do not make sense. But it was the position I liked best and the only one I claimed I could play with any skill. We had no catcher's mitt built for left-handers, of course. We were lucky to have any kind of mitt. I'd use the regular catcher's mitt on my left hand, receive the throw from the pitcher, take off the glove, and throw it back to him left-handed. When I had to throw to a base, trying to catch a runner, I'd throw the glove away, grab the ball with my left hand and heave it with everything I had.

Occasionally Brother Matthias would move me around to various positions, infield and outfield. But the first time he put me in the box to pitch came when I displeased him. He put me in to show me up. I was fourteen or fifteen and we were playing a game in which we were taking a terrific beating. One pitcher after another was being knocked out of the box, and finally it seemed funny to me. When our last pitcher began to be hit all over the lot, I burst out laughing at him. I guess I said a few things too.

Brother Matthias called time immediately and walked over to the catcher's box.

"What are you laughing at, George?" he asked me in his strong but gentle way.

"That guy out there . . . getting his brains knocked out!" I howled, doubled over with laughter.

Brother Matthias looked at me for a long time. "All right, George, you pitch," he said.

I stopped laughing. "I never pitched in my life," I said. "I can't pitch."

"Oh, you must know a lot about it," he said casually. "You know enough to know that your friend isn't any good. So go ahead out there and show us how it's done."

I knew he meant business. I put aside my mask and catcher's mitt, borrowed a finger mitt and walked out to the mound. I didn't even know how to stand on the rubber, or how to throw a curve, or even how to get the ball over the plate.

Yet, as I took the position, I felt a strange relationship between myself and that pitcher's mound. I felt, somehow, as if I had been born out there and that this was a kind of home for me. It seemed to be the most natural thing in the world to start pitching—and to start striking out batters. I even tried a curve or two, and, kidlike, curled my tongue to the corner of my mouth while doing it. It became a habit that I carried into the major leagues with me, and I couldn't break it until Bill Carrigan, my first big-league manager, convinced me that I was "telegraphing" every curve with my tongue.

Brother Matthias saw to it that I didn't get far away from the pitcher's box during my last two seasons at St. Mary's. But he knew there was a time for play and a time for work. I could never duck a class to get to the ball field, never pass up any of the work I had to do in the tailor shop. Tailoring was to be my trade, the trade that would take me away from the water front when, at twenty-one, I would leave St. Mary's and try to make my way in the world. But baseball won out. Through baseball, I got the second break of my life. The first break, it will always seem to me, was the fact that I met Brother Matthias. He was the father I needed.

In this great land today baseball is providing breaks for other youngsters, some of them as hard and unknown as I was. It is a great calling for a boy, but it is only one of countless fields which an American boy can enter and try his hand at.

Too many youngsters today believe that the age of opportunity has passed. They think it ended about the time people stopped reading Horatio Alger. There are more opportunities today than when I was a boy. And all of these opportunities are open to every type of American. The greatest thing about this country is the wonderful fact that it doesn't matter which side of the tracks you were born on or whether you're homeless or homely or friendless. The chance is still there. I know.

There are half a dozen stories about my "discovery." Perhaps several of them are true, for events took place which seemed to have no connection with me and therefore went unnoticed by me.

Rodger Pippen, an old friend and playing mate who is sports editor of the Baltimore

309

News-Post, insists that Jack Dunn, boss of the Baltimore Orioles, and my first boss in organized baseball, signed me without ever seeing me play. Dunn told Pippen in later years that he had made up his mind about me early in 1914, when, during a visit to St. Mary's, he saw me skating on a frozen path in the yard.

Dunnie is supposed to have said, "I can tell from the way that kid handles himself that he's a natural athlete." Perhaps he did see me sliding around the yard. I sure did it often enough, when the ice was right. But if that was so, it made no more impression on me than any casual bystander would make on any other kid concentrating on a bit of fun.

There is another story, told by some of the Xaverian Brothers, that Brother Gilbert, my late old friend and adviser, who at that time was teaching at Mt. St. Joseph's, tried to lift me out of St. Mary's to help his ball club at the Mount get past a tough series. When Brother Paul, superintendent at St. Mary's, refused to let me pitch for the swank school up the road, Brother Gilbert became mad as a hornet and told his friend Paul that, just for that, he'd persuade Jack Dunn to sign me up and remove me not only from St. Mary's "varsity" ball club but from the school itself. That doesn't sound much like Brother Gilbert, but as I say, it is a story that Xaverians still tell.

The other story, which probably has some truth in it, is that Brother Gilbert had promised Jack Dunn to turn over a player to him for the 1914 season, and Dunn, holding him to his promise, asked for a boy named Ford Meadows. Meadows was all for accepting, but Brother Gilbert wanted him to finish his school work at the Mount, and, I guess, also wanted his services that season with the Mount team. Dunn was disappointed, but Brother Gilbert remembered me, urged Dunn to look at me and brought him down to St. Mary's.

Whatever the preliminaries, my first knowledge that I was going to be a professional ballplayer instead of a tailor came in the middle of February, 1914. I was throwing a baseball around the still-frozen yard at St. Mary's—dressed in tight-fitting overalls, by the way—when Brother Gilbert, Dunn, Brother Matthias and Brother Paul appeared. Brother Gilbert introduced Dunn to me.

Dunn had "heard about me," he said, and, to my complete surprise, asked me if I'd like to sign with the Orioles. To me, it was as if somebody had suddenly asked me to join the United States Senate.

I looked up at Brother Matthias for an ex-

planation, and he turned to his superior, Brother Paul. Brother Paul spoke to Dunn.

"George is supposed to stay here at St. Mary's until he's twenty-one," Brother Paul explained. "We would all be happy to see him given an opportunity to prove himself in baseball, but there are certain legal difficulties. You would have to become his legal guardian and be responsible for him."

Dunn looked me over and said he'd take a chance. Then he said, "Now, about his salary —"

"You mean you'd pay me?" I gasped. My voice cracked, and he laughed.

"Sure, George. I'll start you out at six hundred a year."

It made me as lightheaded as if I had been hit on the head with a bat.

"You mean six hundred dollars?" I asked him, unable to believe that I was the one they were talking about.

"That's right," Dunn said. "And if you're as good as Brother Gilbert and the others say you are, you'll be earning more than that in a short time."

I had some great moments in the years that followed that, including the day I signed a contract for $80,000 a year with the New York Yankees. But none of my later thrills ever topped the one I got that cold afternoon at St. Mary's when $600 a year seemed to me to be all the wealth in the world.

Dunn seemed content to wait until he took me to the Orioles' spring training camp at Fayetteville, North Carolina, before he took a good look at me. He signed the papers which made him accountable to a Maryland court for my welfare, and on February 27, 1914, he came to the barred gate at St. Mary's to claim me. What few clothes I had had been packed for days and I had said good-by dozens of times to every boy I knew in the school. Now I said good-by to Brother Matthias, Brother Paul and Brother Albert, who was our sports supervisor. The barred gate was unbolted and I walked out to join Dunn. I was nineteen and the proudest, greenest kid in the country. I stood a little over six feet tall and weighed less than 160. I could chew nails.

I'll never forget the ride to the railroad station the day I left Baltimore. The whole thing still seemed like a dream to me. There were moments when I felt as if I were sitting on the top of the world, and moments when my stomach turned over, wondering if I could make the grade, and fearful that I'd fail and be forced to come back to St. Mary's. And that wasn't because I didn't like St. Mary's. I just couldn't have stood the shame of coming back, after saying good-by and after hearing Brother Matthias tell me in his quiet way, "You'll make it, George."

There were other players on the railroad platform—players who knew each other well, and talked and moved with great confidence. Few of them paid any attention to me. But that didn't matter. The important thing was that I was going with them to spring training camp, and going on a train. It was my first trip out of Baltimore; my first ride on a train.

I couldn't sleep that night, wondering what it would be like in the morning and all the days and months after that. There was another reason I couldn't sleep. One of the older players, a catcher named Ben Egan, had easily talked me into the oldest gag in baseball. He told me, as dumb rookies before and after me have been told, that the little clothes hammock that reached from one end of my berth to the other was put there in order for me to rest my pitching arm. I held the arm up in this uncomfortable position all night because I wanted to act like a pro. The train pulled into Fayetteville early the next morning with the first Oriole injury of the 1914 season. A rookie named Ruth had a cramped and sore pitching arm, thanks to the "rest" he had carefully given it.

I got to some bigger places than Fayetteville after that, but darn few as exciting. It still made me dizzy to think about making $600 for that season. True, there wouldn't be any money coming to me, in $100-a-month payments, until after the regular 1914 International League season began. But I was like a guy who has just been told he's the chief beneficiary of a new will that his 100-year-old rich uncle has just made. The money was as good as mine.

That wasn't all. Jack Dunn took me aside, just before we got to Fayetteville, and slipped me five dollars in advance, and it was more money than I had ever had in my pocket before.

But miracles kept happening. We went to our hotel for breakfast, and while I was studying the menu I heard a player near me say, "Order anything you want, kid. The club pays our feed bills during spring training."

I looked at him, unable to believe it. "You mean I can eat anything I want, and it won't cost me anything?" I asked him.

"Sure. Anything."

I was on my third stack of wheat cakes and third order of ham, and hadn't even come up for air, when I realized that some of the other fellows were watching me. I looked at them silently and kept chewing.

"I wouldn't have believed it if I hadn't seen it," Rodger Pippen, one of the Orioles, said.

I grinned at him. "A guy's got to be strong to play ball," I said.

Dunn dropped by my table and took a look at the ruins. He smiled at me and put his hand on my shoulder. "We've got twenty-seven other fellows on this club, George," he said. "Leave them a little food, will you?"

I got the name Babe during those first few days in Fayetteville. It came out of a couple of incidents. Even in those days Dunn already had a reputation for picking up very young players and developing them. Some of his older players used to kid him a lot about the baby-faced kids he concentrated on, and the first time they saw me with him—on the field—was no exception.

On that day, Dunn practically led me by the hand from the dressing room to the pitcher's box. I was as proud of my Oriole's uniform as I had been of my first long pants. Maybe I showed that pride in my face and the way I walked.

"Look at Dunnie and his new Babe!" one of the older players yelled.

That started it, I guess. But the clincher came a few days later. It had got to be a joke, the way I walked around wide-eyed all the time. I used to get up at five in the morning and walk down to the station to see the trains go through, but I always got back to the hotel in time to be first in line for the opening of the dining room.

The hotel elevator was just about the greatest piece of mechanism I had ever seen. I'd ride up and down on it by the hour, just for the ride and to watch how the Negro operator worked it and how close he'd come to getting the thing on a level with the floor stops. Finally, one day, I couldn't keep my hands off the control another minute. I gave the operator most of the money I had left from what Dunnie had given me, and bribed him to let me handle it myself.

My playing days, in fact my life, nearly ended a few minutes later. I left a door open on the third floor and was rubbernecking up and down the corridor while I made the elevator go up another flight. Suddenly a player screamed at me to pull my fool head inside, and I did . . . just in time to keep it from being crushed.

Dunnie bawled me out until the stuffings ran out of me, and what he didn't say to me the older players said for him. But finally one of them took pity on me, shook his head and said, "You're just a babe in the woods."

After that they called me Babe.

At Fayetteville, Dunnie saw to it that we took things easy for a long time, and when we did finally have a game, it was one of those intrasquad games. Dunnie picked the teams and named one side the Sparrows and the other the Buzzards. I played shortstop for the Buzzards for half the game, then finished in the box.

Late in that game I hit the first professional home run of my life. I hit it as I hit all the others, by taking a good gander at the pitch as it came up to the plate, twisting my body into a backswing and then hitting it as hard as I could swing. The ball cleared the right-field fence and landed in a cornfield beyond. I don't have to tell you what it did to me, inside, but the effect on Dunnie and the others was easy to see too. They estimated that it had carried about 350 feet. I guess that doesn't sound like much in these days of the stitched golf ball, but they thought it was pretty sensational for me because I was, first of all, a pitcher, and next a raw rookie.

We had a funny season in Baltimore in 1914.

That year the Federal League came into town and they put up a field right across from Dunn's park. Dunn tried to fight the Baltimore Federals by putting together one of the best teams that ever has represented a minor-league club. I know our 1914 players could have beaten many second-division clubs I have seen since in the majors. But the town turned its back on us. Baltimore had had National and American League teams in the past and it swallowed the Federal League team hook, line and sinker. The Baltimore Feds would play to 20,-000 and we'd play to twenty. I am not kidding. I was a Baltimore kid, winning almost every time I pitched, and hitting pretty well for a pitcher, but they wouldn't come out to see me. For I was on the minor-league team.

I still have the box score of my first International League game, played in Baltimore on April 22, 1914. We met the Buffalo club and I shut them out with six hits, the Orioles winning, 6-0. After the game was over, Dunnie slapped me on the back and said, "Nice going, kid! Keep pitching like that and no one can stop you from getting into the big leagues."

"Looking into People" has been a popular department in *Cosmopolitan* magazine. It gives sociologists' findings in different fields. Including baseball? Naturally.

From "Looking into People"

AMRAM SCHEINFELD

WHAT'S HE GOT that I ain't got?" the bush-leaguer may ask as he watches the big-league player. Probably, it's "personality and character," according to Dr. John La Place, coach of New York's City College baseball team and himself a onetime pro shortstop. His study of fifty major and sixty-five minor-league players revealed these differences: Big-league players as a group are more self-disciplined, more temperate in their habits, and better at teamwork. They are more dependable, they don't "blow up" as easily, and they pull out of slumps more quickly. Those who play in the minor leagues—often men with top basic ability—tend, by contrast, to be more neurotic and erratic, and less ambitious. "Virtually all big-league players," Dr. La Place told us, "are high-school graduates, and a big percentage are college men. What's more, emphasis on character is now so great that big-league scouts, before signing up a recruit, visit his home and look carefully into his background."

THIS is from Mr. Schwed's book, *How to Watch a Baseball Game,* which, like most good writing, is better reading than it is advice. Nobody can tell you how to watch a baseball game. Nobody can tell you how to keep score either. The best scoring system I know was devised by a nine-year-old in my house. He went to a game and came back with a filled-in score card under which he had preinscribed the following legend: "SO—Struck Out. GO—Grounded Out. FO—Fly Out. SAC—Sacrifice Out. FOO—Foul Out. O—Out on no explanation."

How to Keep Score

FRED SCHWED, JR.

CONSIDER A NOT unfamiliar afternoon. It is a miserable afternoon, too hot, or too cool, and also too windy. The two poorest teams in the league are playing a meaningless contest late in the season. There are less than a thousand spectators. In the vast stands they appear rarer than raisins in the most disappointing raisin bun, and half of them haven't paid their way in. And among those who haven't paid for tickets is the official scorer. He will pay strict attention, even though no one else does, even though one team makes seven runs in the first inning alone, and the other team finally makes one in the last half of the eighth.

He will note down, ineluctable and accurately, Everything. All the triumphs and all the disasters.

After that he will not airily toss away his notes, as most fans chuck away their carefully kept score cards. Far from it. The next day, through publishing devices as complex as New York Stock Exchange transactions require, his notes will appear in hundreds of newspapers all over the land. True they will engage less than six square inches of type; they will be intensely abbreviated, and cryptic. They will then become the "box scores." Only the sophisticated will be able to decipher them. The number of people with the special knowledge to do this is limited, on this continent, to a bare forty or fifty million.

This game being so insignificant, it is likely that no more than half a million newspaper readers took the trouble to notice that Celewiskey, the new third baseman for the losing team,

made three errors and did not improve matters by coming to bat four times and making no hits. If it had been a World Series game, fifty million readers would have studied the box score. (For a Series game, the box score is printed in much bigger type because a lot of baseball illiterates will be trying to decipher it. Several millions of them, examining this type of information for the first time, will learn to understand it. They will become members of a huge scholarly society—the habitual studiers of box scores.)

The baseball box score is the pithiest form of written communication in America today. It is abbreviated history. It is two or three hours (the box score even gives *that* item to the minute) of complex activity, virtually inscribed on the head of a pin, yet no knowing reader suffers from eyestrain. If you know how to read a box score completely you can pretty well find out what happened without reading the lyric sentences that precede it.

The box score, for brevity, is to the *Reader's Digest* what the *Reader's Digest* is to a book titled *Primary Trends in Modern Retail Merchandising.* The box score also has many times the readers of the *Reader's Digest,* which of course has more readers than anyone else.

In a box score nearly everything is abbreviated except the remorseless numerals. The hapless Celewiskey, for example, on perhaps the only day in his life when he got his name (and his shame) into several hundred metropolitan newspapers, finds himself referred to as "Sel'sky, 3b." But under H, it says clearly enough "o" and under E it says "3." This deplorable biography, for anyone who is interested, will be available for reference until the day before Judgment Day. "You Could Look It Up,"* as James Thurber titled one of the best of fantasy baseball stories.

This chapter is not going to explain what each of the abbreviations, a few of them quite puzzling, means. To do so would be entirely wrong, just as it would be wrong to produce a didactic piece explaining to young men how to whistle at young women. If you don't know how to do it, but wish to learn, you should learn by yourself, not read up on it in the public library. If by chance you do not know how to read a box score, just start studying some box scores. If you are a boy I do not think you should ask anyone for help, except perhaps your father. (It will tickle your old man, but be sure he knows the answers before you ask him.) If you are a girl you may ask any man, if you choose. But this is the easy way, and also the flirtatious way.

The first thing you must do, and practically the last, is to procure a copy of a metropolitan newspaper, turn to the sports section, select a box score, and gaze at it. The form differs a little from paper to paper. *The New York Times,* as usual, is perhaps the most explicit. Reading in the usual order, the abbreviations at the top mean at bats, runs, hits, put-outs, assists. Errors are sometimes a sixth column, sometimes underneath, according to the whim of the sports typesetter.

At bats are important because of batting averages. If a man is at bat five times and makes two hits, his batting average for that game is .400. If he is at bat only four times and makes two hits it comes to .500. Such figures are commonplace in box scores, but for the whole season nobody ever bats .500 and the last to bat .400 was Ted Williams a long time ago.

It is feasible for an athlete to come up to the plate five times, swinging a big bat, and in the next day's box score have a zero under AB. This would happen, for instance, if he were walked twice, made a sacrifice fly and a sacrifice bunt, and got hit by the pitcher the last time. This may seem kind of ludicrous, but anyone who studies up on batting averages will learn that there is precise justice here, aimed at, and very nearly arrived at. Anyway a lot more precise than Blackstone's *Commentaries.*

The other item worth noting is the chancy field of "errors." Although errors are committed by the fielding side, they have a lot to do with batting averages. (There are such things as fielding averages but no one pays any attention to them.)

The point is, of course, that if a batter hits the ball, and arrives safe at first (or any other base), and the official scorer says an error was committed, the batter does not get credited with a hit, only another accursed time at bat. So what is an error? This has never been entirely satisfactorily settled. It is clearly an error if a ball comes cleanly to a fielder, and he for some reason, perhaps because the sun is in his eyes, perhaps because of marital problems at home, just drops it to the ground. But this obvious type of error does not happen much in big-league ball.

It is the debatable errors which are the scorer's headache. The batter hits a sharp grounder to the right of the shortstop, the more difficult side. The shortstop bobbles it a tiny moment, comes up with it, but cannot pivot and throw fast enough so the batter just beats it out. Now if the shortstop had been Honus Wagner, or even himself five years younger, he would undoubtedly have made the play successfully. What should the scorer call it? Such is the general philosophy of the game that he will probably call it a hit. Sometimes he will call it an error and then the batter will not talk to him for a month. For the batter has been robbed of a hit, and, as has often been observed, hits are a ballplayer's bread and butter. (Exception: they are not normally a pitcher's bread and butter; strike-outs are. Exception to the exception is, as usual, Babe Ruth. He hit so well that he gave up being a pitcher, and then his hits became his little crackers and caviar.)

Batting averages are terribly important to a player's reputation and salary, but fielding averages are scarcely regarded. The reason for this is somewhat curious. Fielding averages are the percentage of errors to chances. But again we must ask, what is an error? Only one thing is sure. A fielder is not charged with an error if he does not touch the ball. This may often happen because the fielder is daydreaming, or is slow of foot, or of mind, or has stationed himself a couple of yards wrong for this batter on this pitch. None of these four things is a recommendation for a ballplayer. But if he doesn't manage to touch the ball he cannot, under anybody's scoring rules, be charged with an error.

---

* The place to look this up, or anything else up, is in *The Official Encyclopedia of Baseball,* by Hy Turkin and S. C. Thompson (New York: A. S. Barnes & Co., rev. ed., 1956), 583 pages. There is also an inexpensive pocket edition, but I prefer to consult the one that weighs several pounds.

All he can be charged with is not being a particularly valuable ballplayer. A speedy, heads-up player can get to difficult balls, grab at them, almost have them, and muff them. So it is the good fielder who gives himself extra chances to make errors. That is why good managers and knowledgeable fans do not give a hoot if a fielder's average is .992 or .981.

Runs batted in (RBI) is an important statistic, and it has puzzling aspects. It is not unusual to find that a .310 batter has batted in only fifty runs in the season, while a .270 hitter has batted in about a hundred. This can be accounted for in many ways, none of them necessarily correct. It may be as simple a matter as being first man up. First man up has no opportunity in the first inning to bat in anybody but himself. (A home run counts as batting yourself in.) It may be the difference between a long-ball hitter and a "spray" hitter, who is a useful person to have on the team, but who only hits two home runs a year because he is not big and strong enough.

It may have to do with the imponderable matter of whether he is a "clutch" hitter. ("Clutch," in the baseball sense, will not be found in many dictionaries. It is likely a wild aberration on the word *crucial*, or *crux*, or both.) Certain famous players are renowned for being good in the clutch.

A reasonable view of this matter would be that it doesn't exist. It is reasonable to assume that a professional player would do his best to get a hit every time he comes to bat, regardless of the importance of the situation, or even if the game is only in spring training. If the situation is tremendously important, with fifty thousand bellowing their hopes and fears, he may try even harder. (This may be his undoing.) So one might reason that if he can get one of his hits in a crucial situation, swell! If he can't, that is too bad, but after all, he has also failed to hit in thousands of unimportant situations. The average player gets only one hit in three times or four times.

However, this rational view is not a correct view. The records do not show it with any precision, but there are such things as clutch hitters, and there are other hitters with high batting averages who are pretty dismal in the clutch. The usual conclusion about this is that the clutch hitters have courage, or guts, or intestinal fortitude. My own theory varies somewhat.

I think it is a matter of temperament. There are some men who mightily enjoy being in the eye of a hurricane; they enjoy it even more if the whole world is watching. On such occasions their red corpuscles go racing around joyously inside of them. They would rather be up there with the bases full, two out, and big money riding on the next pitch, than anywhere else in the world. (Ruth was one such.) There are, however, other men who secretly would rather be elsewhere. Is it correct to call such men yellow? Or is it perhaps to call the brave men eager exhibitionists? There is a record that baseball does not and cannot keep. Of the clutch hitters who can look a skillful pitcher in the eye, how many of them can look other critical situations in life in the eye? But it is not a statistic I want to see added to the box score.

The box score is full of little curiosities, if you have the eagerness to hunt them out. Take this runs-batted-in business. It seems simple enough. But not always. If you are at bat and you hit a fly that is caught, or a foul even that is caught, and there is a man on third who "tags up" and scores, then even though you are out you get credit for an RBI. You can also "bat in" a run without striking the ball at all. The bases are full and you get a base on balls. Perhaps you never even hit a foul, or even took the bat off your shoulder.

At first glance this seems unfair. A little old lady could do the same thing. Maybe she could, and maybe she couldn't, especially if she happened to be an overeager old lady as many of them are. It takes a good eye and good judgment to get a base on balls with the bases loaded.

The other reason why this scoring law exists is more practical and has less to do with blindfolded justice. A box score must "prove" like double-entry bookkeeping. Every run must be accounted for and so must everything else. A run has been scored. Who batted it in? What more likely candidate than the batter who didn't do any batting? Whom would you suggest—the third-base coach who signaled him to "wait the pitcher out"? That might be correct but it happens that neither the coaches' nor the managers' names ever appear in the box score.

On the defensive side, the bookkeeping is no less severe. Sometimes when the umpire calls "infield fly" no infielder bothers to catch the high short pop-up and it falls to the ground. Yet the runner is automatically out. Who put him out? The scoring rules state that it is the infielder who was nearest to the ball. This might appear to be a picayune ruling, but it isn't. When a team takes the field for nine full innings, the total of putouts must be twenty-seven. (Nine times three equals twenty-seven.) So some fielder must be given that putout or the box score will not prove.

When I was a lad the "infield fly rule" was discussed as much as the high and low tariff. By this time most fans have gotten accustomed to it and understand its peculiar necessity.

The game of baseball was played for generations without any need for so unnatural a rule as the infield fly. Then a thought occurred to one player—I believe it was that intellectual second baseman Eddie Collins. Lying sleepless one night in, I like to think, an alien hotel room (and in those days a bum one) he reviewed in his remarkable mind a familiar situation. There are runners on first and second and less than two out. The batter hits an easy pop-up to him and he easily catches it. The two runners do not move or even consider doing so. The batter is out. That is the way this routine play has been enacted for three quarters of a century. One man, and only one man, out.

But tossing on his thin, not too clean mattress, I like to think, he suddenly gets an inspiration worthy of Tom Watt. "Eureka," he cries to himself, "suppose I don't catch it? Suppose I drop it on purpose? Then the force is on both runners. I pick up the ball and throw to third and the third baseman throws to second. The batter gets safe to first, but *two* men are out. I've made the easiest double play in history."

He was of course absolutely right in his strategy. The runners are helpless if this is perpetrated on them. The very next day, I like to think, he tried out this caper with stunning success and all the Solons in baseball looked at each other in dismay. They finally solved it with a peculiarly unnatural rule. When a pop fly is hit up under certain conditions, the umpire yells, "infield fly." Then the batter is automatically out. The infielder nearest the ball may catch it if he enjoys catching flies (he usually does, especially at a time like this when there is nothing at stake), but if he wishes to he can disdain even reaching for the ball. The batter is just as out as if he had either caught it or muffed it.*

If you make a daily habit, not just a World Series habit, of studying box scores you will find all sorts of nuances in them (if that is the sort of thing that interests you). For instance,

the very last item is the attendance. When there is a double header, it only gives the attendance for the first game. It assumes that nobody got up and went home before the second game. When each team uses more than one pitcher it gives the winning and losing pitcher (WP and LP). But when a pitcher pitches the whole game this item is omitted. It is redundant, and some dozen letters of type are saved.

When a succession of pitchers are used the question of who is the WP and who the LP sometimes comes up, sometimes practically unsolvably. In a majority of games a child could make the pronouncement, but not in all.

If you want to know the exact legislation on this point, get any rule book, or, better and less expensive, ask an old-time fan. He will tell you a lot of stuff about (when a new pitcher comes in) that it is the new pitcher's game "to win or lose" according to the score at the moment of his baptism into the lineup. This is all quite right.

But in one of those dipsy-dopesy games, where each team uses above five pitchers, and the final score is 14-11, and nobody pitches well, and nobody pitches perceptibly worse than anyone else, the case is different. Nobody really deserves to be credited WP, and nobody should be assigned LP. Everybody pitched just lousy.

But the records are sacrosanct, as they should be. If a game is won, there must be a winning pitcher to account for it, and vice versa. To award this laurel and this badge of shame, it would be acceptable to examine the entrails of a sacramental goat, as the Greek soothsayers did. Actually this practice is still occasionally used, without the goat.

There are a good many cases where the winning pitcher only threw one ball. He came in with his team behind and a man or so on base. He threw his one ball, which resulted in a double or triple play, and the side was retired. Then he was lifted for a pinch hitter, went and took his shower, and his team came on to win. A pitcher who only throws one ball does not seem like a likely candidate for WP; but who seems more likely, since everyone who came after him did nothing so effective?

It is possible to dream up a case of a winning pitcher who never threw a pitch at all. He comes in with men on base and two out.

---

* Further research into this difficult subject seems to show that the history of the rule may not be precisely as I have set it down here. But the precise version, whatever it may be, is probably no more interesting than what I have set down, so what the heck.

His first throw (not a pitch) is to a baseman and he picks a runner off.[*]

You can make a daily habit of studying your favorite team's box score *before* you read the thrilling account in prose that goes above it. You will eventually get so proficient at this that you can pretty well find out what happened in the prose recital. Of course you can't go all the way. You can tell if a batter was hit by a pitcher and who they both were, but you cannot find out how badly the batter was hurt. This kind of early-morning doodling I find in the class of crossword puzzles and daily bridge problems. One more bit of advice: If you try this little recreation out, and find you don't care for it, just give it up.

The matter of keeping score on the score card that you purchase is another thing you should not do if you do not enjoy doing it. Millions of people just love it; they had a distant ancestor who was a bookkeeper.

A friend of mine name of Rudyard Kipling once remarked:

There are nine and sixty ways of constructing tribal lays,
And each and every one of them is right.

This is also true of keeping score. You can keep it the right way, whatever that is, or any of the other ninety-five ways. If you are a perfectionist you will only find peace of mind by keeping it the right way, but if you are a perfectionist you already know how to do it better than I do. For instance, it is customary, when a batter strikes out, to put the letter K in the appropriate little box. Why it is K, instead of S, I shall never know until some stranger writes me a sharply worded letter explaining it. I often go to games with a perfectionist friend of mine, a former professional ball reporter. He puts the K in all right when the batter strikes out swinging, but when the batter just stands there with the bat on his shoulder for the third strike, looking silly, my friend prints the K in back-

wards, as it appears in a mirror. Actually a lot of other scorers do this also, but do not count me among them.

After the meticulous scorers have done all this they usually throw the score card away. Occasionally, if it has been a memorable game, they take the card home with them, put it carefully away somewhere, and never look at it again for the rest of their lives. It is hard for me to imagine anyone, on a frosty December evening, sitting before the fire with the score card of a game played the previous June, and recreating the game, batter by batter and inning by inning. However, it has undoubtedly happened. In baseball, as has been mentioned before, everything eventually happens. Another thing I can't imagine is a wife saying to her husband as he departs for the game without her, "Be sure to bring back your score card, dear, I want to read it."

The genuine reason for the nonprofessional scorer keeping score is for the period of the game itself. It will allow you to note, toward the end of the game, that the batter coming up has struck out all three times before, once swinging. Better yet, you can speak up and give this information to the people sitting near you, who will consider you a pretty profound character, which as it happens, you are.

In order to keep score, you must assign a number to each player. The pitcher is 1, and the right fielder is 9. First be sure to underline the starting pitchers and catchers when the batteries are announced over the loud-speaker. Underline them firmly. This may break the point in the lead pencil you just purchased for five cents. Since you don't happen to have a pencil sharpener in your pocket, you can no longer keep score, but will just have to sit back and enjoy the old ball game. Don't be downhearted; if there are points of very recent history you want to know there will be plenty of scorekeepers about who will be happy to inform you.

[*] I don't know if this ever happened. I am not going to bother to look it up either.

HERE is *Time* magazine's cover story of May 28, 1956.

The Whole Story of Pitching

DICK SEAMON

MOVED ONE DAY by intimations of mortality, that bibulous philosopher, W. C. Fields, looked back on his arid boyhood home and chose his modest alternative to death: "On the whole, I'd rather be in Philadelphia."

The 20th century's beneficiaries of William Penn's "Holy Experiment" in "Virtue, Liberty and Independence" might even share this sentiment. A sip of their chlorine-loaded tap water and they understand why Fields shunned the liquid all his life; a trip downtown and they know why he hated the city's narrow, cross-hatched streets. A baseball park should be a place to get away from all this, but these days even a trip to Connie Mack Stadium is seldom a pleasure. The Philadelphia Phillies, now the only major-league team in town, are stumbling through their 1956 schedule with all the grace of corporation lawyers cutting up at a church picnic.

Yet Philadelphia's tiny army of baseball fans can still look the world in the eye. The Phillies may not add up to much of a team, but for the moment it is more than enough that they boast the best pitcher in baseball. This season, as for many a long summer, Philadelphia's oft-punctured pride rides high on the strong right arm of a visiting Middle Westerner named Robin Evan Roberts.

The muscular (6 ft. 1 in., 190 lbs.), 29-year-old fugitive from the chores on an Illinois farm is almost too good to be true. Ever since he came up to the Phillies in 1948 after two brief months in the bush leagues, he has plodded out to take his pitching turn with every-fourth-day regularity. Dedicated to the old-fashioned notion that he is getting paid for throwing the ball over the plate, and not for demonstrating some trick delivery or practicing some offbeat vaudeville act for the TV cameras, Roberts has performed his job with an efficiency deadly to (1) opponents and (2) baseball records. In his third major-league season he won 20 games—a record no other Philly had even flirted with since the hard-drinking days of the late great Grover Cleveland Alexander. Now, six years later, he has yet to fall back below the 20-game mark. No major-leaguer has done so well since the days (1925-33) of the Philadelphia Athletics' Lefty Grove.

Aside from 1950, when he pitched the Phillies to the National League pennant, Roberts has been playing for a club that has never wound up better than third. But over the years he has started, finished and won more games than any other active major-league pitcher. And always, even losing, he has found the plate with such grim routine that in an astonishing total of 2,272 innings of big-league ball, he has been charged with only 500 walks (less than two a game), has made only 19 wild pitches, hit only 28 batters. He has thrown 1,179 strikeouts.

For a while, such heady success seemed too rich for Philadelphia's blood. The monumental indifference that was ultimately to run Connie Mack's old Athletics all the way to Kansas City was far from dissolved by Roberts' effortless and somehow unexciting pitching. And if winning ball games was not enough, off the field the young man was about as colorful as the third fellow from the end in the class picture. The few real fans in town felt like Huck Finn trying to warm up to the Widow Douglas: "It was rough . . . considering how dismal regular and decent the widow was in all her ways." Robin Roberts was an earnest young man interested only in giving the enemy its lumps, while the fans, as one of them explains it today, were looking for a player "who can give us lumps in the throat."

Unfortunately the rest of the team also cried out for color. There are men who still insist that Owner Bob Carpenter was desperately hoping to find some headline-catching shenanigans when he hired a private eye to shadow some of his players two years ago. At any rate Millionaire Sportsman Carpenter learned nothing that he has not known for years: all his money has yet to buy him a polished team.

Still, in the 1956 Phillies, the nucleus is there. Behind the plate, crafty Veteran Andy Seminick makes up in pure baseball savvy what he lacks in hitting; Granny Hamner at short is a real pro; Richie Ashburn and Del Ennis belong in any man's outfield. As for pitchers, though, unless Southpaw Curt Simmons gets back his "bonus baby" form and until the trade for the Cardinals' Harvey Haddix pays off, Robin Roberts is the Phillies' only reliable performer.

The Philadelphia fans have learned to appreciate him, and now they understand what his opponents mean when they call Righthander Roberts an old-fashioned pitcher. He never bothers with fancy stuff but makes do with what he has: a dinky curve, a sneaky but unspectacular fast ball, and a frustrating change of pace. He offers no single dramatic talent—he has no counterpart of Carl Hubbell's spectacular screwball, Walter Johnson's terrifying fast ball, Bobby Feller's strike-out touch. Pitch for pitch, many of his contemporaries have what the trade calls "more stuff," pitches that are harder, faster, or trickier. But better than any of them now on the mound, Robin Roberts can put the ball where he wants. There is one precious-diamond word for him—control.

In this era of short fences and hopped-up baseballs, Roberts' achievements are not easily come by. Managers flash their signals from the bench and teammates bawl their encouragement. But pitching is a loner's art. Once a man places his forefoot on the white rubber slab and takes aim at the plate 60 ft. 6 in. away, he is on his own. Only his craft and strength can whip the ball safely past the waiting batter.

Time was when pitchers got a better break. Before Babe Ruth taught club owners that home runs and high-hitting games mean cash customers, the game was played with a dead ball. Often when a home team took the field for the first time they used a "refrigerator" ball, carefully chilled in the clubhouse icebox to make it even deader. There was no rule against spitballs, so with a cud of chewing tobacco or a wad of slippery elm, a clever man could keep the ball hopping all afternoon. After roughing up one side of the ball, pitchers used to shine the other side on a part of their uniform heavily dosed with paraffin. Thus treated, the ball would really dance.

Unlike modern games, where dozens of new balls are used in nine innings, the games of the memorable days of Cy Young and Rube Waddell, Rube Marquard and Jeff Tesreau and Ed Cicotte used the same ball inning after inning. Batters pounded it until it was brown and hard to see, pitchers doctored its horsehide; everything was stacked against the hitter (everything, that is, except for the occasional inspirations of such old-timers as the pre-World War I Phillies' Otto Knabe and Mike Doolan, who once broke up a game with the Giants by swabbing the ball with capsicum salve, an irritant that sent Spitballer Jeff Tesreau to the showers with painfully swollen lips after only three innings).

Today occasional pitchers may still get away with an occasional outlawed spitter, but that dangerous pitch has all but vanished. Just about the only survival from baseball's rowdy youth is the "accidental" beanball, the close pitch that keeps a batter honest by forcing him back from the plate, that keeps him from taking a toe hold and getting set to powder the ball. If the Phillies' Coach Whitlow Wyatt, who learned his baseball manners as one of Leo Durocher's Dodgers, had his way, Philly pitchers would put the brush-back pitch to constant use. "I think you ought to play it mean," says Whit, "like Durocher did. They ought to hate you on the field." Pitcher Roberts does not fill Coach Wyatt's prescription. "He won't knock down a batter," complains the coach. "Says it don't do him any good, doesn't help him any. Well, it sure helped me. Hell, if it was my own brother, I'd knock him down as soon as I would anyone else. It's my meat and bread he's trying to take away."

In his stubborn refusal to toss beanballs, Roberts resembles the late great Walter Johnson of the lackluster Washington Senators. The "Big Train" was a self-confident competitor who occasionally went so far as to serve up fat ones to hitters suffering from nerve-racking slumps. But throwing at a batter was unthinkable. Johnson never even waited for the umpires to discard scuffed balls; as soon as he saw one he tossed it aside, for fear it might force him to throw his fast one wild and injure the man at the plate.

Even an intentional walk is alien to Robin Roberts' kind of pitching. He plays the percentages, counts on his control to put the ball where the batter can hit it, but not safely.

"Take a .333 hitter," says the Phillies' Coach Wally Moses. "Well, he's only going to get a hit once out of three times. Take Willie Mays; he comes up about 500 times a season, and he hits 50 homers. Hell, that's only one in ten. It'd be silly to walk him. Well, Roberts figures those are pretty good odds."

The odds would be even better if Roberts were willing to throw a few close ones to keep hitters loose. But his opponents know that he won't, so they occasionally scrounge off him. They step into the batter's box with complete confidence that he will put the ball near the plate ("The inclination is just to say 'Strike! Strike! Strike!'" says Umpire Jocko Conlon. "He's so close you gotta watch him like an eagle.") If the hitters happen to be hot, they can dig in and hammer him unmercifully. This refusal to throw anywhere but over the plate has earned him at least one unenviable record: last year he allowed 41 home runs, a major-league record.

A calm man, Roberts recovers quickly from even the most awesome shellfire. This season, after winning his first three games, he was beaten in the next three, knocked out of the box twice. Another pitcher might have wondered whether that inevitable slide down had begun. Not Roberts. One night last week, with his cool and easy motion on the mound and his reckless behavior on the base paths, he beat the league-leading Milwaukee Braves almost single-handed, 2-1. He struck out ten men, allowed only eight hits, tore home from second on an eighth-inning infield single, slid head first into big Del Crandall at the plate, jarred the catcher loose from the ball and scored the run that tied up the game. When Roberts took his turn again, four days later, the red-hot sluggers of the Cincinnati Redlegs sighted in on his polite pitching and beat him handily, 5-1. There was never a sign of wildness; it was just one of the days when the percentages ran against him.

Such hell-bent base running—something of a rarity among pampered pitchers who figure that their only work waits for them on the mound—is typical of Roberts' attitude toward baseball. He loves every minute of the game. He is a better-than-average fielder, can knock down the line drives that whistle back from the batter's box, moves fast and surely to field bunts. Despite his dainty, mincing style at the plate, he is a competent (.250) switch-hitter. "I'm happy as can be out there," he says. "I enjoy all of it—fielding and swinging at bat and all that stuff. If you enjoy baseball and are out there playing when you're a kid, you can become all-round."

Robin Roberts began the rounding-off process early. By the time he was seven he was nourishing a well-developed dislike for his allotted chores on the Roberts farm near Springfield, Ill.; everything came second to learning how to play games—basketball, baseball, anything at all. "He never had a ball out of his hand," his mother Sarah Roberts remembers. "Ah well," says his proud Welsh father Tom. "He could've done a lot worse."

But at the time young Robin's gold-bricking held less appeal to a man who had come up the hard way from the back-breaking labor and pocket-pinching strikes of a Lancashire coal mine. Father Roberts recalls his barely controlled anger the day Robin deliberately broke a hoe to avoid work. The outraged father took a fly swatter to his son's well-padded bottom ("It don't hurt your hand and it don't mark the kid"). But Robin went right on playing. When he couldn't talk one of his three brothers into playing catch, he would prop an old mattress against the garage door and fire away for hours at a hole in the middle. All the while, the braying porch radio kept him up to date on Chicago Cubs ball games. "If people knew what I thought about pitching," says Roberts now, "they'd think I was nuts. They make it so complicated. They're always saying I studied control from the time I was a little kid. That's silly. It's just that it's tough to play catch when nobody's around. I threw to that mattress for fun. I never thought about control at all. It just never entered my mind that the purpose of pitching wasn't to get the ball over the plate."

Impartially athletic, Robin switched to basketball with the season. When his mother would try to get him to do some work around the place, he would put her off: "Naw, Mom, I'm a ballplayer. You just wait till I get into the major leagues. Then I'll build you a house." Even Tom Roberts came to respect his son's determination. "You just had to go along," he says today. "He wouldn't do nuthin' else."

On the way to bigger things, Robin stopped off at Springfield and Lanphier high schools, where he pitched and played third, was a competent end on the football team and a promising shot-putter. When he went to Michigan State in the fall of 1944, he was good enough to earn a basketball scholarship the next year. (He majored in physical education, graduated in 1948 with a B.S. degree.)

When Roberts tried out for the State baseball team, his hitting was too weak for an infielder, so he asked Coach John Kobs for a chance to pitch. "I liked his motion," says Kobs. "He threw it someplace around where the catcher held his glove, and that made sense."

An unspectacular success as a college pitcher, Roberts got his big break when the University of Michigan's baseball coach Ray Fisher took him to New England in the summer of 1946 to play in the old Northern League. Roberts balked often out of sheer awkwardness, fell down fielding bunts, was so eager he threw before he got the catcher's sign. But Fisher saw things worth working on—a tireless arm, an indomitable will to win. As an ex-major-leaguer (with the New York Yankees and Cincinnati), Fisher put the finishing touches on the boy.

Fisher did so well that by the end of his second season in New England, Roberts had excited the scouts of half a dozen big-league clubs. The St. Louis Browns offered him $225 a month to play Class B ball. A few days later the Phillies offered him $10,000. Roberts hesitated and the Phillies raised the ante to $15,000, then to $25,000. Roberts signed. "I would've signed for $2,500," he admits now, "only they didn't know it. When they got up to $25,000, I knew I was going to be able to buy a pretty good house for Mom, so I said yes. She really got a belt out of that house."

Now, nine successful years away from those awkward summers in Vermont, Robin Roberts still turns for help to the man who polished him up for the Phillies. Last fall Roberts surprised his old coach by stopping off in Ann Arbor and asking permission to work out with the Michigan pitchers. Puzzled, Fisher said, "Sure." He watched Roberts throw a few. Fisher saw right away that the familiar three-quarters motion had been replaced by a sidearm delivery; Roberts was unconsciously favoring a sore arm. Fisher walked over. "Robby," he said, "you've changed your delivery, haven't you?" Roberts smiled with relief. "That's what I wanted to know," he said. "You know, in Philadelphia I'm Robin Roberts, and they won't tell me anything."

Roberts' first season with the Phillies earned him an unexciting record (seven won, nine lost), but it also earned him the confidence of his manager and teammates. And it convinced him that he had been right all along: baseball was all he wanted out of life. The small kid who had cried over lost basketball games took naturally to the habits of grown men who sat around and brooded, morose and silent, after a defeat on the diamond. Like all baseballers before and since Ring Lardner's busher, he learned the tired routine for killing time on the road, "the one bad thing about baseball," says he. He went to every movie in town ("I don't care what's playing; I like 'em all"), slept for long hours, read the sports pages, stared blankly out of bus and train windows, sat slack-jawed in hotel lobbies.

By the time he got home that fall, Robin had begun to suspect that there might be something else besides playing ball. He asked his sister Nora if she knew any girls he might ask for a date. Nora fixed him up with a young grade-school teacher fresh from the University of Wisconsin, a pretty brunette named Mary Ann Kalnes. Mary had never seen a big-league game; Robin could talk only about baseball. So the happy couple went to the movies, where conversation is sometimes helpful but not compulsory. "We evidently got along," says Robin. Little more than a year later they were married.

Today the Robin Robertses live on Robin Hood Road in the Philadelphia suburb of Meadowbrook with their two children (Robin Jr., 5, and Danny, 2) and a 3½-year-old Welsh corgi presented to Robin by an upstate New York fan. Mary Ann, who dutifully goes to Connie Mack Stadium when Robin is pitching a home game and turns on radio or TV when he performs on the road, still makes no pretense of being a baseball buff. She admits to knowing precious little about how the other players are doing, is sure only that so far this season has been all slump for the Phillies. "I don't even bother to check the standings," says Mary Roberts.

Roberts professes to be unconcerned with the fact that he is using up his career pitching for a losing club. "Getting traded or staying isn't a deep ingrained thing with me," he says. "This club always could potentially win the pennant. Especially when I pitch, it isn't a fourth-place club. Usually they get the runs for me."

Last year, in fact, from the All-Star game to Labor Day, the Phillies were perhaps the best in the National League. Then Third Baseman Willie ("Puddinhead") Jones was hurt. First Baseman Stan Lopata was beaned, and the team faltered. "You look back on a season," says Roberts, "and you see two or three games, here and there, that if you'd won might have made the difference."

Mild-mannered Manager Mayo Smith agrees. "If we had another like Roberts," says Smith, "it would make a tremendous difference. I agree with Connie Mack that pitching is 70 per cent of the game. If you have it, you're always in the game. Even if you haven't the power hitting, as we haven't, you can work things like the sacrifice, the stolen base and the hit-and-run."

Smith and the Phillies' management are sure that in Roberts they own baseball's biggest bargain. Even in front of a losing team he wins so often that he more than earns his salary (about $60,000, including income from endorsements)—and incidentally disproves Indiana Humorist Kin Hubbard's snide crack: "Knowin' all about baseball is just about as profitable as bein' a good whittler."

To Roberts' slowly growing collection of hot fans, his own success seems adequate denial of his own most cherished belief: that pitching is essentially a simple art. "Anything is simple to an artist," snorts Umpire Larry Goetz. "For the rest of us," echoes Outfielder Ashburn, "there must be more, or everybody would bat .400 and win 20 games a year." But Robin Roberts insists that it is all much simpler than that: "I've been given credit for stuff I don't do. I don't even divide people into the tough and easy. It's never the same. With Willie Mays, for example, I don't put on anything special. I just try to mix up the pitches on him. I can't pinpoint what I pitch. I pitch the same to everybody—low and away, or high and tight.

"You don't have to make a fantastic proposition out of anybody. I live and pitch by a few basic rules. You don't have to make a big study of batters beforehand. When I have good stuff I throw four fast balls out of five pitches. You can basically confuse yourself by typing each hitter or worrying too much about righthanders and lefthanders. I don't have any special trouble with lefthanders."

If he has any trouble at all, says Roberts, it is his shallow curve. "I'm always hoping I can improve that curve, I must have changed that curve nine or ten times. I'll see Maglie throw and say, 'Gee, it'd be nice to have that curve.' But if I try to throw it that way, it hurts my arm. Mainly I try to count on a good fast ball that moves.

"Anyway, when you take up a hitter in a clubhouse meeting, no matter what his weakness is, it's going to end up low and away or high and tight, and the curve ball must be thrown below the belt. That's the whole story of pitching.

"It don't do me a bit of good to tell people this. I try to tell people and they just won't believe me. They want to believe you have everyone taped and baseball is like mathematics or something. But I'm telling the truth. It's like I say, keep your life and your pitching real simple and you'll get along."

Courtesy *Sport* Magazine. ©

"Those three runners you left on . . . they scored."

California Always Was in the Majors

HAROLD SHELDON

CALIFORNIA, though it has just made a place for itself in big-league ball, has been making a name for itself in the majors for years.

Gold wasn't the only California export that glittered during all the time the East and the Middle West had a monopoly on the big-league marts.

"Go East, young man" was advice that had to be accepted by Native Sons if they wanted a place in baseball's top levels. The major scene would have been far less spectacular without them—the likes of Harry Heilmann, Joe DiMaggio, Lefty O'Doul, Ted Williams, Joe Cronin, Lefty Gomez, Hal Chase, Larry French, Chick Hafey, the Meusel brothers, and dozens of others.

California was known for its baseball stars even before it became famous for movie stars. Bill Lange, Frank Chance, Hal Chase and Orvie Overall were among the first to put a glowing Golden State brand on the big leagues.

But it is in the last 25 years or so that Californians have made an impact that is the envy of every other state. Fifty years ago, ten states ranked ahead of California as a source of established major-leaguers. California's output of seven looked mighty puny alongside the 47 from Pennsylvania, 36 from Ohio, 28 from New York, 17 from Massachusetts and 15 from Illinois.

Within a quarter-century, though, California led them all in sheer weight of numbers. Then it moved ahead in production not only of the most, but also of the best.

The Baseball Writers Association began making its all-big-league selections in 1925 and, in the first seven years, only one Californian ranked among the top stars. Joe Cronin was the shortstop choice in 1930 and 1931. Since then, California has had more than twice as many all-stars as any other state—56 out of 285. Pennsylvania is a weak runner-up with 24, followed by New York with 21, then Missouri and Illinois, 19 each. California was the only state with more than one spot for 1957, placing indestructible Ted Williams of the Red Sox in the outfield and the Yankees' Gil McDougald at shortstop.

California now has title to one fourth of the National League franchises yet, ironically, it won't get to see the bulk of its native-born big leaguers.

For some reason, American League clubs have had far more success than the National's in signing up Golden Staters. Of almost 40 Native Sons in the majors on a regular or semiregular basis last season, all but five were in the American League.

So the homecoming for established players will be limited to Duke Snider and Don Drysdale of the Dodgers, newly based in Los Angeles; Marv Grissom of the other new enterprise at San Francisco, Del Crandall of Milwaukee and Lee Walls of the Cubs.

Still far from the native scene, along with Williams and McDougald, are such eminent American Leaguers as Jackie Jensen, Bob Lemon, Jack Harshman, Frank Sullivan, Mike Garcia, Don Mossi, Ray Boone, Gus Triandos, Billy Martin, Andy Carey, Joe DeMaestri and Lou Berberet.

Williams, with his .350 career average, is the best hitter California has produced and that is saying a lot, for these other notable swingers also came from that state:

Lefty O'Doul, .349 for his big league competition; Harry Heilmann, .342; Bill Lange, .336; Joe DiMaggio, .325; Chick Hafey, .317; Lew Fonseca, .316; Emil Meusel, .310; Bob Meusel, .309; Ernie Lombardi, .306; Duke Snider, .303; Joe Cronin, .302; Stan Hack, .301; Frank Chance, .297; Hal Chase, .291.

Not so high in the averages but also ranking among the all-stars for long-range swatting or all-around excellence were Joe Gordon, Bobby Doerr, Bob Elliott, Dom DiMaggio, Harry Danning, George Kelly, Dolph Camilli, Gavvy Cravath, Tony Lazzeri and Willie Kamm.

If California hasn't had its share of Hall of Fame pitchers, compared to Pennsylvania, New York and Ohio, the Golden State has had several who have ranked with the best of their eras.

Foremost are Lefty Gomez, with 189 victories and only 102 defeats for his career; comebacking Bob Lemon, slowed by an ailing arm to a 6-11 record for Cleveland last season for a lifetime tally of 207-127, and Larry French, 197-171. The Indians' Mike Garcia is another Californian who has ranked among the best in recent years.

Others have been noteworthy for briefer periods: Bill James, one of the "big three" who pitched the Braves to their 1914 miracle; Dutch Ruether, who had a talented left hand in pennants for the 1919 Reds, the 1925 Senators and the 1927 Yankees; Remy Kremer, who was 31 before he reached the big leagues and still was able to pile up 143 victories (he lost 85), with championship results for the Pirates of 1925 and 1927, and Jim Hughes, a four-year sensation around 1900.

Two or three of the editor's forenotes, like this one, discussed in the first *Fireside Book of Baseball* the problems sports writers have in composing good stories against instant deadlines. It is a talent that I think is immensely underrated. Here is another example: a bulletin wire-service lead on a game that had just about everything, including an ending that is very hard to describe—visiting team leads by one run, then both teams score 3 in the ninth. Exciting, but adds up to same difference.

The 1957 All-Star Game

HOWARD SIGMAND

THE AMERICAN LEAGUE just barely shook off its recent years of frustration today by putting down a hair-raising ninth-inning rally to edge the National League, 6 to 5, in the 24th All-Star Game.

Dramatically and desperately, manager Casey Stengel dug into his bull pen for help in the critical ninth and relief whizzes Don Mossi and Bob Grim came in to snuff out a last-stand three-run rally by the Nationals which fell one run short.

The American League's own three-run splurge in the top of the ninth proved the difference as Stengel's team won the dream game for the first time since 1954 and only the second time in the last eight years.

Grim got Brooklyn's muscular Gil Hodges on a liner to left fielder Minnie Minoso for the final out, stranding the tying run on second base.

The fates were kind to grizzled old Stengel today. The practically peerless leader of the world-champion Yankees had his crystal ball and everything else working in fine fashion as he sought his second All-Star triumph in seven tries.

A sun-baked crowd of 30,693 fans at Busch Stadium was treated to some masterful early pitching by Detroit's Jim Bunning and Baltimore's Billy Loes and some fine late-inning relief by Chicago's Billy Pierce, Mossi and Grim.

The Americans collected 10 hits off five National League pitchers, and a run-scoring double to center by Chicago's Minnie Minoso in the ninth off Clem Labine proved to be the winning blow.

Bunning, a gritty 25-year-old right-hander making his first All-Star appearance, set nine bewildered Nationals down in order in the first three innings and was credited with the victory.

The slim, six-foot-three Tiger pitcher's efforts were followed by three innings of scoreless three-hit hurling by Loes.

Things weren't so bright in the National League corner. Curt Simmons of the Phillies, manager Walt Alston's starter in the game, failed to last the second inning.

The fast-balling southpaw, who was off in his control, yielded a single to Mickey Mantle and then walked Ted Williams.

Vic Wertz singled across the first run and when Simmons walked Yogi Berra, Milwaukee's Lew Burdette was called on to stop the threat.

Burdette, the big fellow whom players in his own league accuse of being the "king of the spitballers," put out the fire, but not before another run registered when he walked Harvey Kuenn with the bases loaded.

Casey's own Yankees made it 3-0 in the fifth. Moose Skowron doubled, moved to third on a wild pitch by Rookie Phillie right-hander Jack Sanford and scored on a single by Yogi Berra.

The hit gave baseball's highest-salaried catcher the distinction of driving in his first All-Star run in nine appearances in the classic.

So it was 3-0 in favor of the Americans after

6½ innings, and it began to look as if Swami Stengel had found a way to stunt his league's growing inferiority complex.

Stengel stuck to his rights. He called on his third right-hander of the afternoon, 37-year-old Early Wynn of the Indians. Casey was wrong this time.

Willie Mays, dynamic New York Giants' center fielder, who contributed some of his usual dazzling fielding to the game and whose triple touched off his team's last-breath battle at the end, singled to left with one out in the seventh.

Catcher Ed Bailey, one of five Redleg starters, advanced the Say Hey Kid to third with another single. Then Gus Bell, the fellow Commissioner Ford Frick "vetoed" off the starting team, pinch hit for teammate Frank Robinson and scored two runs with a booming double to left.

Wily Casey decided to go left. And he summoned Pierce.

This was a novel way for Billy "The Kid" to get into the dream. The White Sox southpaw ace had been the AL starter in three of the last four summer spectaculars.

Stengel hoped that Pierce would finish this time and Billy almost did.

He got Ed Mathews on a grounder and struck out Ernie Banks to stop the rally and then set the side down in order in the eighth.

But the 2-hour-and-43-minute struggle was to see a hectic ninth inning—on both sides.

A baseball rarity, an error by Red Schoendienst, figured in his team's downfall. The usually redoubtable Milwaukee second baseman booted a bounder by Gil McDougald after Pierce had opened the inning with an infield hit.

Nellie Fox moved the runners up with a sacrifice bunt and Al Kaline, Detroit's magnificent right fielder, capped a sensational day for himself with a two-run single to center.

Labine, Brooklyn's relief specialist, was tagged for another marker as Minoso blasted a double to center field.

Kaline turned in the fielding play of the game when he leaped high against the right-field wall to rob Schoendienst of at least a double in the sixth and his spectacular one-hop pickup of a liner by Mathews in the fifth resulted in a force-out of Robinson at second.

With the score at 6-2 even the most ardent NL partisans in the crowd could not hope to see the "home" team pull this one out in the bottom of the ninth. Pierce appeared to be too strong.

The crowd stirred only slightly when Stan Musial, its incomparable native son, opened the ninth with a walk. The Man, appearing in his record 14th All-Star Game, had received a roaring ovation when he doubled in the fourth during a threat that failed to materialize.

Now, it seemed, a walk meant nothing. Mays then rapped Pierce for a drive down the right-field line. As Kaline chased the ball into the visiting bull pen, Musial raced home and capless Willie flew to third.

Mays scored when Pierce uncorked a wild pitch. Stengel discussed the situation with Pierce and decided to stick with him.

Pittsburgh catcher Hank Foiles hit for Bailey and singled sharply to center. When Bell walked, Stengel decided Pierce was through. He called in Indian southpaw Don Mossi.

The speedball-pitching lefty struck out Mathews for the first out. Stengel looked like a genius again. Casey needed some help on the next play and he got it from Minoso.

Banks singled through third-baseman Frank Malzone but a rifle throw from Minoso caught Bell as he tried to make third on the hit. While all this was going on, Foiles came across with the fifth National League run and Banks, representing the tying marker, perched himself on second.

Alston called on his first baseman, big Gil Hodges, to try to save the day for the Nationals. Stengel made it a family argument by summoning his relief specialist Bob Grim. Hodges lined to Minoso, and the AL had its 14th win in 24 All-Star games.

FROM the book *Baseball Stars of 1958*, edited by Ray Robinson, comes this tale of an exceptional ballplayer. Many are the experts who believe Henry Aaron will prove to have been one of baseball's all-time greats.

Hank Aaron

AL SILVERMAN

WHAT DO YOU WANT to know about Henry Aaron? Ask Don Newcombe, he'll tell you.

The bristling Dodger right-hander had kind of an off season last year but he's still one of the real good throwers in the game today. Ask Newcombe about Henry Aaron. He'll tell you.

This one happened in Milwaukee last summer. Don Newcombe was on the mound for the Dodgers and having a pretty fair time of it, except for Henry Aaron. In two previous times up, Aaron had doubled and been robbed of a hit. His third time up facing Newcombe, the count went to two strikes. Then Big Newk came in with a waste pitch, low and outside, which the book says is the way you should pitch to Aaron; let him fish for it. Henry fished all right, and connected, and the ball spattered into right center. Aaron landed on second base with his second double of the game.

Then the fun began.

With time called the burly Newcombe strode out to second base and aimed a few well-chosen words at Aaron. This extraordinary gesture on the part of an enemy ballplayer was misinterpreted by the Milwaukee fans, who started booing Newcombe. But Hank just stood there at second base laughing and brushing off his uniform and laughing some more. Newcombe shuffled back to the mound talking to himself.

What had Newcombe said to Aaron out there? Henry was still laughing when he came back to the dressing room after the game. "He said to me, 'Next time I'm going to throw the blamed thing *under* the plate to you.' "

Ask Don Newcombe about Aaron. He'll tell you.

Ask those American League winners, the Yankees, about Aaron, too. They'll tell you—

under their breath. In the seven-game World Series, Hank started off kind of slow, "fishing a little, instead of waiting for my pitch," is how he put it. But he warmed up in time to finish with 11 hits, one less than the World Series record and high for both clubs; the most home runs (3); and the most runs batted in (7). While the Braves as a team were hitting a rather anemic .209, Hank's .393 was tops for both clubs. Ask the Yankees about Aaron. They'll tell you.

Ask the Braves themselves about Aaron; they'd be delighted to tell you. Manager Fred Haney: "The most relaxed hitter I've ever seen." Veteran Red Schoendienst: "The greatest right-handed hitter I've ever seen and he's got more power than the greatest left-hander, Musial."

The only one who won't talk about Henry Aaron (unless pressed) is Aaron himself. Ask Aaron about Aaron and you sometimes come away talking to yourself.

For instance, early this year Aaron was telling all who would listen that he was no home-run hitter, that if he hit in the low 30s, he'd be doing very well. Well, all the no-home-run hitter did was lead both leagues in the number of homers hit in 1957, 44; at the same time driving in the most runs, 132. The batting title he had won a year earlier was sacrificed to power—Hank was going after the long ball for most of the season—and the sacrifice paid off in a pennant, and then a world championship for the Milwaukee Braves.

His 43rd home run, incidentally, was the biggest hit of his life. That was the one that gave the Braves the pennant. It came on September 23, against the challenging second-place Cardinals, in the last of the 11th with the score tied 2-2, two out and a runner on first. It earned outfielder Wes Covington the right to pour champagne over Aaron's head in the dressing room after the game. It was, said Aaron at the time, the biggest thrill of his life.

But he's had others—four and five-hit days, game-winning blows, etc.—and the slim, trim 24-year-old belter who is regarded by most experts right now as *the* best hitter in the league and likely to be the best hitter for years to come, will enjoy many such days.

One nice trait of Aaron's is his impartiality as a batsman. In each of his four years in the majors Henry has hit home runs in every National League ball park—and no other major-leaguer, past or present, can make that statement. Also in the last two years, he has hit home runs against every club in the league, both at home and on the road. As for his 132 RBIs, the significant thing about that healthy total is that in 50 of the games he played in he batted in the unproductive second position. Hank had another handicap, too, last year, in that he was forced to play center field for half the season because of an injury to the regular center fielder, Bill Bruton. Hank is a right fielder by trade but he handled himself like a man in center, although he is a long way from being a Willie Mays as a fielder. "He doesn't look like he hustles out there with that long loping gait of his," says Fred Haney, "but you'll notice he always seems to get to a fly ball when there's any chance of making it."

Because of his limitless potential, Aaron has been subjected to as many words of advice and criticism as praise. The experts see such a brilliant future in the young man that they almost automatically feel constrained to offer words of advice. It was the same with Ted Williams when he was a kid and batting over .400. The authorities still felt need to counsel him.

Rogers Hornsby, one of Aaron's milder critics, says that Aaron does have a weakness at bat—"a pitch with something on it right across the letters and in close." But Hornsby is quick to add that this is a batting weakness shared by every great hitter. Presumably, Hornsby was thinking about himself, too, because they don't come much greater.

Stan Musial, who staged a marvelous comeback last year to take away the hitting title from Aaron, once described the Braves greyhound-built outfielder as an "arrogant" hitter. "He thinks there's nothing he can't hit," says Musial, "but there's still some pitches no hitter can afford to go for."

Aaron is generally considered to be a bad-ball hitter—the saying goes that he's the best

bad-ball hitter to come along in the National League since Joe Medwick. "Sure he's a bad-ball hitter," says Bobby Bragan, who had ample opportunity to observe Aaron when Bragan was managing the Pirates. "It would be a bad mistake to change him, though," Bragan thinks.

When Aaron first came up to the majors his philosophy of batting was stated this way: "I just go up swinging. I like to swing at everything that looks good to me." Now it's different. Today he says, "I wait for my pitch," and that is, after all, the measure of a new maturity in the man.

Even though Aaron was swinging for the long ball last year, he might still have won the batting title (he finally finished fourth in the league with a .322 average) if it weren't for the isolated times when he began to press and lash out at everything instead of waiting for his pitch. The circumstance that perhaps hurt him the most came late in the season when he made some unfortunate public remarks to the effect that a certain St. Louis pitcher, among others, was throwing in the general direction of his noggin. To be perfectly fair to Hank, the accusation was made when the Braves were laboring hard and faltering a bit in their pennant efforts. And much of the hitting burden at the time was on Aaron. For quite a few games after that, Hank had trouble regaining his stride, as if the weight of his remarks had laid a heavy hand on his bat.

At any rate, if there is one thing that Aaron is not, it is a pop-off artist. In fact since coming to the majors, he's earned a reputation for his reticence and for his sparseness of conversation, which is not altogether justified, either. While Aaron is no pop-off, neither is he a primitive.

Mr. Aaron of Mobile, Alabama (the town gave him a whopping welcome-home reception after the World Series, choosing to ignore the fact that he now makes his home in Milwaukee) is an undistinguished figure in a baseball uniform. He stands 5-11½, weighs 175 and everybody wonders how he gets the power to hit to all fields the way he does. When he moves from the ondeck circle to the batter's box, he does so in indolent fashion, loping along slowly on bouncy heels. Once he is set in the box, he gives the impression of being rather bored with life. But when the pitcher gets set to fire the ball, Aaron is ready. "He may not look it," says Fred Haney, "but he's always ready to hit. Ever notice how he holds that bat away from him? You have to be a great wrist hitter to do that in the big leagues."

Most baseball experts agree that Aaron has

the best wrists in the game today. It is this wrist action, along with the power in his forearms, plus perfect eyesight and an uncanny sense of timing that make Aaron the best hitter in baseball. Teammate Warren Spahn once remarked how amazing it was to see Aaron stand there and wait for a pitch before making up his mind about swinging. "It's like giving him an extra strike," Spahn says in awe.

Since jumping from Class A baseball to the majors in 1954 (a feat of considerable dimensions in this day and age) all Aaron has done is take his place directly behind Stan Musial in the matter of active National League players with the best lifetime hitting percentage. His first year up with the Braves Henry hit a respectable .280. In 1955 he jumped to .314, including 27 home runs and 106 runs batted in. And in 1956 his league-leading average was .328, with 26 homers and 92 RBIs. He was the only major-leaguer to get 200 hits that year. Last year his 198 hits were two behind the major-league pace-setter, teammate Red Schoendienst.

Ever since he was a kid watching the big-league ball clubs sneak into Mobile for a day on their way north from Florida, Henry hungered for the time he would be traveling with them, as a major-leaguer. Later when he became a member of the Braves, and presumably more sophisticated, he set three other goals for himself—to win the most-valuable-player award (which he did in 1957), to lead his league in hitting, to play in a World Series. Today only 24 years old, Henry Aaron has come just about as close as any man in attaining his aims in life.

Henry is the third oldest boy in a family of eight that includes four other brothers and three sisters. His father, who was a shipbuilder worker in Mobile, also did some ballplaying on the side, but he wasn't playing much ball when Henry was born, February 5, 1934, in the shank of the depression.

In his sandlot days in Mobile, Aaron started out as a catcher, then switched to shortstop—he was always a hitter. He played shortstop for his Central High softball team (the school couldn't afford the equipment for baseball) and also starred in football. When he graduated from Central High at age 17 he played semipro ball with the local Negro baseball team. One day the big-city Indianapolis Clowns came in for an exhibition and the 150-pound Aaron rapped three hits. The Clowns, being a practical aggregation, took the local youngster with them.

But they didn't hold on to their prodigy long. Henry was batting about .450 that early

summer of 1952 and the scouts began converging on Sid Pollet, the Clowns owner. Pollet had all but completed a deal for Aaron to play for the Giants' farm at Sioux City, Iowa, when Dewey Griggs, the Braves scout, happened along. He won Aaron's hand. "The Giants wanted to give me an A contract and a C salary," is how Hank explains his signing with the Braves. He reported directly to Eau Claire in the Northern League and in 87 games established himself as a comer. He hit .336, was named league all-star shortstop and was voted rookie of the year.

The next year with Jacksonville in the Class A Sally League, Aaron completed his lower education. This is what he did for Ben Geraghty's pennant-winning team: Lead the league in hits (208); runs (115); runs batted in (125); average (.362); putouts and assists. He also hit 22 home runs and was second in the league in triples. Naturally, he won the league's most-valuable-player award hands down. "It was," said Ben Geraghty, "one of the greatest one-man performances I ever saw. Henry just stood up there flicking those great wrists of his and simply overpowered the pitching."

The next year the Braves figured that if Aaron made it to Triple A he would be accomplishing something. After all, he was only 20 years old, with but two years of minor-league seasoning behind him. The front office ticketed him for their Toledo American Association club, but in the spring he went to Bradenton, Florida, to work out with the old pros. There he proved that among other things he was also an opportunist.

Henry had played winter ball in Puerto Rico and had his eye when he reported to the Braves in the spring of '54. The Braves put Aaron in the outfield. They figured he would never make it as a shortstop in the majors. Aaron said at the time that it was all right with him because it meant he wouldn't have to do as much thinking (he likes to give people the impression, slightly erroneous, that he isn't a thinking man). Henry hit well all spring and then when the newly acquired Bobby Thomson broke his ankle, the way was clear for Aaron to stay up with the Braves. He had a fine season, finishing second to Wally Moon in the voting for Rookie of the Year. He might have caught Moon in the stretch because he was coming on as a hitter when he got into an accident. Playing a double-header late in the season he collected five straight hits. On the fifth hit he slid into third base and broke his ankle. But that fracture did nothing more than postpone the inevitable, which came in 1955—the establishment of Henry Aaron as an uncommonly gifted ball-player.

Hank is married to the former Barbara Lucas and the Aarons have two children, Gail Elaine, who is five, and Hank Jr., ten months. Henry moved to Milwaukee over the winter to accept a public-relations job with a local brewery, along with some of his Braves teammates.

He should do all right in the public-relations line. Off the field, Henry is a very friendly young man who likes to swim and play pool and eat seafood, especially shrimp. He has a good sense of humor, although it ordinarily has to be drawn out of him because he doesn't care to talk unless spoken to. Teammate Del Crandall describes Aaron as being "dumb as a fox." Once in his rookie year Aaron hit a home run against Robin Roberts and when he returned to the bench he exclaimed in wonder, "Is that really Roberts out there?"

Another time in the off season he was attending a banquet when the Braves' boss Lou Perini got up and in the course of things began extolling the virtues of Henry Aaron. Henry, who looked as if he was dozing through the speech, nudged teammate Bill Bruton and whispered, "Does he mean that before or after I sign?"

One of Hank's lengthiest declamations came when he hit that pennant-winning home run against the Cardinals. Sitting in the dressing room after the game, Milwaukee's good beer sopping through his uniform, he said, "My first thought was Bobby Thomson's homer. That's always been my idea of the most important homer. Now I got one myself. For me to get the hit myself—am I excited! I'm excited for the first time in my life!"

WALT DITZEN

Courtesy National Newspaper Syndicate © 1957 by Walt Ditzen

FAN FARE

BOTH *Fireside Books of Baseball* have included first-person stories from the exciting series "My Biggest Baseball Day," which was put out under the direction of sports-editor John P. Carmichael of the Chicago *Daily News*. In this one Carmichael takes over as ghost for the wondrous Al Simmons—and it's no more than proper that, of all the players, Simmons' greatest day in baseball turned out to be both games of a double-header!

1930:
Philadelphia Athletics 7, 8,
Washington Senators 6, 7

AL SIMMONS
as told to JOHN P. CARMICHAEL

WHEN THAT 1930 season was over and we had won our second straight pennant I understand Clark Griffith told Connie Mack: "I went back and checked up on Al Simmons this year. He hit 14 home runs in the eighth and ninth innings and every one figured in the ball game. We were never the same after he licked us in that double-header." So Connie gave me a three-year contract for $100,000, which he didn't intend to do at all. But that's more like the end, not the beginning, of this particular day. . . . Memorial Day, 1930!

The Senators were in town for morning and afternoon games. They were leading the league by four games and we were second. What's more, they wanted to make so sure of knocking us off twice and really getting a stranglehold on first place that they'd sent Pitchers Ad Liska and "Bump" Hadley into town 48 hours ahead of the team to get fully rested for the big day. Liska worked the opener against "Lefty" Grove, but we weren't particularly worried, because Mose never had lost a morning game in his career . . . that's a fact . . . and he always asked to pitch them.

Well, we were brand-new world champions, of course, and we had a good crowd on hand, but we weren't doing so well near the end of the affair. Liska was one of those semiunder-hand pitchers with a little of this and that and not much of anything, but he had us off stride and was ahead 6-3 into the ninth with two out, nobody on base and Grove up. Naturally Grove didn't hit. Connie sent Spencer Harris up to swing for him and he got a single. Then Dibs Williams hit safely and old man Simmons was on the spot. I'd already gone four for the collar and those Philly fans could be tough every so often. Some of 'em were yelling "Three out" and "How about another pinch hitter?" and I was thinking, "Boy, we better win that second game," when Liska cut loose.

The ball was right in there and didn't break and I really swung. It landed in the left-field seats, the score was tied and the customers were all for me now. We couldn't do anything more and went into extra innings. I got a double in the 11th, but we didn't score. I singled in the 13th and didn't get home. In the 15th I hit another two-bagger . . . four straight hits, mind you, after going out easily four times in a row. Jimmie Foxx came up and hit a twisting roller down the third-base line . . . topped the ball. He beat it out by a half-step and on the play I went to third and rounded the bag as if I might try to score. I got caught in a run-down. Well, there I was, scrambling around and cursing myself for blowing a chance to get the game over, but finally I dove for third and was safe. Just as I lit I felt something go haywire in my right knee.

Standing on the bag I could feel it swelling up under my uniform and by the time "Boob" McNair singled and I scored the winning run it was becoming stiff. We went inside and got the clothes off and the damn thing was twice its normal size. Connie Mack couldn't believe his eyes. "How did you do it?" he kept asking. I didn't know myself . . . didn't hit anything but the ground. He put in a call for Dr. Carnett, our club physician. I can't remember his first name . . . and he's dead now . . . but he was one of the outstanding doctors in the East and a great ball fan. He came in and immediately ordered cold compresses on it.

"You've broken a blood vessel," he said, "but it'll be all right eventually."

We didn't have so much time between games, because that opener had taken too long, so there was nothing to do but sit around and order a little lunch. The outgoing crowd was all mixed up with the incoming customers and, of course, a lot of those who figured to see only the morning game were so het up that they turned right around outside the gates and bought their way back in again. Meanwhile the swelling in my knee was going down, but it hurt and finally Mr. Mack said to Carnett: "He can't play any more today, I suppose," and Doc said no. "You'll probably want to take him to a hospital," said Connie and Carnett agreed.

"But not today," he said. "I came out here to see a double-header and I'm going to see it. You . . ." and he addressed Mr. Mack . . . "can put him back in a uniform and let him sit on the bench. He can't run, but he might come in handy as a pinch hitter. What's more . . ." and he was laughing at Connie . . . "if a spot

comes up, I want him in there, too. I'll take care of the knee later, but at the moment I'm a rabid fan and assistant manager."

Out we went for the second game and the fans were in a great state when they saw Harris going to left instead of me. Only a few knew anything had happened and they couldn't understand why I was benched after driving in three runs and scoring the last one. I think George Earnshaw was going for us and Hadley for them and he got off just as good as Liska had in the first game. Came the seventh inning and we were behind 7-3. We sent up a pinch hitter for Joe Boley and he got on and then there was a base on balls and a hit and the bags were loaded. Suddenly I saw Connie look down the line and crook that finger at me.

"Looks like this is the time and the place," he said. "This is what Dr. Carnett meant and you know what he said. Walk around the bases if you can."

I picked out a bat and there I was for the second time in the same day in the clutch. Hadley told me afterward: "I never wanted a place to put somebody so much in all my life, but we were full up." He seemed to take a long time and finally pitched and it was outside for a ball. He tried another in the same spot and I let it go. Then he changed up on me and tried for a strike.

My bat caught it just right . . . where you know that even if the ball is caught, you've hit it solid. This one came down in the left-field stands, too, and the score was 7-7. I hobbled around the bases and got back to the bench and Connie was sitting up straight, his eyes bright like a bird's, and he said: "My, that was fine, Al!" We won in the ninth and down came Carnett and lugged me off to the hospital.

A REGULAR feature in *The Saturday Evening Post* has been the frequent exploring of baseball's rule-book catacombs by Harry Simmons, author, and Willard Mullin, cartoonist. In the following three examples, the problem is stated textually by Simmons, then restated pictorially by Mullin. Finally the answer.

So You Think You Know Baseball!

HARRY SIMMONS *and* WILLARD MULLIN

SOMETIMES BASEBALL RULES appear illogical. Take this simulated major-league scramble, based on a play which actually occurred elsewhere last year.

Say the New York Giants and Milwaukee Braves are tied, 3-3, as the Giants come to bat in the last of the eighth. Henry Thompson is walked. Willie Mays slams the ball far and deep into center field. The outfielder chasing it slips and falls heavily. The ball bounces to the clubhouse and caroms about before the Braves right fielder reaches it.

Meanwhile Thompson crosses the plate with Mays behind him. But the Giants' first-base coach waves Thompson back to second, for the coach noted that he failed to touch that base. Thompson obliges, carefully touching home plate and third on the way back. He reaches second safely as the ball is returned to the infield. Mays is already in the dugout.

A big question arises. Can a runner score when a player ahead of him in the batting order is still on base?

If you were umpiring, would you let Mays' run count?

A ruling by the Official Playing Rules Interpretations Committee was necessary on this one. Under it, Mays would be out. No runs count. Section 7.12, which reads in part: "Unless two are out, the status of a following runner is not affected by a preceding runner's failure to touch a base," was held inadequate in this case.

An 1897 rule, dropped from the books in 1931 for no apparent reason, would have covered the situation. It provided: "No base runner shall score a run to count in the game ahead of the base runner preceding him in the batting order, if there be such preceding base runner who had not been put out in that inning."

Oddly, if Thompson had been thrown out

while attempting to regain second base, Mays' run would have counted.

* * *

A player who tries, by word or sign, to incite a demonstration among spectators can be banished from the game and playing field under Rule 4.06. Use of this rule in an actual game last year created a remarkable situation. Here is what happened, and what resulted from it:

Detroit, batting in the top of the sixth inning, leads Boston 3-0. With one out, Bill Tuttle doubles. He holds his base as Frank Bolling flies out to right field. Red Wilson grounds an infield fly behind second. Tuttle scores on a very close play at the plate. The Boston catcher sharply challenges the decision. So does Manager Pinky Higgins. The umpire won't be budged, of course. In disgust, the catcher lobs the ball into center field. For this, the umpire thumbs him out of the game under Rule 4.06. The Boston outfield makes a play on the ball.

Wilson, standing near first, starts around the bases. As Wilson rounds third, the umpire bends over to dust off the plate. He wields his whisk broom so long that Wilson has to hold up briefly before stepping on the plate. Boston promptly protests the run.

If you were umpiring, would you let the run count?

The umpire allowed Wilson's run.

The Boston protest was based on two contentions:

That Boston had only eight men on the field after the catcher's ouster, thus precluding legal play.

That there must have been a time-out while the umpire dusted the plate.

Both claims were rejected by the League of-

fice. A new 1957 rule clarifies the first situation, by permitting a "disqualified" player to remain in the game until the immediate play is complete. Whether an umpire ought to dust off home plate with a runner circling the bases is, however, still being argued.

* * *

A base runner who is out but has not yet left the diamond, must avoid confusing or hindering a play on another runner. Here in a hypothetical major-league setting is an unusual mixup resulting from this situation.

Say the Dodgers lead the Cardinals, 4-1, as the Dodgers come to bat in the last of the seventh. Junior Gilliam laces a single to left. As Charley Neal comes to bat, hit-and-run is signaled. Gilliam starts off with the pitch. Neal slaps the ball and heads for first, but his hit is a foul pop. Catcher Hal Smith pulls it in. Noting Gilliam far off first, Smith pegs the ball there in a try at a double play. But the ball hits Neal in the back, as he sprints down the three-foot lane toward first base, and rebounds into the Dodger dugout.

Is Neal guilty of interference? If so, Gilliam, also, is out.

If you were umpiring, how would you call it?

Send Gilliam to third base. (See Section 7.05g.)

Neal, properly running in the three-foot lane, may not be charged with interference. If he had been outside or astride the lane when struck by the ball, Gilliam would have been out because of Neal's hindrance. (See Section 7.09f.) But a Case Book Note permits a batter or runner to advance properly even when out. It says: "He shall not by that act alone be considered as confusing, hindering or impeding the fielders."

IN the exact sense, this isn't a profile at all. It's merely an account of one night in the life of outfielder Hank Bauer, who at the time this piece appeared was charged with hitting another man in an off-the-field brawl. Bauer subsequently was completely exonerated.

Gentlemen, This Is a Man!

BILL SLOCUM

I WAS RAISED among major-league baseball players and all other things being equal I'd rather know a delicatessen owner, anytime.

But a fellow was arrested, fingerprinted, mugged, and paroled the other day and he is something special. His name is Hank Bauer, of course, and I suppose this is a character reference. Mr. Bauer needs a character reference from the likes of me like Tommy Manville needs another wife.

Anyhow, I can't give Mr. Bauer a character reference. I never met him. But, gentlemen, this is a man!

This is not a baseball story. It's not a night-club fight story. And, it's not a story about Mr. Bauer's two Purple Hearts, 11 campaign ribbons, two Bronze Stars, and 23 attacks of malaria.

This is a story about a night in September of 1955 and it occurred before all of 400 people at the Polo Grounds. As you may know, the amputee veterans have a baseball team. This night the wounded heroes were playing a team of TV celebrities for charity.

The Yanks were in town. They were in a terribly trying fight with Cleveland and Chicago. The pennant and $10,000 per man was hanging on every game. That day the Indians had licked the Yankees and Mr. Bauer had gone five-for-o!

You must know ballplayers to know what happens to their good manners and their class when they go to bat five times in an important game and can't get a hit. And now the game is lost, to boot.

The nicest of them won't speak to anybody. The others . . . well, I don't think "raging beasts" quite paints the picture.

Several Yanks were to grace the amputee-TV celebrity game. Mr. Bauer and Jerry Coleman showed up.

Mr. Bauer had had a ghastly afternoon at the Stadium but Mr. Bauer was there that night. In fact, Mr. Bauer was everywhere that night. He was all over the field during practice and in and out of the stands between innings.

He was having a ball with the amputees. I don't have to tell anybody how those unlucky baseball fans felt about Mr. Bauer.

Now, when Mr. Bauer plays at the Stadium before 70,000 fans he speaks to nobody. Not even to the Hollywood and Broadway celebs who have the front-row seats. But, at the Polo Grounds, before 400, he spoke to everybody he could. If the amputees couldn't get to him he got to them.

Mr. Bauer knew the amputees were trying to win (as they did) and he never insulted their courage by clowning during the game as he played on the TV team. He got a scratch hit and he ran it out. And beat the throw to first.

I explained to the lady at my side that Casey Stengel, George Weiss, Dan Topping and the entire Yankee ball club would turn pale at the spectacle of their great outfielder risking his legs in a game that wasn't for money. If Mr. Bauer were hurt the Yanks would probably blow the pennant and the $10,000 it meant to each Yank.

As I talked, John Daly lashed a feeble grounder to first. Mr. Bauer lit out for second and the one-armed first baseman made his play there. When you have but one arm it is terribly strong. The first baseman hit Mr. Bauer squarely on the back of his head.

He went down. And the Yankee pennant chances were on the Polo Grounds basepaths. Mr. Bauer got up and sort of tottered to second as he would in a big-league game. It was an exquisite compliment to the amputees.

I had been growling to the lady beside me about two or three veteran ballplayers who had made one token appearance and then left although they had nowhere to go. Now, Mr. Bauer had a legitimate excuse to get out of there and avoid further injury that would be disastrous to his own pocketbook, to say nothing of his teammates' bank balances.

Mr. Bauer finished the long game, his hat at an odd angle to accommodate an egg-sized lump on his skull.

When the Polo Grounds lights went dim and then flickered out Mr. Bauer was still around talking to amputees. He stood there; hot, sweaty, his head throbbing. He was a very tired man after a long day's disappointing work.

But, Mr. Bauer was there as long as anybody in a wheelchair wanted an autograph, a handshake, or just a few light words.

I've always wanted to tell this story and perhaps I've taken advantage of Mr. Bauer's position and predicament to tell it.

I hope I'm the only one taking advantage of Mr. Bauer's position and predicament.

JOHN GALLAGHER

"Oh, oh—Here comes Windy."

HERE is part of a chapter from Ken Smith's definitive book, *Baseball's Hall of Fame.*

The Pioneers

KEN SMITH

THE PERSONALITIES enshrined in the Baseball Hall of Fame represent a whole gamut of fictional characters and idiosyncrasies. Reading about them, and recalling their varied accomplishments and triumphs is like losing oneself in the great adventure classics of literature. Heroics, tragedies, derring-do, comic relief . . . all of that and more is there, personified by the occupants of the hallowed Hall.

Bold, brilliant, powerful, quick, wise, gay in play or administration of the game, each acted his own role and then gave over the stage to the next scene in the endless cavalcade of baseball.

Alexander Joy Cartwright was one of a group of young gentlemen of the professional, financial and business set of New York City in 1842, who used to lay their waistcoats neatly aside and enjoy a few rounds of the newfangled ball game played on a diamond-shaped surface. Sides were limited to eleven and an out allowed if a ground ball was fielded and thrown to a teammate with his foot on the base, ahead of the runner. This was brand-new in those days, supposedly having been brought down from Cooperstown.

They played "uptown" on Twenty-seventh Street where the original Madison Square Garden was built later. After three years of informal recreation, Cartwright organized the "swells" into a social and baseball club known as the Knickerbockers. The date was September 23, 1845. Duncan F. Curry was president. This was the first baseball team ever formed. A similar group known as the New York Club was organized in another part of town, comprising some gentlemen named Winslow, Murphy, Ransom, Trenchard, Davis, Johnson, Lalor, Thompson and Case. (At least six of these names appeared in modern box scores. Could it be that some of these early New Yorkers were their ancestors?)

The Knickerbockers challenged them and on June 19, 1846, the first baseball game ever played between two definite nines transpired at Elysian Fields, in Hoboken, New Jersey.

Cartwright's friends introduced the first baseball uniforms when they gathered for practice in April, 1849 (without benefit of spring training in the South!). They sported long woolen trousers of blue, white flannel shirts and straw hats. Mohair hats were substituted in 1855. The last Knickerbocker team appeared in 1858. Harry Wright, who later became manager of the Cincinnati Red Stockings, was on that pioneer team. The early Knickerbockers wouldn't play an unproved or nondescript nine when common workingmen began organizing teams, but, in American fashion, the game soon became democratic with skill the sole criterion. Wright's team then took on all comers.

Having organized the first team and having helped promote the first game, not to mention having a hand in the first uniform, Cartwright earned his niche in the Hall of Fame then and there. But the point for which he is best remembered is his establishment of the fundamental rules that prevail today. While Doubleday is credited with inventing the diamond and the theory of put-outs and with limiting the number of players, Cartwright is the man who turned this rough outline into its permanent form of nine innings, nine men on a side and particularly the 90-foot base lines (then called forty-two paces) as he and his Knickerbocker friends put the rules on paper. He headed west in a covered wagon during the gold rush of 1849, taking the game with him. He stopped to play along the way, through the Middle Western valleys, over the Rockies into California and thenceforth to Hawaii. A white-haired and long-bearded old frontiersman in his later years, he lived to see the game grow up. Cartwright, who was born in New York April 17, 1820, died in Hawaii in 1892, maintaining his interest in the game until the end.

Henry (Father) Chadwick, elected to the Hall of Fame with Cartwright in September, 1938, created the first system of scoring games and recording results. He compiled the first rule book in 1859. The first baseball writer, he was pre-eminent for a half-century as publicist, statistician, historian and in keeping diamond affairs in order. Chadwick invented the box score and was chairman of the rules committee of the first nationwide baseball organization. The forerunner of the Sid Mercers, the Ring Lardners, Damon Runyons and the countless baseball reporters who made the National Game big news, Chadwick deserves his place among baseball's elite.

He was born in England in 1833 and came to America when he was thirteen. At twenty-five he became a writer for the New York *Clipper,* with which he was associated for thirty years. While in his fifties Chadwick wrote baseball for the Brooklyn *Eagle.* For the last twenty-seven years of his life, which ended in April, 1908, he was editor of *Spalding's Guide,* and he corresponded for various publications. It was he who established such an intimate relation between the game and the unsubsidized press. He was personally acquainted with the Knickerbockers and followed the sport through the start of the twentieth century. He waged a winning fight against gambling and rowdiness; was a stickler for accurate statistics and presented facts to the public with an interesting literary touch.

George Wright is known as the lead-off man in the Hall of Fame, for he was the first player chosen when the Centennial Commission assembled to pick the Builders of Baseball. He reflected the personality and keen mind that is always associated with stardom on the diamond. Wright was the scintillating hitter and fielder, the star attraction of the historic Cincinnati Red Stockings, first professional team. Wright, in 1869, sparked the Red Stockings to a record that has never been equaled—a full season without a defeat. The victories totaled 57. The streak was extended into the next season when 24 more wins were registered for an unbroken skein of 81 before defeat finally interrupted the mighty display of skill and power.

Wright was born January 28, 1847, in Harlem, New York City. His people came from England, where his father was a cricket player of wide repute. George played baseball with the Gothams of New York City when he was nine-teen and, in 1867, as a government employee, played with the Nationals in Washington. There were no leagues and no salaries—just clubs. As a member of the New York Unions in 1868, he played against the Red Stockings at Cincinnati, then managed by his brother Harry. George's work was so impressive that Harry persuaded him to join Cincinnati the next year.

Harry predated George as organizer, manager, player and press representative of the first professional team, and they might start with him when they mention prominent people left out of the Hall of Fame. Eighty-odd years since Harry's prime, broadcaster Ernest Harwell was in there pitching for him as the first manager to win four pennants in succession, first to use hand signals in coaching, first to see the advantages of Southern spring training, first player to be honored with a "day" and the first chief of umpires. 'Way back he was the first manager to adopt knickerbockers in place of pantaloons. Adept at handling players, he helped steer the game safely through the first channels of professionalism. He is sometimes credited with development of the change of pace and playing the hitter. One of his big accomplishments was projecting George into stardom.

Those Red Stockings of 1869 were a proud, daring team and it was considered a high honor to wear their uniform. They were the first club to discard long pants in favor of knickerbockers. They caught public fancy and played before enormous crowds, sometimes as many as 20,000. There was no admission—generous contributions poured into a passed hat. Players were paid from $700 to $1,400, with Wright in the highest brackets. The entire team sported long whiskers. Traveling east and then from coast to coast, they returned to Cincinnati at the end of the 1869 season with a standing of 1.000. While batting averages were based on standards vastly different from today's, Wright's percentage of .630 is worth noting.

Wright was a great shortstop. He amazed the spectators constantly with his speed, quick thinking and fielding skill. He had a great arm and could play any position. He was a fine catcher. The Red Stockings disbanded in 1870, possibly in remorse because the Brooklyn Atlantics beat them 8 to 7 in eleven innings!

George and Harry joined the Boston Red Stockings in the new National Association, the first professional league, in 1871, and they won pennants in 1872, '73, '74 and '75. When the National League was organized in 1876, the

Boston club was a charter member and shortstop Wright played for three years. The team won the pennant in 1877 and '78. He managed the Providence Nationals in 1879 and won the championship. It was the seventh flag he had helped win in nine seasons. Pitching rules changed in 1879 to the overarm style (contrasting the compulsory underhand throw), and George never did master it. He was a good golfer, played football expertly, and cricket was a natural heritage.

While playing with Boston, he operated a sporting-goods store, later taking on a partner to form the Wright & Ditson Company. A. G. Spalding, who pitched for Wright's Boston team, and A. J. Reach, who played second base for Philadelphia, also organized sporting-goods companies that became familiar to all American boys. The three firms merged in later years.

A fine, intelligent citizen, George Wright helped give baseball a good name from the start. Nor was his pioneering limited to baseball. It was he who is credited with having played the first game of golf in New England and probably in the United States, and he was the first to import and manufacture tennis equipment in this country.

He maintained high interest in the game throughout his life and unknowingly helped start the Hall of Fame when he served on the commission that settled upon Cooperstown as the birthplace of baseball. Wright was seen in the Boston ball parks during the 1930s amusing himself scouting players who performed with the pep and dash of his day. Wright held the first big-league lifetime admission pass issued to ten-year men. On his Boston team was a utility player whose last name was Beals. Blessed with two daughters and two sons, Wright named one of his sons Beals. He, with his brother Irvin, became a national tennis star.

George Wright died in Boston at the age of ninety.

When the National League was formed in 1876, one of the eight clubs was the Hartford Charter Oaks whose president was a brilliant 39-year-old bank president, lawyer and Civil War veteran named Morgan G. Bulkeley. A ringleader and influential voice in organizing big-league baseball, it was because he identified the diamond with a high plane in public life that he was placed in the Hall of Fame. Each occupant in his own way made a certain contribution and his was frankly as a "front." He placed the first permanent major league on solid ground while acting as the first National League president, then, after one year in office, turned over the reins to William A. Hulbert, of Chicago.

Bulkeley then moved up the ladder of a distinguished career. He became president of the Aetna Life Insurance Company in 1879 and four years later was elected Mayor of Hartford, serving eight years. He was Governor of Connecticut from 1888 to 1893 and United States Senator from 1905 to 1911. He always remained close to the game and, while in the United States Senate, he served on the commission that investigated and authenticated the origin of baseball.

Bulkeley was born December 26, 1837, in East Haddam, Connecticut. His father was the first Aetna Company president. The young man studied and practiced law in Brooklyn and served under General George McClellan in the Civil War. He received a Master of Arts degree at Yale and an LL.D. at Trinity. He died November 6, 1922. Baseball has often been pictured as the typical American sport where the banker sits beside the bootblack to cheer, fan and eat peanuts. Bulkeley was probably the banker they had in mind.

Busher

LYALL SMITH

THEY CALLED HIM a "busher" when he was announced as manager of a major-league team.

He was almost 40. His baseball background was minor league. Half his life had been spent on dusty, clay-ribbed diamonds down in the sticks.

When he wasn't bouncing around in buses, he was riding a day coach. He ate at greasy-spoon cafés in the tank towns. A night to remember was one when a fan invited him and other players to a home-cooked meal.

He was a bush-league player who kept waiting for the call to be brought up to the big time for the chance that seemed to come to everyone else but him.

He was recognized as just a good busher, one of the thousands who had what it took for the sticks but not enough of it for the majors where Pullmans replaced buses, where steaks substituted for stew, where pay checks contained four digits and sometimes five instead of only two or three.

But he stuck it out as a cocky, determined little guy who was Irish in more ways than just his name. The big leagues finally noticed him. They made him a manager down on the farm.

He bounced around still more. He played for a while and managed at the same time. Then he stopped playing and just managed. Years went by and he still was minor league.

They weren't looking for his type in the majors. They wanted the boys with the big names and the fancy big-league backgrounds for their big-time managers to go along with all the other ones with years of major-league experience.

Finally he was given his chance. The man he succeeded had been one of the big-name managers with a long career, both as a player and a pilot.

His team had finished in the second division.

The owners wanted a better ending for the new year. So they dipped down and picked up a man who never had played a major-league game in his life.

His name rang no responsive chord when he was unveiled in the big time. Newspapers had to pick up the threads of his background and weave them into a story to let the fans know who he was.

It hadn't been necessary with the man who had preceded him. Everybody knew of him, but not this new manager. He wasn't a complete unknown. But he was the next thing to it.

When he was brought in, he was told by his owners that he was to put some spark and hustle into a team which had shown flashes of greatness the previous year but had sagged when it counted.

He was hired under a "get tough" policy. He put in new rules during spring training. He cracked down on some of the playboys. He rode herd on a couple of players who were front-office favorites but hadn't produced.

He had jibes poked at him from training-camp dugouts when he popped out to argue with umpires. "What's YOUR name?" they would holler. "How are things down in the sticks?"

Some of the fans looked over their noses at him when the team had a poor exhibition-season record and then lost the first game of the regular season.

"That's what we get for hiring a guy with no big-league experience," they grumbled. "He's strictly bush . . ."

But the little Irishman proved them wrong. He stuck around and proved that a "busher" could be big league even though he was nearly 40 when he hit the big time.

In fact, Joe McCarthy, who won nine championships and seven World Series, has made the Hall of Fame.

THE great pennant back-in of our time—the Phillies in 1950—is here recaptured, at its climactic moment, by the incomparable Red Smith.

1950:
Philadelphia Phillies 4,
Brooklyn Dodgers 1

——————————— RED SMITH ———————————

THE TALLEST, steepest, swiftest, dizziest, daredevil, death-defying dive ever undertaken by a baseball team came off with a rich and fruity climax yesterday when the Phillies toppled headlong into the World Series.

For thirty-five years the Phillies struggled to win a National League pennant. For the last twelve days they battled mightily to lose one. Then in the tenth inning of the 155th game of their season, all snarled up in a strangling tie with the team that had closed eight laps on them in a fortnight, they were knocked kicking into the championship by the bat of Dick Sisler.

George Sisler, probably the greatest first baseman who ever lived, whose .400 hitting couldn't get him into a World Series, sat in Ebbets Field and saw his big son slice a three-run homer that shattered the pennant hopes of the Dodgers, whom George now serves.

Sisler's hit won the game, 4 to 1. Minutes earlier, lustrous pitching by Robin Roberts had saved it, after the Dodgers had come within a dozen feet of the victory that would have closed the season in a tie and brought Philadelphia and Brooklyn together for a play-off.

"There hasn't been such a finish," said Mr. Warren Brown, the noted Chicago author, "since sporting British officials carried Durando over the line in the 1908 Olympic marathon."

On September 19 the Phillies had the pennant won in every sense save the mathematical one. They were seven and one half games ahead of the Boston Braves, and Brooklyn was third, nine games off the pace. The Dodgers won fourteen of their next seventeen games,

the Phillies three of their twelve. So when they showed up yesterday before Ebbets Field's largest gathering of the year, the Phils' lead was exactly one game, with one game to play.

They had neither won nor lost the championship, but they had qualified handsomely for off-season employment—substituting for the diving horse in Atlantic City.

They had also brought gold pouring in a bright yellow stream into the Brooklyn box office. Instead of leasing out their park for family picnics this weekend, the Dodgers sold 58,952 tickets for the last two games, many of them to customers who stood outside the bleacher gates all Saturday night.

By four A.M., cars were pulling into parking lots near the field. By six-thirty, there were 5,000 or 6,000 persons in line. By one P.M., all gates were closed and nobody without a reserved-seat ticket was admitted. Cops estimated that 25,000 were turned away. It was bigger than many World Series crowds in Brooklyn, and properly so, for this was bigger than a World Series game, where even the losers gather much loot. The losers of this game got the winter off.

In spite of everything, the Phillies managed a surface appearance of confidence. Before the game the Philadelphia manager, Eddie Sawyer, was asked to name his pitcher for the first play-off game today.

"That's one thing I never do," he said mildly. "Announce my pitcher for the day after the season closes."

For what seemed an interminable time, though, there was reason to doubt that the season ever would close. Big Don Newcombe was rocking back on his hind leg, waggling a big spiked shoe in the Phillies' beardless faces, and firing his service past them. They had at least one base runner in every inning after the first, but these Phils are kids still damp from the nursing bottle, and this was hard stuff Newcombe was serving.

Roberts, who passed his twenty-fifth birthday watching the Phillies lose on Saturday, was pouring an even more poisonous potion. In seven innings the only Dodger to hit him was Peewee Reese, who was to make three of Brooklyn's five hits and the only Dodger run.

This was the run that tied the score in the sixth inning when Peewee sliced a ball which got jammed in a chink on the top of the right-field wall, at the base of the screen that surmounts the wall. Ground rules specify that a ball lodging where this one did remains in play for an Oriental homer.

To say tension was growing is to abuse the mother tongue. Things reached such a pass that when a bug flew into the eye of Mike Goliat, the Phillies' second baseman, Mr. Babe Alexander, of Philadelphia, cursed. "Those Dodgers," he said, "have adopted germ warfare."

But things were practically lethargic then compared with the Brooklyn ninth, when the Dodgers put their first two batsmen on base and Duke Snider lashed what had to be the deciding hit into center field. Richie Ashburn fielded the ball on one hop, threw swiftly and superbly to the plate, and Cal Abrams, coming home with the winning run, was out by twelve fat feet.

Nobody ever saw better pitching than Roberts showed then. With runners on second and third and one out, he walked Jackie Robinson purposely to fill the bases, then reared back and just threw that thing through there. Carl Furillo popped up. Gil Hodges flied out.

Ken Heintzelman and Ken Johnson ran all the way from the bull pen to shake Roberts' hand. Eddie Sawyer patted Robin's stomach. Those were gentle hands. Sisler and Roberts felt others later.

Sawyer watched his operatives pummel this pair when their great deeds were done. Then he announced that the Phillies would take today off. Most of them to rest. Roberts and Sisler to anoint their bruises.

HERE is the story of the man who, as Robert Smith points out in this chapter from his engrossing book *Baseball*, "probably made as sharp an impress on the game of baseball, when it was still growing up, as anybody who ever played for money." Latham died only a handful of years ago, in his nineties.

The Freshest Man on Earth

ROBERT SMITH

ARLIE LATHAM, although his name does not seem to have echoed quite so far in the spoken history of the land as those of a few of his great contemporaries, probably made as sharp an impress on the game of baseball, when it was still growing up, as anybody who ever played for money. When his name is mentioned nowadays, it is often used in an essentially libelous manner. "Giving it the Arlie Latham" means, to an infielder, making a half-hearted pass at a ground ball, without any real attempt to field it. But "giving it the Arlie Latham," if it had been used back in the seventies and eighties, would have meant pouring every last ounce of physical and nervous energy into the game at hand. For Arlie was a boy who played baseball at top speed all the time. He was a fine fielder, a swift runner, a crafty batter, an acrobat on the base lines, and, above all, a tireless "coacher."

Arlie is the man who practically invented the characteristic chatter of the ball diamond, the endless lilting encouragement which an infield gives to the pitcher, the glad shouts and gestures of the coaching box, the raucous ribbing of opponents, the earnest advice offered to base runners.

There probably never was a boy more deeply in love with the game of baseball than Arlie Latham was when, in 1877, at the age of seventeen, he played professional ball in Pittsfield, Massachusetts. The game thrilled him to his bones, uplifted him, turned him inside out, drove from his mind everything but the glad and hot desire to win.

In the many years since then that Arlie has played or coached the game he never, according to his own story, once sat down. He could not bear to be on a bench or chair while the game was moving. He wanted, when he was not playing on the field, to be in the coaching box, beseeching some beloved teammate to come through with a hit, warning a base runner that a throw was imminent, reminding a batter that a walk was as good as a hit, ragging the opposing third baseman, shouting happy replies to the fans who tried to heckle him.

It was not considered good form in those gentle days for a man to comport himself so noisily on the ball field. The better folk, who undoubtedly saw little baseball and played even less, were repelled by the spectacle of a young man in a straggly mustache capering, as Arlie did, to the accompaniment of an endless chirp and chatter.

A ball crank in Pittsfield once offered to outfit Arlie in silk socks and undershirts if he would keep quiet through one complete game. The man showed Arlie a box of the stuff, which to a seventeen-year-old looked like something looted from a castle.

"I'll be quiet," Arlie promised. "I won't say a word."

The only way Arlie could be sure of himself that day was to lie flat on the ground, behind the other seated players—what time he was not actually needed on the field—and hold both hands tight over his ears. The sounds of the game and the cries of the spectators reached him but faintly. Once or twice he felt his muscles contract and caught himself in the act of bounding to his feet to see what the clamor was about. But he managed to hold perfectly still until the ninth inning, when the winning run was on base. He held his breath and tried to pray the run in. He listened for the bat meeting the ball; but only a subdued murmur came through his tightly pressed fingers. Then there was a crack. The fans under the trees began to scream. A hit! Arlie jumped to his feet. "Go it! Go it!" Then he clapped his hand over his mouth. He was . . . Oh to hell with that rich-man clothing! He leaped out onto the grass and shrieked louder than any of them, as his teammate scurried home with the victory.

Arlie's capering was not confined to the side lines. He was an able tumbler (he may have developed this skill in Pittsfield, where he sometimes had to leap from a high window when his courting was interrupted by the return of an irate father). Once, in a game with Chicago, Cap Anson was fielding one of Arlie's bunts on the first-base line; and in the minds of Anson, the spectators, and both teams, Arlie was out by a mile. But the little man simply flew head first over the stooping Anson, landed on hands and shoulders, and flipped himself quickly erect and onto first base. He stood there with both feet on the base and saluted the Chicago captain. "How do, Anse," he said. Anson, while the crowd yelled and laughed, glumly tossed the ball to the pitcher and returned to his position without a smile, a nod, or even a noise.

Arlie's career as an active player was shortened by a foolish sort of accident to his throwing arm which caused it, as he grew older, to tighten up so he could not straighten it at all. He had to impel the ball across the diamond by pushing it as a shot-putter puts the shot. He was on his way out to the ball park in St. Louis one day, in company with Bushong, the catcher, and Manager Charles Comiskey. Comiskey put a point on an argument about throwing ability by offering a hundred dollars to the one who could throw the farthest. Arlie, who was always straining at the leash, could hardly wait to get his coat off and start firing the ball into the distance. He had a wonderful arm and loved to work it. This time, however, he failed to loosen it up beforehand and he worked it just too hard. On the throw which won the hundred dollars he pulled a muscle, and his arm was never the same.

Toward the end of his career his poor crippled arm stood him in such bad stead that he became the butt of current wise guys among players, fans, and sports writers. It was then the phrase "giving it the Arlie Latham" came into being.

It is commonplace nowadays for a well-coached and well-knit team to offer the world a sample of the *real* Arlie Latham by "talking it up" all through a game. You can hear on any ball diamond the continual chant with which the infielders help maintain the pitcher's morale, the singsong encouragement that "we're all behind you, boy. We're all behind you." Or the man in the coaching box will loudly announce his faith in the batter, encouraging that individual with the assurance that he *can* hit, that he needs only to "stay loose," to "wait for the one you want," to "make him pitch to you," to "make him work."

Hear the catcher sometime as he earnestly invites the pitcher to "hit the dicker," to "work easy," or to "make a hitter out of him," insists that there is "no hitter up there," or queries the team as to which one is going to "get the leading lady."

This monotonous chirping may seem dreary and meaningless to a spectator, but it can steady a nervous pitcher, rejuvenate a player discouraged by his own blunders, or provide just the stimulant a man may need to pull him through the last few minutes of a tense game.

So the entire game of baseball, from the sand lots to the stadiums, can take a minute off sometime to acknowledge its debt to a gnarled little man named Latham, who first shook off the silly convention of polite silence and helped turn baseball into a rollicking, noisy, exciting effort where a man can learn to appreciate his kinship with his fellows.

Some part-time bard once wrote a rhyme about Latham, "that man from Lynn, whom no one can approach." Said the verse: "He can scrape 'em, he can scathe 'em, this hustling player Latham!" Undoubtedly that was Arlie's middle name: "Hustle." He liked to hustle between seasons, too. One winter he traveled through New England with a group of ball-players and other athletes who played a game they called "ice polo" and also gave demonstrations of base stealing, sliding, and throwing. Arlie would illustrate the fine art of cutting bases (Mike Kelly's stunt) or show the small-town folk how to make a base safely by sliding between the baseman's legs. In this way he added a little lining to his pockets, won a few more addicts for the national game, and contrived an excellent excuse for continuing to play baseball right through the year.

After his muscles gave out, Arlie turned to umpiring and learned to take with wry equanimity the brutal riding which umpires were subject to in the late nineteenth century. Later he became a coach for the New York Giants, and in 1946, at the age of eighty-six, he was still in the big leagues—in charge of the press boxes at the Yankee Stadium and the Polo Grounds.

When he was at his best, there were not many men more sought after than Arlie Latham. He was the first man to be invited on the round-the-world trip organized by A. G. Spalding in 1889. He had to refuse because he had already been booked to appear with a show called *Fashions,* in which he capered and sang a song written especially for him:

I'm a daisy on the diamond,
I'm a dandy on the stage,
I'd ornament a horsecar,
Or look pretty in a cage. . . .

I'm a Hustler from Hustletown,
The Freshest Man on Earth!

HARRY LYONS

Courtesy *Sport* Magazine. ©

". . . and now, fans, your post-game sponsors,
Mirakleen Soap, bring you another
great television first . . ."

Our Boarding House

OPENING day at San Francisco . . . April 15, 1958, . . . the day that, in the words of Commissioner Ford Frick, big-league baseball became "truly national" for the first time.

1958:
San Francisco Giants 8,
Los Angeles Dodgers 0

BOB STEVENS

THEY WROTE the perfect script for the perfect play and the San Francisco Giants enacted it without a single cue from the wings yesterday.

A capacity Seals' Stadium crowd of 23,448, loud, colorful and enchanted, sat in whispering winds and under nursery-blue skies to welcome major-league baseball to the shores of the Pacific, and got a show even a Barnum wouldn't have dared to conceive.

The Giants, proud and powerful in their soft white uniforms, battered into submission the Los Angeles Dodgers, 8-0, behind the magnificent six-hit pitching of slender Ruben Gomez, the Puerto Rican cutie, and whistling home runs by veteran shortstop Daryl Spencer and rookie first-baseman Orlando Cepeda.

The gray-clad Dodgers, partners with the Giants in the historic transplantation from the streets of Flatbush and the foot of Coogan's Bluff, were formidable-looking as they paraded heads high in the pregame ceremonies.

Shortly thereafter they were homogenized by the pounding Giant bats and the twisting, darting, corner-cutting screwballs from the thin fingers of the kinky-haired right-hander from Santurce.

In less than four innings their great Don Drysdale, who deals wickedly from the side, had been swept out of the box, on the ground of which were little piles of white dust blasted from the resin bag as he slammed it down in disgust and frustration.

By the end of the fourth, the Dodgers were thoroughly beaten, 6-0, but the Giants kept relentlessly on their tail, scoring twice more and turning back with a brilliant, flawless defense every little Los Angeles run they made at the half-smiling, half-scowling Gomez.

Only one Dodger got as far as third base. Six of them struck out. One of them, right fielder Carl Furillo, nearly brained himself crashing into the cement wall of the bleachers trying to flag down the 390-foot shot unloaded by Cepeda, a drive only a paying customer had the remotest chance in the world of handling.

Not an extra base hit leaped off the bats of the club that has been popularly selected as a second-placer with an outside chance for the pennant.

Only two Giant blows went for distance, but where they went nobody could bring them back. And on both sides and in between those home runs were scattered nine singles that kept in constant torment Drysdale and his unsuccessful successors, Don Bessent and Ron Negray.

From any angle you care to view it, this was

a most unforgettable moment in the history of baseball in San Francisco. A minor-league town since 1903, the Queen of Western cities wore robes of pure gold as she showed to the world her readiness to have and to hold National League—major-league—baseball.

The thrill of reality, the fulfillment of the historic Westward Ho movement, came shortly after 1:30 P.M. when the pattern of the first big-league game ever played on this side of the Rockies was established. Gomez struck out native-born Gino Cimoli.

From there on the action was grim, furious and spectacular as these age-old rivals from the faraway East struggled in this 77th National League opener.

Gomez was first to feel the serious threat of a dangerous challenge. In the second, Charlie Neal and Dick Gray opened with singles, only to die on the trail as Ruben wiped out Carl Furillo on a grounder to Spencer, and struck out Rube Walker and Drysdale.

Again, in the third, the Dodgers mixed up a storm when Peewee Reese and Duke Snider, he with the tightly bandaged knee hinge, walked. But Ruben eliminated Gil Hodges on a foul loft to Cepeda and got Neal to ground routinely to the massive Orlando at first base.

Drysdale, with his exploding sidearm hummer, breezed through the first six Giants. Then the house cat went wild.

In the bottom of the third, the lanky man from Van Nuys walked Danny O'Connell on a 3-1 pitch, and passed Valmy Thomas on a full-count 3-2 cast. The infield crept in, expecting a bunt from Gomez, but the cutie from the Caribbean squared off in mock pose, drew back and slammed a high bounder down third.

Gray fled back to his station, a few feet behind the last turn, and waited in abject frustration for the ball to come down. By the time it did, all hands were safe and the assembly line of victory was in full throttle.

Rookie Jimmy Davenport, playing his first major-league game, ripped a long fly to right and Furillo, playing in shallow, turned his number to the crowd back of the plate and took off, reaching at the last moment to haul down what might have been a triple. The sacrifice fly scored O'Connell and the Giants led the National League.

But the rally was to live a while longer. Jimmy King, the ex-St. Louis Cardinal, singled sharply to right and Thomas, the electronics

student from the Virgin Islands, fled home for 2-0.

The destruction of Drysdale became complete in the fourth after Gomez had authored a double play to wipe out an incipient Dodger threat at the top of the round. Cepeda went out to left, and so did Spencer . . . all the way out.

The shortstop with the fullback build snapped a home run into the pavilion at the 364 mark and, engulfed in a triumphant smile, slowly and with great dignity circled the bases, his gleaming spikes carrying him along the first home run trail in San Francisco major-league history.

It was a surprise to Daryl to learn he received a standing ovation.

"No kidding?" he said afterward in the clubhouse. "A standing ovation? I didn't notice. I was so darn happy I didn't notice anything but that ball sailing into the crowd!"

O'Connell went out infield, and then the rally flared anew. Thomas walked and was passed-balled to second, whence he checked in for 4-0 on a Gomez ripper to center. Davenport singled Gomez to third and Dodger manager Walter Alston, head on chest, came out and got Drysdale. He brought with him Don Bessent.

Bessent walked King and the bases were loaded. Willie Mays shot a line drive past the mound that second-baseman Neal, on a breath-taking try, partially stopped. The ball rolled into shallow center, and Gomez and Davenport rolled home. Willie tried to get to second, but was thrown out, Neal to Bessent, but there were four runs on the board and how're we doin'?

With one away in the fifth, the Giants struck again. Cepeda, the son of Pedro, the beegest hitter in all Puerto Rico history, crashed a low, wind-tortured liner to right and Furillo took off for the wall, turned, crashed face on into it, crumpled and it was all vain. Orlando, in his first major-league game, had cleared the 350-foot sign and it was 7-0.

Negray escaped a bases-loaded situation in the seventh, but was punctured for a run in the eighth. King walked, Mays singled infield, Reese lurching far to his left to arrest the ball's flight into center, and Willie Kirkland, playing in his first major-league game, singled over Neal's head to score King and complete the rout of the Dodgers.

Gomez, now wearying, had two away in the ninth when Los Angeles made with the muscle for the last time. Pinch-hitter Junior Gilliam walked, and Cimoli singled strongly to center. The Giant bull pen exploded with action. Gomez took one disdainful look to the right-field corner where the firemen were working, tugged at the cuff of his pants, and went to work on Reese.

Peewee struck out with the gun on his shoulder and the period to the perfect script was plunged home.

JOHN GALLAGHER

Courtesy *Sport* Magazine. ©

"*Nice slide, kid!*"

THIS piece appeared in *The Atlantic* magazine in 1949, while the redoubtable Mr. Tebbetts was still an active major-league catcher. An active catcher with an active mind, you're bound to agree. Did you know, for instance, that signals can be stolen off the *catcher's* motions?

I'd Rather Catch

BIRDIE TEBBETTS

A MASCOT'S uniform with a large zero on its back can inspire a nine-year-old boy to swaggering ambitions. Mine did: I first made up my mind that I was going to be a catcher and play baseball in the major leagues when I was mascoting for the Nashua Millionaires. The team was operated by Francis Parnell Murphy, later twice governor of New Hampshire, who had the special uniform made for me. And of course I was going to be a catcher for the Millionaires just like my idol Bill Haefner, an outlawed catcher from the Pittsburgh Pirates who later played with the New York Giants. He was replaced on my pedestal by Clyde Sukeforth, successor to Haefner and present Brooklyn Dodgers coach.

In my sand-lot playing, in grammar school, and later at Nashua High School, I copied Haefner and Sukeforth. I watched and studied their every move: their handling of pitchers, throwing, work behind the plate, and batting. By the time I graduated from high school I had gained enough proficiency to receive offers from six major-league teams. But no one of the six was the Boston Red Sox, the team of my heart. So I went with Detroit.

The Detroit Tigers helped me through Providence College after accepting their scout Jean Dubuc's report. I graduated in 1934, and after two years in the minors with New Bedford, Massachusetts, Springfield, Illinois, and Beaumont, Texas, I began catching for the Tigers under Mickey Cochrane, the game's greatest competitor. In my first major-league game I caught Elden Auker, the old submarine pitcher with the underhand delivery. We won. And with true beginner's luck I made a hit which figured in scoring the winning run.

It was four years before I played in my first and only World Series. Bobo Newsom, one of baseball's great characters and travelers, sparked us to the pennant by winning twenty-one games. We played the Cincinnati Reds and lost after seven dismal games. I told myself I wasn't nervous in my first game of that series. But I was, as I realized when I attempted a pick-off with Dick Bartell, but threw the ball into center field.

Our manager, Del Baker, one of the brainiest men in baseball, was a great sign-stealer. But in that World Series sign-stealing didn't help. We knew every pitch the Reds' pitchers were going to throw, yet lost. Catcher Jimmy Wilson was giving away the pitches by twitching his forearm muscles when he called a curve. When the muscles were still, the pitch was a fast ball.

Signals are very important but they must be simple. They are of no value if they are so difficult they tend to take the pitcher's mind off the situation. They can be given with the hand, fingers, glove, feet, from the count on the scoreboard, or by the pitcher. When I was with Detroit, Tommy Bridges and Schoolboy Rowe used to give me signs for many of their pitches. I have caught pitchers whom I knew so well through careful study that we could have worked a whole game without signals.

The catcher must be alert to spot the opposition's stealing his signs; he must also watch his teammates so that they won't give away the signal by shifting their weight; but most important, he must watch his manager maneuver his teammates into different positions for each batter, and from these moves anticipate his manager's desires.

I try to let every player know what pitch I have signaled for. The second baseman and shortstop get the sign when I signal the pitcher.

The second baseman relays the sign to first baseman, right and center fielders, while the shortstop relays it to the third baseman and the left fielder. It takes just a couple of seconds for everyone on the team to know the pitch. There's an advantage in giving them an added jump on the pitched ball.

I also try to prepare an umpire for a pitch. In a close game with the count three and two on a batter such a tip-off prepares him for what is coming and he will be set to make the call. Because I work next to the umpire, my relationship with him is an honest one. My beefs are legitimate and I try not to prolong them. Umpires are sensitive and proud of their work.

Of course every catcher tries to take advantage of the batter. For that reason we have a great reputation for heckling. Most of the chatter at the plate is conversational, but sometimes a word here and there may produce the desired result. In a game early this summer at Fenway Park, Paul Campbell of the Tigers took an extremely good pitch for ball four. Later he worked the count to three and two, and I said, "Paul, you've got to swing at those good pitches. That pitch you took for ball four last time was mighty good." The next pitch was a bad ball, but he swung and missed.

In a series against the White Sox, Cass Michaels, a push hitter who causes us a lot of trouble, was at bat and the count went to two balls and no strikes. "Well, Cass," said I, "here's a chance for that first home run." The next pitch had to be good. It wasn't though. Cass swung wildly and popped out.

It is surprising how many major-league catchers develop faulty habits which tip off pitches to the opposition. To protect himself a catcher must be absolutely sure that every movement he makes—after coming out of the sign-giving crouch—is exactly the same for every pitch.

A good catcher has many ways of assisting his pitcher. For example, a right-handed pitcher who has a tendency to hang a curve ball may be helped by having the catcher shift his weight to the right just as the pitcher is about to release the ball. This shift of weight will make the pitcher realize the ball must be thrown with the catcher's shift, and to the catcher's new position. It also will help him to hold on to the ball long enough to correct the hanging of the ball.

If an experienced catcher realizes his pitcher is having trouble controlling his low pitch, and it is costing him strikes, he will catch from a higher position to help correct this normal error. A low ball is always caught up; a high ball is always caught down. Every ball should be caught in the strike zone if it is possible. A curve ball which might have been low could very well be called a strike if a catcher reached out and caught it in a strike zone, rather than wait for the ball to complete its full curve.

Pitchers' tempers are gaited. They react differently to situations. Catchers can criticize some pitchers and they take it graciously and make an attempt to better themselves. Others don't like it: they are sensitive and touchy. They sulk and cry. These pitchers require special treatment.

In a game early this summer one of our young pitchers fell behind by only two runs in a game, became discouraged, and assumed an "Oh, what the heck" attitude. I had to keep after him, telling him he was still in the game, and we could break it wide open any time. He settled down and pitched well, and Vern Stephens smacked a homer to win the game in the ninth.

The easiest pitcher I ever caught was Elden Auker. His underhand deliveries came over the plate nice and soft. The toughest pitchers for me to catch were Hal Newhouser and Dizzy Trout when they were breaking in with the Tigers. They had plenty of stuff, but were extremely wild. I think that Maurice McDermott, our fine-looking prospect with the Red Sox, will also fall into that category.

The best pitchers I have caught are the right-handers Bridges and Rowe, and the southpaw Newhouser. Bridges, who is close to forty-three, is still pitching in the Pacific Coast League. He was a great curve-ball pitcher, an earnest workman, and had fine control. It was reported that the Yankees offered him $5000 to pitch one of the games in the final series against the Red Sox last year. He refused. Rowe had everything, including a smart head. Newhouser overcame his wildness to become one of the game's great pitchers. I used to get a thrill out of working with him. Now I get a thrill out of batting against him.

* * *

When a catcher throws off his mask to catch a foul fly, the first thing he must do is to get under the ball as fast as he can. His next thought is to catch the ball on the tip of his nose. If he starts to whirl and becomes confused, he should immediately focus his eyes on the ground and then look up. The dizziness will stop and he will locate the ball. Jim Hegan of Cleveland is today one of the best at catching foul balls. He is also the finest defensive catcher in the American League. He is tall, fast, has a good throwing arm, and is an able receiver. Yogi Berra of the New York Yankees is the best-hitting catcher and Les Moss of St. Louis hits the longest ball.

A catcher fielding a bunt scoops the ball into the mitt with his bare hand, instead of attempting to pick the ball up without the aid of his mitt. This habit saves many fielding errors during the course of a season. I attempted a barehand pickup on a bunt off the bat of Pete Suder of the A's in a game at Shibe Park last year, couldn't find the handle after three tries, and finally sneaked up on the ball and trapped it with my mask. Believe me, it's much easier using the mitt.

The pick-off is, of course, a defensive aid to the team. The catcher should try to use it without a pitchout. For example, with a man on first base, and a pull hitter at bat, the catcher gives the sign to the first baseman and then signals for a pitch which the batter cannot hit into right field. Many a time the base runner will be forced at second because of his slow start after the attempted pick-off.

I will always remember a bawling out I received from Jack Flynn, my college coach, for throwing the ball into left field on an attempted pick-off at third base in a game in which we were leading, 8-0. He pointed out that my blunder cost our pitcher a shutout. The catcher should never attempt a pick-off with one or no outs unless he has a better than fifty-fifty chance to get the man. If the man advances on a bad throw, he can score on an outfield fly. But there should be no fears with two outs. The catcher may get the pitcher out of a hole, and if not, the error will not be too costly.

With men on first and third bases, and a possibility of an attempted steal, it is the catcher's job to figure out his play. His judgment will be influenced by the score, the type of runner, and the type of opposition. For example, with men on first and third, a tie score, and two out in the ninth, there is little reason for a catcher to throw to second base, because the man on second is not important. He might, therefore, fake a throw to second, and attempt to catch the man at third.

But suppose it's this way: men on first and third; the man on first is fast, the man on third is slow—the score is irrelevant. The ball should be thrown through to second base as fast as possible. The catcher can handle the runner on third. If the man on third were the fast man, the catcher would first fake the man back to third

and then throw to second base. The ability of the pitcher to hold the man on base is a determining factor in all types of these plays, along with the score of the game.

Another important play is the cutoff on throw-ins. Different systems are used, usually to take advantage of the infielder possessing the best throwing arm. On our Detroit pennant winner of 1940, Bartell handled all extra-base-hit throw-ins from the outfield because he had a great arm. The keyman on the cutoff is usually the first baseman. He cuts off throw-ins on directions from the catcher and makes the throw to the different bases. The pitcher backs up the play. Cutoff plays will win many games over the season when properly executed. When they are not, they can be very costly.

A catcher should use the pitchout purely as a benefit measure for the team: for defensive purposes when he has definite knowledge that the runner is going to try to steal; or to upset the running style of the opponents. For instance, a catcher is playing against a team which uses the hit-and-run quite frequently. At the first opportunity where it will not hurt his pitcher's effectiveness, he should call for a pitchout. This can be a defensive maneuver to determine the running strategy of the other team. At the same time it is a bold stroke toward upsetting the opponents' running game. There will be a question in their minds for the remainder of the game as to when he is going to use the pitchout. The question may be sufficiently strong to stop the team from using its usual tactics and make it play an unnatural game.

Luke Appling, the White Sox shortstop, is the best hit-and-run man in the game, and I take keen delight in trying to outsmart him. On one occasion in Chicago, Luke put the hit-and-run on with the count two strikes and no balls, and men on first and second. I thought only a guy like Luke would try anything so crazy, and called for a pitchout. He swung and missed, and I got the runner on third.

In another game against the Chisox, the tying run was on first base. Rowe was the pitcher, and up came Appling with one out. The guessing game started again. I called for four straight pitchouts. The runner stole second on the second pitchout, Luke finally struck at a pitch over his head, and I threw out the runner going into third. Whew!

* * *

The problem of protecting home plate against the runner who is attempting to score is a simple order. The catcher's job is to get the ball and tag the runner. It is foolish, in my opinion, for any catcher to attempt to block the plate unless the throw carries the catcher into the runner's path—and then he is not deliberately blocking the plate. If it is a question of the runner or the ball, get the ball. If the catcher doesn't have the ball, the man is safe. So, get the ball.

That man Appling is in again for a story that happened at home plate in a game against the Chisox at Fenway Park last year. Luke came tearing into the plate as I took a throw from the outfield. I hipped him and he went sprawling to the right of the plate. I then went over and tagged out the highly chagrined Luke, and he was boiling. "If you were anyone else," said Luke, "I'd sock you." The Fenway Park crowd roared its approval of my play.

A few days later the St. Louis Browns came to town with two Negro players. One of those players, Willard Brown, came rushing toward the plate as I awaited a relay from the outfield. The throw was tardy, and again I tried the hip on Brown as he slid in. He went sprawling but managed to tag the plate before I got the ball. Now it was my turn. The crowd cheered Brown and gave me a large round of boos for spilling the Negro.

Immediately following World War II, an alien group of fans took over Briggs Stadium in Detroit from the regular Tiger fans, than which there are few better in the country. This group booed Hank Greenberg, Al Benton, and me out of Detroit. Detroit's postwar fans were not the only ill-behaved crowds in the majors. Joe DiMaggio was booed unmercifully in New York, Ted Williams in Boston, and other name stars got it in their respective parks. The crowds are now back to prewar levels—well behaved and appreciative.

But the alien fans in Detroit crucified me. The boos really hurt, for I felt that the crowd was unfair. I was still rusty after missing four years while in the service and most of spring training because of an ulcer.

I developed rabbit ears. My batting average dropped to .243, and finally General Manager Joe Cronin of the Red Sox was able to obtain my services from the Tigers on May 20, 1947, in an even swap for Catcher Hal Wagner. I had nothing against the Tigers' management, but hated the fans' abuse and was extremely happy to move to Boston.

While most of the big stars were getting booed by the unruly postwar crowds, Ted Williams got a thorough going-over from the Boston fans and press way back in 1942, after leading both major leagues in batting with a .406 mark the year before. He didn't bat .400 in '42, but his .356 average was good enough to lead the American League. The fans thought he should have done better. The boos soured Ted on the fans and the press. He hasn't recovered from them to this day.

I think Williams is the best player I have ever seen. He is an outstanding team player and a great man up at the plate in the clutch. He is not demanding on his teammates as some of the game's other high-priced players are. He minds his own business, is highly popular with the team, and doesn't ask for extra consideration. He can run and throw with speed and accuracy, and is the best left fielder in the game.

Ted calls everyone "Bush." But it is not a derogatory name with him, it's a term of affection. He will call Stephens, our slugging shortstop, "Bush," then turn around and call the newest and greenest rookie by the same name.

I believe Ted would break Babe Ruth's record of sixty home runs in a single season if he were playing at Yankee Stadium, Briggs Stadium, or Sportsman's Park, where the right-field barriers are short. Fenway Park's short left-field wall (315 feet from the plate) is a haven for right-handed batters, but it takes a good poke to get a homer to right.

The Yankee Stadium right-field barrier is extremely short, and Chinese homers are frequent there. Because fans sit behind the right-field fences in New York, Detroit, and St. Louis, it gives the illusion that the fences are farther away. Fenway Park's high left-field wall, with no fans behind it, looks as if it were directly behind third base. The only park that really tests a batter is Chicago's Comiskey Park, where the left- and right-field fences are equidistant from the plate.

If I were called upon to pick my American League All-Star team from 1936 to the present, I would choose Lefty Grove, Newhouser, Charley Ruffing, Bob Feller as pitchers, with Johnny Murphy in relief. The catchers would be Cochrane and Bill Dickey. The infield would have Greenberg, Charley Gehringer, Cronin, and George Kell, with Lou Boudreau as utility man. The outfield would be made up of Williams, Joe DiMaggio, and Earl Averill, with Jimmy Foxx as utility man. My All-Star manager would be Joe McCarthy, with Art Fletcher and Del Baker the coaches.

Cochrane and Dickey were great inspirations

to their respective teams. Cochrane had a dynamic personality. He worked his pitchers hard and was the greatest catcher I have seen at blocking the plate. Dickey was one of the best clutch hitters. He was always cool and at ease. Both Cochrane and Dickey were blessed with superior pitching staffs.

The average catcher's major-league career is longer than the average of any other position, and because of this longer experience, he becomes more valuable to his team. The average career of a major-league catcher is approximately ten years. Mike Tresh of Cleveland has been in the majors ten years, Hegan of Cleveland eight years, Buddy Rosar of Philadelphia eleven years, Bob Swift of Detroit ten years, Al Evans of Washington nine years, and I have thirteen years of service.

Dickey, Cochrane, Rick Ferrell, Luke Sewell, Rollie Hemsley, Ray Hayworth, Merv Shea, Frank Pytlak, Frank Hayes, catchers who have retired in recent years, had from twelve to twenty years of service. The catcher who takes care of himself lasts a long time in the majors. He must do stretching exercises in the off season and quite often remedial exercises to improve his speed. The continual crouching can cause an enlargement of thighs with the resultant loss of speed.

I love baseball and get a challenge out of every game I play. But catching is not a breeze. It is a big job and a self-effacing one. It is a good catcher who remembers that the pitcher is the one who must look good and not himself. It is a great catcher whose spirit and determination will lend confidence to his pitcher as he faces the different issues during the course of a game. He alone sees the entire baseball field, he alone is in front of the pitcher, and from his actions the pitcher will get the feel of those players whom he cannot see. He must always remember that the pitcher and the entire baseball team are looking at him on every pitch, and his actions can either lift a ball club up to its desired key, or let it down. He must know that a game is over only when there are three men out in the ninth inning and his team has won or lost.

That is a large order, and I lay no claims to greatness. But it is a great game.

THE old and the new—Christy Mathewson in 1905, Lew Burdette in 1957. Both of these great World Series pitching performances are chronicled in this book. Here is the Burdette story, vividly told by the expert Joe Trimble.

1957:
Milwaukee Braves 5,
New York Yankees 0

JOE TRIMBLE

MILWAUKEE BREWED the miracle yesterday —winning the world championship with a crashing 5-0 victory over the Yankees at the Stadium. Standing heroically on the mound, Selva Lewis Burdette Jr. lifted the Braves to victory in the seventh game—his second successive blanking of the Bombers and his third triumph in the Series.

The 31-year-old right-hander's magnificent seven-hitter brought the title to Milwaukee just five years after the franchise shift from Boston. It served as the trigger for the wildest civic demonstration a baseball-batty burg ever has had. Burdette, the outstanding player in the classic, could be elected chief braumeister of the city—which is better than being mayor.

In Milwaukee, they use the word "gemütlichkeit" to describe a feeling of satisfaction, contentment and good cheer. So, yesterday was the day of days, when the beer flowed most merrily and the town, after being tied to TV sets for two and a half hours, went absolutely wild.

So did the Braves here, piling on top of and pummeling Burdette in a mass demonstration of affection as Eddie Mathews tagged third base for the final out. The infielder grabbed a smoking smash by Bill Skowron with the bases full, skipped lightly toward the base and jumped on it with a leap of joy.

Yes, Skowron. That's right. The Yankees went down with their big boys trying to avoid the last thrust. Skowron, sidelined with a bad back since the second inning of the opener, went in as a pinch hitter and finished the game at first base. Mickey Mantle played the full game, too, though unable to throw because of a damaged shoulder.

The Braves deserved to win. The Yankees deserved to lose. The 61,207 fans showered Burdette with cheers at the finish. Earlier, they had jeered the Yankees, who presented the unusual and pathetic picture of a team beating itself. For the first time in their proud history, the pin-stripe perfectionists lost a World Series with their fielding.

They blundered into three errors yesterday, the most damaging one a wild throw by Tony Kubek, who had been one of the more brilliant Bombers in the early games. That ruined an easy double play which would have gotten Don Larsen out of the third inning. He got out, in an unhappier way, as the Braves blasted through the opening for four runs.

The other score came in the eighth, when catcher Del Crandall boomed the eighth Milwaukee homer of the Series, one more than the Yankees made. That, too, might have been caught with a better fielding effort by Enos Slaughter, who went back a bit too slowly for it, then dropped it off the end of his mitt at the railing of the left-field stands.

Strangely, poor New York glovework figured in all three of Burdette's victories. The Yanks gave the Braves two runs in Lew's 4-2 win here in the second game and Jerry Coleman's booboo set up the only score as he won the fifth game, 1-0, in Milwaukee.

It's a good thing they weren't handling the money which piled up in this richest Series in history, which was seen by more people paying more money than ever before. The totals for the seven games were: 394,712 spectators and $2,475,978.94 at the gate, after taxes. Highest previous figures were the 389,763 fans who saw the Yanks and Dodgers in 1947 and the "take" of $2,337,515.34 in the '55 set between the same two clubs.

This was the third Series in succession to end in a seventh-game shutout, Johnny Podres of the Dodgers finishing off the Yanks in 1955 and Johnny Kucks returning the compliment last year.

Burdette is the third pitcher to toss two shutouts in the same Series. Bill Dineen of the 1903 Red Sox blanked the Pirates twice and Christy Mathewson held the A's runless in three games in 1905.

The Yankees didn't get a runner to third until the ninth inning as they went down to their sixth Series loss against 17 championships. Burdette, pitching with only two days of rest, had held them to four hits as he went into the final round. Then, tired and straining, he was clipped for a one-out single by Gil McDougald and, after another out, a hit by Coleman. Tommy Byrne, last of five Yankee pitchers, went up to bat because he is a good hitter.

Byrne rapped a hard grounder between second base and Felix Mantilla, the baseman. The Puerto Rican dove at the ball and stopped it, though unable to make a play as it caromed off his glove. His bellywhop did save the shutout, however, McDougald being forced to stop at third.

Skowron, batting ninth after having pinch hit for one of the pitchers earlier, drove a one-bounce liner toward third and Mathews, whose fielding was superb all through the Series, made a smart stop and leaped on the bag for the final out.

The Yankees, being unable to hit Burdette, tried to upset him. In the seventh inning, it took Casey Stengel two minutes to get Elston Howard up to the plate as a pinch hitter for pitcher Tom Sturdivant. Burdette, a nervous, fidgety individual, stood the strain pretty well.

Then, before Howard took his stance, he demanded that plate umpire Bill McKinley examine the ball. Burdette is known as the pitcher with the "moistest" on the ball and is suspected of throwing a spitter. Earlier in the game, in the second inning, he actually spat into his glove while going out to the mound. McKinley could find nothing wrong with the ball and returned it to the pitcher. Burdette, not a bit upset by the byplay, fanned Howard for the second out. Skowron then grounded out, stranding Kubek, who had opened the round with a single.

Larsen, starting his first Series game since the perfect game on Oct. 8, 1956, fanned two in the first inning and got out of a jam in the second after the Braves put two on, Hank Aaron with a single and Frank Torre with a no-strike walk as Don pitched carefully to the big lefty batter. Mantilla flied deep to left, Aaron moving to third, then Crandall forced Torre.

The Yankees blew a big chance in the first inning when Hank Bauer set a record by opening with a double which hit the left field foul line. The rugged outfielder became the first batter to hit safely in 14 consecutive Series games.

Then came a play on which the Dodgers formerly had the copyright—two men on the same base. Slaughter hit back to Burdette, who trapped Bauer off second. The Braves mishandled the rundown and Hank escaped back to the base only to find Slaughter sliding in on him. Shortstop Johnny Logan tagged both as the crowd roared with laughter. Umpire Joe Paparella ruled possession for Bauer and Slaughter ran off the field wearing a red face.

Mantle, his shoulder aching, bounced back to Burdette, who threw him out, Bauer sticking close to second this time. Yogi Berra was intentionally passed as the fans booed and McDougald popped up to Mathews.

The Braves helped Lew with two fine fielding plays in the second. Mathews backhanded Kubek's sharp rap and threw him out. Coleman then topped a ball to third and Mathews' hurried throw into the dirt was scooped stylishly by Torre.

Burdette fouled out to open the third, then Bob Hazle ripped a single to left, his first hit in 11 times up. Logan bounced to Kubek and the third baseman made a terrible throw with an easy double play in hand. It pulled Coleman far off second base. Jerry completed the throw to first, but Logan beat that and both runners were safe. The Yankees protested that Logan's foot had hit that of Joe Collins, the first baseman, and not the bag, but umpire Augie Donatelli ruled against them. Logan said afterward that his foot half hit Collins and half hit the base.

That was the break of the game—and the

Series. The Braves poured through. Mathews pulled a double into the right-field corner, scoring both runners. Bauer had to wait for the ball to roll to him as it hugged the curving fence and Logan just did beat the relay by Collins. Joe's throw was high and Berra couldn't make the tag.

Stengel derricked Larsen and brought in Bobby Shantz, who was clipped for a single through the middle by Aaron, Hank's 11th hit of the Series and one short of the record. Mathews scored with the third run and Aaron brought in the fourth a bit later. He took third on Wes Covington's looping hit over short and scored when the Yanks were unable to make a double play on Torre's slow grounder to second baseman Coleman.

Art Ditmar was pitching in the fourth when Hazle singled after two were out and McDougald made a bad throw to second after fielding Logan's grounder. Ditmar got out of the sick mess with luck, Mathews lashing a liner right at Mantle. Berra made the third Bomber bobble in the fifth, flubbing Aaron's bunt a few feet in front of the plate. The next three men grounded out, the fans mock-cheering the Yankees as they executed ordinary fielding plays.

Hazle, reputedly a poor fielder, retired the side with three catches in the fourth, his running grab of McDougald's bloop to short right being a good one.

The Yankees had a fair shot at Burdette in the sixth, after Mantle singled with two out. Berra came up and the crowd stirred in expectation of a homer which would put the Yanks in contention. Instead, Yogi tapped a nubber to third, which Mathews fumbled as he grabbed at it with his mitt hand while stumbling around nervously. This gave McDougald a chance, but Gil topped one of Burdette's "SS" pitches (sinker or spitter?) and forced Mantle at third.

Byrne was on the mound in the eighth when Crandall hit into the left-field seats after two were out. Slaughter started slowly, then went full tilt and crashed into the fence as the ball flicked off his mitt.

Burdette went through Bauer, Slaughter and Mantle without trouble in the eighth and the crowd began to sense that the reign of the Yankees was about over.

Berra popped to Torre to start the ninth and the fans cheered. McDougald lined a single to center before Kubek's fly to center brought more applause. Then came the Coleman and Byrne hits, Mathews' final stop and stomp, and the miracle had been wrought. And by a pitcher the Yankees had given up six years ago in a trade with the then Boston Braves. Burdette was sent to Boston along with $50,000 in exchange for Johnny Sain on Aug. 29, 1951, when the Bombers needed a bit of pennant insurance.

It took six years for the deal to backfire and then it cost the Yankees the world championship. Burdette held his former teammates to two runs in 27 innings and none over the final 24, in the most dominant pitching performance in a Series since Matty's three shutouts in 1905 —a half-century ago.

Bridegrooms Wallop Beaneaters

— FRANK C. TRUE —

MAJOR-LEAGUE BALL CLUBS have picked up some strange—and sometimes colorful—nicknames in the past 100 years. Do you remember the Bridegrooms and the Beaneaters, currently known as the Dodgers and Braves?

In case you're under the impression that in the distant past groups of stockholders spent hectic nights around a table concocting monikers for their athletes and held christening ceremonies at home plate, we have news for you.

The truth is the names of most major-league teams were derived from circumstances almost as casual as the naming of an Indian papoose—the first object the parents' eyes fell upon. But behind this revelation lies the puzzling fact there are no official league records of when, how or where nicknames so familiar today originated. To find out it has been necessary to dig deeply into faded newspaper files and ransack the archives of the Hall of Fame at Cooperstown.

Take the New York Giants. They were called many things, some of which weren't complimentary, when they came into the National League in 1883. Then along came Jim Mutrie to manage the club in 1885. On his first day out, he looked over the players and blurted: "These blokes are giants." A newspaperman overheard the remark. Thus were the Giants christened.

In many cases a club owner's right to name his own team has been usurped by sports writers. Otherwise the Philadelphia Phillies would be known today as the Bluejays. From the beginning—1883—the team was dubbed Phillies by baseball writers, for lack of a better name. Philadelphia, of course, is known as "Philly"—hence the Phillies.

When Bob Carpenter bought the club some years ago he dedicated himself to finding a better name. He sponsored a contest, with a substantial award offered to the fan submitting the best name. The prize-winning "Bluejays" was hooted at by sports writers, who regarded it as "silly," and wound up in the wastebasket at newspaper offices.

Years ago, when Brooklyn was in the old American Association, a yellow newspaper clipping proclaims, "The streets around the ball park have been made hazardous by these new-fangled street cars, and if a person isn't an alert dodger his chances of reaching the park intact are doubtful." Despite all the other names the Brooklyn team has been called—Bridegrooms, Superbas, Bums and what not—it's still the Dodgers and will be, at least, until it's moved.

The Milwaukee Braves, who migrated to Wisconsin by way of Boston, originally were called Red Stockings, simply because that was the color of their hose; then Doves (after George B. Dovey, former president of the club); Redcaps and Beaneaters. But it remained for a Tammany Hall New Yorker to apply the name that stuck. He was James E. Gaffney, president of the club, who couldn't resist the sentiments of the Wigwam, as Tammany Hall is known. So Braves it was.

The Chicago Cubs, believe it or not, began life as the White Stockings in 1876. Then they became more frisky and were the Colts. Later, when it looked as if they were to be without a park, they became the Orphans. At the turn of the century, bustling, civic-minded Chicagoans insisted the team should have a name indicative of "bear-like strength and a playful disposition." Whereupon some fast thinker, whose name has been lost to posterity, came up with Cubs.

The first team to discard long pants in favor of knickerbockers, the Cincinnati Red Stockings, who date back to 1869, had an opportunity to show their flaming red stockings to admiring fans and promptly were named by sports writers. Later the name was shortened to just Reds. Communism was responsible for the contraction being changed back to Redlegs —though a good many fans still refer to them as the Reds.

Pittsburgh is the only major-league town whose citizens had no voice in naming their team. It was forced upon them—and they accepted. When Pittsburgh came into the National League in 1887 it proceeded to raid other clubs for talent. A loud yell of protest went up throughout the circuit. "Pirates!" they were called.

Because the New York American League park originally was on one of the highest points in Manhattan, plus the fact that the club's first president was Joseph W. Gordon and the Gordon Highlanders was the best known regiment in the British Army at that time, the team became known as the Gordon Highlanders. But that name was too long for newspaper headlines. So one day Jim Price, of the old *New York Press,* became angry and called them the Yankees.

When the late John J. McGraw, of the Giants, referred to the team Connie Mack and Ben Shibe had put together as a "white elephant," sports writers pounced upon the idea and eventually a white elephant appeared on Philadelphia uniforms. But the name Athletics, derived from the old Quaker City professional team of 1876, weathered the storm.

After being known as the Somersets (from Charles Somers, owner), Puritans, Plymouth Rocks and Speed Boys, the Boston American League item quickly grabbed the name Red Sox when the rival National League club in that city decided to adopt white stockings as "less dangerous to players suffering spike wounds."

Washington, D. C., citizens also voted in vain on a name for their team. They preferred Nationals, but sports writers would have none of it. They liked the more distinctive Senators better.

When Charles A. Comiskey brought the St. Paul, Minn., team to Chicago as an American League entry in 1901, newspapermen, who always had liked the name White Stockings, now abandoned by the Cubs, didn't even wait for Comiskey to think of a cognomen. They had it ready and waiting.

The late George T. Stallings put black and yellow striped hose on his Detroit team in 1899. Philip J. Reid, Detroit newspaperman, announced ironically they looked like "tigers." Stallings agreed with him, and Tigers they've been ever since.

The Baltimore Orioles, who began life anew as a big-league team in 1954, received their name from the most obvious of sources—the Baltimore oriole.

Cleveland has seen many names come and go for its Indians. They once were known as the Spiders, later as the Naps, after Napoleon Lajoie, manager from 1905 to 1909. The fact that several nearby teams were known as Redskins finally evolved into Indians.

The St. Louis Cardinals first were known as the Browns because of the trimmings on their uniforms, then later as the Maroons for the same reasons. The color again was changed in 1899 and the Cardinals were born. It was as simple as that.

FROM "My Biggest Baseball Day," drama incarnate: Spittin' Ed Walsh
pitching to the one and only Nap Lajoie when the chips were down!

1908:
Chicago White Sox 3,
Cleveland Indians 2

ED WALSH
as told to FRANCIS J. POWERS

DID YOU EVER see Larry Lajoie bat? No. Then you missed something. I want to tell you that there was one of the greatest hitters—and fielders, too—ever in baseball. There's no telling the records he'd of made if he'd hit against the lively ball. To tell you about my greatest day, I'll have to go back there to October, 1908, when I fanned Larry with the bases full and the White Sox chances for the pennant hanging on every pitch to the big Frenchman.

That was Oct. 3 and the day after I had that great game with Addie Joss and he beat me 1 to 0 with a perfect game; no run—no hits—no man reached first. There was a great pitcher and a grand fellow, Addie. One of my closest friends and he'd been one of the best of all time only for his untimely death two years later. That game was a surprise to both of us for we were sitting on a tarpaulin talking about having some singing in the hotel that night, when Lajoie, he managed Cleveland, and Fielder Jones told us to warm up. A pitcher never knew when he'd work in those days.

I don't think there'll ever be another pennant race like there was in the American League that year. All summer four teams, the Sox, Cleveland, Detroit and St. Louis, had been fighting and three of 'em still had a chance on this day. When Joss beat me the day before it left us two and one-half games behind the Tigers and two behind the Naps (as Cleveland was called in honor of Lajoie). And we had only four games left to play.

It was a Saturday, I remember, and the biggest crowd ever to see a game in Cleveland up to that date jammed around the park. Jones started Frank Smith for us and we got him three runs off Glenn Liebhardt and were leading by two going into the seventh. I was down in the bull pen, ready for anything because as I said, we had to win this one.

As I recall it George Perring, the shortstop, was first up for Cleveland and he went all the way to second when Patsy Dougherty muffed his fly in the sun. I began to warm up in a hurry. Nig Clarke batted for Liebhardt and fanned and things looked better. Smith would have been out of trouble only Tannehill fumbled Josh Clarke's grounder and couldn't make a play. Clarke stole second and that upset Smith and he walked Bill Bradley. I rushed to the box and the first batter I faced was Bill Hinchman. Bill wasn't a champion hitter but he was a tough man in a pinch. I knew his weakness was a spit ball on the inside corner so I told Sully (Billy Sullivan) we'd have to get in close on him. And I did. My spit ball nearly always broke down and I could put it about where I wanted. Bill got a piece of the ball and hit a fast grounder that Tannehill fielded with one hand and we forced Perring at the plate.

So, there were two out and Larry at bat. Now if the Frenchman had a weakness it was a fast ball, high and right through the middle. If you pitched inside to him, he'd tear a hand off the third baseman and if you pitched outside he'd knock down the second baseman. I tried him with a spit ball that broke to the inside and down. You know a spit ball was heavy and traveled fast. Lajoie hit the pitch hard down the third base line and it traveled so fast that it curved 20 feet, I'd guess, over the foul line and into the bleachers. There was strike one.

My next pitch was a spitter on the outside and Larry swung and tipped it foul back to the stands. Sully signed for another spitter but I just stared at him; I never shook him off with a nod or anything like that. He signed for the spitter twice more but still I just looked at him. Then Billy walked out to the box. "What's the matter?" Bill asked me. "I'll give him a fast one," I said, but Billy was dubious. Finally, he agreed. I threw Larry an overhand fast ball that raised and he watched it come over without ever an offer. "Strike three!" roared Silk O'Loughlin. Lajoie sort of grinned at me and tossed his bat toward the bench without ever a word. That was the high spot of my baseball days; fanning Larry in the clutch and without him swinging.

Well, we came home to finish out the season with three games against the Tigers. We still were in the race but we needed three straight for the flag. We got the first two. In the opener, Doc White beat the Tigers 3-1 and held Cobb and Claude Rossman hitless. I pitched the second and beat 'em 6-1 and allowed only four hits and that was my 65th game and 40th win of the season. And that left us a half game out of first and Cleveland was out of the race when it dropped the first game of a double-header to the Browns.

That brought it down to the final day of the season. We heard that Hughie Jennings and Harry Tuthill (Detroit trainer) had sat up to 4 o'clock in the morning putting hot towels on Bill Donovan's arm, trying to get it in shape to pitch. At game time we weren't sure Bill would pitch for he was visiting under the stands with Joe Farrell when Jennings came by and told him to warm up.

Most of us thought Jones would start Smith against the Tigers for he really had them handcuffed and always could be expected to pitch

his best against them. We were startled rather than surprised when Jones said "Doc" White would pitch.

When Jones came in, I said: "Are you going to pitch Doc?" He said "yes." Then I said, "that's a great injustice to a fine young man. You know White needs his full rest to be effective. I'll pitch if you want me to (I'd pitched in 65 games, my arm felt great and another game wouldn't hurt me). But the man you should pitch is Smith . . . but you're mad at him."

I couldn't argue Jones out of starting White and "Doc" didn't last long. I'll never forget that first inning. Matty McIntyre singled. Donie Bush was hit by a pitched ball but the umpires wouldn't let him take first because he hadn't tried to duck the pitch. Then Donie fanned. There was a crowd around in the outfield and Sam Crawford hit a terrific drive into the fans for two bases. And then Cobb—Cobb the man who never could hit White—tripled, cleaning the bases.

I got down to the bull pen in time to get warmed up a bit and after Cobb's hit, Jones sent me to the box. The Tigers scored two more before I could stop them and then I pitched through the fifth. Then when I came to the bench, I threw my glove in the corner. "What's the matter with you?" Jones asked. "I'm through," I said. "Now you'll have to pitch Smith, the man who should have started." Smith finished but the Tigers beat us 7-0 and there went the pennant. Donovan allowed only two hits and fanned nine and we dropped to third place when the Naps won from St. Louis.

I like to think back to the White Sox of those days. In 1906, we won the pennant and beat the Cubs in the World Series. Next season we were in the pennant race until the last days of September and in 1908 we fought them down to the final day of the season. There never was a fielding first baseman like Jiggs Donahue in 1908 when he set a record for assists. Sullivan was a great catcher, one of the greatest. It was a great team, a smart team. But the tops of all days was when I fanned Lajoie with the bases filled. Not many pitchers ever did that.

HERE is a disquieting—and distinguished—short story. Sometimes, Pulitzer Prize-winner Warren points out, the people back home find it hard to get to know the local boy once he has made good—or bad.

Goodwood Comes Back

ROBERT PENN WARREN

LUKE GOODWOOD always could play baseball, but I never could, to speak of. I was little for my age then, but well along in my studies and didn't want to play with the boys my size; I wanted to play with the boys in my class, and if it hadn't been for Luke, I never would have been able to. He was a pitcher then, like he has always been, and so he would say, "Aw, let him field." When he was pitching, it didn't matter much who was fielding, anyway, because there weren't going to be any hits to amount to anything in the first place. I used to play catcher some, too, because I had the best mitt, but he pitched a mighty hard ball and it used to fool the batter all right, but it fooled me too a good part of the time so I didn't hold them so good. Also, I was a little shy about standing close up to the plate on account of the boys flinging the bat the way they did when they started off for first base. Joe Lancaster was the worst for that, and since he almost always played on the other side, being a good hitter to balance off Luke's pitching, I had to come close, nearly getting scared to death of him braining me when he did get a hit. Luke used to yell, "For Christ sake get up to that plate or let somebody else catch for Christ sake that can!"

Joe Lancaster wasn't much bigger than I was, but he was knotty and old-looking, with a white face and hair that was almost white like an old man's, but he wasn't exactly an albino. He was a silent and solemn kind of boy, but he could sure hit; I can remember how he used to give that ball a good solid crack, and start off running the bases with his short legs working fast like a fox terrier's trying to catch up with something, but his face not having any expression and looking like it was dead or was thinking about something else. I've been back home

since and seen him in the restaurant where he works behind the counter. I'm bigger than he he is now, for he never did grow much. He says hello exactly like a stranger that never saw you before and asks what you want. When he has his sleeves rolled up in the summertime, and puts an order on the counter for you, his arms are small like a boy's, still, with very white skin you can see the veins through.

It was Joe hit me in the head with a bat when I was catching. Luke ran up toward the plate, yelling, "You've killed him!"—for the bat knocked me clean over. It was the last time I played catcher; the next time I came out bringing my mitt, which was a good one, Luke said, "Gimme that mitt." He took it and gave it to another boy, and told me to go play field. That was the only thing I didn't like about Luke, his taking my mitt.

I stayed at the Goodwood house a lot, and liked it, even if it was so different from my own. It was like a farmhouse, outside and inside, but the town was growing out toward it, making it look peculiar set so far back off the street with barns and chicken yards behind it. There was Mr. Goodwood, who had been a sheriff once and who had a bullet in his game leg, they said, a big man one time, but now with his skin too big for him and hanging in folds. His mustache was yellow from the chewing tobacco he used and his eyes were bloodshot; some people said he was drinking himself to death, but I'll say this for him, he drank himself to death upstairs without making any fuss. He had four boys, and drink was their ruination. They say it was likker got Luke out of the big league, and none of the Goodwoods could ever leave the poison alone. Anyway, the Goodwood house was a man's house with six men sitting down to the table, counting the grandfather, and Mrs.

Goodwood and her daughter going back and forth to the kitchen with sweat on their faces and their hair damp from the stove. There would be men's coats on the chairs in the living room, sometimes hunting coats with the old blood caked on the khaki, balls of twine and a revolver on the mantelpiece, and shotguns and flyrods lying around, even on the spare bed that was in the living room. And the bird dogs came in the house whenever they got good and ready. At my house everything was different, for men there always seemed to be just visiting.

Luke took me hunting with him, or sometimes one of his big brothers took us both, but my mother didn't like for me to go with the grown boys along, because she believed that their morals were not very good. I don't suppose their morals were much worse than ordinary for boys getting their sap up, but hearing them talk was certainly an education for a kid. Luke was as good a shot as you ever hope to see. He hunted a lot by himself, too, for my folks wouldn't let me go just all the time. He would get up before day and eat some cold bread and coffee in the kitchen and then be gone till after dark with his rifle or his shotgun. He never took anything to eat with him, either, for when he was hunting he was like they say the Indians were in that respect. Luke reminded you of an Indian, too, even when he was a boy and even if he was inclined to be a blond and not a brunette; he was long and rangy, had a big fine-cut nose, and looked to be setting his big feet always carefully on the ground, and came up on his toes a little, like a man testing his footing. He walked that way even on a concrete walk, probably from being in the woods so much. It was no wonder with all his hunting he never did study or make any good use and profit of his mind, which was better than most people's, however. The only good grades he made were in penmanship, copybooks still being used then in the grammar-school part of school. He could make his writing look exactly like the writing at the top of the page, a Spencerian hand tilted forward, but not too much like a woman's. He could draw a bird with one line without taking the pencil off the paper once, and he'd draw them all afternoon in school sometimes. The birds all looked alike, all fine and rounded off like his Spencerian writing, their beaks always open, but not looking like any birds God ever made in this world. Sometimes he would put words coming out of a bird's bill, like "You bastard," or worse; then he would scratch it out, for he might just as well have signed his name to it, because the

teachers and everybody knew how well he could draw a bird in that way he had.

Luke didn't finish high school. He didn't stop all at once, but just came less and less, coming only on bad days most of the time, for on good days he would be off hunting or fishing. It was so gradual, him not coming, that nobody, maybe not even the teachers, knew when he really stopped for good. In the summer he would lie around the house, sleeping out in the yard on the grass where it was shady, stretched out like a cat, with just a pair of old pants on. Or he would fish or play baseball. It got so he was playing baseball for little town teams around that section, and he picked up some change to buy shells and tackle.

That was the kind of life he was living when I finished school and left town. We had drifted apart, you might say, by that time, for he didn't fool around with the school kids any more. I never found out exactly how he broke into real baseball and got out of what you call the sand lot. My sister wrote me some big man in the business saw Luke pitch some little game somewhere and Luke was gone to pitch for a team up in Indiana somewhere. Then the next year he got on the sport page in the papers. My sister, knowing I would be interested in the boy that was my friend, you might say, used to find out about the write-ups and send me clippings when the home paper would copy stories about Luke from the big papers. She said Luke was making nine thousand dollars playing for the Athletics, which was in Philadelphia. The papers called him the Boy Wizard from Alabama. He must have been making a lot of money that year to judge from the presents he sent home. He sent his mother a five-hundred-dollar radio set and a piano, and I admired him for the way he remembered his mother, who had had a hard time and no doubt about it. I don't know why he sent the piano, because nobody at his house could play one. He also fixed up the house, which was in a bad shape by that time. Mr. Goodwood was still alive, but according to all reports he was spending more time upstairs than ever, and his other three boys never were worth a damn, not even for working in the garden, and didn't have enough git-up-and-git to even go fishing.

The next year Luke pitched in the World Series, for the team that bought him from the Athletics, in Philadelphia, and he got a bonus of three thousand dollars, plus his salary. But he must have hit the skids after that, drink being the reason that was reported to me. When he was home on vacation, my sister said he did some fishing and hunting, but pretty soon he was drunk all the time, and carousing around. The next year he didn't finish the season. My sister sent me a clipping about it, and wrote on the margin, "I'm sure you will be sorry to know this because I know you always liked Luke. I like Luke too." For a matter of fact, I never saw a woman who didn't like Luke, he was so good-looking and he had such a mixture of wildness and a sort of embarrassment around women. You never saw a finer-looking fellow in your life than he was going down the street in summer with nothing on except old khaki pants and underwear tops and his long arms and shoulders near the color of coffee and his blondish hair streaked golden color with sunburn. But he didn't have anything to do with girls, that is, decent girls, probably because he was too impatient. I don't suppose he ever had a regular date in his life.

But the next year he was back in baseball, but not in such a good team, for he had done some training and lived clean for a while before the season opened. He came back with great success, it looked like at first. I was mighty glad when I got a clipping from my sister with the headlines, *Goodwood Comes Back*. He was shutting them out right and left. But it didn't last. The drink got him, and he was out of the big-time game for good and all, clean as a whistle. Then he came back home.

It was on a visit home I saw him after all that time. I was visiting my sister, who was married and lived there, and I had taken a lawn mower down to the blacksmith shop to get it fixed for her. I was waiting out in front of the shop, leaning against one side of the door and looking out on the gravel street, which was sending up heat-dazzles. Two or three old men were sitting there, not even talking; they were the kind of old men you find sitting around town like that, who never did amount to a damn and whose names even people in town can't remember half the time. I saw Luke coming up the road with another boy, who didn't strike me as familiar right off because he was one of those who had grown up in the meantime. I could see they were both nearly drunk, when they got under the shade of the shed; and I noticed Luke's arms had got pretty stringy. I said hello to Luke, and he said, "Well, I'll be damned, how you making it?" I said, "Fine, how's it going?" Then he said, "Fine."

After they stood there a while I could see the other boy wasn't feeling any too good with the combination of whisky and the heat of the day. But Luke kept kidding him and trying to

make him go up to the Goodwood house, where he said he had some more whisky. He said he had kept it under a setting hen's nest for two weeks to age, and the other boy said Luke never kept any whisky in his life two days, let alone two weeks, without drinking it up. It was bootleg whisky they were drinking, because Alabama was a dry state then, according to the law, even after repeal; Luke must have been kidding too, because he ought to know if anybody does, whisky don't age in glass whether it's under a setting hen or not. Then he tried to make the boy go up to Tangtown, which is what they call nigger town because of the immoral goings-on up there, where they could get some more whisky, he said, and maybe something else. The other boy said it wasn't decent in the middle of the afternoon. Then he asked me to go, but I said no thanks to the invitation, not ever having approved of that, and Tangtown especially, for it looks like to me a man ought to have more self-respect. The old men sitting there were taking in every word, probably jealous because they weren't good for drinking or anything any more.

Finally Luke and the other boy started up the road in the hot sun, going I don't know where, whether to his house or off to Tangtown in the middle of the afternoon. One of the old men said, "Now, ain't it a shame the way he's throwed away his chances." One of the others said likker always was hard on the Goodwoods. Luke, not being any piece off and having good ears even if he was drinking, must have heard them, for he stooped down and scooped up a rock from the road like a baseball player scooping up an easy grounder, and yelled, "Hey, see that telephone pole?" Then he threw the rock like a bullet and slammed the pole, which was a good way off. He turned around, grinning pretty sour, and yelled, "Still got control, boys!" Then the two of them went off.

It was more than a year before I saw him again, but he had been mentioned in letters from my sister, Mrs. Hargreave, who said that Luke was doing better and that his conduct was not so outrageous, as she put it. His mother's dying that year of cancer may have quieted him down some. And then he didn't have any money to buy whisky with. My sister said he was hunting again and in the summer pitching a little ball for the town team that played on Saturday and Sunday afternoons with the other teams from the towns around there. His pitching probably was still good enough to make the opposition look silly. But maybe not, either, as might be judged from what I heard the next time I saw him. I was sitting on the front porch of my sister's house, which is between the Goodwood house and what might be called the heart of town. It stands close up to the street without much yard like all the houses built since the street got to be a real street and not just a sort of road with a few houses scattered along it. Some men were putting in a concrete culvert just in front of the house, and since it was the middle of the day, they were sitting on the edge of the concrete walk eating their lunch and smoking. When Luke came along, he stopped to see what they were doing and got down in the ditch to inspect it. Although it was getting along in the season, there were still enough leaves on the vine on my sister's porch to hide me from the street, but I could hear every word they said. One of the workmen asked Luke when the next game would be. He said Sunday with Millville. When they asked him if he was going to win, he said he didn't know because Millville had a tough club to beat all right. I noticed on that trip home that the boys talked about their ball club, and not their ball team. It must have been Luke's influence. Then one of the men sitting on the curb said in a tone of voice that sounded righteous and false somehow in its encouragement, "We know you can beat 'em, boy!" For a minute Luke didn't say anything; then he said, "Thanks," pretty short, and turned off down the street, moving in that easy yet fast walk of his that always seemed not to be taking any effort.

It was a couple of days later when I was sitting in my sister's yard trying to cool off, that he came by and saw me there and just turned in at the gate. We said hello, just like we had been seeing each other every day for years, and he sat down in the other chair without waiting to be asked, just like an old friend, which he was. It wasn't long before he got out of the chair, though, and lay on the grass, just like he always used to do, lying relaxed all over just like an animal. I was a little bit embarrassed at first, I reckon, and maybe he was, too, for we hadn't sort of sat down together like that for near fifteen years, and he had been away and been a big-league pitcher, at the top of his profession almost, and here he was back. He must have been thinking along the same lines, for after he had been there on the grass a while he gave a sort of laugh and said, "Well, we sure did have some pretty good times when we were kids going round this country with our guns, didn't we?" I said we sure did. I don't know whether Luke really liked to remember

the times we had or whether he was just being polite and trying to get in touch with me again, so to speak.

Then he got to talking about the places he had been and the things he had seen. He said a man took him to a place in some city, Pittsburgh, I believe it was, and showed him the biggest amount of radium there is in the world in one place. His mother having died of cancer not much more than a year before that day we were talking must have made him remember that. He told me how he shot alligators in Florida and went deep-sea fishing. That was the only good time he had away from home, he said, except the first year when the Athletics farmed him out to a smaller team. I was getting embarrassed when he started to talk about baseball, like you will when somebody who has just had a death in the family starts talking natural, like nothing had happened, about the departed one. He said his first year in Pennsylvania he got six hundred dollars a month from the club he was pitching for, plus a little extra. "Being raised in a town like this," he said, "a fellow don't know what to do with real money." So he wrote home for them to crate up his bird dogs and express them to him; which they did. He leased a farm to put his dogs on and hired somebody to take care of them for him, because he couldn't be out there all the time, having his job to attend to. Then he bought some more dogs, for he always was crazy about dogs, and bought some Chinese ring-neck pheasants to put on his farm. He said that was a good time, but it didn't last.

He told me about some other pitchers too. There was one who used to room with him when the club went on the road. Every time they got to a new city, that pitcher made the rounds of all the stores, then the boxes would begin coming to the hotel room, full of electric trains and mechanical automobiles and boats, and that grown man would sit down and play with them and after the game would hurry back so he could play some more. Luke said his friend liked trains pretty well, but boats best, and used to keep him awake half the night splashing in the bathtub. There was another pitcher up in Indiana who went to a roadhouse with Luke, where they got drunk. They got thrown out of the place because that other pitcher, who was a Polak, kept trying to dance with other people's women. The Polak landed on a rock pile and put his hand down and found all the rocks were just the size of baseballs, and him a pitcher. He started breaking windows, and stood everybody off till the cops came. But Luke was gone by that time; so the police called up the hotel to tell Luke there was a guy needed two thousand dollars to get out of jail. So he and three other players went down and put up five hundred apiece to get the fellow out, who was sobered up by that time and wanted to go to bed and get some rest. Luke didn't know that fellow very well and when the Polak went off with the team to play some little game and Luke didn't go, he figured his five hundred was gone too. The fellow didn't come back with the team, either, for he had slipped off, so he figured he had really kissed his five hundred goodbye. But the night before the trial, about three o'clock in the morning, there was a hammering on the hotel-room door and before Luke could open it, somebody stuck a fist through the panel and opened it. And there was the Polak, wearing a four-bit tuxedo and patent-leather shoes and a derby hat, and his tie under one ear, drunk. He fell flat on the floor, clutching twenty-three hundred dollars' worth of bills in his hands. That Polak had gone back to the mines, having been a miner before he got in baseball, and had gambled for three days, and there he was to pay back the money as soon as he could. Luke said he wouldn't take money from a man who was drunk because the man might not remember and might want to pay him again when he got sober; so he got his the next morning. The fine and expense of fixing up the roadhouse wasn't as much as you'd expect, and the Polak had a good profit, unless a woman who got hit in the head with a rock and sued him got the rest. Luke didn't know how much she got. He said all pitchers are crazy as hell one way or another.

He told me about things that he saw or got mixed up with, but he said he never had a good time after he had to give up the farm where he had the dogs and the Chinese ring-neck pheasants. He said after that it wasn't so good any more, except for a little time in Florida, shooting alligators and fishing. He had been raised in the country, you see, and had the habit of getting up mighty early, with all that time on his hands till the game started or practice. For a while he used to go to the gymnasium in the mornings and take a workout, but the manager caught on and stopped that because he wouldn't be fresh for the game. There wasn't anything to do in the mornings after that, he said, except pound the pavements by himself, everybody else still being asleep, or ride the lobbies, and he didn't have a taste for reading, not ever having cultivated his mind

like he should. Most of the boys could sleep late, but he couldn't, being used to getting up before sun to go fishing or hunting or something. He said he could have stood the night drinking all right, it was the morning drinking got him down. Lying there on the grass, all relaxed, it didn't look like he gave a damn either.

He had his plans all worked out. If he could get hold of a few hundred dollars he was going to buy him a little patch of ground back in the country where it was cheap, and just farm a little and hunt and fish. I thought of old Mr. Bullard, an old bachelor who lived off in a cabin on the river and didn't even bother to do any farming any more, they said, or much fishing, either. I used to see him come in town on a Saturday afternoon, walking nine miles in just to sit around in the stores looking at people, but not talking to them, or, if the weather was good, just standing on the street. But Luke probably liked to hunt and fish better than Mr. Bullard ever did in his life, and that was something for a man to hold on to. I told Luke I hoped he got his farm, and that now was the time to buy while the depression was on and land was cheap as dirt. He laughed at that, thinking I was trying to make a joke, which I wasn't, and said, "Hell, a farm ain't nothing but dirt, anyway."

After lying there some more, having about talked himself out, he got up and remarked how he had to be shoving on. We shook hands in a formal way, this time, not like when he came in the yard. I wished him luck, and he said, "The same to you," and when he got outside the gate, he said, "So long, buddy."

About six months later he got married, much to my surprise. My sister wrote me about it and sent a clipping about it. His bride was a girl named Martha Sheppard, who is related to my family in a distant way, though Lord knows my sister wouldn't claim any kin with them. And I reckon they aren't much to brag on. The girl had a half-interest in a piece of land out in the country, in the real hoot-owl sticks, you might say, where she lived with her brother, who had the other half-share. I guessed at the time when I read the letter that Luke just married that girl because it was the only way he could see to get the little piece of ground he spoke of. I never saw the girl to my recollection, and don't know whether she was pretty or not.

I have noticed that people living way back in the country like that are apt to be different from ordinary people who see more varieties and kinds of people every day. That maybe accounts for the stories you read in papers about some farmer way back off the road getting up some morning and murdering his whole family before breakfast. They see the same faces every day till some little something gets to preying on their mind and they can't stand it. And it accounts for the way farmers get to brooding over some little falling-out with a neighbor and start bushwhacking each other with shotguns. After about a year Martha

Sheppard's brother shot Luke. My sister wrote me the bad blood developed between them because Luke and his wife didn't get along so well together. I reckon she got to riding him about the way he spent his time, off hunting and all. Whatever it was, her brother shot Luke with Luke's own shotgun, in the kitchen one morning. He shot him three times. The gun was a .12 gauge pump gun, and you know what even one charge of a .12 gauge will do at close range like a kitchen.

HAL SHERMAN

"There goes Crinshaw, misjudging another one!"

THE following was written a few years before Bobby Bragan's article on page 46, but that does not alter the tenor of its conclusions. In addition to enjoying Joe Williams' piece by itself, you should find it of interest to compare some of his thoughts with those of Bragan on the same subject.

Managers Are a Dime a Dozen

JOE WILLIAMS

IT WAS the last days of the season and the Giants had clinched the pennant by hanging another crushing defeat on the Dodgers. The crowd, with mixed emotions, was emptying out of Ebbets Field and this particular fellow, very likely a Brooklyn fan, stopped and glared at his companion. "I grant you Alston's no John McGraw, but don't try to sell me Durocher. Last year he was a bum. This year he's a genius. How come? He's no different. His ball club is."

Making due allowance for the gentleman's obvious distress and dismissing some of the impact of his remarks as typical of outraged frustration, I nevertheless found myself agreeing with him in substance. To say that the Giants won the pennant because Leo Durocher was in the dugout is an abstraction which carries no more force than to blame the Dodgers' failure wholly on Walt Alston. Managers simply aren't that important. The Giants won because they had better players (for the course of the one season, at least) and more of them and, specifically, because Johnny Antonelli won the big games the Giants needed, Willie Mays hit and fielded gloriously, Al Dark played a solid shortstop, and Marv Grissom and Hoyt Wilhelm were two of the best relief pitchers you could ever hope to see. Manager Durocher managed the same in 1953 and 1954. He flopped in '53 because he didn't have enough material. He made it in '54, in a tighter league without one dominant team, because he had more and better material.

Bob Hope can get only as many laughs out of his lines as his gagwriters put in them. It is the same with baseball managers. They stand or fall on the quality of their material. Naturally, some managers are quicker on the uptake

than others and, as is true in any other field, the manager with superior attributes is going to be more successful than others less gifted. Even so, he isn't going to win pennants unless he has the players.

This has always been true, for the elementary reason that it has to be, but only in recent years have fans and club owners got around to recognizing it. The fantasy that a manager was somehow capable of a special kind of dugout sorcery which pulled championships out of empty uniforms had a long run and dates back to the early 1900s when pennant achievement was concentrated in a few metropolitan areas, a fact which seemed to give the baseball writers of the period a loose sense of values. Thus Frank Chance of the old Chicago Cubs became the "Peerless Leader," John McGraw the "Little Napoleon," and Connie Mack the "Slim Strategist." Apparently it was much too great a challenge to the imagination to hit upon a title suitable to Hughey Jennings' qualities of leadership, for no stirring monument of inventive nomenclature was erected to his memory except his own ear-shattering battle cry, "Eeeyah!" Or perhaps, even then, the baseball writers were beginning to suspect that a manager who had a Ty Cobb playing for him did not have to be the most brilliant man in North America in order to win pennants, and the Tigers under Jennings (with Cobb at bat) won three non-stop.

At no other time in baseball history were managers so glamorized, and with Jennings winning three in a row, Mack having a run of four out of five with the Philadelphia Athletics, Chance enjoying a similar streak with the Cubs, and McGraw making the Giants a household

word in New York, it is not hard to understand
how they became so awesome in stature as to
betray critical minds into inflated appraisals. It
had to be the managers, for didn't they win
and win and win again? Not only Jennings,
Mack, McGraw and Chance, but Fred Clarke,
too. With three pennants back to back in Pittsburgh, he also was an Olympian. To appreciate
better what a forceful impact these managers
made on public and press box, it should be
noted that from 1901 through 1913, Clarke,
Chance and McGraw accounted for every National League pennant. Less extended but no
less pointed was the AL domination of Jennings
and Mack from 1907 through 1914, a string
broken only by the 1912 Boston Red Sox
under Chick Stahl, who, as a consequence, became something of a baseball curiosity.

The background, as you can see, was persuasive to indiscriminate acclaim and extrava-
gant rating. It did not seem in those days at all
preposterous to rank the manager over the
players. As a matter of fact, at that particular
time the manager was in a very real sense
more important than the players. Not for his
contributions as a field boss but as a builder.
In those days he pretty much ran the whole
works. This, of course, was before the farm
system had been invented, and before scouting
was systematized. I'm not positive but some
clubs may not have had any scouts at all. Most
clubs had only one. Two at the outside. The
managers leaned heavily on information from
old friends and former players who had settled
around the country. As an example, a wealthy
lumberman in Louisiana tipped off McGraw to
Mel Ott, the 16-year-old catcher. And Frank
Baker, the home-run king of the deadballers,
alerted his old boss, Connie Mack, to Jimmy
(Double X) Foxx.

The managers of yesteryear not only put
their teams together, for the most part, but they
made the trades and in many cases handled the
payroll and salary disputes. Today all such
matters are the function of the front office presided over by the general manager, who hires
the scouts, assigns them, acts on their recom-
mendations, decides the size of bonus, if any,
to be paid a youngster, draws up the spring
schedules, and so forth. Naturally, the general
manager will respect his manager's judgment on
players to be used as trading material and
lend an attentive ear to proposed player pur-
chases; at the same time, he must be convinced
the manager isn't giving up too much or getting
too little. And there will be times when the
general manager will make deals wholly on the

strength of his own convictions. In the business, this is known politely as making up the
manager's mind for him.

Casey Stengel blew a gasket when he learned
the Yankees had sold Vic Raschi to the St.
Louis Cardinals in 1954. Maybe he didn't blow
the gasket in public, because ol' Case finally
consented to the trade, but he sure bellowed in
private consultations that he couldn't afford to
lose big Vic. When, after a season of pitching
problems, Casey failed to corral his sixth
straight pennant, one of the fingers of blame
pointed to the Raschi trade. Of course, Vic
didn't burn up the league in St. Louis. But,
either way, whether his absence did or did not
contribute to the Yankee failure, blame (or
credit) for the action belonged to the front
office, not to the manager. It was just another
case of the manager doing what he was told.

In midsummer of 1950 Horace Stoneham
was somewhat startled to find Jim Hearn's
name on the waiver list. At $10,000 the Giants'
president felt the St. Louis Cardinal pitcher
would be worth a gamble. Leo Durocher, his
manager, didn't. It would be like throwing
money away and The Lip knew of many more
fascinating ways to do that. But once in a New
York uniform, all Hearn did was lead the National League pitchers in earned runs and the
following season post 17 wins to help bring
the Polo Grounders their first championship
since 1937. And in the World Series the big
right-hander pitched a winning four-hitter
against the Yankees.

While these transactions are on the minor
side, they do represent front-office influences
that were not common in the old days. Such
matters would not have gone beyond the manager, who, like mother, was deemed to know
best. If the manager kicked one, he had to assume the full responsibility. Once in a while,
even now, a manager is given the green light
to trade or sell as he sees fit, but when this happens it usually turns out the front office's blank
check was the product not so much of infinite
confidence in the manager's judgment as in
lack of judgment in his own.

Something like this happened when the
Detroit Tigers okayed a major deal Red Rolfe
negotiated with the Boston Red Sox, trading
George Kell, Dizzy Trout, Hoot Evers and
Johnny Lipon for Walt Dropo, Don Lenhardt,
Fred Hatfield, Bill Wight and Johnny Pesky. A
number of critics promptly expressed the wry
belief that Rolfe's talents in this field were
somewhat less impressive than those claimed
for David Harum, and when Walter (Spike)

Briggs, Jr., president of the club, was asked if he thought his manager had made a good deal, he snapped: "It had better be a good one." The Tigers were to finish eighth that season for the first time in the club's history and Rolfe was to be replaced before the curtain fell.

It is not conceivable that a deal of such magnitude could have been made by any contemporary manager in an organization where the front office makes it a business to keep minutely informed as to player values. It is precisely this shift in functions and authority that explains the reduced status of the present-day manager. Where the old-line manager used to be responsible for putting the players on the field, this is now the obligation of the front office, and since it is the players who win the pennants, not the managers, the front office has become the lifeline of baseball success. In a word, the better the front office, the better the team you will have.

This is simply a manifestation of progressive expansion. It never should have been the manager's chore to assemble talent. He has enough to do to train, develop and direct. But in baseball's early, sprawling days there was neither the economy nor the time for divisional labors and specialized departments, all operating under a central control. The front office handled the finances, the managers the rest. A pioneer sport, almost, under pioneer management. Today the modern, far-flung, efficient baseball operation is conducted along the same disciplined lines as General Motors, A&P and A.T.&T.

Just when the change from the general-store concept to big-business principles first made itself felt in baseball is speculative. Easier to mark, historically, is the spot where the illusion of managerial omniscience first began to show its slip. This was a tiny cell (now a shrine, no doubt) in Branch Rickey's brain where the farm system was spawned. There can be no doubt that Rickey, a leader in so many things, including the art of advanced circumlocution, was the first to demonstrate the wisdom and practicality of going to the source for material and bringing it along by degrees and in quantity. This patently was a job the manager on the field could never handle. Who else, then, but the front office?

From the day the farm system began to prove itself, the vision of the manager as the man around whom the team's fortunes sank or swam shrank in dimension. And the club Rickey was then associated with, the St. Louis Cardinals, lost no time in reacting accordingly.

Over a stretch of five years the Cardinals had five managers. In 1926 Rogers Hornsby led the Cardinals to their first pennant in history, defeated the mighty Yankees of Ruth's time in the World Series—and was fired a month later. Bill McKechnie brought the Cards their second championship in 1928 and was bounced the next season. Gabby Street added an enduring chapter by winning in 1930 and repeating in 1931. He lasted one more season before getting the gate midway in the 1933 season. A total of four pennants in six years, the combined work of three managers, each of whom was rewarded with the precipitous boot. Inferentially, what Rickey and Sam Breadon, the club owner, were telling the baseball world was: "Managers are a dime a dozen."

Actually, long before the farm system was reaffirming the first basic truth of the game, which is that no manager can win unless he has the players, an amiable, gregarious gentleman who used to run a pleasant taproom in Peoria, Illinois, was making a mockery of the managerial myth, though not by design, in Chicago. You know him now as Clarence (Pants) Rowland, former president of the Pacific Coast League and now vice-president of the Chicago Cubs.

Rowland never played ball in his life unless it was sandlot or obscure semipro. He got to be manager of the Chicago White Sox because Ban Johnson, president of the American League, and Charley Comiskey, owner of the club, patronized his place on hunting junkets during the winter. One of these days I must ask Rowland the details of this fantastic event. How the matter came up, what made him feel he could handle a big-league club, and the like. It should make absorbing telling and reading. Certainly it was the most daring experiment a club owner ever made. But, astonishingly, it proved to be a stroke of genius. In his first year Rowland moved the White Sox from sixth place to third. The next year he had them in second place and the third he was beating John McGraw and his swashbuckling Giants in the World Series, a performance chart no manager of that or this era would have disowned.

If ever proof was needed that any person with even man-in-the-street knowledge of baseball can win if he has the players, Rowland provided it for the record, and I imagine that if he happens to read this he will readily agree. On second thought, perhaps Comiskey made no daring experiment, after all. More likely, he felt that with the material he had the team couldn't possibly miss, and to prove his point and at the same time repay an old friend for many hours of sociability, he gave the manager's job to a man nobody in baseball had ever heard of. Or it may be that when Comiskey came to the next morning and realized what he had done, there was no alternative but to go through with the contract.

In any case, these were the White Sox that many observers, including the author, still rate as the best team baseball ever saw, a team which later, as I happen to know for positive fact, couldn't lose even when five of the regulars, soon to be known scornfully as the Black Sox, were trying to throw games for the gamblers. This was the team that had such remarkable players as Eddie Collins, Joe Jackson, Happy Felsch, Buck Weaver, Ray Schalk, Eddie Cicotte, Red Faber and Lefty Williams. In the 1917 World Series they beat one of McGraw's better teams. Collins hit .409 and Faber won three of the six games needed for decision. About all Rowland had to do was to make out the batting order and name the starting pitcher, although when he had to make pitching changes or send up pinch hitters, it seemed to me that his judgment was every bit as sound as that of other managers held in greater awe.

This, of course, had really been a front-office success, though it would be laughable to use the term in the sense that we now know it, for it was little more than a one-man operation. Comiskey had been a great player and manager and, like McGraw, Mack and other contemporaries, had friends who served as volunteer scouts. He was lucky in that many of the tips he got paid off. The modern front office invites luck but doesn't depend on it. The overall mechanics are geared to a constant production of first-rate ballplayers, and while the processes haven't been reduced to an exact science, the end result can safely be counted on to show more hits than misses year after year. The Yankees are a sound, solid example.

Casey Stengel is the only manager in the history of baseball to win five successive pennants with World Series flags to match. Hence the records describe him as the greatest manager baseball has ever had, and, statistically, he is, because his record is unmatched. And yet George Weiss is ten times as valuable to the Yankees as Stengel, for Weiss is the front office. It is therefore much closer to the truth to say that Weiss won the five straight than it is to credit Stengel with the epic achievement. Weiss, through his organization, developed the players and made the deals which enabled Stengel to win the pennants. I'm fully aware

that these passages may seem to demean Stengel's ability as a manager. Nothing could be more distant from my intentions. My regard for Stengel as a baseball man has always been high. I have spent too many hours in his company not to appreciate his talents.

Paradoxically, Stengel's success with the Yankees was the most devastating document of debunking that the masterminds have ever been called on to rebut. The very force of his unprecedented victory march stripped away the last vestige of fiction that it is the manager who wins the pennants. Prior to coming to the Yankees, Stengel managed eight years in the majors and not once was he able to get his club out of the second division. Indeed, on one implausible occasion, he was paid for not managing. Some great mind in Brooklyn evidently believed Stengel would be of more value to the club if he stayed away from the park. Even in the minors he was not always a ball of fire. Once, with Toledo, he finished last.

It is just as easy to explain Stengel's lack of success as his success, and the same explanation is applicable to all such upside-down experiences. Stengel couldn't win in Brooklyn or Boston because he didn't have the players; he didn't lose in New York for five years because he got the players and it seemed that there were always more where they came from. Stengel was just as competent a manager in Brooklyn and Boston as he has been in New York; maybe he was even better in those days because he had to work harder and couldn't afford the luxury of coaches like Bill Dickey, Frank Crosetti and Jim Turner.

It was Jimmie Dykes, as everybody knows, who called Joe McCarthy a "push-button" manager, implying that all McCarthy had to do was press a button and George Weiss would respond with a Spud Chandler, a Charley Keller or a Joe DiMaggio. It was, to be sure, an amusing exaggeration, but not without some truth. When Dykes was dropped by the Athletics, I wrote: "No one would seriously argue that Stengel could win with the Athletics in their present state, and by the same reasoning, few would want to bet that if the positions were reversed Dykes couldn't win with the Yankees."

A manager has to be more than good. He has to be lucky in the jobs he gets.

When the Yankees failed to get No. 6 in 1954, you knew that Casey would be tagged with a substantial portion of the rap. This genius of five years running had suddenly lost his touch, people said. He was guilty of over-managing, moving so many players in and out of the game that even he lost track. More blame was given to his two-platooning, which had worked for five years, than credit was given to an improved Cleveland club. In the final analysis, the Yankees lost because they hadn't improved, had, in fact, lost some strength as veterans like Rizzuto, Reynolds and Sain faded, and had not picked up the slack enough. And the Indians had improved all over the lot, in the infield, in the outfield and on the mound. Wasn't Al Lopez as nice a fellow this year as last? Sure, only Larry Doby got key hits; Al Smith solved the left-field problem; Houtteman, Newhouser and a trio of rookies backed up the Big Three on the mound; and Westlake, Majeski, Mitchell, Wertz, Glynn and Pope gave them the best bench in the league. Having a strong bench was long a Yankee secret. Once the Cleveland front office gave Lopez the horses, he out-Stengeled Stengel.

It becomes more and more evident with the passing years that club owners no longer attach paramount importance to the managerial post. So long as they are sure their manager has integrity, a certain amount of presence, is intelligent enough to get along with the press and knows how to handle men—all exemplary qualities but not rare—they are satisfied.

The truth is that there have been few managers who were outstanding as personalities. McGraw probably stood alone in this respect. McCarthy wasn't far behind. George Stallings, who led the Miracle Braves of 1914, was an individualist. Stengel is unique because he lives and talks baseball day and night. Leo Durocher has a flash quality that gives him a certain specious distinction. With deeper concentration, Dykes could be the best manager now around. Ty Cobb was another McGraw, lacking only his flinty shrewdness. Ty, incidentally, was a better manager than the records show. Mickey Cochrane was on his way to marked respect when he got hit in the head with a baseball. Bill McKechnie could manage for anybody but was handicapped because he lacked the false values of color and showmanship, empty virtues which blind emotional fans and, in times of box-office stress, are distorted by club owners to conceal their own shortcomings or those of their players.

This brings me to a final and vital point. If managers don't win pennants, why fire them because their players aren't good enough? Bringing the limitations of managers into proper perspective is common sense. But once this is known and front offices agree that ballplayers, not managers, win pennants, no club owner is justified in firing a manager for doing the best he could with what he had. Too many club owners make this a practice. It is their way of kidding the fans, of putting up a show that they are trying to help the team. There was a time when the fans would rise to the bait, just as there was a time when the fans believed managers had a magic touch. But this is a more enlightened age. Nobody has bought the Brooklyn Bridge in years.

You might believe, upon first glancing at the title to Mr. Wind's story here, that this one is about golf—especially because the author also edited *The Complete Golfer*, which I am informed is the best book of its kind. End of discussion about golf. Here's a real good baseball story.

The Master's Touch

HERBERT WARREN WIND

CALVIN COWLEY SHEPARD was methodically going through the mail stacked on his desk. He owned the largest desk in organized baseball—a foot longer and nine inches wider than Branch Rickey's by actual measurement. It was a fine July morning, the air exceptionally cool and dry for the Atlantic seaboard in summer, Shepard was thinking as he savored a testimonial from the local Elks Club to the effect that C. C. Shepard was the smartest man in the major leagues.

Reluctantly, he went on to the next letter, a routine report from the secretary of the Redlands farm team. The weather suddenly changed. The severe granite contours of his face became sharper and deeper as Shepard impatiently jabbed at a buzzer on his desk.

By the time his secretary, Ray Bell, came hurrying in, Shepard looked like the Old Man of the Mountain after a rough storm.

"You're not ready to see the press yet, are you?" Ray asked. He was a slim young man in his early thirties, who spoke, as did Shepard, with slight traces of a Vermont twang.

"No, my boy, I'm not ready to see the press," Shepard said with what was supposed to be elegant sarcasm. "I see them at ten o'clock. I know that. I don't need any coaching." He paused for a moment. "I've just been reading the report from Redlands. Do you know what Walter Eamons is batting?"

"It was .274 on last month's report," Ray answered. "Probably up around .280, .285 by now. I wouldn't worry about Eamons."

"Well, for your information," Shepard said slowly, "our Mr. Eamons is now pounding the ball at a robust .221. That boy ever hit below .340 for us?"

Ray fingered his brow. "No. He was over .370 those two years in the Kitty League. Last year at Redlands, let's see—" He broke off. "Think it was .362."

Shepard leaned over and pushed one button in a battery of sixteen attached to his desk. A glass panel at the far end of the office was jerkily lighted by fluorescent tubing. At the top of the panel, *Redlands* was printed in red; beneath the name of the club, in black, the roster of players. Fifteen similar panels, each devoted to a different farm team, formed unbroken murals along the two windowless walls of the office. The installation of this equipment had been one of Shepard's first moves after he'd bought his major-league franchise, and he derived a sense of power from pressing his buttons and watching the panels light up like a pinball machine in the hands of a true artist.

"I've won three pennants in the five years I've been in baseball," Shepard resumed, slightly appeased by the panel's obedience to his wishes. "How did I do it? By building up the best organization in the game. Not a single personal relation of mine is on the payroll. How come, then, I'm only now getting word that the best prospect we own is miles off the beam?"

"You saw that note about Eamons, didn't you—the one in last month's report from Redlands?" Ray asked him. "That line about possible woman trouble."

"Woman trouble!" Shepard cut in scornfully. "How can you live and not have woman trouble! That doesn't tell me a thing. It seems that any time I want the dope on anything, I've got to get it myself. Add Redlands to the itinerary on tomorrow's trip. Tell McCrillis to get packed. I'll want both of you. And *now* you may show the gentlemen of the press in."

*   *   *

Late Friday afternoon, Shepard and his aides deplaned at San Bernardino and proceeded directly to the Arrowhead Springs Hotel, a plush oasis perched on the foothills of the mountains above the arid valley. Shepard had been pushing himself hard for three days but his labors had paid off in results. In Topeka, Shepard and McCrillis, his chief scout, had watched Whitey Kravchek pitch a four-hit shutout. Sid Sandler, the young left-hander with Portland, had also impressed them as having the stuff to make the big jump to the majors.

As McCrillis put it, both youngsters had a little more to learn before they were finished pitchers, but just as they were, they would probably help the club a lot more than those two base-on-balls philanthropists, Al Marineau and Blitz Baker.

With his pitching problem nicely under control, Shepard took things easy during dinner and limited himself to two long-distance calls. In addition, he made one local call, instructing Emil Hochstetter, the old Cincinnati outfielder who managed Redlands, to meet him at nine o'clock sharp on the hotel's outdoor terrace. After lighting his old cherrywood pipe, Shepard felt so pleasantly in tune with his private universe that the thought of calling a conference of the local sports writers never entered his mind.

Somewhat under the spell of the palms and a few planter's punches, Shepard and his entourage, supplemented by Hochstetter, relaxed contentedly on the terrace. They did not stop talking baseball, however, until their attention was arrested by the entrance of a tall, handsome girl whom the headwaiter guided to a table directly across the dance floor from theirs. She wore a white dress over her tan, and had whatever it is that makes people rest their drinks on the table and stare. The four baseball men looked her over as closely as they would a promising left-hander.

"Now there's the sort of girl I like!" Shepard exclaimed.

"That's very big of you," Ray said. "I thought you were an antiglamour man, boss. That girl's loaded with it."

"*Honest* glamour," Shepard said, correcting him. "That tan, for example. That isn't one of those beauty-parlor jobs. None of that grapefruit-colored hair, either. There're a lot of other tips if you know what to look for. I can tell you all about that girl."

"Like what?"

"Well, first, she's in the movies."

"That's like saying that a guy who's just fanned Kiner, Musial and Robinson is in baseball."

Shepard refused to be thrown off stride. "She's obviously an outdoor girl," he continued calmly. "Plays good tennis, rides horseback well. She's an intelligent girl, levelheaded. Probably from a solid middle-class family. I'd guess that she comes of good old New England stock."

Ray whipped out a notebook and pretended to take notes.

"I don't see what's so amusing," Shepard said to him. "I happen to be able to judge women as accurately as I can judge ballplayers. I can sense these things, just the way I knew that Eamons belonged in center field, not at shortstop."

At almost the exact moment his name was mentioned, Walter Eamons was making his way through the tables at the far end of the terrace. The four baseball men, spotting the rangy towhead immediately, watched him pick a zigzag path to the table where the levelheaded girl from the solid New England family was sitting. She and the outfielder greeted each other with the sort of kiss that can be seen nowadays only in foreign movies.

"I can see it all now," Shepard said, beaming benevolently. "It's as simple as two and two. The boy's in love. No wonder he's not hitting."

"With a dish like that around, he's lucky to be able to find his way to the ball park," Ray said.

"Don't be cynical," Shepard said. "I wish all my players picked girls like that! Say, Emil," he said, turning to Hochstetter, "the next time you people refer to 'woman trouble' in a report, you've got to be more specific—much more specific."

"Would you like to meet her, Shep?" Hochstetter asked.

When Shepard said he would, Hochstetter padded slowly across the dance floor and returned shortly with the model young couple, smiling, in tow.

"I recognized you, all right, Mr. Shepard," Walter Eamons said as Shepard and his aides stood up to welcome him. "I didn't think you'd remember me. That's why I didn't come over."

"Of course I do," Shepard assured him. He

grasped the outfielder's hand. "It's nice seeing you, Walter. Who's the lovely young lady?"

"Mr. Shepard, I'd like you to meet my fiancée, Priscilla Summers," Eamons said awkwardly, as if he had memorized the line. "We're engaged," he explained.

Miss Summers, who had been restricting herself to a smile of general cordiality, turned on the full wattage as she received the congratulations of the three baseball men. "My, you have a strong grip!" she purred to Jim McCrillis.

"Used to catch," McCrillis replied shyly.

"I've heard a lot about *you*, Mr Shepard," Priscilla Summers continued. "You look much younger than your pictures."

Shepard took the compliment gracefully. "You're an extremely fortunate young man, Walter," he said, dropping his voice to a judicial pitch. "When's the big day?"

Eamons looked at his fiancée for guidance. "Sometime after the end of the season," she answered for them.

Shepard thought that was fine, just fine. "You kids run along now," he said. "No sense spending your time with a bunch of old fogies when you've got better things to do. I'll see you at the ball park, Walter."

"Peach of a girl," Shepard said approvingly to Hochstetter, when the young couple had gone off to dance. "Real New England type. It's a pity, though, they couldn't have fallen in love during the off season. That's a small matter, really. Next spring the boy will be himself again."

"I don't think so," Hochstetter said shortly.

Shepard stiffened. "You don't think what?"

Hochstetter looked at his boss as if Shepard were a pitcher to whom he was going to have to break the bad news that he was yanking him. "I don't think Eamons will be any good next year, or the year after, or any year, if he marries that girl."

"Emil—" Shepard's smile was patronizing—"I don't think you know women."

"I don't claim to, Shep. But I know a hell of a lot more about this customer than you do. I wanted to tell you about her, but you didn't give me a chance. Get the picture now. She comes down to this hotel from Hollywood for the weekend. This is five, six weeks ago. She's with another actress friend. They decide they'll kill the afternoon by watching a ball game. They get themselves a couple of box seats, in the section where the players' wives sit. I got this from Lefty Blake's wife. She was sitting in the row behind them. To make a long story short, this Summers babe spots Eamons and she goes for him—"

"But he wasn't hitting," Shepard objected.

"From a woman's point of view, Eamons ain't a good outfielder or a lousy outfielder or any other kind of an outfielder," Hochstetter said. "He's a big, good-looking kid with a build. Well, round about the fourth, when he's leaning against the bat rack, she stands up and looks him over like he was a bull at a country fair. Then she announces to her friend, just as cool as you like, 'I think I want that boy.' Blake's wife told me all about it."

Shepard stared for a long minute at his pipe. "What do you know about this girl's background?" he finally asked.

"Nothing much," Hochstetter replied. "All I know, Shep, is the kid's been no good to the team since she got hold of him. She's down here every weekend, so he can't keep his mind on his work Friday, Saturday or Sunday. Tuesday and Wednesday he's still in a fog, dreaming about the weekend. Thursday he's off on a new fog, counting the hours till she shows up on Friday."

Shepard sat silent for several minutes. Then he turned, as he did whenever his intuitive powers had let him down, to the extreme opposite pole of operation: the meticulous collecting of facts and figures with which his problem could be worked out as unemotionally as an algebraic equation. "Ray," Shepard snapped in a weak imitation of his best bark, "I want you to get up to Hollywood immediately and dig up a full dossier on Priscilla Summers. I want you back by nine tomorrow night."

"You mean you want me to leave right now?"

"That's exactly what I mean. Now get moving."

On Saturday, Shepard pushed himself through, what was, for him, an unsatisfyingly slow morning. He leafed through the special reports his office had airmailed: the team was just barely holding on to third place—something he didn't need to be told. He conferred with McCrillis on minor problems that had arisen at Topeka and Portland, and, after a short call at Lefty Blake's house on the way to the ball park, lunched with the club secretary and was interviewed by the local reporters. After lunch he tried to rouse himself from his lethargy by okaying plans for a new scoreboard and taking batting practice with the team, but his mind was not on his work. Just before game time he motioned Walter Eamons over to his box.

"You weren't getting much of that ball during batting practice," Shepard said, in a more severe tone than he had meant to use.

"Yeah, I was kinda poppin' 'em up," Eamons

said. His face took on a look of concern. "You feeling all right, Mr. Shepard?"

Shepard stared at him.

"You don't look so good as last night," Eamons went on. "You eat something that didn't agree with you?"

"I'll worry about my own digestion," Shepard sputtered. He tried to calm himself. "I'm certain I'd feel a hundred per cent better, Walter, if you started to play the ball we know you're capable of. Do you know you're batting .221?"

"I just can't seem to get a good piece of the ball," Eamons answered. He broke out in a grin, as if a very funny thought had just struck him. "That ball keeps getting smaller and smaller, Mr. Shepard. Right now it looks about as tiny as . . ."

Eamons' voice trailed off as his eyes focused on something over Shepard's left shoulder. He blew a kiss in that direction. Shepard turned. Priscilla Summers, her fingers pressed against her lips, was undulating down the aisle. Shepard scrutinized the faraway look in Eamons' eyes as Priscilla walked toward them. The boy was a goner, Shepard realized, scarcely recognizable as the same lean athlete who had shown such spirit at the training camp that Shepard had soberly appraised him to a newspaperman as "one of those aggressive, old-time ballplayers who can hit, field, throw and run those bases; a true competitor, possibly another Cobb." In the shape he was in, Eamons wasn't fit to carry Cobb's Coca-Cola stock, let alone his glove.

Shepard held his guard high. He just grunted when Priscilla greeted him with a warm smile and repeated her observation that photographs failed to do justice to his youthful appearance. "Walter," Shepard said curtly, as Eamons rested his elbows on the railing before the box, "I think you'd better get out in center field. The game's ready to begin."

"Now, darling," Priscilla cautioned the outfielder, patting him on the hand, "it's a terribly hot day, so don't play too hard. I've got a wonderful evening planned for us, and I don't want you to be all worn out. We're—"

"Walter, you're holding up the game," Shepard interrupted. "Miss Summers," he continued firmly, as Eamons trotted out to center field, "I don't know if you realize this or not, but all this high living and late hours—well, it's hurting the boy. I don't think you have Walter's best interests at heart."

"I think I'm a better judge of what's good for Walter than you are," Priscilla answered. "Anyhow, I don't see how what happens between Walter and me is any business of yours."

"It most certainly is my business," Shepard said. "Women like you don't care who you fool around with. It doesn't mean a thing to you that you're ruining the career of one of the best young ballplayers in the country. No, I can see it doesn't."

Priscilla measured Shepard coolly. "Get this through that great brain of yours, Grandpa," she said. "I don't give a damn about you and your precious baseball. If I want to marry that outfielder of yours or whatever he is, I'm going to, and there's nothing you or anybody else can do about it. Do I make myself clear?"

"You won't talk so bold tomorrow," Shepard fumed. "I've got a man in Hollywood getting the dope on you right now. You won't marry Walter Eamons. I'll see to it you won't."

"Like to bet on that?"

Shepard, barely in control of himself, pushed by Priscilla and marched out of the box.

◦   ◦   ◦

Ray Bell knocked on the door of Shepard's suite and walked in.

"You're back earlier than I expected," Shepard said. "Let's have it."

"She was easier to check on than I thought she'd be. Everyone in Hollywood seems to know Priscilla Summers," Ray explained as he riffled through his notebook. "You were right on some things and wrong on others. Her real name *is* Priscilla Summers. She *does* come from New England. Worcester, Mass. After that, your diagnosis isn't so hot."

"I'm not paying you to tell me how stupid I am," Shepard growled. "Cut the baloney and get on with it."

"Okay. I'll give it to you quick. She's been in Hollywood not quite two years. Been in two movies. They haven't been released yet, but everybody who's seen the previews says she's going to get somewhere. Clean-cut sex appeal. Okay, going back to the beginning. Born Worcester, 1927. Father managed a movie house. Nothing but the usual studio fiction on her till 1946, year she hit New York. Made a big splash as a model. She was a blonde then. That's not important, but I thought you'd like to know. The tan is real, though. She's been on location the last six weeks, making a Western."

"*Private* life," Shepard said.

"Just coming to that. She's been married twice. First time to a light-heavyweight fighter I never heard of. Lasted less than a year. Second time to a pro football player. She's known about town as a pretty predatory gal. Specializes in athletes, the way other women do in artists or millionaires. Just now getting around to baseball, I guess. Let's see, what else? Well, she's five-six and weighs one-nineteen and—"

"Bats right-handed and throws with both hands," Shepard broke in. "That's enough, Ray." He made an effort to smile that didn't quite come off. "I don't want any cracks out of you about how I ought to stick to judging ballplayers," he muttered. "I can handle this baby. Watch me."

Shepard paced the floor for a minute or two, and then directed Ray to summon Jim Mc-Crillis to the room.

"All right. I've got it all figured out," Shepard announced when McCrillis arrived. "We're going to call up Kravchek and Sandler. We'll send Marineau down to Topeka. They need a pitcher. I was going to give Portland Blitz Baker in exchange for Sandler, but I'm going to bring Blitz to Redlands instead. In a hot, dry climate, Blitz has a better chance of getting his arm back. Get the paper work started on this, Ray. One other thing: We're going to bring up Eamons."

Ray jerked his head up from his note-taking.

"I don't see what else we can do," Shepard said defensively. "I suppose we could transfer Eamons to one of the other farms, but I'd feel safer having him where I can keep an eye on him myself. We're dealing with a pretty unscrupulous woman." A new thread of anxiety crept into his voice: "Jim, you go out and round up Eamons right this minute. Get a double room in the hotel for tonight and stay with him. We're starting home first thing tomorrow, and I want that boy on the plane."

*   *   *

On Labor Day, C. C. Shepard's team propelled itself into a tie for first place by taking both ends of a double-header. Sandler and Kravchek were the winning pitchers. They had led the team's drive to the top, and the pro-Shepard press cited their arrival in the nick of time as one further evidence of C.C.'s peerless masterminding. As was to be expected, the reporters who didn't like Shepard glossed over the remarkable showings of Sandler and Krav-chek—they had won eight games between them—and lambasted Shepard for bringing up Walter "Cantaloupe" Eamons, who had succeeded in losing two games all by himself and could easily have lost more if he'd been given the opportunity.

In an important game against Boston, for example, Eamons had been inserted in the line-up in the seventh inning for defensive purposes. In the ninth, although the sun had been down for twenty minutes, for some reason he was still wearing his sunglasses. This may have accounted in part for the improbable demonstration he had put on in attempting to field a hard-hit drive that the average big-league outfielder could have handled with little or no trouble. Eamons had misjudged the sinking liner, and the ball had skidded between his legs on its first low bounce, hit the fence behind him, and rebounded right through his legs a second time.

Eamons had previously been relieved from his pinch-hitting duties after popping up three times and fanning twice. He reminded very few people of Cobb.

Off the field, Eamons dwelt in a similar fog. During his first weeks in the East, it was simply the usual haziness that enshrouds the lovesick. Then it thickened into a depression. During the last two weeks in August, Eamons, who had been hearing from Priscilla at least once a day, received no word whatever from her. His increasingly desperate phone calls to the West Coast had also gone unanswered. Jim McCrillis did everything he could to cheer up the forlorn outfielder. Assigned by Shepard to stay on as Eamons' twenty-four-hour companion, McCrillis took him to a Western movie each night and dined him at the best rathskellers. In their hotel room, he listened patiently to the boy's lamentations.

On Labor Day evening, McCrillis reported to Shepard that the situation had become impossible. "And damn' unpleasant, too," he added. "I can't tell the boy why he hasn't heard from that girl. I think he knows she's dropped him. He just can't bring himself to face it."

"He'll have to eventually. Then he'll start to mend," Shepard told him. "Stick with it, Jim."

The Saturday after Labor Day, Eamons pulled another "Eamons," as his boners were now being called. In the fourth inning, he was sent in as a pinch runner, a seemingly foolproof assignment. Eamons found a way, though. No one told him to steal second, but on the third pitch he was off like a hare.

He flashed down the base line with a terrific burst of speed, and had the base stolen before the catcher went through the motions of making his throw. The only trouble was that second base was already occupied by a teammate. This teammate, of course, was not prepared to jump for third, and Eamons was tagged for the rally-killing out. If there was a bright side to the incident, it was that Eamons didn't have to be used again in the game.

Shepard witnessed this "Eamons" from the center-field bleachers. He made it a practice to mingle with the fans in the bleachers from time to time in order to get, as he phrased it, "a true and undistorted picture of the real fan's attitude toward the team and the administration." On these expeditions, Shepard disguised himself in a baggy suit and dark glasses, and pulled the brim of an old hat down low over his forehead. Now and then a fan penetrated Shepard's disguise, but for the most part his identity went unsuspected. It was a bittersweet triumph. It pleased him to be a successful masquerader, but at the same time he was always hoping that, in spite of his efforts to conceal his face and figure, he would be so well known to an adoring public that they could spot him in a suit of armor with the visor shut.

"Mr. Shepard," he heard a voice saying in hushed tones as he sat in the bleachers, wondering when the fans would quiet down about Eamons' latest blunder and stop accusing C. C. Shepard of throwing away a pennant. He turned his head cautiously. It was Ray.

"Priscilla Summers wants to see you," Ray whispered excitedly in his ear. "She's up at the top of the bleachers."

Shepard's jaw sagged.

"She showed up at your box," Ray went on. "I would have brushed her off but I was afraid she'd get to Eamons."

Shepard tugged the brim of his hat down and followed Ray up the aisle of concrete steps. His mind worked furiously to bring this unsettling turn of events into some sort of focus.

Priscilla Summers sat, with her legs casually crossed, in the last row of the bleachers. She was wearing dark glasses, too. They hid the expression in her eyes, but the line of her mouth showed she was in an aggressive mood.

Shepard removed his hat in an elaborate gesture of mock courtesy. "I hope you didn't come all this distance," he said, "just to tell me I'm looking much more handsome than my recent photographs."

"Is that a nice way to speak to one of your greatest admirers?" she cooed. They faced each other like ancient foes. "I just happened to be in town," she went on coolly. "Publicity. One of my pictures opens here next week. We're greasing the wheels."

"And you came all the way out to the ball park to give me a pair of free tickets."

"Ah, you're a cute boy," she laughed. "No, I've got news for you. Personal news. I wanted to tell you I'm going to marry one of your players next Wednesday."

Shepard tried to steady himself by clutching wildly for Ray's arm.

"I knew you'd be delighted to hear that," Priscilla smiled.

"How'd you ever work that, young lady?" Shepard sputtered feebly. "You haven't seen Eamons for a month. You haven't written him in over two weeks. You—"

"Oh, I'm not marrying Walter," she interrupted. "I'm going to marry Blitz Baker."

Shepard's instinct told him to cover up, fast. The important thing was for Priscilla to believe she had triumphed gloriously and completely. He made a titanic effort not to register the feeling of relief that surged through every fiber of his body. It was only Blitz Baker. A washed-up pitcher. Won four, lost nine. Whew! A cheap price to pay when it could have been Eamons.

"I've got to hand it to you," he said, as if he were standing gallant in defeat. "You're a faster worker than I bargained for."

"Just call me Shep," Priscilla said with frosty sarcasm. She stood up to leave. "How do you like finishing second, Grandpa?"

Shepard watched her as she disappeared down the runway exit. He shocked Ray by leading him back to the office for a good stiff drink. When his nerves had slowed down to a bumpy trot after he'd had three fingers of Scotch, Shepard peeled off his disguise and climbed back into his regular clothes. The telephone rang just as he was leaving for home. It was McCrillis, calling from the players' dressing room. He wanted to know if Shepard had seen the story in the afternoon papers about Blitz Baker and Priscilla Summers.

Shepard described the meeting in the bleachers. "I was going to call you, Jim," he said, his voice still husky with tension. "Do you think we should tell Eamons or try to keep it from him?"

"He knows about it," McCrillis said. "Somebody showed him the paper."

"How'd he take it?"

"Hard, Shep, awful hard. He's been in the shower for over a half hour. I think he's waiting till everybody goes."

"Watch him close," Shepard said to McCrillis. "Don't let him out of your sight."

*　　*　　*

Refreshed by a good night's sleep and some glowing write-ups in the morning papers, Shepard arrived at the ball park shortly after nine on Sunday morning. His footsteps, the only sound in the vast hush of the stadium, echoed strangely as he strode through the rotunda where, three hours later, thousands would be clamoring around the ticket booths. He unlocked a gate next to the turnstiles, and was striding down the passageway under the stands when he was startled by what seemed to be the sound of bat meeting ball. He heard it again as he hurried up the nearest ramp. Probably some kids who'd stowed away over Saturday night.

He stopped short when he came to the head of the ramp, behind first base, and tried to make some sense out of the baffling scene on the diamond below him. Jim McCrillis stood on the pitcher's mound, with thirty or so practice balls scattered around him. He was pitching to Eamons. *Whack!* Shepard watched a long belt sail all the way to the wall in right center. That's the way he used to cut, thought Shepard. McCrillis picked up another ball. Into the motion. *Whack!* Shepard lowered himself into a chair and gazed at the ghostly batting practice.

Eamons slammed the last pitch against the scoreboard in dead-center field and hustled down the first-base line and on into the outfield. He picked up a ball near the wall, wheeled, and fired it in to home plate, where McCrillis stood. Eamons picked up another ball, wheeled and fired again.

McCrillis had just handled the fourth throw from the outfield when, out of the corner of his eye, he caught sight of Shepard making his way through the boxes. McCrillis cupped his glove and bare hand to his mouth and hollered to Eamons to hold it up.

Shepard clambered awkwardly over the railing and onto the field. "What goes on here, anyway?" he shouted as he walked toward the plate.

"He wanted some practice," McCrillis said, panting a little. He looked as if he had just caught both games of a double header. "Got me out of bed at—"

"Watch your head!" Eamons' voice carried pugnaciously from the far reaches of the outfield. A rifle-shot throw kicked off the turf near the pitcher's mound. McCrillis and Shepard hit the dirt just in time, and the ball banged against the backstop. The two men dusted themselves off and moved a safe distance down the first-base line.

"He's been like that all morning. You can't do anything with him," McCrillis grumbled as the bombardment of baseballs continued. "One extreme to the other. Last night, he was like a wounded deer. Pitiful. Fell asleep right after supper. He couldn't eat any. Fell asleep with all his clothes on, in a chair. This morning— whango! I'm living with a madman. He pulls

me out of bed at six o'clock. Yanks the blankets off and tells me to shut up when I ask him what's the matter. He needs some practice, he tells me; we're going to the ball park. We've been out here three hours. He wouldn't even let me get some breakfast."

A bounding ball zipped by McCrillis' knee. He started to yell something to Eamons and then decided it was a waste of time. "When he comes in now," McCrillis complained, "I'll have to pitch that whole batch to him again or hit him fungoes. I don't mind that. But he's got no right to be sore at me. I'm not Priscilla Summers."

"I think you hit it there," Shepard said absently. He had been listening with one ear, trying to put the parts together. "He's going to take it out on everyone for a while, Jim. He's going to show the world."

Shepard and McCrillis were collecting the balls in front of the backstop and rolling them toward the pitcher's mound when Eamons came jogging in from the outfield. Shepard greeted him warmly: "Good morning, Walter."

Eamons glowered at Shepard for a moment. He spat a slug of tobacco juice an inch over Shepard's shoe and walked on to pick up a bat.

Shepard dug an elbow into McCrillis' ribs. "We've got a ballplayer again," he said.

During the week that followed, Eamons treated opposing pitchers with no more respect than he had Shepard. He delivered twice as a pinch hitter, and was given a crack at the starting line-up. In the final six games of the team's home stand, he collected twelve hits in twenty-six times at bat, stole three bases, and was impeccable in the field. His one-man rampage was the spearhead of the drive that sent the team four full games in front as it headed west to play the last twelve games on the schedule.

*   *   *

"And that, gentlemen," C. C. Shepard announced with a crackle of self-congratulation, "is how it worked out—precisely as we planned it." He watched the faces of the reporters whom he had summoned when the news had come through from Chicago that his team had clinched the pennant. Even his severest critics, Shepard could see, had been impressed by his account of how he had coped with his difficult midsummer problems.

Shepard basked for a moment in the admiration of his audience. "I just happen to have the ability to size up women," he went on. "Five minutes after I met this actress, I had her number. I knew Blitz Baker was exactly the type she'd go for. That's why I sent Blitz to Redlands. In two weeks she had forgotten all about Eamons. You know the rest, gentlemen. Last week she and Blitz were married. I'm afraid this will mean the finish of Blitz's baseball career. My guess, gentlemen, is that he'll be lucky to be pitching Class-D ball next year."

Ray, standing beside his boss, studied Shepard's face as he warmed up to the subject of Walter Eamons' great future. It struck Ray that he had never seen Shepard's craggy features composed in an expression of such radiant bliss.

The telephone rang, and Shepard motioned for Ray to take it.

"Who was it?" Shepard asked as Ray hung up.

"Nothing important, Mr. Shepard," Ray answered casually.

"Well, who was it?" Shepard asked again.

"Just Hochstetter," Ray said. "Nothing urgent."

"He wouldn't call me up just to congratulate me on the pennant," Shepard persisted. "What was on his mind, Ray?"

"Just some news about Blitz Baker."

"What did he do? Quit the team?" Shepard asked with a wise twinkle.

"Well, if you must know," Ray said, as if he were being pushed into something against his better judgment, "Hochstetter wanted to tell you that Blitz just pitched a no-hitter and struck out eleven men."

"As I was saying, gentlemen," Shepard resumed quickly, "this Eamons will be even better next year. With proper handling, I predict he'll develop into another Cobb. You can quote me on that."

IN the first *Fireside Book of Baseball,* a piece something like the following appeared and proved a high point in the book. Reviewing the book in *The New York Times,* Mark Harris wrote that the Japanese box score "knocks me out—why, I don't know, since I can't read it." The hell with it.° Here's another one.

1955:
New York Yankees 6,
Japanese All-Stars 1

YOMIURI MORNING PRESS

二回三塁走者とサインを交したコールマンが初球のカーブを二ゴロしてスクイズまないの先取点をもぎとった後、全大阪は右中間二塁打とわずかの希望をもたせた一瞬、送球をはじいたマーティンが杉山の上に折重って倒れ三進を阻むと

いう巧みさで切抜けた。先発阿部は高めの捕球に低めのカーブを生かす用心深い投球だったがヤンキースは三回サーヴの3点大本塁打などで長短打を浴びせた。これは軸足とする後足を少し曲げて弾力性を持たせ軸足でタイミングを合わせてほとんどステップしな

い打撃が巨大なエネルギーと結びついてすばらしい猛襲となったもので理想的な変化球攻法の成功と言えよう。

しかし以後全大阪は中村、山下、西村一の継投、とくに八回から西村一の低めをつくシュートで三振を奪う出色の大好投を織込んで注目を浴びた。この間六回には山下、吉田のコンビで二塁走者ケーリーを刺す堅実な

ネット裏から

端をのぞかせ七回コールマンの野選から吉田の中前適時打で一点をむくいるなど根気強く食い下がったのがせめてもの慰めだった。=観衆一万五千=（浅利）

西村は素晴らしい

ステンゲル監督「西村は素晴らしいピッチングだったがいつも回数が少ないのは残念だ。一度良い回数を投げるのをみたいものだ」

マントルに感嘆
ホームラン競争

全大阪が藤村兄（阪神）戸倉（阪急）飯田（南海）ヤンキースはサーヴ、スコーロン、マントルの六選手がホームラン競争を行なった。アメリカでも公式試合の前に時々行われるが、ヤンキースのマントルとレッドソックスのテッド・ウィリアムスの打合いが一番興味深かったそうだ。強打者ウィリアムスとこの日の素晴らしい当りを見せ右で4本、そ

リカでも公式試合の前に時々行われるが、ヤンキースのマントルとレッドソックスのテッド・ウィリアムスの打合いが一番興味深かったそうだ。強打者ウィリアムスとこの日の素晴らしい当りを見せ右で4本、そ

のうち場外が2本、左で1本計5本をたたき偉大なるスイッチ・ヒッターの威力をみせた。
○…アメリカでは一試合に右打席と左打席でホームランを打分けた記録がたった二つ残っているが今シーズン、マントルがこれを破って話題をさらった。「腰の動きが実にスムーズだ。フォームのまねはできるとしてもあれだけの体格からの馬力はとうていわれわれには…」とパ・リーグの強打者飯田選手もたじろいだ。シタをまくばかり。
○…スコーロン選手の8本が最高だったが、このスコーロン選手の四十二オンス（三〇匁）のバットはア・リーグでも一番重いもの。結局マントルの5本にサーヴ

◇ヤ軍第7戦先発陣容

【ヤンキース】	【全パシフィック】
(右)バウアー	(二)パルボン (阪)
(二)マーティン	(一)榎 本 (毎)
(遊)マクドガルド	(左)山 内 (西)
(捕)ベ ラ	(三)西 田 (南)
(一)スコーロン	(中)飯 田 (西)
(左)ハワード	(右)大 鬘下 (西)
(中)サ ー ヴ	(遊)吉 田 (西)
(投)ケ ー リ ー	(捕)ルイス (毎)
(投)ホ ー ド	(投)榧 本 (阪)

が4本とヤンキースは計17本、全大阪は藤村の5本をトップに飯田が3本、戸倉が1本の計9本で問題にならない。

セーフ　ヤンキース・全大阪３回裏、２死１塁に白坂をおき渡辺博の投ゴロをターレー１塁に投げたがセーフ（１塁手スコーロン、２塁手コールマン）＝大阪電送

第6戦にも快勝

ヤンキース 全大阪に6—1

【西宮発】ニューヨーク・ヤンキースの来日第六戦は二十九日午後二時五分から快晴の西宮球場に約一万五千の観衆を集め、在阪の

セ・パ四球団から選抜した"全大阪"との間で行われた。ヤンキースは三回サーヴの中堅四百フィートの豪快な３点本塁打などで早くも５点を奪う力強い攻撃をみせた。一方全大阪も先発のターレー投手によく食い下がり六回まで３四球、３安打で四、六回を除いて毎回走者

を出したが、速球に極められて後が続かず、七回代ったグリム投手に小玉の右前安打から野選をまじえて吉田の右前安打で一矢をむくいたのみだった。なおヤンキースの遠征での第三戦、全パシフィックとの試合はきょう三十日午後二時から西宮球場で行われる。

全大阪　000 000 100 ｜ 1
ヤンキース 014 000 100 ｜ 6

【ヤンキース】	打	得	安	打	三	四	犠	盗	失
(左)クーレン	5	0	1	0	1	0	1	0	0
(遊)マーティン	4	1	2	0	1	0	0	0	0
(中)サベージ	5	2	3	3	0	0	0	0	0
(捕)ハワード	2	1	1	0	0	1	0	0	0
(捕)シルヴェラ	2	0	1	1	1	0	0	0	0
(一)スコーロン	2	1	1	0	0	0	0	0	0
(二)レージ	3	0	1	0	1	0	0	0	0
(右)ハワード	5	0	3	1	0	0	0	0	0
(二)コールマン	5	0	1	1	2	0	0	0	0
(三)ケーリー	3	0	1	0	1	1	0	0	0
(投)ターレー	3	1	1	0	1	0	0	0	0
(代打)マン	1	0	0	0	0	0	0	0	0
(投)グリム	0	0	0	0	0	0	0	0	0
計	40	6	16	6	7	3	0	0	0

【全大阪】	打	得	安	打	三	四	犠	盗	失
(二)白坂(神)	1	0	0	0	0	0	1	0	0
(二)白岡(南)	2	0	0	0	0	1	0	0	0
(遊)吉田(毎)	3	0	1	1	1	1	0	0	0
(右)渡辺博(神)	3	0	2	0	0	0	0	0	0
(中)堀井(南)	3	0	0	0	0	0	0	0	0
(中右)飯田(南)	2	0	0	0	1	0	0	0	0
(一)宮倉(神)	2	0	0	0	2	0	0	0	0
(左)渡辺(阪)	2	0	1	0	1	0	0	0	0
(三)杉山(南)	2	0	1	0	1	0	0	0	0
(三)河野(近)	2	0	2	1	2	0	0	0	0
(三)小玉(近)	1	1	1	0	0	0	0	0	0
(捕)木樽(南)	2	0	0	0	0	0	0	0	0
(捕)松井(南)	1	0	0	0	0	0	0	0	0
(投)西村(神)	2	0	0	0	0	0	0	0	0
(代打)藤村兄(神)	1	0	1	0	0	0	0	0	0
(投)阿部(南)	0	0	0	0	0	0	0	0	0
(代打)中村(近)	1	0	0	0	1	0	0	0	0
(投)武智(近)	1	0	0	0	1	0	0	0	0
(代打)山下(近)	1	0	0	0	1	0	0	0	0
(捕)徳網(神)	2	0	0	0	1	0	0	0	0
計	34	1	7	1	9	3	0	0	0

▽併殺 ヤ1 大1 ▽本塁打 サーヴ（1号・阿部）▽三塁打 ハワード ▽二塁打 杉山、サーヴ、マーティン ▽勝投 ターレー ▽敗投 阿部

HERE is a grieving, bitter piece by a great baseball writer. I envy him his restraint. Mike Gaven died the day the story appeared in the New York *Daily News* of March 11, 1958.

Dateline: Miami

DICK YOUNG

A FELLOW LIES gravely ill in the hospital here. He is a sports writer named Mike Gaven, and he was stricken at the ball park yesterday, and maybe that's a good way for a baseball writer to get it, if there is a good way to get it—with his boots on, in the ball park, covering the team that was his.

The doctor said it was a stroke, caused either by a ruptured blood vessel in the head, or a clot. I'm sure that's right. I'm just as sure that there was a lot of aggravation mixed in, and a lot of heartbreak.

Three weeks from now, Mike was to lose his team, the one he had covered for the past 13 years. They were going on to Los Angeles, and he was going back to New York. He kidded about it, and every time he kidded about it, he got sicker.

It wouldn't have been much for them to have made the last three weeks pleasant. Instead, they planned to make it miserable, just as they had made the previous three miserable. They hadn't singled out Mike, but they had bunched him with the rest of the New York writers in this colony of discarded souls, and I guess Mike just felt it a little deeper than the rest of us. He usually did. He's a sensitive Irisher, and he tried always to hide his hurt behind a big laugh.

Mike wished, more than anything else, to feel that he belonged and was wanted. Here, in the Dodger camp this spring, that is the last thing a Brooklyn writer felt. They made it vividly clear that we no longer belong, and are not wanted. Day after day, in coming across all the little details that used to be so routine, we were told that we were not included in the plans, and would have to shift for ourselves. They are petty things, but the petty things hurt most, because a premeditation is required to be petty.

Like this: In past years, a press bus was made available for those who desired to use it between the hotel and the ball park. Some did, some didn't, but it was there—and it was thought up. This year, no bus. The club hired a couple of cars and placed them at the disposal of the Los Angeles writers, who are writing the kind of stories that will sell tickets where tickets are being sold. The difference in cost between two cars and one bus would have been so small. Instead, the club was so small.

And like this: On Thursday, the Dodgers are scheduled to fly from Vero Beach to Bradenton for a game with the Braves. This is one of the more difficult trips on the citrus circuit. It is followed by a return to Miami after the game. Unless you fly, it is virtually impossible to make the two-legged tour, and cover a ball game between. In past years, space on the same plane was reserved for Dodger writers. This year, there are two groups of Dodger writers—those who belong, and those who don't.

Yesterday, those who don't were told that there would be no space on the flight to Bradenton. How were we to cover? That's our worry.

"Chee," said Mike Gaven on the field before the game, "I hope we can get somebody to cover for us over there. Just in case something unusual happens."

Then, Mike waxed philosophical, and laughed. "Well, at least I covered the Dodgers when they were a great team," he said. "They'll never be that great again. And at least I covered baseball in the days when it was a pleasure. They can't take that away from me."

It was something a guy says, with no possible way of knowing what is to happen to him several hours later. And yet, as you recall it, you get goose flesh. It was as though he had a premonition.

I would like to make a point here that not all members of the Dodger front office subscribe to the picayune practices that have been such a dominant factor of this camp. There are those who are embarrassed when confronted with the tawdry situations, and they almost apologize for the crude policy which tossed over the Brooklyn writers as though they were "last year's wives." There is no sense naming these class exceptions because that would only serve to embarrass them further, or expose them to reprisal by an organization that has proven itself capable of such.

Besides, there are so few. They grow fewer all the time, as the Dodger organization, once virile with ideas and individual expression, decays into a body of "yes men." Time was when to have an idea or a thought was considered to be of some value; now, if you dare suggest that the "party line" policy is out of whack, you had better be ready to face the music.

Mike Gaven used to have a word for it.

"Government radio," he'd say. I'm not talking about newspaper criticism in this particular case; I'm talking about the exchange of free opinion in Dodger meetings—something which is of so much value in all organizational meetings, but which is being increasingly stifled in Dodger sessions.

And so, I say to you, Walter O'Malley: Rid yourself of your yes men—you know who they are—or pay the price of a decadent organization.

And I say to you, sports writers of Los Angeles and other cities: When a club official comes to you and says, "Why don't you be a nice fellow; after all, you're like one of us," never for a moment believe that you are one of them, because you are merely tolerated—and then only for as long as they feel they can use you and your paper. You belong to your readers, and to them alone.

And to you, Mike: You were so right. You covered baseball, and the Dodgers, in the golden era—and they can't take that away from you.

Index of People

Aaron, Barbara, 332
Aaron, Henry (Hank), 76C, 329-32, 359-60
Abrams, Cal, 344
Adams, Bobby, 299
Adams, Charles (Babe), 181, 183
Adams, Myron, 1-6
Adcock, Joe, 48, 49, 51, 204B
Addington, L. H., 11
Agannis, Harry, 72
Albert, Brother, 310
Alexander, Babe, 344
Alexander, Grover C., 7-9, 29, 140A, 181-84, 319
Allen, Johnny, 153, 159, 202
Alston, Walter, 52, 170, 327-28, 351, 371
Ames, Leon, 258
Amoros, Sandy, 270, 285-86
Anson, Adrian (Cap), 10, 18, 346
Antonelli, Johnny, 371
Aparicio, Luis, 143-44
Appling, Luke, 355-56
Ashburn, Richie, 49, 320, 323, 344
Auker, Elden, 100, 101, 102, 353, 354
Averill, Earl, 225, 356
Backman, Lester, 34
Bailey, Ed, 328
Baker, Del, 24, 353, 356
Baker, J. Franklin (Home Run), 130, 240-42, 372
Ball, Neal, 22
Banks, Ernie, 49, 51, 328
Barnes, Donald, 122, 224-25
Barnes, Virgil, 184
Barnhart, Clyde, 12, 23
Barr, George, 187
Barrett, Charles (Red), 190, 288
Barrow, Edward, 154, 158, 159, 161, 163, 191, 212
Barry, Jack, 130
Bartell, Dick, 163, 226, 353, 355
Bauer, Henry (Hank), 150, 285-86, 337-38, 359-60
Bavasi, E. J. (Buzzy), 197, 270
Beamon, Charlie, 305
Bearden, Gene, 28-29
Bearden, Henry, 28-29
Bell, Gus, 328
Bell, Herman, 182-83
Bender, Charles (Chief), 242, 258, 272-73
Bennett, Charlie, 69

Bennett, Dr. George, 191
Benny, Jack, 194
Benton, Al, 356
Benz, Joe (Butcher Boy), 12
Berberet, Lou, 325
Berg, Moe, 13, 14
Berger, Wally, 255
Berra, Lawrence (Yogi), 142, 147, 169, 170, 280, 282, 284, 295, 327, 355, 359-60
Bessent, Don, 270, 350-51
Bevens, Bill, 197
Bissonette, Del, 11
Blackburne, R. (Lena), 131
Bleeker, Marty, 128
Bluege, Oswald (Ossie), 226
Boeckel, Tony, 69
Boley, Joe, 334
Bolling, Frank, 336
Bonham, Ernest (Tiny), 72, 86
Boone, Ray, 325
Bottomley, Jim, 22, 182-83
Boudreau, Lou, 60, 76B, 143, 144, 356
Bradley, Alva, 297
Bradley, Bill, 363
Bragan, Bobby, 46-54, 227, 288, 330, 371
Branca, Ralph, 236B, 270
Brandeis, Justice, 115
Brannick, Eddie, 161
Breadon, Sam, 373
Brecheen, Harry, 288
Bresnahan, Roger, 258, 271, 273
Bridges, Tommy, 102, 191, 288, 353, 354
Bridwell, Al, 259
Briggs, Walter O., 226
Briggs, Walter O., Jr. (Spike), 226, 373
Broaca, John, 159, 161
Brodie, Steve, 258
Broun, Heywood, 259
Brower, Frank, 22
Brown, Mace, 186
Brown, Walter (Jumbo), 161, 162
Brown, Warren, 343
Brown, Willard, 356
Browne, George, 273
Browning, Pete, 12
Brucker, Earle, 223
Brush, John T., 35, 258
Bruton, Bill, 330, 332
Bryant, Clay, 185
Bulkeley, Morgan G., 341

Bunning, Jim, 327
Burdette, Selva L. (Lew), 288, 297, 298, 327, 358-60
Burns, Ed, 8
Burns, George, 22
Burnside, Peter, 30
Busby, Jim, 150-51
Bush, Donie, 130, 364
Bush, Guy, 153, 154
Bush, Joe, 274
Bushong, Albert (Doc), 346
Butcher, Max, 255
Byrne, Tommy, 142, 147, 359-60
Camilli, Adolph (Dolph), 191, 254, 326
Campanella, Roy, 50, 69, 270, 285-86, 294, 299, 300F
Campbell, Paul, 354
Carey, Andy, 285, 286, 325
Carlson, Hal, 72
Carnett, Dr., 334
Carpenter, Bob, 319-20, 361
Carrigan, Bill, 309
Carroll, Ralph, 274
Cartwright, Alexander J., 339-40
Caruthers, Robert, 271
Casablanca, Luis M., 140
Case, George, 192
Casey, Hugh, 26-27, 194, 196
Cassidy, Joe, 71
Castleman, Clydell (Slick), 163
Cavaretta, Phil, 186
Cepeda, Orlando, 350-51
Cerv, Robert, 144
Chadwick, Henry, 340
Chance, Frank, 60-61, 212, 325, 371, 372
Chandler, A. B. (Happy), 76, 107-114, 116-118, 128
Chandler, Spurgeon (Spud), 374
Chapman, Ben, 153, 154, 159, 161-62, 225
Chapman, Ray, 72, 130
Chase, Hal, 127-28, 325
Chase, Judge, 110-11, 113
Cheney, Larry, 7
Chesbro, Jack, 154, 288-89
Chico, 141
Cicotte, Eddie, 127, 129, 320, 374
Cimoli, Gino, 270, 351-52
Clark, Jay (Nig), 363
Clarke, Fred, 372
Clarke, Josh, 363

Clarkson, John, 271
Clemente, Bob, 48, 54
Coan, Gil, 192
Cobb, Ty, 36, 41, 84, 88, 103, 130, 155, 192, 279, 296, 364, 371, 375
Cochrane, Gordon (Mickey), 100, 101, 102, 353, 356-57, 375
Coffman, Samuel (Dick), 162, 163
Cole, Dick, 298
Cole, Leonard (King), 71
Coleman, Jerry, 60, 337, 358-60
Coleman, Joe, 288
Collins, Eddie, 240, 242, 317, 374
Collins, James (Rip), 101-02, 186, 300D
Collins, Joe, 170, 359-60
Combs, Earl, 95, 153, 159, 161-62, 182
Comiskey, Charles, 127, 129, 151, 346, 362, 373-74
Comiskey, J. Louis, 85
Condon, David, 131
Conlon, John (Jocko), 321
Consolo, Billy, 144
Cooke, Allen (Dusty), 96
Cooke, Bob, 190
Cooney, Jim, 22, 23
Cooper, Mort, 172A, 194
Cooper, Walker, 172A, 298
Corbett, James J., 272
Corridon, Frank, 288
Courtney, Clint, 298
Coveleski, Stanley, 183, 287
Covington, Wes, 330, 360
Craft, Harry, 254-55
Craig, Roger, 170, 270
Crandall, Del, 321, 325, 332, 358-60
Crandall, Otis, 241
Cravath, Clifford (Gavvy), 326
Crawford, Sam, 364
Cronin, Jack, 258
Cronin, Joe, 86-87, 223, 224, 325, 356
Cronin, Mildred, 87
Crosetti, Frank, 41, 60, 153, 154, 159-62, 374
Cross, Lave, 258
Crowder, Alvin, 102
Curry, Duncan F., 339
Cuyler, Hazen (Kiki), 254
Dahlen, William, 273
Dahlgren, Ellsworth (Babe), 70
Daily, Edward, 71
Daly, John, 337
Danning, Harry, 326
Dark, Alvin, 371
Daubert, Jake, 7, 71
Davenport, Jimmy, 351
Davis, Harry, 242
Davis, James, 90
Dean, Jerome H. (Dizzy), 14, 99,

100-102, 172A, 186, 295, 300D
Dean, Paul (Daffy), 101, 172A
Deets, Jim, 194
Delahanty, Ed, 72
DeLancey, Bill, 69, 71, 102, 300D
DeMaestri, Joe, 325
Demaree, Frank, 153
Demeter, Don, 270
Derringer, Paul, 24, 226
De Shong, James, 159
Devens, Charlie, 14
Devlin, Arthur, 258, 273, 291
Devore, Josh, 241
Dickey, Bill, 27, 86, 97, 153, 159, 161-63, 203, 356-57 374
Dickson, Murry, 288
Didrickson, Babe, 172C
Dillhoefer, William (Pickles), 71
DiMaggio, Dominic, 157, 172A, 326
DiMaggio, Joe, 24, 27, 36, 37, 38, 41, 69, 89, 94-99, 140A, 147, 155, 157-63 172A, 300, 325, 356, 374
DiMaggio, Vince, 38, 157, 172A, 281
Dineen, Bill, 359
Ditmar, Art, 360
Doby, Larry, 145-46, 375
Dockins, George, 293
Doerr, Bobby, 326
Dolan, Patrick (Cozy), 71-72
Donahue, John (Jiggs), 364
Donald, Atley, 86
Donatelli, Augie, 359
Donlin, Mike, 34
Donnelly, Arthur, 279
Donovan, Bill, 364
Dooin, Charlie, 130-31
Doolan, Mike, 320
Dorish, Harry, 53
Doubleday, Abner, 339
Dougherty, Patrick (Patsy), 363
Dovey, George B., 361
Doyle, James, 72
Doyle, Larry, 241
Dressen, Charley, 196, 215, 301
Dropo, Walter, 142-43, 146, 372
Drysdale, Don, 204B, 325, 350-51
Dubuc, Jean, 353
Duffy, Jo Ann, 302
Dugan, Joe, 182
Dugey, Oscar, 295
Duggleby, Bill, 258
Dunn, Jack, 310-12
Durocher, Leo, 46, 47, 53, 82-83, 84, 100, 102, 103, 191-94, 196, 214, 223, 227, 254, 279, 296, 300D, 320, 371, 372, 375

Dyer, Eddie, 155
Dykes, Jimmy, 85-86, 212, 297, 298, 374-75
Earnshaw, George, 288, 334
Easter, Luke, 143
Eckstein, Buck, 140
Edwards, Bruce, 50
Egan, Ben, 311
Ehrhardt, Welton (Rube), 256
Eisenhower, Dwight, 145
Elberfeld, Norman (Kid), 290
Elliott, Bob, 326
Engel, Joe, 86-87
English, Elwood (Woody), 153, 254
Ennis, Del, 320
Erickson, Paul, 193
Erskine, Carl, 215, 270
Essick, Bill, 158
Etten, Nick, 129, 215
Evans, Al, 357
Evans, Billy, 212
Evers, John, 60-61, 69, 259
Evers, Walter (Hoot), 372
Faber, Urban (Red), 131, 287, 374
Fain, Ferris, 60
Farrell, Joe, 364
Faust, Charlie, 298
Feller, Bob, 24, 69, 76, 76B, 203, 225, 226, 296-97, 320, 356
Felsch, Oscar (Happy), 374
Ferrell, Rick, 357
Fields, W. C., 319
Finn, Cornelius (Mickey), 72
Fisher, Ray, 322
Fitzsimmons, Fred, 162-63, 274
Flack, Max, 281
Fletcher, Art, 241, 356
Flynn, Jack, 355
Foiles, Henry (Hank), 328
Fondy, Dee, 51, 302
Fonseca, Lewis, 85-86, 325
Ford, Edward (Whitey), 49, 142-48, 149, 298
Foster, John B., 35
Fothergill, Robert (Fatty), 99
Fowler, Art, 288
Fox, J. Nelson (Nellie), 146, 298, 328
Fox, Pete, 97
Foxx, Jimmy, 161, 202-03, 204A, 216, 333, 356, 372
Frank, Judge, 111, 113, 116-17
Frankhouse, Fred, 288
Fraser, Charles (Chick), 258
French, Larry, 325, 326
Frey, Benny, 71
Frey, Lonnie, 50
Frick, Ford, 60, 83, 108, 129, 282, 287, 288, 328
Friedlander, Sid, 198
Friend, Bob, 47
Friend, Hugo, 128

Frisch, Frank, 100, 101, 102, 279, 281, 295, 300D
Fullis, Charles (Chick), 101
Furillo, Carl, 270, 285, 344, 350-51
Gabler, Frank (Gabbo), 162
Gaffney, James E., 361
Gandil, Charles (Chick), 127
Gantenbein, Joe, 195
Garcia, Mike, 325, 326
Gardella, Daniel, 107-14, 116-20
Gardner, Jerry, 141
Gardner, Larry, 9
Garibaldi, Art, 281
Gastall, Tom, 72
Gaven, Mike, 83, 197, 386-87
Gehrig, H. (Lou), 38, 69, 70, 153, 159-63, 182, 215, 256, 279, 300
Gehringer, Charles, 12, 14, 97, 102, 297, 356
Gelbert, Charlie, 69
Geraghty, Ben, 331
Gharrity, Edward (Patsy), 88
Gilbert, Billy, 258, 273
Gilbert, Brother, 310
Giles, Warren, 281, 288
Gilliam, Jim (Junior), 270, 282, 285, 336, 352
Gionfriddo, Al, 140A, 197
Glazner, Charles (Whitey), 12
Gleason, William (Kid), 14, 131
Glenn, Joe, 159
Glynn, William, 375
Goetz, Larry, 323
Goliat, Mike, 344
Gomez, Ruben, 204B, 350-52
Gomez, Vernon (Lefty), 153-54, 157, 159, 161-63, 191, 203, 216-17, 224, 295-96, 298, 325, 326
Gonzales, Mike, 281
Goodman, Ival, 255
Goodwin, Marvin, 70
Gordon, Joe, 27, 38, 60, 326
Gordon, Joseph, 362
Gorman, Tom, 147
Goslin, Leon (Goose), 102
Gowdy, Hank, 184
Graham, Charles, 157, 158
Graham, Frank, 127-28
Grasso, Newton (Mickey), 228
Gray, Dick, 351
Gray, Pete, 236A
Greenberg, Henry (Hank), 24, 86, 102, 297, 356
Griffith, Clark, 86-87, 88, 223-25, 227-28, 333
Griggs, Dewey, 331
Grim, Bob, 327-28
Grimes, Burleigh, 153, 287-89
Grimm, Charlie, 60, 153
Grissom, Marv, 288, 325, 371
Groat, Dick, 52
Gromek, Steve, 288, 298

Groth, John, 39
Grove, Robert (Lefty), 147, 161, 224, 274, 319, 333, 356
Gumbert, Harry (Gunboat), 162
Hack, Stan, 186, 325
Haddix, Harvey, 320
Hadley, Irving (Bump), 161, 162, 333-34
Haefner, Bill, 353
Hafey, Charles (Chick), 69, 182-83, 325
Haines, Jess, 182, 184
Hale, Sam, 87
Hall, Dick, 48
Hall, Marcus, 72
Hamlin, Luke, 254-55
Hammer, Granny, 320
Hand, Learned, 111-12
Handley, Lee (Jeep), 70, 186, 297
Hanlon, Ned, 258
Harder, Mel, 296
Harridge, William, 108, 288
Harris, Dave, 13
Harris, Mark, 384
Harris, Spencer, 333-34
Harris, Stanley (Bucky), 87, 153, 197, 226, 228
Harshman, Jack, 325
Hartnett, Charles (Gabby), 153, 154, 185-87
Harum, David, 372
Harwell, Ernest, 236D, 340
Hassett, Buddy, 254
Hatfield, Fred, 372
Hatter, Clyde, 72
Hawley, Emerson (Pink), 14
Hayes, Frank, 357
Haynes, Joe, 228
Hayworth, Ray, 357
Hazle, Bob, 359-60
Hearn, Jim, 372
Heffner, Donald (Jeep), 159
Hegan, Jim, 354, 357
Heilmann, Harry, 88, 325
Heintzelman, Ken, 194, 344
Hemsley, Rollie, 357
Hemus, Solomon (Solly), 298
Henline, Walter (Butch), 197
Henrich, Eileen, 42-43
Henrich, Thomas, 26, 27, 36-43, 89, 95, 98-99, 156
Herman, Billy, 60, 153, 186
Herman, Floyd (Babe), 300
Herman, George, 184
Hershberger, Willard, 72
Herzog, Charles (Buck), 241
Higgins, Michael (Pinky), 336
Hildebrand, George, 288
Hill, Jesse, 159
Hinchman, Bill, 363
Hoag, Myril, 159
Hoak, Don, 204C
Hoblitzel, Richard (Doc), 275

Hodges, Gil, 50, 51-52, 84, 270, 282, 285-86, 297, 298, 299-302, 327-28, 344, 351
Hodges, Joan, 301
Hofman, Artie, 259
Hogan, Frank, 122
Hogsett, Elon, 12, 102
Holke, Walter, 22
Hooper, Harry, 9, 275
Hopp, Johnny, 196
Hornsby, Rogers, 22, 36, 121-22, 153, 155, 182-83, 204A, 299, 330, 373
House, Frank, 298
Householder, Charles, 71
Houtteman, Arthur, 375
Howard, Elston, 140C, 169, 359
Hoyt, Waite, 181-84
Hubbard, Kin, 323
Hubbell, Carl, 99, 149, 151, 162, 163, 292, 320
Hudson, Johnny, 254
Huggins, Miller, 48, 72, 153, 182, 184
Hughes, Jim, 326
Hulbert, William A., 341
Hurst, Tim, 258
Hutchinson, Fred, 143, 147-48, 155, 281, 282
Hyland, Dr. Robert, 193
Irvin, Monte, 53
Jackson, Joe (Shoeless), 12-13, 128, 374
James, Bill, 326
Jamieson, Charles, 23
Jansen, Larry, 147-48, 288
Jennings, Hugh, 50, 103, 290, 364, 371-72
Jensen, Jack, 147, 186, 325
Jethroe, Sam, 53
Johnson, Ban, 257, 373
Johnson, Ken, 344
Johnson, Walter, 151, 183, 184, 320
Jones, Fielder, 363-64
Jones, Oscar, 258
Jones, Willie (Puddinhead), 322
Jorgens, Arndt, 159
Joss, Adrian (Addie), 69, 70, 363
Judd, Oscar, 222
Jurges, Billy, 60, 153, 186
Kaline, Al, 145, 328
Kamm, Willie, 326
Kase, Max, 83
Kazin, Alfred, 243
Keefe, Tim, 271
Keeler, Willie, 50
Kell, George, 39, 356, 372
Kelleher, Frank, 53
Keller, Charles, 27, 374
Kelly, Emmett, 300F
Kelly, George, 326
Kelly, Mike, 346
Keltner, Ken, 24, 297
Kenna, Ed, 15

Kenna, John E., 15
Kilduff, Peter, 22
Killefer, Bill, 8, 29
Kinder, Ellis, 288
Kiner, Ralph, 299
King, Clyde, 197
King, Eddie, 274
King, Jimmy, 351
Kirke, Jay, 43
Kirkland, Willie, 351
Kissam, Samuel, 90
Klem, Bill, 100-101
Kline, Ronnie, 47
Kluszewski, Ted, 48, 51
Knable, Otto, 320
Knickerbocker, Billy, 87
Knoll, Charles (Punch), 71
Kobs, John, 322
Koenecke, Leonard, 72
Koenig, Mark, 153, 181-84
Koy, Ernie, 191, 254
Kremer, Remy, 326
Krichell, Paul, 163
Kroh, Floyd, 259
Kubek, Tony, 358-60
Kucks, Johnny, 170, 359
Kuenn, Harvey, 145, 146, 327
Kurowski, George (Whitey), 196
Labine, Clem, 270, 327-28
Lajoie, Napoleon (Larry), 274, 362, 363-64
Lake, Edward, 39
Landis, Kenesaw Mountain, 42, 76A, 100, 101, 102, 115, 128, 129, 132, 191, 193, 227
Lane, Frank, 151, 288
Laney, Al, 97
Lange, Bill, 325
Lanier, Max, 107-109, 112, 116, 119
La Place, Dr. John, 313
Lardner, Ring, 12, 215, 243, 322
Larsen, Don, 46, 140C, 280, 282, 284-86, 358-60
Latham, Arlie, 345-47
Lavagetto, Harry (Cookie), 197, 254
Lazzeri, Tony, 140A, 153, 159-63, 181-83, 186, 326
Lee, Bill, 185-87
Lee, Cliff, 22
Lee, Thornton, 151
Leiber, Henry (Hank), 69, 162
Lemon, Bob, 288, 325, 326
Lemon, Jim, 145
Lenhardt, Don, 372
Leonard, Hubert (Dutch), 9
Lerian, Walter, 69-70
Lewis, George (Duffy), 9
Liebhardt, Glenn, 363
Lindell, Johnny, 195
Lipon, Johnny, 39, 372
Liska, Ad, 333-34
Livingston, Thompson (Mickey), 50

Lobert, Hans, 50
Lockman, Carroll (Whitey), 293
Loes, Billy, 298, 327
Logan, John, 49, 359-60
Lollar, Sherman, 149, 150
Lombardi, Ernie, 254-55, 325
Long, Dale, 47, 48, 145
Lopata, Stan, 322
Lopez, Al, 281, 375
Lord, Bristol (Briscoe), 273
Lutzke, Walter, 22
Lynch, Pat, 83
Lyons, Ted, 156
Mack, Connie (Cornelius Mc-Gillicuddy), 13, 76A, 96, 222-23, 228-29, 240, 242, 258, 274, 295, 319, 323, 333-34, 362, 371, 372, 374
MacMillan, Roy, 236C
MacPhail, Leland (Larry), 185, 191, 227
Magerkurth, George, 196
Maglie, Sal, 49, 148, 284-86, 288, 294, 323
Mahon, Jack, 160
Majeski, Henry, 375
Malarkey, Jack, 258
Mallette, Mal, 215
Malone, Perce (Pat), 153, 154, 159, 161, 162, 163
Malzone, Frank, 328
Mantilla, Felix, 359
Mantle, Mickey, 49, 108A, 145, 150, 170, 190, 214, 215, 216, 257, 285-86, 327, 358-60
Mapes, Cliff, 40
Marberry, Fred, 102
Marion, Marty, 143, 155, 296
Marquard, Richard (Rube), 240-42, 320
Martin, Alfred (Billy), 60, 170, 285, 298, 325
Martin, Fred, 107-109, 112, 116, 119
Martin, John (Pepper), 41, 100, 101, 102, 300D
Marty, Joe, 186
Masi, Phil, 76B, 150
Mathews, Ed, 49, 51, 204C, 328, 358-60
Mathewson, Christy, 8, 127-28, 181, 183, 184, 240-42, 258, 259, 271-73, 274, 298, 358, 359, 360
Matthews, Wilson, 33
Matthias, Brother, 308-11
Maxwell, Charlie, 144-45
May, Frank (Jakie), 153, 154
Mayer, Jim, 9
Mays, Carl, 72
Mays, Willie, 30, 49, 51, 52, 191, 216, 270, 278, 292, 321, 323, 328, 330, 335-36, 351, 371
Mazeroski, Bill, 52
McBride, George, 88

McCarthy, Joe, 70, 89, 97, 153, 154, 158-63, 183, 191, 225, 342, 356, 374-75
McConnell, Amby, 22
McCormick, Frank, 24, 226, 255
McCormick, Harry (Moose), 259
McCullough, Clyde, 298
McDermott, Maurice, 354
McDougald, Gil, 76C, 149, 281, 282, 285, 325, 328, 359-60
McGann, Dan, 258, 290
McGinnity, Joe (Iron Man), 256-59, 272
McGowan, William, 144
McGraw, Bob, 256
McGraw, John J. (Muggsy), 32-35, 50, 70-71, 97, 128, 184, 240, 241, 257-58, 272-73, 290, 295, 298, 362, 371-75
McGraw, Mrs. John, 292
McHenry, Austin, 71
McInnis, John (Stuffy), 212, 274
McIntyre, Matthew (Matty), 364
McKechnie, Bill, 24, 373, 375
McKinley, Bill, 359
McLean, John, 32
McMullin, Fred, 131
McNabb, Edgar (Texas), 71
McNair, Donald (Boob), 334
Meadows, Ford, 310
Medwick, Joe (Ducky), 100-102, 300D, 330
Meeker, Roy, 72
Melton, Cliff, 298
Mercer, George (Win), 71
Merriwell, Frank, 86
Merkle, Fred, 241, 259
Mertes, Samuel (Sandow), 258, 273
Merullo, Leonard, 204B
Meusel, Bob, 161, 181-84, 256, 325
Meusel, E. (Irish), 97, 325
Meyers, John (Chief), 241
Michaels, Cass, 354
Miksis, Eddie, 197
Miller, Eddie, 24
Miller, Otto, 22
Minoso, Orestes (Minnie), 327-28
Mitchell, Clarence, 22
Mitchell, Dale, 146, 282, 284-85, 375
Mitchell, Jackie, 172B
Mize, Johnny, 95, 192
Monroe, Marilyn, 172C
Montgomery, Alvin, 70
Moon, Wally, 331
Moore, Al, 97
Moore, Eddie, 14
Moore, Joe, 163
Moore, Ray, 288
Moore, Terry, 94, 281
Moore, Wilcy, 153, 154

Moran, Pat, 7-9, 69
Moriarty, George, 296
Morris, Ed, 70
Morrison, John, 12
Moses, Wally, 321
Moss, Les, 355
Mossi, Don, 325, 327-28
Munger, George, 46
Murphy, Dannie, 242, 273
Murphy, Francis P., 353
Murphy, John, 70, 117, 118, 159, 161, 162, 163, 356
Murphy, Mike, 275
Murray, Jim, 300
Musial, Lillian, 155
Musial, Lukasz, 155, 156
Musial, Stan, 49, 51, 52, 155-56, 214, 328, 329, 330, 331
Mutrie, Jim, 361
Myatt, Glenn, 23
Myer, Billy, 274
Myers, Elmer, 274
Nabors, Johnnie, 274-75
Neal, Charley, 336, 351
Negray, Ron, 350-51
Nelson, Lindsey, 191
Nelson, Olof, 140
Neun, Johnny, 23
Newcombe, Don, 48, 169-71, 270, 294, 298, 329, 344
Newcombe, Mrs. Don, 170, 171
Newcombe, James, 169-70
Newcombe, Norman, 170
Newhouser, Harold (Hal), 354, 356, 375
Newsom, Henry, 223, 226
Newsom, J. R., 223-24
Newsom, Louis N. (Bobo), 70, 202-03, 222-29, 353
Nieman, Bob, 236A
Noonan, Pete, 35
Nuxhall, Joe, 298
O'Brien, John, 52, 71
O'Brien, Thomas, 71
O'Connell, Daniel, 49, 298, 351
O'Connor, Jack, 290
O'Day, Henry (Hank), 259
O'Dea, June, 154
O'Doul, Frank (Lefty), 19, 325
O'Farrell, Bob, 182-84
O'Loughlin, Frank (Silk), 364
O'Malley, Walter, 294, 387
O'Neill, Steve, 143
O'Rourke, James (Orator Jim), 11-12, 14
Orsatti, Ernest, 102, 162, 300D
Ott, Mel, 83, 95, 99, 162, 204A, 287, 372
Overall, Orval, 325
Owen, Arnold (Mickey), 26-27, 140A
Owen, Marvin, 100-01, 102, 103, 297
Padgett, Ernie, 22
Padgett, Howie, 140

Page, Joe, 288
Painter, Earle, 160-61
Paparella, Joe, 359
Parnell, Mel, 89, 144, 151
Parrott, Harold, 82-83
Passeau, Claude, 24, 280
Patkin, Max, 236A
Patterson, Arthur, 192
Paul, Brother, 310
Paul, Gabe, 49
Pearson, Ike, 192-93
Pearson, Monte, 161, 162, 163
Peckinpaugh, Roger, 130, 183, 184
Peitz, Henry (Heinie), 14
Pennock, Herb, 181-82, 184
Perini, Lou, 332
Perring, George, 363
Pesky, Johnny, 372
Peters, John, 11
Pfeister, Jack, 259
Phelps, Ernest (Babe), 254
Philley, Dave, 195
Picinich, Val, 274
Pick, Charlie, 274
Pierce, Billy, 53, 146, 149-52, 327-28
Pierce, Gloria, 152
Piersall, Jim, 146, 199-201, 296, 298
Pinelli, Mabel, 278, 281
Pinelli, Ralph (Babe), 194, 278-83, 285
Pipgras, George, 153, 154
Pippen, Henry (Cotton), 281
Pippen, Rodger, 309-10, 311
Pitler, Jake, 270
Pittinger, Charley, 258
Plank, Eddie, 258
Podres, Johnny, 270, 359
Poles, George, 305-06
Pollet, Sid, 331
Pope, David, 375
Porter, J. W., 305
Potter, Nelson, 288
Povich, Shirley, 13
Powell, Jake, 161-63
Power, Vic, 140C, 298
Pressnell, Forest (Tot), 255
Price, Jim, 362
Priddy, Jerry, 60
Purcell, William (Blondie), 13
Pytlak, Frank, 357
Quezada, Carlos, 140
Quinn, John, 287
Raffensberger, Ken, 191
Raimondi, Billy, 279
Raschi, Vic, 372
Raymond, Arthur (Bugs), 32-35
Reach, A. J., 341
Reardon, John (Beans), 281
Reese, Harold (Peewee), 50, 170, 193, 196-97, 215, 216, 270, 280, 285, 297, 301, 302, 344, 351-52

Reeves, Bobby, 87
Reid, Philip J., 362
Reiser, Harold (Pete), 140B, 190-98
Reynolds, Allie, 53, 375
Reynolds, Carl, 186
Rhodes, James (Dusty), 30, 293, 298
Richards, Paul, 46, 47, 53, 150, 151, 295
Richardson, Nolem, 159
Rickey, Branch, 11, 12, 14, 49, 50, 52, 71, 82-83, 156, 190-91, 197, 227, 297, 373
Rickey, Branch, Jr., 83
Riggs, Lew, 254-55
Rigler, Cy, 41
Rigney, Bill, 293
Rikard, Culley, 196-97
Rios, Benny, 140
Ripple, Jimmy, 162, 226
Rixey, Jeptha, 9
Rizzo, Johnny, 186, 194
Rizzuto, Phil, 53, 60, 130, 236C, 298, 375
Roberts, Mary Ann, 322
Roberts, Nora, 322
Roberts, Robin, 48, 319-23, 332, 343-44
Roberts, Sarah, 321, 322
Roberts, Tom, 321
Robertson, Charlie, 285
Robinson, Aaron, 39, 151
Robinson, Frank, 49, 51, 305-06, 328
Robinson, Jackie, 52, 76, 170, 215, 270, 280, 282, 285-86, 297, 299, 344
Robinson, Wilbert, 224, 256-57
Roe, Elwin (Preacher), 270, 288
Roebuck, Ed, 170
Rogell, Billy, 101, 102, 297
Rolfe, Robert (Red), 26, 159, 161, 162, 163, 372-73
Rooney, Gus, 212
Roosevelt, Franklin D., 162, 226
Root, Charles, 153, 154, 186
Rosar, Buddy, 357
Rossman, Claude, 364
Roth, Allan, 48, 49
Rothrock, Jack, 101, 102, 300D
Rowe, Lynwood (Schoolboy), 100, 102, 288, 297, 353, 354, 355
Rowland, Clarence (Pants), 373, 374
Ruark, Robert, 225
Ruether, Walter (Dutch), 157-58, 326
Ruffing, Charles (Red), 153, 159, 160, 161, 162, 163, 225, 356
Ruppert, Colonel Jacob, 159, 163
Ruth, George H., 307, 308

Ruth, George H. (Babe), 14, 36, 37, 38, 41, 48, 69, 84, 96, 143, 153, 154, 155, 158, 159, 160, 161, 162, 181-84, 236D, 256, 279, 287, 307-12, 315-16, 320, 356
Ruth, Kate, 307, 308
Ryan, John (Blondy), 159
Sain, Johnny, 76, 360, 375
Saltzgaver, Otto (Jack), 159
Sanchez, Raul, 288
Sanford, Jack, 327
Sarni, Bill, 69, 71
Sath, Johnny, 76C
Sauer, Henry (Hank), 30
Sawyer, Eddie, 343-44
Schacht, Al, 87-88, 263, 297
Schalk, Ray, 131, 132, 374
Schang, Wally, 274-75
Schanz, Charley, 196, 279
Scharein, George, 195
Schevill, James, 16
Schmidt, Harry, 258
Schmitz, Johnny, 288
Schoendienst, Albert (Red), 155, 298, 328, 329, 331
Schulte, Frank, 38
Schumacher, Garry, 83, 190, 300
Schumacher, Hal, 162, 163
Score, Herb, 149
Scott, Everett, 130
Segar, Charley, 60
Selkirk, George, 159, 161-63
Seminick, Andy, 320
Sewell, Joseph, 153
Sewell, Luke, 357
Shannon, Paul, 212
Shantz, Bobby, 360
Shaughnessy, Frank, 287
Shea, Merv, 357
Shean, Dave, 212
Sheehan, Tom, 274
Shellenback, Frank, 287
Shepard, Jack, 53
Shibe, Ben, 362
Shocker, Urban, 69, 70
Shore, Ernie, 8, 9
Shotton, Burt, 49, 50, 51, 82, 156, 197
Simmons, Al, 333-34
Simmons, Curt, 320, 327
Sington, Fred, 185
Sisler, Dick, 343-44
Sisler, George, 69, 84, 130, 212, 343
Sivess, Pete, 14
Skinner, Bob, 53
Skowron, William (Moose), 144, 170, 327, 358-59
Slattery, Jack, 122
Slaughter, Enos, 84, 95, 170, 193, 204D, 280, 358-60
Smith, Al, 375
Smith, Earl, 141

Smith, Edgar, 24
Smith, Elmer, 162
Smith, Frank, 363-64
Smith, Hal, 336
Smith, Mayo, 323
Snider, Edwin (Duke), 49, 51, 147, 190, 216, 270, 280, 285, 299, 325, 344, 351
Snodgrass, Fred, 183, 184, 241, 242
Sockalexis, Louis, 11
Solano, Claudio, 140
Somers, Charles, 362
Soule, Asa T., 1, 2, 5-6
Southworth, Billy, 155
Spahn, Warren, 331
Spalding, A. G., 341, 347
Speake, Bob, 143
Speaker, Tris, 29, 94, 97-98, 158
Spence, Jack, 140
Spencer, Daryl, 350-51
Stahl, Charles (Chick), 69, 372
Stahl, Jake, 22
Stallings, George, 295, 362, 375
Stanky, Eddie, 83, 155, 204B, 280, 301
Stengel, Charles (Casey), 28, 37, 46, 47, 53-54, 72, 170, 257, 288, 298, 327-28, 337, 359-60, 372, 374-75
Stephens, Vernon, 142, 354, 356
Stephenson, Cuyler, 153
Stephenson, Joe, 22
Stewart, Bill, 301
Stirnweiss, George (Snuffy), 38, 89
Stobbs, Charles (Chuck), 144
Stoneham, Charles, 121-22
Stoneham, Horace, 83, 190, 292, 372
Storke, Alan, 72
Strang, Sammy, 258
Stratton, Monty, 69
Street, Charles (Gabby), 224, 373
Stricklett, Elmer, 288-89
Sturdivant, Tom, 359
Sturn, John, 26
Suder, Pete, 355
Suhr, Gus, 155, 186
Sukeforth, Clyde, 353
Sulik, Ernie, 14
Sullivan, Billy (Sully), 363-64
Sullivan, Frank, 325
Sullivan, Ted, 131
Summa, Homer, 23
Sutcliffe, Sy, 71
Swift, Bob, 357
Taft, William Howard, 188
Talcott, Edward, 90
Tamulis, Vito, 159, 254
Tannehill, Jesse, 363
Tavener, Jack, 23

Tebbetts, George (Birdie), 52, 117, 172, 288, 298, 305, 353-57
Temple, Johnny, 298
Terry, Bill, 103, 155, 159, 162, 163
Tesreau, Jeff, 320
Thevenow, Tommy, 181-83
Thomas, Frank, 51, 53
Thomas, Ira, 242
Thomas, Valmy, 351
Thompson, Henry, 335
Thompson, S. C., 315
Thomson, Bobby, 53, 236B, 292, 331, 332
Thorpe, Jim, 263
Thurber, James, 315
Tierney, James (Cotton), 22
Tinker, Joseph, 60-61, 259
Tinning, Lyle (Bud), 154
Todd, Al, 186
Tolan, Eddie, 76
Topping, Dan, 337
Torre, Frank, 359-60
Trautman, George, 108, 116
Travis, Cecil, 24
Tresh, Mike, 357
Triandos, Gus, 325
Trimble, Joe, 215
Trout, Paul (Dizzy), 354, 372
Trucks, Virgil, 288
Turkin, Hy, 315
Turley, Bob, 46
Turner, Jim, 374
Tuthill, Harry, 364
Tuttle, Bill, 336
Van Atta, Russell (Sheriff), 159
Vance, Arthur (Dazzy), 256
Vander Meer, Johnny, 254-55
Van Haltren, George, 258
Vaughan, Joseph (Arky), 24, 186, 227
Veeck, Bill, 19
Vernon, James (Mickey), 143
Vico, George (Sam), 39
Virdon, Bill, 48
Vitt, Oscar, 129, 131, 296-97
Waddell, George (Rube), 32, 320
Wade, Gale, 298
Wagner, Charles (Heinie), 22
Wagner, Hal, 356
Wagner, Honus, 315
Wakefield, Dick, 39
Walker, Al (Rube), 301, 351
Walker, Fred (Dixie), 95, 117, 196, 227, 300
Walker, Hal, 12
Walker, Harry, 155
Walls, Lee, 325
Walsh, Edward, 32, 289, 363-64
Walters, Al, 212
Wambsganss, Bill (Wamby), 22
Waner, Lloyd, 23, 172A, 186
Waner, Paul, 23, 172A, 186

Warneke, Lon, 153, 154
Warren, Benny, 50
Weafer, Hal, 223, 224
Weaver, George (Buck), 127-32, 374
Weiss, George, 288, 337, 374
Welsh, Jimmy, 122
Wertz, Victor, 39, 298, 327, 375
Westlake, Waldon (Wally), 375
White, Guy (Doc), 364
White, Joe, 70
White, Joyner (Jo-Jo), 102
Wight, Bill, 372
Wilcox, Ralph, 141
Wilhelm, Hoyt, 371
Willaman, Bob, 39
Williams, Claude (Lefty), 374
Williams, Davey, 71

Williams, Denny, 72
Williams, E. Dibrell (Dib), 28, 333
Williams, Ross, 28
Williams, Ted, 24, 142, 145, 146, 147, 155, 172, 215, 216, 225, 305, 315, 325 327 330, 356
Wilson, Hack, 204A
Wilson, Jim, 288, 353
Wilson, Robert (Red), 336
Wiltse, George (Hooks), 242
Witt, Lawton (Whitey), 274-75
Wolfe, Bob, 169-70
Woodward, Frank, 13-14
Wright, Beals, 341
Wright, George, 340-41
Wright, Glenn, 22, 86

Wright, Harry, 339, 340
Wright, Irvin, 341
Wrigley, P. K., 224
Wyatt, Whitlow, 24, 193, 320
Wynn, Early, 328
York, Rudy, 38, 228
Young, Denton (Cy), 320
Young, Dick, 302
Young, Lemuel (Pep), 186
Young, Ross, 69, 70-71
Yvars, Sal, 280
Zauchin, Norm, 143, 298
Zeller, Jack, 227
Zimmer, Charles (Chief), 14
Zimmerman, Henry (Heinie), 13, 128
Zuverink, George, 84

About the Editor

CHARLES EINSTEIN'S *last addition to the literature of baseball was, of course, the first* Fireside Book of Baseball. *Before that, Mr. Einstein calculates that he had written more than four million words about the game, first as baseball editor of the International News Service, and later as a free-lance writer. His articles and short stories have appeared in more than forty magazines. His books on the game have included the novel* The Only Game in Town, *and a collaboration with Willie Mays on the latter's autobiography,* Born to Play Ball.

He is not only a ranking authority on baseball, deeply familiar with its literature, but, naturally enough, a Giant fan as well.

Mr. Einstein is a graduate of the University of Chicago. He has spent the greater part of his life to date in and around New York City. Two years ago, he and his wife moved from Ardsley, New York (a half-hour drive to the Polo Grounds, where the Giants played), to a desert mountain home in Scottsdale, Arizona (a half-hour drive from Phoenix, where the Giants train). More recently, and timing it to coincide with the transfer of the Giants franchise to San Francisco, he moved to that city, where he is feature columnist for the Examiner.

DAWN OF A NEW ERA... Opening Day, 1958 at the Los Angeles Coliseum.